BRITISH INTERVENTION IN GREECE

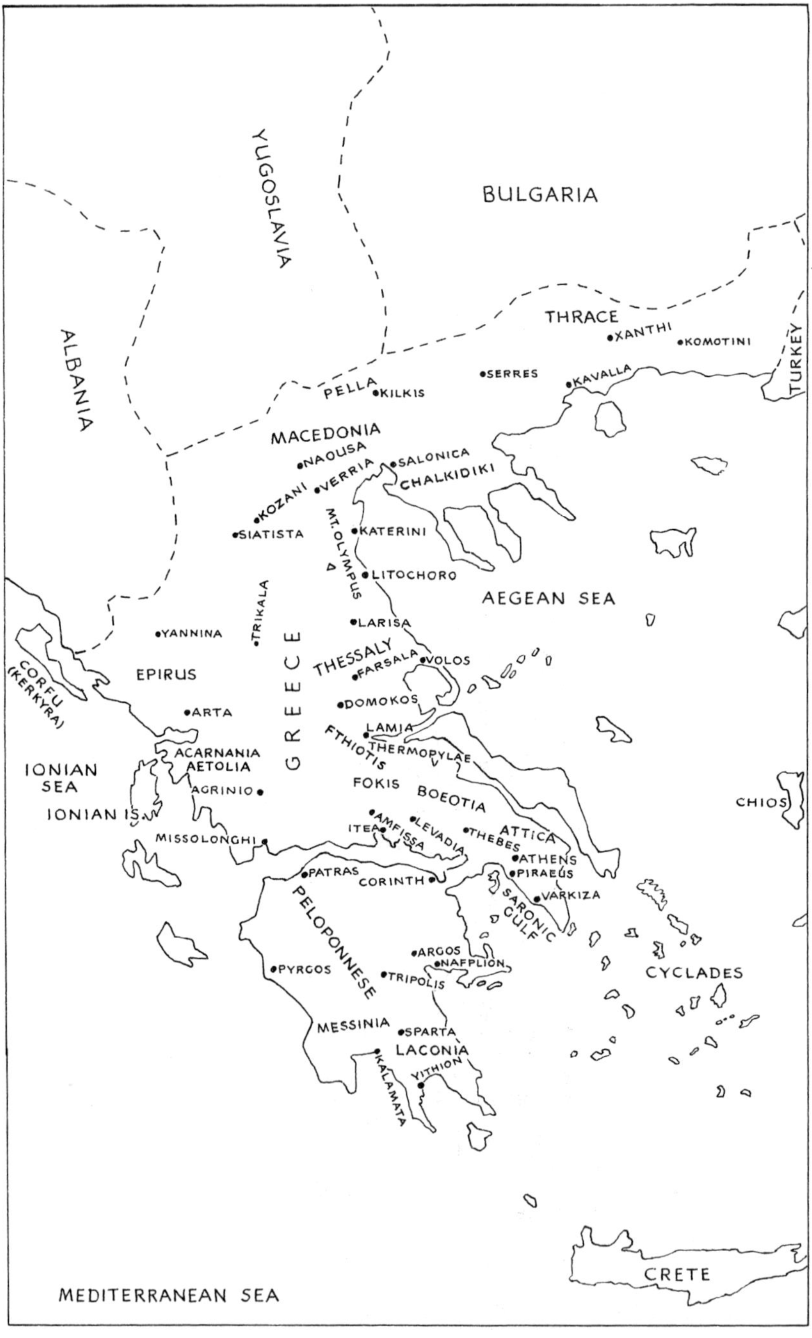
YUGOSLAVIA
BULGARIA
ALBANIA
THRACE
XANTHI
KOMOTINI
TURKEY
SERRES
KAVALLA
PELLA
KILKIS
MACEDONIA
NAOUSA
SALONICA
VERRIA
CHALKIDIKI
KOZANI
SIATISTA
KATERINI
MT. OLYMPUS
LITOCHORO
AEGEAN SEA
TRIKALA
LARISA
YANNINA
CORFU (KERKYRA)
THESSALY
VOLOS
FARSALA
EPIRUS
GREECE
DOMOKOS
ARTA
LAMIA
FTHIOTIS
THERMOPYLAE
ACARNANIA
AETOLIA
IONIAN SEA
AGRINIO
FOKIS
BOEOTIA
CHIOS
IONIAN IS.
ITEA
AMFISSA
LEVADIA
THEBES
ATTICA
MISSOLONGHI
ATHENS
PIRAEUS
PATRAS
CORINTH
VARKIZA
PELOPONNESE
SARONIC GULF
ARGOS
NAFPLION
PYRGOS
TRIPOLIS
CYCLADES
MESSINIA
SPARTA
LACONIA
KALAMATA
YITHION
CRETE
MEDITERRANEAN SEA

BRITISH INTERVENTION IN GREECE

From Varkiza to Civil War

February 1945 to August 1946

HEINZ RICHTER

Translated by Marion Sarafis

MERLIN PRESS
LONDON

First published in 1985
by The Merlin Press Ltd
3 Manchester Road
London E14 9BD

© Heinz Richter 1986

British Library Cataloguing in Publication Data

Richter, Heinz
    British intervention in Greece: from Varkiza
to Civil War. February 1945 to August 1946.
    1. Greece—Politics and government—1935-1967
    2. Greece—History—Civil War, 1944-1949
    3. Great Britain—Foreign relations—Greece
    4. Greece—Foreign relations—Great Britain
    I. Title
    949.5'074   DF849.5

ISBN 0-85036-301-5

Maps by Walter Kemsley

Jacket design by Louis Mackay

Printed in Great Britain by
Whitstable Litho, Whitstable, Kent

Typesetting by Hems & Co.
The Old Brewery, Tisbury, Wilts.

CONTENTS

Introduction	vii
The Armistice	1
The British White Paper and the TUC Delegations Report	21
From the Armistice to the Varkiza Peace Negotiations	49
The Peace Negotiations at Varkiza	57
Varkiza: Compromise or Capitulation?	71
From Varkiza to the Fall of Plastiras	79
The First Voulgaris Cabinet, April–August 1945	109
Implementing the Varkiza Agreement – The White Terror	125
The Second Voulgaris Government	177
Greece's Economic Development, March–September 1945	201
From the Return of Damaskinos to the Resignation of Voulgaris	221
The Evolution of the Left from Varkiza up to October 1945	235
Kanellopoulos' Cabinet	289
The Sofoulis Government	323
Greece at the UN Security Council	387
Election Preparations	405
The Elections	441
From the Seventh Party Congress to the Second Plenum, October 1945–February 1946	457
The Second KKE Central Committee Plenum, 12th–15th February 1946	477
From the Second Plenum to the Elections and Litochoro	497
The Escalation of Violence	519
Acronyms	543
Bibliography	545
Foreign Office and Public Record Office Reference Concordance	557
Varkiza Agreement (text)	561
Index of Proper Names	565

ACKNOWLEDGEMENTS

This study could not have been written without the help of the Deutsche-Forschungsgemeinschaft which granted me a three year post-graduate fellowship.

Next I would like to thank Professor Dr Dieter Groh, Panayotis Kanellopoulos, the late Komninos Pyromaglou, Evangelos Averoff, the late Dimitrios Partsalides, Leonidas Kyrkos, Professor Evangelos Spyropoulos, Mrs B. Janssen, Mrs Lilli Mutschler and Mrs Danae Coulmas.

The following libraries have given invaluable help: The Heidelberg University Library (especially Dr Willer), the Command Reference Center Library of HQ USAREUR in Heidelberg, King's College Library, the Library of the London School of Economics, the Labour Party, the Trades Union Congress, the Gennadius Library, the Vivliothiki tis Voulis (Parliamentary Library) in Athens, Otto Steiner and the staff of the Max Planck Institut für ausländisches öffentliches Recht und Völkerrecht in Heidelberg. The Public Record Office have also given their permission for the quotation of documents in their custody.

For the English edition I would like to thank the Cork County Library, Robert Macdonald of CBC, Mrs Betty Papworth, Mrs Diana Pym and finally Mrs Marion Sarafis whose cooperation has extended far beyond the normal brief of a translator.

Heinz Richter

INTRODUCTION

At 10.30 p.m. on the 11th January 1945, representatives of the National Popular Liberation Army ELAS (Ethnikos Laikos Apeleftherotikos Stratos) and General Ronald Scobie, commander of the British intervention forces, signed an armistice which provided for cessation, from 1 a.m. on 15th January, 1945, of the hostilities which had broken out on the 4th December 1944. This armistice was to prepare the way for negotiations between the National Liberation Front EAM (Ethniko Apeleftherotiko Metopo) and the Greek government, thus putting an end to one of the most tragic chapters in Greece's recent history, a chapter recorded in that history as the *Dekemvrianá* (December Events).[1]

The *Dekemvrianá* were not—as has until now been repeatedly asserted—the long-prepared communist revolution; rather they were the result of an intervention to crush the whole Greek Resistance in order to restore the semi-colonial dependence of the past, an intervention carefully prepared at both the diplomatic and the military levels by Churchill since the summer of 1943.

This intervention in Greece was part of a British policy for re-establishing the Empire and for the safeguarding of its communciations, together with the erection of an anti-communist bastion against the Soviet Union. In the framework of this policy, the Mediterranean and more especially Greece in its important strategic position played a central role. Whilst Churchill's policy for the Western Mediterranean was conditioned by the presence of American troops and the existence of an active US policy which he had to take into account and which imposed caution on his political manoeuvring, in the Balkans in general and in Greece in particular the restricted nature of US interest almost completely removed that obstacle. But against this he had to take into account Soviet interests at that end of the Mediterranean which were reinforced by Red Army successes. In contrast to the US which, on principle, rejected a 'spheres of interest' policy, the Russians were in no way averse to this tradition of foreign policy nor to the traditional means of applying it—by intervention, though out of consideration for US scruples they did not themselves raise the issue.

Thus the initiative for the 'spheres of interest' policy devolved on Churchill. The first step was the conclusion of an Interim Agreement on the Balkans in July 1944 for a period of three months. In the following months the advance of the Red Army and the gradual withdrawal of the *Wehrmacht* from the Balkans enabled Stalin on the one hand to take over the sphere allotted to him; whilst Churchill, on the other, was forced to remain a passive spectator of these developments, since lack of troops meant that a landing in Greece would be possible only after a German withdrawal. The Interim Agreement was in danger of running out without any advantage to Churchill. It was under these circumstances that he decided to act.

On the 9th October 1944 he concluded with Stalin the ill-famed Percentage Agreement on the Balkans. In his Memoirs—which until recently were the only first-hand source for these events—Churchill stated that these measures too were only valid for the duration of the war and that the final solution to all problems would have to be reached at the peace conference. In his telegram of 11th October to President Roosevelt, in which he informed the latter somewhat imprecisely of the results of his negotiations, he spoke likewise of a provisional agreement.[2] In fact, Churchill's published version bears signs of internal contradiction. From the Soviet side the existence of a 'spheres of interest' agreement has been categorically denied, with the result that non-communist historians have accepted Churchill's version; whilst communists until recently believed the Soviet *démenti*.[3] Checking of the actual content of the agreement, for example in the files of the Public Record Office, has not so far been possible since the relevant files are missing. This gap has recently been closed by Daniel Yergin's book *Shattered Peace*.[4]

Yergin came by chance upon the official British Minutes of the meeting of 9th October 1944 amongst the papers of General Hastings Ismay.[5] Their publication throws a completely new light on this agreement and its implications—never to be under-estimated—gain enormously in significance. At that session of 9th October Churchill and Stalin reached a 'gentlemen's agreement' *of unrestricted duration*. Stalin showed great understanding for British claims to hegemony in the Mediterranean and gave the British a virtually free hand in Greece; in return for which Churchill sanctioned what was about to happen in Romania. Finally it was mutually agreed to conceal the real content of the agreement from the US. However, when Eden and Molotov discussed the Percentage Agreement again on 10th October, there were differences of opinion,[6] but there was no further change to the substance of what had been agreed. Churchill and Stalin, in a bilateral agreement behind the back of the US, had divided the Balkans into permanent spheres of influence.

Gabriel Kolko, to whom the actual content of the Percentage Agreement was unknown, therefore attached little importance to it. According to him, Churchill returned from Moscow with more or less empty hands.[7] As regards the Polish question this is certainly correct. But, in regard to Churchill's Mediterranean policy and under the prevailing political and military conditions, the Moscow result could not have been bettered. Without this agreement, Churchill would have had to carry through his intervention in Greece in the face of united opposition from the Americans and the Russians—if he had been able to carry it through at all. For Stalin, on the other hand, this agreement was the first step to recognition of his empire-building gains. For the sake of such gains both participants were ready to abandon their former supporters to their fate. For Stalin this secret agreement was to form the basis of his Balkan policy for the next few years. During the *Dekemvrianá* and until 1946 he never once intervened against the execution of British policy in Greece and even afterwards, as we shall show, he abstained from any direct action since he wished to avoid confrontation with the Western Allies. For Churchill, however, the conclusion of this agreement was an instant solution which would make intervention in Greece a possibility, whilst not preventing him, during his remaining tenure of office, from following a contrary line in conjunction with the US, so that a year and a half later he could condemn this policy of division in the sharpest terms in his Fulton speech.

This stabilised system of spheres of interest was subsequently disrupted by Tito who, despite Soviet pressure, was not willing to have his post-war political and social regime determined by Churchill; later also by the US; and, after Churchill's electoral defeat, by the Labour government which, in all probability, had likewise never been informed by Churchill of the existence of this 'gentlemen's agreement'. We shall return to this in the context of foreign policy developments in 1945. Here, this is what must be emphasised: at the end of the Second World War, the first to enforce a political system of his own preference on a liberated European country was Churchill; Stalin only copied him within his own sphere of influence, and in the choice of enforcement methods he was frequently less brutal than his exemplar.

After this parenthesis on the international implications of the *Dekemvrianá*, let us return to the events themselves. We stated at the outset that the *Dekemvrianá* were not a long-prepared communist revolution but a carefully-prepared military intervention by Churchill to crush the Greek Resistance in order to restore the semi-colonial dependence of Greece on Great Britain. At the same time, the *Dekemvrianá* were to be the springboard of a civil war waged by the dominant Greek oligarchy against the democratic camp in its widest terms. In this way too they constitute a phase in the great internal conflict which began in Greece in 1916 and which is still to-day unresolved, the conflict which has brought the very nature of the Greek political regime into question. In December 1944 the alternatives were not dictatorship of the proletariat or a free democracy; they were national independence, popular sovereignty and democratic socialism or a client state under oligarchic rule. However, in 1944 these clear alternatives were to a certain extent overlaid and blurred by other factors which had arisen during the Second World War as a result of historical processes.

The active participation of the Greek monarchy in the fascist regime imposed on 4th August 1936 had, after the break-up of the latter at the German invasion of 1941, brought the constitutional question to the fore again. The overwhelming majority of the Greek people, from the 'old-school' politicians to the masses, regarded the king as responsible for the dictatorship and therefore demanded a post-war republic. Only fanatical royalists and the followers of the fascist regime supported the monarchy and both these factions compromised the monarchist cause by their collaboration with the Occupation authorities. The republicans on the other hand could not achieve any organisational unity. The old-school politicians would not join the organised Resistance and tried to promote their aims by wasting ink on futile statements. The Resistance itself was split into different movements of which EAM was the strongest. Nevertheless, in summer 1943, there was a general consensus that the post-war state would be a republic.

Against this, there was no general consensus on the post-war form of government. The old-school politicians naturally aimed at the re-establishment of their oligarchic rule within a republican framework. The theoretical proposals evolved by the various Resistance groups were rather vague; but, in the liberated areas, EAM–ELAS put into practice a system of local self-government, culminating in 1944 in a provisional government, which opened new perspectives. A new democratic state, a socially just state, was growing up from the grassroots and signalling a renaissance of the Greek polity. In this the Communists certainly played an important part but the danger of a communist takeover did not exist. In contrast to Tito, KKE (the Greek Communist Party) held formalistically to the orthodox theory of revolution which at that time prescribed a bourgeois republic for Greece. Quite the contrary, KKE regarded many of these radical democratic reforms with the greatest distrust and made every effort to restrain those voices in EAM–ELAS which demanded acceleration of the process of social change. In particular, KKE set itself against any efforts which could lead to a confrontation with the British. A post-war Greek state erected on these foundations would have been a liberal, democratic and socially just state. Its foreign relations, that is its relations with Great Britain, would have been conducted in a spirit of equal partnership. The new Greek state would no longer have been ruled by an oligarchy and its semi-colonial dependence on Great Britain would have been relegated to the past.

This trend first became apparent in August 1943 when a unified republican opposition, drawn together from the government-in-exile, the old-school politicians and representatives of the Resistance, raised its head against restoration of the Greek monarchy. It was from this date that

Churchill, who saw the Greek King George II as the guarantor of British interests,[8] began preparing the military intervention. Simultaneously, he began trying to split the republican camp by trumpeting the communist threat. Although this threat was non-existent, he succeeded by working on the pathological anti-communist fears of the Greek bourgeoisie in convincing the latter and thereby in bringing about a *rapprochement* between the monarchist and the republican factions of the oligarchy. In this endeavour he was assisted by the KKE leadership's mistakes. Finally, the *Dekemvrianá*, which he had himself provoked, furnished a 'proof after the event' of the communist threat; whilst the conference at Christmas 1944, by shelving the constitutional question through the appointment of Archbishop Damaskinos as Regent, removed the last obstacle to the reconciliation of the two bourgeois camps. British propaganda—which during the Occupation had been seconded by an almost identical German effort—had secured a complete victory. The British military intervention opened the way for the Greek Right to regain its former position of power. The Left had indeed suffered a military defeat in December but it was still a moral and political force throughout the whole of Greece. It is the annihilation of this moral and political potential which will be examined in the following chapters.

NOTES

1. The best English account of the December events is that given by John Iatrides, *Revolt in Athens: the Greek Communist 'Second Round' 1944-45*, (Princeton N.J.: Princeton University Press 1972). For an eye-witness testimony see W. Byford-Jones, *The Greek Trilogy: Resistance, Liberation, Revolution*, (London: Hutchinson, n.d. [1947]); and for a fuller analysis: Lars Baerentzen, 'The Demonstration in Syntagma Square on Sunday, the 3rd December, 1944', *Scandinavian Studies in Modern Greek*, 2, (1978), pp. 3-52; see also Heinz Richter, *Griechenland zwischen Revolution und Konterrevolution 1936-1946*, (Frankfurt: Europäische Verlagsanstalt, 1973); also 'O rolos tou G. Papandreou kata tin Apeleftherosi', *Anti*, Vol. II, Nos. 58-61, (Nov.-Dec. 1976); 'Ta praktika tis "Megalis Syskepsis",' *Athina*, 26-27 Dekemvri '44. *Ibid.*, Nos. 61-62, (Dec. 1976-Jan. 1977).
2. Robert G. Kaiser, 'Churchill-Stalin accord reported on East European takeover', *International Herald Tribune*, 25 August, 1977.
3. Most recently: Panayis Koutoulas, 'Mia palia kai nea theoria "Sfaires epirroïs kai yperdynameis",' *Kommunistiki Epitheorisi*, (May, 1975), pp. 45-56. Koutoulas, a dedicated adherent of the Moscow-aligned KKE, 'proves'—on the principle that what ought not to be, is not—the non-existence of the Percentage Agreement: spheres of interest policy is an exclusive characteristic of imperialist powers.
4. Daniel Yergin, *Shattered Peace: Origins of the Cold War and the National Security State*, (Boston: Houghton Mifflin, 1977). For an account of the whole process documented from British sources see Elisabeth Barker, 'Greece in the Framework of Anglo-Soviet Relations 1941-1947', in *Greece: From Resistance to Civil War*, M. Sarafis, ed. (Nottingham: Spokesman, 1980), pp. 15-31.

5. Yergin, *op. cit.*, p. 60.
6. Anthony Eden, *The Eden Memoirs: The Reckoning*, (London: Cassell, 1965), p. 483.
7. Gabriel Kolko, *The Politics of War: The World and United States Foreign Policy 1943-1945*, (New York: Vintage Books, 1970), p. 145. Kolko erroneously assumes that Churchill actually sent the Memorandum of 11th October to Stalin. It is much more likely that he drew up this Memorandum, which he let the US ambassador, Averell Harriman, read, just as he drew up the telegram to Roosevelt and Hopkins, to reassure the Americans and conceal the real content from them.
8. For the most recent account of the British obsession with the restoration of George II see Procopis Papastratis, *British policy towards Greece during the Second World War 1941-1944*, (Cambridge University Press, 1984), *passim*.

THE ARMISTICE

The armistice negotiations between ELAS and the British, 9th–11th January 1945, represent one strand in the new British political tactics initiated on 25th December 1944. On that day Churchill had yielded to the united opposition of Macmillan, General Alexander, Eden and Ambassador Leeper and accepted Macmillan's proposed change of tactics. This policy did not differ from Churchill's in its goal: Greece must remain a British client state. But, in contradistinction to Churchill, Macmillan had understood that this goal could not be reached by Churchill's route of enforced Restoration. The available British military forces might perhaps prove sufficient to drive ELAS out of Athens and Piraeus, perhaps even to gain partial control of the northern and central plains but the German Occupation had proved that a more far-ranging result was impossible. Moreover, a long drawn-out armed conflict would do even more to arouse public opinion in the US and the Commonwealth against British policy since, in these quarters, the British plan to impose Restoration was seen as the cause of the conflict. In addition there were problems at home: Churchill had twice had to submit himself to massive criticism from a section of the House of Commons and the wartime all-party coalition government was threatened with dissolution.

Macmillan's purpose was to remove the stumbling-block, the problem of the king's Restoration, by the establishment of a Regency. By this he hoped to deprive EAM of its main propaganda weapon and at the same time hive off the moderates within EAM from the revolutionary core of KKE. Parallel with the establishment of the Regency, the republican General Plastiras should form a 'non-political' government, that is one of indeterminate party complection. For this position Plastiras was the most suitable candidate. Both nationally and internationally, he was known as one of the protagonists of Greek republicanism; whilst at the same time his Supreme Command of the Greek Expeditionary Force against the Russian Revolution had made him an implacable opponent of communism. As a professional officer, he was a law-and-order man and, having been in exile for ten years, he had no party base in Greece and would therefore be dependent upon the Regent. The Regent himself, Archbishop Damaskinos, was an anglophil, definitely anti-Left and, what was more ready to exercise his function in agreement with the king. All moderate forces would therefore concentrate around the Regent and Plastiras and the bourgeois camp would re-unite. If the Left chose to continue the conflict, they would be isolated and the world would see that it had really been a case of communist revolution. Macmillan's aim was to end the armed conflict on conditions favourable to Great Britain. Genuine reconciliation was not under discussion. Churchill's last reservations as to the correctness of this policy disappeared after his meeting with Archbishop Damaskinos on board the cruiser *Ajax* on the evening of 25th December.

On 26th and 27th December this new policy was wheeled out for world public opinion.[1] Leeper was instructed to invite leading Greek personalities to a conference in the Athens Foreign Ministry. In order to demonstrate to public opinion Churchill's conciliatory intentions, to damp down American criticism and to forestall possible criticism from Russia; likewise to demonstrate to EAM that even the Soviets agreed with this course of action, the US Ambassador MacVeagh, his French colleague Baelen and the head of the Soviet Military Mission, Colonel Popov, were all invited. The latter conducted himself during the conference in complete accord with Stalin's policy of non-intervention and played a strictly non-speaking rôle.

The course and proceedings of the two-day conference themselves constitute the clearest proof that it had no real task. The chairman, Archbishop Damaskinos, guided procedure so skilfully that its sole result was the ratification of the British decision establishing the Regency, a result with which all political trends except the extreme royalists agreed. Just how far this conference was programmed in advance became apparent when, at the end of the second day's session, the EAM–ELAS delegation tabled a proposal for the solution of the current crisis. This was the moment when the real work of the conference, the negotiation of a compromise, should have begun. Instead, the Archbishop adjourned the conference *sine die*. So its only result was what had already been decided— his own nomination as Regent and the replacement of Papandreou by Plastiras. The winners at the conference were the British and their Greek allies: the losers were EAM–ELAS. They had been ready to participate in the conference so as to find there a political solution to the crisis; instead of this they had contributed to the ratification of Churchill's and Macmillan's decisions. Their pre-condition for the start of negotiations, a Regency, had indeed been achieved but their suggested solutions for the political crisis were not even discussed. For world public opinion, the central problem, that of the Regency, had been solved. Macmillan's calculations had worked out: Churchill had demonstrated to world public opinion that Great Britain was prepared to compromise. Were the conflict to continue—or the projected armistice and peace negotiations to fail— this could then be attributed to communist extremism.

During the whole course of the battle for Athens, there had been contacts between Scobie and EAM-ELAS during which armistice terms had been discussed. On 12th December, Scobie, personally instructed by Churchill to drive a hard bargain, had defined the following terms: in accordance with the Caserta Agreement, ELAS must carry out his orders and withdraw from Attica; all ELAS members in Athens and Piraeus must cease resistance and hand over their weapons to the British; when these conditions had been complied with, Field Marshal Alexander would announce the end of the current conflict and restore to all Greeks, irrespective of their political convictions, their democratic liberties; for this the first step would be the disbanding of all private armies.[2] In other words, Scobie required ELAS to place its fate at the discretion of Alexander's good will.

The replies of EAM-ELAS of 14th, 15th and 18th December, signalled a readiness to compromise but also indicated the Left's need for security, understandable in the circumstances. It was stated that the responsibility for the maintenance of order and for the restoration of liberties—in other words for the solution of the political crisis—belonged to the Greek government alone. For this reason it would be necessary, first to establish a Regency and then to form a government of national unity. Faced with such a government, ELAS would be ready to lay down its arms. In the meantime it was ready to evacuate Athens and Piraeus on the condition that the opposing forces would withdraw from Attica too. The gendarmerie must be disarmed and its members sent on home leave. The former collaborationist forces must be disarmed and interned to await trial. The British forces must refrain from intervening in internal Greek affairs. As soon as a government inspiring mutual confidence had been formed, ELAS would be prepared to disarm its members in Athens and Piraeus on the condition that its opponents did likewise with regard to their adherents. Finally, as a matter of principle, arms could only be laid down to a Greek government.[3] On the 27th December, at the conference, the EAM-ELAS delegation repeated these conditions and, on the 28th December, they sent a memorandum of corresponding content to Churchill. On the British side however, for reasons already explained, there was no interest in a conciliatory solution of this sort.[4]

Meanwhile, the political and military situation was evolving. On 30th December 1944, George II signed the decree appointing Archbishop Damaskinos Regent and the Papandreou government resigned. On 1st January 1945, Damaskinos issued an appeal for unity to the Greek people and called on them to lay down their arms. In the afternoon of the same day, an ELAS delegation led by Zevgos approached Scobie and pressed him to put an end to the fighting—ELAS had accepted Scobie's terms. But, when the delegation demanded a guarantee that the opposing forces would be disbanded at the same time, Scobie declared that this could only be done after ELAS had laid down its arms and referred them to the

Greek government which had yet to be formed. This again delayed the start of armistice negotiations. The reason for Scobie's delaying tactics is to be sought in the successes of the British forces, which had so far cleared two-thirds of Athens and Piraeus of ELAS and were now re-grouping for a further offensive due to start on the 3rd January. At the same time Scobie wanted to withdraw his previous armistice terms and to send ELAS an ultimatum.[5]

The ELAS delegation thereupon addressed itself in vain to Archbishop Damaskinos who simply referred it to the government, suggesting that ELAS could, in the meantime, suspend hostilities. On the 2nd January Archbishop Damaskinos appointed Plastiras Prime Minister and on the 3rd January the latter formed his Cabinet[6] which, with the exception of the Foreign Minister, Ioannis Sofianopoulos, consisted by and large of conservative Liberals. On the same day EAM addressed a memorandum to Damaskinos, stressing again its readiness to negotiate and demanding a start to negotiations; but EAM received no reply.

Macmillan and Alexander turned down the ultimatum suggested by Scobie and Leeper and cabled the relevant instructions. On the 4th January Macmillan flew to Athens to take personal charge. Scobie informed him that in Patras the situation was critical—the brigade there must either be reinforced or evacuated—and Macmillan notified Alexander accordingly. On the 5th January rumours reached the British that an ELAS delegation had set out to negotiate for an armistice. Macmillan decided that, if they actually arrived, they should be presented with the original armistice terms. Damaskinos agreed. In the evening Alexander arrived in Athens and told Macmillan that he had ordered the reinforcement of the Patras garrison.[7] In the meanwhile, the British offensive had had its first successes. By the evening of the 5th January Athens and Piraeus had been almost completely cleared of ELAS and the British forces were preparing to drive the retreating ELAS troops beyond the city boundaries next day. The British successes would soon render the previous armistice terms obsolete.

But not only Scobie and Leeper were pursing a hard line—so was the Greek government. As we already pointed out Plastiras, the professional officer, was set to impose law and order. Already on the 12th December 1944, shortly after his return from exile, he had given an interview to the *Times* Special Correspondent in which he had expressed the opinion that the situation could only be cleared up by the use of force and had completely excluded the possibility of compromise.[8] During the Christmas conference, too, he had given proof of his intransigent attitude and his sharp rejection of the EAM–ELAS delegation's proposals had contributed decisively to the result that these were not even discussed.[9] On the 4th January 1945, in a second interview with the *Times* Special Correspondent, he affirmed that he stood by his original statement that he would include no representative of the Left in his Cabinet; and not only Athens, but also the rest of Greece would be cleared of ELAS by force of arms. This, he said, could be carried out without great difficulty by the new National Guard (armed units provisionally drafted during the December fighting)—since EAM-ELAS controlled their members by terrorism, most of ELAS would go over to the advancing National Guard.[10]

At the same time the Greek Cabinet introduced administrative measures for the suppression of EAM-ELAS. During the Cabinet meeting of Saturday, 6th January, it was decided to purge the public services (telephone, gas, water, electricity, etc.) of followers of the Left. The Military Governor of Athens, Brigadier Pavsanias Katsotas, ordered any Athens citizen who had given refuge to an ELAS fighter to hand him over to the police on pain of being regarded as an accomplice. The *Times* Special Correspondent concluded from this that the government did not intend to grant an amnesty, but was seeking a solution by force.[11] On the 9th January the *Times* reported that police notices for the arrest of Zevgos, Porfyrogenis, Siantos, Ioannidis, Partsalidis, Svolos, Tsirimokos and Aris Velouchiotis and for another 150 so-called 'leaders of the revolution' had been posted. Anyone had the right to arrest the 'wanted' men. The government had also issued an order for the purging of the public services, the police and the judiciary; and three high-ranking police officers had already been arrested for collaboration with the rebels. The press was full of shrill demands for far-reaching reprisals or, at least, for condign punishment of all who had participated in the revolution.[12] Although the next day the Athens Police Chief, Evert, denied that he had given this information to the press, and the Foreign Affairs and Information Minister, Sofianopoulos, spoke of a misunderstanding, the whole affair remained highly ambiguous.[13] On the most lenient interpretation, it had been shown that the Greek government and its subordinates were pursuing an ambivalent line. The reason for this lack of clarity was a renewed British intervention.

Macmillan, in concert with Alexander, had been following political developments closely; and on the morning of the 6th January further British tactics were discussed. It was concluded that, as a result of the military situation, the previous armistice terms had become obsolete. But, in opposition to Leeper and Scobie, Macmillan and Alexander had recognised that an ultimatum was impossible, both for political and for military reasons. An ultimatum would merely harden the attitude of the EAM-ELAS leadership and might indeed extend the conflict to the whole of Greece. Such a development would be most undesirable in view of the restricted British forces available and the precarious situation in Northern Greece. Militarily, therefore, the armistice conditions only allowed for insignificant alteration.[14] Politically, too, a hard line was excluded: an ultimatum would have again roused public opinion in the US and in Britain—which, though somewhat appeased by the Christmas conference, remained very critical—since the British government had categorically declared that it was seeking a compromise solution.[15] Moreover, the measures of the Greek government had found a critical response from the Western press. Under these circumstances, Macmillan decided for a careful re-drawing of the line in two directions: he wanted to withdraw the previous armistice conditions and make the Greek government alter its course.

To this end, Macmillan drafted a *communiqué* which, as he emphasised, 'was titivated up with a view to the British and American press', and which would be published in Scobie's name.[16] In this *communiqué* it was merely stated that the previous armistice terms were withdrawn but no new military conditions were defined. On the other hand the *communiqué* contained new, potentially explosive elements which were cited as the reason for the withdrawal of the previous conditions: both sides had in the meantime taken prisoners and, despite allegedly repeated demands from Scobie and the International Red Cross, ELAS had refused permission for inspection of the detention camps and had not given any assurance that these were being conducted according to the recognised conventions. The *communiqué* went on to say that the future truce must therefore contain a clause dealing with the whole question of prisoners. Moreover ELAS had taken hostage a large number of Greek and a smaller number of British civilians and was continuing to do so. The taking of civilians as hostages was a direct contravention of the rules of civilised warfare. The future truce would have to cover this situation as well.[17]

Macmillan's intentions in drafting this *communiqué* are transparent. The mention of the taking of hostages by ELAS was intended to distract attention from the fact that the actual armistice terms were not announced. At the same time he was opening a psychological attack on the Left which was difficult to answer and which would certainly cost it public sympathy in the US and in Britain since, at that time, hostage-taking was regarded as on a par with German reprisals in the occupied countries. Events proved Macmillan's calculations sound. The international press took up the hint about the hostages and no longer questioned the military terms of the armistice.

But before Macmillan could get down to working out the armistice terms in detail, Plastiras too had to be made to change his line. In his memoirs, Macmillan writes somewhat vaguely that he wanted to bring the Greek government to discuss all the elements of the crisis and in this context he lists the Greek armed forces, the police, the gendarmerie, the collaborators and an amnesty; the aim of this policy being to isolate the communists within EAM–ELAS.[18] In other words he wanted to induce Plastiras to be more flexible and bring him on to his own line. This seems to have succeeded at a conference between Macmillan, Alexander, Scobie, Damaskinos and Plastiras on the evening of the 6th January.[19] The cancellation of the arrest warrants against the EAM–ELAS leaders came as first proof of this new policy. On the 7th January the new armistice terms were worked out, which provided for the withdrawal of ELAS from Boeotia, Attica and the Peloponnese, or its disarming in these regions and also for the evacuation of the Cyclades. Silence was agreed in regard to these conditions and even London was not informed. When, on the 10th January, the content became known there, there was anxiety that the new conditions—if they became known before the conclusion of negotiations—might produce negative results.[20] But London's anxieties were groundless: EAM–ELAS negotiators had reached British HQ on the 8th January.

The actual armistice negotiations did not begin till the 10th. The reason for this was the British attempt to win time to push its offensive as far north as possible. Another reason was that Macmillan and Alexander, who had in the meantime returned to Italy, had reserved the right to authorise publication of the armistice terms and only gave this on the 10th January[21] when it had become clear that the EAM–ELAS delegation seriously intended to negotiate.[22]

The British negotiating team was led by Brigadier Mainwaring, appointed by Macmillan and Alexander to replace Scobie's former Chief-of-Staff. EAM–ELAS was represented by Partsalidis and Zevgos and the ELAS majors, Makridis and Athinellis. Zevgos acted as spokesman. At the start of negotiations Mainwaring repeatedly emphasised that only the purely military conditions could be discussed; political problems were a matter for the Greek government and must be discussed with it. The armistice conditions which he eventually proposed amounted to the equivalent of an ultimatum and contained a series of highly political demands. After a first attempt by Mainwaring to surprise the EAM–ELAS delegation into blanket acceptance of the conditions had been frustrated by Zevgos' negotiating skill,[23] the four topics of radical disagreement which would frequently threaten to wreck the negotiations began to crystallise.

Article 1 of the armistice document stated that the armistice was being concluded in order to open the way for negotiations with the Greek government. Zevgos declared that EAM–ELAS was ready for such negotiations but he noted the lack of any comparably binding consent on the part of the Greek government: if the government refused to negotiate, would this mean a resumption of hostilities on the part of the British?[24] Zevgos' attitude of mistrust was understandable in view of the repressive measures of the Greek government. Mainwaring referred him to relevant statements by Plastiras.

In fact Plastiras had made a statement on the 10th January in which he defined his government's policy. The army would be reorganised on the basis of universal conscription. The gendarmerie and the police would be reconstructed with the help of a British Police Mission. The collaborators would be brought to account. The workers would regain their rights to trade union organisation. His government aimed to improve the country's economy. General elections and a referendum would be held as soon as possible and he would have no objection to supervision of these elections by allied observers. He appealed to all Greeks of good will to support him in carrying through this programme which contained all the demands of the insurgents. If the insurgents were honourable patriots, they would now lay down their arms and cooperate in the realisation of the programme. He gave categorical assurances that there would not be any proscriptions. But those who had offended against common law or against the internationally acknowledged rules of war would be brought to trial.[25]

In this statement the hand of Macmillan was clearly apparent. The moderate members of EAM were to be separated from the hard core of communists. There was no mention of amnesty and the announcement of a judicial epilogue to the December events was in itself a bad omen. It is not known whether this statement came to the knowledge of the EAM–ELAS delegation. But Zevgos declared himself satisfied with Mainwaring's commentary.

The second controversial issue was definition of the armistice boundary-line. Mainwaring demanded that ELAS withdraw behind a line drawn from Itea through Amfissa, Lamia, Domokos, Farsala and north of Volos to the sea-coast.[26] ELAS units to the south and east of this line (that is within the future British zone) must surrender their arms to the British and disband. After some hesitation the EAM–ELAS delegation agreed to this line and, when Makridis pointed out that those ELAS units now still within the zone could, by a march through the mountains, withdraw behind the line, Mainwaring accepted this solution.[27] This held for the ELAS units in Attica and Boeotia; but for the ELAS units in the Peloponnese British control of the Isthmus of Corinth rendered it impracticable, since this would have meant that these units must disband, a solution which the EAM–ELAS delegation rejected for various reasons.

Zevgos pointed out to Mainwaring that, during their first discussion of armistice terms on the 1st January, he had demanded specific guarantees for the safety of EAM supporters in Athens in the event of an ELAS withdrawal; that this had been refused and that now thousands were obliged to flee for their lives from right-wing persecution. He insisted that a similar tragedy must be avoided in the Peloponnese.[28] When Mainwaring's threats failed to break Zevgos' resolute stand, the former consulted Scobie and produced a compromise which Zevgos again rejected as it in no way solved the original problem.[29] Eventually, on the 11th January, the solution was found. ELAS units which originated from the Peloponnese should withdraw south of a line from Pyrgos to Argos; whilst units which did not originate from the Peloponnese should withdraw to the mainland behind the line of demarcation. Any units from the Peloponnese on the mainland would be withdrawn there behind the Pyrgos–Argos line.[30] This solution, acceptable to both parties, was arrived at only because Zevgos did not yield to Mainwaring's massive pressure and resolutely defended the safety of EAM supporters in the Peloponnese. Probably he had noticed early on that Mainwaring's hard line was a large-scale bluff and that he could not afford to risk a breakdown of the negotiations. Whilst in this instance Zevgos' brinkmanship—he, too, repeatedly threatened to break off negotiations—secured at least a temporarily favourable result for EAM-ELAS, on the third and fourth of the controversial issues he secured only a partial success, in fact a Pyrrhic victory.

These issues concerned the delicate matter of the prisoners and hostages. The armistice draft provided for the release of prisoners and hostages by ELAS. Zevgos commented on the relevant clause as follows:

'Certainly we must envisage the liberation of military prisoners. The liberation of prisoners, however, is generally made on the basis of parity, and I see no safeguard in this article for the prisoners you hold from ELAS. With regards [sic] to civilian hostages, we have already commenced the liberation of women, children and the aged. Hundreds and thousands of people in the same category have been taken, and are still being taken here. When I was coming down myself I found the British forces were seizing large numbers of the refugees from Athens. . . Further numbers are being seized daily by the Greek government, and other organizations and individuals. The mere fact of the publication recently of an order forbidding this practice proves it is widely in use.'[31]

What Zevgos stated was correct as to content and his demand for parity was reasonable but the form he gave it amounted to a serious blunder in negotiating tactics: he owned in so many words that the Left had taken hostages. Before we proceed with the account of negotiations on this problem, a brief retrospect on how it arose may be in order.

The taking of prisoners and hostages during the December events was a by-product of the ambivalent character of that conflict. The December events were, as has been repeatedly emphasized, on the one hand an armed struggle between ELAS and the British, and on the other a civil war between the Greek Right and the Greek Left. On the British side, alongside the British forces, there fought a regular Greek Army unit, the Third or Mountain Brigade, as well as gendarmerie and police units, all designated as combatants by their uniforms. In addition the Greek government put up a number of so-called National Guard battalions whose members were to be denoted by blue arm-bands since there were not sufficient uniforms. These battalions accepted all volunteers indiscriminately, from the members of right-wing secret associations and those of the former collaborationist units to the criminal scum of the capital.[32] In addition to these, groups from right-wing anti-communist organisations, like Colonel Grivas' 'X' participated in the fighting, likewise without uniforms; and there were even many private individuals who took part in one way or another.

On the ELAS side, the brunt of the fighting was born by the Athens–Piraeus ELAS Reserve, also distinguished by armbands. Of the regular ELAS units who, with more or less complete uniforms, would have been more easily recognised as combatants, few participated. The ELAS fighters were reinforced by a large number of EAM members and those of organisations directed by EAM as well as by individual sympathisers. In general, therefore, only the British forces and the armed forces of the Greek government were manifestly recognisable as combatants.

The nature of the fighting intensified this problem. The British and Greek regular units were trying to clear ELAS out of the districts it was holding and in this process they took prisoners by criteria similar to those the *Wehrmacht* had employed in dubious cases: anyone who in any way seemed suspicious was arrested, even if it was only that he happened to be in the conflict area. By the end of the fighting the British had, in this way, taken approximately 15,000 prisoners of whom 8,000 were transported to the Middle East. Leeper himself acknowledged that only about 8,000 were actually members of ELAS.[33] The treatment of these prisoners was not always in accordance with regulations for prisoners of war but their lives were not directly in danger.[34]

In contrast, the irregular bands carried out a campaign of extermination. Fanatical supporters of the Greek Right hunted out their political opponents. Former members of the collaborationist units (the Security Battalions) sought to rehabilitate themselves by particular brutality and to prove, *post facto,* that they had all along been fighting the real enemy. All this was compounded by acts of vengeance, personal vendettas and the lust to kill. The consequence was uncontrolled taking of prisoners, mass arrests of sympathisers with the Left, outrages and massacre. Contrary to the British, who arrested wholesale because they had no means of checking identity, the irregular Greek bands—who generally operated in their own districts—knew their opponents from the days of the Occupation and could engage in individual pursuit of left-wing sympathisers. The Greek police units, who also participated in this pursuit, had likewise the advantage of local knowledge acquired under the Metaxas dictatorship and during the German Occupation.

From this we can safely conclude that both the British and the Greek regular forces took non-combatant civilian prisoners; for which we can acknowledge, at least at the start, a degree of military necessity; whilst the later arrests and especially those by the Greek auxiliary units were nothing but a politically-motivated reprisal. These civilian prisoners were certainly not hostages in the sense that the *Wehrmacht* had taken hostages whose lives were directly threatened. But that did not alter the fact that they were human bargaining-counters and exposed to reprisals, and therefore also hostages.

ELAS had, on the other hand, until the middle of December restricted itself to the taking of military prisoners and in this they faced the same problem as their opponents: with the exception of the British and the Greek regulars, these opponents were not in uniform and, for this reason, civilians were arrested on exactly parallel criteria. But mass arrests of right-wing sympathisers came only as a reaction to corresponding measures from the other side. On the 18th December, following a decision by the Political Bureau of the KKE Central Committee, the EAM Central Committee decided that their side too would take non-combatant prisoners.[35] The more level-headed on both sides seem to have been unhappy about this development. From a document of 28th December addressed by the EAM Central Committee to Damaskinos it emerges that, even before this date, the EAM leadership had made contact with him in an effort to arrange mutual release of civilian prisoners but had encountered a similar counter-proposal. In the document itself, the EAM Central Committee renewed its appeal to Damaskinos[36] but there was no reply. On the 29th December, the ELAS Central Committee issued a *communiqué* in which it called on the other side to put an end to persecutions and arrests. ELAS declared itself ready to cease arresting and to release all those arrested so far with the exception of those charged with common law crimes, provided its opponents did the same. As an earnest of intent, it had already begun to release those against whom there were no charges.[37]

The opposing side did not react, but rather increased the tempo of arrests. The consequence of this was that the Left, too, began to arrest civilians again. On the 29th December the *New York Times* demonstrated that both sides were holding civilian hostages.[38] About the same time ELAS began to withdraw from Athens and the resulting confusion had most unpleasant consequences. Since ELAS had hardly any motorised transport at its disposal, it marched its prisoners off towards Thebes on foot which, in the wintry weather, had fatal results for many of them. Furthermore, in the last days before the withdrawal, ELAS, facing defeat, had turned again to wholesale arrests in the middle-class districts of Athens, accompanied by acts of extremist violence.

These undisciplined arrests of civilians, carried out under the pressure of defeat, proved to be a decisive blunder and gave the British and the Greek Right a propaganda weapon morally disastrous to the Greek Left. Immediately following on ELAS' withdrawal, a well-organised press campaign got under way. Stavrianos reported:

'In order to neutralise enraged world opinion British "public relations" experts were sent to Athens, where they immediately began to pour out stories about the barbarity of the EAM fighters and especially about their uncivilised practice of taking civilian hostages.[39]

To prevent independent-minded correspondents reporting with objectivity how matters really stood, the British imposed censorship which led to protests from American reporters.[40] At the same time Leeper began to collect reports of ELAS atrocities and sent them to the Foreign Office which compiled them into a White Paper. But, before we deal with the background to the creation of this White Paper and the subsequent development of the propaganda offensive against EAM-ELAS, we must return to the armistice negotiations concerning the prisoners and hostages.

We have shown how Zevgos made a serious tactical blunder when he admitted that ELAS had taken hostages. Mainwaring brushed his arguments aside and demanded unilateral release of ELAS' prisoners and hostages. Zevgos held out for mutual release—this was of the greatest political importance. Mainwaring pointed out that a military armistice was under discussion and that it was customary for those who sought the armistice to hand over their prisoners. Zevgos rejected this and asked why EAM-ELAS should hand over their civilian hostages whilst their opponents continued to hold theirs. Mainwaring riposted: 'You have this evening admitted to me that you have taken hostages, and that you have already returned women, children and the aged. *The British forces have no hostages.* It is, therefore, not necessary, and would be unthinkable in any British document, to make allusion to hostages being detained by British forces.'[41] But, even when Zevgos drew Mainwaring's attention to the mass arrests and the deportations to the Middle East, the latter maintained his stand that the British forces had no hostages, at the most a few who had been unjustly arrested and that these would soon be released. The British demand for the unilateral release of hostages remained in force; and on this point and the demand for withdrawal from the Peloponnese, the negotiations were in danger of breaking down.

After consultation with Scobie and Leeper, Mainwaring declared that the British army was prepared to exchange prisoners of war with ELAS on a mutual basis. But that as, unlike ELAS, they had no hostages, there could be no mutual hostage exchange.[42] Faced with this, Zevgos maintained that most of the hostages had been taken by the Greek gendarmerie and the former collaborationist troops and that he could not understand why EAM-ELAS should release their civilian prisoners whilst their opponents could keep theirs. He agreed to the solution in regard to prisoners of war, but the question of the civilian prisoners was between EAM-ELAS and the Greek government.[43] Mainwaring conceded this point but maintained that the Greek government insisted on release of the hostages.[44] Zevgos persisted in his demand for mutual release and added:

> 'Let us be cautious in the use of the word "hostages" in the sense that the Germans use it, and in the sense that we ourselves were formerly hostages under the Germans. We commenced this practice only when the authorities here commenced to seize hostages on a large scale.'[45]

The question of the civilian prisoners was in essence a question between EAM-ELAS and the Greek government, since ELAS had no British civilian prisoners. Mainwaring could not disentangle himself from this argument and left the matter pending.

On the 11th January, Mainwaring introduced a new argument: ELAS did have some British civilians among the hostages and these must be released with the prisoners of war. Zevgos accepted this at once. Mainwaring then repeated the demand for the release of all hostages and stressed again that the British army had no hostages. Zevgos, who had in the meantime realised the significance attached to the word 'hostages', replied:

'Hostages, in the sense of prisoners whose lives are in danger if any condition is not fulfilled, do not exist in our hands, although on this side [government side] executions are believed to have taken place. We hold supporters of the fascist faction, and possible re-inforcements for them, who, in some cases, are war guilty during the period of occupation.'[46]

Mainwaring, recognising that this definition of the term 'hostage' exactly fitted the civilian prisoners taken by the British and by the Greek government—if in an opposite sense—avoided the issue by transferring his argument to the moral plane:

'As a soldier, I am not prepared to listen to any discourse on the categories of hostages which ELAS troops have taken: it grieves me very much to sit in a room with another soldier who mentions the word "hostages", which should never be mentioned by a man in my profession.'

What followed was near to moral blackmail:

'All I want to know is whether you are prepared for the negotiations to break down, and for it to be known to the world that they have broken down on the point of hostages—when it is well known that it is against all rules of warfare for anyone to have hostages in their possession.'[47]

Zevgos skillfully evaded this pressure by taking over Mainwaring's main argument that the British had taken no hostages. He maintained that ELAS, as a purely military organisation, had likewise taken no civilian prisoners nor did it hold any. Civilians had been arrested by the EAM Police, the EP (Ethniki Politofylaki) for which reason this question could not be dealt with by a military armistice. ELAS' prisoners were prisoners of war and would be exchanged.[48]

Mainwaring's efforts to refute this argument and to resort again to moral pressure were countered by Zevgos with the comment that purely military negotiations were apparently about to break down for political reasons and he repeated his position. Mainwaring changed the subject.[49]

After further hard bargaining, punctuated by repeated consultations between Mainwaring and his superiors, the following clause concerning the prisoners was eventually agreed:

> 'All service personnel of whatever nationality including Greek police or gendarmerie captured by ELAS will be returned. This will include all Greek personnel taken by ELAS while they were bearing arms. This will not include civilians detained by the EAM Civil Police. An equivalent number of ELAS prisoners will be released by the British authorities in exchange.'[50]

Now that this controversial issue had been cleared up, the armistice was signed, to come into force one minute past midnight on 15th January 1945.

At first sight, the result of the negotiations would seem to be a practical compromise. Hostilities were to cease. The armistice line, as it had evolved from negotiation, was also in the nature of a compromise. A mutual exchange of prisoners would follow. The problem of the civilian prisoners would be settled in the course of negotiations with the Greek government. It looked as though the armistice could form a basis for reconciliation of the opponents. But already the way in which the Greek and British governments published this result signalled an unremitting pursuit of the propaganda campaign against EAM–ELAS.

In London the British government announced that, whilst it approved of the armistice, hostage-taking was a barbarous custom condemned by international law. The armistice could not last or evolve towards a peace unless the hostages taken by ELAS were released.[51] Damaskinos declared himself deeply shocked that ELAS had refused to release thousands of innocent hostages; but he was prepared to arrange a meeting between ELAS and the Greek government and to mediate.[52] Finally, the Greek government welcomed the British statement with which it found itself in complete agreement.[53] Alongside these official statements of position, there began a massive press campaign against EAM to which we shall return later.

The carrying out of the armistice terms also showed that only EAM–ELAS really envisaged reconciliation. ELAS withdrew behind the armistice line on time. Directly the armistice was signed, it released its prisoners of war and began the unilateral release of civilian prisoners.[54] The British, on the other hand, kept to the letter of the armistice and in doing so belatedly revealed a serious omission on the part of Zevgos. The armistice provided for the exchange of an equal number of ELAS members and British soldiers. ELAS had taken 1,170 British prisoners of war. But the British were in no way prepared to comb through their Middle East camps, or even their prisoners in Athens, on a strictly comparative basis, but simply released an equal number of their Athens prisoners.[55] The result was not only that these included non-combatants, old people and children; but also that many genuine ELAS members, including high-ranking officers, remained in British custody.[56] These remaining prisoners

(5,500 in Athens and Piraeus) were investigated by specially appointed Greek government commissions to ascertain whether any charges were pending against them. By mid-March 2,840 prisoners had been released as innocent, whilst the residue of 2,500 remained in detention.[57] In the Middle East things were more complicated. There, according to official information, the British were still holding 4,000 prisoners from the disturbances in the Greek army-in-exile in spring 1944,[58] the investigation of whose cases had not yet been concluded. To these were now added 8,000 ELAS prisoners who were also to be checked by a Greek government commission. The first repatriation convoy of the innocent was announced in March 1945.[59] The numbers afford further proof of the extent of British arrests and further demonstrate that the British attached no importance to genuine conciliation. Potential opponents of their policy were to be kept out of circulation for as long as possible. Thus, the armistice became a further weapon to annihilate the Greek Left.

This aim to annihilate was even more obvious on the Greek Right. For the Right, which—as we shall go on to show—was at least at that time not yet fully identified with the Greek government, there could be no discussion of compromise, reconciliation or power-sharing. For them the December events had been an anti-communist crusade with no quarter given which—had the British allowed them—they would have pursued throughout the length and breadth of Greece. This was most clearly shown in the case of the civilian prisoners. The Right did not arrest its opponents, as the Left had done, from fear of reprisals, but in order to destroy their opponents' organisation by terrorising individuals. The Right saw its civilian prisoners not even as human negotiating pawns to be exchanged under suitable conditions, but as criminals who would inevitably remain in prisons or detention camps. Thus the arrests did not end with the signing of the armistice but were pursued at such an increasing tempo that, on the 16th January, Leeper found himself forced to protest against this to the Greek government.[60] But his intervention brought no improvement. Whether it was that the Greek government made no effort or—more probably—that it was unable to impose its will, the arrests continued. The prisons acted as sieves: thousands were arrested and investigated; those with nothing outstanding against them were released; those known to be of the Left remained in prison to await sentencing at a later date. These arrests—carried out also by the right-wing clandestine organisations—were based and undertaken on purely political motives and their justifications were such that at the beginning of March Leeper protested again and again without success.[61] As we shall show, this was only the beginning of the judicial 'coming to terms with' the December events.

But, before we concern ourselves with the propaganda campaign which distracted attention from these happenings and served to mask them, let us look again at the hostage problem from the viewpoint of EAM–ELAS.

We have characterised Zevgos' negotiating achievement as a Pyrrhic victory. In fact the negotiations had faced him with an insoluble dilemma. Were he to accept the return of the civilian prisoners, the Left would lose a negotiating counter and still remain exposed to the charge of having taken hostages; were he to refuse unilateral release—as he did—this would make sense only if EAM-ELAS were prepared to take a hard line, in other words for an eventual continuation of the conflict. In January such a line was still a possibility. The loss of Athens and Piraeus had been a tactical, not a strategic defeat. As during the Occupation, ELAS could have continued the fight from the mountains and eventually won a compromise or even participation in the Government. This would have required that EAM-ELAS had really been fighting for power. But this was just what they did not do. During the December events, they had been fighting not for the installation of a left-wing dictatorship but in defence of the positions they had won during the Occupation. At the same time they were suffering from illusions about the real balance of forces and about the aims of their opponents. They looked on the British as their true opponents with whom they had to find a compromise; and they overlooked the fact that the Greek Right—which had been extremely weak during the Occupation—had, since the return of the government-in-exile, been progressively working its way back into positions of power and had no intention of compromising. The leadership of the Left interpreted the mass arrests of its sympathisers as hostage-taking and did not realise that its opponents were set on annihilation. It was over-estimation of the British and under-estimation of the Greek Right which caused them to seize upon the mistaken weapon of hostage-taking which on the one hand compromised them and on the other proved itself useless. They did not comprehend the real alternatives: submission or a struggle for power and therefore inevitably led the Left into defeat. All Zevgos could achieve at the armistice negotiations was to reduce its extent. The EAM leadership was working for conciliation; its opponents for annihilation.

NOTES

1. Heinz Richter, 'Ta praktika tis "Megalis Syskepsis", Athina 26-27 Dekemvri '44', *passim*.
2. Richter, *Griechenland zwischen Revolution und Konterrevolution*, p. 527.
3. *Ibid.*, pp. 528-30.
4. *Ibid.*, pp. 551-3.
5. *Ibid.*, p. 557.
6. The Ministries were allocated as follows:
   General Nikolaos Plastiras: Prime Minister, Minister for War, Navy, Air Force and Merchant Navy.
   Ioannis (John) Sofianopoulos (Agrarian Party): Foreign Minister and temporarily Minister for Information.

Petros Rallis (moderate Populist): Minister of the Interior and temporarily Education and Labour Minister.
Georgios Sideris (Liberal): Finance and Public Services Minister.
Nikolaos Kolyvas (a conservative): Minister for Justice, Welfare and Health.
Ioannis Glavanis (Liberal): Minister for Agriculture and temporarily Minister for Trade.
General Loukas Sakellaropoulos (a conservative): Minister for Public Works and temporarily Telecommunications, Posts and Transport Minister.
General Leonidas Spaïs: Assistant-Minister for the Army.
Naval Captain Th. Koundouriotis: Assistant-Minister for the Navy.
Squadron-Leader Petros Vilos: Assistant-Minister for the Air Force.
Georgios Melas (Liberal): Assistant-Minister for Foreign Affairs.
Michaïl Mavrogordatos (Liberal): Assistant-Minister to the Prime Minister. The Assistant-Ministers had Cabinet rank.
Alkiviadis Provatas, *Politiki istoria tis Ellados 1821-1980: Nomothetika kai ektelestika somata*, (Athens, 1980), p. 570.
7. Harold Macmillan, *The Blast of War, 1939-1945*, (London: Macmillan, 1967), pp. 634 ff.
8. *The Times*, 6th January, 1945.
9. Richter, 'Ta praktika', p. 33.
10. *The Times*, 6th January, 1945.
11. *Ibid.*, 8th January, 1945.
12. *Ibid.*, 9th January, 1945. It was eventually explained as the mistake of a police interpreter, *Hansard*, 19th January, 1945, col. 606.
13. *Ibid.*, 10th January, 1945.
14. Alexander intended to secure a good defensive position at a suitable distance from Athens, behind which the Greek government could acquire strength. *Report by the Supreme Allied Commander Mediterranean to the Combined Chiefs of Staff on Greece, 12th December 1944 to 9th May 1945*, (London: HMSO, 1949), p. 15.
15. Thus Eden on 20th December in the House of Commons; *The Times*, 9th January, 1945, where the most important points were again summarised.
16. Macmillan, *op. cit.*, p. 636.
17. *The Times*, 8th January, 1945.
18. Macmillan, *op. cit.*, p. 635.
19. *New York Times*, 6th January, 1945; *The Times*, 8th January, 1945. Macmillan does not report this meeting.
20. Foreign Office to Leeper 10th January, 1945 (R 765/4/19), See note on F.O. documents, p. 557.
21. Macmillan, *op. cit.*, p. 637.
22. Record of Meeting with Representatives of EAM Committee at Headquarters of Land Forces and Military Liaison, Greece (R 3400/4/19, pp. 4-9).
23. Mainwaring rejected counter-proposals by the EAM-ELAS delegation and demanded either acceptance or rejection of the conditions. Zevgos replied: 'You mean agreement to the text as it stands.' Mainwaring: 'I would like confirmation that you are in general agreement with what has been put down— merely leaving slight modifications.' Zevgos: 'General agreement on the form of the present text is impossible. We have counterproposals we wish to make, and we would like to make these in the form of observations.' (R 3400/4/19, p. 15.)
24. *Ibid.*, pp. 11, 15, 16.
25. *The Times*, 11th January, 1945.
26. This line went much further than that suggested by Macmillan and Alexander (Itea-Thermopylae). Macmillan, *op. cit.*, p. 637.

27. R 3400/4/19, p. 14.
28. *Ibid.*, pp. 18, 21. In fact, from the start of the December fighting, as ELAS withdrew from one Athens district after another, this was followed by an intensive hunt for left-wing sympathisers. The events in Kallithea and Petralona, where 'X' followers liquidated numerous left-wingers, achieved a tragic notoriety.
29. *Ibid.*, pp. 23, 24. Scobie allowed a longer time limit for the withdrawal from the Peloponnese. Against this, Zevgos maintained that most of the units there were from the Peloponnese itself and that their future should be decided at the conference with the Greek government (p. 26).
30. *Ibid.*, p. 25; Stefanos Sarafis, *ELAS: Greek Resistance Army*, (London: The Merlin Press, 1980), p. 516.
31. R 3400/4/19, pp. 18 ff.
32. William Hardy McNeill, *The Greek Dilemma: War and Aftermath*, (London: Victor Gollancz, 1947), pp. 181 ff; Richter, *Griechenland zwischen Revolution und Konterrevolution*, p. 532.
33. Richter, *loc. cit.*, pp. 386, 478. In his telegram of the 16th January 1945 (R 1193/4/19) to the Foreign Office, Leeper reported: '12,000 ELAS prisoners held by us here and in Middle East divide roughly into two categories. Approximately 8,000 can be identified as belonging to recognised ELAS fighting formations. Remainder are ELAS supporters or persons captured during the battle in circumstances in which presumption was that they had been, or intended to be, involved in hostile acts. But in house to house fighting it is of course impossible always to obtain satisfactory proof of this.' On the 8th March 1945 he was even more precise in a further telegram to the Foreign Office (R 4905/4/19): '. . . on 11th January there were in British custody approximately 5,600 Greek males and 1,100 females in Athens, and 8,000 in the Middle East. These were all taken during operations as being members of ELAS forces or their civilian supporters. They included however, a number of people who are innocent but were arrested by British troops in the course of house to house fighting with ELAS troops in civilian clothes and a further number seized by the Greek police in street fighting and because of breaches of regulations.' An American report mentioned that more than 15,000 ELAS members had been deported. Telegram from Halifax to F.O. 13th March 1945 (R 5073/4/19). The excessive arresting by the British was carried out with Churchill's express approval (*Hansard*, 18th January, 1945, col. 470).
34. Those deported were detained in concentration camps. For the detention conditions of those arrested in Athens, see the report of the *News Chronicle* editor, Gerald Barry, who undertook investigations on the spot from the 18th January to the 1st February and reported as follows: 'I visited prisons. . . and found. . . conditions which could readily be turned to propagandist advantage by the other side.' Gerald Barry, *Report on Greece*, (London. News Chronicle Publications: 1945), p. 5.
35. Dimitris Vlandas, *'1950-1967': Tragodia tou KKE*, (Athens, 1976), p. 34; National Liberation Front E.A.M., *White Book, May 1944-March 1945*, (New York: Greek American Council), p. 106 (this is the English edition of Ethniko Apeleftherotiko Metopo, *Lefki Vivlos, Maîs 1944-Martis 1945*, (Trikala, 1945), pp. 89 ff).
36. National Liberation Front, E.A.M., *White Book*, p. 106; EAM, *Lefki Vivlos*, p. 90.
37. *Op. cit.*, p. 107, p. 91.
38. *New York Times*, 29th December, 1944.
39. Leften S. Stavrianos, 'Greece. The EAM White Book', *Nation*, 161 (15th

December, 1945), p. 662.
40. On the 11th January 1945 the *New York Times* reported that eleven out of twelve US correspondents were protesting against the censorship which meant that they could not present the EAM viewpoint. 'General Scobie, according to John Nixon of the BBC, ruled that war correspondents should not be allowed to interview representatives of ELAS the grounds being that ELAS should be treated in every respect as an enemy.' In: *Greek Diary* (R 1643/4/19, p. 108). See chapter 2, footnote 30.
41. R 3400/4/19, p. 20. Author's italics.
42. *Ibid.*, p. 27.
43. *Ibid.*, p. 29.
44. *Ibid.*, p. 31.
45. *Ibid.*
46. *Ibid.*, p. 36.
47. *Ibid.*
48. *Ibid.*, pp. 37 ff.
49. *Ibid.*, pp. 38 ff.
50. *Ibid.*, pp. 48 ff.
51. *The Times*, 15th January, 1945.
52. *Ibid.*
53. *Ibid.*
54. National Liberation Front, E.A.M., *White Book*, pp. 86-8, 108-11.
55. Leeper to Foreign Office 16th January, 1945 (R 1193/4/19); also Leeper to Foreign Office 13th March, 1945 (R 4905/4/19).
56. National Liberation Front E.A.M., *White Book*, pp. 86-8.
57. Leeper to Foreign Office 8th March, 1945 (R 4905/4/19).
58. In spring 1944 the creation of PEEA caused unrest among the Greek forces-in-exile which was confined to political manifestations, such as the demand for a Government of National Unity. Churchill, however, interpreted this in his own way as mutiny and had it rigorously suppressed. The two Greek army brigades and the Greek naval forces were thoroughly purged and the 'mutineers' sent to concentration camps in Eritrea and Sudan. The remnants of the army were re-organised in the Third (Mountain or Rimini) Brigade.
59. Lord Killearn (Cairo) to Foreign Office 6th March, 1945 (R 4452/4/19); Foreign Office to Leeper 8th March, 1945 (R 4469/4/19).
60. Leeper to Foreign Office 17th January, 1945 (R 1325/4/19).
61. Leeper to Foreign Office 8th March, 1945 (R 4905/4/19), where he reported: 'Arrest of persons suspected of complicity in the rebellion did not, however, cease with the signature of truce. Large scale arrests continued (1,500 of both sexes were arrested in Athens and Piraeus during week ending 2nd February and 940 for week ending 21st February) and, although releases on a fairly wide scale are taking place there were reported on 27th February to be still 4,500 of both sexes in prison, and intake of arrested persons has greatly exceeded the output of innocent. Very few trials have so far taken place. . . General Scobie and I have been making strong representations to General Plastiras in the following sense: a) that powers of arrest should be limited to police. . . b) that ground for arrests should be limited to: i) crimes in contravention of penal code, ii) acts considered contrary to the usages of war and committed before signature of the truce, iii) collaboration with the enemy.'

Demarcation line between ELAS and British forces, Armistice of January 1945.

THE BRITISH WHITE PAPER AND THE TUC DELEGATION'S REPORT

EAM–ELAS's uncompromising stand on the hostage question during the armistice negotiations was regretted by Macmillan for the sake of the victims; but he recognised its political propaganda value—it was a weapon which, in Great Britain, would put ELAS politically beyond the pale.[1] As has been explained, it was Macmillan's policy to drive a wedge between the moderates in EAM and the revolutionary core of KKE and in this way to isolate the latter. This policy he had not only expounded in British circles but he had introduced it to the Greek government during the conference on 6th January. But, since the desired result, the splitting of EAM, was not forthcoming by the start of the armistice negotiations, it had to be helped.

During the Athens fighting a quarrel had erupted in the Salonica EAM on the issue of civil war. Some self-declared leaders of the ELD [Union for Popular Democracy] (Enosi Laikis Dimokratias) issued a statement at the beginning of January in which they condemned both the civil war and KKE and announced their breach with EAM. The British consul in Salonica, Rapp, noticed this and began to do what he could to foster this divisive tendency which was so completely in accord with British policy. After agreement with the four dissidents, he sent the statement to Leeper and to the Foreign Office. At the same time he announced the impending final breakaway of ELD from EAM, in which it would be joined by two more parties, the Socialist Party of Greece SKE (Sosialistiko Komma tis Ellados) and the Agrarian Party AKE (Agrotiko Komma Elladas), so that EAM would remain synonymous with KKE.[2]

In Athens Leeper was enthusiastic and suggested to Plastiras that he take one of the dissidents into his Cabinet, which would prove that EAM had ceased to exist. Since Plastiras rejected this, Leeper came up with a new suggestion: the dissidents were to arrive in Athens on the 11th January; Plastiras should receive them, praise them for their stand and recommend that, together with their comrades in Athens, they should issue a statement that EAM was dissolved and that they themselves fully supported the Greek government. This Plastiras accepted.[3]

Leeper's 'promptings' were immediately translated into action on the Greek side: on the 10th January he received a visit from a delegation of Greek trade union representatives with a long-winded condemnation of communist action and thanks to the British for rescue from communist tyranny.[4] On the 12th January he reported that five representatives of ELD, SKE and AKE from Salonica had visited him: these three socialist parties had all broken with EAM which had thereby ceased to exist.[5] The Foreign Office Press Department edited Rapp's and Leeper's telegrams and, together with a similar SKE statement, issued them to the press on the 11th January. These published versions could not but give the impression that the two socialist parties had officially broken with the communists and left the EAM coalition; that the Greek workers organised in the trade unions also opposed EAM and that in Salonica AKE had broken away from EAM, with the result that EAM had become a wholly communist organisation.[6]

Since the supposition that EAM was in dissolution was to play a central part in the forthcoming parliamentary debates, we must throw a more searching light on these three 'documents'. The published version of the so-called ELD statement produced the impression that it had been issued by the ELD Central Committee in Athens; whereas in fact it originated— as we have seen—from a few individuals in Salonica whose relationship to ELD was not wholly clear. Even Leeper had second thoughts on reading the British press reports and warned the Foreign Office.[7] But London kept on course and, on 16th January, Churchill himself requested detailed particulars of the dissidents since the pro-EAM press in Britain was raising doubts about them.[8] Leeper replied that the Opposition press did not know the names of the dissidents—who were actually not very important people—and that therefore it was easy for them to cast doubts on their significance.[9] In other words, Leeper knew that the ELD statement was worthless. A few days later, this statement was disavowed by the ELD leader, Ilias Tsirimokos, in a speech at Patras;[10] but by then it was too late: the impression that ELD had broken with EAM remained in force. ELD did in fact later break away from EAM, but as late as mid-March 1945.[11] However, Leeper's warning caused London to be more cautious in its handling of the ELD issue and instead to stress the importance of the SKE statement of the 11th.

Like ELD, SKE was not a party in the West-European sense but rather a patronage-and-clientèle group typical of the Greek political landscape, in other words the personal clientèle of the party leader of the moment.[12] Since the founding of the Greek Communist Party, there had no longer been a socialist party of any significance. ELD and SKE were new growths of the Occupation period. However, there was another tiny group which laid claim to the name SKE but did not belong to EAM.[13] The leaders of SKE were Dimitrios Stratis and Alexandros Svolos. The provenance of the SKE statement is even more obscure. As a result of research, Sir Richard Acland, MP, was able to state on 30th January, that none of the signatories had been even a local SKE leader.[14] In fact SKE too broke away from EAM in March 1945 and shortly afterwards amalgamated with

ELD.[15] Further, the supposition that AKE had split off from EAM was absolutely without foundation, seeing that AKE was a peasant equivalent of KKE.

These facts were known to the British government since the Foreign Office had a personalities index from which Acland's information could be readily verified.[16] Nevertheless, the Foreign Office held to its thesis about the disintegration of EAM and Eden made this his central argument in the House of Commons debate on the 19th January.[17] He did, however, confine himself to the political parties and made no mention of the trade union statement. The reason for this was very simple: unlike contact between the Labour Party and the Greek socialists, contact between the TUC and the Greek trade unions had never been completely interrupted and the TUC knew something of the people involved and was therefore in a position to react with immediate criticism of the press statement of the 11th January. Professor Harold Laski characterised the Greek trade union representatives as 'phoney'.[18] This is not the place to examine the problem of the Greek trade unions which will be dealt with in connection with the TUC delegation: here we will only record the relevant results. Both the information available and the reaction from Labour and TUC circles caused the Foreign Office to desist from further efforts to maintain its thesis that the Greek trade unions too had broken away from EAM and to restrict itself to the thesis of a split amongst the political parties.

Parallel with this well-aimed disinformation policy, there began a general press campaign against EAM–ELAS. Stereotype letters from British soldiers in Greece, with a varying number of signatures, were published in local and national newspapers, all effusively justifying Churchill's policy and therefore suggesting official inspiration.[19] Nevertheless, despite the censorship, up to the 18th January British press reporting had been relatively objective, of which Leeper had more than once bitterly complained.[20] On the 15th January he made detailed suggestions as to how the situation in Athens should be interpreted and commented:

'The only way that peace can be restored throughout Greece is not by a compromise with the Communists but by the authority of the Greek government being imposed everywhere... I am sure... that the very unintelligent foreign correspondents here will fasten on every defect they can find in the handling of the situation by the Greek government. They have no background knowledge or understanding of these people. What is more American correspondents are not even likely to recall the aftermath of their civil war; nor have British correspondents now here any recollection of the bloodshed in Eire by Irish Government–I.R.A. after rebellion was over.'

And he went on to recommend a hard line in the forthcoming House of Commons debate.[21] So as to supply the Foreign Office with the relevant material, he sent a telegram in which he reported one case in which ELAS had taken British civilians hostage, adding recommendations as to how this could be most effectively exploited.[22] Further telegrams contained a report on the experiences of two British prisoners of war, another on the northwards march of the Greek civilian prisoners and one on the discovery of corpses in the Athens suburb of Peristeri. Apart from the personal experiences of the two soldiers, all this information was second-hand.[23] Thus primed, Churchill and Eden faced the House of Commons.

Churchill began his report on British policy in Greece with a review of developments since mid-December. Then he went over to the attack. He quoted Leeper's telegram (R 1148/4/19 of 15th January) in such a way that the passage in which Leeper made recommendations about interpretation appeared as a factual report. When Aneurin Bevan demanded that the entire text be submitted to the House, Churchill refused on national security grounds and tacked on the report of the northwards march of the Greek civilian prisoners and the discovery of corpses at Peristeri.[24] The reactions of the House are best illustrated by Churchill's telegram to Leeper:

'Do not go worrying too much about public opinion here or the Opposition Press. You will never satisfy the confirmed E.L.A.S.-ites. We have, however, I think isolated and discredited them. Your telegrams about various atrocities read out by me in the House today produced a great sensation, and the Foreign Secretary will add to them tomorrow. Mr. Aneurin Bevan claimed that having quoted these documents we should publish them as a White Paper. We shall certainly do so with alacrity and add to them any further reports that come in. It is, however, absolutely vital that they should be well-founded and that the names of those responsible for them should be given... Not one voice was raised today in favour of the retention of hostages and Mr. Greenwood, who spoke for the non-Ministerial members of the Labour Party, was outspoken in his repugnance at this form of cruelty.'[25]

After Churchill had thus succeeded in destroying the moral integrity of EAM–ELAS, the Tory member Quintin Hogg, later Lord Hailsham, called for 'unity of all democrats': the Labour members should distinguish themselves clearly from the small radical clique amongst them who took the side of EAM.[26] On the 19th January, the Commonwealth MP Acland tried to pull things together again. He rejected Churchill's propaganda about atrocities and maintained that, in a civil war, it was irrelevant who had committed the greater cruelties. The decisive question was which side had pushed matters beyond the point where discussion and compromise were still possible.[27] Churchill's speech was only intended to split the Labour Party, some of whose members were always ready to run a hundred miles or more if one could convince them that there was a communist anywhere in their vicinity. Then Acland pointed out that not one single known non-communist EAM leader had detached himself from EAM. Finally he pointed out that the trade union delegation which had visited Leeper had been composed of extremely dubious elements.[28] But for lack of information even Acland could not refute Churchill's atrocity stories, he could only reduce their impact. At the end of the debate, Eden made further unscrupulous use of the government's advantage in regard to information, documenting the dissolution of EAM from the so-called SKE statement and suggesting in addition that ELD and AKE had also seceded from EAM.[29] The Opposition members could only cast doubts on this supposition but could not directly disprove it (though Acland did so convincingly on the 30th January). The result was that the impression left on public opinion was that EAM was a band of communist murderers from which all decent elements had seceded. To keep this impression firm and not have it shaken by critical press reports, the censorship established at the beginning of December was maintained into February.[30]

During the House of Commons debate on the 18th January, Churchill had promised that he would publish the documents quoted in his House of Commons speech as a White Paper. In his telegram of the 19th to Leeper, he mentioned a plan to send a British Enquiry Commission to Athens, to investigate the ELAS atrocities; at the same time he urged Leeper to carry on with the exhumations of atrocity victims and send him further reports.[31] The incoming reports from Leeper and from AGIS (Anglo-Greek Information Service, an organisation coming under the Political Warfare Executive)[32] were so featureless as to have little propaganda value;[33] and moreover the Opposition Members were insisting that *all* the documents from November onwards must be published.[34] Since this could have proved embarrassing for the government, it was decided only to publish the documents quoted by Churchill, plus a few others. This was done at the beginning of February.[35]

So the White Paper contained only these documents. Leeper's suggested interpretations of the 15th January were quoted at length but the fairly extensive omissions were not marked (by the use of dots). To these were added a few telegrams from Consul-General Rapp retailing rumours, a doctored version of the EDES charter and the text of a resolution passed at a mass meeting of Athens right-wingers on the 14th January.[36]

Churchill could relax and now had no need for the publication of a further White Paper on EAM–ELAS extremism. He had found a way to get the required reports compiled by witnesses who would be above suspicion, by a TUC delegation under the leadership of Sir Walter Citrine.[37] How this delegation which should have concerned itself with Greek trade union problems was re-oriented by Churchill for his political purposes is a story probably unique in international trade union history.

It began in September 1944, when the Assistant-Minister for Finance in Papandreou's government-in-exile, Angelos Angelopoulos, (one of PEEA's ministers) was in London for negotiations with the British government. A representative of the international trade union movement made unofficial contact with him and suggested that a Greek trade union delegation should come to London and perhaps take part in the World Trade Union Congress planned for February 1945. The trade union leaders Kalomoiris, Theos and Laskaris were suggested as possible delegates.[38] The next contact was at the beginning of November 1944, when the British Embassy transmitted an invitation from the General Confederation of Greek Labour (GSEE, Geniki Synomospondia Ergaton Ellados, from now on referred to as GCL), signed by Kalomoiris and Theos, through the Foreign Office to the TUC, to send representatives to Greece, to investigate German depredations.[39] But before an answer could be sent, the December conflict broke out and prevented further contact.

After the December events, the first contact with Leeper had come when the trade union delegation visited him on the 10th January. This deputation represented seventeen unions from Athens, Piraeus and Mytilene. Its spokesman was a certain Krokos representing the British and American oil companies' personnel. After their address of thanks, they told Leeper the following: that the GCL Executive had instructed all unions which under existing circumstances were in a position to do so, to form provisional committees and proceed within ten to fifteen days to elections. They hoped to be able to call a GCL Congress within six months at which all the provinces, including those at present under ELAS, would be represented and which would elect a new Executive. Leeper then went on:

> 'Furthermore, they expressed an earnest hope either that a deputation formed from among themselves might go to England, in order to renew their contacts with the Trades Union Congress, or, better still, that a delegation of the latter body might come to Greece, in order to study the conditions on the spot. They had heard a rumour that Kalomoiris and Theos and some of their colleagues were intending to go to London in an effort to influence the British Labour Party. They wished it to be generally known in England that these men were not entitled to speak on any matter on behalf of the Greek trade unions whose fully accredited representatives they themselves were.'[40]

The TUC's reaction to this statement was extremely reserved. So the Foreign Office asked Leeper for more information,[41] which he supplied during the next few days.[42] We have said that the content of Leeper's telegrams was such as to make the Foreign Office very cautious in its handling of the trade union issue. On the 15th January there was discussion in Downing Street with the Labour leaders Arthur Greenwood, Professor Harold Laski and Aneurin Bevan on British policy in Greece, though no information is available as to the result of this. But it can be assumed that amongst other things the possible despatch of a TUC delegation was discussed. Whatever happened, the next day, when the General-Secretary of the TUC, Sir Walter Citrine, visited Churchill, it was definite that he would lead a delegation to Greece.

Churchill made use of this conversation to outline Citrine's task. He was to concern himself with Greek trade union problems and help in rebuilding the Greek unions. To this end he would have free access to Leeper and Scobie, who would also arrange his contacts with the Regent, the Prime Minister and other ministers. But it was neither part of his job to inform the British government about the political situation, nor to make suggestions how present difficulties could be overcome. At the same time, however, Citrine naturally was to form personal impressions which he, Churchill, would be extremely interested to hear. He, personally, was of the opinion that Citrine should not cross the demarcation line into ELAS territory since this had nothing to do with his particular mission.[43]

Churchill then told Eden that Citrine had understood what it was about and should be supplied with some background briefing.[44] On the 17th January Eden and Citrine had a talk which Eden described as good. Eden got the impression that Citrine wanted to be helpful. He had agreed that, given the long period during which the Greek trade unions had been non-existent, it was not surprising that the names of the trade union leaders were unknown in Britain. Addressing himself to Leeper, Eden recommended the greatest possible care: 'If I may suggest it, I feel sure he will respond to any attention you can give him'—a recommendation which was to find a positive response.[45]

In other words: the British government laid down the framework within which Citrine was to operate; he was forbidden to concern himself with political issues or to speak to the opposing side. Citrine, for his part, by his remark to Eden, signalled that he would pursue a helpful line. Citrine's sphere of action became extremely restricted.

The delegation arrived in Athens on the 22nd January and returned to London on the 3rd February. During this whole time Citrine had adhered rigorously to Churchill's instructions. In contrast to the editor of the *News Chronicle,* Gerald Barry, who was investigating in Athens at almost exactly the same time (18th January–1st February) and who took pains to talk to all sides,[46] Citrine restricted his talks to the government side. He refused to speak with representatives of the political parties and, with the exception of one discussion with the trade union leaders Kalomoiris, Stratis, Theos and Mariolis on 27th January, had no contact with the Greek Left. In accordance with Churchill's instructions, Citrine's delegation confined itself to trade union problems and to such 'unpolitical' topics as the morale of the British troops, the corpses exhumed at Peristeri, the hostage question and the prisoners of war.

Citrine's programme had been skilfully organised by Leeper. On the 23rd January the delegation visited Damaskinos and questioned him about the truth of the suggestion that the Greek government had arrested a great number of people who were being treated as hostages. Damaskinos denied this indignantly and stressed the strictly constitutional behaviour of the government. During the following visit to the Minister for Justice, the TUC delegation received the same answer: owing to organisational problems, the housing of the detainees was under somewhat straitened and difficult conditions, but access to a prison would be readily permitted. In contrast to Gerald Barry, the TUC delegation expressed itself satisfied with its prison visit (on 24th January): the Greek government was doing its best to improve conditions of detention and to release as soon as possible those who had been unjustly arrested. Citrine expressed himself completely re-assured when he heard that the Greek government had invited a British Police Mission to help in re-organising the Greek police.[47]

For 'variety', Leeper organised an interview with Greek hostages recently released by ELAS. Citrine noted their poor clothing and listened to their reports of mistreatment by the ELAS guards.[48] The delegation was then taken to Peristeri and shown the graves with the already decaying corpses. This horrible sight had its expected effect—the delegation uncritically accepted the official version that the corpses were murdered ELAS hostages. Interviews with relatives of the victims strengthened the impression that here was a case of organised mass murder. The delegation's report spoke of 10,000 murdered—the figure Damaskinos had quoted.[49]

We have dealt elsewhere with the problem of the shooting of hostages;[50] here we will summarise as follows. The theory that there were wholesale mass executions can no longer be sustained. There is no doubt that KKE's secret police, OPLA (Organosis Perifrourisis Laikon Agonon, Organisation for the Safeguarding of Popular Struggles) did proceed to executions during the second phase of the December fighting, though it is not certain whether this was done on authorisation from the Political Bureau or not.[51] People's courts were also functioning and sentencing notorious collaborators.[52] The actual number of their victims is unknown. The figure given by Damaskinos is greatly exaggerated since British service reports of that date speak of 1,500 corpses found.[53] Moreover, many of those found dead at Peristeri and elsewhere were not murdered but had died a natural death or had been killed during the fighting and were only posthumously mutilated and transported there by right-wing bands.

It is still to-day extremely difficult to obtain reliable information about these 'murders'. When the author tried to research this during the Junta period, no one except the former EDES Resistance leader and left-liberal politician, Komninos Pyromaglou, proved ready to supply information. But even Pyromaglou asked the author not to mention his name, not because he feared trouble for himself, but because through him his witness —at that time still a serving police officer—could have been traced. Pyromaglou told the author that in 1958, when he was elected to parliament as an EDA deputy, he was one day visited by this police officer, who, under the seal of secrecy, gave him the following sworn statement: during the Occupation he had served as an officer in the Security Battalions; at the end of December 1944 it had been suggested to him that he could re-habilitate himself if, during the next nights, he would exhume the dead who had died either from natural causes or as a result of the fighting in Athens and had been temporarily buried in the park behind the parliament building and transport them by lorry to Peristeri. This task he had carried out with a number of former Security Battalion men. At Peristeri the corpses were then mutilated and thrown into those mass graves where Citrine saw them. Since that time, these events had been on his conscience and, to free himself, he was telling Pyromaglou. The author has no reason to doubt this report since, after the fall of the Junta, he himself came across two cases of eye-witness testimony from people who were forced to identify relatives who had died a natural death during the December fighting and had been buried amongst the murder victims at Peristeri. Marion Sarafis, too, writes of two similar cases known to her in her introduction to the English edition of *ELAS*. Obviously, Colin Wright, a member of the British intervention force, was right when he wrote in a letter of 13th March 1945:

'. . . Investigations into the atrocity stories are being carried out by EAM and I think we will find that most of it has been pure moonshine. Some frightful tricks have been perpetrated, it is alleged, by the Right against the Left. People who have died from natural causes have been exhumed, noses and ears cut off, eyes removed and genitals interfered with, and corpses shown as ELAS atrocities. People have come forward and declared on oath that relatives' graves have been tampered with. . .'[54]

In this context it is significant that the *New York Times* was all along very reserved about the alleged ELAS victims.

British press censorship was maintained in force and Churchill refrained from sending the Enquiry Commission about which he had told Leeper. The Embassy reports, including eye-witness testimonies to the atrocities, are remarkably vague;[55] and finally the press reports of the ELAS massacres ended as abruptly as they had begun, with the publication of the TUC Report. Whilst there is unquestionably a grain of truth in the massacre reports, one is nevertheless left with the impression that the actual murders were multiplied by Greek and British sources out of all proportion so as to blacken EAM-ELAS in the eyes of world public opinion.

The presence of Citrine, who had no experience of this type of Greek intrigue, was a happy coincidence and his testimony was far more convincing than, say, Leeper's reports. At the same time he was far more credulous than hard-bitten war correspondents of independent newspapers. Moreover, to make quite sure of the desired result, Leeper had assigned to Citrine as interpreter a certain Roxane Sedgwick who came from an extremely conservative Greek family and was married to the 'ultra-reactionary' US correspondent A.C. Sedgwick whose provocative articles had at that time raised protests in New York.[56]

In contrast to Gerald Barry, who had also visited Peristeri and interviewed hostages and who also condemned EAM–ELAS extremism but nevertheless sought for motives and explanations, Citrine after his visit felt only horror of the Greek Left. Addressing an audience of British paratroops detailed by Scobie next day, he toed Leeper's line exactly. By asking loaded questions he provoked his audience to violent attacks on the British press and the Left of the Labour Party. He let himself be told of ELAS' unfair fighting methods and accepted the assertion that ELAS had not fought the retreating Germans; had the British troops not intervened against ELAS, there would have been a massacre of gigantic proportions; the mistake had been that the troops were brought into action too late.[57] According to the TUC Report, not a single voice testified to understanding for EAM–ELAS. Scobie's stage-management had been a complete success.

On the 26th January, the delegation at last found time for its real task—Greek trade union problems. At a banquet organised for the TUC delegation by Greek trade unionists, Citrine made a speech in which he sternly lectured the British press. Leeper was delighted.[58] As Citrine himself acknowledged, the Greek trade union situation was somewhat confused and he decided that on this, too, he would follow Churchill's policy and do nothing to change the *status quo,* in other words, here too he took a stand against the Greek Left.

But before we proceed with the Citrine delegation's activities in regard to the trade union question, we need to take a bird's eye view of the Greek trade unions.[59]

The roots of Greek trade unionism stretch far back into the 19th century but the unions' importance in national political life dates from 1909 when a section of the labour movement took part in the Goudi revolution. The liberal bourgeoisie, who came to power under the leadership of Eleftherios Venizelos, was worried about the attitude of the workers and lower middle class at future elections and feared the development of class conflict on the Western European model which, given the political unreliability of the army, could threaten its position. Use was therefore made of a two-fold strategy: on the one hand a series of social welfare laws sought to mitigate the worst effects of nascent capitalism; on the other a successful effort was undertaken to bring the trade union movement under State control. For this reason, the Ministry for Economics, established in 1911, acquired a Department of Labour and Social Affairs which was to have the final word in all labour conflicts and which could, by administrative measures, control the internal affairs of the trade unions. To round off this paternalistic system, Venizelos had one of his party members organise the first Trades Council, the Athens Labour Centre. This institution, organised on the French *(bourse du travail)* model, became in its turn the model for the whole of Greece. During the course of the following years and parallel with growing industrialisation, similar Trades Councils were established in many provincial towns. Venizelos' paternalistic treatment of the trade unions could not prevent socialist ideas from finding an ear in individual unions and so the first conflicts arose. The situation became sharper during the Balkan Wars and in 1914 the government was obliged to make some concessions to the trade unions.

Law 281/1914 accorded workers the right to organise. But the State still retained certain prerogatives: a trade union could only attain legally recognised status when it had submitted its charter to a Court of First Instance for approbation. But even after that, government inspectors and provincial Prefects[60] could intervene in internal union affairs and, for example, remove a union official who was not doing his job properly. A union pursuing aims which exceeded those sanctioned by its charter could be dissolved by court order.[61] Although the trade unions had the right to organise beyond strictly local limits, the movement remained in general decentralised until 1918. The role of the state as arbiter in labour disputes still held. Legal regulations determining state control of the trade unions were later repeatedly modified but remained substantially in force until the end of the Second World War.

Modifications were made to this system by the first All-Greek Trade Union Congress in October 1918. Here it became obvious that amongst the unions there were three political trends. There were the supporters of the former paternalist system, who called themselves Reformists and enjoyed government support. The two other groups represented the right and left wings of the socialistically-inclined trade unions. The socialist movement had, at that time, not yet split[62] and socialist delegates had a majority amongst the Congress participants. Therefore they could carry through their political line. Whilst the Reformists maintained that the unions should only fight for better working conditions and higher pay and should abstain from all political activity, the socialist unionists put forward as the central plank of their future programme the advancement of the class struggle and defence against every form of state intervention. The text of the Greek Confederation of Labour's (GSEE) founding resolution shows that the socialists had won their point.[63]

But the socialist success in no way meant that the Greek trade unions had emancipated themselves from State guardianship. The GCL did indeed acquire a hierarchy consisting of an Executive Committee, a Secretariat and a Trade Union Congress meeting at regular intervals which together put an end to the extreme localisation of the Greek unions; and the foundation of ten Pan-hellenic Federations indicated a readiness on the part of the unions to consolidate more closely. But, as regards basic control by the state, nothing was changed. The system for the supervision of individual unions, laid down in Law 281/1914, remained in force. Law 2151 of 1920 gave the state even greater potential control. The result, which held good until the end of the Second World War, gives the following picture.

The basis of the Greek trade union movement continued to be the individual unions in which the various trades were organised according to local conditions. Of these there were in all Greece more than one thousand. The unions in any one town came together in the local Trades Council of which, in the inter-war years, there were over forty. Parallel with this structure, there were the Federations in which related trade unions came together at a national level. Since affiliation to these Federations was voluntary, even for unions representing the same trade, the Federations did not become—as one might have expected—agents for unification of the Greek trade unions, but only contributed to their further splintering, as these in their turn were independent competing organisations. However, the decisive obstacle to the development of big, powerful and militant unions was the method of election for the national Trade Union Congress.

The GCL statutes provided that each individual union should send at least one delegate to the Congress; whilst even the biggest unions and the Federations could not send more than seven.[64] The significance of this unrepresentative, undemocratic system can be judged from two concrete examples: a union with 3,500 members had seven representatives at the GCL Congress, against which the same number of workers organised in local mini-unions might control over one hundred representatives; and, whilst thirty local unions—with no more than 5,000 members between them—would have thirty representatives, an organisation with 100,000 members based on the industrial centre of Athens and Piraeus would send only seven representatives.[65] The consequence of this system was an increase in the number of individual unions (at the founding GCL Congress there had been forty-four participating unions representing approximately 75,000 organised workers)[66] which in no way represented the increasing industrialisation of Greece but instead demonstrated that each political group took pains to create its own trade unions, be they never so small, so as to secure a majority at the GCL Congress.[67]

The reason for this struggle for the Congress majority was because Congress elected the Executive Committee and the Secretary. In sharp contrast to the *Deutsche Gewerksschaftsbund* or the TUC, the GCL leadership had rights of control over the individual unions. It laid down policy for the Greek trade union movement and individual unions which got out of line could be excluded from the GCL. This position of the GCL leadership was strengthened by the fact that, until 1935, the Greek trade unions did not have the right independently to bargain wage agreements. Every wage agreement reached by a local union—no matter how insignificant—had to be submitted through the GCL leadership to the Ministry for Labour, for vetting and ratification. Thus, the GCL leadership acquired the functions of a pressure group and therefore directly invited state intervention in the composition of its membership. In this way the Ministry for Labour came to play the central role in the settling of labour disputes. The results of this system were highly unsatisfactory.

Within the GCL, the unions were transformed into unofficial State unions; and the leadership was subjected at all levels to the favouritism so well-known from Greek political party life—nepotism and *rousfetism* (patronage and favouritism). Corruption and position-hunting became characteristic traits of many GCL officials whose only anxiety was to retain their posts at any price. To put it briefly, the GCL was completely integrated into the political system of inter-war Greece. Thus splintered and decentralised, the Greek trade union movement was not an opponent those centralised state agencies which looked after the interests of Greek industry needed to take seriously.

The disunity of the Greek working class likewise contributed to the splintering of the trade union movement initiated and fostered by the state. Despite these divergent tendencies, at the first Congress a split had been avoided by the election of an Executive Committee with representatives from all three trends. But the foundation of the Socialist Workers' Party of Greece (SEKE) a few days after the end of the Congress brought the inner tensions to the surface. A section of the Executive Committee supported cooperation with SEKE, whilst the so-called Reformists demanded independence of political parties. At an emergency Trade Union Congress in 1919, summoned with the help of the well-organised Macedonian unions, the SEKE supporters were able to prevail and this led to the withdrawal of the conservative Reformists and the founding of a competitor organisation. The Venizelos government realised the danger to the existing system presented by a revolutionary socialist GCL and had its leadership deported. The unions thereupon called a general strike which, by reason of the low level of organisation, proved unsuccessful but nevertheless has gone down in history as the first politically-motivated strike of the Greek trade unions.

In April 1920 came the second SEKE Congress which decided to affiliate to the Third International and to change the party's name to SEKE(K) (for communist). This resulted in resignations and a splitting off of social-democrat orientated groups and personalities, and in the splitting of the socialist camp within the trade unions. In mid-September 1920 the second GCL Congress met in Athens, only to be confronted, a few days later, with a competing Congress held by the Reformists in

Piraeus. Both Congresses claimed to represent the GCL. At the Congress called by the progressive forces it came to an open breach between supporters of the Second and Third Internationals; whilst the Reformists' Congress resolved to abstain in future from all forms of political activity. The following years were characterised by a three-cornered conflict between these trends which made it possible for the government to clamp down by means of its control system.

In 1926 when they realised how far political divisiveness had reduced the efficiency of trade union work, all three trends decided to hold the third Trade Union Congress jointly like the first one in 1918. This had been preceded by the third Emergency Congress of SEKE(K) in December 1924, at which the party changed its name to Communist Party of Greece (KKE) and ratified the Comintern's Macedonian policy according to which the Slavonic-speaking part of Greek Macedonia was to be incorporated in a future Macedonian state. This mistake, loaded with disastrous implications, was deeply wounding to the feelings of all Greek patriots and indicative of the complete submission of the Greek Communists to the Comintern. This and the mistaken steam-roller tactics of the KKE trade union representative at the GCL Congress, had the effect of producing a voting alliance between the Reformists and the socialists which secured the majority at this Congress. Faced with repressive measures on the part of the state (the Pangalos dictatorship) against KKE, including a series of arrests of communist trade union leaders and brutal suppression of strikes by the police and the courts which threatened to paralyse all trade union activity, the Congress—after a further State intervention when communist delegates were arrested off the Congress floor—found it convenient to abstain from all political activity for the future. After the conclusion of the Congress, the Executive Committee, which—though the Socialist Dimitrios Stratis was General-Secretary—was controlled by the Reformists around Ioannis Kalomoiris, decided to sever the contacts existing since 1920 with the Comintern's trade union organisation and affiliate to the Amsterdam IFTU. At the same time, it began to expel communist-orientated trade union formations (amongst them forty organisations representing 45,000 tobacco workers), despite the fact that the third Congress had renewed the second Congress's decision for cooperation with KKE. The communist-orientated trade unions under the leadership of Kostas Theos thereafter directed their main effort to the grassroots and built up revolutionary fractions within the local unions which should unmask the 'social fascists' (socialists and Reformists) and function as cadres for projected new communist trade unions.

At the fourth Trade Union Congress in May 1928 communist and non-communist delegates actually came to blows and, when some of those who caused the disturbance were excluded from further participation in the Congress, all 170 communist delegates left in protest, denouncing the remaining 282 socialists and Reformists as fascists. The fourth KKE Party Conference in December 1928 resolved to intensify the attack on the 'social fascists' and to work for the creation of a new, revolutionary trade union organisation. Finally, in February 1929, the Unifying GCL (Enotiki GSEE) was founded, representing 300 unions with about 70,000 members, the majority of whom were the tobacco workers expelled in 1926.

This organisational split in the Greek trade union movement enabled Venizelos' government to pick off the communist unions by legal action. Over the next years such unions and Federations and communist-led Trades Councils were dissolved and their leading activists imprisoned or deported. A further measure to bring the unruly unions under state control was the institution of the Ergatiki Estia (*lit.* Labour Hearth), a sort of trade union fund financed by business and by the government and administered by a tripartite committee of business men, GCL leaders and the Ministry for Labour. The relevant law provided that unions which pursued activities directed against the government would receive no contributions.

But disagreements developed between socialists and Reformists as well. The socialist, Dimitrios Stratis, elected General-Secretary by the third Congress and confirmed in office by the fourth, who had been elected to the newly-formed Second Chamber, the Senate, in 1929 as representative of the GCL, turned against the increasingly open state intervention in internal union affairs and began, for his part, to build up socialist groups within the trade unions. At the fifth GCL Congress in 1930, it came to a clash between socialists and Reformists (the communists did not participate) and the government openly sided with the Reformists. Ioannis Kalomoiris became the new General-Secretary. Thereupon the socialist unions left the GCL and formed their own organisation, the All-Greek General Confederation (Panelladiki Geniki Synomospondia). This reduced the GCL to a Venizelist party trade union. At the sixth GCL Congress in 1932 neither socialists nor communists participated.

The effects of the world economic crisis, the rise of fascism in Germany, the internal power struggle in which Panayotis Tsaldaris defeated Venizelos, the fear of an impending military dictatorship and KKE's change of line to a Popular Front strategy, combined to bring about a *rapprochement* between the three trade union organisations from the grassroots and against the opposition of the GCL leadership. Accordingly at the seventh GCL Congress in 1934, voices were heard demanding reunion of the movement, resulting in a joint declaration against fascism in October of that year.[68] In 1935, the socialist confederation dissolved itself and some of its members returned to the GCL which for that reason—and because the Venizelists were now the Opposition—began to take an antigovernment line: together with the Unifying GCL strikes were organised.

At the start of 1936, negotiations began between the two GCLs at base level with the aim of creating a new, independent GCL. The government's repressive measures which reached a high point of brutality in the forcible suppression of the strike of 9th May 1936, strengthened the pressure of the rank-and-file on the GCL leadership and in July 1936 it was decided to call a Unification Congress and to organise a 24-hour General Strike for the 5th August. The *coup d'état* of Metaxas and George II on 4th August put an end to both these plans.

Like early Italian fascism, Greek fascism had certain 'socialist' traits. Metaxas announced a minimal 'social' programme which corresponded to some long-term demands of Greek labour but in point of fact served to exploit the workers more thoroughly. Then he set about 're-organising' the trade unions. He appointed as Minister for Labour Aristidis Dimitratos, a former communist trade unionist who had gone over to the right-wing of the Reformists in the twenties. Dimitratos proved himself the right man for this programme of *Gleichschaltung* (Nazi term for enforced uniformity). First, he appointed people who enjoyed his confidence as officials in all trade unions and opposition union leaders were either arrested and deported or forced to amalgamate their unions with the GCL. Then he called a GCL Congress and had himself elected General-Secretary. At the same time the right to strike and the right to found new unions were abrogated. In 1938 Law 1435 recognised the system of state trade unionism. From then on the minister had the right to recognise a union of his own choice as sole legitimate representative of each trade union or profession. This union alone had the right to negotiate with the ministry over wage contracts—as far as these still existed. Thus, the Labour Ministry not only controlled, as before, relations between unions and employers but even the unions themselves. To reinforce this control, Dimitratos introduced compulsory membership of the respective trade union and the payment by each member of compulsory dues, to be deducted by the employer from the pay packet and paid into the Bank of Greece where it was administered and distributed by the Minister for Labour and the GCL leadership. At the same time individual unions were forbidden to put aside money, for instance a strike fund, without permission from the ministry, even if they had the means available. The funds which the GCL put at the disposal of the individual unions were administered by the Trades Councils who thus became another force for control and acquired an importance far in excess of that of the Federations. In addition, Dimitratos reserved to himself the right to intervene in internal union administration whenever he wished and to sack officials of whom he did not approve. This right was also extended to regional Governors-General and provincial Prefects. The system was completed with the introduction of a Labour Corps on the German *Reichsarbeitsdienst* (Nazi state labour service, a compulsory pre- and paramilitary labour organisation) model. Briefly, the fascist system introduced by Dimitratos mirrored fairly faithfully its pattern, the *Deutsche Arbeitsfront* (a Nazi organisation uniting workers and employers) but, unlike its model remained almost completely in force until the mid-sixties and its inventor had later (as Labour Minister in the Karamanlis government of 1958-61) the opportunity to see how well it still worked.

Paradoxically, it was the occupation of Greece by the Axis which first brought life into this rigid system of control. Shortly before his flight to foreign exile, Dimitratos had handed back his post as General-Secretary of the GCL to Kalomoiris, who had lain low during the period of the Metaxas dictatorship, inactive but by no means in opposition. Kalomoiris at first collaborated with the Germans but later—probably opportunistically—joined EEAM (Ergatiko Ethniko Apeleftherotiko Metopo, the EAM Trade Union Liberation Front). The trade union mechanism set up by Dimitratos continued to function under the Occupation: the compulsory dues were further raised and the officials saw to it that the unions functioned smoothly, this time in the service of the occupying powers. Had it depended only on the fascist regime's trade union officials, nothing would have disturbed this good understanding. But, on the 16th July 1941, on KKE's initiative, EEAM was founded with the participation of all political trends within the Greek trade union movement, with the exception of the fascists. Woodhouse describes these developments as follows:

'There was a clear-cut division between collaborating puppets on the one side and EEAM on the other; there were no fine shades, no indeterminate borderline occupied by ambiguous adventurers anxious to keep a foot in both camps. Outside EEAM there was no organised body at the time that could claim to represent the workers. After the liberation of Greece a new such body was formed by official action, and led successively by Hadjidhimitriou and Makris; but neither represented any serious section of opinion, and their group was not even in being before the early months of 1945. During the occupation, therefore, Greek labour was exhaustively represented by the coalition of Theos, Kalomoiris and Stratis.'[69]

Although EEAM was created by the communists, it never became a mere creature of KKE. On the Central Committee, Kalomoiris' followers had nine seats, those of Theos four and those of Stratis two. EEAM in fact became the means of re-uniting the Greek working class. Its activities were highly successful. EEAM organised sabotage and several major strikes and its resistance was responsible for the failure of Saukel (Hitler's Minister of Labour) to recruit forced labour in Greece.

By 1944 EEAM had penetrated the whole of the old trade union movements and had built up its own organisational structure which, by the end of the Occupation, numbered 200,000 members. As ELAS liberated the

Greek mountains, so EEAM units liberated the eastern working class suburbs of Athens so that, from summer 1944, they were outside the control of the occupying power and the Quisling government. Simultaneously with the creation of PEEA (Politiki Epitropi Ethnikis Apeleftherosis, Political Committee for National Liberation)—EAM's provisional government in the liberated Greek mountains—the EEAM Central Committee transferred its seat to the mountains and decided to re-name EEAM as GCL, to constitute itself the provisional GCL Executive Committee and to call the eighth Trade Union Congress at latest in six months' time. This removed all legitimacy from the collaborationist GCL under its General-Secretary Simos Hajidimitriou. The new GCL Executive decided that, as the Germans withdrew, it would take over the Trades Councils, which indeed it did, thereby evoking cries of protest from the former GCL leadership.

On the 30th October 1944 the new GCL leadership under General-Secretary Stratis sent a circular to all trade union organisations suggesting that they hold general meetings to which the presently serving leadership (including the collaborators) should render account and which should elect committees to supervise Executive elections for each union. The former GCL Executive under Hajidimitriou realised that, if the elections were properly carried out, it had no chance of re-election and began to protest against this procedure. Though knowing better, it denounced the new leadership as communist and took its stand on the charge that the new measures were not legally valid. Meanwhile, on the 10th November, the new GCL leadership issued its second circular with further instructions: the elections were to take place on 1st December. Hajidimitriou thereupon appealed to the Labour Minister Miltiadis Porfyrogenis, a communist, and demanded that he use his prerogative to nominate a committee which should also include representatives of Hajidimitriou. Porfyrogenis rightly rejected this on the 28th November, basing himself on the government-in-exile's Law 3127 of 31st October 1942, which had repealed Metaxas' trade union decrees and restored the *status quo ante*. He officially appointed the new GCL leadership under Stratis as provisional Executive with the task of summoning the eighth Trade Union Congress within six months. At the same time it was made clear that there could be no valid objections from basic individual unions. The Council of State (Symvoulio Epikratias—supreme court for administrative issues) certified the legality of the ministerial order. Hajidimitriou now tried to proceed against this order through the courts, alleging that the law of the government-in-exile had not been published in the *Government Gazette* in Greece and was therefore invalid but, before this could be cleared up, the EAM ministers had resigned, the December fighting broke out and the GCL leadership under Stratis retired behind the ELAS lines.

Hajidimitriou seized his opportunity and addressed himself to Prime

Minister Papandreou who instructed the Ministry for Labour to round up some trade union officials who could elect an anti-Executive Committee. Nineteen were found, who elected a General-Secretary—Hajidimitriou, and an Executive Committee—themselves.[70] It seems superfluous to add that all of them were collaborationists from the state trade unions of the Metaxas regime. This was indeed known to the new Labour Minister in the Plastiras Cabinet, Georgios Sideris, but the pathological anti-communism of Greek bourgeois politicians no doubt caused him to see these dubious GCL representatives as a 'lesser evil' and he confirmed them and a few others of their sort in office. It was seventeen of these dubious trade union representatives who formed the delegation which visisted Leeper on the 10th January. The spokesman was Krokos, at one time Dimitratos' right-hand man, since Hajidimitriou was presumably too well-known as a representative of trade union collaboration. But on 14th January he took part in a victory demonstration of the Athens Right and signed the resolution it passed as General-Secretary of the GCL.[71] On 17th January he sent a circular to his trade unions instructing them to hold elections.

This was the situation when Citrine began his investigations. Although he was informed about the part played by Hajidimitriou and had known Kalomoiris personally for years,[72] he accepted the clique installed during the December events as the legitimate GCL leadership. Whether this was through his own anti-communism, or through his wish to carry out Churchill's instructions, or whether he fell victim to his own uninformed credulity is hard to say. On 27th January, in Levadia, the TUC delegation eventually met Stratis, Kalomoiris, Theos and Mariolis (another communist trade unionist). The EAM trade unionists informed Citrine and his colleagues in detail about the situation in the Greek trade unions: it was they who represented the real unions and the legitimacy of their leadership rested on Porfyrogenis' decree. Citrine replied that the present GCL made the same claim in regard to its nomination by Sideris. By saying this, Citrine implicitly accepted and sanctioned the right of the Greek state to intervene in the unions' internal affairs. Thus, a fresh start and a fundamental reform of the Greek trade unions was obstructed. At the same time Citrine made it clear to his interlocutors that there would be no general amnesty for all participants in the December events. In other words, Citrine went completely over to Leeper's line, as the latter had defined it on the 27th January:

'I think it important to make distinction between *pacification* and *reconciliation*. Pacification means the right political tact to achieve as much disarmament of ELAS as possible. In my view this is the object of the coming conference here. Reconciliation is quite unreal and I never use the word with the Greek Government. For example, Siantos and company may get an official amnesty, but if they were to appear thereafter openly in the streets of Athens they would be very quickly bumped off.'[73]

The euphemism 'pacification' concealed the intention to achieve total subjugation of the Greek Left. It is worth noting here that the German Occupation authorities had similarly announced their projects for subjugation as 'pacification measures'. In fact, the parallel with subsequent developments is shattering.

At this time, in the political sphere, the preliminaries for the peace conference were being transacted and Citrine organised a similar conference for trade unionists. He knew as well as Leeper that EAM—and the EAM trade unions—represented a very large proportion, if not the majority, of the population—or in the latter case the working class, and that the communists in both were in the minority. It was impossible to exclude the workers organised in EEAM from the new GCL under construction, since the Hajidimitriou group had hardly any followers. Therefore the EAM trade unions must be brought to sit down with the Hajidimitriou group and to take part in the elections ordained by the latter. Then, on past precedent, these elections would give the desired result, Hajidimitriou's nomination would be legitimised 'after the event' and the EAM trade union leaders would be deprived of their base in the rank-and-file.

To achieve this, Citrine organised a conference on the 29th January in which representatives of both groups and the Labour Minister participated. The EAM union leaders showed themselves ready for compromise: they did not insist on clearing up the legality of Sideris' nomination of the provisional Executive, although this was just as questionable as the nomination of the previous one by Porfyrogenis (the relevant law of 31st October 1942 was only published in the *Government Gazette* on 25th May 1945, long after the conclusion of the Varkiza Agreement); they restricted their demands to a temporary postponement of the new elections. In detail, the agreement reached at this conference covered the following:

In Article 1 it provided that trade union elections must be shown to have been in conformity with the pre-Metaxas legislation.

In Article 2 the same would hold for future elections, which must be conducted as free and democratic ballots.

In Article 3 to guarantee this, they should be observed by judges.

In Article 4 a committee consisting of one representative of the present provisional Executive and one of the former—who must not have been an EAM member—and one from the TUC should supervise the elections which would be held before the 15th February.

In Article 5 the elections were to be restricted to a maximum of twenty unions from Athens and Piraeus.

In Article 6 further elections would be held in other towns as soon as these were under Greek government administration.

In Article 7 as soon as peace was established, the present provisional Executive would be reconstituted in order to represent all trends of the working class. As soon as conditions of tranquility were restored a writ would be issued for fresh elections in all the country's trade union organisations. The Labour Minister took note of this agreement and would give its application his support.[74]

This agreement was signed by the TUC delegation, by the representatives of the Hajidimitriou group and by the interpreter, Roxane Sedgwick. The representatives of the EAM trade unions at first refused to sign on the grounds that no elections should be held before the signature of a peace treaty between EAM and the government. But, when Sideris insisted that elections must be held in the twenty most important unions so that industry could be got going again, they accepted this argument but demanded that further elections should not take place until the thousands of arrested EAM workers and those in hiding had returned to their homes. The GCL representatives would not accept this, whereupon the EAM trade unionists refused to sign the agreement. Instead, they signed a postscript, stating that they would have signed had this condition been accepted.

On the 3rd February the TUC delegation returned to England. On the 9th they published their report. As *The Times* remarked in its commentary of the same date, the report corresponded exactly to the line expounded in the Foreign Office Command Papers. It neither made any contribution to clarifying the causes and background of the December conflict, nor did it show any prospects for the future; the attacks on the reporting by the British press were not substantiated. Its real significance lay elsewhere: this report, from a source apparently independent of the government, appeared to confirm fully Churchill's case about the ELAS atrocities. The TUC Report made the previously planned publication of a second White Paper superfluous since, with its appearance, the EAM cause finally lost all moral stature as far as the general British public was concerned. Nor can its internal political effect in Greece be over-estimated. It sanctioned the restoration of the pre-war regime in the Greek trade unions. All later disagreements over the control of the trade unions, on which we shall have more to say, represented a fighting retreat by the Left and alter nothing to the fact that, by the so-called Citrine Agreement, the Greek Right had once more seized power in the unions. Citrine had fulfilled Churchill's expectations and the TUC boss had willingly allowed himself to be misused as a tool of British imperialism.[75] Leeper's 'guided tour' had proved successful.

Meanwhile in Britain a grassroots protest movement was growing up. Already in 1943, Greeks working in London had formed the Greek Unity Committee in which the Federation of Greek Maritime Unions played an important part. The chief sponsor of this Committee was the well-known British author and philhellene, Sir Compton Mackenzie. Its aims were the formation of a Government of National Unity and enlightenment of British public opinion about the Greek Resistance. The latter was highly necessary to counter Churchill's advice to the BBC in spring 1944 to report nothing favourable to EAM–ELAS.[76] The December events nullified the Committee's first aim but, at the same time, showed how little British public opinion understood what was happening in Greece, which given wartime censorship was not surprising. Therefore the Committee was replaced by a News Agency, Maritpress (later the Greek News Agency), again initiated by the Federation of Greek Maritime Unions.

When it became clear that the Labour government, elected in summer 1945, was not going to change British policy towards Greece, the League for Democracy in Greece was founded in October 1945, under the presidency of Sir Compton Mackenzie and with the support of over eighty Labour Members of Parliament.

Whilst the News Agency addressed itself to the press, the League directed its efforts mainly at the trade union base of the labour movement. The News Agency produced regular bulletins with news not reported by official agencies. The Federation addressed its occasional *Greek Trade Union News* to TUC circles and this was later replaced by the League's *Greek News,* of wider scope, and by its pamphlets on trade union and other topics.

All these publications reached a wide readership amongst trade unionists and members of the Labour Party. An informal pressure group like the League could not succeed in influencing British policy but at a lower level its influence was certainly felt. Its members were well-informed on Greece and this meant that, during the civil war, the appeals by the League for intervention on behalf of persecuted democrats found wide response and contributed effectively to reducing the number of executions in Greece.

This pressure from below had a further illuminating result. When, in 1948, the Director of the Greek Information Office in London, S.L. Hourmouzios, addressed himself to Citrine's successor as TUC General-Secretary, Vincent Tewson,[77] and suggested a reprint of the Citrine Report, his suggestion was turned down flat. Clearly, the TUC leadership had in the meantime realised the true character of this report.[78]

NOTES

1. Macmillan, *op. cit.,* p. 640.
2. Rapp to Leeper 10th January, 1945 (R 767/4/19).
3. Leeper to Foreign Office 10th January, 1945 (R 775/4/19).
4. *The Times,* 12th January, 1945.
5. Leeper to Foreign Office 12th January, 1945 (R 956/4/19).
6. *The Times,* 12th January, 1945.

7. Leeper to Foreign Office 13th January, 1945 (R 1048/4/19).
8. Foreign Office (Prime Minister) to Leeper 16th January, 1945 (R 1250/4/19).
9. Leeper to Foreign Office 17th January, 1945 (R 1302/4/19).
10. Leeper to Foreign Office 25th January, 1945 (R 1905/4/19). In this telegram Leeper gave vent to his anger at having been misinformed, describing Tsirimokos as a 'poor-spirited creature', 'who has been terrorised by the communists and prefers the role of a gramophone record to risk of being shot by them'.
11. Enosi Laïkis Dimokratias, *Theseis ya ta Dekemvriana. Apofasi tis Kentrikis Epitropis tis 15 Martiou 1945,* (Athens, 1945), p. 1.
12. On the Greek political parties see Richter, *Griechenland zwischen Revolution und Konterrevolution,* p. 50.
13. C.M. Woodhouse, *Apple of Discord: A Survey of Recent Greek Politics in their International Setting,* (London: Hutchinson & Co., n.d. [1948]), p. 60. *Sosialistiko Komma tis Ellados, To kommounistiko kinima 1944-1945,* (Athens, 1945), deals with the attitude of the non-EAM SKE to the December events. This was a tiny party, hardly meriting the title.
14. *Hansard,* No. 407, cols. 1417-22.
15. Enosi Laïkis Dimokratias, *Theseis ya ta Dekemvriana,* Apofasi tis kentrikis Epitropis tis 15 Martiou 1945, (Athens, 1945), p. 1.
16. *Hansard,* No. 407, col. 1420.
17. *Ibid.,* cols. 598-602.
18. Foreign Office (Prime Minister) to Leeper 16th January, 1945 (R 1250/4/19).
19. *The Manchester Guardian,* 11th January, 1945.
20. Leeper to Foreign Office 12th January, 1945 (R 936/4/19).
21. Leeper to Foreign Office 15th January, 1945 (R 1148/4/19).
22. This was the only case of British subjects (a Mr and Mrs Henderson) detained by ELAS as civilian prisoners. Leeper to Foreign Office 15th January, 1945 (R 1154/4/19). 'To secure the maximum publicity, it would be best to arrange for a Question in the House whether the Foreign Minister had any information about British hostages. This could be answered quite shortly. Editors could then be relied on to cable their correspondents for full details when we would release the whole story here. . .' Leeper's previous career in the Press Department of the Foreign Office and in the Propaganda Service of SOE (PWE—Political Warfare Executive) bore fruit. For further details on the Henderson case see *The Times,* 20th January, 1945.
23. Printed in *Documents regarding the situation in Greece,* January 1945, (London: HMSO, 1945, Cmd. 6592), pp. 3-7.
24. *Hansard,* No. 407, cols. 408-12.
25. Foreign Office (Prime Minister) to Leeper 19th January, 1945 (R 1621/4/19).
26. *Hansard,* No. 407, cols. 452-67.
27. *Ibid.,* col. 554.
28. *Ibid.,* cols. 560-2.
29. *Ibid.,* cols. 599-602.
30. *Ibid.,* cols. 2053 ff.
    American journalists addressed a protest to MacVeagh for transmission to Washington, saying: 'Lt.-Gen. Scobie has put into force, on grounds of military security, regulations which make it impossible for American correspondents to interview and make known to the American public the political views of EAM leaders who are opposing him. The correspondents have asked, in the public interest, to be permitted to interview EAM leaders with British officers present. Gen. Scobie, replying to this request, has forbidden all contact with the "enemy". We ask that the U.S. Government take all required steps to ensure that American correspondents may be freed from the restraints named, in order

that the deeply interested American public may be enabled rightfully and without any infringement of British military security to hear occasionally part of the EAM view of the present conflict.' This remarkable letter was signed by M.W. Fodor, Farnsworth Fowle, Clay Gowran, Joseph Harrison, Reg Ingraham, Guthrie Janssen, Dimitri Kessel, Panos Morphopoulos, Constantine Poulos, James Roper and George Weller, that is to say, by all the American correspondents save one, A.C. Sedgwick *(New York Times)*, who dissociated himself from the protest. The English newspapers for which at the time American correspondents were writing, included *Observer, News Chronicle* and *Daily Express.* From: Richard Capell, *Simiomata: A Greek Notebook 1944-1945*, (London: McDonald, 1946), pp. 129-30.

Constantine Poulos of the Overseas News Agency sent the following report on British Censorship home:
'Athens, Jan. 16. (ONA)— It is becoming increasingly difficult to tell the story of developments in Greece honestly and completely. To the carefully-schooled British military censorship has been added the blue pencil of the British Embassy here.
The policy of not permitting correspondents to see EAM or ELAS representatives, even in the presence of British military authorities, is still in force.
Military censors, determined to protect British policy in Greece against criticism, take it upon themselves to recommend strictly political changes in stories. The necessity of maintaining cordial relations with censors forces many correspondents to make requested alterations.
Sometimes the censors make slight changes in dispatches, such as substituting one descriptive word for another. With a daily word limitation to think of, the correspondents select words carefully and the one word that the censor may change may be, and usually is, very significant.
Now the correspondents have to contend with a British Embassy official also. Stories which the military censors feel should be checked, even when not for military or political reasons, are 'referred' to the Foreign Office man. Today I discovered, in the file of my stories at the Censor's office, one despatch marked "Okayed by Osbert Lancaster", the press attaché at the British Embassy.'
From: *Challenge to Freedom: The Story of what happened in Greece. From the Reports of Leland Stowe and Constantine Poulos,* (New York: The Greek American Council, March 1945), pp. 29-30.

So as to be able to send his first uncensored radio report on the December events, the American radio reporter Leland Stowe had to fly from Athens to Rome (Leland Stowe in a letter to the author). He represented the Blue Network (ABC), see Leland Stowe, *While Time Remains,* (New York: Alfred Knopf, 1947), pp. 246 ff.

31. Foreign Office (Prime Minister) to Leeper 19th January, 1945 (R 1621/4/19).
32. Until 1943 Leeper had been its head. See footnote 22.
33. Leeper to Foreign Office 7th February 1945 (R 2743/4/19; R 2662/4/19; R 2874/4/19; R 2900/4/19).
34. *Hansard,* No. 407, cols. 2051-53.
35. The Foreign Office advised the British Embassy in Washington not to give the White Paper any special promotion nor to arrange a special distribution in the US. Foreign Office to Washington Embassy 30th January, 1945 (R 1962/4/19).
36. *Documents regarding the situation in Greece.* For the EDES charter see 'Ethnikos Dimokratikos Ellinikos Syndesmos (EDES), Idrytikon (1941), Programma (1943), Ya mia nea politiki zoï (1943)', reprinted in *Ellinika Themata,* Athens, 1974. The version published in the British White Paper does

THE BRITISH WHITE PAPER & THE TUC DELEGATIONS REPORT 45

not bear even a remote relation to the original text.
37. C.M. Woodhouse, *The Struggle for Greece 1941-1949*, (London: Hart-Davis, MacGibbon, 1976), p. 134. 'That [the White Paper] might not have been decisive but for the almost accidental part played in the destruction of illusions by British trade-unionists.'
38. Greek Unity Committee, *Greek Diary*, January 17, 1945 (R 1643/4/19).
39. Leeper to Foreign Office 15th January, 1945 (R 1164/4/19).
40. *The Times*, 12th January, 1945.
41. Foreign Office to Leeper 14th January, 1945 (R 770/4/19).
42. Leeper to Foreign Office 15th January, 1945 (R 1164/4/19); Leeper to Foreign Office 16th January, 1945 (R 1234/4/19); Leeper to Foreign Office 18th January, 1945 (R 1415/4/19).
43. Draft of a letter from Churchill to Citrine, 16th January, 1945 (R 1415/4/19).
44. Prime Minister's Personal Minute 16th January, 1945 Serial No. M 80/5 (R 1642/4/19). How compliant Citrine was is further illustrated on p. 125 of the *TUC Report 1945* which mentions only the invitation of the 10th January.
45. Personal telegram Eden to Leeper 18th January, 1945 (R 1141/4/19).
46. Barry, *Report on Greece*, p. 2.
47. Trades Union Congress, *What we saw in Greece: Report of the T.U.C. Delegation*, (London, 1945), pp. 16 ff. Further details of the TUC delegation's visit can be found in the Appendix to *I ekthesi ton anglikon syndikaton. O syndikalismos kai ī katastasi stin Ellada meta tin katochi*, (Athens: Sideris, 1977), which consists of extracts from the newspaper *Kathimerina Nea* of the period.
48. *Ibid.*, p. 17.
49. *Ibid.*, p. 16. The figures quoted by Mathiopoulos (20,000 murdered, 60,000 hostages) have no foundation in fact. Basil P. Mathiopoulos, *Die Geschichte der Sozialen Frage und des Sozialismus in Griechenland (1821-1961)*, (Hannover: 1961), p. 146. Verlag für Literatur und Zeitgeschehen.
50. Richter, *Griechenland zwischen Revolution und Konterrevolution*, pp. 561-3.
51. Dominique Eudes, *Les Kapetanios: La guerre civile grecque 1943-1949*, (Paris: Fayard, 1970)), p. 294. English edition *The Kapitanios*, (London: New Left Books, 1972), pp. 219-20. Eudes, however, does not give his source.
52. *Ibid.*, p. 297; p. 222 in English edition. Such a people's court sentenced Eleni Papadaki, the well-known actress and mistress of the third collaborationist Prime Minister, Rallis, to death. See also Kenneth Mathews, *Memories of a Mountain War*, (London: Longmans, 1972), pp. 54, 96-9.
53. *New York Times*, 16th January, 1945.
54. Richter, *Griechenland zwischen Revolution und Konterrevolution*, pp. 562 ff; Stefanos Sarafis, *ELAS:* p. LXXVII; Colin Wright, *British Soldier in Greece*, (London: Lawrence & Wishart, 1946), p. 60; and for further information Eudes, *op. cit.*, pp. 219 ff.
55. R 2662/4/19.
56. '. . . It is interesting to note that the NYT has sent A.C. Sedgwick back to Greece. Sedgwick is perhaps the most openly reactionary correspondent the Times has employed since Mr. Carney smeared the Loyalists from Franco's side during the Spanish civil war. It wasn't a coincidence, either, that the British in Greece, in January, 1945, chose Mrs. Sedgwick, a Greek by birth who comes from a banking family of very conservative political views, to act as interpreter and guide for the Citrine Mission.' 'News from Greece', *The Nation*, 17th January 1948, p. 60; *New York Times*, 26th January, 1945. Roxane Sedgwick (née Sotiriadis), was the daughter of an archaeologist, and had served the British Embassy before the war as an interpreter-guide for visiting notables.
57. TUC, *What we saw in Greece*, pp. 14 ff; Barry, *Report on Greece*, pp. 4 ff.

58. Leeper to Eden 27th January, 1945 (R 2291/4/19). 'Citrine made a speech in which he gave British press a pretty good dressing down. . . It is refreshing. . . to watch how the British visitors rapidly align themselves with the policy of His Majesty's Government once they see the situation on the spot.' See also: *I ekthesi ton anglikon syndikaton*, pp. 54–6.
59. The only account in English is Christos Jecchinis' *Trade Unionism in Greece: A Study in Political Paternalism,* (Chicago: Roosevelt University, 1967). Jecchinis was an active trade unionist from 1949 to 1955 and from 1948 to 1951 an official of the Marshall Plan administration in Greece. At that date, both these functions are proof of his anti-Left attitude. The book is more or less a paraphrase of the ILO Report *of 1949.* International Labour Office: *Labour Problems in Greece: Report of the ILO Mission to Greece October–November 1949,* (Geneva, 1949).
60. Before the Second World War, regional administration in Greece was organised in ten provinces. But these were simply administrative divisions, not regional self-governing bodies in the West-European sense. The provinces of Macedonia, Epirus, Thrace and Crete had a special status under a Governor-General appointed by the king, with a three-member council for economic affairs, finance and justice. There was no elected legislative body alongside the Governor-General. The provinces were divided into *nomoi,* each under a *nomarch.* These corresponded more or less to a French *département.* Just as the French prefects have been appointed from Paris, so the *nomarchs* were appointed in Athens and just as in the provinces, so in the *nomoi,* there was no legislative body. The *nomarchs* were the representatives of the government and exercised full executive powers under instructions from Athens (except in the judicial and military spheres). The *nomarch* was served by his administration and by the police of his *nomos.* Below the *nomoi* were the *eparchies,* or sub-provinces under an *eparch,* similar subordinate executive agencies. In other words, a highly-centralised, undemocratic system.
61. For the latter see: Internal Situation of Greece, September 1945. Labour and Trade Unions in Greece (R 18945/4/19); and for the text of Law 281 of 21-25 June 1914: Antonios Malagardis, ed., *Geniki kodikopoïsis tis ischyousis ellinikis nomothesias apo tis systaseos tou ellinikou kratous mechri simeron* Vol. 7, (Athens, 1934), pp. 624–38.
62. The Socialist Workers' Party of Greece (Sosialistikon Ergatikon Komma tis Ellados) was founded a few days after the Trade Union Congress. After initial hesitations and negotiations with both the Second and Third Internationals, in 1920 it joined the latter and changed its name to Socialist (Communist) Workers' Party of Greece. The moderate socialists split off and formed their own party which joined the Second International in 1923. In contradistinction to the later KKE, this Socialist Party had only a shadowy existence during the inter-war years.
63. For the text of the founding resolution see Mathiopoulos, *op. cit.,* pp. 86 ff.
64. Jean Meynaud, *Les forces politiques en Grèce,* (Montreal, 1956), p. 186. For the text of Law 2151 of the 21st March–6th April 1920 see pp. 638–44.
65. Nikolaos Stavrou, *Pressure Groups in the Greek political setting,* (unpublished thesis: The George Washington University, 1970), pp. 175, 188.
66. Jecchinis, *op. cit.,* p. 42.
67. A change in this undemocratic electoral system was first introduced by Law 4361 of 2nd September 1964, when G. Papandreou's Centre government undertook a few cautious modifications. *Efimeris tis Kyverniseos (Government Gazette)* I, No. 1499, 2nd September 1964, pp. 729–31. These modifications were abrogated later by the Junta government. Stavrou, *op. cit.,* pp. 179–93.

For further developments see Kostas Seferis, *Elliniko syndikalistiko kinima 1860-1975*, 2nd edition, (Athens: Neo Syndikalistiko Kinima, 1976). The communist version of trade union history was given by Kostas Theos, *Ta ellinika syndikata stin pali enantia sto fasismo kai ya tin anexartisia tous*, (Athens, 1947).

68. Kommounistiko Komma tis Elladas, *Episima Keimena, Vol. IV, 1934-1940*. (n.p.: Politikes kai logotechnikes ekdoseis, 1968), pp. 90-2.
69. Woodhouse, *Apple of Discord*, pp. 33-4. The report of the British Labour Attaché to the Embassy (see footnote 61 above) characterised Hajidimitriou as 'a corrupt and incompetent place-seeker'.
70. Leeper to Foreign Office 18th January, 1945 (R 1415/4/19).
71. *Documents regarding the situation in Greece*, p. 14.
72. *The Times*, 30th January, 1945.
73. Leeper to Foreign Office 27th January, 1945 (R 2291/4/19). Author's italics.
74. TUC, *What we saw in Greece*, pp. 22 ff.
75. Compare the commentary in: *Fourth International*, April 1945, p. 101.
76. Prime Minister to Lord Moyne 27th April, 1944 (R 6627/3/19).
77. Letter of 1st June 1948 and reply of 8th June 1948 (TUC archives).
78. The League continued its activities after the end of the civil war, campaigning for an amnesty for prisoners and internees and collecting funds for relief. During the Junta dictatorship it was again intensely active, this time with the total support of British public opinion. The archives of this admirable organisation can be found today in the Department of Byzantine and Modern Greek Studies in King's College, University of London.

FROM THE ARMISTICE TO THE VARKIZA PEACE NEGOTIATIONS

Before the back-drop of this propaganda campaign and of British intervention in the Greek trade unions' internal affairs, the preliminary negotiations for the Varkiza peace conference began. It has already been shown that the Plastiras government rejected a political solution to the country's internal problem and aimed at military annihilation of EAM-ELAS. It was Macmillan's intervention which first produced, on 6th January, a partial deflection in the British line. But even after this the Greek government's policy was not consistent; nor was British policy—represented on the spot by Leeper and Macmillan—monolithic. But both had a common aim: the subjugation of EAM-ELAS. Reconciliation or compromise were not under discussion.[1]

On the 11th January, after the signing of the armistice, Damaskinos had given the ELAS plenipotentiaries a message for the ELAS Central Committee[2] in which he expressed his deep distress at their refusal to release the hostages and declared himself ready to organise a conference between representatives of ELAS and of the Greek government.[3] The EAM-ELAS leaders who feared a re-opening of hostilities pressed for the earliest possible start to negotiations. On the 15th January the ELAS Central Committee replied that a five-member delegation from the EAM Central Committee was ready to open negotiations and asked the Regent to initiate the necessary steps for the delegation to come to Athens.[4] Since no answer was received, the ELAS Central Committee repeated this message on the 18th January.[5]

Meanwhile, Alexander and Macmillan had returned to Athens on the 16th January. Both knew that Damaskinos and Plastiras were still seeking a military solution and in this they were supported, up to a point, by Leeper. However, they were determined to carry through to a conclusion the policy they had initiated in December. Therefore, on the very day of their arrival, they held a meeting during which they laid down the programme to be followed and informed London accordingly in a joint telegram.[6]

On the 17th January they visited Damaskinos, who informed them of the ELAS Central Committee message of the 15th. Macmillan writes:
'The F.M. began by giving a rather defeatist account of the military future. He emphasised the great difficulty in the mountains if it were necessary to clear out the rebels by force. He also explained the need

to reduce his military commitments to Greece to the minimum, in view of the need to send divisions to the Italian and perhaps to the Western Front. The purpose of this was to deflate the Greek attitude a little. But the Archbishop did not react very favourably. I then developed my political thesis and here also had rather a frigid reception.'[7]
Macmillan's demand for an amnesty, in particular, met with obstinate resistance from Damaskinos. Eventually, the following procedure was agreed on:

Damaskinos would again inform EAM of his readiness to organise a conference. But a date would not be mentioned to EAM—though 24th or 25th January was under consideration for the opening. The invitation to EAM would say 'as soon as possible'. The conference would not be chaired by Damaskinos, as Macmillan had apparently suggested. The government would not be represented by Plastiras but by the left-liberal politician Sofianopoulos, a more flexible negotiator, and Periklis Rallis. The place might perhaps be Lamia, certainly not Athens. The central topic would be the disarming of ELAS. There would be no question of a general amnesty; an amnesty could not include insurgents who had committed crimes which had no connection with military operations. Macmillan was apparently satisfied with this provisional solution.[8]

On the 18th January, as agreed, Damaskinos sent a telegram to the ELAS Central Committee in which he confirmed receipt of the ELAS telegram of the 15th and stated that he would bring the five EAM delegates into contact with representatives of the Greek government. As soon as place and date had been decided, a further message would be sent.[9] On the morning of the same day Leeper visited Sofianopoulos and demanded an explanation of a report which had appeared in the newspaper *Kathimerina Nea* on the 16th January, to the effect that the government had issued 150 arrest warrants against leaders of the rebellion. Sofianopoulos denied responsibility and maintained that his *démenti* of the 8th January still held good. However, it was more difficult to get rid of a statement by Plastiras to a reporter from that paper. According to this, Plastiras had stated that the leaders of the rebellion would be heavily punished and that there was no question of an amnesty.[10] Sofianopoulos asked Leeper to intervene with Plastiras to obtain a denial of this statement. He also agreed that Leeper should extract from Plastiras the cancellation of the plan to nominate Stylianos Gonatas Governor-General of Macedonia because his name had been connected with organising Security Battalions.[11]

The subsequent conversation between Macmillan, Leeper, Plastiras and Alexander cleared up the outstanding problems. Plastiras took back his statement and adopted Macmillan's concept of an amnesty. The planned appointment of Gonatas was cancelled. The conference preparations would be carried out in close cooperation with the British. No statements on future political intentions would be issued before the start of the conference.[12] The next days were marked by two parallel lines of political activity. Macmillan was negotiating conference matters with Damaskinos and Sofianopoulos whereby agreement was reached on all points. The only point on which the Greek side wanted more information was a clarification as to how far the British were prepared to commit themselves militarily in Greece for the future. The negotiating position of the government delegation depended on the answer to this question. If the British were prepared to give the Greek government some form of military guarantee, then the government delegation could take a much harder line. To clear this up, Macmillan sent a detailed report to London and asked for a decision.[13] However, London was not prepared to give a far-reaching guarantee which would have implied a resumption of hostilities against ELAS in the event of the failure of the conference. Instead, it confined itself to a statement of faith in a positive outcome for the conference and affirmed that British troops in sufficient strength would remain stationed in Greece until the new Greek army was built up. Requests for weapons and other equipment for the Greek army in excess of its agreed maximum strength of 40,000 men would be sympathetically examined but, in view of present conditions, were unrealistic.[14]

Parallel with this, an internal Greek controversy developed over the composition of the EAM delegation. On the 18th January Damaskinos had accepted the presence of a five-man delegation at the negotiations. Whether it was that he had been informed of its composition; or that he wanted to restrict its size because the government delegation was to consist of only three members (Sofianopoulos, Periklis Rallis and the recently nominated Agriculture Minister Ioannis Makropoulos) and apparently no other minister was considered qualified for the negotiations; or whether he genuinely feared endless negotiations resulting from a bigger delegation; whatever it was, on the 19th January he let the ELAS Central Committee know that the conference would start on the 25th January and that the EAM delegation should consist of only three members: the ELAS Central Committee should inform him of the names so that the necessary preparations could be made.[15]

This telegram did not reach the ELAS Central Committee till the 21st January, when the EAM delegation—to lose no time—had already set out from Volos. The ELAS Central Committee informed Damaskinos of this the same day and named the delegates: Dimitrios Partsalidis, Miltiadis Porfyrogenis, Ilias Tsirimokos, Kostas Gavriilidis, Georgios Georgalas and Alexandros Svolos (the last already in Athens). With the delegation, in addition to their assistants, was a GCL delegation (Kostas Theos, Ioannis Kalomoiris, Dimitrios Mariolis and Dimitrios Stratis) who were to negotiate with the TUC delegation. The ELAS Central Committee regarded the participation of these as essential but, if Damaskinos insisted on only three, then the delegation would select the three among themselves.[16]

On the 21st January the EAM delegstion reached Levadia where it was held up by the British. In Athens its composition had produced a worried reaction both from the British and Damaskinos—it represented all the parties and groups constituting EAM[17] and thus proved *post factum* that the supposition that ELD, SKE and AKE had withdrawn from EAM had been merely a propaganda gambit: the participation of the known non-communist Tsirimokos must at all costs be prevented. The British authorities now inevestigated whether—as they suspected—the EAM delegation really knew nothing of the restriction on numbers. When this had been confirmed, Leeper discussed further action with Sofianopoulos and later Damaskinos, too, joined in. They came to the conclusion that the conference only made sense with the communist leaders and, on the 23rd, the Regent sent a telegram in this sense to the ELAS Central Committee insisting that the three EAM delegates must be communist leaders.[18] At the same time instructions were sent to detain the EAM delegation at Levadia and to give the press no reason for this delay.[19] The EAM delegation protested at these measures and, when Damaskinos too repeated his earlier demand,[20] they returned to Trikkala having achieved nothing.

In the meantime, the Greek government had received the limited British guarantee and having noted the outcome of the House of Commons debate of the 19th January, was even less inclined to admit Tsirimokos to the negotiations where his participation would expose Eden's statement about EAM's alleged dissolution,[21] and also their own lies. Macmillan, who had returned to Naples on the 21st January, was told by Harold Caccia that 'the conference was unlikely to meet without great delay, if at all'.[22] Therefore he returned to Athens on the 25th January. Meanwhile, the Foreign Office had realised that the opening of the conference was blocked by the Regent's last-minute objections and that ELAS was justifiably critical.[23] Macmillan's presence brought about a compromise. On the 26th a telegram reached Athens from the EAM Central Committee in which they expressed their astonishment at Damaskinos' behaviour and their doubts as to the government's readiness to negotiate.[24] Macmillan, who had become impatient, thereupon intervened with Damaskinos and told him it was quite sufficient if Siantos participated representing KKE.[25] Damaskinos yielded and on 29th January informed the ELAS Central Committee that he insisted on the sending of Siantos and Partsalidis; Sarafis could participate as military adviser.[26] Thereupon the EAM Central Committee nominated Siantos (Secretary of KEE), Partsalidis (General-Secretary of EAM) and Tsirimokos as delegates and Sarafis to function as military adviser; Gavriilidis, Georgalas and Stratis would belong to the delegation but would not participate in the negotiations.[27] Macmillan agreed to this composition and brought Damaskinos to accept it likewise, when all of a sudden Sofianopoulos protested strongly against Tsirimokos' participation. Damaskinos thereupon changed his mind and returned to his original demand that all the EAM delegation must be communists. Macmillan had to exercise massive pressure on Sofianopoulos and Damaskinos to bring them back into line, the only concession that Sofianopoulos achieved being the sending back of Gavriilidis, Georgalas and Stratis.[28]

This was the situation in which Damaskinos had Tsirimokos brought to Athens for a talk on the 1st February. This was an astute chess move on his part. In their two conversations on the evening of the 1st and the morning of the 2nd February Tsirimokos informed the Regent that his colleagues were ready to conclude peace. Then he revealed the demands they would put forward and gave assurances that, on two basic questions— general amnesty and participation in the government—he would vote against the communists. Furthermore, he wrote Damaskinos a letter in which he declared his resignation from the delegation, at the same time warning that—were it accepted—Siantos and Partsalidis would let the conference break up. He added that he was ready to persuade Siantos and Partsalidis to write a letter to Damaskinos—which he himself would countersign—in which it would be stated that his appointment to the delegation had not been for the purpose of causing difficulties but that, as it was now a fact, any change would involve delay.[29]

Damaskinos was highly satisfied and informed Macmillan and Leeper as to the content of the conversations. Sofianopoulos, with whom Damaskinos, Macmillan and Leeper conferred on the morning of the 2nd, was not informed. Now that the last obstacle to the start of the peace conference had thus been swept away, on the evening of the 2nd Macmillan and Sofianopoulos again went over the details of the latter's opening address and Macmillan formulated with him a summary of the programme which he was to present to the conference in the name of the Greek government. No doubt on account of the after-effects of British threats, Sofianopoulos accepted it without question. The Foreign Office commented on this programme as follows:

'If the ELAS representatives accept, this will be equivalent to complete surrender on their part and will mean the end of ELAS control in any part of Greece.'[30]

Before we proceed to describe the conference itself, first a few words about Tsirimokos. Ilias Tsirimokos, the son of a bourgeois politician, born in 1907, belonged to the younger generation of Greek politicians and was elected a Liberal member of parliament in 1936. Unlike most of his older colleagues, he was not prepared to wait out the German Occupation in a respectable passivity, and in 1941 founded ELD and joined EAM. He became a socialist because, at that time, socialism was in fashion but in reality he remained a Liberal and his party differed little in structure from the traditional type of Greek party: it was just another patron-and-clients set-up. But his adherence to EAM gave him a significance which he would never have acquired merely as leader of ELD. He became a member of the EAM Central Committee, was a representative of EAM at the Cairo conference in 1943 and was Secretary for Justice in the PEEA. Later in 1944 he became Economics Minister in the Papandreou Cabinet. Tsirimokos was not a 'fellow-traveller' as many wartime inactivists described him, neither was he an adherent of that fanatical, sterile anti-communism represented by Metaxas and his henchmen. He was an upright democrat prepared to cooperate on an equal basis with communists. Certainly, he did not understand how to keep his end up adequately with his communist colleagues in the EAM Central Committee. Briefly, had the situation developed peacefully, Tsirimokos could have continued to play a most honourable role in EAM. On the outbreak of the December fighting, he woke up to find himself in no-man's land. He accepted neither the British intervention nor KKE's line. His dilemma was that he neither wanted to join the 'nationalist' camp nor, in such a critical situation, to desert EAM. It was by no means what his critics supposed: that he did not cross the lines for fear of the communists.[31] He did not change sides because his opposition to KKE policy by no means implied that he supported British policy and that of the Greek government. His behaviour on the 1st and 2nd February and during the conference can be assessed as an attempt to free himself from the KKE line and return to a more independent one,[32] which he eventually achieved at that ELD Central Committee meeting of 15th March 1945.[33] But, objectively, his actions before and during the peace conference helped the British and the Greek Right.

NOTES

1. On the 12th January Leeper telegraphed to the Foreign Office (R 936/4/19): 'We have forced the Regent to agree to a conference with these men if they express their desire for it but I wish to make it clear from the outset that there can be no understanding between the Greek Government and the hard core of irreconcilable communism that is left of EAM. There can be no compromise with them on internal or external policy. As the Regent said last night, the two sides represent two different worlds. . . This struggle can only end in victory of the vast majority of the Greek people. . .'
2. The ELAS Central Committee was established in February 1942 to direct ELAS before the formation of GHQ. It was re-established in December 1944 to guide the Athens fighting.
3. Text in: Leeper to Foreign Office 24th January, 1945 (R 1904/4/19).
4. *Ibid.*, and National Liberation Front, E.A.M., *White Book*, p. 112.
5. National Liberation Front, E.A.M., *White Book*, pp. 112 ff.
6. Text of the programme in: Macmillan, *The Blast of War 1939-1945*, (London: Macmillan, 1967), pp. 736-9. With the exception of some stylistic changes, this version is identical with R 1216/4/19.

FROM THE ARMISTICE TO THE VARKIZA PEACE NEGOTIATIONS   55

7. Macmillan, *op. cit.*, p. 641 and Macmillan to Foreign Office 17th January, 1945 (R 1321/4/19), where the fact that the speedy raising of a large number of Greek troops was excluded due to equipment problems, is added.
8. Macmillan, *op. cit.*, p. 642.
9. R 1904/4/19. See footnote 3 to this chapter and National Liberation Front, E.A.M., *White Book*, p. 113.
10. *The Times*, 17th January, 1945.
11. Leeper to Foreign Office 18th January, 1945 (R 1373/4/19). Gonatas was an old friend of Plastiras. His appointment was an aspect of Plastiras' patronage policy by which he hoped to influence developments in his own preferred direction. This method showed up Plastiras as a 'politician of the old school' and at the same time it proved utterly useless under the political conditions of 1945.
12. Leeper to Foreign Office 18th January, 1945 (R 1376/4/19). For Macmillan's amnesty plans see Macmillan, *op. cit.*, p. 737.
13. Leeper to Foreign Office 21st January, 1945; telegrams nos. 275, 276, 277, 278 (R 1575/4/19).
14. Prime Minister's Personal Minute D 39/5 of 21st January 1945; Draft Minute to the Prime Minister from the Secretary of State 22nd January 1945; Draft of telegram to Mr. Leeper from Secretary of State (undated); C.R. Price (Offices of the War Cabinet) to D.F. Howard (Foreign Office) 22nd January 1945, C.O.S. 131/5; all in R 1575/4/19. See also Macmillan, *op. cit.*, p. 644.
15. National Liberation Front, E.A.M., *White Book*, p. 113; R 1904/4/19.
16. National Liberation Front, E.A.M., *White Book*, p. 114.
17. Partsalidis represented EAM, Porfyrogenis KKE, Tsirimokos ELD, Gavriilidis AKE, Georgalas EPON and Svolos SKE. The four trade union leaders spoke for the three groups in the Greek unions.
18. National Liberation Front, E.A.M., *White Book*, p. 114; R 1904/4/19; Leeper to Foreign Office 23rd January, 1945 (R 1762/4/19).
19. R 1762/4/19.
20. R 1904/4/19.
21. See pp. 23-25.
22. Macmillan, *op. cit.*, p. 644.
23. Howard's Minutes 27th January, 1945 (R 1904/4/19).
24. National Liberation Front, E.A.M., *White Book*, p. 115; Leeper to Foreign Office 29th January, 1945 (R 2162/4/19).
25. Macmillan, *op. cit.*, p. 649.
26. National Liberation Front, E.A.M., *White Book*, p. 115 and R 2162/4/19; see note 24.
27. National Liberation Front, E.A.M., *White Book*, pp. 115 ff.
28. Leeper to Foreign Office 30th January, 1945 (R 2236/4/19); Foreign Office to Embassy in Washington 2nd February, 1945 (R 2236/4/19); Macmillan, *op. cit.*, p. 651.
29. Leeper to Foreign Office 2nd February, 1945 (R 2458/4/19).
30. Author's italics. The text of the programme can be found in Leeper to Foreign Office 2nd February, 1945 (R 2439/4/19). Laskey's Minute 1st February, 1945 (R 2291/4/19). This remark was initialled without comment by all the personnel of the Southern Department, as also by Sir Orme Sargent, the Under-Secretary and by the Foreign Secretary, Anthony Eden.
31. See Leeper's character sketch, footnote 10 to preceding chapter.
32. In a further telegram on 6th February Leeper reported attempts to draw Tsirimokos into the dissident ELD camp (R 2714/4/19).
33. ELD, *Theseis ya ta Dekemvriana*.

THE PEACE NEGOTIATIONS AT VARKIZA

The peace negotiations began at 10 p.m. at a villa in the holiday resort of Varkiza, about 40 km south of Athens on the Saronic Gulf. Sofianopoulos opened the conference by reading the government programme formulated by Macmillan. In his introductory statement he stressed the need to restore national unity: the government was not irreconcilable nor inspired by intolerance but by a spirit of conciliation; then he read the government programme.

The government expected all hostages to be released; this included prisoners who might be charged with crimes. All party and private armies must be disarmed and disbanded, so that a politically independent army, serving only the state, could be built up. This new army would be formed on the basis of regular conscription of certain age-groups. The regular Officers' and NCOs Corps would be integrated, so would already existing units of state forces. A special British Military Mission would assist in building the new army. The police and gendarmerie should remain as they were. Members of these bodies, from the Metaxas dictatorship down to the present, who had shown themselves blameworthy or were unsuitable for the service would be relieved of their posts by a committee. A British Police Mission would supervise the purge and re-organisation. In this way citizens would be able to feel confidence in the state security forces.

In order to guarantee the citizen's freedom of expression the government would protect this and would repeal existing laws from the time of the dictatorship which restricted such freedom. No citizen would be persecuted by the Executive or the judiciary for his political or social convictions, but anyone who used force to impose his views would be brought to trial. As soon as peace was restored to the country, the government would hold a plebiscite on the constitutional issue and elections for a Constituent Assembly. Both electoral processes would be genuine and free. Allied observers would be invited to supervise this.

Freedom of assembly and association would be secured directly after repeal of martial law, which would be the outcome of the pacification expected from these negotiations; and these rights should be based on the legislation in force before the dictatorship. This would apply especially to the trade unions. The government would not retain any right of intervention in their internal affairs. As regards the amnesty, the government did not intend any systematic persecution or general proscription of participants in the rebellion; but those who had committed brutal crimes or transgressed elementary international rules of warfare would feel the full severity of the law. Collaborators would be sentenced and punished as soon as possible.[1]

Sofianopoulos then addressed a conciliatory appeal to the delegation to conduct the coming negotiations in a tranquil and constructive spirit so that a good result could be achieved: and he ended by quoting Herodotus: 'This is the old trouble of the Greeks. Those who cultivated the growth of envy prepared their own destruction. And this is the reason why they are subjected to foreigners.' To this Tsirimokos remarked: 'There is also the converse, too: Because they are subjected to foreigners, they are divided. . .' Sofianopoulos agreed, and Siantos added assurances that the EAM delegation, too, would be guided by the same conciliatory spirit: it realised the dreadful consequences of a continued blood-letting for the nation and therefore likewise sought a speedy and happy conclusion to the conference.[2]

Sofianopoulos really meant his conciliatory words. Born in 1887, John Sofianopoulos could be best described politically as a left-wing Liberal.[3] Before the Metaxas dictatorship he led an Agrarian Party which had secured 1.02% of the votes and one seat in parliament in the elections of the 26th January 1936. Since his visit to the Soviet Union in 1924 he had pursued a policy of good relations with that country. In contrast to most of the other older politicians, who had paid no attention to the rise of fascism in Italy and Germany and had not realised the danger of a fascist takeover in Greece, Sofianopoulos had followed European developments closely and when, in 1936, portents of a fascist *coup* in Greece began to multiply, on the 27th July he joined the Popular Front. Under the dictatorship, he cooperated with those forces which were working for its overthrow. During that time and during the Occupation he had moved leftwards though without becoming a declared socialist. After a few moment's wavering at the beginning of the Occupation he was for resistance and hoped that it would produce a new, socialist Goudi.[4] At first he had sympathised with EAM but, when the latter failed to create an all-embracing popular front including the anti-fascist bourgeois parties and when its class character became increasingly marked, he distanced himself. He wanted a resistance movement which would be above party and for this reason he did not join any of the other, equally party-affiliated resistance organisations. But he did not break off contact with EAM. In 1943 he had founded a rally movement, the New Democratic Union of the Left (Nea Dimokratiki Enosi Aristeron) which he represented at the Lebanon Conference. Sofianopoulos intended this organisation as a sort of receptacle for all the non-communist forces in EAM which wanted social reform of the existing bourgeois system, without destroying the system itself. From an early date he saw that the Greek Right would denounce the entire Resistance as communist. He knew that the founding of EAM had been largely influenced by KKE, but he also knew that the phenomenon of mass resistance reached far beyond KKE's sphere of influence—that the Resistance was a genuine popular uprising.

From 1943 he tried to steer a course between the two extremes. Whenever he thought he saw the bourgeois system in danger, then he opposed EAM. Thus, in spring 1944, he declined the presidency of PEEA (the provisional government established by EAM in liberated Greece). But, whenever the undemocratic bourgeois camp tried to get power into its own hands, then he supported EAM. Thus, at the Lebanon, he strongly advised Svolos against participation in Papandreou's National Unity Government since such participation must end in catastrophe for the progressive forces. From the Lebanon Conference until the outbreak of the December fighting, he endeavoured to unite the democratic forces in the bourgeois camp against the confrontation being sought by the Greek Right and by the British—in vain, since the bourgeois politicians were afraid of being denounced as Leftists.

After the resignation of Papandreou, he entered Plastiras' Cabinet in order to save what could still be saved of the Resistance's democratic potential. He knew that even Plastiras, who had promised him to work for a coalition of all democratic forces, was now himself afraid of being denounced as a Leftist,[5] if he showed a conciliatory spirit. It was Sofianopoulos' aim to keep the extreme Right from power. He wanted to maintain the bourgeois system in place and to save it by re-integrating the democratic and progressive forces. Macmillan's moderate programme may well have expressed his own ideas and therefore he did not press any objections. But his opposition to Tsirimokos' participation is not so easily explained. Given his knowledge of the people concerned, one can hardly assume that he believed in the break-up of the EAM coalition. It would seem more probable that he had been involved in the background activities which produced the various statements of the so-called ELD, SKE and AKE leaders, in the hope of splitting off the non-communist element from EAM. The participation of Tsirimokos and possibly of Svolos and Stratis would have signalled the continued existence of EAM and threatened to bring his plan for the re-integration of the democratic Left and the isolation of KKE to nothing. His sudden change of mood and the abrupt ending of his opposition to Tsirimikos in the late afternoon of the 2nd February could be attributed to the probability that he had been informed from the Greek side of the part the latter was playing.[6]

We said at the beginning that Sofianopoulos really meant his conciliatory words. He wanted reconciliation with the non-communist element in EAM; but he was irreconcilably opposed to KKE—ideological opposition precluded any conciliation there. That is also the reason why he obstinately refused to agree to a general amnesty. Thus, despite his insight into the problems, he forgot that the anti-communist denunciations of the Right attacked all Resistance members indiscriminately—indeed anyone who did not belong to the Right—and would not even stop at his own person. His aims were: to prevent a right-wing counter-revolution, to frustrate the Restoration of the king, and to create that new political organisation of the democratic Left which should absorb the non-communist EAM masses. As we shall show, he was defeated on all fronts. Exactly as Tsirimokos' behaviour objectively aided the Greek Right, so the democrat Sofianopoulos, by the compromise he bargained through with EAM, helped to hand over to the Right—to the persecutors—the only forces which could have restrained that Right. In no case can we accept Kousoulas' theory that Sofianopoulos was playing Siantos' game.[7]

On the second day, the 3rd February 1945, the Secretary of the KKE Central Committee, George Siantos, spoke on behalf of the Central Committee of EAM. He welcomed the fact that it had at last been possible to call the conference: it was the task of the conference to reach an agreement as soon as possible; reconciliation was certainly made more difficult by the fact that, on the very day the conference opened, the government had started trying December fighters by special courts-martial and this was made still more serious by the failure even to start judicial proceedings against the collaborators.[8]

In point of fact, the mass arrests had continued and, on the 2nd February, the trial of sixteen alleged members of OPLA had started before an Athens military tribunal. On the same day, in another trial, two who were accused of high treason and armed resistance to the state were sentenced to death and a third accused—aged only 18—to ten years' imprisonment. A charge of actual murder was regarded as secondary.[9] On the 3rd February, three more who were accused of murder were sentenced to death.[10] All these were to be executed on the 4th February. Macmillan, who had nothing against these trials in principle, but considered them politically untimely, intervened and as a result, Plastiras stopped the planned executions on the 4th February and postponed further trials until after the conference.[11] On the 14th February, he finally annulled the courts-martial verdicts.[12]

Siantos then set out his pre-conditions for peace: the fascist past must be swept away and civil liberties safeguarded for the future; for this EAM required definite guarantees. On particular topics EAM's position was as follows:

Armed forces. EAM agreed to the demobilisation of ELAS. The new national army must be free from suspicion of one-sided party influence, from whatever direction. EAM was particularly concerned as to how the new army would be built up: the composition of the forces' cadre was the decisive criterion; an army whose cadre consisted of men accused of collaboration with the enemy or of fascists, and was composed of so-called volunteers not belonging to the age groups called up in the normal way, would rightly be suspect in regard to the task it was called upon to carry out. EAM therefore demanded that the army should be formed exclusively of conscripts regularly called up from particular age groups without any exceptions. The officers must be men worthy of their position and on no condition collaborators or men with dictatorial ambitions. A purge of the army cadre was therefore urgently necessary. The new army must include the regular cadre, the reserve cadres and the rank-and-file of ELAS belonging to the age groups called up, while the rest must be demobilised and hand in their arms.

Police and gendarmerie. In view of the moral crisis in the country's police forces resulting from the dictatorship and the Occupation, a purge and re-organisation was needed. In future they must not become instruments of suppression in the hands of tyrants; they should be guardians of order watching over the citizens' security. EAM welcomed the government's programme; but a mere re-organisation was not sufficient, EAM insisted on a purge.

Clean-up of the state machinery. Parallel with the purge of the security bodies, the administrative machinery must be purged of all collaborators and fascists. Only thus could the state be democratised. Unfortunately, since the December events, developments had taken the opposite direction: the administration was being purged of left-wing and other democratic elements; this was surely not the government's intention and could assist only those who dreamt of an anti-EAM state.

Reprisals. As far as ELAS was concerned, the hostage-taking chapter was closed. The ELAS Central Committee decisions of 29th December and 14th January had ordered the release of all hostages. As for those who were to be charged with collaboration, EAM had always intended to hand them over to the law. Whilst there had been so much talk about the ELAS hostages, those detained by the opposite side were called prisoners or accused persons and amongst those were young and old people, women and children. The only charge—if any—that could be brought against them was that their political views differed from those of the government. They had been maltreated in the most disgraceful way and were still languishing in miserable conditions in the police cells, in prisons and in concentration camps both in Greece and abroad; in the overseas concentration camps they joined the 15,000 officers and men from the Middle East disturbances of spring 1944. EAM welcomed the government's intention to get this situation under control: an end to this state of affairs would be a further important step towards peace. Finally as regards the crimes mentioned by the government, the other side had also committed numerous crimes, which only too often were committed by those who not long before had been torturing and killing in the name of Hitler. To put an end to mutual denunciations which could only perpetuate and increase the present bitterness, EAM suggested a general amnesty.

Government and elections. Though EAM had nothing against the present composition of the government, the formation of a representative government was important for unifying the country and putting an end to unrest. EAM therefore suggested that representatives of all parties be included in the government. Finally, a plebiscite and elections should take place as soon as possible and a time limit should be fixed now.

This was EAM's programme. Its realisation was the pre-condition for the country's entry upon the road of normal, democratic evolution, reconstruction and progress.[13]

If one compares the government programme with that of EAM, it will be seen that there was agreement on both the issues which the Greek government and the British regarded as pre-conditions for the conclusion of a peace treaty—release of the hostages and demobilisation of the volunteer armies (Resistance armies, Mountain Brigade, Sacred Company).[14] EAM was, as it had been before the December events, ready to demobilise its fighting force provided that other such volunteer forces were also disbanded. The decisive difference between the two positions on re-organisation of the armed forces of the state (army and security forces) concerned how this could be achieved and guaranteed. The Greek government wanted to invite two British Missions for this purpose, thus making the British guarantors and arbiters that this would be done democratically. EAM on the other hand believed that the guarantee it was seeking could be attained by participation in the government and an agreed settlement. Given the precedent of British intervention, the government's view must have given EAM pause for thought. The demand for participation in the government was based on the false premise that the government side and the British were really aiming at reconciliation. Siantos must have sensed this and therefore laid the main weight of his programme on the demand for a general amnesty. In contrast to the government programme which, on the crucial points, was somewhat vaguely formulated, EAM's proposals were moderate, conciliatory and offered a real basis for peaceful development. EAM's demand for guarantees was not a tactical manoeuvre but arose from an elementary need for security, understandable in view of recent persecution of the Greek Left.

On the afternoon of 3rd February came the first clash between Sofianopoulos and Siantos on the amnesty question. Siantos did indeed agree in principle that crimes should be punished but put forward the opinion that, considering the mass hysteria of a civil war, it was impossible to discriminate between real and politically-motivated crimes. He could not imagine any guarantee which would ensure that the government's formula did not—even against its wish—degenerate into a proscription of the Left.[15] Sofianopoulos held to the government's formula. Eventually

THE PEACE NEGOTIATIONS AT VARKIZA

a compromise was found. Rallis and Tsirimokos withdrew from the conference and worked out part of a draft amnesty law.

According to Article 1: an amnesty would be granted for purely political offences committed between 3rd December 1944 and the date when the law was signed. Common law crimes committed in connection with a political offence but not imperatively for its accomplishment would be excepted.

According to Article 2 any dispute or doubt as to the meaning of Article 1 should be irrevocably settled by a council of judges of the Court of Appeal, composed of the President of the Court, four judges, the Public Prosecutor and a secretary. In all cases where such a composition of the council was not possible, a maximum of two of the Appeal Court judges could be replaced by the Presidents of First Instance Courts or by such judges of that Court who shall have completed a term of office of five years and shall be appointed by the Appeal Court President from among judges serving in the town where the Court is situated or failing that serving elsewhere.[16] In addition to this, further clauses were apparently formulated exempting the leaders of the rebels from prosecution even if they would have been guilty under Article 1.[17]

It speaks for Siantos that he did not accept the advantages which this draft-law conferred on him and on the other EAM and KKE leaders but continued to insist on a general amnesty and even threatened to break off the negotiations.[18] Sofianopoulos, for his part, would not yield either and postponed the conference to consult the government.

On the 4th February Sofianopoulos sent Siantos via Tsirimokos a statement in the form of a letter to EAM in which he referred to the draft-law and rejected a general amnesty, though the government was ready to continue negotiating. Now the British, too, intervened again. Macmillan and Leeper did not agree with the draft-law and had informed the Foreign Office: at no point would they have ventured to suggest such wide-ranging demands or such administrative guarantees.[19] The Greek government could not grant a general amnesty, much less now when the world had been told of the atrocities. If the conference was to fail, it would be better that this should be over the amnesty question and not over the question of EAM participation in the government or the admission of the ELAS officers to the national army. Siantos on the other hand could not agree to disband ELAS and hand over his OPLA forces to persecution. The Regent had summoned Tsirimokos in order to make him carry out his undertaking to support the government on the amnesty issue. Leeper and Macmillan would see the Regent afterwards. They were assuming that London did not expect them to bring pressure on Damaskinos for the sake of a general amnesty and communist participation in the government. But in any case they would exert themselves for the continuation of the conference.[20]

At the meeting with Damaskinos, Macmillan and Leeper learned that Tsirimokos had assured the Regent he would press for acceptance of the draft-law. If Siantos and Partsalidis refused, he would break with them openly.[21] Siantos' attitude on the amnesty question was certainly hard, but the government would nevertheless send him a written statement of its own position. He, Damaskinos, expected the conference to continue next day.[22] Macmillan, who feared that the conference might break up, had 'prepared telegrams for the Prime Minister and asked for authority in the last report to threaten Siantos with all our military resources if he did not yield. . . He [Damaskinos] was very grateful for my offer of obtaining further promise of support from Churchill but he thought it not yet necessary. The discussions would not be called off. Like all arguments in Greece they would continue for a long time'.[23]

Despite Damaskinos' reassuring words, Macmillan still thought it necessary to arm himself against a possible breakdown of the conference. Therefore, on the same day (4th February), he sent Churchill a long telegram in which he explained the military situation and asked for a decision whether Scobie should declare the armistice cancelled or not and, in the event of an affirmative answer, what military operations Scobie should plan. With the forces available a situation resembling that of the German Occupation period could at least be set up. Moreover, it would be helpful if Churchill could break his return journey from Yalta for talks in Athens.[24] On the 5th February he turned to Churchill again and urged him to push through Alexander's declared recommendation of an increase in the Greek armed forces to 100,000 with the Combined Chiefs-of-Staff on the favourable occasion of the Yalta conference. This would be of great significance if the negotiations failed and ELAS resumed military operations.[25]

On the 4th February there had been no official conference session at Varkiza but unofficial negotiations had continued. Tsirimokos had that evening handed Siantos Sofianopoulos' statement. Siantos thereupon sought a private interview with Sofianopoulos on the 5th February, which was however refused. At the same time the government made known that court-martial proceedings against ELAS members would for the time being be suspended and that the collaborators who had been flown to Egypt during the December fighting were being brought back and would soon stand trial. Eventually the EAM delegation decided to accept the government's version of the amnesty and informed Sofianopoulos in writing. This news item he communicated to the press on the evening of the 5th. The EAM delegation's text, signed by all three delegates, made clear that the delegation did not agree with the government's viewpoint but that, since insistence on their own would bring about the failure of the conference, which would involve the country in even greater misery, they therefore consented.[26]

The reasons why Siantos yielded are complex. Macmillan's supposition that he hoped for Stalin's assistance in the context of the Yalta conference, then in session, is hardly convincing. Throughout the December conflict KKE had been in radio contact with Tito and Georgi Dimitroff, the latter at that time in Moscow for talks with the Soviet party leadership. On the 19th December Dimitrov had let the KKE leaders know that they could expect no help whatsoever from abroad. On account of a transmission failure this message did not reach Siantos till the 15th January, together with a communication from the Secretary of the Bulgarian Communist Party's Central Committee, Traicho Kostov, that help from abroad was impossible at that point.[27] From this and from the behaviour of the head of the Soviet Military Mission, Colonel Grigori Popov, who had spent the whole of December in the government-controlled zone and had participated in the Christmas conference in a strictly walking-on role, Siantos must have realised that he could not count on Soviet aid. Siantos' reasons were much more probably internal Greek reasons. During the early conference days he had had several personal talks with Sofianopoulos and had got the impression that the latter was genuinely seeking peace. He himself had a horror of terrorism,[28] and since the transgressions of some ELAS and OPLA members were not committed on instructions from the leadership, he was not prepared to risk the break-up of the conference for their sake. Moreover, the ultimatum-style wording of the government text made it clear that they were going to take a hard line on this issue. Nor is it impossible that rumours had percolated to him of Macmillan's offer of 'aid' to Damaskinos. In addition to that, administrative guarantees provided for in the government's draft-law might have coincided with his own bureaucratic cast of mind; and, finally, Tsirimokos' influence should not be discounted. In short, Siantos accepted the government plan. The consequences for the whole Greek Left were disastrous.

In London, the reaction to Macmillan's enquiry of the 4th February as to whether the British Army should in certain circumstances resume its offensive against ELAS was treated with reserve since Siantos' yielding was already known on the 5th and thus there was no longer any immediate danger that the conference would break down. The Foreign Office remembered the decision of the 21st January, when the Chiefs-of-Staff had rejected a further commitment of British troops; and it was expected that Churchill would reach a similar decision;[29] there was surprise that Macmillan apparently knew nothing of this decision.[30] Churchill replied to Macmillan on the 7th February: he reserved his decision until he had seen the situation on the spot—he and Eden intended to visit Athens, with Alexander, after the end of the Yalta conference and he hoped that, in the meantime, a final break-down could be avoided.[31] Thereupon the Foreign Office sent Leeper a telegram in which it expressed its astonishment that Macmillan had not taken note of the January decision.[32] This prompted Churchill to tell Eden on 12th February that Macmillan had been absolutely right, that in no case should British assistance against the communists be excluded until the Greek army was fully trained.[33]

In Athens negotiations were resumed on the 6th February on the military and financial issues. In cooperation with Brigadier Mainwaring, the figures for the arms to be handed over by ELAS were settled and Sofianopoulos agreed that the government would honour the financial obligations (stemming from requisitioning of pack animals, food stuffs, etc.) incurred by ELAS during the Occupation.[34] Negotiations went so smoothly that Greek government circles expected the peace treaty to be signed next day. Parallel with this Tsirimokos, Stratis and Papapolitis were negotiating the unification of the socialist parties in which Leeper played a part which is not wholly clear.[35] Military negotiations continued on the 7th February. EAM demanded that the ELAS officers must be integrated in the national army and that, once the peace treaty was signed, the state of siege should be lifted. The representative of the War Ministry, Assistant-Minister General Leonidas Spaïs, was against blanket integration since only 200 of the 1,700 ELAS officers had been on the pre-war active list, with another 500 officers belonging to the Reserve, and he mistrusted the graduates of the ELAS Officers' Training School. Eventually it was agreed that all officers should prove their qualifications before a committee and this committee would decide on their subsequent service.[36]

On the question of the lifting of martial law and the payment of ELAS obligations and also on the too mild amnesty terms, the Greek government was faced with an internal crisis. The anti-ELAS faction protested, the Finance Minister refused to pay up and Plastiras roundly rejected the lifting of martial law. Since Damaskinos, too, was against this, the conference again risked running aground. Leeper was instructed by Churchill on no account to demand the lifting of martial law.[37] The question remained unresolved. On the other hand, on the 8th February, a solution was found to the problem of how the ELAS arms should be handed over. The British would take them over on trust.

On the 8th February there was great progress: the military issue was finally cleared up; the amnesty would be announced immediately after signature of the agreement; martial law would be replaced by the somewhat milder 'state of emergency law' in which certain articles of the Constitution were suspended; and trials for offences not covered by the amnesty would begin at once before the accessors' courts. Siantos accepted all these points and Damaskinos, too, was in agreement with the solution arrived at; but Plastiras still refused to yield.[38] Therefore, on the morning of the 10th, Leeper intervened and, with the support of Rallis, brought him to acceptance.[39] However, at the session of the 11th February, a last-minute obstacle appeared. The Greek government wanted to maintain the state of emergency until disarmament was completed.

Siantos insisted that the state of emergency, too, should be lifted after signature of the peace treaty.

This 'state of emergency' involved suspension of the following articles of the Constitution:

Article 5. No arrests to be carried out without a warrant; the arrested person to be brought before the competent judge within 24 hours and the judge to decide within three days whether he should be set free or remain in pre-trial custody: if these conditions were not complied with, the arrested person to be set free.

Article 10. Right of assembly. The police can only be present at public meetings. Open air meetings may be prohibited if there is a danger to public order.

Article 12. Inviolability of the home.

Article 20. Inviolability of correspondence.

Article 55. Political offences to be tried before assessors; the same for press offences unless they belonged to the civil law sphere.

Siantos had good reasons for his insistence. He knew that the suspension of Article 5 until the completion of disarmament would lead to a wave of legal arrests throughout Greece lasting many weeks. This had been proved by the mass arrests in Athens and Piraeus after the withdrawal of ELAS and the conclusion of the armistice. Once EAM's followers were in prison, their release would be endlessly delayed and charges for crimes not covered by the amnesty would surely be found. Siantos knew he could not ask the EAM-ELAS members first to lay down their weapons and then to return to their homes in the certainty that they would be arrested there. So he continued to refuse his consent. Macmillan's intervention was needed to overcome this obstacle. He realised that the government had every intention of arresting a great number of suspects before disarmament could be completed and that this was just what Siantos feared. He therefore suggested the following compromise: the state of emergency should be lifted in Athens and Piraeus directly after the signing of the peace treaty; for the rest of Greece only after the completion of disarmament. All parties accepted this formula[40] and thus, at last, in the early hours of 12th February, after a few further problems of wording had been overcome, that document was signed which was to go down in history as the Varkiza Agreement.[41]

Leeper described the agreement as follows, in a telegram to the Foreign Office:

'The signing of this agreement is a victory for the forces of moderation. The Government will be attacked by the Right and Siantos will equally have difficulties with his own people when he returns, but the average person, both here and in the rest of Greece, will be relieved and and thankful.'

After a few words about the positive role played by Damaskinos, there followed a passage which showed a remarkable insight, something rather unusual with Leeper:

> 'The Greeks of the beaten party will have more confidence in us tomorrow than they ever had before. Without us and the guarantee which our presence here affords, they would never have come to terms with their Greek opponents. We therefore have all the heavier responsibility towards Greece because of our success here, which above all things must be regarded as a moral success. I suggest therefore that this agreement should be treated not as a victory for either side in Greece or for the British, but as a victory for Greece. Sophianopoulos [sic] and Siantos in their speeches after the signing of the provisional agreement struck this note in their concluding words "long live Greece". Greeks, in their present battered state, realising too with a shock to their self-esteem how dependent they are on us, will appreciate it enormously with their lively but sensitive intelligence if we hail this agreement in the same words "Long live Greece".'[42]

Reactions in the Greek press were varied. *Eleftheri Ellada,* the official EAM paper, declared that the Left had made every possible concession in order to reach an agreement. KKE's *Rizospastis* expressed the opinion that the peace treaty was fair and honourable for both sides. The Centre papers welcomed the agreement but took an attitude of 'wait and see': if ELAS actually did lay down its arms, then there would really be a chance for a genuine peace. Only the papers of the Greek Right attacked the government for yielding to the Left and called the agreement a left-wing victory.[43] In other words, immediately after the conclusion of the treaty, all moderate and left-wing forces agreed that the Varkiza Agreement was a workable compromise.

NOTES

1. Speech of Ioannis Sofianopoulos (R 2902/4/19). The government's programme coincided almost down to the last word with that formulated by Macmillan. See Leeper to Foreign Office 2nd February, 1945 (R 2439/4/19).
2. Proceedings of the Conference on the Evening of 2nd February Immediately After the Opening Speech of M. Sofianopoulos (R 3226/4/19).
3. The following portrait of Sofianopoulos is taken mainly from the biography by Sotiris Patatzis, *Ioannis Sofianopoulos: Enas epanastatis choris epanastasi,* (Athens, 1961).
4. Sofianopoulos referred to the military rebellion of 1909 at the Goudi barracks which brought the liberal statesman Eleftherios Venizelos to power.
5. Patatzis, *op. cit.,* p. 204.
6. Macmillan, *op. cit.,* p. 652.
7. D. George Kousoulas, *Revolution and Defeat: The Story of the Greek Communist Party,* (London: Oxford University Press, 1965), p. 216. Kousoulas, who teaches in the US, is a militant anti-communist. In 1967 he participated in a symposium in Washington, financed by the State Department and composed of

hand-picked anti-communists, which prepared the ideological ground for the Junta *coup* of 21st April 1967. Stephen Rousseas, *The Death of a Democracy: Greece and the American Conscience*, (New York: Grove Press, 1967), p. 94. Kousoulas' name appears in the last of participants published in *Balkan Studies* Vol. 8, 1967, p. 223. After the *coup* Kousoulas was one of the foremost apologists of the Colonels' regime, was also involved in preparing the Junta's 'constitution' and defended the regime at the US Senate hearings in 1974.
8. Speech by M. Siantos at the Conference, 3rd February, 1945 (R 3227/4/19). Greek text published in 'To Kommounistiko Komma tis Elladas sto polemo kai stin antistasi', *Episima Keimena, Vol. V, 1940-1945*, (Athens: KKE/ESOTERIKOU, 1974), pp. 333-9 (cited hereafter as *Episima Keimena, V*).
9. *The Times*, 3rd February, 1945; *New York Times*, 3rd February, 1945.
10. *New York Times*, 4th February, 1945.
11. Macmillan, *op. cit.*, p. 653.
12. *New York Times*, 5th, 7th and 15th February, 1945.
13. R 3227/4/19. See footnote 8.
14. The Third Brigade, called also the Mountain or Rimini Brigade, represented the remains of the Greek armed forces after the purge of the First and Second Brigades following the Middle East disturbances of spring 1944. See p. 15. footnote 58. The Third Brigade was militantly anti-communist in orientation and mainly royalist. There was also the Sacred Company, a unit composed largely of officers which came directly under the Allied High Command.
15. Macmillan and Leeper to Foreign Office 4th February, 1945 (R 2520/4/19).
16. Leeper to Foreign Office 5th February, 1945 (R 2548/4/19).
17. R 2520/4/19.
18. *Ibid.*, Kousoulas' argument (*Revolution and Defeat*, p. 216) that Siantos was not interested in a general amnesty because he feared that, if the EAM-ELAS members could return home without fear of persecution, they would have turned against the KKE leadership, is simply absurd.
19. R 2520/4/19.
20. Macmillan and Leeper to Foreign Office 4th February, 1945 (R 2541/4/19).
21. R 2548/4/19. See footnote 16.
22. Macmillan and Leeper to Foreign Office 4th February, 1945 (R 2545/4/19).
23. Macmillan, *op. cit.*, p. 653.
24. Macmillan to Foreign Office (Prime Minister) 4th February, 1945 (R 2543/4/19).
25. Macmillan to Foreign Office (Prime Minister) 5th February, 1945 (R 2652/4/19). See p. 51, footnote 14. General Robertson of Allied Forces Headquarters supported Macmillan's request in a telegram to Alexander on 6th February, 1945 (R 2543/4/19).
26. *The Times*, 5th, 6th and 7th February, 1945. The government's statement was in the nature of an ultimatum. See *Episima Keimena, V*, p. 341, and for the text of the EAM delegation's reply, *Ibid.*, pp. 340 ff.
27. *Ibid.*, pp. 324-6.
28. Eudes, *op. cit.*, p. 206; English edition, p. 148.
29. Laskey's Minutes 6th February, 1945 (R 2543/4/19); see also p. 51, footnote 14.
30. *Ibid.*, Minutes by Sir Orme Sargent and D. Howard.
31. Prime Minister to Macmillan 7th February, 1945 (R 2543/4/19).
32. Foreign Office to Leeper 9th February, 1945 (R 2543/4/19).
33. Copy of Prime Minister's Minute 12th February, 1945 (R 2543/4/19).
34. *The Times*, 6th and 7th February, 1945.
35. *Ibid.*, 6th February, 1945; Leeper to Foreign Office 6th February, 1945 (R 2714/4/19).

36. *The Times,* 9th February, 1945. Spaïs' figures must be compared with those given by Sarafis: serving professional officers 700, reservist officers 100, officers from ELAS Training School 1,270, professional officers purged after the republican *putsch* of 1935 or retired by the Metaxas dictatorship 1,500. Sarafis, *op. cit.,* p. 402. The motive underlying Spaïs' reduced figures is transparent.
37. Leeper to Foreign Office 8th February, 1945 (R 2745/4/19); Leeper to Foreign Office 8th February, 1945 (R 2854/4/19); Foreign Office (Prime Minister) to Leeper 10th February, 1945 (R 2855/4/19).
38. Leeper to Foreign Office 10th February, 1945 (R 2969/4/19).
39. *Ibid.*
40. Macmillan, *op. cit.,* p. 652-8.
41. For text, p. 561.
42. Leeper to Foreign Office 12th February, 1945 (R 3053/4/19). Compare: *The Foreign Relations of the United States, 1945, Vol. VIII: The Near East and Africa,* (Washington: US Govt. Print. Off., 1969), p. 114 (hereafter cited as *FRUS 1945, VIII*).
43. *FRUS 1945, VIII,* p. 114.

VARKIZA: COMPROMISE OR CAPITULATION?

Though at the time when the Varkiza Agreement was signed the KKE leadership—with a few exceptions—appeared satisfied with it, it soon began to be criticised and later on it became the cause of a major internal party controversy. Therefore it may be useful to take a closer look at the development of this argument and to analyse whether Varzika was in fact a compromise or a capitulation.

If, soon after the signing of the agreement, criticism began to be heard, this was not directed at the text of the agreement itself but rather at the way in which it was carried out—or more properly was not carried out—by the Greek government. EAM up to its banning at the end of 1947 and KKE up to 1950 restricted their criticism to showing how their opponents had systematically transgressed the terms of the agreement.[1] Critics from the bourgeois camp likewise only criticised the way the agreement was adhered to.[2]

The first time the agreement itself was called in question was in February 1950, by one of its signatories, Dimitrios Partsalidis. Within the framework of a criticism of the KKE General-Secretary, Zachariadis, and of the line followed by the party in the previous ten years, he expressed doubts as to whether the agreement should have been signed at all.[3] In his speech to the Seventh Plenum of the Central Committee (14th-18th March 1950), he formulated his criticism more specifically: up till now the Varkiza Agreement had been regarded as a necessary manoeuvre to permit the regrouping of the popular democratic forces. Even when, at the Fifth Plenum (30th-31st January 1949), Zachariadis had criticised the line followed by the party during the Second World War, he had regarded the Varkiza Agreement as correct, since ELAS—by reason of its political aims and organisational structure—could not have fought on and would have suffered a crushing defeat. Varkiza had given the opportunity for political and organisational re-grouping and for better preparation of the Democratic Army's new uprising. But the fact was—Partsalidis continued—that at the time of Varkiza the party had not yet emancipated itself from the theory that, under the conditions prevailing in Greece, it could achieve nothing on its own if the international situation did not favour decisive support for its struggle from abroad. This had been the party's viewpoint. Nevertheless, he maintained that the Varkiza Agreement had been a mistake: ELAS should not have surrendered its arms and could have continued the struggle outside Athens. KKE should not blame others who had simply advised the party to sign the agreement so as to keep its forces intact. But this is just what the Varkiza Agreement had not achieved. Had the struggle been continued outside Athens, such conditions might have been achieved. It was true that, at that time, the party was burdened with the consequences of a whole series of mistakes, but it was not true that ELAS was in no condition to fight. It had fought both in Athens and in Epirus. What was needed and had been lacking at that time was confidence in the potential support existing both within and outside Greece.[4] At the end of his speech he added an important piece of information:

'It is known that, when we had reached a particular difference of opinion [over the amnesty], and the conference was interrupted for two days, I suggested to Siantos, the leader of the delegation, that we withdraw. Siantos was at that time Secretary of the Political Bureau. I then thought we could say we have the mandate to demand a general amnesty. It is true, I too did not then see the problem of Varkiza as we see it now and I did not get to the point of standing up and withdrawing on my own... The Political Bureau approved the Agreement.'[5]

But Zachariadis stuck to his opinion. In an article written in preparation for the Third Party Conference in October 1950 he expressed the following views: Varkiza was the last link in a chain of mistakes resulting from the party's fundamentally incorrect political and organisational line during the Occupation, the main characteristic of which had been its unconditional support—not of the Allied struggle—but of British imperialist policy. The consequences had been: incorrect orientation of EAM and ELAS, wrong composition and policy of PEEA, wrong organisational and cadre policies, the Lebanon and Caserta Agreements and, finally, the complete lack of preparation for the December conflict which led to defeat. Thus, Varkiza was not an acceptable compromise but an unacceptable surrender. Certainly, in view of the defeat in Athens and of the situation within ELAS itself, an agreement, a compromise with the enemy had to be found; a compromise acceptable for a revolutionary party such as KKE and based on the balance of forces existing at the time, both within Greece and internationally. It was this balance, too, which had compelled the British to seek a compromise. Had the British not been under this compulsion, they would not have hesitated to destroy KKE. Zachariadis went on to specify wholly illusory conditions which should have been incorporated into the Varkiza Agreement: the *andartes* to keep their personal weapons, the granting of an unconditional general amnesty, recognition of the EAM Resistance, withdrawal of British forces from Greece, formation of a government with EAM participation and speedy elections. Such an agreement would have permitted the regrouping of the party's forces; instead, the Varkiza Agreement had been a surrender.[6]

He then proceeded to denounce Partsalidis and Siantos because they had signed that agreement without insisting on the general amnesty and in spite of explicit contrary orders from the Political Bureau. Then he attacked this body itself because it had sanctioned the signing. The Varkiza Agreement had thus confirmed the mistaken political line of the Occupation period. Zachariadis then referred to the Seventh Plenum's criticisms and, without acknowledging it, exactly reproduced Partsalidis' argument when he criticised the resolutions of the Twelfth Plenum (June 1945) and the Seventh Congress because these had characterised the Varkiza Agreement as a tactical move to facilitate re-grouping. All he forgot to mention was that both resolutions had been passed under his chairmanship. Self-criticism was not for Zachariadis. He closed the matter by stating that the Varkiza Agreement had in fact become a serious obstacle to the re-grouping of party forces.

This discussion, which was only one element in the major controversy within KKE after defeat in the civil war, ended for the time being with the expulsion of Partsalidis. In 1956, during destalinisation, it was resumed.[7] Since even an outline of this renewed debate would far exceed the framework of this book and since, moreover, it did not produce many new arguments, it will not be pursued here. Instead, there is another critic to be heard, Svetozar Vukmanović.

Vukmanović (Tito's lieutenant for Macedonia, *nom de guerre* Tempo) regarded the defeat of ELAS in Athens as unimportant. The December fighting had certainly shown that ELAS could not fight regular British units; but, had the fighting continued, it could have become a real revolutionary army able to overcome foreign intervention. The Varkiza Agreement was a capitulation. The masses, too, had been ready to continue the struggle against monarcho-fascism as well as against foreign intervention. The KKE leadership of the time had followed an opportunist policy. In accepting the disarming of ELAS they had offended against a fundamental Leninist principle. Lenin had always maintained that, for a revolutionary movement to be victorious, it was essential that the masses should be armed.. KKE had in fact taken a social democratic line, recommended to them—as to other communist parties—by the Communist Party of the Soviet Union. Vukmanović then pointed to the Communist Parties of Yugoslavia and China as the only parties to have taken a sound line.[8]

These three critiques, representing three ideologically different communist positions, have been often repeated in varying configurations. So it may be useful to take a closer look at them. Though at first glance they differ greatly, they have one factor in common: they criticise the Varkiza Agreement with hindsight—with knowledge acquired from the post-Varkiza and the civil war defeat and thus they make use of criteria, facts and arguments, either non-existent at the time the Agreement was signed or whose significance was not yet apparent. Such an analysis is antihistorical and obstructs recognition of the real problems. In the author's opinion, a sound historical evaluation of the Varkiza Agreement should take into account only such factors as could be known to the participants. Nevertheless, in view of the prominence of the three critics, their arguments may deserve more detailed scrutiny.

Vukmanović's critique is the most radical of the three, but his application of the Yugoslav and Chinese models to the Greek situation does not hold. The geo-political, military, social and ethnological circumstances were too different. A resumption of the fighting pursued until an ELAS victory was excluded: this would merely have anticipated the course of events during the subsequent civil war (1947-49). Moreover, it can justifiably be doubted whether all ELAS units would have been ready to continue fighting. Certainly, some units such as those under Aris Velouchiotis would have gone on fighting, but the majority of ELAS members were not KKE party members and it is questionable whether they would have followed KKE into such a desperate undertaking, especially since ELAS was not psychologically prepared for this new fight against yesterday's ally. Unlike the later Democratic Army of Greece (Dimokratikos Stratos Elladas) of the civil war, ELAS was not a party army controlled by party cadres down to the battle group. Thus, Vukmanović's critique is based on wrong premises and yields equally wrong deductions.

Zachariadis' critique in his 1950 article boils down to an acceptance of the premise that the British would have been forced by their own public opinion and that of the rest of the world to find a compromise. Had the representatives of ELAS driven a harder bargain, they would have obtained much better conditions. But the armed intervention in December 1944 had shown beyond any doubt that this was just not so—even at a time when the British were obviously in the wrong. After the propaganda campaign on the hostage-taking and other acts of extremism, the moral stature of the Greek Left was so diminished that the British had even less need than before to compromise. Thus, Zachariadis' critique, too, is based on an erroneous premise.

Finally, Partsalidis' arguments are similar to those of Vukmanović. Had the EAM delegation broken off negotiations, the British would not have yielded but would have declared the armistice at an end. This would have meant the temporary division of Greece into two. The British would have covered the government-controlled zone and speeded up reconstruction of the army which, with British support, would certainly have gone over to the offensive by summer 1945. In the plains even the regular ELAS units could have achieved nothing in modern pitched battles against such forces equipped with heavy weapons. The result would have been a military situation resembling that of the German Occupation (in late 1943) or the future civil war. At first the government forces would have controlled the plains and the guerrillas the mountains; with growing strength the government forces would have begun drives against the mountain strongholds and the end would have been the same as that of the civil war in 1949—utter defeat.

Partsalidis' hypothesis that to continue the fight would have led to a compromise on better conditions than those of the Varkiza Agreement is wrong from another aspect too. In this fight ELAS would have had no support from abroad, either from Yugoslavia or from the other Balkan socialist neighbours, since in 1945 the Communist Parties in these countries had by no means consolidated their authority. Nor could any help have been expected from the Soviet Union. Continuation of the conflict would thus have meant fighting alone against an opponent who had the support of the British Empire. For the Greek Right and its protecting power there was no question of yielding or compromising, as was to be proved during the civil war when just such compromise proposals were turned down by the government side. Thus, Partsalidis' hypothesis is likewise unsound.

Having dealt with these criticisms from hindsight, we will now try to evaluate the Varkiza Agreement in its context. To begin with, the author agrees—though for different reasons—with the verdict that the Varkiza Agreement was the last mistake in a long chain of mistakes. Partsalidis, as well as Zachariadis, attributed these mistakes to a basic error in KKE's line, to its incorrect policy towards the British. But this is only half of the truth. During the Occupation KKE was not following one line but two, between which it was oscillating in a most inconsistent way. The first line resembled very closely the policies of the other Western European Communist Parties: cooperation with the Allies and eventual peaceful integration into the post-war parliamentary system. This line had the blessing of Moscow. This was reflected in Greece in KKE's cooperation with the British Military Mission from 1942, the National Bands Agreement of early summer 1943, participation in the *andarte* delegation to Cairo in August 1943, the Plaka armistice, the Lebanon and Caserta Agreements and PEEA's entry into the National Unity Government in September 1944.

The other line may, with certain reservations, be called a Titoist line: cooperation with the Allies as long as this did not prejudice the party's post-war aim of establishing a socialist society. Reflections of this line can be seen in the repeated efforts to dissolve the competing Resistance movements EDES and EKKA[9] culminating in the fighting between ELAS and EDES during autumn/winter 1943-44 and the killing of Psarros in spring 1944, the setting-up of PEEA and the National Council and the hesitations about entering the Government of National Unity, the rough treatment meted out to collaborators and finally the armed conflict with the British in December 1944. Whilst on the one hand internal developments pointed to the Titoist option, KKE constantly tried to adhere to what they believed to be Moscow's wishes. As a result they for some time steered a most erratic course which led inevitably to conflict with the British and the Greek Right. Towards the end of the Occupation, however, they returned to the first, or parliamentary course. This was made clear by Siantos in an interview with the *Daily Herald* correspondent in November 1944, apparently never published in that paper.

> 'KKE is for normal democratic solutions and for democratic renewal of the country. If KKE had intended to proceed by force, it could still achieve this today. But no honest person can deny that KKE has put all its forces at the disposal of the National Government and has been the champion of exemplary maintenance of order and of normal development of our political life.'[10]

Even after the December events, directly after the signing of the Varkiza Agreement, Siantos confirmed this course when he was asked at a press conference whether he agreed with Thorez' statement that the French Communist Party would pursue its political activity as a party loyal to the constitution and within the constitutional framework. He replied: 'What Thorez says holds both for France and for Greece.'[11]

If we take both statements as more than mere lip-service (and in fact, as we shall see later, KKE's ideological position obliged the party to follow precisely this course), we arrive at the following conclusions. The December events, as well as the Varkiza Agreement, were the inevitable logical consequences of KKE's incoherent and oscillating policy during the Occupation and thus the last in a long chain of mistakes. However, as KKE finally decided to take the parliamentary road, a compromise of the Varkiza Agreement type was the only option open to them. All other alternatives would have meant a deflection from the chosen course. Given this situation, Siantos had no choice but to decide as he did. Under these conditions his signature to the agreement was the lesser evil. Only thus could he hope to bring EAM's mass political organisation relatively intact into the post-war world. True, ELAS would have to be disarmed and disbanded. However, the party had never seen it as more than an auxiliary force and had under-rated it as a peasant army (revolution could only be brought about by the armed urban proletariat), which had several times been the cause of dangerous Leftist deviations. The only condition the Political Bureau had imposed on Siantos when he left for the negotiations at Varkiza was that he should bargain for a general amnesty. KKE's Political Bureau had indeed estimated the situation correctly. They had noted the wholesale arrests towards the end of the December fighting and wanted to put a stop to this and prevent it from spreading all over Greece.

The question of the amnesty was indeed crucial. Already by the time of the Varkiza negotiations the first steps had been taken towards the judicial aftermath of the December events, the wholesale trials. We shall show later that, in the months to come, this 'legal' persecution by trial assumed proportions which far exceeded the most pessimistic expectations. But this lay in the future and cannot be used as an argument against Siantos. Under the existing circumstances, Siantos negotiated the best possible result. Insistence on the amnesty to the point of breaking off negotiations, as Partsalidis suggested, would have possibly meant resumption of hostilities and would have diverted KKE still further from its political aim—integration into the post-war parliamentary system. There were also other factors which probably influenced Siantos. His negotiating partner at Varkiza was Sofianopoulos, a left-wing Liberal in whose guarantees he could put a certain trust. The text of the Agreement contained important concessions and guarantees on a purge of fascists and collaborators from the state apparatus and on the re-integration of EAM and ELAS members. And there were also the British guarantees. Finally, Siantos himself did not approve of the extremist violence in December and was therefore not wholly opposed to the argument that real crimes must be punished. Last of all, one should not forget the role played by Tsirimokos. Taking all this into account, it becomes understandable why Siantos signed. He believed he had reached an acceptable compromise—the subsequent outcome he could not even imagine; just as in the pre-December days the EAM leadership had not been able to imagine that the British would use force to achieve their ends. Perhaps we should add here that his negotiating partner, Sofianopoulos, too, had never imagined the ensuing degradation of the Varkiza Agreement into an instrument of revenge.[12]

NOTES

1. In June 1945 EAM published a White Book in which it demonstrated in detail how the opposing side was systematically violating the agreement, by circumventing its terms: Politikos Synaspismos ton Kommaton tou EAM, *Lefki Vivlos. Paravaseis tis Varkizas Flevaris-Iounis 1945*, (Athens, July 1945); reprint. (Athens: *Ellinika Themata*, 1975). In October 1945, a further White Book was published in which the growth of fascism in Greece was exposed: Politikos Synaspismos ton Kommaton tou EAM, *Lefki Vivlos, 'Dimokratikos' neofasismos. Ioulis-Oktovris 1945*, (Athens, October 1945); reprint, (Athens: *Ellinika Themata*, 1975). These were followed in 1946 by a Black Book dealing with developments up to the elections: Politikos Synaspismos ton Kommaton tou EAM, *Mavri Vivlos: To eklogiko praxikopima tis 31 Marti 1946*, (Athens, May 1946). In 1947 EAM presented its view of developments in a memorandum to the UN Security Council Investigating Commission: Politikos Synaspismos ton Kommaton tou EAM, *Oi pragmatikes aities tou ellinikou dramatos*, (Athens, January 1947); reprint, *(Athens: (Ellinika Themata, 1974)*. In the three Blue Books of the Provisional Democratic Government there is likewise no substantive criticism: *La verité sur la Grèce Livre Bleu: Sur l'occupation americano-anglaise, sur le régime monarcho-fasciste, sur la lutte du peuple grec*, ed. Ministère des Affaires Etrangères du Gouvernement Démocratique Provisoire

de Grèce, (n.p., August 1948). *For Peace and Democracy in Greece: Second Blue Book. On the Anglo-American Intervention, on the monarcho-fascist regime, on the people's struggle for liberty,* ed. Provisional Democratic Government of Greece, (n.p., August 1949). *For Peace and Democracy in Greece: Third Blue Book. On the Anglo-American Intervention, on the monarchofascist regime, on the people's struggle for liberty,* ed. Democratic Organisations of Greece, (n.p., September 1950).
2. *E.g.* Sofianopoulos himself. Ioannis Sofianopoulos, 'Le problème grec', *Politique Etrangère* 12:4, (September 1947), pp. 390 ff. Sofianopoulos divides the blame for violations of the agreement equally between the Greek Government and the British and stresses: 'L'accord de Varkiza. . . offrait en effet au peuple grec toutes les chances pour une réconciliation nationale et une reconstruction pacifique du pays. . . Mais à conditions qu'il fut respecté des deux côtés.'
3. Dimitrios (Mitsos) Partsalidis, 'Analytiko Simeioma', *Neos Kosmos,* (August 1950), p. 482. This 'Analytic Note' is dated 14th February, 1950.
4. Dimitrios Partsalidis, 'Omilia stin 7i Olomeleia tis KE tou KKE (14–18 May 1950)', *Neos Kosmos,* (August 1950), p. 486.
5. *Ibid.,* p. 492.
6. Nikos Zachariadis, *Deka chronia palis: Symperasmata, didagmata, kathikonta,* (pros ti syndiaskepsi tou KKE), (n.p., 1950), p. 17. This booklet was originally an article by Zachariadis written in preparation for the Third Party Conference of October 1950 and published in *Neos Kosmos,* (August 1950), pp. 397–433, and (September 1950), pp. 509–53.
7. A summary of the further debate on the Varkiza Agreement can be found in the KKE Central Committee's official reply to a reader's question about responsibilities for Varkiza: KKE Central Committee, 'Ap' aformi tis efthynes ya ti Varkiza', *Neos Kosmos,* (February 1957), pp. 93–100. See also Svetozar Vukmanović, *How and Why the People's Liberation Struggle of Greece met with Defeat,* (London: 1950). Reprint (London: Merlin Press, 1985).
8. Vukmanović, *op. cit.,* pp. 16, 25, 29, 49.
9. EKKA, a small resistance organisation confined to Central Greece, was forcibly dissolved by ELAS in spring 1944, when its leader, Colonel Psarros was captured and killed under so far unexplained circumstances.
10. *Episima Keimena, V,* p. 276. The *Daily Herald* Athens correspondent F.H. Salusbury filed his first report on the 8th November.
11. *Ibid.,* p. 351.
12. See p. 502.

FROM VARKIZA TO THE FALL OF PLASTIRAS

The first political event of real importance after the signing of the Varkiza Agreement was the Athens visit of Churchill, Eden and Alexander on their way back from the Yalta conference, on 14th February 1945. During the conference Churchill had noted with satisfaction that Stalin was holding to their agreement of the 9th October—no need to fear Soviet interference with British policy in Greece.[1] During his stay in Athens he could therefore restrict himself to a public speech in Syntagma Square where he received the ovations of the Athenian crowd and to a reception at the British Embassy. On the 15th he flew on to Cairo. The political significance of the visit lay in the conference held on that day in the British Embassy and attended by Eden, Macmillan, Leeper, Alexander, Cadogan, Scobie, the currency expert D. Waley and a number of other high Foreign Office officials and officers of the British forces stationed in Greece. The subject under discussion was future British policy in Greece and the methods for carrying it out.[2] Discussion was based on a paper submitted by Macmillan, the content of which was to be of the greatest importance for future developments in Greece.

Macmillan began by announcing with satisfaction that during the Varkiza peace negotiations all the points important to the British had been established. The guerrilla forces would be disarmed and disbanded; the amnesty was a limited one and KKE had been kept out of the government. British intervention had indeed been successful but it could not end there and must now take on a new form. The Greek government must be assisted in solving its administrative, economic, financial and military problems; and, since the danger of another communist *coup* was not excluded, it would be necessary to keep British forces in Greece for the time being.

The period to follow could be divided into three phases. In the first, which would last two to three months, ELAS would be disarmed and the Greek National Guard would be built up to a point where it could give support to the administration as it gradually replaced ELAS control. British help was absolutely necessary for the reconstruction of the Greek administration. During this period the present strength of the British forces must be maintained. In the second phase, which would be of longer duration, the maintenance of order and tranquillity would indeed pass to the Greek forces but, in the interests of security, one British division would be left in Greece. During this phase the Greek police, gendarmerie and public administration would be re-organised by British Missions. Economic and financial policy would be guided by the advice of British experts. In the third phase the British troops would be finally withdrawn. It would, however, be worth considering whether naval and air force bases should not then be leased from Greece. A lease agreement would be easy to achieve at the right moment.

As soon as the military phase was concluded—it was hoped in the near future—British authority in Greece would revert to a civilian basis, in other words to the Embassy. Since the British ambassador would for a long time have to exercise functions greatly in excess of normal ambassadorial functions, he would in effect have somewhat the character of a High Commissioner, though in deference to Greek susceptibilities, he should not bear this title. He would be responsible for the British Missions (naval, military, air force, police, prisons, possibly even public administration), for supervision of the Greek government's economic and financial policy by expert advisers, for supervision of the British information services and for political guidance to the commanders of British naval, military and air forces.

Since the ambassador would not be able to carry out the work of co-ordination single-handed, he should be given an assistant of ministerial rank. Three committees should be established. The first should consist of the heads of the above-mentioned Missions, the commander of the British forces and the economic and financial advisers. This committee must be kept fully informed of all Foreign Office recommendations. The second committee which would be responsible for economic and financial matters must cooperate closely with the US embassy. Although the members of this committee had not been invited by the Greek government, they would control the economic and financial policies of the Greek government. The third committee, the information committee, should consist of the head of AIS (Allied Information Service), the press attaché and the head of the British Council in Greece. The task of this committee would be to make British policy comprehensible to the Greeks. The minister would need a staff and Macmillan suggested he take over Scobie's political advisers under Brigadier Smith Dorrien and Major Matthews. Harold Caccia would be the Minister.[3]

Alongside this, Scobie submitted a detailed study for further military action. It was the task of the British Army to take over the ELAS arms.[4] It was desirable, of course, to extend the influence of the Greek government to the whole of Greece as soon as possible, but so far it had seemed that Greek administrative reconstruction would be a very slow process and could not keep up with the advance of the British Army. The take-over by the government of the ELAS-controlled regions would thus have to be regulated by the government's ability to control them. He therefore suggested proceeding in two stages: on the 2nd March the forces would advance into South Peloponnese, Fthiotis-Fokis, Larisa-Trikala, Chalkidiki, Thessaloniki (Salonica), Kilkis, Pella, Aetolia and Acarnania. By the 9th March the National Guard would have taken up its positions. By the 16th March the surrender of weapons would be concluded and the Greek administration would be sufficiently established to organise the further call-up for the National Guard. Call-up would be completed by the 23rd March and on the 31st the National Guard would be armed. In the immediately-following second phase, which in principle would take the same course, the rest of Greece would be penetrated. Thus, the disarming of ELAS would hardly be completed before the end of April and the government would not really be in control of the whole country before the 1st June. The first Greek division would not be ready for action before the 15th June. Therefore, withdrawal of a part of the British forces could be initiated at the earliest from the 1st April.

Next, the British currency expert, Sir David Waley, examined existing problems from his own standpoint. It was absolutely essential that the Greek government take some measures to counteract the threatening inflation, perhaps through a wages and prices freeze. The solution of this problem was urgent because the British had tied their Occupation currency to the *drachma* by a fixed exchange rate.

Subsequent discussion yielded the following results: Macmillan's proposals were accepted. On the 1st April Leeper would become 'High Commissioner'.[5] Eden undertook to secure the British government's official *imprimatur*.[6]

Comparison of Macmillan's plan with the Foreign Office views of May 1943[7] show that the basic concept of British policy towards Greece had altered little. Britain did not regard Greece as a sovereign ally but as an occupied country whose sovereignty was suspended just as it was almost totally suspended in occupied Germany or in Italy. The Greek government was to be the executive agency for the 'British High Commissioner', a system very reminiscent of the Axis powers' system of Quisling governments; whilst the British had the further advantage of having in the person of Damaskinos—who in this, too, played the traditional role of the Greek monarch—a viceroy who would control any obstreperousness on the part of the government in British interests so that the latter would not even have to carry out changes of government themselves. In a few words, in the post-Varkiza period, Greece became increasingly like an occupied country.

On the afternoon of the 15th February there were talks between Eden, Macmillan, Leeper and Waley on the one side and Plastiras, Sideris and Sofianopoulos on the other, on the country's economic and financial situation which was indeed extremely critical.

The causes of this crisis stretched back into the Occupation period.

During the German Occupation inflation had been rampant in Greece and, despite German efforts to support the *drachma*, the result was that, at liberation, the currency was practically valueless.[8]

In order to give back to the *drachma* something like the appearance of a currency, Waley advised the creation of a new *drachma* which, whilst on the one hand it bore some definite relation to that up to now current, was on the other hand firmly tied to the British occupation pound.[9] Stabilisation of the currency was only a first step. Production and trade must be got going again. An end must be put to the black market, the price of essential goods be brought down, wages and salaries adapted to the changed situation. Work must be found for tens of thousands and means of livelihood ensured for the families of war casualties and prisoners. The 200,000 refugees, who had not the slightest means to sustain life, must be provided for.[10] Over and above this, some way must be found to provide the government, which could not even pay its soldiers, with an income. Moreover, as the government did not have any reconstruction programme, no one gave the first incentive for reviving the economy. Government and people counted entirely on British help.

That this situation did not end in another catastrophic famine like that of the winters of 1941 and 1942 is to the credit of the British relief service, Military Liaison, which, despite all difficulties, had managed by mid-November 1944 to bring 130,000 tons of relief supplies into the country and, in comparison with the need, even this proved too little. Furthermore, distribution of these supplies was so delayed by lack of transport and—where they could be transported—by the Greek authorities' inability to organise the distribution efficiently that in February 1945 the head of ML was forced to admit that, of the 220,000 tons (of which 170,000 represented foodstuffs) delivered only half had been distributed.[11] The consequence was that on the one hand much of the relief supplies disappeared at once on to the black market; and on the other, the Greek government which would have liked to sell these goods at low prices to obtain revenue, had to abandon this project, since the sale would only have stoked anew the inflation already rising by reason of the shortage of goods; whilst the majority of those who needed the supplies most would have been unable to buy them.

Likewise another measure which could have brought money into the state coffers, the taxing of luxury goods and a high tax on war profiteering, proved ineffective. Finally, the December conflict had destroyed the little national wealth which had survived the Occupation and also what had been newly created. Consequently the government provided itself with funds in the classic way: it printed money. The result was that, at the end of the December conflict, the situation was the same as at the end of the German Occupation, except that inflation had not yet reached comparable heights.[12]

In this situation Sideris, who was both Finance and Supply Minister, came on the idea of curing the Greek domestic economy by resorting to the traditional fiscal nostrum of a foreign loan. In a conversation with Scobie on 26th January he explained that, through lack of inland revenue, he was not able to meet government expenditure without British and American help. The issuing of *drachmas* was not covered by foreign currency and would therefore lead to renewed inflation. In particular, it was essential that the Western Allies should take over the expenses of the Greek armed forces. He suggested that the troops should be paid about two-thirds of what they had received from the British in the Middle East (ten times more than their pre-war pay). The British rejected these demands because, no matter who actually paid, the costs would be such as to stoke inflation.[13] But Sideris stuck to his position that only foreign aid could solve the Greek economic problem.

Two days later, on 30th January 1945, the new Governor of the Bank of Greece, Kyriakos Varvaressos, returned from London where he had had talks with the British on Greek financial problems. Varvaressos put forward the view that Greece was living beyond her means. Given the country's poverty, the present high prices and wages were economically ruinous. From now on the ML supplies should be sold, at reasonable prices, to all but the really poor. The present practice of distributing them free, or at the most at prices covering the cost of transport, must be abandoned. It would also be necessary to control the prices for home produce and to adapt wages to these prices and those of the ML supplies and not to black market prices. He rejected the government's view that only foreign aid could solve the Greek problem. The Greek army must be of a size proportionate to the country's economic conditions: it would be armed by the Allies but he regarded the demand that they should also pay it as ridiculous. Up to now pay had been much too high. The *drachma* was over-valued but, for political and psychological reasons, could not at this moment be devalued. To get production going again, bank credits should be granted at favourable interest rates to firms which would really produce. These firms must be compelled to sell their goods at fixed prices. He had the impression that many entrepreneurs now intended to recoup their wartime losses as quickly as possible. This was unacceptable.[14] The British and American experts agreed with Varvaressos' assessment.

During the talks on 15th February Eden brought up all the outstanding economic problems for discussion in very blunt terms[15] and it emerged that Plastiras had no understanding of such matters and that the other ministers feared to take drastic measures which would make them unpopular.[16] Eden required of the Greek government resolute, speedy and effective remedial measures. In addition he demanded a 75% cut in army pay, retirement of older supernumerary officers and civil servants and dismissal of redundant officials.[17] No written report of the conference results is available but, in the light of later developments, we will probably not be far out in conjecturing that the Greek participants accepted the British viewpoint with the unspoken reservation that they would make no radical change of direction. This would hardly be surprising given the inextricable entaglement of Greek politicians with Greek industrial interests.[18] On 16th February 1945, Eden left Athens.

Two days later, on the 18th, Plastiras took a decision which was to have far-reaching consequences: he appointed his old friend, General Simos Vlachos, Assistant-Minister for Public Order in the Ministry of the Interior and with Cabinet rank. Like his attempt to appoint Gonatas Governor of Macedonia, this was a spectacular example of Plastiras' misguided decisions in the sphere of personal politics. Both cases show that Plastiras was still thinking in terms of the pre-Metaxas period. Politics for him consisted in a placements policy: if he could only fill the key positions with his personal clientele, then political developments would take the direction he wished. Plastiras had a strong sense of loyalty and expected the same of his followers. He mistrusted professional politicians and therefore preferred to appoint officers to important posts. What Plastiras (who had been in foreign exile since 1934) did not realise was that the period of the fascist dictatorship had left its mark on them and that many of them out of fear of the communists had changed camp and become royalists during the Occupation years. This was what had happened in both these cases: Gonatas had been involved in the creation of the Security Battalions and Vlachos had become a royalist.

The real reason for Vlachos' appointment was as follows. The already existing and projected National Guard units, which were to form the nucleus of the future army, did indeed come under the War Ministry which Plastiras himself controlled but, for the transitional period, until the whole country had been subjugated, the National Guard was to carry out police duties and for this purpose would come under the Ministry of the Interior. Plastiras had not succeeded in getting his way on the amnesty question nor over the lifting of martial law and hoped, by creating the Assistant-Ministry for Public Order—attached to the Ministry of the Interior but not subordinate to it—to be able to influence future developments in accordance with his own intentions.

Vlachos had been appointed on the advice of the Chief of the General Staff, General Konstantinos Vendiris. Vendiris had originally been a follower of Venizelos and a republican; in fact, his elder brother was Venizelos' private secretary. In 1935 he was involved in the failed republican *putsch* and was therefore dismissed from the army. In contrast to the convinced republicans like Sarafis, Bakirjis, Psarros—to name only a few—Vendiris' republicanism was obviously not a matter of conviction, since otherwise his attitude during the Occupation and the metamorphosis he underwent at that time would be inexplicable.

At the end of 1941 he belonged to that group of republican officers to which Sarafis turned to build up his resistance organisation. But, confronted with a political programme including certain socialist features, Vendiris rejected this as 'virtually communist' and rejected military action too as 'premature'. Although he thus showed himself a man of distinctly conservative mentality, Sarafis continued trying to get him to cooperate; at least up until October 1942, when, after the arrest of one of Sarafis' republican AAA members, Vendiris declined further involvement.[19]

He had changed sides, having in the meanwhile got together with Major Tsigantes who had returned from the Middle East on a British-inspired mission; and the latter had recruited him as a member of that committee which was to go down in history as the Committee of Six Colonels. This committee was extremely royalist and anti-communist and did not concern itself with problems of resistance to the Occupation, but rather with how the post-war army should be rebuilt, how a communist takeover should be prevented and the king brought back, and how it could itself take control of the post-war state.[20] But Vendiris did not content himself with such military sand-castle games but took very positive steps towards the achievement of these aims: he founded the secret organisation RAN (Roumelia-Avlona-Nisa) with irredentist goals. At the same time he maintained links with the other right-wing secret organisations and, at the end of 1943, he brought RAN into the right-wing umbrella group PAS (Panellinios Apeleftherotikos Syndesmos, Panhellenic Liberation League).[21]

The value attached to Vendiris' activities by the authorities of the time can be assessed from the following facts: after 1943 he was promoted Lieutenant-General and, in April 1944, PAS sent him to the Lebanon Conference as representative of the 'national' organisations. In June 1944 the Papandreou government appointed him commander-in-chief of the Greek army.[22] As such his influence was felt in two directions: he purged the armed forces of all left-wingers and republicans and, within the army, he promoted the right-wing secret societies.

Since 1942 there had been in the Greek army-in-exile a right-wing officers' organisation known as SAN (Syndesmos Axiomatikon Neon, League of Young Officers). To this can be traced the first disorders in the Middle East, those of 1942. Stavrou, referring to a book by General Georgios Karayannis, mentions yet another important secret society, the ENA (Enosi Neon Axiomatikon, Union of Young Officers) and suggests that SAN dissolved itself soon after its founding by Colonel (actually Major) Solon Gikas.[23] In point of fact, ENA never existed and is not mentioned either by so well-informed an authority as Woodhouse or by Tsouderos. The acronym ENA is simply an inaccurate rendering of the actual SAN, with *enosi* substituted for *syndesmos* and altered word-order. To this must be added that Gikas was later a member of the steering committee of IDEA (Ieros Desmos Ellinon Axiomatikon, Sacred Bond of Greek Officers), the organisation which succeeded SAN.[24]

The reason for the founding of SAN had been political. Ever since the failed republican *putsch* of 1935, the army had been wholly royalist. During the Metaxas dictatorship many officers had discovered in themselves an additional affinity with fascism. Republican and democratic officers had been excluded from service in the Albanian campaign and, at the beginning, the army-in-exile too was controlled solely by royalists and fascists. This began to change when republican officers reached the Middle East in increasing numbers, got commands and thus began to threaten the royalist monopoly in the Officers' Corps. When, as a consequence of the Middle East royalist *putsch* (1942), some of the leaders were deprived of their commands and a process of democratisation was initiated by War Minister Panayotis Kanellopoulos, the royalist officers organised themselves in SAN.

The aim of SAN was to prevent this democratising process, by force of arms if necessary. The pretext was the alleged danger of communism.[25] The most urgent task was to be the re-instatement of royalist officers and, so far as the army-in-exile was concerned, this had largely been achieved by liberation, thanks to Vendiris' assistance. In Greece, too, the Right were able to promote their people into a number of important posts. Thus, General Spiliotopoulos, another member of the Six Colonels' Committee, was appointed military commander of Athens at the Caserta conference.[26] After the return of the government-in-exile, Vendiris and Spiliotopoulos were deprived of their commands and replaced by Othonaios and Katsotas, both republicans. But the plot continued to operate: the Assistant-Minister to the War Ministry, Lambrianidis, tried to recruit former Security Battalion officers as officers for the National Guard. After SAN was re-named IDEA, officers from other right-wing organisations were brought in.[27] The IDEA programme shows clearly Vendiris' influence: it demanded a Greater Greece, denounced KKE and demanded that the Officers' Corps be purged of all officers adhering to internationalist ideas or whose nationalist attitude was not beyond question; furthermore, re-integration in the army of former Security Battalion officers—who were after all 'good nationalists'—was to be actively pursued.[28] We do not know whether Vendiris was himself the leader of IDEA. At any rate, through his intrigues with Scobie, he was able to bring Othonaios' military programme to nothing and to provoke the latter's resignation on 13th November 1944.[29] A short time afterwards Vendiris re-appeared as Chief-of-Staff and Plastiras, as Commander-in-Chief, confirmed him in this appointment.

Plastiras could not comprehend this kind of intrigue. He was a courageous soldier who steered a straightforward course and expected that his brother-officers would do likewise. Therefore he followed Vendiris' advice and this was why Vlachos was appointed assistant-minister. In so doing Plastiras took it for granted that Vlachos would obey him and that supervision of police activities would be best entrusted to a soldier. He overlooked two points: the Assistant-Ministry for Public Order had been established by Metaxas, when it had achieved a disastrous notoriety by institutionalising torture; and the assignment of police supervision to Vlachos was interpreted by the Left as a breach of the Varkiza Agreement.

No sooner was Vlachos appointed than Periklis Rallis protested to Damaskinos: by putting his signature to the Varkiza Agreement he had pledged his honour for its correct application as far as concerned public order. Sofianopoulos and Makropoulos supported Rallis. But Plastiras could not be shaken. If no compromise could be found either Rallis or Plastiras would have to resign. Damaskinos informed Leeper on the 19th February and added that Plastiras was still needed. Leeper promised to mediate.[30] But on the same evening Plastiras provoked Rallis to resign.

On the morning of the 20th Leeper again visited Damaskinos. The latter told him that Sofianopoulos and Makropoulos too were determined to resign. Plastiras would have to yield. Should he resign, Damaskinos would appoint Varvaressos to replace him. However the Regent would prefer to keep Plastiras in office for the present but on his conditions. Leeper, likewise, condemned Plastiras' attitude.[31] During the afternoon Plastiras informed the Regent that he was for the time being taking over the Interior Ministry himself. Damaskinos, however, declined to sign the necessary decree. In the evening Sofianopoulos visited Leeper and told him that, as regards his resignation, he would be guided by the Regent's advice. Shortly afterwards Plastiras, Rallis and Makropoulos all came to talk to Leeper and, after supper, Leeper and Plastiras had a private conversation. Leeper reported to the Foreign Office as follows:

'We were both extremely frank with one another. I did my best without success to persuade him to come to an arrangement with Rallis and avoid any resignation at this moment. Plastiras was quite friendly throughout but worked himself into a very exalted frame of mind, declaring that everybody looked to him alone to save the country, that EAM now had complete confidence in him, that the resignation of one politician did not matter as many others could be found, and that I would see everything going quite smoothly in a few days. I warned him I could not share this confidence and that what might seem today to be one small cloud on the horizon might lead to a storm. I therefore pressed him hard to come off his high horse. The only effect of this was for him to warn me in a somewhat theatrical fashion that if the British intervened in what was purely an internal affair they would create a conflagation greater than last December.'[32]

On the morning of the 21st Sofianopoulos and Leeper agreed that the matter should be left to the Regent to settle: he, Leeper, would have no objection if Plastiras learned that the previous evening's conversation was known to Damaskinos and Sofianopoulos. The result was that only Rallis resigned and Damaskinos signed Plastiras' decree. But the latter was so furious with Leeper that, on the same morning, he called a press conference for Greek reporters and gave himself free rein on the subject of British interference in Greek internal affairs. However, towards the end, he realised that he had gone too far and asked that his remarks should be regarded as off the record. Unfortunately, however, some of it leaked through to a foreign press correspondent; thus the affair became known in Greece, too,[33] where it became apparent that a great part of Greek public opinion subscribed to the same view.

The Foreign Office, too, had been following developments attentively and had instructed Leeper that the resignation of the three moderate ministers must be prevented; otherwise Plastiras would have to be deposed. Damaskinos had indeed—so the comments ran—avoided a rupture, but sooner or later it was bound to come.[34] Leeper, for his part, had not forgotten Plastiras' rebuff. In a telegram of the 23rd to the Foreign Office he expressed ambivalent views: despite all his weaknesses as Prime Minister and the bad influence of his circle upon him, Plastiras should be kept in office for the time being; he had forgiven him and would let him enjoy his triumph; but it would not be long before new difficulties would arise and then public opinion would accept a change; he himself would in many ways have preferred it if Plastiras had gone, but it had been proved that this would be too risky; for the moment it was important to strengthen the Regent's position and to build up a non-communist left-wing block, perhaps under the leadership of Kafandaris.[35] In other words, Leeper knew that, for political reasons, he had to keep Plastiras in office; but this did not hinder him from giving free rein to his personal animosity and from using every political opportunity to intrigue against Plastiras in order to bring about his fall.

The opportunity arose a few days later. His success over Vlachos had encouraged Plastiras to continue appointing his clients to a number of high posts in the provinces and departments. He went on to place his officer clients in army commands. In the military section of the Varkiza Agreement it had been agreed that a military commission would be established which would investigate the qualifications of the officers who were to be taken into the new army. This provision had been introduced in order to guarantee the intake of ELAS officers, or rather to prevent political discrimination. Whilst Plastiras had no very marked interest in the recruitment of former ELAS officers, he attached great importance to securing key-posts for a considerable number of his republican followers. But he knew that his candidates would be at a serious disadvantage before the commission. Many of them were too old for active service and even the younger ones often lacked military skills because all but the more junior republican officers had been excluded from the Albanian campaign and those who had acquired their military expertise later in the Second World War had done so either in the Resistance or in the armed forces in exile. The former he himself distrusted and the latter had in the majority been purged after the Middle East disturbances of spring 1944. The remainder were those who had sat out the war in inactivity. Plastiras knew that, if he left the intake to the commission, the key army posts would be filled with royalists. IDEA's machinations were at that time known to no one and the existence of SAN was only revealed by Tsouderos in April 1945.[36]

The commission was to meet in a few days and to select fourteen out of fifty-seven available generals for future commands. Plastiras thereupon decided to act. Without consulting the General Staff, he chose fourteen of his own followers, none of whom had fought in the Albanian campaign and many of whom had long been retired. This measure alerted the royalist officers who feared that the appointment of colonels would take the same course and that they would lose power. Leeper was informed and turned to the Foreign Office: it was surely not British policy that the republicans should take over control of public administration and of the army; for political reasons it was certainly inopportune to bring down Plastiras on these issues and it would be unacceptable as a *fait accompli*; the inevitable collision with Plastiras would be so grave that he did not want to undertake any action without London's advice and he strongly recommended the presence of Macmillan and Alexander.[37] One would have to discuss the present problems openly with Plastiras in the presence of the Regent and make clear to him the nature of Anglo-Greek cooperation; Damaskinos and Sofianopoulos gave the British full latitude for intervention since this was in Greece's interests; if Plastiras would see this, he could remain Prime Minister for the time being, otherwise he would have to be relieved of his office. 'If we take the gloves off with these people they will understand and they will respect us for it. The time for plain speech has come.'[38]

But it was not only in Athens that the fall of Plastiras was being engineered. In London, the former ambassador, D. Kaklamanos, addressed himself to the Foreign Office: Plastiras was surrounded by a group of flatterers who wanted to turn him against Great Britain and towards the US.[39] This group was supported by B. Vlavianos, the publisher of *Ethnikos Kiryx (National Herald)*. They wanted to get their people into all the key posts and replace Sofianopoulos by Alexandris. The aim was to set up in Greece a regime controlled by Venizelist officers. Bankers would have to be excluded from any change which would otherwise appear as a conflict of competing financial interest groups. Anglo-Greek friendship must be put, once and for all, on a solid basis.

The Foreign Office was very impressed and Eden commented that this text must be brought to Leeper's attention as soon as possible.[40]

Kaklamanos' information was partly correct. Efforts were in fact, at that time, being made to free Greece from its relation of dependence on Great Britain, or at least to neutralise British influence by a corresponding American influence. Sofoklis Venizelos and, to a certain extent, Emmanouil Tsouderos, were behind these endeavours. American financial interests too were more than ready to bid for concessions in Greece. On the other hand, Kaklamanos belonged to that group of Greek politicians who saw unconditional cooperation with Great Britain as the only salvation.

In the meantime, in Athens, Leeper was preparing for the collision with Plastiras. On the 1st March he secured for himself the support of Sofianopoulos.[41] On the 3rd March he got his instructions from the Foreign Office: it was agreed that Plastiras' clientele policy must be restrained but clever tactics must be used; if Plastiras were confronted at once with Macmillan and Alexander, he would certainly resign and this was not at present desirable since there was no suitable successor in readiness. Confrontation was a last resort; Leeper's suggestion of a National Council was likewise rejected.[42]

On the 3rd March Macmillan arrived in Athens. Alexander could not accompany him on account of other duties. Macmillan's visit was supposedly for information purposes and to work out plans for future action.[43] In his discussion with Plastiras on the composition of the new Greek army, for which he had armed himself with a directive from Alexander, he struck resistance. Plastiras regarded the precise wording of the Varkiza Agreement as of little importance. Macmillan thereupon drafted with Leeper the text of an agreement which should regulate future relations between British and Greeks. To Churchill he maintained that only a written agreement could provide a solid basis for British influence.[44]

This agreement, the need for which he substantiated at length and with the content of which Damaskinos agreed, consisted of two sections. The first, generalised, section was intended for possible publication; the second was to remain secret.[45] The powers of control included by the British in the second section would have made Greece not only *de facto* but also *de jure* a British protectorate. The British Military Mission was to function as a consultative authority for the Greek War Ministry and General Staff, without whose consent no appointment could be made. The missions attached to the navy, the air force and the police would have comparable authority. For public administration a corresponding committee should be created which would be advised by a representative of the British Embassy: a British Administrative Mission might even be considered. The Greek Finance, Economics and Labour Ministries would have the support of British advisers. The other ministries' cooperation with the British authorities would be ensured by the attachment of British liaison personnel. If differences of opinion arose between the Greeks and their British advisers, the British ambassador would be informed and he would settle these on a friendly basis with the Greek Prime Minister of the moment. These regulations would appertain until the elections.[46] After his return to Caserta, on 7th March, Macmillan told Alexander of the content of this agreement and he gave his approval in a telegram to Churchill.[47]

Macmillan's suggested agreement was received with scepticism in the Foreign Office. D.S. Laskey was of the opinion that no Greek government could sign such an agreement which deprived it of any power and made Greece into a British protectorate. Such an agreement would serve as a precedent for the Soviet Union in Romania, Bulgaria and Hungary and for the French in Syria and Lebanon. It would provoke criticism in Britain and the USA and in Greece the people would certainly reject it. Moreover, it would be of little use. Obviously, for the immediate future Britain would be treating Greece as a protectorate, but this did not require a general government treaty, it would be sufficient if the powers of the individual Missions were settled by pact.[48] Sir Orme Sargent likewise rejected the agreement: Leeper should make his prestige and his personal influence felt, as Lord Cromer had done in Egypt in the 1880s.[49] Alexander Cadogan and Eden too were against concluding an agreement.

On the 7th March Churchill replied to Macmillan:

'The extrusion of Plastiras at the earliest convenient moment seems to me most desirable on the merits, and would be greatly welcomed here. Any move Leeper or you may take in that direction will have my cordial support. It would be wise however to decide beforehand on his successor. Whom have you in view?'

Eden he said would reply to the question about the agreement, but Macmillan should bear in mind Napoleon's saying: 'a Constitution should be short and obscure'.[50]

Meanwhile Leeper had come through again. On the 7th March he telegraphed that Plastiras was intending further appointments with which Damaskinos was not in agreement. The Regent had therefore more or less decided to make Admiral Petros Voulgaris the new Prime Minister. Voulgaris was in full agreement with Damaskinos on all political questions and would gladly accept British advice. It was true Voulgaris was an officer but Damaskinos intended surrounding him with the following ministers: Sofianopoulos as Vice-premier and Foreign Minister, Varvaressos as Finance Minister, Petros Rallis as Interior Minister, General Othonaios as War Minister, Konstantinos Triandafylopoulos as Minister for Justice, Konstantinos Tsatsos as Education Minister and Themistoklis Tsatsos as Governor of Macedonia.[51] To bring about Plastiras' fall, the Regent made the following suggestion. Directly Macmillan had returned to Athens, Plastiras should be confronted with Macmillan's cooperation agreement, which he would certainly not accept and over which he would resign. Then Damaskinos would propose the Voulgaris Cabinet and at the same time summon a National Council under the chairmanship of the Liberal leader, Themistoklis Sofoulis. In this National Council each of the thirty-six departments would be represented by that one of its deputies who had been elected to the 1936 parliament with the greatest number of preference votes, with the addition of party leaders, representatives of the trade unions, universities, chambers of commerce, etc. This National Council would have about one hundred members. The Communists would be represented by Siantos (the acting party leader) and Partsalidis (deputy for Kavalla in 1936).

Leeper took a favourable view of Damaskinos' plan and asked the Foreign Office to support Macmillan and himself by accepting the co-operation agreement.[52] The Foreign Office clearly realised that such a Cabinet would be under the Regent's control. Its composition was welcomed but the National Council was regarded with scepticism. However, the means by which Leeper wanted to bring about Plastiras' fall were rejected on tactical considerations and the suggested cooperation agreement had already been ruled out. Even if Plastiras resigned over this, it would have to be submitted to Voulgaris for signature, which would lead to his denunciation as a British puppet; nor could the agreement be dropped after Plastiras' fall, as then the whole affair would appear as a transparent manoeuvre to bring about that fall. Moreover, after the fall of Plastiras, such an agreement would no longer be needed; nor was it the only tactic which could inevitably bring about his resignation. His conflict with Damaskinos over the appointments could also provide a handle.[53] Churchill was much attracted by the idea of a Voulgaris government and requested that Damaskinos should be supported on this issue.[54]

On the 9th March Eden informed Leeper of the Foreign Office attitude. The change of government was welcomed as Plastiras' replacement had for some time been necessary. If no action had so far been taken, this had been because there was no suitable successor available. The Voulgaris solution would strengthen the Regent's influence. Nevertheless, the co-operation agreement must not be used to bring about the change: he would go into this problem in a future telegram, but there were numerous points of conflict between Damaskinos and Plastiras over which the latter's resignation could be provoked.[55] On the 11th March, there followed the Foreign Office's rejection of the cooperation agreement.[56]

Meanwhile, in Athens, Leeper had found a further important reason for removing Plastiras. The Left had carried out its obligations undertaken at Varkiza and was now occupied in exploiting the mistakes of Plastiras and of the Right by skilful propaganda, presenting itself as the victim of the new dictatorship so as to regain the public sympathy forfeited as a consequence of the December events. Leeper had hitherto been of the opinion that Plastiras should be left in office until public opinion could accept a change without too great a shock. This was no longer the case since Plastiras was steadily forfeiting confidence. As far as he himself was informed, the Regent had decided to depose Plastiras.[57] But during a conversation between Leeper and Damaskinos on the evening of the 8th March, it became obvious that the latter was hesitating, not wanting to take the first step himself and preferring to leave the decision to the British.[58]

On the 11th March Leeper reported on the attitude of the political parties to the forthcoming fall of Plastiras, which was now the talk of the day in Athens. The Left favoured a change of government, hoping for participation in the new one. The result of this was that Kafandaris and the Liberals advocated the retention of Plastiras. The Populists were indeed against Plastiras but, out of fear of the Left, wanted to keep him in office for the time being. Leeper himself was for a change, for practical reasons, and had hoped that Damaskinos would take the initiative without British intervention. The latter was hesitating on account of the attitude of the political parties and would only act under pressure which he (Leeper) would naturally not apply. In the meantime he had received the instructions concerning the cooperation agreement and suggested a policy of wait and see.[59]

After his return to Caserta, Macmillan re-appeared, recommending Churchill to keep Plastiras but on a tighter rein. Churchill, however, preferred Leeper's plan,[60] to which the Foreign Office likewise agreed. There was to be no direct and open intervention to get rid of Plastiras.

'The whole essence of our position in Greece is that our authority must be exercised behind the scenes. It does seem to me, however, that an early change of Prime Minister is still the most desirable and now that the possibility of a change has become common gossip in Athens, I do not think that the present Greek Government can last very long... In the past we have never found any difficulty in producing changes...'[61]

Direct intervention was therefore not necessary but, during the rest of his time in office, Plastiras had to be prevented from carrying on with his previous clientele policy.[62] Leeper was instructed accordingly.[63] One cannot tell exactly how far these cautious tactics of the Foreign Office were due to the favourable attitude of the State Department towards Plastiras.[64]

Macmillan flew back to Athens on the 12th March, to support Leeper in putting through this policy for direct control of Plastiras and also to discuss on the spot the other problems of the moment: adherence to the Varkiza Agreement, withdrawal of a part of the British forces,[65] change-over from ML to UNRRA, imminent transfer of responsibility for Greece from the military to the diplomats. Available sources do not permit us to establish the time-table of his visit or to reconstruct his conversations but we can ascertain the topics which were discussed.

It seems that Macmillan and Leeper investigated the possibility of restricting Plastiras' sphere of manoeuvre by Cabinet changes. When this proved too complicated, they decided to leave things as they were and on 15th March they informed the Foreign Office that for the moment a change of government was not required and that, in general, the situation had improved. They had told Damaskinos that, for the present, they did not want to intervene in the change of government but that they would follow future developments closely. Provided that the Greek government did nothing to necessitate a British intervention and that it did not come to a purely internal Greek crisis, they were for the present prepared to cooperate with Plastiras. Damaskinos was greatly relieved at this and left any further decision on Plastiras' fate to the British.[66]

Macmillan used the occasion of an official dinner given by Plastiras in his honour, at which US diplomats, too, were present, to make an afterdinner speech inciting Plastiras to a moderate policy and to maintenance of the Varkiza Agreement.[67] The reason for this public criticism is to be found in the repeated complaints of the EAM leaders that the government was violating the Varkiza Agreement. On the 7th March Siantos, Partsalidis and Tsirimokos had visited Leeper and had informed him about the violations.[68] Leeper asked them to submit these in writing and thereupon on the 10th March the EAM leadership handed him a detailed memorandum which was also sent to Damaskinos, Plastiras and the US and French ambassadors.[69] On the 14th March Macmillan received a further memorandum from Siantos, Partsalidis and Tsirimokos addressed to the governments of Great Britain, the USA, the USSR and France. In this further detailed complaints were formulated and the establishment of an inter-allied Control Commission was requested in accordance with the Yalta Declaration.[70]

Here, we shall not go into the problem of the violations of the Varkiza Agreement but only report the immediate political results of these memoranda.

Macmillan—certainly no friend of EAM—had to admit that some at least of the EAM leadership's complaints were justified, especially in regard to Plastiras's clientele policy in the armed forces and security apparatus.[71] Furthermore Macmillan feared that too obvious violations of Varkiza could on the one hand lead to questions in the House of Commons and on the other provoke EAM to renewed disturbances in confronting which the Greek government could not be wholeheartedly supported.[72] The result of all this was the above-mentioned public criticism.

At this time too the plebiscite and elections began to be discussed, though it is not clear who provided the initiative. But the mere fact that Macmillan was concerning himself with these matters was sufficient to give rise to hectic political activity. The Liberals split. Sofoulis expressed himself for a republic. Venizelos and Gonatas joined the royalists. The Populists too united under royalist leadership. But this was not so much a question of the form the constitution should take as a question of power. The party leaders had the impression that the British were in favour of an early plebiscite and they hoped, by taking up their positions in good time, to achieve personal advantage at the elections. The king would again—as in the past—become the leader of certain political constellations.[73] George Papandreou was the most obvious example of this attitude. He advised Leeper that the plebiscite should be held as soon as possible as this would bring in a big majority for the monarchy. In addition he recommended that, after the king's return, a Constituent Assembly should be summoned which would alter the Constitution so that the Prime Minister would in future be directly elected by the people for a term of three years and could only be removed by a two-thirds majority. In this way the king would be protected from day-to-day political controversy. Papandreou's motives in making these suggestions were obvious. He was reckoning on a certain victory for the monarchy and hoped to be entrusted by the king with the holding of elections and thus become the first Prime Minister with the new extended powers.[74]

Damaskinos, for his part, wanted to know what policy the British were intending to pursue in this regard. He saw the following alternatives: either the plebiscite would take place as soon as possible, in which case the king would certainly return in triumph but, in view of the opposition to him, would have to rely on only one party (the Populists);[75] or the present regime would be maintained in power for a time, in which case Plastiras would have to be replaced within the next two or three weeks. In addition, the National Council should be summoned to act as a kind of parliamentary safety-valve.[76]

After some discussion, the Foreign Office inclined to the second alternative, as had both Leeper and Macmillan, the latter having returned to Italy on the 17th March. On the 25th March Leeper was instructed accordingly: the change of government should be brought about with the least possible delay.

'You need only stop short of forcing the Regent to act against his own best judgment, since in the last resort we must be guided by him as regards effects and timing.'

A date for the plebiscite was not yet decided.[77]

The suddenly renewed urgency to overthrow Plastiras was also a result of the plebiscite discussion. We have already mentioned that Gonatas and Venizelos had gone over to the royalists. On the 20th March Gonatas founded a new royalist party, the National Liberal Party (Komma Ethnikon Fileleftheron). This brought about a breach with Plastiras who at once appointed the republican General Konstantinos Manetas Governor-General of Macedonia, a post which he had so far been keeping open for

Gonatas. On the 21st Plastiras informed the Regent that he had decided to appoint Sideris Vice-premier, although Sofianopoulos was against this. Since this was just before Greek Independence Day (25th March) and Damaskinos had still not received any answer to his enquiries from the British about the plebiscite, he decided to wait.[78]

On the 26th March Leeper told Damaskinos of the Foreign Office's attitude on the plebiscite. Damaskinos agreed to the postponement and recommended the establishment of the National Council. Then Leeper gave him to understand that London wanted Plastiras overthrown. Damaskinos understood but a cause would have to be found which would sound plausible to public opinion. For the moment he had no solution to this problem.

In his report to the Foreign Office, Leeper put forward a suggestion how this problem too could be solved: the National Council should be established even before the fall of Plastiras and he should be forced to resign through this very Council. In this way it would be possible to achieve a change of government without a crisis. In the present situation it would be best to proceed slowly. He would put this suggestion to Damaskinos.[79]

In London there was irritation at Damaskinos' delaying tactics[80] and on the 29th March Leeper was instructed accordingly: there was understanding for Damaskinos' search for a convincing pretext to get rid of Plastiras but Leeper had more than once been made aware that a speedy change was hoped for; there were maximum reservations about the National Council which could only become a focus for intrigue amongst Greek politicians; it would be dangerous to give this Council too great powers; the present priority was for a strong government; the Voulgaris solution appeared reassuring.[81]

On the 28th March Leeper met Damaskinos and put to him the plan to act through the National Council. Damaskinos agreed and promised to work on Plastiras through Sideris to accept this institution. Damaskinos then returned to the subject of plebiscite and elections. He would prefer to hold the elections first but the royalists were pressing for an early plebiscite. Such were the instructions they had received from the king through Spyros Markezinis.[82]

In his report to the Foreign Office, Leeper asked whether this direct contact of the king's with his followers behind the Archbishop's back was either correct or wise since such behaviour made him a participant in party politics.[83]

After a personal intervention by Churchill in favour of the king,[84] the Foreign Office rejected the priority of elections and told Leeper that the king was within his rights in conducting his own electoral campaign.[85]

On the 31st March Damaskinos informed Leeper that for the moment he was not intending to provoke a change of government. Varvaressos had refused to become Finance Minister and Sofoulis and Kafandaris had publicly aligned themselves with Plastiras; he (Damaskinos) would not dare a head-on collision with the country's two most important republican leaders and, in Greece's financial situation, a Cabinet without Varvaressos was unthinkable. In the matter of the plebiscite he would conform with British wishes.[86] On the 1st April Leeper once more took up a position on the question of the plebiscite date. In a personal letter to Sir Orme Sargent he recommended that the plebiscite should not be held too soon. In view of the unstable situation, there was a danger that, if the king returned too early, he would again establish an authoritarian regime, in which case the whole process would repeat itself. However, as long as the British had direct responsibility for Greece, it must not come to extreme right-wing domination.[87] To this Leeper added, when informing the Foreign Office about the content of this discussion, that in view of their attitude, he would leave the National Council question open. In London Damaskinos' decision was only grudgingly accepted.[88]

On 4th April Damaskinos and Leeper again discussed the problem of the plebiscite date. Leeper put forward the opinion that it could not be held before the end of the summer but that this would depend on future developments. Damaskinos undertook to seek advice from the Ministry of the Interior but in the meanwhile there was increasing pressure from those who wanted the earliest possible date. He was expecting an imminent offensive by the Populists, who were not interested in elections but hoped to take over the government after a plebiscite resulting in a verdict favourable to the monarchy. If Damaskinos hesitated, the Populists would blame him for each financial crisis. For the moment, however, he was playing for time; meantime, Papandreou too had joined the royalist camp.[89]

Outwardly, it seemed that in this way Plastiras' position was secure, at least for the next few weeks. Certainly, both the British and Damaskinos were of the opinion that he must be replaced as Prime Minister in due course but immediate action against him was not on the programme. Internal political developments seemed set for a period of relative tranquillity when, on the 5th April, a newspaper of the extreme Right, *Ellinikon Aima* (Greek Blood) published a compromising letter from Plastiras of the 16th July 1941 to Pierre Metaxas, the Greek ambassador in Vichy, which shook the Greek political scene to its foundations and gave the pretext for Plastiras' overthrow.

The content of this letter has been described in detail elsewhere.[90] The occasion for digging it out of archival oblivion was a press statement by the Quisling Prime Minister, John Rallis, who had been on trial for collaboration since 21st February. In this Rallis indignantly rejected the charge of collaboration, stressed that he had prevented the communists from taking over power in Athens after the German withdrawal and threatened revelations which would be highly compromising for leading politicians, even for those in the present government.[91] This threat prompted Edward Warner, the official responsible for secret operations at the British Embassy, to recall the letter—in 1941 Warner had held the Greek desk in the Southern Department of the Foreign Office and that letter of Plastiras, as well as a series of others, had passed through his hands.[92] When, in summer 1943, the possibility of an SOE operation to evacuate Plastiras by submarine from Occupied France had been ventilated in Cairo, Warner had again been involved.[93] He now realised the possibilities of the letter and on the 7th March telegraphed to Laskey to look it up in the archives and send him a copy. As far as he remembered this letter showed Plastiras in a somewhat ambivalent light.[94]

At the Foreign Office there was no difficulty in finding Plastiras' letter, but at the same time D.F. Howard of the Southern Department warned against using it to set a snare for Plastiras. He hoped that the Embassy had only asked for this letter in order to discount any attacks on Plastiras.[95] In his reply, in which he wrote that the letter in question and also an additional MI5 report of 1942 on Plastiras' activities in France had been despatched by courier, Laskey transmitted Howard's warnings to Warner and added that the British themselves were far too involved in Plastiras' appointment for it to be advisable to resurrect these old charges. Moreover, Eden had defended Plastiras from just such attacks in the House of Commons.[96]

During the following days the British Secret Service learned further details concerning Rallis' threats. He was going to implicate Plastiras and to demonstrate that his own behaviour under the Occupation had been no worse—if not in some respects better—than that of Plastiras. Rallis maintained that he had approached Altenburg (Hitler's plenipotentiary in Greece) and suggested that Plastiras be made Prime Minister in order to counteract growing communist influence amongst former refugees from Asia Minor. (After the 1922 catastrophe Greece had to integrate more than one and a half million; as this proved difficult, communist votes were proportionally much higher amongst the former refugees.) Altenburg had agreed to bring this matter up in Berlin. Meanwhile Rallis had made contact with Gonatas so that the latter should inform Plastiras. Gonatas had written a letter which had been transmitted to Plastiras *via* the German authorities in Paris. Plastiras had replied by the same route, refusing on grounds of ill-health but at the same time appointing Gonatas his official representative. Gonatas had passed this letter on to Rallis in whose possession it still was. This letter showed that Plastiras had taken the same view of the communist danger as Rallis. So it was only his illness which had saved him from becoming an Occupation Prime Minister.[97] The British Secret Service report contained two further 'revelations', but these were much vaguer.

The Foreign Office knew that these 'revelations' had some factual basis but no great attention was paid to them[98] as it was known that the charges in question would not stick.[99] Plastiras had as a matter of principle consistently refused to collaborate with the Germans. Two points should however be borne in mind. Rallis' 'revelations' were well known in Athens,[100] where there is scarcely anything which does not become public knowledge; and secondly, during the Occupation Rallis had not only been in contact with the Germans but also with the British.[101] As the Secret Service report demonstrates, even now when Rallis was on trial, this contact had not been broken.

But the events which led up to the publication of the letter are still obscure. There are no relevant documents in the Public Record Office in London. The reaction of Leeper and the Foreign Office to publication would seem to indicate that official diplomatic circles were not involved. But this raises two questions: why was this letter published just at that moment? and who leaked it to *Ellinikon Aima*?

The answer to the first question is relatively simple. The publication was part of the major Populist offensive, under Konstantinos Tsaldaris, for the earliest possible plebiscite date, as mentioned by Damaskinos to Leeper on 4th April. On the 2nd there had been a head-on collision between Plastiras and Tsaldaris over the question of the date. On the 3rd the royalist press opened a campaign against Plastiras. On the 4th the Populist Supply Minister, Chatziskos, resigned on the pretext that the Cabinet had not yet discussed the plebiscite date, forgetting that he himself, a member of the Cabinet since the 10th January, had not raised this topic either.[102] The plan of action was obvious: Plastiras' Cabinet was to be forced to resign. Publication of Plastiras' letter came as the culminating point of this offensive.

It is harder to answer the second question. In 1941 there were four copies of the letter, in the following hands: Plastiras, the Vichy ambassador, Tsouderos and the Foreign Office. The fact that Warner requested a copy suggests that, in 1945, there was no copy easily available in Athens.[103] This leads to the inference that the British Secret Service leaked the letter to *Ellinikon Aima*.[104] Whilst it is unlikely that any source will ever be found to show how the letter made its way from Warner's desk to the editorial office of *Ellinikon Aima*, a more than merely probable guess can be hazarded that Plastiras' fall was staged by British Intelligence. But the question remains how it came about that Leeper, and even the Foreign Office, were obviously taken by surprise. This suggests an analogy with the CIA. Just as, years later, American ambassadors did not know what the local CIA operative was planning, so Leeper may really not have been informed—or at least not officially.

In the Foreign Office publication was greeted with mixed feelings. On the one hand there was relief that the pretext of Plastiras' overthrow had been found; on the other hand it was realised that, if Plastiras' resignation were based on the publication of this letter, it could create an unpleasant situation for the British as it would be impossible to deny all knowledge of it. A cautious attitude would have to be taken with the Press. Eden regarded the issue of the letter as secondary, since it had been intended to get rid of Plastiras anyway.[105]

Immediately on publication of the letter, Leeper had turned to Damaskinos. During the conversation he declared himself ready to receive the necessary explanations from Plastiras. A further conversation with Plastiras brought no result. Plastiras remained calm. He rejected the charge of collaboration with the Germans and said that he himself would publish the letter in full. Leeper went back to the Regent:

> 'I told him I was not shaken as regards the honesty of Plastiras but his stupidity was so dangerous that he must not remain any longer in office. I must therefore ask for an immediate change of Government. I left him to choose the reason for the change but I suggested Voulgaris should take his place.'

Damaskinos agreed.[106]

The 6th April was a day of hectic activity. Sideris paid an early morning visit to Damaskinos who told him he should inform Plastiras that the Regent was awaiting his resignation. When Sideris objected that Plastiras had no thought of resigning, Damaskinos instructed him brusquely to transmit the message, adding that Leeper was in agreement. When Sideris tried to see Leeper, he was rebuffed. Shortly afterwards Sofoulis visited Damaskinos and assured him of his support. Kanellopoulos told the Regent that he and Papandreou—who was ill—were both of the opinion that Plastiras must go. When Sideris came back and told Damaskinos that Plastiras was objecting, Damaskinos showed him the door. In the late afternoon Damaskinos called in Leeper—whom he had kept informed of developments through his private secretary throughout the day—to show him the letter to Plastiras demanding his resignation.[107] Still later, Sideris returned to Damaskinos and asked him to postpone the resignation for a week so as to save Plastiras' face. Leeper rejected this.[108]

On the morning of the 7th Damaskinos received Plastiras. Conciliatory in manner but in point of fact inexorable, he rejected any postponement of the resignation, making Leeper's pressure on him responsible. Plastiras refused to resign under these circumstances: Damaskinos must deprive him of his office and thus assume his responsibility before history; but if he did this, he would be the cause of a new civil war.[109] In the late evening of the same day, Damaskinos sent Plastiras the letter removing him from office[110] and Plastiras accepted. On the morning of the 8th Damaskinos swore in Voulgaris as the new Prime Minister.

The deposing of Plastiras was a watershed. Let us recapitulate here the decisive points in the Plastiras government's evolution. Plastiras took over as Prime Minister at a moment when British prestige had sunk to an all-time low in world public opinion. By winning over Plastiras with his reputation as an upright democrat and convinced republican the British were able to mask their real aim: the restoration of the monarchy and the return of Greece to its semi-colonial dependency, and prove to world public opinion that their military intervention had been directed only at the suppression of a communist *putsch*. They knew Plastiras' anti-communism and that, as a soldier, he thought in terms of law and order. His many years' absence from Greece was also an advantage. He had no party political cohorts at his disposal. These characteristics likewise proved extremely useful during the period of peace negotiations. Plastiras' hard line against the Left prevented Sofianopoulos from making too great concessions and the British could restrict themselves to the role of mediators. But during Macmillan's first phase—the disarming of ELAS and the penetration of the country by British forces and the Greek National Guard—Plastiras began to shake off British control and follow his own policy. At the beginning of April 1945, this first phase was nearing its conclusion. In the next phase Leeper was to take over as a 'British High Commissioner' for Greece and for that there was need of a Greek Prime Minister who would carry out British orders unquestioningly. Plastiras was not suited to this and must therefore go: he could only have survived as a British puppet.

The question must be asked whether Plastiras could have found a way of neutralising British influence whilst remaining in power. Two conditions would have been necessary for this. In foreign policy, as Plastiras himself rightly realised, he should have leaned more heavily on the US and the latter would have had to be prepared to risk at the very least a limited clash with the British. Such a policy demanded close relations with the Americans which could not be built up in so short a term of office; whilst the Americans, on their side, were not prepared for such a clash. In internal matters, he should have secured—as towards the end of his term in office he did attempt to secure—the support of the most important Liberal Party leaders. That is Plastiras should have tried to change the character of his service government by taking in the party leaders to create an all-party Cabinet. Liberals and republicans would certainly have welcomed such an effort; whether the royalists would have participated in such a Cabinet is more than questionable. But the Archbishop and the British would most certainly have taken such an enterprise as a reason to hasten Plastiras' fall.

After the signing of the Varkiza Agreement the fall of Plastiras was therefore only a matter of time. His mistakes were not the reason for his overthrow; at the most they supplied the pretext and facilitated it. But, objectively, these mistakes were of assistance to the Greek Right and to the British. His most disastrous mistake, his clientele policy, was a result of his oligarchic attitude of mind. In principle, it was right that he tried to counteract royalist influence by appointing republicans: his mistake lay first in choosing the wrong people but also in making far too few changes. The first was a result of his prolonged absence and the second showed that he saw Greek political life in terms that were suited to the twenties but that in 1945 had become obsolete.

Plastiras did not realise that, during his absence, the power structures had altered. To control the machinery of the Greek state, it was no longer sufficient to fill the key posts in Athens with a few nominees; the machinery had to be controlled by suitable people at all levels. The Greek Right had realised precisely this and began energetically to push its followers into these subordinate posts. Democratic personnel for even these lower posts was available amongst the membership of EAM-ELAS. Their recruitment to the Greek administrative machine would have prevented the domination of the Right. But this integration was impeded by Plastiras' anti-communism. Thus he opened the door to the Right and unintentionally promoted the counter-revolution. It is the personal tragedy of Plastiras that he—the upright democrat and uncompromising republican—contributed to the crushing of the democratic potential established by the Resistance during the Occupation.

NOTES

1. On the 8th February 1945 the following dialogue on Greece had taken place.
   'M. Stalin said that he had heard many rumours about Greece. He had no intention of criticising, but would like to know what was happening.
   The Prime Minister (Churchill) hoped that peace would come soon on the basis of an amnesty except for acts contrary to the laws of war. He doubted whether a Government could be formed which contained all parties, because they hated each other so much they could hardly keep their hands off their opponents.
   Marshall Stalin suggested that perhaps they had not yet got used to discussions.
   The Prime Minister said that he would much like to inform Marshal Stalin. He had asked Sir W. Citrine. . . to go to Greece. They had made a report which he had not seen himself, but he would try to get a copy. The British had had rather a rough time and he was much obliged to Marshal Stalin for his attitude to this matter.
   Marshal Stalin repeated that all he wanted was information and that he did not wish to interfere.'
   Protocol of the fourth Plenary Session, 8th February, 1945 (R 3460/4/19).
2. Up to now the only sources for this conference were the very vague allusions by Leeper, Macmillan and Eden. Sir Reginald Leeper, *When Greek meets Greek*, (London: Chatto & Windus, 1950), pp. 155-7; Macmillan, *op. cit.*, p. 662; Eden, *op. cit.*, p. 520.
3. Discussion on Greece at the British Embassy, Athens, 15th February, 1945 (R 3559/4/G) [G = 19].
4. Appreciation from the point of view of Commander, land forces and military liaison, Greece, of the future British military commitment in Greece in the event of disarmament of ELAS (R 3559/4/G) [G = 19]. Here Scobie mentioned the following figures agreed at Varkiza. He stressed that these figures represented

75 per cent of ELAS' actual weapons. ELAS in fact handed over considerably greater quantities (figures in brackets). See Sarafis, *op. cit.*, p. 525.

Rifles	41,500	(48,973)
Automatic rifles	850	(713)
Submachine guns	1,050	(1,412)
Machine guns	315	(419)
Light mortars	108	(138)
Heavy mortars	55	(81)
Artillery of various types	32	(157)
Radios	15	(17)

5. Meeting held at the British Embassy, Athens, 15th February, 1945 (R 3669/4/19).
6. This he did on 5th March. Greece. Memorandum by the Secretary of State for Foreign Affairs (R 3559/4/G) [G = 19]. W.P. (45) 138.
7. Richter, *Griechenland zwischen Revolution und Konterrevolution*, p. 324.
8. For economic and financial policy see Richter, *loc. cit.*, pp. 195-7, 390 ff, 468 ff, 500 ff.
9. Six hundred new *drachmas* or 20 million millions old *drachmas* to one B.M.A. pound. Byford-Jones, *op. cit.*, p. 104.
10. Byford-Jones reported: '. . . Greeks were selling English cigarettes, . . . tinned fish, milk and meat; toffee, bars of chocolate, soap, toilet requisites, lace and bread, all at black market prices. . . Many of the goods had come from the Red Cross relief, having been sold to enable the poor purchasers to buy food more useful to them.' *Op. cit.*, p. 102. And 'On 27th October I saw [in Athens shops] innumerable luxury goods, many of which were not obtainable in England. . . Leica cameras, fountain pens, silver pencils, Dunhill lighters, gold and silver watches, diamond rings, smart ladies' shoes, clothes, suits, even silk stockings; . . . American dollars or British pounds being more popular than any other foreign currency.' *Ibid.*, p. 103.
11. British Embassy *aide memoire* for the Greek Government 15th February, 1945 (R 3659/4/19). ML was an allied operation whose correct title was AML (Allied Military Liaison). It was the forerunner of UNRRA. But in Greece the Americans had withdrawn from AML shortly before liberation, so that this remained a purely British undertaking. On 29th November 1944, by an agreement with UNRRA signed at Scobie's headquarters, ML was placed under Scobie's command so that it was henceforward controlled by him. Constantine Poulos, 'Rule Britannia', *Nation*, 159 (23rd December, 1944), p. 773.
12. Woodhouse, *Apple of Discord*, p. 206.
13. *FRUS 1945,VIII*, pp. 195 ff.
14. *Ibid.*, pp. 196 ff.
15. Eden, *op. cit.*, p. 521. 'I am afraid that I was blunt to the verge of rudeness on the need for Greeks to bestir themselves.'
16. Leeper, *op. cit.*, p. 155.
17. R 3559/4/G. [G = 19].
18. After the end of the conference, Sideris, who did not agree with the proposed economic policy, suggested to Plastiras that Eden's behaviour had been an affront to his person. On the 16th Plastiras complained to Damaskinos who reassured him. Damaskinos asked Leeper to act as go-between and the latter agreed. Leeper told Eden that he would put the problems to Plastiras in military terminology so that he could understand them. Leeper to Eden 16th February, 1945 (R 3769/4/19).
19. Sarafis, *op. cit.*, pp. 39, 46.
20. Thus, C.M. Woodhouse in an autobiographical article series published in

Akropolis in 1965; see also Sarafis, *op. cit.*, p. 50; Richter, *Griechenland zwischen Revolution und Konterrevolution*, p. 263.
21. Richter, *op. cit.*, p. 346.
22. On the appointment of Vendiris: *Poios einai poios eis tin Ellada. Viografiko lexiko*, (Athens, 1958), p. 52. At the Myrofyllo-Plaka conference in February 1944 it had been agreed that the republican General Othonaios should take this post. Sarafis, *op. cit.*, p. 256. But this was later opposed not only by PAS but by the British, although the latter had been co-signatories at Plaka. 'Fortunately' for both, Othonaios became ill and Vendiris was able to take over. Christos Zalokostas, *To Chroniko tis Sklavias*, (Athens: Estia, n.d., 2nd ed.), p. 243. Zalokostas was one of the main voices for these right-wing secret societies, see Richter, *op. cit.*, pp. 347 ff., 493.
23. Georgios Karayannis, *To drama tis Ellados 1940-1952*, (Athens, 1964); Stavrou, *op. cit.*, pp. 219 ff.
24. *Ieros Desmos Ellinon Axiomatikon (IDEA)*. Vol. 1. *Apokalypseis tou typou (1951-1952)*, (Athens: *Ellinika Themata*, 1975), p. 65.
25. Stavrou, *op. cit.*, p. 223.
26. Richter, *op. cit.*, p. 504. As colonel in command of the second bureau at gendarmerie HQ Spiliotopoulos had issued, on 28th September 1941, an order for the rounding up of British soldiers stranded in Greece and for the punishment of those supplying them with fake identity papers. National Liberation Front, EAM., *White Book*, pp. 13-4.
27. *Ieros Desmos Ellinon Axiomatikon*, pp. 53 ff.
28. Stavrou, *op. cit.*, pp. 229, 243 ff. A typical example of the reintegration of Security Battalion members is the later Junta leader of 21st April 1967, Georgios Papadopoulos, who had belonged to IDEA since 1947. Spyros K. Theodoropoulos, *Ap'to 'Dogma Truman' sto 'Dogma Chounta': I 'Pax Amerikana' strangalizei tin Ellada*, (Athens: Papazisis, 1976), p. 103; and Georgios Karagiorgas, *Apo tin IDEA stin Chounta, I pos fthasame stin 2li Apriliou*, (Athens: Papazisis, 1975), p. 12.
29. Sarafis, *op. cit.*, pp. 479-82. It would be interesting to ascertain how far IDEA members were involved in the massacre of 3rd December 1944.
30. Leeper to Foreign Office 19th February, 1945 (R 3472/4/19). Plastiras' biographer, Peponis, reports that Periklis Rallis also promoted the penetration of the police and gendarmerie by followers of the right-wing secret societies who were pursuing their own campaign against the Left. Plastiras had wanted to put a spoke in this by the appointment of Vlachos. Ioannis A. Peponis, *Nikolaos Plastiras sta gegonota 1909-1945*, (Athens, 1947), Vol. II, pp. 681-4.
31. Leeper to Foreign Office 20th February, 1945 (R 3517/4/19).
32. Leeper to Foreign Office 21st February, 1945 (R 3564/4/19).
33. Leeper to Foreign Office 21st February, 1945 (R 3566/4/19); *The Times*, 23rd February, 1945.
34. Minutes. Greece. General Plastiras (R 3566/4/19). Eden commented: 'Plastiras struck me as courageous but wooden and stupid.'
35. Leeper to Foreign Office 23rd February, 1945 (R 3734/4/19).
36. *The Times*, 21st April, 1945.
37. Leeper to Foreign Office 26th February, 1945 (R 3902/4/19).
38. Leeper to Foreign Office 27th February, 1945 (R 3950/4/19).
39. Besides Gonatas, Kaklamanos named the following: Apostolos Alexandris, Foreign Minister in the Revolutionary Committee of 1923, then a follower of Venizelos' Liberal Party which he however left to become leader of the deceased Michalakopoulos' Reformists. In Poulitsas' service government and in the first Tsaldaris Cabinet he was Economy Minister, in the third Tsaldaris Cabinet he

was Minister without Portfolio and in Maximos' Cabinet Minister of Justice. Vilos, Assistant-Minister in the Air Force Ministry (shipowner) and closely connected with Dimitrios Chelmis. Chelmis was a rich businessman with financial interests in Egypt and the US. He was a Populist and, after the withdrawal of the Liberals in 1944, had become minister in Papandreou's Cabinet. Alexandros Zannas, a close colleague of Eleftherios Venizelos in Salonica in 1916, founder of the Air Force Ministry and Air Force Minister 1929-32. Liberal member of parliament in 1933, 1936 and 1950. Working with the International Red Cross 1941-2 and from 1945 chairman of the Greek Red Cross. Letter from Dimitrios Kaklamanos to the Foreign Office 23rd February, 1945 (R 4229/4/19).

40. *Ibid.*, Minutes.
41. Leeper to Foreign Office 1st March, 1945 (R 4036/4/19). On the 28th February he had addressed himself to Macmillan and Alexander and asked for support. Macmillan, *op. cit.*, p. 664.
42. Foreign Office to Leeper 3rd March, 1945 (R 3950/4/19). With this National Council, Leeper had wanted to exercise a kind of 'parliamentary' control over Plastiras.
43. Macmillan's memoirs do not mention this first visit; both visits are treated as one. Macmillan, *op. cit.*, pp. 644 ff.
44. Macmillan to Churchill 5th March, 1945 (R 4386/4/19).
45. Macmillan and Leeper to Foreign Office 5th March, 1945 (R 4386/4/19).
46. Macmillan and Leeper to Foreign Office 5th March, 1945 (R 4385/4/19).
47. Special unnumbered signal from Caserta 7th March, 1945 (R 4385/4/19).
48. Relations between HMG and the Greek Government. Minutes (R 4385/4/19).
49. *Ibid.*
50. Prime Minister to Macmillan 7th March, 1945 (R 4386/4/19).
51. Leeper to Foreign Office 7th March, 1945 (R 4562/4/19). This Cabinet list was very subtly balanced: Voulgaris was a right-wing republican who had achieved a tragic notoriety by his putting down of the Greek naval disturbances in spring 1944 and had in the meantime become a royalist. The two 'leftists' Sofianopoulos and Othonaios were counterbalanced by the moderate Populist Rallis and the conservative Liberal Konstantinos Triandafyllopoulos (Justice Minister in 1926 and 1932). The Tsatsos brothers, on the other hand, belonged to Damaskinos' personal following. Konstantinos Tsatsos was married to Ioanna, the sister of the poet George Seferiadis (Seferis), Damaskinos' political bureau chief. She entertained close personal relations with Damaskinos. Such a Cabinet would have given the impression of a centre-left government but in point of fact would have been a government of the Right under the close control of Damaskinos.
52. *Ibid.*
53. Laskey's Minutes which represent his opinion and that of Sir Orme Sargent (R 4562/4/19).
54. Copy of Minute by Prime Minister 8th March, 1945 (R 4562/4/19).
55. Foreign Office to Leeper 9th March, 1945 (R 4562/4/19). Churchill, too, took this line. Prime Minister's Personal Minute Serial No. M 198/5 (R 4562/4/19).
56. Foreign Office to Leeper 11th March, 1945 (R 4385/4/19).
57. Leeper to Foreign Office 9th March, 1945 (R 4644/4/19).
58. Leeper to Foreign Office 9th March, 1945 (R 4652/4/19).
59. Leeper to Foreign Office 11th March, 1945 (R 4771/4/19).
60. Prime Minister's Personal Minute Serial No. M 182/5 9th March, 1945 (R 4653/4/19). Eden agreed with Churchill's opinion.
61. Laskey's Minutes 12th March, 1945 (R 4771/4/19).
62. Howard and Sir Orme Sargent were also in favour of waiting.

63. Foreign Office to Leeper 16th March, 1945 (R 4771/4/19). 'The initiative for a change of government must therefore come from the Greeks themselves.'
64. In a conversation between Foy D. Kohler and a representative of the British Embassy in Washington, the former had expressed himself in favour of Plastiras remaining in office. British Embassy in Washington to D.F. Howard in Southern Department 2nd March, 1945 (Ref. 22/63/45 R 4665/4/19).
65. *FRUS 1945, VIII*, p. 118. On 12th March Scobie replied to an enquiry from Alexander that some units could be withdrawn on the 7th April at the earliest.
66. Macmillan and Leeper to Foreign Office 15th March, 1945 (R 5072/4/19); Macmillan, *op. cit.*, p. 665. The Foreign Office realised that Damaskinos wished to withdraw from the affair and Leeper was instructed that he must bring him to take a strong line towards Plastiras. Foreign Office to Leeper 17th March, 1945 (R 5072/4/19).
67. *FRUS 1945, VIII*, p. 120.
68. Leeper to Foreign Office 7th March, 1945 (R 4451/4/19).
69. EAM Central Committee memorandum of 5th March, 1945 (R 5443/4/19). *FRUS 1945, VIII*, pp. 116-8.
70. EAM Central Committee memorandum of 12th March, 1945 (R 5617/4/19).
71. Macmillan to Foreign Office 17th March, 1945 (R 5191/4/19). Up to this date no former ELAS member had been taken into the army, police or gendarmerie.
72. Laskey's Minutes 19th March, 1945 (R 5191/4/19).
73. Leeper to Foreign Office 15th March, 1945 (R 5105/4/19).
74. Leeper to Foreign Office 17th March, 1945 (R 5192/4/19). Leeper commented: 'My recent experience of Greek politics often leads me to regret the absence of Papandreou who has imagination about the future not only of his country but of his own career.'
75. Leeper to Foreign Office 19th March, 1945 (R 5268/4/19).
76. Foreign Office to Leeper 25th March, 1945 (R 5268/4/19). The actual telegram with Damaskinos' suggestions could not be found.
77. *Ibid*.
78. Leeper to Foreign Office 22nd March, 1945 (R 5498/4/19).
79. Leeper to Foreign Office 27th March, 1945 (R 5757/4/19).
80. Sir Orme Sargent commented: 'It looks as [if?] the Regent [is?] shirking the task of turning out Plastiras and intended to build up the National Council to do it for him. I don't think we ought to allow him to evade his responsibilities in this way.' Minute of 29th March, 1945 (R 5757/4/19). Laskey and Howard also rejected Leeper's idea.
81. Foreign Office to Leeper 29th March, 1945 (R 5757/4/19).
82. Leeper to Foreign Office 28th March, 1945 (R 5825/4/19).
83. *Ibid*.
84. Churchill to Eden 29th March, 1945 (R 5825/4/19). Churchill rejected the postponement of the plebiscite and demanded plebiscite and elections at the earliest possible date. If the king got a large majority, this would justify the British intervention *post facto*. Moreover, the king had the right to correspond privately with his subjects.
85. Foreign Office to Leeper 30th March, 1945 (R 5757/4/19) and Foreign Office to Leeper 30th March, 1945 (R 5825/4/19).
86. Leeper to Foreign Office 31st March, 1945 (R 5989/4/19). Inflation was gaining strength again; and Plastiras had moreover succeeded in securing Alexandros Mylonas (leader of one of the agrarian parties) as a future Finance Minister.
87. Leeper to Sir Orme Sargent 1st April, 1945 (R 6868/4/19).
88. Laskey, Howard and Sargent, Minutes (R 5989/4/19).
89. Leeper to Foreign Office 4th April, 1945 (R 6176/4/19). Papandreou had

written to the king recommending himself as a future Prime Minister (R 8080/4/19 for the text of this letter).
90. On the 16th July, 1941 Plastiras had reported to the ambassador on his reactions to a German offer of mediation in the war between Greece and Italy, made to him in November-December 1940 and on his own vain efforts to make contact with the Greek Government, to try to forestall a German invasion. Richter, *op. cit.*, pp. 164 ff, 571.
91. Leeper to Foreign Office 19th March, 1945 (R 5857/4/19). This telegram of Leeper's contains the report on the trial from its opening until 8th March, 1945.
92. On the 2nd September 1941 Warner had entered in the Southern Department archives a letter from Plastiras to Ioannis Moatsos (Jean Moazzo) intercepted by the Imperial Censorship in Bermuda. In this letter of the 19th July 1941, Plastiras reported details of his row with the consulate in Nice, the legation in Vichy and the government-in-exile in Johannesburg, in the course of which he had sent the letter to Pierre Metaxas (R 8205/4078/19, 1941). In October 1941 the Southern Department received the letter itself from Tsouderos (R 9006/4078/19, 1941). In December the Southern Department received a letter from Stelios N. Pistolakis to Plastiras of 16th October 1941 containing further details about this matter (R 8205/4078/19, 1941).
93. Letter from Edward Warner to P.J. Dixon 20th June, 1943 (R 5657/4/19, 1943).
94. Warner to Foreign Office (Laskey) 7th March, 1945 (R 4563/4/19).
95. Howard's Minutes 14th March, 1945 (R 4563/4/19).
96. Foreign Office (Laskey) to Warner 15th March, 1945 (R 4563/4/19). In a further telegram of 16th March, 1945 Laskey even certified Plastiras' integrity (R 4563/4/19).
97. AIS Report (R 5702/4/19).
98. Hayter's Minute to this report 28th March, 1945: 'I don't think these disclosures are very damaging. They sum *[sic]* that the General may have used some accommodating phrases, perhaps not unnatural in occupied Europe [but] in fact [they] are pretext and he managed to avoid working for the Germans.'
99. SIS agent's report of 1st April, 1944: Attempted exfiltration of General Plastiras (R 6174/745/19, 1944). In this report further German efforts to recruit Plastiras as Prime Minister are mentioned. Plastiras, however, rebuffed them all. In spring 1944 he considered the communist peril non-existent.
100. Foivos Neokosmou Grigoriadis, *Istoria tou Emfyliou Polemou 1945-1949 (To deftero andartiko)*, (Athens, n.d.), Vol. II, p. 514.
101. Richter, *op. cit.*, p. 247. On the 11th April 1945 Rallis told the court that the Intelligence Service had suggested to him to take over as Prime Minister. *Rizospastis*, 27th April, 1945.
102. Peponis, *op. cit.*, p. 696. Sofianopoulos' absence at the UN foundation session in San Francisco may have influenced the timing of the publication.
103. Tsouderos was abroad at the time.
104. *Rizospastis* reported that the royalists had had the letter in their hands for ten days and had got it from Gonatas. Whilst the timing agrees well with the date of the letter's arrival in Athens, the source seems unconvincing. Whence should Gonatas have got the letter?
105. Laskey's Minutes of 6th April, 1945 (R 6244/4/19). Cadogan commented: 'We must not be so simple as to think that Plastiras' removal will not be connected with the letter, though we can ask that the letter should not be given as the acknowledged reason for the dismissal.' Eden: 'I agree with Sir A. Cadogan. This is a troublesome business. But we *did* want to get rid of Plastiras anyway

and the letter is in this sense secondary. This should be our line, I suppose, if he does go.' Foreign Office (Eden) to Leeper 6th April, 1945 (R 6244/4/19).
106. Leeper to Foreign Office 6th April, 1945 (R 6244/4/19).
107. Leeper to Foreign Office 6th April, 1945 (R6317/4/19), on which Churchill commented on 8th April: 'I approve very much. WSC.' *Ibid.*
108. Leeper to Foreign Office 6th April, 1945 (R 6318/4/19).
109. Peponis, *op. cit.*, p. 699.
110. Text, *ibid.*, pp. 699 ff.

THE FIRST VOULGARIS CABINET, APRIL-AUGUST 1945

Admiral Petros Voulgaris' assumption of office coincided almost exactly with the handover of supreme British authority in Greece by Scobie to Leeper, who now became *de facto* British High Commissioner for Greece,[1] and with the replacement of ML by UNRRA. As always during the past three months whenever important decisions had to be taken, Macmillan was again on the scene. By the 8th April Voulgaris had formed a Cabinet consisting almost exclusively of naval officers and professors.[2] All it had in common with the Voulgaris Cabinet suggested at the beginning of March was the person of its leader and that of Konstantinos Tsatsos. Whilst the suggested Cabinet had had a left-centre character, the real one could at best be described as right-centre, with a clear preponderance of the Right.

On the 10th April Macmillan arrived in Athens and 'advised' Voulgaris on the final assignment of ministries.[3] This presented an immediate problem of finding suitable people since the Cabinet was to have the character of a politically neutral 'service government'. Macmillan's original idea of a super-ministry under Varvaressos covering the responsibilities for Finance, Economics, Trade and Reconstruction struck an obstacle in the latter's absence in London.[4] The result was a Cabinet consisting of Voulgaris' naval cronies and of colourless personalities without political influence, under a royalist premier. Outwardly—after the recruitment of further ministers—it had a liberal appearance, but in fact it was completely controlled by Damaskinos (through Tsatsos) and by the British.

This was helpful to Leeper in his role as 'High Commissioner' but at the same time made it possible for the Greek Right to infiltrate the administrative machinery at all levels. By reason of its weakness, Voulgaris' government became a government of reaction and counter-revolution. Leeper realised this weakness and tried to raise the government's prestige by recommending London to issue a statement on the Dodecanese in favour of Greece.[5]

In addition, the Americans were beginning to take an unfriendly attitude. As has been mentioned, Greek-Americans and American business interests were trying to get economic concessions in Greece. The climax of this process had been the signing by Plastiras of an airline agreement with American Airways who would thus have secured a dominant role in air traffic with Greece had not the British annulled this agreement.[6] Now, on

10th April, it came to an open confrontation. The Athens press reported with maximum publicity that the US Secretary of State, Stettinius, had stated at a press conference on the 9th that the US ambassador in Athens, Lincoln MacVeagh, had not been consulted by Damaskinos about the change of government, in contrast to Leeper whose advice had been sought. The Athens press interpreted this as open criticism of British behaviour by the Americans: had Damaskinos consulted MacVeagh, there would have been no change of government. The liberal *Athinaïka Nea* opined that Stettinius' statement was manifestly expressed American disapproval of what had happened.[7]

Damaskinos was worried and sent his private secretary, Ioannis Georgakis, to MacVeagh to justify retrospectively the overthrowing of Plastiras: the new government was politically neutral and would not give preference to the Right; moreover the Cabinet members had been personal friends of the founder of the Greek Republic, Alexandros Papanastasiou; if he had not consulted MacVeagh, it was because he regarded the change of government as a purely internal Greek matter. MacVeagh accepted the explanation and promised to inform Washington. In this report MacVeagh expressed the opinion that Plastiras' enforced resignation could with a little patient restraint have been avoided; in any case the 'dynamic' Prime Minister inspired far less confidence than his predecessor.[9] Washington replied with a *démenti*: Stettinius' remark had been mis-reported.

Macmillan's two-day stay in Athens is of basic importance for future developments. On 10th April Scobie officially handed over responsibility for Greece to Leeper and was replaced by a Corps commander whose task it would be to take command of the British troops remaining in Greece. Major-General Smallwood, Admiral Turner and Air Commodore Tuttle took over as heads of the Military, Naval and Air Force Missions. Sir Quintin Hill succeeded Sir David Waley as financial adviser. Harold Caccia became assistant-ambassador and coordinator and Leeper 'High Commissioner' for Greece. On the 11th a meeting took place in the British Embassy with Voulgaris, Leeper, Caccia and Macmillan participating. Voulgaris willingly accepted the system of cooperation suggested by the British. British officers and civil servants 'would be assigned to the Athens ministries and to the provincial administrative centres'. In regard to economic policy, Voulgaris acknowledged that he did not understand much about it. But Macmillan had the impression that he understood more than he admitted which in view of his close connection with the Greek armaments tycoon, Bodossakis Athanasiadis, was not surprising. Voulgaris recommended early elections but feared that technical difficulties would not permit these before autumn. For that reason he recommended the establishment of the National Council. He promised to pursue a moderate policy and to apply the Varkiza Agreement, but he sharply condemned KKE. In general Macmillan was very satisfied with the new Greek Prime

Minister:[10] Voulgaris would collaborate most happily with Leeper.

The conversation over, Macmillan and Leeper each sent the Foreign Office a statement of position and a programme which contained and co-ordinated the results of the Athens talks. Macmillan's report dealt with the military and Leeper's with the internal political problems. Macmillan's purpose was to counteract Allied Forces HQ's demand for withdrawal of the British troops from the 1st July.[11]

Macmillan went on to recall the economic discussions of 15th February and demonstrated that the realisation of the plan was ahead of schedule.[12] By 1st April the whole of Greece had been re-occupied by British troops. The disarming of ELAS had been concluded earlier than expected; but, though ELAS had handed over more weapons than had been demanded, it had still retained and concealed a certain number—a fact which must not be overlooked. Greek administration had also been installed sooner than was expected and the programme for the setting up of local National Guard units was on time. But the formation of the first mobile, regular division would not be completed till the end of September on account of training problems, especially in regard to technical personnel; whilst the second division would not be available as a mobile reserve before the end of December and Major-General Smallwood regarded even these dates as optimistic. The transfer of authority to Leeper had gone through successfully and the 46th Division would be withdrawn from Greece by the end of April. His original plan had provided for leaving only one division in Greece during phases two and three of the takeover by government forces but this would have to be modified on account of the delay in forming the first Greek division and on account of the forthcoming plebiscite and elections.

As regards the plebiscite and the elections, it was under no circumstances possible to conclude the necessary preparations before November. The existing political situation in Athens, and indeed in the whole of Greece, meant that the elections would be an occasion for bitter conflict. An attempted pre-election *putsch* by either Left or Right was improbable but, after the elections it could well be imagined that the losers would accuse the winning side of fraud and would try to correct the result by force of arms. To prevent this, more than one division would have to be left in Greece: the situation of the past December must not be allowed to repeat itself. Either all troops should be withdrawn before the elections or two divisions should be stationed in Greece until at least two months after the elections. Both he and Leeper were for the second alternative. In view of the sacrifices made so far, the desired result must be obtained. In addition, on account of the confused situation in south-east Europe, the strategic position of Greece and also on account of the Middle Eastern situation, it was of importance that two divisions should be kept available in Greece for a longer time as an intervention reserve. He hoped that

London would agree with this programme.[13]

Leeper recommended that the present government should be kept in office until the elections which could not take place for another six months. It would have the support of moderate royalists and of the Liberals; public confidence in the government was increasing and only the Communists opposed it. But confidence in the government depended on the solving of two problems.

The first was the economic and financial problem. In the past three and a half months the Greek government had accumulated a deficit of ten billion *drachmas*. Circulation of banknotes had doubled since the 1st March and now amounted to over twenty billion *drachmas*. It had risen by 3,600 million in March and by 6,300 million in the first two weeks of April. This was partially due to a loan for agriculture and industry but the real reason was the alarming rate of inflation[14] which became known to the public through the steady rise of the *drachma*-sovereign rate and the rise in prices.

This situation could only be rectified by the following measures: a drastic tax increase combined with revision of the whole taxation system; rigorous economy, stabilisation measures such as fixed prices and wages. But these would only work if administrative efficiency could be improved. Pressure must therefore be brought to bear on Voulgaris to tackle the financial problem at once.

The second problem was the maintenance of law and order. Since the signing of the Varkiza Agreement there had been remarkably few incidents in the provinces, but order and tranquillity were by no means restored and the danger of an armed rising or at least a revival of 'banditry' had by no means been excluded. This had negative repercussions on the revival of trade and of the economy. At present, except for Athens and Piraeus, police duties were carried out by the willing but unqualified National Guard and the problems could be solved only with the establishment of regular gendarmerie units. The despatch of the British Police and Gendarmerie Mission was therefore urgently necessary.

Further, the Greek government was hindered in its task by a chaotic administration. Officials and civil servants were too generously remunerated and there were far too many of them. There was no central control of the public service and even within the departments of a ministry order and co-operation barely existed. Assistant-ministers had to do the jobs of civil service heads of department and changed with every change of government. A reduction in the number of civil servants and appointees was urgently required for reasons of economy. Moreover, the public service must be made more efficient and that would mean a fundamental reformation. He would do what he could, particularly to achieve coordination with the centres of internal policy making. Economic, financial and labour policy should be coordinated by a central council under Varvaressos.

Except for the gendarmerie and the police, all this was of course a problem for the Greeks themselves to solve. The British contribution should consist of leaving two divisions in Greece and drawing up a financial plan. It would have to be determined which financial expenditures would have to be repaid later and which not. A solution would have to be found which was not in excess of Greek ability to pay. Great Britain should manifest a long-term interest in Greece, for example by making a statement about the Dodecanese. Supplies of consumer goods should be stepped up by better organisation of transport. A British representative should be speedily assigned to UNRRA since otherwise there was a danger that what ML had achieved would be undone. This seemed to him a minimum programme for the next six months. Only if this programme were carried out could a stable Greece, well-disposed towards Great Britain, be ensured.[15]

Until the elections there were two possible types of government: an all-party government or a 'service government'. As long as the passions aroused by the civil war had not cooled, the former was impracticable. A fresh attempt was now being made with the latter. If this attempt were also to fail, the Regent would probably not be able to form another service government and, in that case, the Right would take power. In such a case, Plastiras—whose fall had already won back for him much of his former popularity and prestige—would again carry great weight. There were rumours that, if the present government were to fail, Plastiras would demand the resignation of Damaskinos and the establishment of a Regency Council consisting of Sofoulis, Maximos and Kafandaris, with himself as Prime Minister. Since the king would hardly approve such a Regency Council, it could come about only through a revolutionary *coup* which could plunge the country into renewed civil war. In view of these dangers, the present government should be kept in office.[16]

His new position had inspired Leeper with a remarkable insight and a realistic assessment of part of the Greek problem. Just as in 1943, when he took up his post as ambassador, he subjected the existing situation to a reasonably objective analysis and clearly recognised various weaknesses of the prevailing system.[17] That he did not recognise the second basic problem—the re-integration of the Resistance, in other words the application of the Varkiza Agreement—or did not want to recognise it is not to be wondered at in view of his political orientation. He regarded the excesses of the National Guard against the Left, common at that time, with indulgence as an understandable reaction to the December events. To all appearances, as in 1943, within the framework of his own political outlook, Leeper was quite prepared to steer a course which, if he had held to it, could have had constructive results for the evolution of Greece's internal situation. At the very least this policy would have prevented the total penetration of the Greek administrative machinery by the Right.

But again, as in 1943, London applied the brake to Leeper's independent impulse and he again sought the line of least resistance, loyally adapted himself to London's demands and let things take their course.

For Eden and Churchill the possibility of an early plebiscite was not yet excluded. In telegrams of the 30th March and 6th April Eden had pointed out to Leeper that it was British policy that plebiscite and elections should take place as soon as possible and that no predictions about possible consequences should be allowed to deflect from this. On 8th April he added, addressing himself to Churchill, that the earliest date could be in three or four months' time. It should be suggested to the Regent that he make a statement to the effect that it was his and the government's policy to hold the plebiscite and the elections as soon as circumstances would permit; and he should name a date in three months' time. This would certainly have a positive effect in Greece and would damp down the extreme royalists who wanted to hold the plebiscite in the next two weeks. If Churchill agreed, he would instruct Leeper accordingly.[18] But Churchill's answer was long in coming.

The reason for the delay was the sudden death of President Roosevelt on 12th April. Churchill had at first planned to attend the funeral himself, but had then decided that Eden should go. Therefore, on the 13th April Churchill took over, in addition to his other tasks, the supervision of the Foreign Office. Just as in spring 1944, during the disturbances in the Greek Middle East forces, and on the 4th December when he sent his Balfourian 'don't-hesitate-to-shoot!' telegram,[19] the fact that Churchill was in immediate control of British foreign policy was to have grave consequences for Greece.

On 17th April a telegram had arrived from Leeper in which he complained of the Americans' continued unfriendly attitude. Their press was presenting Plastiras as the victim of British intrigues in favour of the royalists. Plastiras had given an interview to the correspondent of *PM* in which he openly accused the British ambassador of having forced the Regent to dismiss him. In addition there were widespread rumours in American circles that the British had leaked that letter to *Ellinikon Aima*. The American air transport command had been reinforced by a high-powered public relations officer who had at once invited two well-known *Fortune* feature writers who were to prepare a series of articles on the future of American civil aviation in the Eastern Mediterranean. Greek broadcasts by the Voice of America had been stepped up to once a day from the previous three times a week, and their content was propaganda for the benefits already conferred or to be conferred on Greece by America. AIS reported a negative attitude on the part of the OWI (Office of War Information) towards British policy. In addition, OWI was planning the establishment of a high-powered information service which would provide the Greek press with up to the minute news, photographs, articles, etc. on a scale which the British might well find difficult to match.

The first fruits of this propaganda had been the Stettinius statement and the way in which, on the occasion of Roosevelt's death, the latter had been presented in a very positive way at the expense of Churchill. The Greeks hardly believed any longer in the fact of British–Soviet friendship. If the Americans continued this policy, it would be impossible to maintain belief in the three great powers' common cause.[20]

On the 20th April Churchill replied. Leeper should not worry too much about this sort of thing. Undoubtedly there was conflict with the US about the breakdown of the Chicago Air Conference and it was quite possible that some angry decisions were taken against Great Britain in this special sphere, of which the activities in Greece were only one of many instances. Roosevelt's death had been a great shock to him of course but his health had been ailing for some time and 'I am not sure that the telegrams I received from him were in many cases his own'. With Truman this would be different and Eden, during his stay in Washington, would clear up the differences with the US.

'You should therefore work hard for our simple policy of the full, free, unfettered secret ballot, universal suffrage and the expression of the will of the people in three or four months at the worst.'

In regard to internal Greek policy, he advised Leeper not to involve himself too much in matters of detail.[21]

On the same day Sir Orme Sargent sent a telegram to Sir Alexander Cadogan, who was with Eden in Washington. In it he recommended that Eden should take the matter up personally with Stettinius. An exchange of opinion on Greece with the US would be welcome.[22] Leeper was delighted with Churchill's answer and telegraphed his reply on the 21st. Since Plastiras' resignation, he had held himself aloof from details of Greek policy and discussed only practical problems with the new Greek government. Meanwhile he had made his peace with Plastiras. With MacVeagh he had close and friendly contact; but MacVeagh was 'frightened by every wind that blows and winds blow pretty often here'. Anglo–US cooperation was extremely important. He would do his best, but Washington must give strict guidelines to its weaker vessels in Athems. Finally, Leeper referred to his telegram of 18th March and underlined the request made therein.[23]

In the meantime Macmillan's and Leeper's telegrams of the 18th April had reached the Foreign Office. Hayter and Howard noted far-reaching agreement with their contents. The War Office had agreed that British troops should remain in Greece until after the plebiscite and the elections but with the understanding that these should take place in August. Now their consent to the postponement would have to be sought. Macmillan's view that the elections could take place at the earliest in November was disappointing. During his visit to London (on his way to San Francisco),

Sofianopoulos had spoken of four months. Leeper should be asked if the date could not be pushed forward somewhat. At the same time the suggestion of a Greek government statement on the elections could be put to Leeper, who should also be asked to submit suggestions for the planned Three Power supervision. As regards the life expectancy of the present government, Sofianopoulos had given it three months, which spoke for an early election date. Leeper's suggestions concerning financial and economic policy were acceptable. On the Police Mission, the Treasury was at present investigating how this should be paid for. Leeper's proposals for administrative reform were agreed and his recommendations were awaited concerning financial settlement with the Greek government. As regards a statement on the Dodecanese, the US and the USSR were being consulted. Improvement of supplies would be discussed with the relevant minister. Finally, the suitable person had not yet been found for British UNRRA chief. If these points found general agreement, a suitable telegram could be sent to Leeper. But, as Eden was absent, that must be discussed with Churchill.[24]

Sir Orme Sargent expressed strong reservations about the late election date and rejected the idea of a statement by the Greek government since, in view of the later date, this would have the contrary effect. He agreed to the drafting of the telegram but added that Leeper should be instructed to justify the postponement.[25] The draft telegram subsequently contained the gist of Hayter's and Howard's thinking as well as Orme Sargent's reservations.[26]

Meanwhile Churchill had seen Leeper's telegram of the 18th April and reacted characteristically. On the 22nd April he drafted the following instructions to Leeper:

'Your 999 [Leeper's first telegram of 18th April] does not at all accord with the instructions you have been given which aim at a maximum of four months before the plebiscite. It is not part of our policy to enter so deeply into every aspect of Greek life as your telegram indicates. Your acquiescence in the six months period is therefore not accepted. Your 1000 [Leeper's second telegram of 18th April]: We shall of course support His Beatitude [Damaskinos], and if he felt like banishing Plastiras to some island, he should not be deterred from doing so...'[27]

At the Foreign Office Sir Orme Sargent tried to blunt the edge of this telegram in the following memorandum to Churchill:

'Before seeing your draft telegram to Leeper, serial No. T.586/5, we had drafted a telegram to him replying to his telegrams Nos. 999 and 1000... I attach copies of these telegrams and our draft reply. You will see that we also were surprised and disappointed at his estimate that the plebiscite and the elections cannot be held before November and had pressed him to advance the date. Our draft telegram sets out the case in full and so it also deals with the other points in his telegram, I should still like to send it if you agree. As regards paragraph 2 of your serial No. T.586/5 Leeper has now made his peace with Plastiras and perhaps it is not necessary to send this. . .'[28]

Churchill reacted with irritation:

'You must not put so many words into my mouth. Pray send my telegram, T.586/5 with the amendments I have put in to meet your view. You will note that you should draft for me the special points not dealt with in my telegram in a short memorandum, which he will receive from you. Let me see it.'[29]

Thus, on 24th April Churchill's telegram was despatched to Leeper.[30] Sir Orme informed Churchill accordingly and submitted the draft Churchill had asked for.[31] Churchill approved the draft text without any amendment and on the 25th it was sent to Athens. Comparison with Sir Orme's original draft shows that it in the main adhered to the original version.[32]

Churchill's reply to Macmillan was markedly more moderate: he expressed his regret that there could not be an earlier election date and assured Macmillan that two British divisions would remain in Greece until the end of the year.[33] Churchill's dissatisfaction with Greek developments led him to concern himself more closely with that country's situation. A telegram of 19th April from Sir Orme Sargent aroused his attention. Sir Orme had told Leeper about an article by Christopher Lumby in *The Times* of 17th April, strongly critical of the present state of affairs in Greece.

This is not the place to go into the content of this criticism. That will find place in our general review of the violations of the Varkiza Agreement. Here we will deal only with what is relevant in the present context. From a previous telegram of Leeper's, Sir Orme had got the impression that Lumby's comments were not without foundation and urged Leeper to express an opinion how far it could be hoped that the extremists of both sides might be prevented from influencing the Greek government's policy or even getting control of the situation. One way to curb the Right would be to persuade the Greek government to take more drastic measures against the former collaborators:

'Your recent reports suggest that membership of E.A.M. tends to be considered a greater crime than collaboration with the Germans. You should take every opportunity of emphasising our view that assistance to the enemy is regarded by His Majesty's Government as much worse than membership of the E.A.M. and should be met with prompt and condign punishment. I am by no means satisfied that adequate purge of gendarmerie and other state services has been carried out or is being seriously undertaken.'[34]

On reading this telegram, Churchill sent the following memorandum to Sir Orme Sargent:

'. . . I do not agree at all with your last paragraph. It seems to me that the collaborators in Greece in many cases did the best they could to shelter the Greek population from German oppression. Anyhow they did nothing to stop the entry of liberating forces, nor did they give any support to the EAM designs. The Communists are the main foe, though the punishment of notorious pro-German collaborators, especially if concerned with the betrayal of loyal Greeks, should proceed in a regular and strict manner. There should be no question of increasing the severities against the collaborationists in order to win Communist approval. Their approval is not worth having, and will only be given in cases where they feel they have gained an advantage for themselves. It will never be given in a manner to strengthen any Government but their own. . . . Our policy is the plebiscite within three or four months, and implacable hostility to the Communists whatever their tactics may be.'[35]

In the Southern Department there was considerable perplexity. Hayter commented:

'I should have thought it self-evident that collaboration with Germany was a worse crime than Communism, even in Greece. It seems to me that it could make us look rather foolish if we suggested the contrary to Mr. Leeper.

But apart from the merits of the case, I cannot help feeling that the Prime Minister's suggestion is bad tactics. It is surely our policy to build up the moderates in Greece against the extremists of either side. At the moment the extremists of the Right, mostly ex-collaborationists, are on the crest of the wave and the Communists in the trough. If we now allow it to be thought that the ex-collaborationists of the Right have our support it will not be long before they are in a position to control the whole of the Greek state. Once in that position they will no doubt abuse it and provoke a swing to the Left, which will give the Communists their opportunity and make the position of the moderates impossible.'[36]

Howard, too, expressed concern at Churchill's crude thinking:

'Are we really to tell Mr. Leeper that the Communists are the main foe and should be treated worse than the ex-collaborators? It seems to me out of the question. It is not, however, a question of increasing the severities against the collaborationists in order to win Communist approval. We suggested it because the delay in punishing the collaborationists was causing concern and in order that a fair balance should be maintained, so that the moderates might be strengthened.'[37]

Sir Orme Sargent had a memorandum drawn up in this sense which he sent to Churchill on the 24th April and in which he added that the Greek government had in the meantime begun to take suitable action against the collaborators. He hoped that, in view of this fact, Churchill would agree to regard the matter as settled.[38]

We have no documentary evidence whether Churchill's views on the collaborators reached Athens or not. But this has little significance since exactly that policy was in practice there. The only result of Churchill's intervention in diplomacy was, as we have already pointed out, to incline Leeper to let things take their course.

His reaction to Churchill's intervention was characteristic. He addressed himself to the Minister for the Interior, Konstantinos Tsatsos, and asked for a report on progress to date. Tsatsos hoped to hold the plebiscite in five months' time. As reasons for delay he mentioned the non-existence of electoral lists, the dispersal of the population throughout the country and the disorganised administration which would have to be rebuilt and that at a time when the strictest economy was needed. He had explained the position to the royalists and suggested they should send a representative to observe the preparations so that they could convince themselves that everything possible was being done. In addition to this, as Leeper informed Churchill, internal security was still far from guaranteed. It would be the height of irresponsibility to announce a date for the plebiscite under these circumstances. The earliest this could be carried out would be when the gendarmerie had been built up and had taken over control. Public administration was in such a chaotic state that no Greek government, of whatever composition, could get an earlier result. At the end of this self-justification, he appended a 'declaration of loyalty': he was carrying out British government instructions to the letter, but he regarded it as his duty to point out that only if the administrative difficulties could be overcome would an earlier date be possible and that only the solution of the security problem would allow a really free electoral choice.[39]

Churchill's intervention was the signal for a radically different assessment of the methods by which Great Britain should control Greek political life. On the aim—the return of Greece to semi-colonial dependence on Great Britain—Churchill, the Foreign Office, Macmillan and Leeper were all in agreement; but their views on how this should be achieved were diametrically opposed. Churchill's recommendation to Leeper not to interfere in details of internal Greek politics represented traditional British policy towards Greece: Greece should be kept on the right line by British influence on the king, or at the moment on the Regent; whilst at the same time close contact was maintained with the pro-British section of the Greek oligarchy: should there be deviations, an intervention at the highest level would be sufficient to bring Greece back into line.[40] This method had stood the test of time for over a hundred years but its precondition was that Greek political life should be controlled by the people to whom British policy addressed itself. At any rate this method had proved both efficient and extremely economical. However, Macmillan had realised that this traditional British policy towards Greece was no longer practicable, since the groups which had hitherto been its targets were themselves no longer in full control of the Greek state. The two potential new ruling groups, the Left and the extreme Right, he rejected for ideological reasons. Thus in order to restore British hegemony Macmillan wanted, for the moment, to penetrate the Greek state machinery at all levels,[41] and bring it under British control. Once the old power structure had been restored, then direct British influence could be reduced and brought back to the traditional system of control at the highest level and intervention when necessary.

One may ask if Macmillan's concept was capable of being realised and this question gains interest from the failure of a similar US effort two years later, despite the abundant resources in finance and personnel at its disposal. The author's opinion is that Macmillan's plan did stand a chance. In contrast to the situation two years later, in 1945 political structures had not yet solidified. The old power structures from the period of the Metaxas dictatorship and the German Occupation were still in existence but their position was relatively weak. The Greek state was in a phase of reconstruction and British influence could have inspired a sense of direction which might have altered the character of the post-war Greek state towards the political centre. The old power machine would of course have offered passive resistance and corruption would have hindered the reorganisation process but these difficulties could have been overcome. However, this would have pre-supposed determination in the British authorities to act speedily and consistently and to extend their control to all spheres.

Instead, the whole area of public administration was not even touched, the Police and Gendarmerie Mission arrived only when the Greek security forces had already been almost completely re-built so that their character could no longer really be changed and, finally, Churchill's intervention stopped all British initiatives. The problem of British policy towards Greece after April 1945 lay not in the fact of penetration of the Greek state but in its inconsistency which allowed the extreme Right to take over control of the state apparatus.

NOTES

1. Macmillan, *op. cit.*, p. 667.
2. The Cabinet consisted of the following:
   Admiral Petros Voulgaris: Prime Minister, Navy, War and Air Force Minister.
   Georgios Mantzavinos (banker): Finance Minister.
   Rear-Admiral Spyridon Matesis: Merchant Navy Minister and temporarily Communications Minister.
   Professor Dimitrios Balanos: Education Minister and temporarily Food Minister.
   Dr. Nikolaos Sbarounis-Trikorfos: Health Minister.
   Professor Anargyros Dimitrakopoulos (civil servant in the Public Works Ministry since 1911): Public Works and Post Office Minister.

THE FIRST VOULGARIS CABINET, APRIL–AUGUST 1945

Professor Konstantinos Tsatsos: Welfare Minister and temporarily Justice and Interior Minister.

Professor Grigorios Kasimatis (professor of civil law since 1936, Assistant-Minister for Economics in the Demertzis–Metaxas Cabinet): Economics Minister and temporarily Labour Minister.

Professor Dionysios Zakynthinos (professor of Byzantine studies since 1939): Assistant-Minister for Press and Information.

Naval Captain Georgios Lambrinopoulos: Assistant-Minister to the Prime Minister.

3. The alterations were as follows:

Professor Konstantinos Tsatsos: Minister of the Interior.

Sotirios Soliotis (judge): Justice Minister.

Andreas Zakkas (civil servant in the Economics Ministry since 1935): Labour Minister.

Professor Tryfon Karandasis (chemistry professor, former head army pharmacologist): Transport Minister.

Professor Petros Koutsomitopoulos: Agriculture Minister.

Dr. N. Sbarounis-Trikorfos: Health and Welfare Minister.

Professor Grigorios Kasimatis: Economics Minister and temporarily Supply Minister.

Konstantinos Kambas: Assistant-Minister for Welfare.

Wing-commander Georgios Alexandris: Air Force Minister.

Michail Pesmazoglou: Assistant-Minister for Finance.

Ioannis Paraskevopoulos (appointed 16th April): Supply Minister.

Lieutenant-General Markos Drakos (appointed 16th April): Assistant-Minister for War.

Ioannis Sofianopoulos (sworn in on the 16th April by the US Orthodox Archbishop): Foreign Minister.

See Provatas, *op. cit.*, pp. 576 ff.

4. *FRUS 1945*, *VIII*, p. 122. For the facts which 'hindered' Varvaressos' appointment see pp. 83, 210.
5. Leeper to Foreign Office 10th April, 1945 (R 6532/4/19). The Dodecanese was ceded by Italy to Greece in 1947.
6. Macmillan, *op. cit.*, pp. 666–7. 'There is an additional complication due to the Americans having rather "taken up" Plastiras. They have been showing him a lot of attention lately and sending over all kinds of people from the U.S. on various excuses.'

On the 10th April Leeper reported to the Foreign Office: 'I have noticed during the last few days a marked irritation on the part of the Americans on disappearance of Plastiras. . .' (R 6525/4/19). See also Foreign Office to Ambassador in Washington 13th April, 1945 (R 6569/4/19).
7. MacVeagh to Secretary of State 11th April, 1945. *FRUS 1945*, *VIII*, p. 123.
8. *Ibid.*, pp. 124 ff.
9. Secretary of State to MacVeagh 13th April, 1945. *Ibid.*, p. 125.
10. Macmillan, *op. cit.*, p. 668. It was probably on Macmillan's advice that on the 12th April Leeper advised abandonment of the National Council project. Leeper to Foreign Office 12th April, 1945 (R 6653/4/19).
11. Alexander Kirk to Secretary of State 15th April, 1945. *FRUS 1945, VIII*, pp. 125 ff. Kirk was the political adviser to the Supreme Commander of the Mediterranean Theatre, General Alexander.
12. See pp. 83–4.
13. Resident Minister, Central Mediterranean (Macmillan), Caserta, to Foreign Office 18th April, 1945 (R 6972/4/19).

14. Exchange rate of the *drachma* against the gold sovereign:

1st February 1945	4,300
17th April	8,600
23rd April	9,000
24th May	26,000
28th May	17,000
3rd June	Devaluation
9th June	12,800
14th June	11,000
14th July	11,000
21st July	14,000
27th July	15,700
28th July	15,000
4th August	18,000
13th August	16,500
27th August	19,500
28th August	22,800
1st September	21,100

15. Leeper to Foreign Office 18th April, 1945 (R 7055/4/19).
16. Leeper to Foreign Office 18th April, 1945 (R 7056/4/19).
17. Richter, *op. cit.*, p. 228.
18. Eden's Minute 8th April, 1945 (R 5989/4/19).
19. W.S. Churchill, *The Second World War*, (London: Cassell, 1954), Vol. VI, p. 252; Richter, *op. cit.*, pp. 401, 521.
20. Leeper to Foreign Office 17th April, 1945 (R 6914/4/19).
21. Prime Minister to Leeper 20th April, 1945. Prime Minister's Personal Telegram Serial No. T 539/9 (R 6914/4/19).
22. Foreign Office to Embassy in Washington 20th April, 1945 (R 6914/4/19).
23. Leeper to Foreign Office/Prime Minister 21st April, 1945 (R 7165/4/19).
24. Hayter's Minutes 20th April, 1945 (R 7055/4/19).
25. Sargent's Minutes 21st April, 1945 (R 7055/4/19).
26. Draft Telegram to Leeper (R 7055/4/19).
27. Prime Minister to Leeper 22nd April, 1945. Prime Minister's Personal Telegram Serial No. T 586/5 (R 7055/4/19).
28. Sir Orme Sargent to Churchill 22nd April, 1945 (R 7055/4/19).
29. Prime Minister to Sir Orme Sargent 23rd April, 1945. Prime Minister's Personal Minutes Serial No. M 384/5 (R 7055/4/19).
30. The only alteration was: 'Your 1,000. We shall of course support His Beatitude in dealing with Plastiras as may be necessary.' Foreign Office to Leeper 24th April, 1945 (R 7055/4/19).
31. Sir Orme Sargent to Churchill 24th April, 1945 PM/OS/45/26 (R 7055/4/19).
32. Foreign Office to Leeper 25th April, 1945 (R 7055/4/19).
33. Foreign Office to Resident Minister's Office Central Mediterranean, Caserta, 23rd April, 1945 (R 7280/4/19). This telegram was also sent to Leeper.
34. Foreign Office to Leeper 19th April, 1945 (R 6325/4/19).
35. Churchill to Sir Orme Sargent 22nd April, 1945. Prime Minister's Personal Minute Serial No. M 382/5 (R 7423/4/19).
36. Hayter's Minute 23rd April, 1945 (R 7423/4/19).
37. Howard's Minute 23rd April, 1945 (R 7423/4/19).
38. Draft Minute to the Prime Minister from Sir Orme Sargent 24th April, 1945 (R 7423/4/19).
39. Leeper to Foreign Office 25th April, 1945 (R 7408/4/19).
40. On the principles advanced by Rosenau (James N. Rosenau, *The Scientific*

Study of Foreign Policy, (New York: Free Press, 1971). John G. Iatrides defines this intervention policy as follows: 'Traditionally "intervention" refers simply to occasional efforts by one state to coerce another into modifying its internal or external policy. It usually occurs at the highest level of governmental authority and policy making and does not affect the bureaucratic operations of the state which is the object of intervention.' John G. Iatrides, 'The Truman Doctrine: The beginning of United States penetration in Greece', in Theodore Coloumbis and Sallie Hicks, (eds.) *U.S. Foreign Policy towards Greece and Cyprus: the clash of principle and pragmatism,* (Washington: Center for Mediterranean Studies and the American Hellenic Institute, 1975), p. 12.

41. Iatrides calls this type of political control penetration and defines it as follows: 'Penetration. . . has been defined as the process whereby members of one polity serve as participants in the political process of another and implies a much greater depth of systematic involvement in the internal politics of another state.' *Ibid.*

IMPLEMENTING THE VARKIZA AGREEMENT—THE WHITE TERROR

His analysis of 18th February shows that Leeper had fully understood the two major problem areas of Greek internal policy—the economic and financial problems and the law and order problem. Although these two areas impinged upon each other at many points, for the sake of clarity they will be dealt with separately. First, the problem of law and order. This subject goes beyond the issues of security forces' organisation and re-organisation of the public service raised by Leeper; it also includes civil liberties, legal matters, trade union rights, treatment of collaborators, reconstruction of the armed forces, etc.; in short, the law and order problem coincides exactly with the content of the Varkiza Agreement and this is why we will present Greece's internal evolution up to summer 1945 in terms of the articles agreed at Varkiza.

Article 1 of the agreement laid down:
'The government will secure in accordance with the Constitution and the democratic principles everywhere recognised, the free expression of the political and social opinions of the citizens, repealing any existing illiberal law. It will also secure the unhindered functioning of individual liberties such as those of assembly, association and expression of views in the Press. More especially, the government will fully restore trade union liberties.'[1]

For the government the first step to securing civil liberties should have been the repeal of those restrictive laws left over from the past. The oldest of these was an Emergency Law of 1917 (No. 755/1917) penalising anyone who publicly expressed opinions subversive of public order or likely to disturb the citizens. However, this law was not only not repealed but was used as the legal basis for repressive measures.[2] The ill-fame *Idionymo* law on *sui generis* offences of 1929 (No. 4229/1929) which made agitation against the existing social system a criminal offence, had been repealed by a law of the government-in-exile. But, after the return of that government, the abrogating law was not re-published in the *Government Gazette* and this gave the prosecuting authorities a pretext to regard the *Idionymo* as still in force.[3] Law 1075/1938 of the Metaxas dictatorship on social and political convictions, applied by the then Assistant-Minister for Security in the form of the notorious Certificates of Unimpeachable Socio-political Convictions, for which the Security Service (Asfalia) had amassed long lists of suspects, continued to be enforced in exactly the same way; as was the law of the same period on press censorship (No. 1092/1938).[4] The laws of the Quisling governments remained in force and not until summer 1949 did the government promulgate a law which made it possible to repeal individual laws after strict investigation and a lapse of six months.[5] On the 24th February, the Plastiras government had ordered that the laws promulgated by the government-in-exile be published in the *Government Gazette* to validate them for Greece. But, as Tsouderos stated in a letter to Voulgaris of 16th May, this had not been done, although a Statutory Law of 23rd March had made the Varkiza Agreement valid Greek law.[6] The government did nothing and the judicial apparatus went on issuing judgments according to the Metaxas legislation and that of the Quisling governments. This ensured continued persecution of the Left.

Freedom of the Press. The very day after the signing of the Varkiza Agreement the Greek Right began its systematic attack on the press. On the 13th and 14th February, followers of 'X'[7] stormed and laid waste the offices of *Eleftheri Ellada* and *Rizospastis* (the EAM and KKE dailies) in the centre of Athens. But as these operations took place before the eyes of foreign correspondents and produced a negative reaction, the Right changed its tactics in the direction of undermining the circulation of the Left press. The methods used included the following: police confiscation of newspapers, a prohibition on sales by the gendarmerie commander in certain Athens suburbs, beating up the newsvendors by the police, destruction of papers at the newsagents by the National Guard, police threats to newsvendors, denunciation of readers employed in the public services to their superiors, threats to purchasers. It was only in working class suburbs that the left-wing press circulated more or less freely.

On 26th February an EAM delegation consisting of Partsalidis, Porfyrogenis and Georgiou complained to Plastiras who promised to give instructions that the left-wing press be allowed to circulate unhindered. The only effect was that, in Piraeus, the officer in command of the 162nd National Guard Battalion obstructed the distribution of the left-wing press for days on end. On the 6th March Vlachos told journalists that he disapproved of such behaviour and had ordered that the left-wing press be allowed to circulate freely. But the persecution continued. On the 7th March, as we have already described, Siantos, Partsalidis and Tsirimokos visited Leeper and complained about violations of Varkiza. On the 10th Partsalidis submitted EAM's complaints in writing to Damaskinos, Plastiras and the ambassadors of the three Western powers. This report made clear that the advance of the British and the National Guard into the countryside had been accompanied by an extension of this press persecution throughout the whole of Greece, and that in the provinces the persecutors hardly needed to restrain themselves, since foreign correspondents were mostly unwilling to go there to report on the situation. EAM printing presses were destroyed and their editorial offices ransacked. The EAM White Book gives places and dates (Volos 1st March and 14th March, Kalamata 29th March, Patras 12th April, Agrinion 14th April, Yannina 16th April, Thebes 27th April, Salonica 5th March, Chios 17th April, Larisa 1st May, Kalamata 10th May, Pyrgos 31st May, etc.), showing the extent of the attacks. The Plastiras government reacted on 31st March with the announcement of a law (245/1945) penalising obstruction of the free circulation of the press which, as the above dates make clear, proved ineffective. On 17th April, Interior Minister Tsatsos announced further measures, but the attack on the left-wing press continued.[8]

William Hardy McNeil, at that time Assistant Military Attaché at the US Embassy in Athens, wrote as follows:

'Despite the handicaps under which they labored once the National Guard had come to town, EAM and Communist newspapers generally continued to appear as before. A favorite pastime of some of the National Guardsmen came to be breaking up the leftist printing shops. On many occasions a group of soldiers in their off-duty hours invaded the premises where the printing was done, scattered the type founts and smashed as much as they could of the presses. The editors, if caught, were beaten.'[9]

On 29th April Assistant-Minister Zakynthinos told press representatives that he had the assurance of the Defence Minister (Voulgaris) and of the Army Chief-of-Staff (Vendiris) that the army would keep a watch on press freedom. But the army's watch evolved in the spirit of Big Brother. Local army commanders themselves began to censor the press or prohibit it, citing Law 1092/1938. Meanwhile, attacks by the National Guard and the Right continued.[10]

The final result of this systematic campaign of suppression against the left-wing press was that, whereas at liberation there had been an EAM newspaper in practically every major Greek town, during 1945 the number of left-wing provincial papers steadily declined. In Athens the left-wing dailies *Rizospastis* and *Eleftheri Ellada* continued to appear and this was used as a proof for foreigners that press freedom reigned in Greece. Circulation of the left-wing press was undermined by more subtle means. The Twentieth Century Fund's observation team reported in January 1947:

'It must be borne in mind that in few places would anyone buy a Communist paper for fear of police, who, if they do not actually witness the purchase, soon hear about it from some patriotic neighbour. This is true even in Athens and extends to Liberal papers as well. Once for example a working man sat in a café reading *Eleftheria*[11] when a policeman passed by and gently flicked the paper with his fingers, saying "I prefer to read *Ethnos*" (a royalist paper). This kind of moral intimidation had the effect of censorship. Our team was having lunch in a Salonica restaurant when a boy came in with the Athens papers. Everyone bought papers, and everyone looked around to see what others were reading. Nearly all the patrons of the restaurant bought *Kathimerini* [royalist, in 1947 the top circulation paper] — when one man took *Vima* [a liberal paper] there was a perceptible tension.'[12]

The Fund's team reported other practices obstructing the circulation of papers unpopular with the government. Newsprint supplies were on a rationed basis, distributed to the papers in proportion to their circulation, and this had resulted in a newsprint 'grey market' in which bribery and corruption were rampant. Then there was an agency in Athens which undertook distribution of the Athens press in the provinces and it often so happened that opposition papers reached it too late for the outgoing bus. Taken together, all this makes it possible to say that, from the day of the signing of the Varkiza Agreement, freedom of the press was systematically dismantled. This process terminated with the prohibition of *Rizospastis* in October 1947.

The trade union question. The trade union liberties guaranteed by the Varkiza Agreement fared no better. Article 7 of the Citrine Agreement provided that, after conclusion of the peace negotiations, the provisional Executive Committee of the GCL should be re-constituted so as to represent all trends amongst the workers, and as soon as tranquillity was restored new elections should be proclaimed in all the country's trade union organisations. The TUC delegation had assured the Greek trade unions of further assistance in the re-establishment of their movement. This was why a second TUC delegation arrived on the 20th February, under the leadership of Vincent (later Sir Vincent) Tewson and with Bert Papworth and Victor Feather as members. These TUC representatives had presumed their main task would be the supervision of the elections and now found themselves suddenly confronted with the problem of reconstructing the Executive Committee. This problem had priority since the Executive would have considerable influence on the correct conduct of elections in the individual unions and the Trades Councils.

The first talks between the representatives of the EAM trade unions (Stratis, Theos and Kalomoiris) and the Hajidimitriou group (Hajidimitriou, Makris, Volotas, Vasiliadis) were held on the 20th February in the Athens Ministry for Labour under Tewson's chairmanship. The only apparent result of these first talks was the invalidating of the previous election results.[13] Negotiations during the next few days clearly demonstrated the conflicting positions: Hajidimitriou was fighting solely for a majority whilst the EAM delegation based its position on that of the International Trade Union Congress in London: that no fascists should sit on the future Executive Committee. EAM demanded an equal number of seats for both groups, whereupon Hajidimitriou maintained that he represented three groups (Dimitratos, Kalyvas[14] and his own) and demanded that the present twenty-one members should be augmented by two additional members for Theos and Stratis and three for Kalomoiris. But the EAM representatives stuck to their original proposal and referred to Article 7 of the Citrine Agreement which required reconstruction, not enlargement of the Executive. When Tewson intervened, Hajidimitriou offered a new division of seats (EAM was to have five out of the twenty-one), but the EAM delegation rejected this, saying it was more interested in the character than in the numbers of the Executive.[15] In other words Hajidimitriou was trying to strengthen his position by getting additional fascist and collaborationist elements on to the Executive.

On the 25th February the TUC delegation reported to Sideris its failure to reach a compromise so far: they would make one more effort, then the minister would have to take over. Sideris stated that, in that case, he would carry out the Citrine Agreement.[16] On the 26th February agreement was achieved and the following accord was signed by all groups: the Executive Committee would be re-constituted; the Minister for Labour would undertake this in accordance with Article 7 of the Agreement and after discussion with both the parties; for the rest, the other articles of the Citrine Agreement were accepted; the elections would be carried out as quickly as possible so as to solve the problem of representation of the various groups in the GCL leadership; both parties would be represented on the supervisory committee provided for by Article 4 of the Citrine Agreement, and would work with the TUC delegation and the other groups until the elections were concluded.[17]

Sideris expressed agreement and readiness to start discussions with both parties. But Hajidimitriou did not agree with the result which he felt could threaten his leading position and demanded that, in assigning places on the new Executive Committee, Sideris include representatives of the Dimitratos and Kalyvas groups as well as of the independent and Trotskyist trade unions.[18] On 1st March Sideris began negotiations and on the 6th he nominated the new Executive Committee.

It consisted of: two representatives of the Theos group, two of the Stratis group, four from Kalomoiris, one Trotskyist, one independent and eleven of the Hajidimitriou-Makris group. Presumably the EAM trade unions had accepted this because they were assured of victory in the forthcoming elections (appointed from the 9th March in Attica). But in the meanwhile there had been serious developments which led to a hardening of the EAM representatives' attitude. Sideris had promised—in conjunction with the signing of the Citrine Agreement—to bring Laws 211/1914 and 2151/1920 back into force at once and thus to exclude all possibility of state intervention in internal union affairs. But the Prefect of Patras had deposed the leadership of the Trades Council, which had been correctly elected by sixty-four out of seventy-five unions, and had replaced them by two former adherents of the Metaxas unions,

Kouloumbis and Antypas. Kouloumbis had already been chairman of the Trades Council during the Metaxas dictatorship. This action had been approved by the GCL leadership, then still under Hajidimitriou's control. The GCL leadership itself deprived the chairmen of the Athens and Piraeus Trades Council of their posts and appointed in their place the chairmen of the Occupation period, Tsakos and Kouzentzis. Both these actions contravened Law 3127/1942 of the government-in-exile which had repealed the enabling legislation of the Metaxas period which allowed a higher level trade union authority to depose a subordinate one. However, as this law of the government-in-exile had also not been published in the Athens *Government Gazette,* Hajidimitriou was acting within his rights. Theos criticised these proceedings in an open letter to Sideris[19] but this did not prevent Hajidimitriou from deposing the properly elected leaders of individual unions and of other Trades Councils (Salonica, Larisa, Volos, Trikala, Kerkyra).[20]

The new Executive met on the 8th March under Tewson's chairmanship to elect the Secretary-General and the six-member Secretariat. The EAM trade unions suggested that

'apart from whoever was elected as Secretary-General [and that it would be Hadjidimitriou was a foregone conclusion] the remainder of the Executive should be divided three and three between the two main Groups',

as this would accord with the spirit of the Citrine Agreement. Hajidimitriou rejected this, the matter was settled by vote and the suggestion turned down. 'The ballot proceeded and the Hadjidimitriou group, in the light of their superior numbers, took all the offices.'[21] As to ensuing events, we have two reports. According to *Rizospastis* and Theos, the EAM trade unionists protested against this and Hajidimitriou called in 'X' men who used force against them, with the result that seven resigned at once. Kalomoiris, being an opportunist, remained with the new GCL leadership.[22] According to the TUC Report, after the above meeting there was

'a demonstration by about a score of widows who commenced abusing the leaders [of the EAM trade unions]. A very tense scene ensued. Crowds assembled and the British representatives had to see [them] away'.[23]

On the 10th March the EAM trade unionists saw the British representatives. They alleged that the demonstrations by the widows had been organised, with which the TUC representatives agreed. They added that 'a fleet of cars had also brought between 80 and 100 gun-men'. This was not accepted by the British representatives.[24] Then the EAM delegates declared that under these circumstances (they spoke of fascism), no further cooperation was possible with the Hajidimitriou group. The only way out of the impasse would be to adopt their suggestion of a Secretariat of three from each side with the Secretary-General in the Chair. Finally they once more demanded conformity with the decisions of the International Trade Union Congress in London.[25]

Meanwhile, the commission for supervising the elections, in which both parties were cooperating under Tewson's chairmanship to prepare the trade union election for Attica, continued its work. On the 14th March it was decided to hold the election during the next weeks on the basis of the pre-Metaxas legislation and under judicial supervision. In the provinces elections would be held when administrative order was restored. Tewson was of the opinion that the election results would solve the problem of the Executive's composition.[26] However, during the following weeks Hajidimitriou continued his manoeuvring to replace the elected committees. The TUC Report of 1945 had this to say:

> 'Under the law the Provisional Committee of the Confedreration were entitled, with the agreement of the Ministry of Labour, to appoint Provisional Committees in Working Centres (like our Trades Councils) and even in Unions. As the Confederation was now representative of one Group only it was evident that there was some justification for the claim of the representatives of the Old Committee that, in the main, Hadjidimitriou was appointing his own supporters in these new Provisional Committees.'

The Report then stated that the new Minister of Labour (Nikolaïdis) supported this action.[27] When, at the beginning of April, the TUC representatives tried to overcome the difficulty over the 'arbitrary appointments' and intervened with the minister, he requested them to submit their opinion 'in writing', which was done.[28] The purpose of these manoeuvres is transparent: Hajidimitriou was trying to influence the election results.

On the 30th March the EAM trade union leaders reacted to this and to Kalomoiris' defection by founding their own trade union federation ERGAS (Ergatikos Antifasistikos Synaspismos, Anti-fascist Workers' Alliance). Its aims were the restoration of trade union liberties, independence of the trade unions from all state intervention, abolition of the system of appointed Executives, re-establishment of workers' right to elect and control their own representatives and, finally, action to prevent the introduction of state-controlled corporate unions of fascist type.[29] The communists, most of the socialists and some followers of Kalomoiris participated in ERGAS.

Early in April elections began to be held in Athens and Piraeus. They were conducted according to the laws and the trade union statutes valid before 1936, which led to an artificial revival of the old union structure. Although Hajidimitriou—who had in the meantime been elected GCL General-Secretary by the votes of his faction—tried by every means, including the introduction of armed 'X' men, to manipulate the electoral process, he suffered a humiliating defeat.[30] In Athens and Piraeus ERGAS was the undoubted victor. Then, too, at the May Day celebrations in the Olympic stadium in Athens on 10th May 1945, for which a political truce had been declared, it was apparent that ERGAS had the working masses on its side. Hajidimitriou, on the other hand, could hardly drum up any following. This, together with the election results, alarmed Hajidimitriou and his group, Labour Minister Zakkas and the TUC delegation. Hajidimitriou therefore declined to continue the elections beyond the boundaries of Attica unless he could first appoint new Executives to all the trade unions and Trades Councils.[31] In this way he hoped that he could still influence the election results to his own advantage. But in the meantime opposition to his line had raised its head within his own faction and Kalomoiris reverted to ERGAS. Some individual unions were now on strike. All these factors—and probably also Feather's advice (Tewson had returned to Britain on the 19th April and Papworth left Greece on the 27th)—persuaded the new minister Zakkas to publish the Tsouderos government's Law No. 3127/1942 on the restoration of trade union liberties in the *Government Gazette* of 25th May.[32] On the 29th May Theos demanded an end to the 'appointments' and the removal of those already appointed from their posts.[33] On the same day an ERGAS delegation, with representatives of Kalomoiris, visited Zakkas and demanded that the GCL Executive be re-constituted. Zakkas agreed.[34] According to the 1945 TUC Report, which is unfortunately not completely clear, apparently a new agreement about the future composition of the Provisional Committees was even signed, providing for representation on the following basis: Hajidimitriou nine seats, Kalomoiris five, Theos four and Stratis three. The nominations were submitted to the Minister of Labour.[35] But before this re-constitution could be effected there was a 'palace revolution'[36] within the Hajidimitriou group and he was replaced by the TUC delegation's new discovery, Fotis Makris.[37]

Fotis Makris had been at the head of a union of telephone workers during the Metaxas dictatorship. During the Occupation he had worked with the GCL and when, towards the end of the Occupation this seemed opportune, he had joined EEAM. After liberation he had returned to Hajidimitriou's old fascist clique. This opportunist with strong fascist inclinations became Hajidimitriou's successor in the right-wing trade union faction and soon after General-Secretary of the GCL which he was to remain until 1964.

Meanwhile negotiations continued between ERGAS, its allies and the Labour Minister on the one side and the Hajidimitriou-Makris group on the other. The result was a supplement to Law 3127/1942 agreed on the 9th June and coming into force on the 21st, which permitted the Labour Minister to appoint a new provisional Executive.[38] Finally, on 26th June, in the presence of Feather, the two trade union groups concluded the following agreement: a new provisional GCL Executive would be formed on which the Makris group would have eleven and the left-wing trade unions ten seats; Makris was to be General-Secretary; this committee would organise the elections so that the Eighth Trade Union Congress could be held at the latest on 10th September. Should the Congress not take place, the committee would automatically cease to exist on that date and would be replaced by a new committee consisting of an equal number of delegates from the Trades Councils of Athens, Piraeus, Salonica, Volos and Patras. This committee's only task would be to complete the elections and call the Congress.[39] It would be for the future GCL leadership to replace the present union and Trades Council leaderships in the provinces by new ones in which all trade union trends were represented.

The purpose behind this is clear. Makris hoped in this way to win a majority in the provincial leaderships as well and to emerge as victor from the elections. The Left accepted because they were sure of the election results.[40]

On 3rd July, therefore, Labour Minister Zakkas issued a decree appointing the new provisional GCL Executive, consisting of eleven Makris representatives, four from Theos, four from Kalomoiris and two from Stratis. Makris became Secretary-General; Kalomoiris, Stratis, Theos and one other Makris nominee the officers of the confederation. The Executive was made responsible for the completion of the trade union elections within the time limit specified by the supervising committee under the chairmanship of the TUC representative.

'Pending elections taking place, the appointed Executives of all Federations and the most important Working Centres (definitely Patras, Volos, Salonika, Athens and Piraeus) must be reconstructed [in conformity with the above numbers] in order to include representatives from all groups. A president and two secretaries of equal rank must be elected by these reconstituted bodies, and from any other group no more than one official shall be elected. The Election Committees in those Unions in which elections have not already taken place must include representatives of all groups and, during the ten-day period in which elections for Union Executives must be taken, this all-group Election Committee will take complete charge of the Union.'

All these appointed committees, including the GCL Executive itself, would forego their offices by 20th *(sic)* September or the date of the Congress, whichever was earlier. Forty (forty-five) days' grace might be granted on the request of at least five-sevenths of the confederation Executive, to allow for the completion of Congress arrangements in the event of unavoidable delay; however, should the Congress not be summoned before 20th September (plus the days of grace) responsibility would then be assigned to a fifteen-member committee elected by the five Trades Councils mentioned above, the Athens Trades Council to act as convenor. Finally it was stated that this was to be the last re-constitution.[41]

This seemed to clear the way for holding the elections. But Makris had no interest in elections because he knew that the Left would emerge victorious as it had in Athens and Piraeus. Moreover, his group lacked the funds for a campaign. To this end the enforced trade union contributions of the Metaxas period had been re-introduced in April. The money raised was handed over to the GCL leadership who passed it on to the 'appointed' subordinate executives.[42] But, even there where the new executives had already been appointed, Makris's followers did all they could to hinder the holding of elections. They accused their opponents of multiple voting or found other formal pretexts. In towns where they had no base at all, they prevented the elections by declaring a boycott. In Salonica they went so far as to ensure themselves of security assistance. On the 4th August, the Salonica security commander, Major Georgios Stefanakis, informed the Ministry for Northern Greece that he had forbidden the holding of trade union elections because, in the existing situation, the communists would win and thus yet one more Trades Council would fall into their hands.[43]

In Athens and Piraeus most of the elections had been held by the middle of August and the new provisional GCL Executive decided to call the Athens Trades Council delegate conference for the 19th. It was also decided to appoint mixed control commissions for the provincial elections and to hold these before the 15th September. Having achieved that much unity, Makris, Kalomoiris, Theos and a representative of Stratis (Laskaris) took themselves off to Salonica where the elections were to be held after all.[44]

Meanwhile, the Athens trade union election results had become known and gave the Makris group serious pause for thought. In the absence of their leader, they turned to the remaining members of the GCL Executive and, under a pretext, proposed a postponement of the delegate conference till the 26th August. The Executive accepted and, after some opposition from ERGAS, this date was agreed.[45] As the 26th approached, panic on the Makris side grew: ERGAS started a poster campaign and Makris' only come-back was with the photographs of four trade union leaders allegedly murdered in December. On the 25th developments reached crisis point. Behind Theos' back, Makris, Kalomoiris and Laskaris sent the GCL Executive a telegram demanding a further postponement of the Athens conference on the grounds that ERGAS was proving intransigent in Macedonia. On the advice of a high official of the Labour Ministry (Panayotis Pavlakis), acting behind Zakkas' back, the provisional Executive of the Athens Trades Council which was also Makris-dominated demanded postponement and declared its resignation. At Zakkas' suggestion, the police proceeded to close down the Trades Council in order to forestall a possible occupation by ERGAS and to 'prevent disturbances'.[46]

At the same time the Makris group instructed its delegates to abstain from the conference due to begin the next morning.

On the morning of the 26th a large number of delegates assembled in the Central Theatre. Of the 620 elected about 400 had appeared. Directly the conference began, a speaker from the Makris faction instructed his followers to leave the conference, whereat two or three delegates left the auditorium. Of the remaining 397, 370 belonged to ERGAS. Despite the boycott, the conference sat since it was rightly held that those present represented the majority of the Athens workers, and a new Executive was elected, controlled by ERGAS.

In the meantime, the Makris group went into action. They addressed themselves to Zakkas and to the British labour attaché: the delegate conference had been manipulated by ERGAS which had created phoney unions in order to secure a majority—an imputation at least as applicable to the Makris faction. Moreover they maintained that the conference had been unconstitutional since it was held without the presence of the Trades Council chairman, a Makris man who had resigned on the 25th; nor had there been a magistrate present. The labour attaché took a reserved attitude, but Zakkas acted: he refused the new Executive official recognition.[47]

The Piraeus Trades Council's delegate conference was to be held on the same day. At first the police, at the Makris group's instigation, tried to obstruct it but there too an Executive was later elected without participation by Makris' followers. But, since the provisional committee had not resigned, there were now two Trades Council leaderships in operation. Here, too, Zakkas refused official recognition. Likewide in Kalamata and Levadia ERGAS-controlled Trades Council leaderships were elected and were not recognised.[48] In this way the Makris faction succeeded—even where it was clearly in the minority—in enforcing its will and torpedoing the preparations for the Trade Union Congress.

In this they were supported by Labour Minister Zakkas. After the failures in Athens and Piraeus he considered whether he should send a magistrate to the two Trades Councils to select a new Executive representing all trade union groups. Such a committee would then hold a re-play of the delegate conference. It was only with difficulty that the British labour attaché talked him out of this: so open an intervention could produce a negative reaction in Britain.[49] The labour attaché had also to intervene to get the Athens Trades Council re-opened after it had been closed by the police. On the 27th August, when the attaché wanted to visit the building, he found it had been occupied by armed police. On orders from the newly arrived British Police Mission these forces were withdrawn but two plain-clothes men remained behind. When Makris returned to Athens he complained about the withdrawal of the police.[50]

Even when Theos, Makris, Kalomoiris and Laskaris had all returned, nothing changed. In the Trades Councils where ERGAS had the majority and the Makris faction was non-existent (*e.g.* Salonica, Kavalla, Xanthi, Komotini and Serres), the ERGAS-controlled executive committees refused to form a new one consisting of representatives of all the trends. In smaller towns, wherever the Makris faction allegedly had a majority, they likewise refused to re-constitute. The result was an all round stalemate and on the 20th September the term of office of the provisional GCL Executive would end with its task unfulfilled. The GCL was leaderless.

Until after the return of the four GCL leaders from Macedonia Zakkas had not really intervened openly in the proceedings, but had more or less restricted himself to the role of a spectator, looking with a benevolent eye on the Makris faction's activities. Now, under pressure from Kalomoiris, he decided to intervene directly.

Instead of starting negotiations with the trade union groups themselves, he turned to the 'proven' method of regulation by law. At the beginning of September he worked out with Kalomoiris a draft law on trade union elections which had a double purpose: on the one hand the elections should be supervised by magistrates, in other words they would be under state control; on the other a complicated and cunningly devised electoral system of indirect list voting with transferable preference votes would break ERGAS predominance and give the other groups a disproportionate allocation of votes and seats in the various leaderships. Nominally, this was supposed to render the trade union leadership more representative, but in reality it was a political manoeuvre to weaken the Left. Even the British labour attaché was alarmed and criticised the draft law

'(a) for being a political measure to keep down communism, (b) because it may reduce the unions to impotence through insistence of mixed committees, (c) might sap vitality of the unions through too much nursing by the state.'[51]

Since the law also provided for the annulling of the elections already held, including those supervised by the TUC, the Foreign Office was nervous, expecting protests from that quarter. On the 23rd September it expressed its grave doubts as to the wisdom of the law.[52]

Meanwhile, on the 18th-19th September, Zakkas had started negotiations with the provisional GCL Executive in which the British labour attaché also participated. Since the provisional GCL Executive's term of office was about to end, this was the first problem for discussion. Kalomoiris and Stratis proposed that a new committee should be formed in which the groups were represented in proportion to their strength. Makris rejected this because he had the majority on the previous committee which he demanded should remain in office. Theos also rejected it as the proposed distribution of seats did not represent the real proportionate strength of forces resulting from the Athens and Piraeus elections. Since no agreement could be reached negotiations were broken off without result.

Faced with this confused situation and acting on the advice of the labour attaché, Zakkas temporarily refrained from signing his law. The situation was further complicated by an over-zealous magistrate who declared the Athens elections invalid; whilst, from the provinces, news came in of further massive ERGAS victories. Moreover, the International Labour Conference was due to open in Paris and, without a GCL leadership, the Greek trade unions could not be represented. Zakkas therefore saw it as his most urgent task to re-constitute the GCL Executive. To this end he promulgated Law 581 of 29th September 1945.[53]

This law renewed the Labour Minsiter's right to appoint a provisional GCL Executive, as laid down by Law 393 of 9th June.[54] According to the new law the Labour Minister could, within ten days from its publication in the *Government Gazette,* appoint a new provisional GCL Executive which must then summon a Trade Union Congress within four months at most. Once the law was published, at the beginning of October, Zakkas started negotiations with the leaders of the four trade union groups and submitted to them the following new plan. A provisional GCL Secretariat should be formed, consisting of Makris, Kalomoiris, Stratis and Theos, each of whom would function as General-Secretary for one month. At the same time a conference should be called of all Athens and Piraeus union leaderships which had been properly elected. This conference would elect eleven of its members as a provisional GCL Executive and these, together with the four General-Secretaries, would constitute the new GCL leadership. The members should be elected in proportion to the strength of each group, but no group should hold more than five seats or less than one.[55]

Kalomoiris, Stratis and Theos accepted this proposal. But Makris and his faction rejected it. He demanded direct election of the General-Secretary by the trade union membership and accused the other groups of tolerating government intervention in internal union business—as though he had not so far himself been the chief beneficiary of such intervention: Zakkas obviously intended to hand the unions over to EAM and KKE. On 8th October Makris had his men occupy the GCL offices. Since this coincided with a government crisis resulting from Voulgaris' resignation, he was able to continue the occupation successfully for a few days. This government crisis also prevented the planned re-constitution of the GCL leadership, so that for some weeks chaos reigned.

It only remains to add that, in regard to the restoration of trade union liberties, the Varkiza Agreement—which had become valid law through its publication as Constitutional Act No. 23 in the *Government Gazette* of 23rd March[56]—had been radically violated. During the whole period, from the signing of the agreement to the resignation of the Voulgaris Cabinet, the Hajimitriou-Makris clique had taken pains to revive the system of state-controlled unions of the fascist Metaxas dictatorship. These activities were tolerated by the Greek government and by the TUC delegation and were unremittingly seconded by the underground right-wing organisations and the subordinate authorities. If, by autumn 1945, the unions had not reverted to fascism, this was because the former EEAM members held firmly to their line and did not let themselves be deflected even by right-wing terrorism. It must also be made clear that neither EEAM nor ERGAS was a communist organisation in the sense of being controlled solely by communists and pursuing communist trade union policy. Both organisations were trade union movements drawing on the whole spectrum of democratic parties: just the opposite of the Hajidimitriou-Makris clique which was pursuing the restoration of the fascist system of Metaxas.

Treatment of collaborators. In his opening speech at the Varkiza conference Sofianopoulos had guaranteed that the government would apply the laws concerning collaborators and bring the accused to justice. In accordance with Article 4, EAM had handed over its arrested collaborators to the government who, by the same article, had undertaken the obligation to try them.

The Greek collaborators belonged, in general, to one of three categories: first, the members of the three Quisling Cabinets (under Tsolakoglou, Logothetopoulos and Rallis) who were for the most part in British custody or, like Logothetopoulos, had taken themselves off to Germany. The second group included members of the police, the gendarmerie and officers and men of the Security Battalions *(Tagmata Asfalias),* many of whom had fallen into ELAS' hands. The third group consisted of entrepreneurs, Occupation profiteers, Gestapo agents, informants, Greek Nazis—in other words the scum of Greek society at all levels including that society's upper crust.

The legal basis for trying the collaborators was Constitutional Act No. 1 of 6th December 1944, promulgated by Themistoklis Tsatsos, Minister for Justice in the Papandreou Cabinet and modified by his successor, N. Kolyvas, in Constitutional Acts Nos. 6 and 12.[57] Whilst prior to the December events inclination had been in favour of the Left's demand for a court in which representatives of the people should have the preponderance, later, this popular element was restricted. The president of the tribunal was an Areopagus (Supreme Criminal) Court judge, with four Appeal Court judges and two lay assessors.[58] The trial of the first of the groups began on the 21st February 1945. The defendants were twenty-four former ministers and officers.[59]

The first days were taken up by a sharp exchange between prosecution and defence. The defence maintained that the whole case was illegal. Since Article 91 of the 1911 Constitution forbade the setting up of special courts and since the Constitution did not provide for the Regency in its present form, Constitutional Acts 6 and 12 were invalid. It was only with difficulty and by a somewhat idiosyncratic interpretation of the Constitution that the tribunal was able to circumvent this charge. The defence then fell back on the argument *nulla poena sine lege* (no penalty without a law) enshrined in Article 7 of the Constitution: Constitutional Act No. 12 contravened this by making the holding of government office during the Occupation in principle subject to prosecution, without taking into account how the individual ministers had discharged their office. The tribunal rejected this, maintaining that the present government had the right to amend the Constitution and thus also to condemn actions after the fact, provided these actions could be condemned as immoral and were clearly regarded as such by Greek public opinion. But at the same time the tribunal restricted its own authority: it announced that the sentences to be imposed would require parliamentary ratification since the Constitutional Act itself would have to be ratified by the future parliament. This made it clear that the whole collaboration trial would involve relatively little danger for the accused. John Rallis commented that he was now confident the good God had granted him several more years to live.[60] Even more significant was a further decision of the tribunal: no official protocol of the trial would be drawn up and the unofficial shorthand report of the proceedings would be destroyed after six months.[61]

The trial proper began on the 27th February with the indictment drawn up by the prosecution. The specific charges were: the unauthorised armistice of 1941, the formation of a government, collaboration with the Germans in the economic and labour sphere and the creation of the Security Battalions. The testimony of the first prosecution witness, Themistoklis Tsatsos, showed clearly that, even from this quarter, there was a tendency to put a favourable interpretation on the conduct of the accused. Tsatsos said of the Security Ballalions that their task was to fight communism, not to support the Germans. When he pointed out that, in the Constitutional Act he had drafted as Minister of Justice in the Papandreou Cabinet, participation in a collaborationist government was not regarded as treason, the president of the tribunal gently reminded him that this Act was not in force (probably because it had not been republished in the *Government Gazette*).

Themistoklis Sofoulis' testimony was the most typical: 'His "evidence" was distinguished by its inconclusiveness, even in such a context. To questions of fact he answered that he knew very little about the Occupation Governments; he had not been concerned in politics during that period; he was an old man and did not remember very well. Asked if the Security Battalions had served the Germans, he answered that no Greek would ever consent to serve the Germans. Asked "Did the Occupation Government betray Greece?" he said: "I cannot accept that assumption. I know all the defendants. They are good Greeks. They love their country; and I respect them".'[62]

The other prosecution witnesses, likewise, tried to exonerate the defendants. Panayotis Kanellopoulos was an honourable exception when he said that the mere existence of a government during the Occupation had helped the enemy, as had the mere fact of the existence of the Security Battalions whose creation could only be partially justified by the previous misdeeds of EAM-ELAS. The same series of questions was then put to a number of bourgeois politicians, professors and higher civil servants. It was apparent that the tribunal went out of its way to encourage the witnesses to make general statements and express personal opinions and it is interesting too that there were no witnesses from the Left.[63] Facts were of no interest. Testimony by the prosecution witnesses ended on the 26th March.

The defence opened on the 27th with the examination of its witnesses. On the very first day the testimony of D. Maximos demonstrated the two-handed defence tactic: on the one hand it tried to present the maximum number of members of the 'political world', of the higher ranks of the Officers' Corps and of the civil service as accomplices, as 'in the know' or at least as in silent agreement; on the other hand it tried to prove that many of the defendants had worked secretly for the Greek cause and, wherever possible, for the Allies. Maximos (a Populist) testified that the creation of the Security Battalions had been very useful and had been fully justified retrospectively by the December events. Other former Populist ministers[64] expressed themselves similarly. At the same time, facts were revealed which were extremely embarrassing for the British. Leeper told the Foreign Office:

'A certain regrettable though not excessively detailed publicity has been given to the contacts of British secret organisations with the alleged traitor Ministers, in the attempt to subvert or make use of them.'[65]

On 30th March it came to a trial of strength between the tribunal and the defence. On the 24th Justice Minister Kolyvas had published a law supplementing Constitutional Act No. 6 and, amongst other things, restricting the number of character witnesses to five for each defendant and providing for the arrest of all the accused.[66] The reason for this was the defence's attempt to line up a phalanx of two hundred character witnesses in order to block the proceedings. When the tribunal tried to apply the new law, it was confronted with a united defence protest. Counsel demanded that the law be changed or they would lay down their briefs. After an *entr'acte* during which defence counsel actually withdrew, a compromise was reached. In principle the character witnesses would be restricted to five but in exceptional cases more could be heard. This invalidated the law and the victorious defence resumed its task. It was now in control of proceedings.

After this success, the defence intensified its campaign and set out to compromise members of the government. On the 2nd April Major-General Panagakos testified that all the generals with whom Rallis had discussed the creation of the Security Battalions had recommended this. Amongst others, the second-in-command of the Third Brigade, Papadopoulos, was named as the chief organiser before he was taken off to Cairo. On the 4th April Archbishop Spyridon of Yannina testified that, in 1941, he had recommended capitulation to Generals Tsolakoglou, Bakos and Demestichas and, at their request, had given them a list of honourable Greeks suitable for ministerial posts. The royalist politician, John Theotokis, maintained that the December rising had been a direct consequence of the disbanding of the Security Battalions by Papandreou. The former General Director of the Labour Ministry, Pavlakis, went so far as to suggest that, if the Germans had been unable to mobilise labour from Greece, this was the merit of the Rallis government. Colonel Ilias Zoumboulakis of the Security Battalions testified that, a few days before the German withdrawal, the collaborationist Colonel Bakoyannis had ordered his forces to cooperate with the government's security forces which were to come under General Spiliotopoulos (military commander of the Athens area for the liberation). Another witness testified that another collaborationist, Louvaris, had become a minister on the express advice of Damaskinos. Rear-Admiral Oikonomou testified that the Archbishop had personally given his blessing to Rallis' decision to serve as Prime Minister. In general, the defence tactic seems to have been thoroughly successful and this was aided by the efforts of the accused to devolve responsibility for obviously discreditable acts on to the absent defendants, denouncing these as the real collaborators. These dirty tactics reached their climax in the middle of April, when the former second-in-command of EDES, Komninos Pyromaglou, testified in writing that he had never received any assistance from Rallis and distanced himself from Gonatas and the collaborating EDES Central Committee. Rallis thereupon took up a Mark Antony attitude and produced the Plastiras letter of the 10th January 1944 appointing Gonatas his official representative in Greece and thus showing that he accepted cooperation with him.

This tactic of washing Greek politicians' dirty linen in a public trial (as Leeper described it)[67] continued during the defence pleas which lasted from 16th April to 5th May. These were, in the main, repetitions of what had already been said in the evidence but some new points did arise which throw an interesting light on certain events. For example, the pleas for Tsolakoglou and Demestichas agreed in showing that the editor of *Ellinikon Aima,* Konstantinos Vovolinis, had collaborated, at least during the first half of the Occupation. General Katsimitros, Minister for Agriculture in 1941, expressed his astonishment that he was on trial at all instead of getting on with the reconstruction of the eighth (Epirus) Division, the special job to which he had been appointed in January

1945. Rallis advanced it as a merit that he had been able to modify the German round-up system by which communists and nationalists were arrested indiscriminately as hostages, so that only communists were arrested.[68] In his opinion he had deserved well of his country and his peroration was greeted with loud applause from the audience.[69] Colonel Bakoyannis related how, in November and December 1944, British officers had come to the Averof prison to fetch away Security Battalion officers and men detailed there and incorporate them in the Third (Mountain) Brigade.[70]

Public Prosecutor Papadakis' summing-up on 5th May brought a breath of fresh air to this moral quagmire; the accused were trying to exploit the present confused political situation and the criminal December rebellion for their own purposes; but the December events were one thing and the behaviour of the accused during the Occupation another; this behaviour had been in crass contrast to the heroic resistance of the Greek people both before and after the German invasion; the accused generals had, at first, done their duty, but later had wavered, betrayed their honour, damaged the alliance with Great Britain and ignored the express instructions of the government; the army's morale had been high and statements to the contrary were lies; as ministers they had offered no resistance to German orders; if the civilian mobilisation for enforced labour, ordered by Tsolakoglou, had failed, this was mainly because that section of the population now under persecution by the majority, had offered resistance; Rallis was responsible for the start of the civil war against an organisation [EAM] that had united almost the whole nation against the enemy. Although in some parts of the country this organisation's character had been deformed it remained a fact that—more than anyone else—it had fought the enemy. At this point the accused and their defence counsel protested loudly and furiously and Rallis quoted Churchill's hostile words about EAM. Papadakis went on to deal with the brutality of the Security Battalions against the Resistance and the civilian population and cited details; the responsibility for all this lay with those who had organised these forces, forces armed by the Germans, controlled by them and fighting with them; the prosecution need not concern itself with Constitutional Act No. 6: the accused were responsible for murder and other crimes and the penal code would suffice for sentencing them.

Verdicts were pronounced on the 31st May. Tsolakoglou and Bakos were found guilty of concluding the armistice against the orders of the 1941 government. Bishop Spyridon of Yannina—who was not on trial—was found to share this guilt and that for forming a government. Further, the tribunal found that the three Occupation prime ministers had supported the aims of the enemy but absolved them of acting with premeditation and cleared them of criminal intent. But the most important part of the verdict dealt with the Security Battalions, as follows:

'As is shown by the process of the trial, the formation of the Security Battalions by John Rallis did not aim at the exercise of force against Greeks on account of their activities against the Italians or Germans, nor at the provocation of a civil war, but at the restoration of public order in town and country, which had been dangerously disturbed since the summer of 1942 by the activity of evil-doers who had proceeded to the destruction of authorities, the murder of civilians and those responsible for maintaining order, and the burning of public buildings and other establishments; the result of which disorderly state of affairs was to compel many inhabitants of the rural districts to migrate to the towns for safety. These units were armed by the Germans with other ends in view, that is to say the protraction of the division between Greeks, which assisted their security in Greece; but this was not among the intentions of the Government which formed the Security Battalions, though it unintentionally did, nevertheless, assist the designs of the enemy. Consequently John Rallis and his government stand acquitted as regards the Security Battalions.'[71]

After this monstrous verdict, the next one finding the accused guilty of propaganda for the enemy seemed like a bad joke. Public Prosecutor Papadakis went on to demand heavy sentences, though he recommended that they be carried out only after ratification by the future parliament. The tribunal's sentences constituted a public scandal. Tsolakoglou was sentenced to death with the recommendation that this be commuted to life imprisonment. The two Finance Ministers, S. Kotzamanis and S. Tsironikos, were sentenced to death in absence but with the same recommendation. The two Prime Ministers, Logothetopoulos and Rallis, were sentenced to life imprisonment.[72]

The Athens press reacted characteristically. *Rizospastis* contrasted the verdict on the Security Battalions with BBC broadcasts of 1943 and 1944[73] in which these were condemned and also cited statements by Tsouderos and Eisenhower containing condemnations of the collaborating forces. The clemency towards their creator, Rallis, was regarded as particularly unfortunate and the acquittal of their actual organiser, Bakoyannis, as a provocation. The bitterness felt in the left-liberal camp found expression when *Eleftheria* headlined its commentary on the verdict 'A half a million dead'. The Centre press (*Vima* and *Kathimerina Nea*) commented that public opinion would not be satisfied with these verdicts. The right-wing press was at first silent and then deplored the sentences. Even the Justice Minister in the Voulgaris Cabinet declared that he was not satisfied with the verdict. In point of fact, the verdict was practically an acquittal. None of the death sentences were carried out and the prison sentences were amnestied in 1948. The only prominent collaborator who died in prison was John Rallis, in October 1946. Those sentenced in absence were detained after their return to

Greece (Logothetopoulos in February 1946 and Tsironikos in August 1946) until the 1948 amnesty.

Subsequent trials of collaborators were characterised by similar clemency and in December 1946 they were suspended by Act of Parliament.[74] In November 1945 the former police commander, General Lambou, had been sentenced to death but, except for a few criminal offenders, who had worked with the Gestapo during the Occupation, no one was actually executed. If one compares the trials of the main Greek collaborators with the trials of EAM-ELAS members going on at the same time, in which death sentences were regularly handed out (though not, in general, carried out until 1947-48) and prison sentences really had to be served, it is possible to speak—without distortion—of class justice. Greece was the only country in Europe in which collaboration went, for all practical purposes, unpunished. One cannot know for certain how far the contacts of the accused with British Intelligence operated as a form of Life Insurance; but it cannot be excluded since the sentences for those who lacked these contacts (Logothetopoulos, Tsironikos) were proportionately heavier. At any rate Woodhouse's formulation appears correct: 'In the mood of the time Communism seemed a worse crime than collaboration; and collaboration unlike capital punishment, admitted degrees.'[75]

The National Army. Article 5 of the Varkiza Agreement ruled as follows:

'The National Army, apart from the professional officers and NCOs, shall consist of soldiers of the classes which shall from time to time be called up. Reserve officers, NCOs and other ranks, who have been specially trained in modern weapons, shall remain in service so long as there is a formation requiring them. The Sacred Squadron [Company] shall remain as at present, since it is under the immediate orders of the Allied High Command, and shall thereafter be merged in the united National Army in accordance with the above principle. The effort will be made to extend regular conscription to the whole of Greece in accordance with the technical facilities existing and the necessities which may arise. After the demobilisation of ELAS, those men who belong to classes which are to be called up shall report for enrolment in the units already existing. All men who have been enrolled in the units now existing without belonging to the classes being called up, shall be discharged. All members of the permanent cadres of the National Army shall be considered by the Councils for which provision is made in Constitutional Act No. VII.[76] The political and social views of citizens serving in the army shall be respected.'[77]

Constitutional Act No. 7 regulated the composition of the Officers' Corps and, amongst other things, provided that the republican officers dismissed from the army in connection with the military rebellions of

1933 and 1935 should once more belong to the Officers' Corps. On the other hand those who had participated in the Middle East disturbances of spring 1944 remained excluded as did those who had served in the Security Battalions. All the remaining officers were, however, to be investigated by various special councils for which the Constitutional Act specified the following criteria: military activity, character, moral stature as a commander, conduct during the Occupation, and professional qualifications.[78] With this law, Plastiras had mainly in view the rehabilitation and re-employment of his republican officer friends, but the mention of Constitutional Act No. 7 in Article 5 of the Varkiza Agreement opened the way to army employment to the ELAS officers and NCOs—at least it did so theoretically.

To understand these developments, a brief retrospective on the evolution of the armed forces from the return of the government-in-exile in October 1944 is required. At that point the Greek government's only regular unit was the Third (Mountain) Brigade. Up to the outbreak of the December conflict, fourteen so-called National Guard battalions had been formed by call-up but these dissolved overnight when the fighting started as many of their members were EAM sympathisers. During the Athens fighting another thirty-six battalions were formed, officially from the classes of 1934–40. McNeill, however, reports as follows on their composition:

'Inasmuch as the writ of the Papandreou Government ran only where British arms prevailed, recruits to the National Guard came at first only from the small district in the center of Athens. With confusion so great, the "conscription" amounted to little more than a legal framework for the formation of volunteer units. Nobody looked too closely at the men who offered themselves for service. That they should be strictly within the age limits, nobody cared; nor did anyone examine the past record of the recruits. . . Many roughnecks and criminals hastened to join the new National Guard. Veterans of the Security Battalions did the same. The gendarmes, who had been brought to Athens to be screened, were incorporated into the National Guard in a body without any pretense at checking their individual records for collaboration. . . all the battalions that were raised during the fighting in Athens were rowdy and strongly anti-Communist.'[79]

After the signing of the Varkiza Agreement, the British troops advanced across the armistice line into ELAS-land to take over the arms laid down by ELAS at specified collecting points. ELAS had handed over considerably more arms than had been required, though a respectable supply of weapons was successfully hidden and, fifteen months later, formed the basic equipment of the Democratic Army *(Dimokratikos Stratos)* of Markos Vafiadis.[80] In the wake of the British came the Athens National Guard battalions with a double mission: to establish order and tranquillity and to form new National Guard battalions in the localities they occupied before moving on to continue their work elsewhere. By the 1st April the British had practically completed their task. But it was 15th May before the National Guard was in control of the whole country. By mid-April twenty-two further battalions had been formed. The head of the British Military Mission, Major-General G.R. Smallwood, reported on the character of these units:

'Again, however, it could not be expected that those responsible for their formation would prove entirely impartial in the recruitment of their personnel. Units were being formed to maintain law and order. Those responsible for their formation were inevitably anti-Extreme Left. . . In the view of the battalion commander therefore, danger to law and order was most to be expected from the Extreme Left and any officer who, in such circumstances, enlisted a probably disaffected element into his battalion would have been carrying impartiality to the point of imbecility. . .'[81]

In other words, instead of the planned recruitment of National Guard battalions from the appointed age group, the Athens units recruited them exclusively from local right-wingers.

During the period when the National Guard had sole responsibility for law and order (until July 1945), it staged a counter-revolution. The actual process of take-over soon became stereotyped. The advance British troops reached a certain locality and were received by a more-or-less welcoming EAM demonstration.[82] Then the British commanding officer installed the government-appointed prefect *(nomarch)* or mayor, whilst the British unit collected the arms handed in by ELAS and tried to prevent immediate clashes between the disarmed left-wingers and the local Right. Hardly had the British moved on and the Athens National Guard taken over control than suppression of the Left began. For instance, in Sparta the new prefect at once forbade any form of left-wing activity and released three hundred Security Battalionists from the jail.[83] Then the National Guard began the search for concealed weapons which extended even to torture. Some of these weapons were handed over to the British but the greater part soon found their way into the hands of local right-wingers. Directly the Left was disarmed, followers of the Right denounced local left-wingers to the National Guard command. Every kind of crime was attributed to the Left and the Athens units did not stop to check the veracity of the denunciations but locked up the accused. The liberties guaranteed by the Varkiza Agreement were trampled underfoot. Since no courts were functioning in the provinces, those arrested remained in detention over the next months. The prisons were often in a terrible condition and were soon impossibly overcrowded, so that in summer 1945 the government was obliged to empty them by a series of partial amnesties. In addition, there were personal acts of revenge by the Right against the Left.[84]

As already described, one of the next measures taken by the National Guard was the destruction of the local EAM press and the ransacking of EAM offices. Extremist violence increased proportionately to the distance from Athens and also depended on whether or not there was a British unit in the vicinity to exercise a moderating influence on the Right. This was usually the case in the provincial towns and the arming of right-wingers was done more cautiously there than in the villages where the National Guard commanders were subject to no restraints. Soon nationalist organisations made their appearance in the provincial towns and villages, of which the most important was Colonel Grivas' 'X' which, in autumn 1945, claimed 200,000 members. These organisations drew together local royalists, followers of the Metaxas dictatorship, collaborators and Security Battalion members, as well as members of the right-wing secret groups of the Occupation period. By the end of 1945 these organisations had coordinated at national level. Between them and the National Guard—and later the army and gendarmerie—there were close relations and a personal network which, through RAN, reached up to the General Staff.[85] Briefly, a state was beginning to grow up within the state and increasingly to control the state itself; whilst the official state authorities had little or no influence over it. This is what the Greeks call *parakratos*. In contrast to the EAM state which, by its mass organisations, its propaganda and its demonstrations, lived in the public eye, the Right preferred to work under cover. EAM had established its state as a declared alternative to the existing one: the Right endeavoured through the *parakratos* to control the state itself.

In point of fact, these first months after Varkiza were decisive. Because long months passed with hardly any administrative contact between the capital and provinces, the right-wing fanatics of the Athens National Guard could impose their own law and order in the countryside so that when, in the summer, they were replaced by the gendarmerie, the *parakratos* was firmly established and even had the gendarmerie wished to, it could have made little difference to the new power structures. During the first phase the British had restricted themselves almost entirely to a spectator's role and the Greek government regarded the misdeeds of the Right as an understandable reaction to the previous excesses of the Left and contented themselves with admonitions,[86] which were not attended to.

By summer 1945 one could discern the following regional landscape of suppression: in Athens and Piraeus the police, in cooperation with 'X' members, former followers of the collaborationist EDES Central Committee and other right-wing groups set out to subdue the red working-class suburbs (Kaisariani, Peristeri, Kokkinia, Neo Ionia, etc.). The favourite method, the blockade (a rounding-up operation), was disastrously reminiscent of the German Occupation. Thousands were arrested on the pretext that they had belonged to OPLA, others were detained on the most fantastic charges. There were murders and the murderers went free because they belonged to 'X' and this even though they were known.[87] Nevertheless, in comparison with what went on in the provinces, conditions in Athens and Piraeus were relatively orderly. For a detailed picture of the situation in the provinces, we will take the Peloponnese as representative since for August 1945 we have an excellent source: the report of C.M. Woodhouse of 11th August 1945.[88]

In late July and early August 1945 Woodhouse undertook an extended journey through the Peloponnese and visited all the main towns in order to collect impressions. The reason for this journey lay in alarming reports that ELAS was planning an armed uprising. At the very beginning of his report Woodhouse made it clear that there were indeed grounds for alarm, not from any danger of a left-wing rising but from a danger of the 'obliteration' of justice by the Right. On the journey, he had taken care to talk with the most important government officials in each town and with the British Liaison Officers and had compiled his report on the basis of their information. In the first part of this report, he described some habits and activities of the Left which were not wholly in conformity with the law but to which he himself did not attribute too much importance[89] and went on to formulate the situation as follows:

'The case against the Right, which is identical for most practical purposes with the governing authorities, is very much worse. The following principle faults are noted from the reports of BLOs and the authorities themselves. All testimony from the left-wing, which is naturally more damaging still, has been excluded. What remains is bad enough.'

Under the heading 'Arrests without Warrant' Woodhouse reported some characteristic examples.

'The public prosecutor of Kalamata (Mr Kardaras) pointed out that the National Guard have the right to arrest without warrant. He admitted that this practice is enforced solely against "those accused of crimes during the occupation". (By these he meant EAM–ELAS.) Those accused of collaboration with the Germans are not so arrested... The public prosecutor of Yithion [Gythion] (Mr Kritikos) a well-meaning and simple-minded reactionary, agreed that arrest without warrant had been practiced. I expressed surprise that it was enforced only against EAM, who composed almost the whole of his 290 prisoners. He indignantly replied that they did also arrest collaborationists (though not without warrant), and claimed to have at least 3 under lock and key already... The BLO at Tripolis (Major Orr) reported finding seven men arrested in a nearby village by the local National Guard sergeant, not only without a warrant, but without even a report to his superiors. They would have been held indefinitely if Major Orr had not intervened. No charge was ever brought against any of them... The

Nomarch of Kalamata has ordered the gradual, unostentatious release of such cases, to reduce overcrowding in the prisons. But the prisons continued to fill up daily.'

Everywhere Woodhouse found discrimination against the Left. The NCOs and men of the National Guard abused their position to pursue local vendettas. The officers were either in sympathy or could not keep them under control and restricted their activity to the area of their headquarters. They had no idea what was going on in the villages. Then Woodhouse reached the subject of the prisons.

'In Pyrgos gaol there is a man... who carried in his pocket a certificate signed by Field-Marshal Alexander in recognition of his services during the occupation. He is held for (unspecified) crimes committed during the occupation as a member of ELAS... Wherever any member of EAM is accused of a crime, all the local members of the organisation are liable to be arrested as "morally responsible". I was informed by British officers stationed in Pyrgos the 270 prisoners held there are divided as follows: Convicted felons 36, criminal charges 34, nationalist 1, EAMites held as "morally responsible" 199. These figures were confirmed by the Nomarch, Mr Papadopoulos, an ex-adherent of Zervas who was as disgusted as myself.'

Until shortly before this, warrants for the arrest of collaborators could only be issued by the two Chief Prosecutors for the Peloponnese, in Nafplion and Patras; whilst warrants against left-wingers could be issued by any of the nine prosecutors. Lately, the prosecutors' powers had been extended to cover the former as well, but the documents were still located in Nafplion or Patras and this made arrests impossible.

'Mr Khronaios [Chronaios], deputy Public Prosecutor of Tripolis, informed me that he had been trying in vain ever since his appointment to obtain warrants against two collaborationists... They are known by the entire neighbourhood to have handed over to the Italians a Greek Officer of Force 133... who parachuted into the Peloponnese under my command in 1943.'

The Peloponnese prisons, inhumanly overcrowded, contained 6,000 prisoners of whom more than 90% were detained because of their EAM membership. Moral responsibility for EAM crimes was the normal charge. It would be impossible to deal with all these cases within the year. Woodhouse proceeded to indicate a very interesting aspect of this.

'It follows that a very large number of men who may eventually be acquitted will be disfranchised at the elections if they are held this year. The relatives and friends of these men dare not present themselves for enrolment on the electoral lists for fear of being arrested themselves. Obviously, this makes the prospects of the left wing at the elections hopeless...

'Mr Papadopoulos, Nomarch of Pyrgos, was outspoken in his

criticism of the Government and National Guard for discriminating against the left. He regarded the collaborationists. . . as responsible for the whole of the present situation. He deplored the fact that so few had been arrested, and quoted the case of Major Mitropoulos, formerly an officer of the local security battalion, who had just been promoted Lieutenant-Colonel in the National Guard. . . Colonel Belingratis, OC Gendarmerie at Tripolis, quoted to me a case of armed civilians arresting communists and keeping them under lock and key at a neighbouring village. . . he insisted. . . that this was not an isolated case but a common occurrence. He added that less than 10 per cent of the armed ELAS-ites in the hills are criminals: but they are discouraged from giving themselves up by fear of consequences at the hands of the National Guard.

'Mr Tsambasis, public prosecutor of all collaborationists for the whole of Greece, informed me that in the Peloponnese collaborators were openly protected by the authorities. He cited the public prosecutor of Tripolis and Colonel Papanikolaou, military commander of Patras, as examples. (The former, it seems, has arranged for the removal of his deputy [Chronaios]. . . for "left wing sympathies".) He added that right-wing pressure has prevented him from issuing all warrants for arrest of collaborationists with a few exceptions, and has reduced his own position to that of a cipher.'

Woodhouse dealt next with the inadequate control of local security forces by the administration: whatever command might be passed down from above, one could never be sure that it would be carried out at ground level. The Military Commander at Tripolis openly admitted that he had not a single officer he could trust. The Chief-of-Staff of the Peloponnese High Command in Corinth was not sure whether his commands were executed unless he himself supervised this. Furthermore, there was a confusion of powers between the National Guard and the gendarmerie.

'Most men in authority complacently accept, or even fail to recognise, the irregular situation. They frankly divide all Greeks into Nationalists ("our side") and Communists: these are the actual words of the Mayor of Yithion. Those who have an objective outlook could be counted on the fingers of one hand. They were the Nomarchs of Pyrgos (Mr Papadopoulos) and Kalamata (Mr Kalkandis), the Chief of Police in Tripolis (Colonal Belingratis), and the deputy Public Prosecutor in Tripolis (Mr Khronaios). It was from them that I first heard the suggestion of a general amnesty as a solution.'

The gendarmerie acted more honourably than the National Guard and recognised its limits. Moreover, local authorities would send reports of alleged left-wing acts of terrorism, calculated to provoke panic. Really, these were shameless exaggerations or pure inventions. Many of the local authorities were not at their posts at all, but in Athens. 'During my visit, the following were absent in Athens: the Public Prosecutors of Tripolis and Pyrgos, the Nomarchs of Tripolis and Sparta, the O.C. Gendarmerie of Patras and Kalamata. In addition the Mayor of Kalamata and the military commander of Tripolis were about to leave for Athens.'

Woodhouse's next topic was the armed right-wing organisations. In a village near Kalamata 'X' had set up its own state, controlled several villages and maintained a private police. The National Guard armed its sympathisers everywhere. Former collaborators held leading positions in 'X'. Woodhouse concluded by making suggestions how these deplorable conditions could be remedied.[90]

In the other provinces the situation was little better. In Central Greece and Thessaly, too, the Right had succeeded in wresting control of the villages, with the aid of irregular right-wing bands such as that of the notorious Sourlas. These groups were growing up all over Greece. Their nucleus usually consisted of a few criminals with a long penal record for brigandage. During the Occupation many of these had harassed the ELAS guerrillas on German instructions. After Varkiza, they suddenly discovered their devotion to George II and posed as champions of the monarchy. But in reality they remained criminals pursuing their criminal instincts under a legal mantle of anti-communism, terrorising the countryside and conducting a head-hunt—sometimes literally—against left-wingers. At higher levels these 'allies' were not greatly appreciated and so, at the beginning of May, the military commander of Thessaly and West Macedonia outlawed Sourlas and other bands. But they found support and protection from subordinate authorities and thus were able to continue their reign of terror before the eyes of the National Guard.[91] Indeed, by summer 1945 close cooperation had been established between the National Guard, the nationalists and these bandit groups. Only in the towns where British units were stationed was there any sort of security for the Left.[92]

In Epirus there was an additional factor. Two National Guard brigades had been formed from the EDES units evacuated to Corfu in December 1944 and demobilised in January 1945 and in February 1945 one of these had been transferred to Epirus. Here—in addition to suppressing the Left—it drove the approximately 15,000 strong Albanian minority into Albania on the pretext that the Greek minority in that country was being oppressed.[93]

In West and Central Macedonia, where EAM had first been active and where it had the strongest membership, the Right had great difficulty in establishing a foothold and the result was that here National Guard brutality and excesses were at their worst. The Slavo-Macedonian minority suffered particularly. In Eastern Macedonia and Thrace EAM was often equated with the hated Bulgarians (Eamovoulgaros became a common abusive epithet) and was correspondingly persecuted. In this province, the right-wing Tsaous and Andon group, led by Andonis Fosteridis, had actually signed a pact with the Bulgarian Army of Occupation. This band now seized the towns of Drama and Serres and, until the arrival of the National Guard, established a reign of terror there, even continuing its terrorism until, in summer 1945, it was incorporated into the local nationalist organisations.[94] In conclusion one can say that, up to summer 1945, a wave of White Terror engulfed the whole of Greece and that its most important driving force was the National Guard. Under National Guard protection, the local right-wingers took over power and there arose the *parakratos*—a state within a state. When, at the end of this phase, the gendarmerie assumed control, hardly anything changed, the *parakratos* retained its sway.

We have several times mentioned the fact that, where British units were stationed, there the White Terror had not the same effect. This raises the question of the British role at that period.

An explanation can be found in an article by Hal Lehrman in the Washington newspaper *PM* of 17th June. Amongst other things Lehrman wrote:

'It is not quite correct to say that this (terrorism) is a purely internal affair. The British are training the Greek Army. They are supplying the material, much of it American. Thus they have the wherewithal to exert pressure toward the remedy of manifold evils. In some areas the British are doing a great deal. In Kozani, for example, no arrest may be made by the Greeks without specific British authorization... [In Verroia] a brigadier was advised that certain National Guardsmen had fired bullets into the air to relieve their exaltation during a religious festival. Here is a portion of his order to his subordinate officers: "According to British military law, this action constitutes an offense triable by court-martial and punishable by long terms of rigorous imprisonment. I do not know exactly how the offense is treated under Greek military law, but I remind you that I have warned you against such acts of indiscipline. I now direct that forthwith you investigate and try the offenders, reporting to me the punishment awarded..." If a British Commander at Verroia can display such vigor because of a few shots in the air, it is difficult to understand why, at Larissa, less than a day's unhurried motoring from Verroia, gendarmes should be knocking people's heads together with impunity.'[95]

Halifax, the British Ambassador in Washington, cabled this report with a commentary to London and Athens.[96] The reaction of the Athens Embassy was characteristic. Caccia (Leeper was on leave) regretted the *PM* article '... unfortunately Lehrman is not the type of American correspondent whom it is possible to keep on the lines. We and the censors have had much trouble with him... He made an extensive tour in the north ostensibly with the object of describing the work of U.N.R.R.A. His behaviour in Salonica, where he sought contact exclusively with the extreme Left and made no response to the suggestion that he should call on the British Commander or on the British Consul General, provoked strong protests from these officers. . . . Meanwhile we will try to get New York's correspondent [Sedgwick?] in to do a new article on the present situation in Greece and give some credit to the Greek government for the very real improvement that has taken place in all spheres since they took office in April'.[97]

This British Embassy reaction must be analysed in the light of Leeper's position as 'High Commissioner' since April 1945 and of Churchill's directive of 22nd April that he should not concern himself with all the details of Greek internal politics. The former would in fact have required him to concern himself effectively with details, in this case with implementing the Varkiza Agreement. But, even before Churchill's intervention, Leeper had only to a very limited extent been ready to take action in this sense. In his view this was a conflict with the battle orders reversed. The British Embassy in Athens was, as the former chief of the Australian Relief Team in Greece, Colonel A.W. Sheppard, described it 'the bulwark of conservatism and reaction'.[98] In other words, the British Embassy regarded the Greek Left—which it identified indiscriminately with the communists—as its main foe and, in principle, had nothing against its suppression, unless the measures used by the Greek authorities could—if they became known abroad—directly or indirectly damage British interests. A few typical examples may serve to illustrate this.

On the 5th April Leeper wrote in regard to the implementation of Varkiza:

'It is the Government, which has the responsibility of implementing all positive action under the agreement for the restoration of the country. KKE are left free to criticise with impunity, since the inactive role prescribed for them presents virtually no target on which Government can, from a publicity point of view, effectively retaliate.'[99]

Thus, for Leeper, left-wing criticism of the failure to implement the agreement and of the excesses was merely propaganda. He listed the main points of criticism and took up a position on them: the government had dismissed officials appointed by EAM or who were simply sympathetic to EAM, but this was no breach of Varkiza; National Guard excesses certainly did occur, but the Greek government had issued orders prohibiting these and by punishing or transferring certain officers responsible, had offered convincing proof that it was doing its best; illegal arrests and failure to bring the arrested to trial were due to the slow reconstruction of the judicial system, but it was not in the spirit of Varkiza that the guilty should escape punishment on such formalities as the issue of an arrest warrant; suppression of the KKE press had only occurred once or twice as a temporary measure when it could be proved that the press was threatening law and order; British and Greek troops would soon deal with the failure to disarm all armed bands; and on the other hand it was primarily the KKE bands which were violating these clauses. As regards discrimination against former ELAS members in the recruiting of the National Guard, this was

'true and had been rather unfortunately handled. It is however based on sound military principle that quality of a new unit is largely determined by its cadre; and if the Government recruiting officers were to accept all comers without reference to their record KKE would see to it that their supporters were first to be called up. By forming a nucleus of Nationalists and then accepting other recruits to fill this framework Government considers that rightful thinking elements will absorb and moderate extremists. In the absence of some such procedure reverse might well be the case'.

In general—and in contrast to KKE—the government was holding to the spirit and in the main to the letter of the Varkiza Agreement.[100]

Leeper's inclination to minimalise the significance of right-wing excesses and to justify the Greek government's line becomes even clearer in the context of a critical article which appeared in *The Times* on 17th April. To the *Times'* charge that EAM was being persecuted, Leeper replied that it was unfortunately true that former ELAS members were sometimes beaten up but that this was not happening so often now and was anyway unavoidable in a Balkan country so soon after a civil war. Nor had the arrests without warrant completely ceased, but most of the ELAS members awaiting sentencing had been arrested for real crimes committed before or during the revolution. As regards the dismissals, almost all the public utilities in Greece were in the hands of private enterprise and the dismissals of EAM members were undertaken on the basis that they were redundant, which would be a justification. It was true that there were close links between SAN (IDEA) and 'X'. The aim was undoubtedly royalist domination in the army and this could lead to a *coup d'état* if events did not develop as desired. In the Security Police *(Asfalia)* there were still members of Maniadakis' (Metaxas Minister for Security) secret police, but he was confident that these would soon lose their posts.[101] He for his part would continue to encourage the Greek government to implement the Varkiza Agreement.

On the 1st June Leeper brought the subject up in a talk with Damaskinos: he had expected the reaction to the civil war to lead to some excesses and that the Varkiza Agreement would not be fully observed; the violations of Varkiza were not as bad as KKE made out and complaints from the other side had reached his ears—that British pressure was hindering real punishment of KKE; recent reports indicated however that, in certain localities the National Guard was up to something which could only be described as a reign of terror; this was harmful to the Greek government and it should be put down and those responsible should be punished. Damaskinos did not deny this: the National Guard should be replaced as quickly as possible by the gendarmerie. Addressing himself to the Foreign Office, Leeper added that the arrival of the British Police Mission was urgently necessary.[102]

A report of 24th June from Caccia made it clear that right-wing excesses had gone further and that Leeper's intervention had born no fruit.[103] Furthermore, this report showed that the British Embassy had relied for its reports on Greek government sources and that these were often derived from the imaginings of subordinate officials. Thus, in Caccia's report there was a story of an ELAS band in the Taygetos mountains which terrorised the villages—the invention of a gendarmerie officer.[104] Even the British authorities were not without responsibility for inaccurately informing the Embassy. Colonel Sheppard reports a typical incident:

'When he went to see what had happened at Mandalos [where a guerrilla raid was followed by the usual reports of atrocities] on November 25, 1946, Mr Peck [the British consul in Salonica] told me that the Right-wing newspaper reports were incorrect. But in his weekly report written a few days afterwards he repeated those press reports. When I asked him why he did not report the truth as he had told it to me he replied "There are enough people making propaganda for the Left, why should I. . ." Each week he repeated as fact the allegations made by the various Greek military authorities. . .'[105]

This report does in fact date from 1946, but there is no reason to assume that conditions in 1945 were any different.

The British Embassy in Athens was wrongly informed and, in its turn, wrongly informed the Foreign Office. But it would have been within the bounds of possibility for it to obtain objective information from the British Liaison Officers spread all over the country; and just through these BLOs it could have influenced further developments, once it had realised that the Greek government had hardly any influence over the officers and men of the National Guard. This emerges quite clearly from the report of the Civil Affairs Officers' Pool of 21st June 1945 on the situation in Western Greece:

'When they [the National Guard] have a strong BLO and are near a British commander, they are well behaved, correct and fair; when they are on their own, they act as political partisans, and indulge in illegal arrests, and condonation of, if not participation in, terrorism. . . The most unhappy feature is that acts of violence against Leftists are approved and openly applauded by members of the church and the upper classes.'[106]

But the British Embassy continued its *laissez-faire* policy and left it to the individual British commanders whether they wanted to intervene or not. Therefore the British Embassy bears a heavy degree of responsibility for the wave of counter-revolution which swept over the Greek provinces up to the summer of 1945, since despite the wide range of powers at its disposal it remained a silent spectator of the takeover of power by the Right. It would perhaps be stretching interpretation too far were one to conclude that the British Embassy consciously promoted this process; nevertheless intervention on behalf of the persecuted Greek Left was for the Embassy simply unthinkable. Whoever felt it was their business could take up the cause of the Greek communists, it was certainly not the Embassy's concern.

In late summer 1945, the gendarmerie assumed control and the National Guard was transformed into a frontier force. But even this brought no real change. The British Police and Gendarmerie Mission under Sir Charles Wickham[107] was in complete control of organisation, administration, discipline and training for the gendarmerie but the mere fact that a proportion of the National Guard was integrated in the gendarmerie shows that, at least as regards personnel, there was a certain continuity. The British Mission restricted its activity to the vocational training of the police. A purge of the Security forces, as prescribed by the Varkiza Agreement, was never fully undertaken. The gendarmes who had served under Metaxas and during the Occupation remained on active service. Many members of the Security Battalions were appointed to leading posts and this guaranteed a continuity of political attitude in the Security forces.

In the army the situation was not much better. Regular call-up began early in April 1945. After a few days it became clear that the army command was discriminating against the Left. For example, former ELAS members were rejected on 'health grounds'. The same happened with 'not nationally-thinking elements'.[108] In building up the Officers' Corps, the special commission adjudged that, out of twelve ELAS colonels, twenty-nine lieutenant-colonels and sixty-two majors, only one lieutenant-colonel and four majors were suitable as professional officers. Of the ten ELAS major-generals (among them Sarafis, Mandakas, Bakirjis and Avyeropoulos) none was considered worthy to remain on the active list. They as well as the other officers were placed *en disponibilité*. Nor were any of the lower-ranking ELAS officers taken into the army at the beginning. In contrast to EDES and 'X' NCOs, no ELAS NCOs were admitted for training to the Reservists Officers' School. Approximately eight hundred former ELAS officers were put on the demobilisation list. Against this, former Security Battalion officers were taken on without question.[109] Promotions initiated by Prime Minister Rallis were confirmed and these officers were integrated in the new army. Woodhouse wrote:

> 'Decorations and promotion, denied to Greek Officers who had served in the resistance organisations, were conferred on those who had served in the Security Battalions. When the services of the Commander of the Peloponnesian Security Battalions, Colonel Papadongonas, were cited in the *Gazette (Efimeris tis Kyverniseos)* in connection with his

posthumous promotion by two ranks, the matter became such a public scandal that the order had to be reversed; but more discreet examples passed unhindered.'[110]
The higher ranks of the army and the whole staffing policy was thenceforth controlled by the Chief of the General Staff, Vendiris. At the head of the Security division of the General Staff was General Efstathios Liosis, another leading member of IDEA. A republican renegade, General Christos Avramidis, who had also been involved in raising the Security Battalions, became military commander of Volos. General A. Spanopoulos, involved in the same business during the Occupation, became military commander of Attica. Certainly, the army command did not consist exclusively of right-wingers and IDEA men but Major-General Smallwood's assessment that, out of seventeen generals on the active list, ten were republicans, four royalists, two neutral and one a nationalist, was based on pre-war criteria no longer valid in 1945. There were, of course, still some republicans amongst the generals but the decisive factor was that all were fanatical anti-communists and that the key posts were held by IDEA members. Here we must again add the rider that in Greece, until recently, everyone who did not belong to the Right was accounted a communist and was described as such.

Hal Lehrman was right in his formulation of May 1945:

'The Greek General Staff is methodically welding this army into a political weapon, loading it with royalists from the rank to the top command. Quisling security battalions and monarchist mountain and sacred brigades are being incorporated en masse.'[111]

These developments, accompanied by rumours of preparations for an army *putsch* appearing in the Athens press at the end of May, began to worry even the War Minister, Admiral Petros Voulgaris himself, and he looked for ways to extricate the army from the influence of the Vendiris clique and bring it under government orders. He realised that on his own he could not prevail against the General Staff, so he evolved the following plan: a Supreme War Council would be formed under a civilian minister which would bring the army under government control. However, a pre-condition for the success of this undertaking was General Smallwood's participation. Leeper produced this idea at a Foreign Office meeting in London on 12th June in which representatives of the three armed forces ministries took part. Leeper maintained that, next to the economic problem, the problem of the restoration of order in Greece was the most important.

'It was essential that they should tackle the Greek General Staff who were tending to form an *imperium in imperio*. Right wing extremists like General Vendiris must be removed. . . Unless the British Mission had the powers now proposed, Admiral Voulgaris felt that he would be quite unable to create an efficient and non-political Greek Army.'[112]

After some discussion it was decided to postpone the decision on this extension of the powers of the British Military Mission until after Field-Marshal Alexander's return. The documents available do not indicate when the final decision was taken, but it can be definitely stated that, when the Voulgaris Cabinet was re-shuffled in August, this plan was at least partially carried out.

General Merenditis, a republican and a democrat, became War Minister and announced that, from now on, the army would keep out of politics and that army administration in general and in particular the personnel department would be removed from the jurisdiction of the General Staff, which would henceforward concern itself with purely military tasks. The War Ministry would run the army through an Army Council on which the head of the British Military Mission (BMM) would have a seat. In addition, the General Staff's previous decision regarding appointments would be subjected to review and promotions would be suspended for the time being.[113] There was only one weak point in this programme— General Vendiris remained Chief-of-Staff.

At the beginning of September Merenditis issued an Order of the Day prohibiting any participation in politics or expression of opinion in favour of any political party by members of the armed forces, who were also prohibited from obstructing free expression of civilian opinion. Transgressors were threatened with severe penalties.[114] At the same time the creation of an Army Council and the removal of appointments from the General Staff's competence were under discussion with the BMM. Merenditis even succeeded in flushing out three high-ranking officers from the Second Bureau of the General Staff where they had been responsible for the posthumous promotion of Papadongonas. In mid-September he ordered all former Security Battalion members to render an account of their conduct to the Ministry, after which their cases would be investigated by a Special Commission.[115] In the row between Merenditis and the army command resulting from these orders, the former got no support either from the Greek government or from the BMM and therefore on the 28th September he resigned. His successor, who held office until the 7th October, avoided any conflict and it was only the next Prime Minister but one, Themistoklis Sofoulis, who succeeded in getting BMM consent to the removal of Vendiris from his post. The new Chief of the General Staff was General Spiliotopoulos but even the Sofoulis government could not achieve further personnel changes, let alone a clean-up of the army. The BMM was against any purge for political reasons.[116] Thus the character of the Greek army was determined for decades to come. A purge of the army, as provided for in the Varkiza Agreement, had indeed taken place and continued to operate—but in the oppposite sense. The Greek Officers' Corps became a focus of reaction and fascist plotting, with a tendency to intervention whenever it considered the state to be under threat from communism.

Purging the administrative apparatus. Articles 7 and 8 of the Varkiza Agreement required a purge of the public service and of the security forces (police and gendarmerie). The criteria were to be: professional efficiency, character and personality, possible collaboration with the enemy or abuse of authority in the service of the dictatorship. Anyone who during the Occupation had joined the Resistance was to return to his post and, together with all public servants, he would be investigated by a special commission. These special commissions would have the right temporarily to suspend public servants who had been involved in the December events. Their eventual fate would then be decided by the government which would emerge from elections. No one with previous service should be dismissed on grounds of his political convictions alone.[117]

These provisions, too, were not implemented. Instead of Special Commissions investigating those with previous service, as had been provided, a law of the Metaxas period was given a new application. hundreds of public servants were either retired or dismissed because of their membership of 'anti-national organisations' (EAM) or, in the case of the judicial branch, given punitive postings.[118] Persecution of EAM members extended to all officials even down to Social Security (IKA) personnel. As representative of many cases, we will quote one quite typical example published in the Athens newspaper *Kathimerina Nea* in early June 1945.

'In June 1944 the SS and the Security Battalions were conducting an intensive search for twenty Finance Department officials suspected of Resistance activities. In order to escape the torturing in Merlin Street (Gestapo HQ) and the Kaisariani (Athens suburb) firing squad, they did not present themselves for work but went into hiding. The Economics Ministry of the time demanded an explanation and subsequently dismissed the officials for arbitrarily absenting themselves for over ten days. Then, on 12th October, came the Liberation and the officials returned to take up their work. To justify themselves seemed incompatible both with their personal dignity and the dignity of the liberated State. Nor did the Ministry demand such a justification. In May 1945, however, the Ministry demanded through their superiors that they justify their absence so that they could be investigated by the relevant commission—and dismissed.'[119]

Like the army, the public service was purged of all Resistance members and the same held good for the gendarmerie and the city police. One typical case must represent many similar ones to illustrate conditions in the gendarmerie. On 8th August 1943 the BBC's Greek Service had described the second-in-command of the Siatista gendarmerie, Captain Thomas Venetsanopoulos who, on 2nd February 1943, had taken his whole unit over to ELAS as an outstanding example and had urged all gendarmerie officers to follow him.[120] At the end of April 1945

Venetsanopoulos was arrested and on 15th May he appeared before a court-martial. The charge was that, in February 1943, he had abandoned his post without permission. He was acquitted but was arrested again on the 30th May, this time on the charge that, sometime in April 1943, he had murdered two people and he was detailed in Kozani gaol. Another arrest warrant had already been issued for him from Arta on the 21st January 1945 for another, unspecified murder. Here it must be added that, immediately after liberation, Venetsanopoulos was one of the officers commanding the ELAS police in Salonica where he had contributed in no small degree to the avoidance of armed conflict with the British.[121]

In contrast, gendarmes who during the Occupation had participated in hunting down resisters remained unpenalised. The activities of the British Police Mission were restricted to purely formal police training. The gendarmerie became one more partisan force of the Right, closely collaborating with the *parakratos*. A report of October 1945 from Salonica, according to which five hundred local gendarmes had joined a secret right-wing organisation of fascist type, can be taken as characteristic.[122] In the city police, too, there was the same continuity at all levels. Angelos Evert, who had held this post under Metaxas and during the Occupation, remained Chief of Police.

But the cleansing of the state from all left-wingers was not confined to the administrative apparatus. In March 1945 the Holy Synod sat under the chairmanship of Bishop Spyridon(!) of Yannina. The two 'EAM bishops', Joachim of Kozani and Antonios of Elis, were deprived of their sees and proceedings were initiated against the Metropolitans of Chios and Chalcis on account of their favourable attitude to EAM. No action was taken against bishops who had collaborated.[123] In the universities the following leading EAM personalities were purged: Alexandros Svolos, Professor of Constitutional Law at Athens University, former Chairman of the PEEA and Economics Minister in the Papandreou Cabinet; Angelos Angelopoulos, Professor of National Economy, former Secretary for Economics in the PEEA and Assistant-Minister for Economics in the Papandreou Cabinet; Petros Kokkalis, Professor of Medicine, former Secretary for Social Welfare in the PEEA; G. Georgalas, Academy member, Chairman of EPON; N. Kitsikis, Rector of the Polytechnic.[124] Provincial EAM leaders and high-ranking ELAS officers and capetans were arrested and detained on charges of 'moral responsibility' for ELAS atrocities. Thus, General Psiarris, commander of the Thessaly ELAS Reserve, a former Liberal member of parliament and a member of the National Council, was imprisoned on this charge.[125] The Tripolis Public Prosecutor issued similar arrest warrants for the former ELAS military commander, General Stefanos Sarafis, and two ELAS divisional commanders, Colonel Papastamatiadis and Lieutenant-Colonel Tsiklitiras.[126] No attempt was made to arrest Sarafis but the other two were detained. For the subsequent fate of

Tsiklitiras we have the eye-witness report of three British MPs and we quote this as representative of many other, similar cases.

'Colonel Tsiklitiras had been in command of the ELAS Forces near Kalamata. Major Wilkes, MP, had particularly asked us to look out for him as they had fought together against the Germans. Major Wilkes had a high opinion of the colonel's military achievements and personal integrity. . . In February, 1945, Colonel Tsiklitiras was charged with shooting 135 men. In April 1945, he was arrested and detained in Sparta for 260 days. He was severely beaten up and his arm broken—we saw his scars. He was released in January this year and lived openly in Athens. On April 17 [1946] he was re-arrested and sent to Hadjicosta [an Athens prison]. His trial had been fixed for May 3, although no investigation had taken place when we saw him (April 27). He was charged with murder in a district which he had not visited for years. He met his "accomplices" for the first time in Hadjicosta. His first name and that of his father were incorrectly stated on the charge, in which he was described as a major in the gendarmerie, whereas he was actually in the artillery. . . Since our visit—and representations by Major Wilkes—we now learn that the Colonel has been acquitted.'[127]

It can easily be imagined how other prisoners, who had no British MPs as advocates, must have fared. The most insignificant pretexts were sufficient to justify arrests and, in cases of doubt, denunciations by 'national elements' were sufficient. In April 1945 the lawyer and ELD/SKE Central Committee member, Stratis Someritis, was arrested and detained for six months because an old pistol was found in his possession.[128] In this system of mass arrests of democratic citizens, the member of parliament and later leader of the Centre, Georgios Mavros, told the three British MPs:

'Justice cannot work. Ninety per cent of the judges belong to the extreme Right. They are so fanatical that, without regard to evidence, they will always return a verdict for the Right against the Left. . . In some cases I found that twenty to thirty people had been charged for the same murder. . .'[129]

In 1944 a special court had been established at Patras to try collaborators—in 1945 it was trying former Resistance fighters. For assessors only royalists and followers of the extreme Right were selected. The Patras special court ruled that the killing of a Security Battalionist during the Occupation was murder unless it could be proved that he was killed in the act of collaborating with the enemy.[130] At Larisa Appeal Court there was a public prosecutor who had collaborated in that capacity with the Germans at Preveza and for whom a warrant on this charge was outstanding there. The judges at Larisa Magistrates' Court had served in other towns during the Occupation.[131]

Right-wing excesses reached a high-point at the beginning of June and protests became audible. As leader of the Liberals, Themistoklis Sofoulis warned the government that, unless effective measures were taken against the police, the National Guard and the royalist terror organisations, an anti-government campaign would be started in the Liberal press. On 3rd June, the republican leaders Kafandaris, Plastiras, Mylonas, Rendis, Tsouderos and Mercouris visited Voulgaris and demanded measures. On the 1st June Leeper had warned Damaskinos and on the 2nd Voulgaris that something must be done. Both agreed and set their hopes on the gendarmerie.[132] In the middle of June Interior Minister Tsatsos tried to get control of the situation by administrative measures,[133] which however brought no improvement. In the middle of July Sofoulis and the republican party leaders protested again against the lawless situation which made the holding of elections impossible. Kafandaris demanded that the many thousands imprisoned in connection with the December events should be set free: if the government did not take immediate steps to safeguard the liberty and security of the citizens and the impartiality of the state agencies, he would boycott the elections. Porfyrogenis expressed himself in a similar sense.[134] At the end of July EAM stated in a memorandum, sent to Churchill, Stalin and Truman, at that time in conference at Potsdam, that approximately 30,000 EAM members were in prison.[135] The government contested these figures and gave the total of prisoners as approximately 12,000 of whom 1,100 were collaborators and 2,000 sentenced prisoners, figures confirmed by the British Police Mission.[136]

British parliamentary elections were held on the 28th July and resulted in a victory for the Labour Party. In his first message to Damaskinos, Prime Minister Attlee stressed the need for full implementation of the Varkiza Agreement. Damaskinos agreed. On the 8th August the Labour government suggested a general amnesty for all those arrested in connection with the December events, as a means of improving the atmosphere.[137] On the 14th August the Foreign Office defined this more precisely: the amnesty had been discussed with Leeper and a conclusion reached to make it as comprehensive as possible, taking in both collaborators and former EAM members; it should also be made retrospective and death sentences already passed should be commuted to imprisonment; it should be understood that extreme cases in both categories would be exempted, but what was important was that the amnesty should not be too restricted since, otherwise, critics would be able to say that the number of exceptions nullified the amnesty; it was hoped that the amnesty would be announced as soon as possible.[138] However, Damaskinos and Voulgaris rejected this on the grounds that it would only lead to fresh disturbances. But, on Voulgaris' instructions, the new Justice Minister, Kyriakopoulos, drafted a law providing for more courts to deal with collaboration cases; whilst those imprisoned in connection with the rebellion would be released at once if they had been detained for over six months without trial; offences not connected with the December events but committed before Varkiza would be amnestied; anyone else charged with offences other than murder would be released and brought to trial later; arrests without warrant were to be forbidden on the spot. In this way it was hoped that thousands of prisoners could be freed.[139] The law was promulgated on the 25th August.[140]

On the 2nd September the Justice Ministry announced that, on the basis of this law 1,000 prisoners had been released and 16,225 remained in detention.[141] On the 3rd September another law was promulgated reducing pre-trial detention to two months.[142]

On the 7th September the subject of the prisons came up during a conversation between Foreign Secretary Bevin and Archbishop Damaskinos at the Foreign Office. To Bevin's charge that the real figure for prisoners far exceeded the 18,000 now admitted by the Greek government and that many of those detained were innocent, Damaskinos replied by recalling the communist atrocities, maintaining that, if all those involved in these murders were to be released, this would result in private acts of vengeance; the new laws would free certain groups of prisoners, but a general amnesty was excluded; the problem must be dealt with step by step. When the Minister of State, Philip Noel-Baker, pointed out that many were in prison only because they had been members of EAM, Damaskinos denied this: it would damage Great Britain if the impression was created in Greece that murderers had been released under British pressure. The Regent likewise showed himself unaccommodating in the face of further remonstrances: at present it was difficult enough for the Greek government to prevent disturbances; if these criminals were released, this would become impossible; the only solution was to send more British troops; he agreed, however, that as many prisoners as possible should be released and that the rest should be more speedily brought to trial.[143]

On the 15th September the British Embassy in Athens sent a fresh report: during the period from the 2nd to the 12th September 445 prisoners had been released; according to Ministry of Justice figures the overwhelming majority of the remainder were detained for murder—though the Greek definition of murder was fundamentally different from the British.[144] By the 17th September another 504 had been released, nevertheless there were still 16,700 *[sic]* in prison, of whom 14,152 were awaiting trial.[145] In other words, after the release of nearly 2,000 prisoners, there were still more people detained than before the relevant laws were promulgated.

The Foreign Office realised that the Greek government's measures were achieving nothing and that the Athens Embassy was not prepared to make further suggestions. But the matter could not be left at that. Minister of State Noel-Baker brought up the issue again in taking leave of Damaskinos:

from London one could not, of course, judge the situation in Athens in detail but the fears of the Greek government and the British Embassy of the consequences of an amnesty seemed exaggerated; there were the following alternatives: a date could be fixed by which the releases must be carried out; in this way all those arrested before a certain date and not yet brought to trial would be freed; or all those arrested without warrant, *i.e.* by the National Guard, could be released.[146] On 22nd September Bevin, prompted by Noel-Baker, sent a telegram in this sense to Athens and recommended that the Embassy deal with the matter energetically.[147]

Leeper's reply of 24th September shows that he did not like this change of direction: mass releases could only be achieved by some sort of general amnesty, all other methods were impracticable; if the Foreign Office were really to insist on the release of large numbers of detainees, then it must demand a general amnesty to cover the whole period from 29th October 1940 (date of the Italian attack on Greece) to 12th February 1945, since many of those arrested were detained for offences during the Occupation; he was, however, not sure whether the Greek security forces were in a position to prevent the outbreak of acts of vengeance feared by the government and that would only lead to another wave of arrests; this could perhaps be risked, provided the Greek government was prepared to announce the amnesty: 'I should however warn you that insistence on such an amnesty, which would be condemned by substantial majority of Greeks, will almost certainly provoke the resignation of the Government. I would propose discussion of the matter first informally with the Regent and will then report, but even from the Regent I am likely to meet with strong opposition at first.'[148]

If we discount the unsupported—and unsupportable—contention that the majority of Greeks would reject an amnesty—the majority may well have longed for an end to persecution, Leeper's attitude on this question is in sharp contrast to his previous attitude when the Greek government had to be forced into taking uncongenial action. His intervention on the amnesty question probably had a correspondingly low-key result.

In his talks with Damaskinos after the latter's return his main argument therefore was that, unless a large number of political prisoners was speedily released, there would be massive criticism in the House of Commons. Although Damaskinos continued to reject a general amnesty, on 28th September he declared himself ready to bring pressure on the government for the immediate release of all those detained for 'moral responsibility'. These he assessed as 80per cent [!] of all those detained. All the same, commented Leeper, one would have to reckon with continued obstruction from subordinate authorities; the Right was intransigently opposed to the amnesty and could rely on its own strength.[149] On the 4th October Leeper pointed out to Damaskinos that, unless something happened soon, Bevin would have to be publicly critical in the House of Commons.[150] As a result, on 6th October, Justice Minister Kyriakopoulos and the Assistant-Minister to the Prime Minister visited Leeper. They rejected a general amnesty as this would offend against the sense of justice of the majority of Greeks. The policy of partial amnesty initiated in August would be continued and the outstanding trials would be speeded up. Kyriakopoulos went on to point out that, between January and April, nearly 2,400 detainees had been released (a figure which illustrates once more the extent of mass arrests towards the end of the December events). By the end of September this figure had risen to 3,745; the remainder were all detained on capital charges: of the 11,487 prisoners, 8,767 were charged with murder; certainly, many of these were 'moral responsibility' cases but, according to Greek law, these were considered equally responsible. Then Kyriakopoulos produced a suggestion: Great Britain should send a Legal Mission to Greece to inquire into Greek justice. Leeper supported this in his report to London.[151] Bevin was not satisfied with the Justice Minister's explanations and expressed his hope that Kyriakopoulos' successor would take a more sensible attitude on the amnesty question.[152]

Here it must be stated that the Varkiza Agreement was implemented by the Left, with the single reservation regarding the handing over of arms. For the Greek Right, Varkiza was from the start non-existent. None of the agreement's provisions concerning liberties, amnesty and purging of the state apparatus of fascists and collaborators was implemented. The various Cabinets were unable—and by reason of their hatred of communism even unwilling—to impose implementation. This lack of control led to an alliance between the subordinate authorities and local right-wingers, whilst fascists and collaborators found their way back into—or were never removed from—the key positions. Thus arose the so-called *parakratos* which, by the end of this period, had become so firmly established that it could escape all state control.

The British role was decisive. Between February and April 1945 Macmillan and the British authorities in Athens developed and institutionalised the concept of Leeper's 'High Commission'. This meant that Greece's sovereignty was suspended, that the state apparatus was penetrated at all levels by British 'controllers' and that Greece became *de facto* a British protectorate. To be successful, such a penetration policy needed to fulfill certain premises. The most important pre-condition was consistency in application and this, in turn, demanded not only a clear organisational plan but also a unified political will at all levels of British policy making. But that was just what was lacking.

Organisationally, the British contented themselves with controlling the highest level of Greek decision making by sending out specialists and commissions. They neglected to integrate in this control system the British Liaison Officers who were spread out all over the country, though it was just these who could have prevented many of the negative developments up to summer 1945. A consistent penetration policy would have required attention to details of Greek policy at all levels. The original concept had indeed provided for this. But at least after Churchill's *diktat* of 22nd April to Leeper—not to concern himself with details of Greek policy—this vital premise of a penetration policy was allowed to lapse. After that, what British official would dare to develop any initiative and involve himself in tiresome matters of detail or even to stop such developments?

On the political level matters were not much better. Even if by April Macmillan's and Leeper's thinking had evolved, Churchill held rigidly to his well-known anti-communist and pro-restoration policy which led him to regard even the collaborators with leniency.

It was Churchill's intervention which robbed the original concept of its political and organisational substance and in this way brought about the passivity observed in the British authorities. It was not the penetration policy itself which was responsible for the disastrous developments in Greece, but its inconsistent application which provoked an attitude of *laissez-faire*. This in turn permitted the revival of a fascist Greek state— a development certainly not intended by British policy but the inevitable result of its inconsistency and incoherence, so that the Churchill government must bear responsibility for the subsequent tragedy.

NOTES

1. Diefthynsi Typou kai Pliroforion, *I Symfonia tis Varkizas: ola ta schetika keimena*, (Athens, February, 1945), p. 14. Reprinted: *Ellinika Themata*, [n.d. 1974?] No. 6. For English text see p. 561.
2. On the 22nd February, on the basis of this law, the military commander of Attica issued an order forbidding even indoor meetings. On the 2nd April the Athens Misdemeanours Court sentenced a citizen to three-and-a-half months' imprisonment because he had discussed KKE affairs with three others in his own house. The editor of the Larisa EAM newspaper was arrested because he published the text of a Moscow radio broadcast critical of the Greek government. *Lefki Vivlos: Paravaseis tis Varkizas*, pp. 8 ff, where further examples can be found.
3. The *Idionymo* law of 1929 was put through parliament by Eleftherios Venizelos. Its wording was so vague that quite innocuous efforts at reform, having nothing to do with communism, could be penalised. The first case judged under this law was that of a student who had read the communist youth organisation's (Organosi Kommounistikis Neoleas Elladas—OKNE) newspaper and admitted to the court that he was a Communist. Between 1929 and 1941, more than two hundred dissidents were sentenced on the basis of this law. Giorgis D. Katsoulis, *Istoria tou Kommounistikou Kommatos Elladas, vol. III, 1927-1933*, (Athens: Nea Synora, 1976), p. 111; *Lefki Vivlos: Paravaseis tis Varkizas*, p. 11.
4. *Lefki Vivlos: Paravaseis tis Varkizas*, pp. 10 ff.
5. Taken together, the collaborationist governments had promulgated 4,223 laws.

H. Caccia to Sir J. Anderson 23rd July, 1945 in Report on the Week's Events, ending 22nd July (R 12730/4/19). The result was that many of these laws remained in force for years, some of them until quite recently.
6. *Lefki Vivlos: Paravaseis tis Varkizas*, pp. 12 ff.
7. 'X' was a clandestine organisation of the extreme Right set up during the Occupation. It did not engage in resistance activities against the Germans, rather its relations to the occupying power were ambivalent. 'X' considered communism as Enemy Number One. Towards the end of the Occupation they received arms from British sources with which they fought in the December events. Leader of 'X' was Colonel George Grivas, a Greek Cypriot by birth, who later acquired fame as leader of the underground EOKA movement in Cyprus.
8. *Lefki Vivlos: Paravaseis tis Varkizas*, pp. 15–19.
9. McNeill, *The Greek Dilemma*, p. 199.
10. *Lefki Vivlos: Paravaseis tis Varkizas*, pp. 18 ff.
11. A liberal paper founded in 1945, which in 1947 had achieved the fourth-largest circulation and which was close to the politician George Kartalis.
12. Frank Smothers, William Hardy McNeill, Elizabeth Darbishire McNeill, *Report on the Greeks. Findings of a Twentieth Century Fund Team which surveyed conditions in Greece in 1947*, (New York: The Twentieth Century Fund, 1948), p. 130.
13. *Rizospastis*, 22nd February, 1945.
14. Kalyvas had been Minister for Labour in the Quisling government and was executed by ELAS in February 1944.
15. *Rizospastis*, 24th February, 1945.
16. *Ibid.*, 25th February, 1945.
17. *Ibid.*, 27th February, 1945; *TUC Annual Report*, 1945, p. 128. This supervising committee consisted of the following: H.V. Tewson—chairman; K. Chrysanthopoulos—Ministry for Labour; I. Renzies—Hajidimitriou group; S. Mastroyannakos—Kalomoiris-Theos-Stratis group. *TUC Annual Report, 1945*, p. 132. Despite all difficulties, this committee worked successfully and completed its task by the end of June.
18. *Rizospastis*, 1st March, 1945.
19. *Ibid.*, 6th March, 1945.
20. *Lefki Vivlos: Paravaseis tis Varkizas*, p. 23.
21. *TUC Annual Report*, 1945, p. 129.
22. *Rizospastis*, 9th and 10th March, 1945; Theos, *Ta Ellinika Syndikata*, p. 16.
23. *TUC Annual Report*, 1945, p. 129.
24. *Ibid.*
25. *Ibid.*; *Rizospastis*, 11th March, 1945.
26. *Rizospastis*, 15th March, 1945.
27. *TUC Annual Report*, 1945, p. 130.
28. *Ibid.*
29. Theos, *Ta ellinika syndikata*, p. 17.
30. Throughout April and May *Rizospastis* published election results almost daily and they left no doubt of an ERGAS victory. It was also apparent that the early ERGAS successes increased in May. The figures published by *Rizospastis* show some inaccuracies and contradictions and should therefore be regarded as approximate and merely as indications of relative strength. On the 3rd May *Rizospastis* published the following figures for the elections in fifty Athens trade unions up to the 30th April, 1945:

Votes cast for		
	ERGAS	9,780
	Hajidimitrious	2,764
	Independents	3,261

Athens Trades Council Congress seats	ERGAS	256
	Hajidimitriou	22
	Independents	40
Delegates to the GCL	ERGAS	50
	Hajidimitriou	22
	Independents	11

On the 15th May *Rizospastis* published the following results from sixty trade unions:

Total votes cast		17,591
Votes cast for	ERGAS	11,460
	Hajidimitriou	2,667
	Independents	3,474
Athens Trades Council Congress	ERGAS	125
	Hajidimitriou	38
	Independents	19
Delegates to the GCL	ERGAS	82
	Hajidimitriou	22
	Independents	17

On the 6th June *Rizospastis* published the results for seventy-seven trade unions in Athens up to the end of May:

Total votes cast		21,903
Votes cast for	ERGAS	15,546
	Hajidimitriou	3,188
	Independents	3,654
Athens Trades Council Congress seats	ERGAS	179
	Hajidimitriou	39
	Independents	20
Delegates to the GCL	ERGAS	119
	Hajidimitriou	23
	Independents	18

For fifty-one trade unions in Piraeus *Rizospastis* of the same date gave the following results:

Total votes cast		11,681
Votes cast for	ERGAS	10,120
	The rest	1,241
Piraeus Trades Council Congress seats	ERGAS	123
	The rest	16
Delegates to the GCL	ERGAS	78
	The rest	11

A telegram of Leeper's to the Foreign Office of 8th June, 1945 (R 9925/4/19) gave the results up to the 4th June: out of 25,879 votes cast by ninety-two trade unions in Athens, 18,395 were for ERGAS. The Piraeus results are obviously false. The figures published by Hajidimitriou in *Neon Ergatikon Vima* at the end of April are clearly falsified. Leeper had given these figures in his report to London on the events of the last weeks of April, Leeper to Churchill 1st May, 1945 (R 7954/4/19). Eden then quoted these figures in the House of Commons. *Rizospastis* thereupon published the above figures in an open letter of 6th June to Eden. For Hajidimitriou's attempts at manipulation, see *Lefki Vivlos: Paravaseis tis Varkizas*, p. 24.

31. Theos, *Ta ellinika syndikata*, p. 18.
32. *Efimeris tis Kyverniseos* Vol. 1, Law sheet No. 124, 25th May, 1945, p. 531. This abrogated Law 1435/1938 and brought Laws 281/1914 and 2151/1920 back into force.

THE VARKIZA AGREEMENT—THE WHITE TERROR

33. *Rizospastis,* 29th May, 1945.
34. *Ibid.,* 30th May, 1945.
35. *TUC Annual Report,* 1945, p. 131. The date given, 24th April, is obviously incorrect.
36. Woodhouse, *Apple of Discord,* p. 240. '. . . no lasting effects came about, because there followed an internal revolt in Hadjidimitriou's group, by which he lost the leadership to the equally irresponsible Makris.' On p. 131 the TUC Report of 1945 gives details. '. . . Mr. Hadjidimitriou withdrew his signature, and it transpired later that in signing the Agreement he had done so without the knowledge or consent of his colleagues on the Confederation Executive, and in fact, had omitted the names of most of his colleagues already on the Confederation *[sic]* from the list of nominees put forward for inclusion on the reconstituted Executive. When this matter came to the knowledge of his colleagues, Mr. Hadjidimitriou was compelled to resign the General Secretaryship of the Confederation, his place being filled by the unanimous election of Mr. Fotis Makris, Mr. Makris then took up the negotiations on reconstitution, disclaiming entirely the basis of representation accepted by Mr. Hadjidimitriou.'
37. Jecchinis, *op. cit.,* p. 97. 'As Makris admits himself, he was "discovered" by a top official of the TUC, who like most of the foreign friends of the Greek trade union movement, was looking for a comparatively young and able trade union leader capable to take over the leadership of the non-communists.' In 1967, still General-Secretary of the GCL, Fotis Makris welcomed the Colonels' Junta and collaborated with it until such time as they replaced him with their own nominee.
38. Anangastikos nomos No. 393 of 9th June, 1945. *Efimeris tis Kyverniseos* Vol. 1, Law sheet No. 138, 21st June, 1945, p. 713. At the same time Article 6 of Law 1435/1938 was brought back into force temporarily, till 31st December 1945.
39. *Rizospastis,* 28th June, 1945.
40. *Ibid.,* 4th July, 1945; Theos, *Ta ellinika syndikata,* p. 18.
41. *TUC Annual Report,* 1945, p. 132; Jecchinis, *op. cit.,* p. 90. From him stems the information on the forty days' time limit.
42. *Lefki Vivlos: Paravaseis tis Varkizas,* p. 25.
43. Theos, *op. cit.,* p. 18; text of the document, *ibid.,* p. 38.
44. *Rizospastis* of 18th August published the following results. In 154 unions with 71,082 members, 44,758 voted as follows: ERGAS 31,050, the rest 11,876. Makris reported 158 unions with 66,000 members of whom 38,000 voted. Caccia to Foreign Office 24th August, 1945 (R 14341/4/19). For the inaccuracy see footnote 30.
45. R 14341/4/19.
46. Caccia to Foreign Office 28th August, 1945 (R 14521/4/19); Labour and Trade Unions in Greece (R 18945/4/19).
47. *Ibid.*
48. *Rizospastis,* 3rd September, 1945.
49. R 14521/4/19.
50. Caccia to Foreign Office 29th August, 1945 (R 14623/4/19).
51. Lascelles to Foreign Office 12th September, 1945 (R 15570/4/19). Details of the law in Lascelles to Foreign Office 15th September, 1945 (R 16254/4/19).
52. Foreign Office to Leeper 23rd September, 1945 (R 15570/4/19).
53. *Efimeris tis Kyverniseos* Vol. 1, Law sheet No. 241, 29th September, 1945, pp. 1179 ff.
54. See note 38 to this chapter.
55. General Labour Memo (Greece) No. 12 (R 20571/4/19).

56. *Efimeris tis Kyverniseos* Vol. 1, Law sheet No. 68, 23rd March, 1945, pp. 235–41. Jecchinis erroneously cites Sofianopoulos' introductory speech as the text of the agreement, Jecchinis, *op. cit.*, p. 88. For English text, see p. 561.
57. *Efimeris tis Kyverniseos* Vol. 1, Law sheet No. 12, 20th January, 1945, pp. 26–31; Law sheet No. 24, 7th February, 1945, pp. 69–71.
58. The three assessors were a pathology professor, a doctor and a chemist who were chosen by lot and who all tried by every means to avoid this duty. Leeper to Foreign Office 19th March, 1945 (R 5857/4/19).
59. The defendants were: the three prime ministers, Georgios Tsolakoglou, Konstantinos Logothetopoulos (in absence) and John Rallis; the politicians N. Louvaris, D. Bakoyannis, I. Grigorakis, Pl. Hajimichalis, E. Kanakousakis, G. Karamanos, V. Karapanos, S. Tsironikos (in absence), A. Tavoularis (in absence), G. Pamboukas, S. Gotzamanis (in absence), K. Pournaras, N. Kalyvas*, D. Polyzos and L. Tsirigotis; the officers G. Pyrounakis*, I. Passadakis (in absence), V. Symeonidis, A. Livieratos, E. Loulakakis, K. Bakos*, S. Moutousis, G. Katsimitros, N. Markou, G. Demestichas, A. Rousopoulos, D. Dialetis (in absence), I. Papadopoulos, A. Rangavis. Those marked * had been executed by ELAS during December 1944 or in the case of N. Kalyvas in February 1944.
60. R 5857/4/19. See footnote 58 to this chapter.
61. Leeper to Foreign Office 5th June, 1945 (R 10144/4/19). In view of this, documentary sources for the collaboration trial are defective. The best summaries of the proceedings are the British Embassy reports: Leeper to Foreign Office 19th March, 1945 (R 5857/4/19); Leeper to Foreign Office 5th June 1945 (R 10144/4/19). These reports were compiled from the daily press reports in *Ellinikon Aima, Eleftheria* and *Rizospastis,* supplemented by official information from the Ministry for Justice on particular points. The account of the trial by Lefteris Apostolou, *I parodia tis dikis ton dosilogon kai i aftokatadiki tis Dexias,* (Athens: O Rigas, June 1945), contains many interesting details but is somewhat one-sided.
62. R 5857/4/19.
63. R 10144/4/19. The following were also examined: the professor of international law K. Triandafyllopoulos; the politicians George Papandreou and Alexandros Mylonas; the journalists L. Piniatoglou and Achilles Kyrou of *Ellinikon Aima,* both of whom had been in more than dubious relations with the Germans; the former under-secretary in the Finance Ministry Sbarounis, the former under-secretary in the Foreign Ministry A. Delmouzos and a number of civil servants from various ministries. The two originally listed by the prosecution: Alexandros Svolos and Nikolaos Askoutsis (the latter a liberal and former PEEA minister) were struck off the list.
On *Ellinikon Aima*'s collaboration with the German see Richter, *op. cit.,* p. 571. Another member of *Ellinikon Aima*'s editorial staff was Konstantinos Vovolinis, whose political career culminated when he became under-secretary in the Junta Prime Minister's office of G. Papadopoulos, see *ibid.,* p. 149.
64. For example G. Stratos and D. Yannopoulos; also the former parliamentary Speaker Konstantinos Grapsas and one of the directors of the Copaïs Company, Rodokanakis (R 10144/4/19).
65. On the 27th March Rodokanakis revealed that in August or September 1944 a supply of British arms had been transported from Rafina on the east coast of Attica to Athens with the help of the commander of the notorious motorised police, Colonel Bourandas, where it had been distributed to members of 'X' and of the collaborating EDES Central Committee (R 10144/4/19). On the 2nd April Major-General Panagakos reported that British officers had helped

financially with the forming of the Patras Security Battalions (*ibid.*). On the 11th April Rear-Admiral Oikonomou testified that when, in 1943, the Italians had suggested that he form a government, British officers had encouraged him to do so (*ibid.*).
66. *Efimeris tis Kyverniseos* Vol. 1, Law sheet No. 69, Law 217, 24th March, 1945, pp. 246-8. Some of the defendants were still at liberty.
67. R 10144/4/19.
68. *Ibid.* Here Leeper added in brackets: 'It may be commented that this is an interesting confession as to the part played by agents of M. Rallis in these later wholesale seizures of hostages, in which Greeks wearing masks used to point out which men should be arrested.'
69. *Ibid.*
70. One of the volunteer forces mentioned on p. 62, footnote 14.
71. R 10144/4/19.
72. The rest of the sentences were as follows: life imprisonment A. Tavoularis, I. Passadakis, G. Karamanos; twenty years imprisonment Pl. Hajimichalis, G. Demestichas; eleven years imprisonment A. Livieratos, S. Moutousis, N. Markou; five-and-a-half years imprisonment G. Katsimitros, I. Papadopoulos, D. Polyzos, K. Pournaras, N. Louvaris, V. Karapanos, A. Gerondas. Acquitted: A. Rousopoulos, E. Loulakakis, A. Rangavis, I. Grigorakis, E. Kanakousakis, D. Bakoyannis, L. Tsirigotis.
73. In June 1944 British policy on the Security Batallions changed and instructions were given to stop attacking them. Foreign Office to Cairo, Greek Directive, 22nd June 1944 (repeated to Washington, Telegram No. 5643 R 8041). Apparently it was intended to use them as anti-ELAS auxiliaries.
74. Fairly full information on subsequent collaboration trials appears in *Lefki Vivlos: 'Dimokratikos' Neofasismos*, pp. 22-5.
75. Woodhouse, *Apple of Discord*, p. 241. Originally 22,877 Greeks were charged with collaboration. After preliminary investigation 12,688 cases were not proceeded with, 10,209 were proceeded with. By January 1948 7,027 cases had been dealt with—3,182 defendants were found guilty, 121 were sentenced to death of whom 18 were actually executed. 'Greek Balance Sheet', *New Statesman* and *Nation* Vol. 35:901, No. 901, (12th June, 1948), p. 475.
76. *Efimeris tis Kyverniseos* Vol. 1, Law sheet No. 14, 21st January, 1945, pp. 37-8.
77. *I Symfonia tis Varkizas*, p. 18. See p. 561.
78. *Efimeris tis Kyverniseos* Vol. 1, Law sheet No. 14, 21st January, 1945, p. 38.
79. McNeill, *The Greek Dilemma*, pp. 181 ff.
80. In the Kissavos (Ossa)-Mavrovouni region of Thessaly arms for 800-900 partisans were concealed. In the Oxya district of Mt. Olympus there was equipment for 1,300-1,500 partisans. There were further large arms depôts in the Kalambaka district of Antichasia and in the Karditsa area. Many partisans from the mountain villages were instructed to keep their personal, often valuable, automatic weapons hidden. Even in the towns (Larisa, Tyrnavos, Trikala, Karditsa, Volos) considerable quantities of weapons were successfully concealed from the handover. Giorgis Blanas (Kapetan Kissavos), *Emfylios Polemos 1946-1949 (Opos ta ezisa)*, (Athens, 1976), pp. 35 ff. Although the National Guard, on entering a locality, began a systematic search for arms, they found relatively few. The official figure was 4,000. But, since a large quantity was distributed direct to followers of the Right, this figure may well be too low. McNeill, *The Greek Dilemma*, p. 197. What these figures in general prove is how successfully ELAS had fought during the Occupation.
81. The Political Character of the Greek Army and the National Guard, Report of Major-General G.R. Smallwood, in Leeper to Foreign Office 23rd April, 1945

(R 7716/4/19).
82. Geoffrey Chandler, *The Divided Land: An Anglo-Greek Tragedy*, (London: Macmillan, 1959), gives examples for Megalopolis (p. 60), Kalamata (p. 62) and Sparta (p. 64). Chandler reports a typical incident at Megalopolis. '... the town seemed to wear a sinister aspect. The andartes, most of whom were strangers to the district, were in complete control and the lethargy that we had come to recognise in the mountains as the hall-mark of their occupation was visible everywhere. At the same time it seemed that despite the suppression of all opposition and the consequent difficulty of gauging opinion there was a strong body of genuinely left-wing feeling. EAM and KKE propaganda had done its work well. An old woman sitting spinning on the doorstep of her house said to me that this was just another occupation: after the Italians and the Germans, the British. I reasoned with her with a sharp sense of personal distress, but she sighed the infinitely deep sigh of which Greek women are capable and murmuring "How we have suffered" went on with her spinning.' (p. 61.) Chandler belonged to the Political Warfare Executive and was active in Greece from 1944 to the end of 1946.
83. *Ibid.*, p. 65.
84. McNeill, *The Greek Dilemma*, p. 198 ff.
85. *Ibid.*, pp. 199 ff; see p. 85, footnote 21.
86. Thus Plastiras on 7th March, 1945 and in May Voulgaris. The latter stressed that passing sentences was not the job of the National Guard. *Lefki Vivlos: Paravaseis tis Varkizas*, pp. 51 ff.
87. In *Lefki Vivlos: Paravaseis tis Varkizas* there are five pages (pp. 54-8) of examples of right-wing excesses, mostly taken from reports in the bourgeois press. Stavrianos gives a typical case. 'In June 1945 armed Royalist gangs simultaneously attacked two theatres in Athens. They killed one actor, seriously wounded several others, tried to assault the actresses, and destroyed much property. It was generally known that a certain lieutenant of the National Guard, who had been a notorious Gestapo collaborator during the Occupation period, directed the raids. When protests were made to the Minister of the Interior, Konstantinos Tsatsos, he declared that the raids were caused by the politically provocative types of plays which were being presented. The plays were *The Merchant of Venice* and *Julius Caesar*.' Leften S. Stavrianos, *Greece: American Dilemma and Opportunity*, (Chicago: Regnery, 1952), pp. 154 ff. Compare *The Times*, 23rd June, 1945.
On 25th March, 1945 (Greek Independence Day) *Rizospastis* published the names of the two students, Manolis Glezos and Lakis Sandas, who, on the night of the 31st May, 1941, took down the swastika flag from the Acropolis and hid it. This was a serious mistake. 'X' members tracked them both down and beat them up mercilessly. Constantine Poulos, 'Greek Tragedy 1945', *Nation*, No. 161, (3rd November, 1945), p. 452.
88. Report of Colonel C.M. Woodhouse 'Situation in the Peloponnese', 11th August 1945, to British Embassy in Athens (R 14973/4/19).
89. Woodhouse specified arms depôts in the mountains, refusal of ELAS men to return to their villages for fear of reprisals, delaying tactics towards the administration, and communist control of all left-wing political activity.
90. It is to be regretted that Woodhouse forgot to incorporate this report in *The Struggle for Greece*, (London: Hart Davis, 1976), pp. 163 ff., where he plays down the excesses of the Right. Nor is it mentioned in his latest book *Something Ventured* (London: Granada, 1982). His bibliography likewise shows that he did not make use of the record in *Lefki Vivlos:* Paravaseis tis Varkizas, pp. 62-6.

91. *Lefki Vivlos: Paravaseis tis Varkizas,* pp. 62-6.
92. McNeill, *The Greek Dilemma,* p. 201.
93. *Ibid.*
94. *Ibid.,* p. 202. The British Consul-General, Rapp, reported as follows on the situation in Salonica. 'Situation generally unchanged. Rabid Royalist elements in National Guard are making presence increasingly felt and are in many cases out of control. Good Republicans are, according to Governor General, often beaten up on pretext that they are Communists. Object is to secure return of the King through rightist terrorism. Governor General has remonstrated with General Bitsanis whose reply was that these were the people who had been placed under his command and he could not control them. Although British Military Authorities can and do insist on removal of individual officers, evil is too widespread for them to tackle effectively. . . Judicial authorities are encountering passive resistance from similar elements in Salonica Police Force with regard to execution of warrants of arrest against well-known collaborators.' Rapp to British Embassy in Athens 20th April, 1945 (R 7178/4/19).
95. Quoted from Stavrianos, *Greece: American Dilemma and Opportunity,* pp. 155 ff.
96. Halifax to Foreign Office 24th June, 1945 (R 10743/4/19).
97. Caccia to Foreign Office 26th June, 1945 (R 10743/4/19). This suggestion was welcomed in London. Foreign Office to Halifax 29th June, 1945 (R 10915/4/19). Churchill commented: 'It would be better to leave it alone for a little.' Copy of Minute by Prime Minister 26th June, 1945 (R 10915/4/19). Censorship was still functioning. In October 1945 Constantine Poulos reported: 'There is still a censorship in Greece. It is the well-known "hidden Censorship". Two copies of all dispatches must be submitted at the telegraph office. Efforts to trace the second copies have been fruitless. The trail leads only as far as the director of the telegraph office, who admits there is censorship but doesn't know who exercises it. Inasmuch as the "stringers" who do most of the reporting out of Greece now for American and British newspapers and agencies are Greeks, they cannot report as fearlessly as they would like.' Poulos, 'Greek Tragedy', p. 451.
98. A.W. Sheppard, *Britain in Greece,* (London: League for Democracy in Greece, 1947), p. 10. Colonel Sheppard went to Greece with the Australian Imperial Forces in 1941 and was in command of D Beach (Porto Rafti) during the evacuation. In 1945 he returned as chief of two Australian relief teams and later transferred to UNRRA for which he undertook various missions. From July 1946 to March 1947 he was Director of the Northern Greece Office of the British Economic Mission.
99. Leeper to Foreign Office 5th April, 1945 (R 6249/4/19).
100. Leeper to Foreign Office 5th April, 1945 (R 6325/4/19).
101. Leeper to Foreign Office 22nd April, 1945 (R 7256/4/19).
102. Leeper to Foreign Office 2nd June, 1945 (R 9539/4/19).
103. Caccia to Foreign Office 24th June, 1945 (R 10852/4/19).
104. In Woodhouse's report (see footnote 88) this is referred to. 'Captain Dimas, second in command Gendarmerie at Kalamata told me a long story of ELAS terrorism in Pylia and Taygetos. It was soon apparent that he had never been to either. He had not taken the trouble to confirm the stories personally. . .'
105. Sheppard, *Britain in Greece,* p. 11. The author recently learned from Dr. Yanis Yanoulopoulos that in 1947 the Foreign Office contemplated prosecuting Col. Sheppard under the Official Secrets Act for these revelations but eventually decided that it was not worth while (see PRO 371.67141).
106. Caccia to Foreign Office 27th June, 1945 (R 11283/4/19).
107. Sir Charles Wickham had served in the British Expeditionary Force against

the Red Army at the end of the First World War. Lyall Wilkes, 'British Missions and Greek Quislings', *New Statesman* and *Nation* Vol. 33:832, (1st February, 1947), p. 88. In 1920 he was Divisional Commissioner of the Royal Irish Constabulary and from 1922-45 he had held the post of Inspector-General of the Royal Ulster Constabulary, in which capacity he was involved in the setting up of the Ulster Special Constabulary, the 'B Specials'.

108. *Lefki Vivlos: Paravaseis tis Varkizas*, p. 26. For example, in Agrinion, out of ninety potential recruits of the class of 1939 only fifteen, all known collaborators, were called up. The head of the British Military Mission, Major-General Smallwood, assessed the rejections on 'health grounds' at approximately 12 per cent of the potential call-up (R 7716/4/19).
109. *Lefki Vivlos: Paravaseis tis Varkizas*, p. 27. For example, Colonel Christos Gerakinis, former second-in-command of the Euboea Security Batallions who was involved in the shooting of numerous hostages, and a number of his officers. The organisers of the Corinth Security Batallions, Majors G. Kondostanos and G. Oikonomou, were promoted lieutenant-colonels and taken on. The Chief-of-Staff of Papadongonas' Peloponnese Security Batallions, Major Tavoularis, was also re-appointed. The *Lefki Vivlos* contains long lists of officers who had served in the Security Batallions and were now taken into the army.
110. Woodhouse, *Apple of Discord*, p. 97. Compare *Lefki Vivlos: Paravaseis tis Varkizas*, p. 29. In 1946, in answer to a question in the House of Commons, the Foreign Office had to admit that 228 former Security Batallion officers held commands in the army. Smothers et al., *Report on the Greeks*, p. 34.
111. Hal Lehrman, 'Athens Calling', *Nation*, No. 160, (5th May, 1945), p. 515.
112. Record of a Meeting held at the Foreign Office 12th June, 1945 (R 10667/4/19).
113. Caccia to Foreign Office 27th August, 1945 (R 14710/4/19).
114. Caccia to Foreign Office 17th September, 1945 (R 15829/4/19).
115. Lascelles to Foreign Office 18th September, 1945 (R 16154/4/19).
116. Woodhouse, *Apple of Discord*, p. 257. Vendiris became Chief of the General Staff for a second time in February 1947.
117. *I Symfonia tis Varkizas*, pp. 18 ff.
118. *Lefki Vivlos: Paravaseis tis Varkizas*, p. 33.
119. *Kathimerina Nea*, 3rd June, 1945, as quoted in *Lefki Vivlos: Paravaseis tis Varkizas*, p. 35.
120. *Ibid.*, p. 43; Leeper to Foreign Office 30th November, 1945 (R 20262/4/19); p. 47, footnote 76.
121. R 20262/4/19. Leeper commented: 'This case is one of many outstanding in Greece where people who undoubtedly did good work for the Allied cause are nevertheless accused of crimes against the Greek Penal Code.' The persecution of Venetsanopoulos continued until 1949 with repeated attempts to bring him to trial. *New Statesman* and *Nation* Vol. 38:962, (13th August, 1949), p. 162.
122. Leeper to Foreign Office, draft telegram of 2nd October, 1945 (R 18502/4/19). In contrast to this, by spring 1946 2,000 gendarmes who were unwilling to take part in excesses had been suspended from the service.
123. *Lefki Vivlos: Paravaseis tis Varkizas*, p. 39; Leeper to Foreign Office 17th April, 1945 (R 7363/4/19). For Bishop Spyridon's record, see pp. 141-2.
124. EAM Memorandum 12th March, 1945 (R 5617/4/19).
125. Norman Dodds, Leslie Solley, Stanley Tiffany, *Tragedy in Greece*, (London: League for Democracy in Greece, 1946), p. 20. General Psiarris remained in prison till December 1945.
126. Leeper to Foreign Office 7th May, 1945 (R 9478/4/19). 'Meanwhile the Crown Prosecutor of Tripoli has caused a small-scale flutter by issuing warrants for

the arrest of Ares [Velouchiotis] (which is understandable), General Saraphis, and two former ELAS divisional commanders (Colonel Papastamatiadis and Lieutenant-Colonel Tsiklitaras) as being morally responsible for atrocities. This runs counter to the spirit of the Varkiza agreement, and delegations from both EAM and ELD/SKE have called on Admiral Voulgaris to protest. But to judge from the small measure of indignation shown in the EAM-press, even they do not seem to think that the warrants will be actually executed.' In the case of Sarafis, too, the attempts to bring him to trial were continued in 1947 and 1948. Sarafis, *op. cit.*, pp. LXXXIII, LXXXV.
127. Doods et al., *op. cit.*, p. 12.
128. Lehrman, 'Athens Calling', *p. 516 and Lefki Vivlos: 'Dimokratikos' Neofasismos, p. 26.*
129. Dodds et al., *op. cit.*, p. 49.
130. *Ibid.*, p. 50.
131. *Ibid.*, p. 18.
132. Leeper to Foreign Office 4th June, 1945 (R 9885/4/19).
133. He promised to disband the right-wing para-military organisations. The gendarmerie would be expanded from 7,000 to 16,000 by the 1st July. A committee consisting of the Justice and Interior Ministers and the Assistant-Minister for Finance would investigate the violations of the Varkiza Agreement. The gendarmerie would be brought under the Minister for the Interior. Caccia to Foreign Office 22nd June, 1945 (R 10682/4/19). At the end of July, as a result of the attack by 'X' members on an Athens theatre (see footnote 87), Tsatsos ordered the closing of one 'X' office, but he stopped short of banning 'X' as freedom of political association was presumed to exist. Caccia to Foreign Office 2nd July, 1945 (R 11562/4/19).
134. Caccia to Foreign Office 23rd July, 1945 (R 12730/4/19). Damaskinos admitted to Caccia that the opposition's complaints were well-founded—but directly the gendarmerie took over control this would change.
135. Coalition of Political Parties of EAM Central Committee. Memorandum of 26th June, 1945 (R 11370/4/19). Caccia to Foreign Office 30th July, 1945 (R 13134/4/19).
136. R 13134/4/19. The 'normal' prison population before the war was approximately 8,000.
137. Caccia to Foreign Office 13th August, 1945 (R 13927/4/19).
138. Foreign Office to Caccia 14th August, 1945 (R 13332/4/19).
139. Caccia to Foreign Office 20th August, 1945 (R 14320/4/19).
140. *Efimeris tis Kyverniseos* Vol. 1, Law sheet No. 213, Law No. 525, 25th August, 1945, pp. 1044 ff.
141. Lascelles to Foreign Office 7th September, 1945 (R 15198/4/19). This figure was analysed as follows:

	common law offenders	insurgents	collaborators
convicted	2,458	48	(negligible)
awaiting trial	8,116	5,282	1,246

142. *Efimeris tis Kyverniseos* Vol. 1, Law sheet No. 224, Law No. 533, 3rd September, 1945, pp. 1075-82.
143. Bevin to Caccia 7th September, 1945 (R 15383/4/19).
144. Lascelles to Foreign Office 15th September, 1945 (R 15768/4/19). Homicide, including killing from political motives or under war conditions, was regarded as murder. The British Legal Mission commented: 'Many persons detained for offences alleged to have been committed during the occupation or the Civil War, are accused not of actual perpetration, but of "moral responsibility" for it. Thus for one murder several persons may be accused, one or more of actually

committing the murder and the others of moral responsibility for it. For example the members of an execution squad who shot an alleged traitor during the occupation might be accused of murder and the witnesses who gave evidence against him, and the judge who passed the sentence might be accused of moral responsibility for the killing.' *Report of the British Legal Mission to Greece*, (London: HMSO, 1946), Cmd. 6838, p. 14. In the same way, people who had collected taxes on the instructions of the PEEA administration were accused of theft, robbery or looting. Gendarmes who had gone over to the Resistance were accused of desertion.

145. Leeper to Foreign Office 25th September, 1945 (R 16632/4/19). Leeper's figures for 15th September were: total number of prisoners 16,600 of whom 14,152 awaiting trial.

	common law offenders	*insurgents*	*collaborators*
convicted	2,086	151	231
awaiting trial	5,991	5,796	2,665

Leeper to Foreign Office 24th September, 1945 (R 16303/4/19). Comparison with the figures of 7th September shows that the Justice Ministry's statistics were anything but reliable.

146. Laskey's Minutes 20th September, 1945 (R 15768/4/19). Noel-Baker's suggestions were based mainly on Woodhouse's report of 11th August. Hayter commented: 'This report makes nonsense of the Regent's repeated statements about the dangers of early release on the grounds that private vengeance against the "murderers" would follow. We shall really have to bring him to his senses about this before he leaves, if all else goes well; there is no greater handicap to our Greek policy than this scandal.' Hayter's Minutes, 18th September, 1945 (R 14973/4/19).

147. Bevin to Leeper 22nd September, 1945 (R 15768/4/19).

148. Leeper to Foreign Office 24th September, 1945 (R 16303/4/19).

149. Leeper to Foreign Office 2nd October, 1945 (R 17133/4/19).

150. On the 3rd October Sir Orme Sargent telegraphed to Leeper: 'He [Bevin] feels that the Regent has let him down. He has done everything possible to meet the Regent's wishes as regards the internal situation and his chief request in return was that some thing should be done about the amnesty. But in fact nothing has been done and the number of prisoners is actually increasing. Feeling here on this subject is getting really dangerous and I am afraid that if the Prison scandal is allowed to continue we may have to revise our whole policy. . .' Foreign Office to Leeper 3rd October, 1945 (R 16631/4/19). On the same day Bevin himself sent a telegram to Leeper in which he urged him sharply to bring massive pressure to bear on Damaskinos on the amnesty issue. Foreign Office to Leeper 3rd October, 1945 (R 16631/4/19).

151. Leeper to Foreign Office 7th October, 1945 (R 17081/4/19).

152. Bevin to Leeper 10th October, 1945 (R 17081/4/19).

THE SECOND VOULGARIS GOVERNMENT

After this extended parenthesis on the failure of successive Greek governments to implement the Varkiza Agreement—or rather on the creation and seizure of power by the *parakratos*—it is time to return to internal political developments. The manner of Plastiras' deposition had led to a passive refusal of cooperation by Greek politicians and Voulgaris at first had difficulties in finding enough personalities willing to enter his Cabinet. But in talks with the various party leaders he eventually managed to reduce their resistance. Even the KKE leadership assured him that it had changed its attitude to the government, provided that the government really would take effective measures to ensure a normal evolution. Svolos and Tsirimokos of ELD-SKE declared that, whilst in principle they were against a service government, this would not prevent them from being the first to welcome the government's steps towards ensuring freedom and prosperity and towards controlling the military leagues and the paramilitary organisations.[1]

However, parallel with the abnormal conditions resulting from the excesses of the National Guard and developments in the army, opposition to the Voulgaris government revived. In the middle of May the Liberals and the Left demanded the formation of an all-party government: only a coalition could prevent the situation from deteriorating. On the 23rd May this movement suffered a severe setback when the Populists declared that they rejected such a solution.[2] At the beginning of June came the protests of the Liberals and other republicans against growing right-wing excesses in the provinces.

In the middle of June the increasing polarisation of Greek political life became apparent. The Populist leader, Konstantinos Tsaldaris, nephew of the pre-Metaxas Populist Prime Minister Panayotis Tsaldaris, openly espoused the monarchist cause. Emmanouil Tsouderos pronounced for a republic: during the exile period he had recognised George II as head of the nation; but in peacetime the monarchy was divisive of the nation.[3] The Liberals and other republicans for their part demanded that, contrary to the provisions of the Varkiza Agreement, elections for a constituent assembly should precede the plebiscite. EAM associated itself with this demand. On the other hand the Populists, now joined by Papandreou, supported—in this instance—the strict implementation of the Agreement.[4] On the 28th June Voulgaris, to avoid the difficulties menacing him from both sides, stated that it was still uncertain which would be held first; nor was the electoral system yet decided. Moreover, restoration of order and tranquillity and revision of the electoral lists were necessary pre-conditions for the holding of elections; presumably the revision would be completed by October.[5]

On the 6th July Kafandaris, Sofoulis, Mylonas, Plastiras and Tsouderos demanded of Voulgaris the resignation of General Drakos (Assistant-Minister for War) and of the Minister for the Interior, K. Tsatsos: the army was completely under the control of the Right and Tsatsos was doing nothing against right-wing terrorism. Voulgaris rejected the demands as unjustified but he nevertheless enacted a law against illegal possession of arms and brigandage which, as we have already seen, had no effect.[6] On the 17th and 19th July came the Liberal and republican protests against the right-wing terror,[7] in which they were joined by KKE. On 20th July the Central Committee's Political Bureau published a statement to the effect that, despite the official denial, the state was in the hands of the royalists and their armed terrorists; the worst element in this situation was that the British could radically alter it within 24 hours if they so wished; were the Greeks allowed to solve this problem for themselves, an all-party government would be formed which would restore order with the cooperation of an inter-allied commission; KKE would support such a government without seeking party advantage; if conditions of freedom were not restored, then KKE would boycott the elections.[8] Voulgaris thereupon stated that he would resign if the Liberals and other republicans did not participate in the elections but that, for the moment, he saw no reason to do so. Damaskinos declared himself of the same opinion.[9]

The crisis peaked on the 22nd July when the Foreign Minister, Sofianopoulos, returned from San Francisco where he had represented Greece at the inauguration of the United Nations, Sofianopoulos reported to the Regent and Voulgaris on his activities over the last three months and submitted his resignation. In an article for the *News Chronicle* he gave his reasons. For reasons of foreign and domestic policy the experiment of a service government should be abandoned and a truly representative government should be formed, including all political parties. Only such a government could deal effectively with the country's internal and external problems. He then referred to the Yalta decisions which demanded just such a solution. If the Plastiras government had been overthrown on the grounds that it was not above party—a supposition which was not justified —then the same held good for the Voulgaris government, since during its period in office the reactionary organisations' power had increased.

> 'The incredible terrorism practised by these organisations has not only become a threat to the security of democratic citizens but has also multiplied the dangers of external friction. If for a moment some justification could be found for passionate feelings in the desire for

revenge on the part of certain victims of the December events, no excuse can be put forward for the responsible Government, which has not only failed to quieten these passions but also to prevent terrorism. And, in this way, failed to fulfill its elementary obligation to secure order and protect the life, honour and property of the citizens. This dangerous situation. . . only a political Government can effectively counter. Such a Government, representing all currents and tendencies in the nation, could possess the necessary authority to master the reaction of the intransigents and the reactionary activities of certain irresponsible organisations. Only such a Government could restore law and order and inspire confidence to [sic] all citizens, and lead them to free and genuine democratic elections, the results of which would be beyond dispute. . .'

In order to give force to these views he was submitting his resignation.[10]

In the article Sofianopoulos added that he hoped that the result of the British elections would have positive effects in Greece and lead the Greek people to a decision for democracy and socialism at the earliest possible opportunity. He hoped that the Regent would draw the necessary conclusions and that the government would make way for one that would be representative.[11]

In a conversation with Caccia on the 23rd July, Sofianopoulos went further and said that during talks with Molotov and with the Australian and New Zealand representatives in San Francisco, he had formed the impression that an all-party government would be the only correct solution. This would be even easier to achieve since KKE had let it be understood that it did not necessarily want to participate in such a government. Such a government would also serve the interests of British policy.[12] Later in the same day Voulgaris visited Caccia and said he was ready to resign as Prime Minister if the British government wished, though this should not be understood as a retreat in face of Sofianopoulos. Caccia then visited Damaskinos who wanted to know what the British government thought of Sofianopoulos' suggestions. He confirmed that Voulgaris was ready to resign, though he saw no internal policy justification for this; any sort of all-party government would be problematic; but considerations of foreign policy had priority; before taking any steps, he wanted to know whether London desired a change of government.[13]

Caccia reported these conservations to London and commented that there were no internal policy reasons for a change of government; that it was true that some republican party leaders and KKE were agitating for a 'political' government; but that there was no sign they had the backing of public opinion; a change of government would be a gratuitous setback to the country's development; for Damaskinos it was a foreign policy question and he wanted a clear answer from London:

'He naturally does not expect that reply will be in the nature of a *diktat* but that it will be friendly prompting from Greece's protecting power who is better placed to know the true interests of this country in relation to her neighbours, than His Beatitude or the Greek government.'

He, Caccia, was awaiting a speedy reply.[14]

In London, Eden and Sir Orme Sargent decided that the government should remain in office, that a respectable politically uncommitted Foreign Minister should be appointed and that the service character of the Greek government should be maintained; furthermore, measures were being considered to strengthen the Regent's position and to put a stop to demands for a change of government.[15]

In this way Sofianopoulos' resignation was rendered ineffective. The Populists (Tsaldaris and Mavromichalis), knowing that time was on their side, decided to enter a coalition government. Sofoulis and Kafandaris set their hopes on a British decision. Thus Sofianopoulos found wholehearted support only from Plastiras and from KKE, which made it easy for Caccia to dispose of the whole project as a communist manoeuvre. Moreover, if Sofianopoulos had not himself agreed, some pretext would have been found to sack him, since at San Francisco he had dared to cast Greece's vote with the Soviet Union and in opposition to the British and Americans, against the admission of what he regarded as the fascist state of Argentina to the UN.[16] All that Damaskinos took seriously was the threat of an election boycott; but even this difficulty could be overcome if the party leaders were informed of the present state of negotiations with the Allies over supervision of the elections. In order to avoid a repetition of the situation at Plastiras' overthrow, Caccia maintained close contact with MacVeagh.[17]

There was to be another set-back to the hopes for a change in British policy towards Greece when, on the eve of the official announcement of the result of the British parliamentary elections Bevin—according to Greek press reports—stated that the Churchill Cabinet's Greek policy had been based on unanimity and warned the Greek workers to pay more attention to their country's reconstruction than to political matters.[18] The continuity of British policy towards Greece was thus apparently guaranteed.

In Athens, however, the campaign for a coalition government continued. On the 27th July Damaskinos addressed himself to Caccia: in accordance with the result of the British elections, he expected that republican demands would be more loudly voiced; he would find himself in difficulties if there was no public indication of guaranteed continuity in British policy towards Greece; Voulgaris was serious in his readiness to resign; but, for practical reasons, an all-party government was impossible; he needed to know whether the British government expected him to carry on on the basis of the telegram from Eden and Sir Orme Sargent; in that case, he asked for a clear—and if possible an immediate—decision. Voulgaris expressed himself similarly.[19]

The first to comment on the effects of the British elections for Greece—and that already on 28th July—was Plastiras: this had solved Greece's constitutional problem; Greece would become a republic. Unfortunately, the state of the electoral lists did not permit of immediate elections; the royalists would be well-advised to persuade the king to abdicate; a change of government was urgently needed and the royalists should participate in the new Cabinet; this would elect a three member committee which would exercise the Regency until the elections, which would produce a new head of state. KKE participation in the government he considered unsuitable.[20]

On 30th July EAM applied for Voulgaris' consent to a mass demonstration in the Athens stadium in favour of a political government. On the 31st Voulgaris rejected this on the ground that, in accordance with the Varkiza Agreement, Article 10 of the Constitution (Freedom of Assembly) was suspended.[21] KKE reacted at once. At the Political Bureau session on 1st August the following resolution was passed. a protest was registered against the prohibition; in the past days both terrorism and economic oppression of the working class had been intensified; the Regent and the government were not only unable, but also unwilling to use their influence for an improvement; they were on the side of the capitalists, the exploiters and the collaborators; the state apparatus was being mobilised to terrorise the people and in support of monarcho-fascist bandits. Then came a new tune: Plastiras' and Sofoulis' plans, if they were realised, would lead to the formation of a pseudo-political and pseudo-representative government, hostile to the democratic Left, which would bring about no real change of situation; KKE condemned the attempt to form a reactionary, anti-popular coalition of the Right; the EAM Central Committee should seize the initiative to form a truly democratic government; in this government all parties and groups supporting democracy should participate, as well as the Resistance.[22]

Meanwhile, Eden's and Orme Sargent's suggestion for relieving pressure on Damaskinos had arrived in Athens. It was the revival of an idea already under discussion in the spring: the formation of a commission on which all political parties would be represented. Even before discussing it with Damaskinos, Caccia rejected this suggestion as unsuitable: the formation of such a commission would certainly reduce the immediate pressure on the Regent, but its consequence would be the postponement of elections and plebiscite to 1946. Damaskinos for his part had found another solution—he would replace the Minister for Justice and the Assistant-Minister to the War Ministry who, unlike the Interior Minister Tsatsos had been deservedly criticised; General Smallwood agreed to the removal of the assistant-minister.[23]

On the 2nd August Sofoulis entered the spotlight again with a press interview: Greece was at present split and would be stifled between the two extremes of Left and Right; the situation could be summarised as follows: 'complete non-existence of security; that is to say, complete non-existence of the State and omnipotence of the armed bands'. Voulgaris had good will and honourable intentions, but the existing situation was beyond his powers; an all-party government must be formed, based on the elections of 1936, that is excluding EAM and ELD–SKE; only such a government could solve the immediate problems.[24] Sofoulis' suggestions released a wave of protest from Left to Right; not even the other republicans approved.[25]

In the meantime the Regent had already received the message from Attlee about the implementation of Varkiza. This, together with the reaction of the Athens press to Sofoulis' statement, brought Damaskinos into action. Though he continued to reject the formation of a coalition government, he realised that, in some way or other, he would have to meet the republican leaders' demands since otherwise he would remain a target for their criticism. Moreover, the public indication of British wishes he had requested had not yet arrived. So, on the 3rd August, he decided to open talks with the party leaders. He informed Caccia and repeated his request for a clear signal. For the moment he gave urgent priority to a definite answer from London on the character of the Greek government: such an answer could, if necessary, be communicated to him confidentially; but it must be unambiguous; facing a confrontation, he must at all costs have British guidelines.[26]

Caccia recommended to London that, in formulating these guidelines, they should not envisage any radical alterations: the present government had certainly failed in the law and order sphere but, against this, there were successes to be recorded in the economic sector; a radical change would call the latter into question and, as regards the first problem, replacement of the War Minister would suffice; were the whole government to be replaced, this would also involve postponement of the elections. MacVeagh, too, shared this view.[27]

On 4th August, Damaskinos began his talks with the party leaders. Sofoulis repeated his suggestions, though in a watered-down form as a result of the negative press reaction. Concluding, he let it be understood that he would also accept the continuation in office of the Voulgaris Cabinet. The Populists sent a delegation (Tsaldaris, Mavromichalis, Theotokis and Stefanopoulos) which rejected the formation of a coalition government and demanded that the Voulgaris government remain in power. On the 5th Gonatas put in an appearance and likewise demanded that Voulgaris remain in office. Plastiras, on the other hand, demanded a coalition government: if the Populists did not want to participate, it should be formed by republicans alone and excluding KKE and EAM. Kafandaris had few constructive suggestions beyond the appointment of Varvaressos as Prime Minister. On the 6th, Tsouderos recommended that

K. Tsatsos be the new Minister for Justice. Papandreou cited 'logical' reasons for the retention of the Voulgaris government and proposed the formation of an all-party home policy committee whose task would be the supervision of law and order. Siantos demanded the formation of a political government, adding that, if this were not possible, EAM and KKE were ready to form one whose programme it would be to proclaim a general amnesty and to purge the army, police, gendarmerie and the state apparatus. Sofianopoulos advocated an all-party government. Kanellopoulos was for the continuation of a service government and Alexandris declared himself of the same opinion.

On the 7th, Svolos and Tsirimokos recommended the formation of a broad-based political government in which the Resistance should be strongly represented; if the Liberals and other republicans did not want to participate in this, it should be formed from the Resistance parties (with the inclusion of KKE). There followed a delegation from some of the parties within the EAM coalition (Gavriilidis and Thanasekos for the Agrarian Party, Loulis and Kyrkos for the Radical Democrats, Kritikas for the Democratic Union, Georgalas and Oikonomou for the Progressive Socialists). They recommended that, if it proved impossible to form a broadly-based government, a Resistance government should be formed.

Kartalis, a centre left politician and former political adviser to EKKA, submitted the most interesting proposal, for which Woodhouse gave his backstage support. The new government should be formed from personalities who inspired political respect and not from party leaders. The Communists should not participate but, against this, there should be leading non-communist personalities from EAM. There would be no objection to the participation of Voulgaris and Varveressos in such a government. A consultative assembly should be formed from representatives of all the parties and of the Resistance. The new government should announce that preparations for the plebiscite and the elections would not begin until law and order ruled throughout the land. This could indeed mean a delay of nine months but, during this time, the consultative assembly would revive the country's political life. The leader of the republican wing of EDES, Pyromaglou, espoused this suggestion. Napoleon Zervas—the last to visit the Regent—spoke of the royalist wing of EDES supporting the retention of the service government.[28]

Kartalis' suggestions would have meant a fresh start. He had realised that the old-school politicians, though they spoke in the name of the great traditional parties, in fact represented only themselves. During the Occupation, the mass of the people had turned away from them and towards the Resistance. Kartalis' solution would in all probability have had the overwhelming majority of the population behind it and would have given the entire post-war evolution of Greece a different direction. It would, of course, also have meant that the traditional parties and their leaders would have lost influence and that British control over Greek political life would have been reduced. In brief, this suggestion could have meant a new edition of the joint Resistance Front of summer 1943,[29] with all its implications. So it is not surprising that, in his report to London, Caccia played down the significance of this suggestion and the personality of Kartalis.

The four days of talks therefore resulted in no real change. Neither an all-party government nor a coalition government from the bourgeois parties would be formed. As planned, Damaskinos would simply instruct Voulgaris to re-shuffle his Cabinet.[30]

At this period the Foreign Office was still considering the need for a new Greek policy and therefore it accepted Damaskinos' decision. On the 9th August it instructed Caccia that Voulgaris should remain in office and the service character of the government should be preserved until the elections; there would be no objection if some incompetent ministers were replaced; Caccia should raise with Damaskinos the proclamation of a general amnesty; this would silence criticism and reduce tension.[31]

Damaskinos accepted these instructions: he would replace the Justice Minister and the Assistant-Minister for War; in principle he agreed to an amnesty but murderers must remain excluded; he would discuss the matter with Voulgaris.[32] On the 9th August he issued a public proclamation in which he asserted that he had toiled in vain to form a 'political' government and told Voulgaris to reshuffle his Cabinet. His desire for instructions from London had prompted Foreign Secretary Bevin to turn his attention to British policy towards Greece. To this end he asked for a detailed memorandum.[33]

This memorandum demonstrated that the following had been the basic principle of previous Greek policy.

'. . . that we require a stable and pro-British government in Greece and the sincere friendship of the Greek people if we are to maintain our political and military position in the Eastern Mediterranean and to safeguard our lines of communication with the East. Since the sentiments of the majority of the Greek people were fervently and genuinely pro-British, our aim will be achieved if we can promote the formation of a government which represents the will of the Greek people.'

Economic assistance to Greece was another important factor. The Greeks had certainly been advised to turn to the US for this, since Great Britain could not meet all Greek requirements; nevertheless Greece's economic needs would for long remain an important factor; whilst in the political sphere Greece would have long-term need of firm guidance from abroad and this Great Britain was almost alone in being able to give, since the Greeks regarded Great Britain as their main protecting power and mentor. This task was rendered more difficult by the Soviet Union which had unleashed a war of nerves against Greece and this threatened not only Greece but also British interests in the Eastern Mediterranean. Therefore the objectives of British policy in Greece were: 1) the maintenance of the pro-British attitude of the population and the creation of a stable and friendly government; 2) democratic decision as to the future of the regime and to future government; 3) support for Greece and Turkey as independent states with close and friendly relations between themselves and with Great Britain. This was an essential component of long-term British strategy in the Eastern Mediterranean; 4) resistance to any attempt by Yugoslavia and Bulgaria (with or without Soviet support) to dominate Greece.

The memorandum went on to deal with the present situation and came to the following conclusions: the Regency under Damaskinos had proved itself and should continue; there was no alternative to the present Voulgaris service government which should therefore be retained; Damaskinos had asked for detailed guidelines but until these were elaborated he should be instructed in the above sense. The memorandum then examined the prospects for the proposed consultative assembly and adjudged them not very promising. In the meantime Leeper had written to the Foreign Office suggesting Damaskinos be invited to London for talks.[34] This would have two advantages: it would gain time and the US ambassador in London could be involved in the talks so that full US support could be secured. The memorandum concluded with an analysis of problems connected with the elections to which we will return in dealing with that topic.

On the 11th August Bevin submitted to the Cabinet a memorandum on policy towards Greece which made the following points:

'1. We should press for the elections and plebiscite to be held in Greece as soon as possible. If it can be arranged, the elections should precede the plebiscite, but this is a matter on which the Greeks themselves must take the initiative and responsibility.

2. The Voulgaris Government should be maintained in power until the elections. All reasonable steps should, however, be taken to meet justifiable criticism by the Left Wing Parties and to ensure that law and order are maintained on an impartial basis.

3. To steady the position in Greece and to assist us in working out a satisfactory Greek policy, the Regent should be invited to visit this country to confer with His Majesty's Government.

4. If Russia continues to press on with her propaganda regarding the position of Greece, it will be necessary to make plain to the USSR our position.

5. We should do our utmost to secure the full support of the Dominions for our whole Greek policy. We should also lose no opportunity of associating the United States in all steps we take.'

Bevin then stated various reasons for this line of action, of which the

following was the most important:
'The most overpowering reason of all this is that we must maintain our position in Greece as a part of our Middle East policy, and unless it is asserted and settled it may have a bad effect on the whole of our Middle East position.'[35]

The Cabinet approved Bevin's statement and on the 16th August he instructed Caccia correspondingly: in addition, he intended to give a statement on British policy in Greece to the House of Commons on 20th August; Caccia should invite Damaskinos for the beginning of September, at which time too the Council of Foreign Ministers would be meeting in London; this would make it possible to invite US Secretary of State, Byrnes, to join in the talks and to gain his support for British policy; furthermore, Damaskinos could have talks with Molotov; Damaskinos should regard the invitation as confidential until 20th August; Caccia should explain to the Regent that Great Britain was aiming at early elections but he should say nothing about the actual timing.[36]

Meanwhile, in Athens the reshuffling of the Cabinet had started on the 11th August.[37] As had been foreseen, the Minister for Justice and the Assistant-Minister for War were dropped. But Interior Minister Tsatsos also had to go, though Damaskinos wanted to keep him. To retain him would have brought Damaskinos—whose relations with the Tsatsos family have already been referred to—into the critical firing line. The Cabinet reshuffle was merely cosmetic surgery: the basic problem of the Voulgaris Cabinet—as we saw in connection with the implementing of Varkiza— remained unchanged.

In his first talk with Caccia on August 13th after the government changes, Damaskinos returned to his wish for a 'visible signal'. Caccia told him that Bevin was planning a statement in the House of Commons. Damaskinos was pleased and expressed his hope that in what he said about the elections Bevin would be reserved and say nothing that could prejudge the issue.[38] When, on the 17th, he accepted Bevin's invitation, he expressed himself again in the same sense: a final decision on the elections should be taken only during his visit.[39] In the following days Voulgaris completed his Cabinet and at the same time the politicians went on discussing the elections issue. The royalists demanded the implementation of Varkiza. The republicans demanded that the plebiscite be held after the elections and that these should be postponed.

On the 20th August Bevin appeared before the House of Commons and gave his expected statement on Greece. First, he made it plain that the Labour government was following the same policy' as Churchill at the liberation of Greece, the policy which he had defended at the Labour Party Conference on 11th December 1944.[40] He went on to speak of the present situation. The Voulgaris government should remain in office until the elections:

'Greece will never recover while her leaders spend their time in continuously, week by week, trying to change their Government. They had better take an example from us. Until the election has taken place, no one can know whether any new Government rests on the sure foundations of the consent of the people or not.'

The elections should be held as soon as possible. The question arose which should be held first, the plebiscite or the elections. According to the Varkiza Agreement the plebiscite should be held first. But he realised that a significant proportion of Greek public opinion wanted the order changed. However, this was a matter for the Greeks and he in no way wanted to prejudice the result; though the question should be resolved with speed. It was to British interest that the solution reached should be accepted by the majority of the Greek people and should lead without delay to firm results.[41] In addition, Bevin expressed his hope that, as a consequence of British support, the gendarmerie would soon be in the position to guarantee law and order. Moreover, he hoped that an amnesty would be proclaimed as soon as possible. He was conscious that this was a difficult problem since it would affect not only criminals (sic) but also collaborators. Nevertheless he believed it would contribute to stabilising the situation if an amnesty were granted and the prisons were emptied.

As regards the elections, the US, French and British governments had undertaken to assist in supervision and he suggested that representatives of the Dominions might also be involved. He regretted that the Russians had refused to participate in the supervision. He was happy to be able to announce that Damaskinos had accepted an invitation to Britain. Finally, he hoped that, after the holding of elections, tranquillity would return to that region of the world.[42] With this speech Bevin gave not only the public, but also the left-wing of the Labour Party to understand that there was continuity in British policy towards Greece.

The speech had been preceded, at the beginning of August, by a statement from the Chairman of the Labour Party National Executive, Professor Harold Laski, that British policy towards Greece would be completely revised.[43] In the parliamentary debate on the 16th August Churchill had taken heated issue with Laski's version and had attacked Bevin on the grounds that not he but Laski was deciding foreign policy.[44] The Commonwealth MP Ernest Millington (Chelmsford) counter-attacked as follows:

'I listened with extreme interest to [Churchill] who gave us an alarming picture of the "police state" throughout the Balkans. . . While he was talking I thought to myself, "surely [Churchill] is thinking about Greece, our ancient Ally, the prototype now of all police states, whose Government has put this year into prison, without trial, 17,300 people for doing no more than fighting our struggle against Nazi domination during the course of the war. This is the Government which in the past derived support from the Government of Great Britain when we were in Coalition, and this is the Government which receives no support from any accredited democratic institution throughout the whole of the country of Greece. His Majesty's Government today must realise that fact. They must realise the responsibility that the British people owe to the Greek people. His Majesty's Government must do all that it possibly can in deeds and not merely in fulsome and specious words, to give every possible opportunity for the freely expressed will through some democratic machinery of the Greek people, to prevail in the polls".'[45]

In the debate following Bevin's speech on 20th August, the Labour MP Major Lyall Wilkes (Newcastle-upon-Tyne, Central)—who had personal knowledge of conditions in Greece—took up this thread; in Greece Goebbels' propaganda thesis that war between Great Britain and the Soviet Union was imminent was being taken at its face value. The British Embassy had up to now done nothing to disturb this illusion, despite the fact that, wherever he appeared, the British ambassador was greeted with cries of 'To Sofia!' and sometimes even 'To Moscow!'. There was a danger that, in Greece, pro-Russian and pro-British parties could come into existence, something which—given Greece's geo-political situation—must be avoided at all costs.

Major Wilkes went on to speak of the partisan character of the Greek army and demanded a remedy. He welcomed international supervision of the elections but thought it important to make clear to the Greeks that Great Britain was not a member of some new anti-Comintern pact and that the excesses of the Greek Right did not have British government approval. A statement of this sort should have been made long ago. The Greek royalists had interpreted the British government's silence as consent. He then turned to the problem of the prisoners and of the re-integration of the collaborators into the state apparatus. Here, too, he noted the lack of British intervention. Before the December events the British authorities had intervened on every possible occasion so as to forestall arbitrary action by ELAS. Since January 1945 British units had instructions from the highest level not to intervene in internal Greek affairs. Therefore to-day the British forces in Greece no longer acted as umpire and the consequence of this had been that the Varkiza Agreement was a dead letter. For the British authorities the possibility of changing the present situation existed, as had been shown by the intervention against EAM-ELAS. He hoped that the British government would contribute to stopping the excesses of the royalists and fascists who controlled the Greek state.[46]

After Major Wilkes, Eden spoke. When he came to Bevin's statement there was the following interchange:

'*Mr. Eden:* He [Bevin] and I served a few years together in the War Cabinet.

Mr. Churchill: Five.
Mr. Eden: Well, I was not in the Cabinet all the time. During that period there were many discussions on foreign affairs, but I cannot recall one single occasion when there was a difference between us. I hope I do not embarrass the Foreign Secretary by saying that.
Mr. Bevin: No.
Mr. Eden: There were no differences on any important issue of foreign policy. My right hon. Friend helped me during those critical war years, and in the same spirit I should like to try to help him now. . . He [Bevin] said, in reference to the Mediterranean and the Middle East. . . that this was one of the most vital areas affecting the British Empire and Commonwealth. We entirely associate ourselves with that remark.'[47]

In other words, British policy towards Greece remained the same under Bevin as under Eden. Michael Foot proved mistaken when he formulated the position thus:

'a few words. . . might have a good effect in warning reactionary elements in Greece that a great change had taken place in this country, and that the foreign affairs of this country were no longer conducted by persons who had a vested interest in securing the return to his throne of King George of the Hellenes—a vested interest in order to justify a long campaign which they waged on behalf of King George. . . and which. . . is partly responsible for the unhappy state of Greece today'.[48]

How far this continuity went was demonstrated on 22nd August, when Bevin slapped down some critical questions from Seymour Cocks MP, just as Eden had done in the debate in December 1944.[49]

In one respect one could say that Michael Foot was right: Bevin was not trying to restore George II at all costs and he did try to insist on an amnesty. But in all else there was continuity.

In Athens reactions to Bevin's statement varied. Royalist circles were satisfied since Voulgaris would remain in office and the elections would be held soon. The Liberals and the Left stated that, under present conditions, free elections were impossible and that they would boycott them; there was, however, hope that, during the Regent's visit to London, it would be decided that the elections should be held first. The EAM parties condemned Bevin's statement.[50] In the following days Voulgaris completed his Cabinet reshuffle by appointing A. Merenditis Army Minister (22nd August) and P. Gounarakis Minister of the Interior (30th August). At the same time the Regent held talks with the party leaders in preparation for his visit to London. On the 24th August he informed Caccia of the results to date.

The republicans would boycott the elections unless there was to be a considerable interval between these and the plebiscite—five years had been suggested. In view of the fact that the constitutional problem had tormented Greece for the past thirty years and its final solution was urgently needed, this demand seemed only mildly exaggerated. If the plebiscite was held too soon, the result would certainly be called in question and give grounds for prolonging the controversy. He therefore asked that a decision on this should not be taken before his visit to London. Republican demands must be taken seriously; an election boycott would turn the elections into a farce. As regards the date, he saw no possibility before mid-December. This would certainly not please the British government but his premise was that the British government attached importance to at least reasonably valid electoral lists. If the compilation of these lists was unduly hurried, there was a danger that the republicans—in agreement with the majority of the population—would exercise a boycott. The royalists would not oppose this solution if they knew it was backed by Great Britain. The way they had behaved on the National Guard issue, in arming civilians and on the economic programme deserved no further encouragement. It was necessary they should be somewhat deflated. Finally, Damaskinos asked for complete confidentiality.[51]

Caccia recommended to the Foreign Office that the change of priorities should be left to Greek initiative. The Regent should not receive any directions. Unless there were strong reasons against it, such an initiative should be supported. As regards the election date, he was afraid the Regent was right. He would contact MacVeagh.[52]

During the next days Damaskinos continued his talks with the party leaders. The royalists demanded strict implementation of the Varkiza Agreement, that is priority for the plebiscite. On the 4th September Papandreou presented a memorandum making the same demand: as, irrespective of the outcome, it would anyway lead to a conflict either with the royalists or the communists (here Papandreou equated the republicans with the latter), it would be preferable that the communists should suffer.[53]

In London, even before Bevin's statement, a decision had been taken to hold the elections first. But, as Damaskinos had asked that nothing should be pre-judged in advance of his visit, Bevin had—on the recommendation of the Southern Department—refrained from mentioning this in the House of Commons.[54] Instead the Americans were informed and were recommended to take the same line. The State Department let the Foreign Office know that, in principle, they were in agreement but wanted to be told the exact date of the elections.[55]

Therefore, on the 1st September, Secretary of State Byrnes telegraphed to MacVeagh, asking him to discuss confidentially with Damaskinos a Greek initiative for the priority of the elections; the State Department had for a long time been of the opinion that this was the only way to stabilise the Greek situation; there was understanding in principle for the British procedure but for reasons of 'good housekeeping' details of the time

THE SECOND VOULGARIS GOVERNMENT

schedule were needed; a long interval between elections and plebiscite was, however, rejected since this would mean either a protracted stay for the American supervisors or the sending of a second contingent which had not been planned for; MacVeagh should get into contact with Damaskinos about this.[56]

MacVeagh informed Damaskinos of the State Department's attitude and, on 4th September, Damaskinos received the British and US ambassadors. He gave them a brief summary of his talks with the party leaders and explained that in London he would present a memorandum with the following content: the plebiscite should be postponed to a fairly distant date, on the other hand the elections should be held as soon as possible; this could not be before the end of December 1945 or the beginning of January 1946; they should be held on the majority system so as to achieve clear majorities; they would not be for a constituent assembly nor for a simple parliament but for a 'revisionary assembly'. Elections for a constituent assembly would resemble a pre-empting of the plebiscite and a simple parliament's powers would be too restricted. A 'revisionary assembly' would have the following advantages: there could be more deputies which would ensure that all leading personalities were represented in it; it could undertake certain constitutional changes, though not in matters of principle such as the form of the state.

The plebiscite should be postponed for a long time: an interval of three to five months was useless; an interval of three to five years had been suggested to him. He stressed most emphatically that this was the key issue of the whole programme; if the elections were only to be a curtain-raiser to the plebiscite, then the order in which they were held was immaterial (this MacVeagh evidently did not report to Washington). If his programme were accepted, it was of central importance that it should be supported by a public declaration from the British and US governments. This declaration should state clearly that, after hearing the Regent, and wishing to give Greece internal tranquillity, both governments recommended the Greek people to accept this programme. Such a procedure would not give offence in Greece, as it would have the form of a recommendation and not of a *diktat.* It would also strengthen his own position for the remainder of his term of office and save him from the charge of having chosen this solution for personal and party-political reasons. The bourgeois parties would accept this programme, if both the ambassadors supported it. He himself intended to resign at the earliest opportunity and the Regency could then be exercised by a Regency Council.

As regards the American reservations, it would be helpful if the election observers arrived at the beginning of December. The presence of the observers was less important than the cooperation of the parties. Should this not be guaranteed, the result would be many individual abstentions—

even if not an organised election boycott—which would make the election results appear dubious in the eyes of the people. If his suggestions were for any reason rejected, he could see no sense in any further effort either by the US and British governments or by himself to solve the present problems. In this case one should let matters take their course. Caccia reported Damaskinos' peroration as follows:

'The affliction that had cursed Greece for 30 years would not be cured and there would be no hope of stability. We should be under no illusion on this point. If the constitutional issue were not postponed for a considerable period unrest and disorder were certain.. He had had innumerable suggestions put before him and had wrestled with this problem day after day before deciding what he must propose for the good of his country to the British and United States Governments. He saw no other possible way out.'

Both MacVeagh and Caccia urgently recommended their governments to accept Damaskinos' proposals.[57]

The Foreign Office had already decided that the elections should be held first. But on the question of the interval between elections and plebiscite no decision had yet been reached. Caccia's telegram of the 30th August gave rise to further discussions. Laskey did not doubt that postponement of the plebiscite for a long time would be the best solution, but the final decision must come from the Greeks themselves and in view of royalist opposition, it would be very difficult to achieve this; he hoped that the solution could be found during Damaskinos' visit to London; one solution would be to leave the exact date of the plebiscite open until after the elections: If the republicans won, the postponement would present no problem; if the royalists were victorious, it would be difficult to prevent an early plebiscite. Hayter agreed with this view and Sargent feared the plebiscite would not come about except in the form of a *coup d'état*.[58] Damaskinos' proposals of 4th September were discussed on the 6th in a specially summoned session, by Laskey, Sir Orme Sargent, Leeper and Hayter.

Leeper explained that he fully supported Damaskinos' line: if one adhered to the procedure provided for in the Varkiza Agreement, the monarchy would certainly be restored but renewed unrest—if not even civil war—would be the inevitable consequence; if one decided for postponement of the plebiscite, this postponement must be a considerable one—six months was not enough. The Greek parties must be brought to regard the constitutional question as for the time being an open one; only thus could that question be removed from the electoral arena; therefore it would be necessary for all the Greek parties to come to a relevant agreement which would have British and US government support; it was of course possible that the two extremist parties, the Populists and the Communists, would try to hinder this, but the risk must be taken.

Such a course would mean a breach of the agreement reached with George II in December 1944; in this event the Greek king would refuse his consent and cancel the Regency, which would put Damaskinos in a difficult position; perhaps Damaskinos might have to try to persuade George II. Moreover, the latter could order his supporters to boycott the elections. In any case, after the withdrawal of the British troops, the extreme royalists would try to carry out the plebiscite with army assistance; for that reason the army must be de-politicised before the elections. If Damaskinos' proposals were to be accepted, the date of the plebiscite must not be left open; a decision must be taken now that the plebiscite would be held on a definite date in three or five years' time. If this programme was clearly formulated and supported by the British and US governments, then it was unlikely that the royalists would achieve a majority; but, if they won, there would be difficulties. This question must be discussed with the Regent.[59] Since no common line could be agreed on, the session was adjourned.

On the next day (6th September) Damaskinos arrived accompanied by Caccia who was leaving Athens to take up a post in the Foreign Office. Next day he visited Bevin. Not only the Greek ambassador in London, Agnidis, but Leeper and Philip Noel-Baker, the Minister of State, were present at the conversation. Damaskinos made basically the same points as he had made on the 4th in his talks with Caccia and MacVeagh. The only difference was in regard to the interval between elections and plebiscite: he suggested no precise date but explained that, if the British and US governments would recommend that the elections be held first and that the plebiscite be indefinitely postponed, this would be accepted by the Greek parties. To this Bevin replied that for both the British government and the Americans intervention was problematic since the Varkiza Agreement was a purely inter-Greek accord. He thought it better for the Greeks to take the initaitive and then to ask the two Allies to back this decision. Damaskinos pointed out that this would be very difficult since the Populists would come out in favour of implementing Varkiza. Without a pressing recommendation from the British and the Americans it was unlikely that they would change their attitude. Bevin went on to speak of George II. Damaskinos pointed out that the king's consent must be obtained to the proposed postponement of the plebiscite and hinted that Bevin should undertake this. If the king's consent were obtained, the situation would evolve smoothly; otherwise there was danger of serious unrest; if it came to a clash with the king, he (Damaskinos) would lose his position of neutrality. Finally, it was agreed that the Regent should submit his wishes to the Foreign Office in writing.[60]

On the same day Sir Orme Sargent officially informed the US ambassador in London, Winant, of what was intended for Damaskinos' London visit: the Regent was in London for talks with the British government; as the Foreign Ministers' Council was in session at about the same time, he hoped that Secretary of State Byrnes would find an opportunity to talk with Damaskinos, though in general his visit should be regarded as completely independent of the Council session. The Greek government was now in favour of a postponement of the plebiscite but was very uncertain of the length of interval; he himself was of the opinion that the interval should not be too long, as this would involve difficulties with the Greek king. In any case, a meeting between Damaskinos and George II was both desirable and necessary.[61]

A conversation between Hayter and US diplomats on 11th September demonstrated that the British were still undecided about the length of interval and had reached no conclusion: they wanted the State Department's opinion.[62] The 13th was, for Greece, the most portentous day of Damaskinos' visit to London. In the morning he met US Secretary of State Byrnes at the American Embassy. We have no record of what was said, so we can only report the result. Byrnes accepted Damaskinos' suggestion to postpone the plebiscite but the proposed three years' interval seemed to him too long; in his opinion a year was enough.[63] In the evening of the same day there was a conversation between Damaskinos and George II who had returned to London from Scotland for this purpose.

George II demanded that, in regard to elections and plebiscite, the sequence provided for in the Varkiza Agreement should be maintained. Varkiza had put an end to a civil war; any violation of Varkiza would lead to a new civil war; Greeks must settle their constitutional problem promptly and no longer lay themselves open to foreign intervention. Damaskinos objected that, if the plebiscite were to be held under present conditions, the republicans would boycott it; he regarded postponement of the plebiscite as essential; Bevin was of the same opinion and had assured him that, in his next statement on British policy towards Greece, he would make this quite clear. George II held to his viewpoint that the whole matter should be solved without foreign intervention; Damaskinos' view was erroneous; he could assure him that, if the elections were held first, the Right would boycott them. Although the conversation lasted till late in the evening, there was no *rapprochement*.[64]

On the same day, the lack of any clear concept of a British policy for Greece prompted Minister of State Philip Noel-Baker to submit to the Foreign Office a ten-point programme entitled 'A New Start for Greece': if these ten points were simultaneously applied in Greece, there could be hope for a really fresh start. Noel-Baker's points were as follows:

'1. The announcement that fair elections for a 'revisionary parliament' would be held soon, while the plebiscite on the monarchy would follow when conditions of tranquillity have been restored. . .

2. Strengthening of the Voulgaris government. There are young and able men, anti-communists but known in the Resistance movement,

who could be brought into the government.
3. Emptying of the prisons. All innocent of crimes should be released in batches as soon as possible. Every day they are kept in makes them and their families and friends more angry and makes it more certain that they and large sections of the public will abstain from elections.
4. Return of the Varvaressos policy, i.e. taxation of the rich, increase of wages, control of prices. Unless this is done, inflation will be very difficult to avoid.' He personally believed that the markets were 'rigged' to turn Varvaressos out of office, and that it might be right to bring him back.
5. Strengthening the UNRRA administration in Greece...
6. Return of Mr Caccia to Athens...
7. Strengthening of transport...
8. Release of additional coasters for the Greek government...
9. Borrowing 4,000 tons of olive oil from the Italian government.
10. 'The return of Cyprus to Greece. There is no doubt that the population of Cyprus ardently desire to rejoin Greece, and that feeling is beginning to run high.'

To suit Bevin, Noel-Baker added the following justification:

'I believe the adoption of this policy would (i) kill Communist hopes of obtaining power by civil war; (ii) render possible a fair election, in which all parties would take part, within a period of months; (iii) give such impetus to democratic movements in Greece that a stable Government would result from this election, so that the British troops could come away; (iv) bring H.M.G. great success in the House of Commons, and the Labour Party outside; (v) greatly strengthen your hands in your efforts to check Russian imperialist plans in the border countries; and (vi) greatly raise the prestige of H.M.G. in the United States...'

All ten measures would sooner or later have to be taken but, if they were taken singly one after another, they would prove ineffective. The Regent's visit must be seen against the background of the dangerous situation in Greece.

'An inflation has begun which may get out of control and which, if it did, would lead to unforeseeable results. The large number of innocent prisoners in the prisons, and their families and friends outside, are a festering centre of discontent. The excesses of the Royalists under the name of the National Guard have convinced many anti-Communist Democrats that the present Government is incapable and not impartial. The Communist extremists want civil war; the Royalist extremists could welcome it hardly less. An economic collapse might well lead to further fighting in which it would be very difficult for the British troops not to be involved.'

He added that the Regent's visit would be either a great success or a serious defeat for the Regent himself and for the British government and hoped that his proposals could contribute to a successful conclusion.[65]

Noel-Baker's document received a mixed reception in the Foreign Office. The points which agreed with the Foreign Office line were accepted; others—for example his suggestions about Resistance representatives and Cyprus—were rejected.[66] Had they been accepted, Noel-Baker's suggestions would certainly have brought about a partial improvement in Greece but they would not have meant a completely fresh start. This would have demanded a fundamental change in British policy towards the Greek Left. The crucial weakness in Noel-Baker's concept was that of the Foreign Office too: that neither was prepared to adopt Damaskinos' proposal for a three year interval between elections and plebiscite. This became clear at the second meeting between Bevin and Damaskinos on 17th September.

Damaskinos informed Bevin about his talk with George II and asked him to take up a clear position. Bevin showed him the text of a draft statement to be issued by the three Western Allied governments. The decisive passage read as follows:

'The Regent informed the three Governments that after taking into consideration the views of all parties in Greece, he has reached the conclusion that it is desirable to hold the elections for a revisionary assembly as soon as possible. It is hoped that it will be possible to arrange the elections before the end of the year.

'As a result of these elections the Regent considers that it should be possible to form a Government which would be based on popular and parliamentary support. The formation of such a Government would facilitate the restoration of conditions of normal tranquillity in Greece. Only when these conditions are firmly established will it become possible to hold a free and genuine plebiscite to decide on the future form of Government for Greece. The three Governments are in full agreement with the programme outlined by the Regent. . .'

Damaskinos objected that it emerged from this statement that the initiative for postponement of the plebiscite came from him. This would make his position untenable. The statement must be so formulated that the initiative appeared to come from the Western Allies. Moreover, he considered the question of the interval very important: only a longer interval between elections and plebiscite could prevent the elections being loaded with the constitutional question.

Bevin told Damaskinos that he had discussed this question with Byrnes who had refused to include the two or three year interval in the statement. He therefore could not agree to the mention of a particular time limit; but one could find a formula which would give the impression that the interval would be of considerable duration. Damaskinos agreed and Bevin promised to put this point to Byrnes and the French Foreign Minister, Bidault. Meanwhile the Regent should work out with Leeper a version of the statement which would meet his wishes.[67]

The altered version read as follows:

'The three Governments hold the firm opinion that elections for a revisionary assembly should be held as soon as possible. They hope that it will be possible to arrange elections before the end of the year. Thus a Government would be formed which would be based on the wishes of people and parliament. The formation of such a Government would facilitate the restoration of conditions of stable tranquillity in Greece. Only when these conditions are in due course firmly established will it become possible to hold a free and genuine plebiscite to decide on the future regime in Greece. The three Governments in full agreement hope and recommend that all parties in Greece with the interests of their country before them will collaborate sincerely and willingly in the execution of this programme which in their judgement represents the best hope of orderly and democratic development.'[68]

In a conversation with Bevin on 18th September, Byrnes agreed to this formulation and, on the evening of the same day, Damaskinos informed George II who 'under massive pressure' eventually found himself able to agree that the elections should have priority.[69] The Foreign Office was satisfied and, on the morning of the 19th, the above statement was simultaneously issued in London, Paris and Washington. On the same day Damaskinos travelled to Paris where he was received by De Gaulle and on the 22nd he was back in Athens. On the same day, in London, George II addressed three identical messages to Bevin, Byrnes and Bidault. He protested at the way the statement had been produced: the postponement of the plebiscite violated the Royal Act of 29th December 1944 and the Varkiza Agreement, both of which had been drafted in accordance with British advice; but he did not want to obstruct Allied policy in any way.[70]

Bevin replied that he had taken note of the king's views and was glad that he did not want to cause difficulties; he himself regarded the policy recommended in the statement as the most suitable for Greece.[71] At the same time he got in touch with Byrnes and Bidault who, at the beginning of October, answered George II in the same vein.[72]

Leeper had already returned to Athens on the 20th September. His first impressions after his three months' absence were that the situation had deteriorated.[73] In particular, the country's economic situation was extremely critical. So, before we continue our chronological account, we must pause for a short retrospective description of Greece's economic development up to this date.

NOTES

1. Leeper to Foreign Office 1st March, 1945 (R 7954/4/19).
2. Leeper to Foreign Office 28th May, 1945 (R 9518/4/19).

3. Caccia to Foreign Office 22nd June, 1945 (R 10682/4/19).
4. Caccia to Foreign Office 25th June, 1945 (R 11161/4/19).
5. Caccia to Foreign Office 2nd July, 1945 (R 11552/4/19). The Liberals, the other republicans and the Left demanded proportional representation. The Populists advocated a majority system.
6. Caccia to Foreign Office 9th July, 1945 (R 11825/4/19).
7. *Cf.* p. 162, footnote 134.
8. Caccia to Foreign Office 23rd July, 1945 (R 12730/4/19); *Rizospastis,* 20th July, 1945.
9. *Ibid.*
10. John A. Sofianopoulos, 'Greece needs an all-party Government to end terrorism', *News Chronicle,* 28th July, 1945.
11. *Ibid.*
12. Caccia to Foreign Office 23rd July, 1945 (R 12416/4/19).
13. *Ibid.*
14. Caccia to Foreign Office 24th July, 1945 (R 12416/4/19).
15. Sir Orme Sargent to Caccia 26th July, 1945 (R 12416/4/19).
16. Patatzis, *op. cit.,* pp. 222-8; Caccia to Foreign Office 30th July, 1945 (R 13134/4/19); Caccia to Foreign Office 28th July, 1945 (R 12732/4/19).
17. Caccia to Foreign Office 24th July, 1945 (R 12458/4/19).
18. Caccia to Foreign Office 30th July, 1945 (R 13134/4/19).
19. Caccia to Foreign Office 27th July, 1945 (R 12679/4/19).
20. Caccia to Foreign Office 30th July, 1945 (R 13134/4/19). Plastiras' comments were published on the 29th July.
21. Caccia to Foreign Office 2nd August, 1945 (R 13087/4/19).
22. Resumé of the Decisions of the Political Bureau of the KKE Central Committee dated 1st August, 1945 (R 13812/4/19); *Rizospastis,* 2nd August, 1945.
23. Caccia to Foreign Office 31st July, 1945 (R 12875/4/19).
24. Caccia to Foreign Office 3rd August, 1945 (R 13256/4/19). Such a government would have meant a majority for the Liberals. In 1936 the Liberals had 133 seats, the Populists 112 and the Popular Front 15. The remaining 40 seats were divided amongst parties most of which no longer existed in 1945.
25. Caccia to Foreign Office 10th August, 1945 (R 13508/4/19).
26. Caccia to Foreign Office 3rd August, 1945, no. 1635 (R 13105/4/19).
27. Caccia to Foreign Office 3rd August, 1945, no. 1637 (R 13105/4/19).
28. Resumé of the Conversations which the Regent held with the Party Leaders, Caccia to Foreign Office 10th August, 1945 (R 13496/4/19).
29. On this topic see: E.C.W. Myers, *Greek Entanglement,* (London: Rupert Hart-Davis, 1955), pp. 218-227; Sarafis, *op. cit.,* pp. 160-7.
30. Caccia to Foreign Office 6th August, 1945 (R 13166/4/19).
31. Foreign Office to Caccia 8th August, 1945 (R 13166/4/19). See also footnote 137 to the preceding chapter.
32. Caccia to Foreign Office 8th August, 1945 (R 13332/4/19).
33. Draft Note [unsigned and undated] for the Secretary of State (R 13143/4/19).
34. Note by Sir Reginald Leeper on the present situation in Greece (R 13082/4/19).
35. Memorandum by the Secretary of State for Foreign Affairs, C.P. (45) 107 of 11th August, 1945 (R 13846/4/19). In a document of 14th August, 1945 (R 13689/4/19) which served as a basis for Foreign Office discussion, Bevin was even clearer: he himself was in favour of holding the elections first; but he realised that this did not coincide with the Varkiza Agreement and he attached importance to the implementing of agreements; perhaps some consensus could be found with the Greek government. Whatever the decision might be, the elections must be held as soon as possible; only thus would it be possible to

exert pressure for free elections in the other Balkan countries.
36. Foreign Office to Caccia 16th August, 1945 (R 13846/4/19). The same telegram was sent to the British ambassador in Washington with the following addition regarding British Middle East policy: 'You have discretion to omit [it] or water [it] down.' Foreign Office to Washington 16th August, 1945 (R 13846/4/19).
37. Petros Voulgaris: Prime Minister, Navy and Air Force Minister, and temporarily Army, Foreign and Interior Minister.
Petros Gounarakis: Minister for the Interior from 30th August.
Ioannis Politis: Foreign Minister from 18th August.
Alexandros Merenditis: Army Minister from 22nd August.
Kyriakos Varvaressos: Vice-premier, Minister for Supply.
Vasilios Kyriakopoulos: Minister for Justice from 18th August.
Georgios Mantzavinos: Finance Minister.
G.N. Oikonomou: Minister for Education.
Grigorios Kasimatis: Minister for Social Welfare.
Ioannis Paraskevopoulos: Economics Minister.
Andreas Zakkas: Minister for Labour.
Petros Koutsomitopoulos: Minister for Agriculture.
Anargyros Dimitrakopoulos: Minister for Public Works.
Vasilios Voilas: Minister for Health.
Spyridon Matesis: Minister for Merchant Marine.
G. Lambrinopoulos: Minister for Communications.
Dimitrios Machas: Minister for Transport from 18th August.
Vasilios Dendramanis: Minister for Information from 18th August.
Provatas, *op. cit.*, pp. 580 ff.
38. Caccia to Foreign Office 13th August, 1945 (R 13641/4/19). In this conversation Damaskinos expressed interesting views: there was only one political issue which united almost all Greeks and that was their horror of the Metaxas dictatorship, for which the king—and that was a fact—was personally responsible. There was a basic difference between republicans and royalists: the former believed in what they represented and so hated the king that no co-operation was possible; the latter included few real monarchists and even fewer who wanted the return of the present king; for the majority of royalists this was a tactical question and a reaction to the EAM rebellion. Were the king to return on the basis of an anticommunist campaign, that would create difficulties with the republicans and would eventually lead to rebellion. Their opposition to the king would bring the republicans once more into the same camp with the communists which would benefit only the latter. The result would be some sort of royal dictatorship. To prevent this, there was need for a very subtle joint policy and he therefore suggested that a British Cabinet member come to Athens. It was easier to solve problems by direct contact, as they arose.
Caccia saw Damaskinos' analysis as generally correct and concluded that British policy was therefore faced with the following alternatives: either one remained neutral, in which case it would come to a Restoration because the floating vote both feared the Communists and also thought that Great Britain wanted a Restoration; or British policy could express itself clearly in favour of the republicans or at least take care that the elections were held before the plebiscite. The intervening period would enable the Greek voters to convince themselves of the existence or non-existence of a communist peril: the longer the interval, the less would memories of the rebellion influence the outcome. Instead of a British Cabinet member coming to Athens, Damaskinos could be invited to London. Harold Caccia to Sir Orme Sargent 14th August, 1945, received in London 21st August (R 14008/4/19).

39. Caccia to Foreign Office 17th August, 1945 (R 13852/4/19).
40. For Bevin's justification of Churchill's intervention in Greece see especially Alan Louis Charles Bullock, *The Life and Times of Ernest Bevin, Vol. II, Minister of Labour 1940-1945*, (London: Heinemann, 1967), pp. 340-7.
41. *Hansard*, 413, cols. 289 ff.
42. *Ibid.*, cols. 290 ff.
43. *New York Times*, 12th August, 1945.
44. *Hansard* 413, cols. 87 ff.
45. *Ibid.*, col. 220.
46. *Ibid.*, cols. 305-11.
47. *Ibid.*, cols. 312-4.
48. *Ibid.*, col. 338.
49. *Ibid.*, cols. 588-90.
50. *The Times*, 22nd August, 1945.
51. Caccia to Foreign Office 30th August, 1945, no. 1783 (R 14618/4/19).
52. Caccia to Foreign Office 30th August, 1945, no. 1784 (R 14618/4/19).
53. Statement of his views, submitted by M. Papandreou to His Beatitude the Regent 4th September, 1945 (R 15996/4/19).
54. 'The Secretary of State had proposed to say in his speech that H.M. Government would favour holding the elections before the plebiscite. The Department advised against this. . .' Laskey's Minutes 8th September, 1945 (R 13649/4/19). And 'we have already decided that the elections in Greece should precede the plebiscite'. Laskey's Minutes 2nd September, 1945 (R 14618/4/19).
55. *FRUS 1945, VIII*, p. 149.
56. Byrnes to MacVeagh 1st September, 1945 (*Ibid.*, pp. 150 ff).
57. Caccia to Foreign Office 5th September, 1945 (R 15066/4/19); MacVeagh to Byrnes 5th September, 1945 (*FRUS 1945, VIII*, pp. 152-4).
58. Laskey's Minutes 2nd September, 1945; Hayter's and Sargent's Minutes 3rd September, 1945 (R 14618/4/19).
59. Laskey's Minutes 6th September, 1945 (R 15279/4/19).
60. Bevin to Caccia 7th September, 1945 (R 15382/4/19).
61. Winant to Byrnes 7th September, 1945 (*FRUS 1945, VIII*, pp. 154 ff).
62. *Ibid.*, p. 155.
63. Memorandum by the Secretary of State 13th September, 1945 (*ibid.*, p. 157).
64. Substance of the conversation between the King of Greece and the Regent (R 16291/4/19). Leeper did not believe that the Right would boycott the elections and, if they did, this would not be important. The meeting itself was described as 'stormy'. *FRUS 1945, VIII*, pp. 207-10.
65. A New Start in Greece, Memorandum from Philip Noel-Baker to Bevin 13th September, 1945 (R 16249/4/19).
66. Sargent's Minutes 14th September, 1945 (R 16249/4/19).
67. Bevin to Caccia 17th September, 1945 (R 15991/4/19).
68. Statement by the United Kingdom, United States and French Governments (*FRUS 1945, VIII*, p. 158).
69. Winant to State Department 19th September, 1945 (*ibid.*, p. 159).
70. The King of the Hellenes to Mr. Bevin 22nd September, 1945 (R 16589/4/19); the King of the Hellenes to the Secretary of State 22nd September, 1945 (*FRUS 1945, VIII*, pp. 160 ff).
71. Mr. Bevin to the King of the Hellenes 29th September, 1945 (R 16589/4/19).
72. *FRUS 1945, VIII*, pp. 165-7.
73. Leeper, *op. cit.*, p. 180.

GREECE'S ECONOMIC DEVELOPMENT MARCH–SEPTEMBER 1945

The basic problem of Greek reconstruction was the prevailing apathy and the waiting for help from abroad.[1] This passivity was in no way another result of the German Occupation—quite the contrary. The German Occupation had set free hidden resources in the Greek people which found expression not only in armed resistance to the invaders, but also in the creation of a new form of state from the grassroots. During the Occupation, the infrastructure of such a state took shape in free mountain Greece. EAM established schools and hospitals, repaired roads, created a communications network and even opened factories.[2] These activities did not come to an end with liberation but were spontaneously extended to the regions previously under German control. Reconstruction began from the base upwards, without state instructions, under the organising leadership of EAM. British intervention and the subsequent White Terror put an end to all this. In October 1945 the American journalist, Constantine Poulos, reported from Athens as follows.

'The workers and peasants, the class which made up the bulk of Greek emigration to the United States in the early part of the century, wanted to stay in Greece last year. "We will make Greece a good place to live in", they said. This year it is different. The men and women who a year ago were turning coffee houses into schools and community centers are now holed up in their homes. The young men who a year ago were voluntarily repairing roads and rebuilding bridges now stand sullenly on street corners. Today one hears peasants and workers saying, "We must get away. Anywhere. There is no hope in this cursed land. This is not life. It is a terrible thing to say, but we hate our country. They have made us hate it".'[3]

British intervention destroyed the only capital that war-devastated Greece still possessed—the enthusiasm of millions who were ready to take into their own hands the rebuilding of their own lives and the life of the nation. But for this intervention, and with a fraction of the sums spent in vain between the end of the December events and the outbreak of civil war and still more during the civil war, the encouragement of these initiatives from the grassroots could have sown the seeds for Greece to blossom. Naturally, a necessary premise would have been readiness on the part of the British to accept a post-war republic, democratic and socially just, as well as the disappearance of the former political and economic oligarchy. Since this premise did not exist and, instead, the pre-war regime was restored by force of arms, the people's dynamic enthusiasm for reconstruction withered, first into frustrated apathy and then into hatred. The restoration of the old oligarchies benefited only themselves but brought no peace to the country since no reconstruction programme could succeed without popular cooperation.

Finance Minister Varvaressos' analysis of February 1945[4] is therefore subjectively correct but it ignores the decisive factor, the readiness of the people to cooperate in his programme. In examining Greek economic development since 1945 one must not lose sight of this factor.

What characterises economic development up to June 1945 is the virtual non-existence of an economic policy. Up to the beginning of March 1945 economic responsibility rested almost exclusively with Military Liaison (ML). At this point an agreement was reached between ML, UNRRA and the Greek government which provided for the Greek government to take over the distribution of relief supplies from the 15th March and that UNRRA would take over the tasks of ML from the 1st April. This meant that, for a fortnight, from the unloading of the ships until these relief supplies were distributed to the consumers, they were at the unrestricted, uncontrolled disposition of the Greek government which was answerable to no one—a procedure which at this time already seemed dubious to MacVeagh.[5] From another angle he was likewise dubious: he had realised that ML had become an instrument of British policy.

American participation in ML had been most reserved and had amounted only to the detailing of a few financial and economic advisers from the US Embassy in Athens to serve on the ML Advisory Committee. This was on the basis that ML was an Anglo-American organisation, more or less restricted to advising Scobie, which therefore only intervened very indirectly in the Greek government's affairs. Actual developments had however shown that the Advisory Committee was virtually an intervention and control agency. Therefore MacVeagh rejected Leeper's suggestion that, from 1st April, the Americans should participate in a new committee to advise the Greek government, then about to be formed.[6] The State Department agreed with him in this.[7] UNRRA was not to become an Anglo-American political agency, but was to retain its international and neutral character.

Meanwhile, from the beginning of March, the EAM leadership's protests against the violations of Varkiza had been arriving in Washington. Amongst other things, EAM's protests had demanded the sending of an inter-allied commission to investigate the situation in Greece.[8] EAM's complaints and MacVeagh's reports on British intervention policy prompted President Roosevelt to take an amazing initiative. On 21st March 1945 he telegraphed to Churchill.

'What would you think of sending a special mission for developing productive power of Greece rapidly by concerted, nonpolitical action? Such a mission could consist of people like Lyttleton [Oliver Lyttleton was British Production Minister], Mikoyan [the People's Commissar for Foreign Trade of the USSR], and Donald Nelson [Chairman of the US War Production Board] . . . It would not take them long and might have a highly constructive effect on world opinion at this time. I take it that they could meet in Greece in about a month's time. I am not taking it up with the Soviet Government until I get your slant.'[9]

Churchill instructed the Foreign Office to draft a reply. On 22nd March Hayter, Sargent and Howard discussed Roosevelt's suggestion: it was clear that this was purely political; the President had taken initiatives in regard to the Russian-controlled sphere in Romania and thought that—to balance this—he should now take action in the British sphere of influence ('in our Greek parish'). At the same time the suggestion must be regarded as an indirect reply to EAM's proposal; it was important that the answer should not be too encouraging. US assistance was needed for Greek reconstruction and the more the Americans could be involved, the better (here Eden noted in the margin 'I agree'); but Russian participation in reconstruction aid was not needed, especially as they had nothing to contribute. Their participation would therefore be a political gesture. Moreover, the whole idea could only be realised if one could rely on the Russian commission member behaving correctly, which was more than doubtful. At the present moment, when the Russians were excluding the Western Allies from any voice in Romanian affairs, it would be somewhat humiliating to ask them to intervene in Greek matters. Therefore the US suggestion should be welcomed, but Russian participation should be rejected; and at the same time the US should be informed of the new British organisational measures in Greece and be invited to take part in these.[10]

Eden supported this analysis and informed Churchill to this effect but at the same time suggested that, if a US mission were to go to Greece, it would be best if this happened after the re-organisation of British agencies there.[11] On 3rd April he submitted the final draft of the reply to President Roosevelt to Churchill who approved it in the following terms:

'I agree. But—We have had to take all the risk, do all the work, shed all the blood and bear all the abuse, including American abuse. Poor old England.'[12]

The reply to Roosevelt contained the essence of what has been described above but at the same time the US was again invited to participate in the new British policy towards Greece: so far the Greek government had been advised by Scobie and his staff; from 1st April this function would devolve on the British Embassy. It was hoped that the US would be prepared to continue the previous cooperation in Athens in the form of a new committee of experts from both embassies. The Greek government had indeed not yet asked this committee for its advice but it would nevertheless exercise considerable influence on the economic and financial policy of the Greek government. This committee should start its work before any commission was sent to Greece. Only when this committee was working efficiently and ML had been replaced by UNRRA would the sending of a commission have any point. By that time the Romanian problems would have been settled too and the Russians could be invited.[13]

Washington accepted Churchill's arguments against Russian participation but, on the other hand, regarded the setting-up of a bilateral mission as mistaken since it would contravene the Yalta Declaration. On 8th April Roosevelt informed Churchill that he absolutely rejected the official participation of American experts in the planned committee, but that the US Embassy in Athens would be prepared to give unofficial help in particular instances. Greece had, in the meantime, applied unofficially to the US for economic assistance and the US had suggested that they send an economic delegation to Washington for negotiations. Finally, Roosevelt suggested that they abstain for the present from sending an official mission and that Donald Nelson be sent to Greece instead. Nelson would then inform him of the needs and possibilities.[14]

Churchill was clearly irritated by Roosevelt's snub.

'I think it is rather hard that the Americans should come in and take the credit as they no doubt will do. However I do not wish to stand in the way of any economic help that can come to Greece. Therefore I would look towards the least formal and least impressive of the Missions or organisms the President now wishes to set up.'[15]

Eden, too, reacted with some bitterness when, on 11th April, he drafted the answer to Roosevelt. But he too saw no alternative: Roosevelt's suggestion must be accepted.[16] Then, on the 12th April, came the total surprise of Roosevelt's death. When, on the 15th, Eden submitted the revised version of the reply to Churchill, the latter reacted characteristically, instructing Cadogan. 'Let it lie till we have a chaser from the new President. It may well be forgotten for a fortnight.'[17] The future was to show that Roosevelt's suggestion would be forgotten—not for a fortnight, but for ever.

As the Foreign Office had rightly recognised, President Roosevelt's original suggestion was first and foremost a political one. It was an effort to break through the system of 'spheres of influence' established by Churchill and Stalin at the Moscow Conference (percentage agreement) in October 1944.[18] The despatch of an inter-allied commission would not have greatly changed the economic situation, but the mere fact of its existence and its presence in Greece would have made it harder for the British authorities to ignore the violations of Varkiza and would have forced them to restrain the Greek Right more effectively, with the result that there might have been no White Terror and that therefore post-war Greek history might in all probability have evolved differently. The death of President Roosevelt was a catastrophe for Greece.

The decision for UNRRA to replace ML on 1st May (postponed from 1st April) proved problematic in another way as well. MacVeagh adhered to the State Department's instructions of March 1944 that UNRRA was to be regarded as an international organisation, completely independent of US embassies: in no way must the impression be created that the US was trying to dominate UNRRA itself, its personnel or its policy.[19] In accordance with this, he had—as we have described—rejected Leeper's invitation to participate in the new advisory body and had likewise rebuffed a similar suggestion from the American UNRRA representative, Maben. He refused to give official instructions to UNRRA: the US Embassy was, however, prepared to give unofficial assistance.[20] The British Embassy had no such scruples: at the start of 1945 Leeper had told the first UNRRA Mission chief, Laird Archer, that in Greece UNRRA should be an Anglo-American operation in which Russian participation was not desired.[21] In June 1945 MacVeagh had to state flatly that the British saw UNRRA as some sort of continuation of ML rather than as a joint United Nations operation. Thus, in Greece there were fundamental differences of opinion between the British and the Americans over UNRRA. For the British it was an agency of their 'spheres of influence' policy and in fact it was under their total control.[22] The reason for this was partly that the American UNRRA personnel was incompetent[23] and lacked the resolution to resist British pressure[24] and also that the few British UNRRA staff who wanted to act impartially did not dare to oppose direct intervention by high-level British authorities.[25]

In this evolution the decisive role was played by the Joint Policy Committee which in mid-April replaced the Joint Co-ordinating Committee of the ML period. This was nominally under the chairmanship of the Greek Finance Minister. The Greek government had nine representatives (including six ministers), UNRRA four representatives and the British likewise four (including Caccia and Hill). At the first session of this committee it was decided that the Greek government should officially invite British and American advisers to the sessions. This the Greek government did and, though MacVeagh rejected participation by American experts, for public consumption the fiction was maintained that the committee was a tri-lateral one and the British neglected no opportunity to reinforce this impression.[26] In fact, the Joint Policy Committee was the realisation of Macmillan's suggestion—made at the conference on 15th February 1945—for a committee to control the Greek government's economic and financial policy.[27] It was the instrument by which 'High Commissioner' Leeper directed Greek government policy. The fact that this committee was also responsible for all UNRRA affairs only increased its importance.[28]

MacVeagh described the committee as follows:

'Actually the Committee is Anglo-Greek despite attempts to make it look otherwise. The same office building in Athens houses British Military Headquarters, the administrative offices of UNRRA and the four British advisers who serve on the Joint Policy Committee. The latter officials are attached both to the British Embassy and to the Commander of Land Forces Greece, Lt. General Scobie, but in practice they and their staffs have had little other work to do and have devoted almost their full time to advising UNRRA and the Greek Government. The meetings of the Joint Policy Committee are, therefore, simply the outward manifestations of a continuous process by which UNRRA and Greek Government activities are directed to a very considerable extent by a group of able British officials.'[29]

Even when, in June, Varvaressos became Finance Minister and the Committee was renamed Economic Advisory Committee and held its sessions at the Bank of Greece, its domination by the British was in no way altered.

However, the British not only controlled both Greek government and UNRRA policy but they also understood how to exercise a continuous subtle influence on the US representative in UNRRA so that he became a spokesman for their line with the State Department. On 5th May, on a visit to Washington, Maben stressed that it would be a serious mistake for the US Embassy in Athens to maintain its refusal to advise UNRRA officially.[30] The way in which he played down the significance of the Joint Policy Committee showed that either he had failed to understand its function or that he did not want to understand. As a result of Maben's pressure for the US Athens Embassy to pursue a less 'standoffish policy', the State Department told MacVeagh that Washington would have no objection to the Embassy advising UNRRA.[31] In his reply, MacVeagh pointed out that he was ready to take part in informal UNRRA discussions but that he absolutely rejected participation in the Joint Policy Committee.[32] On 18th June he again wrote to the State Department that Maben had renewed his demands that the Embassy should participate in this committee, which he had again refused. He added a detailed description of the actual situation of UNRRA, in Europe generally and in Greece particularly.

'That it [UNRRA] is British-controlled at present is undeniable, and the whole conception of what UNRRA is and stands for is accordingly at stake. Should the United States parallel British action with a more aggressive independent policy of its own in supplying official advice and guidance, it would only duplicate grounds for objection by other UNRRA members. . . What would seem possibly necessary at this time, therefore, is the discovery and institution of practical and effective methods for bringing the UNRRA effort. . . on to the broadest possible international basis, to save UNRRA's own credit and make clear beyond any question the disinterestedness in this great project of both Great Britain and the United States.'[33]

The State Department told the Director-General of UNRRA, Herbert H. Lehman, about MacVeagh's report and urged the latter to make use of the opportunity of Lehman's visit to Athens in mid-July to speak to him openly.[34] In the course of this conversation, Lehman—who had previously been of the opinion that the US Embassy should cooperate with the British Embassy in advising UNRRA—changed his mind after hearing from MacVeagh.

'I explained to him at length the superior position enjoyed by the British here in consequence of their political and military tutelage over the country, and emphasized that American advice can. . . be most effectively rendered if given independently of an association inevitably overshadowing [sic] in Greek eyes. I assured him that the Embassy is ready to support UNRRA unofficially but directly with Mr. Varvaressos or other Greek Government officials whenever asked, the amount of such support being entirely in UNRRA's hands.'

MacVeagh and Lehman concluded that up to now the American UNRRA directors in Greece had shown no individual initiative but had always awaited guidance from the US Embassy. A suitably dynamic personality should be found who would be capable of taking an independent line. They eventually agreed on Lt.-Colonel Harold B. Hoskins, who had already carried out similar missions with success, as future UNRRA director in Greece. Negotiations with Hoskins were prolonged and, thus, for the time being all remained as before and the British continued to make use of UNRRA as an agency of their policy in Greece.

A break in the system came only with Bevin's letter of 29th September to Secretary of State Byrnes in which he recognised the bankruptcy of this policy and recommended that UNRRA should take over direct control of the Greek economy.[35] We shall return to the circumstances surrounding his letter, but for the moment we must analyse the background to this policy failure. When MacVeagh learned that the Greek government was to have complete control over the distribution of UNRRA relief supplies, he expressed himself seriously disturbed. He had been right. In the economic —even more than in the political—sphere power remained in the hands of the old oligarchy. This tiny group of industrialists and financiers had made tremendous profits under the Occupation and, after liberation, sought to increase these still further. Here the Bank of Greece played a decisive role. Although the state had 51% ownership of this bank, it was in effect controlled by a few families of the financial oligarchy bound to each other by inter-marriage, and by two British banks who together owned the other 49%. The Governor normally came from one of these families. Since there was no other significant money market, a few people were able to manipulate the Greek economy to their own personal advantage. Furthermore, there was the usual family network connecting the economic oligarchy with the country's political leadership which prevented the government from taking measures which could have reduced the profits of this clique.[36]

A few examples may provide glimpses through the meshes of this network. The most notorious example of the close ties between government and economic oligarchy was the relationship between the tycoon Bodosakis Athanasiadis—known familiarly as Bodosakis—and Prime Minister Voulgaris. Bodosakis was the typical self-made man. He came from a poor Asia Minor family and himself boasted that he had had hardly any schooling. His innate cunning and unscrupulousness made up for this and he knew how to turn everything into money. He laid the foundations for his fortune during the Asia Minor campaign of 1920-22, delivering supplies to both the Greek and the Turkish armies. When the Greeks were expelled from Asia Minor he was able to save his fortune and he began to build up a new economic empire in Piraeus. By the end of the 30s he controlled the Greek munitions industry which brought him tremendous profits during the Spanish Civil War and the Albanian campaign. He also dominated the Greek shipbuilding and alcohol industries and owned the only Greek artificial silk factory. He had business agencies all over the Middle East.

From the late 20s he had been manoeuvring in the backstage corridors of Greek political life, supporting all the political parties and with many politicians on his payroll. Alongside this he had built up an information service which kept him abreast of all the government's intended economic measures long before they were translated into fact. The consequence was that he could plan his business operations more accurately and that, if the intended measures were against his interests, he could prevent their realisation. He had spent the Second World War in the Middle East and had been involved in the troubles in the Greek armed forces-in-exile. After liberation, he supported the republicans, but did not forget the royalists and to insure his rear he even filtered large sums to KKE. His acquaintance with Voulgaris dated from the failed republican rising of 1935 in which the latter had been implicated. As a consequence, Voulgaris had been compulsorily retired and Bodosakis had taken him on as director of one of his factories—an investment which now paid dividends. Voulgaris would initiate no economic measures which could damage the interests of his former benefactor.[37]

Bodosakis' 'colleagues' resembled him like peas in a pod. Whilst in other European countries, *entrepreneurs* were struggling to reopen their firms and get the economy going again, their Greek equivalents had discovered a much more lucrative source of profit: they 'participated in the distribution' of UNRRA relief supplies. Poulos reports a typical instance. 'Determined to profit regardless of what happens to the Greek people, this same group, with the connivance of the government, is using UNRRA supplies to fatten its pocket-books. A plan for the strict control and audit of raw-wool and cotton stocks brought to Greece by UNRRA and turned over to the Greek government, has been blocked by these people, and much of the finished product appears on the black market at exorbitant prices. The big mill-owners are claiming a 20 per cent shrinkage on UNRRA's raw stocks which they are given to process. Six experts who resigned from the Ministry of Supply this month [October], charging graft, favouritism, and misuse of UNRRA's supplies, say that only a 7 per cent shrinkage is possible, and that the remaining 13 per cent is diverted for sale on the black market.'[38]

Up to the end of March 1945, ML had brought 387,000 tons of food supplies into Greece and, between that date and spring 1946, UNRRA brought in another 1,400,000 tons, [that is approximately four hundred pounds yearly for every single person in Greece, more than a pound a day].[39] Despite this, large numbers of people were starving. If one takes into account that these food supplies were mainly distributed in the urban agglomerations—the peasants in the countryside were regarded as self-supporting—then the mere existence of hunger shows the extent of the inefficiency and corruption attending distribution. Thousands of tons of food supplies disappeared on to the black market or were left to rot in government warehouses.

A further factor influencing Greek *entrepreneurs* to keep their businesses closed was the exchange rate problem. We have dealt with the inflation problem at an earlier stage.[40] One of the reasons leading to renewed inflation was the non-convertibility of the *drachma*. The re-valuation of November 1944 had only determined its relation to the old *drachma* and had quite arbitrarily fixed the rate of exchange against the dollar and the pound at its pre-war level which, at the rate of 150 *drachmas* to the dollar, was pure fiction. The consequences were: first, that in early summer 1945 recipients of currency transfers only received about 10% of their value (in May the purchasing power of the dollar was equivalent to 1,000 *drachmas* and deals took place on the basis of 3,000);[41] second—as during the Occupation—the *drachma* began to lose its monetary character. MacVeagh described the attendant circumstances graphically.

'Practically no one deposits it [the drachma] in the bank or otherwise retains possession or title to this currency any longer than is absolutely necessary. It has no value abroad and even in the case of domestic transactions its use is limited principally to day-to-day purchases of necessities. A sale involving the equivalent of $25 or more is almost invariably calculated in gold. It would not be quite fair to liken the present drachma notes to cigar-store coupons or premium stamps, but it would be reasonably accurate to compare them to a token good for purchase at a company store charging high prices.'[42]

The result was a secondary currency: the British gold sovereign. Anyone who could bought sovereigns with his *drachmas* and this raised the price of gold far above the world market-price. Gold smuggling from abroad became a lucrative business in which even Greek diplomats participated. Anyone who could not obtain gold at least hoarded goods. No one made long-term investments and there was not even a start with industrial reconstruction. Lack of goods led to another leap in inflation and it was the 'little people' who suffered from this as they found no employment, could not pay the black market prices and were therefore dependent on free distributions of UNRRA relief. Who can wonder that public employees sought to augment their frozen wages by taking bribes. Yet in the midst of this wretchedness there was luxury. Just as during the starvation winter of 1941-2, anyone who had money could have everything. Opulent meals were served at exorbitant prices in smart Kolonaki restaurants.[43]

The government made the situation worse by obstructing the flow of foreign currency by exchange control which hindered the export-import trade and prohibited the purchase of spare parts from abroad. Thus, for example, the import of hospital equipment and railway stock was delayed. The reason for this was, first and foremost, that the Greek government relied on UNRRA and believed all these things would arrive *gratis* and moreover—under the influence of the business world—they did not want to expend valuable foreign currency on such mundane goods. In addition, they needed the currency for paying delayed interest on British bank loans, some of them dating from the 19th century—an obligation which accounted for a third of the Greek budget.[44]

The solutions suggested by the Governor of the Bank of Greece, Kyriakos Varvaressos, at the end of January 1945,[45] amounted to a state-controlled austerity programme which had the approval of the British and American ML advisers. In February, Varvaressos had further analysed the economic situation and had stated that, in addition to food supplies, Greece's prior need was for raw materials and industrial goods. In mid-March he told the British and US ambassadors that he wanted to visit London and Washington to inform the authorities there about these problems and to coordinate the relief consignments more effectively. He also hinted that for this purpose he wanted to raise a loan from the US Export-Import Bank. At the same time he told the two ambassadors that the Greek Finance Minister and other members of the government were 'delighted' at the prospect of his journey and had suggested that he also join the delegation to the UN foundation conference at San Francisco. Obviously, this meant rejection of his policy of economic austerity and they hoped to keep him out of the country for a considerable period.[46]

Varvaressos' journey had little success. Practically speaking all he achieved was improved coordination of the work of the foreign relief organisations. The US Export-Import Bank refused to give the Greek government a blanket credit: only when trade was functioning again would it be able to finance particular projects.[47] The US government took the same standpoint: private enterprise trade must be revived. Direct US credits for Greece were excluded for the present and credit for specific projects could only be considered if Congress agreed.[48] Both in London and Washington Varvaressos was under pressure to seek an internal Greek solution.

During his absence the economic situation had deteriorated still further and already by mid-April Leeper was urging Voulgaris to recall Varvaressos,[49] since he realised that Finance Minister Mantzavinos was not prepared to take effective measures to fight inflation. In May, after his return to London, the TUC representative, Bert Papworth, publicly exposed the White Terror and criticised the use of relief supplies of flour by pastry-cooks and of cotton for luxury textiles to be sold on the black market, whilst the Greek people had not the wherewithal to clothe themselves.[50] This criticism and the daily deteriorating economic situation prompted the British to bring pressure on Voulgaris, who thereupon made a few statements about his intentions, but in effect nothing happened. Amongst other things, he mentioned that, in the next months, raw materials and machinery to the value of 200 million dollars would be delivered *gratis* by the Allies:[51] a wholly groundless supposition but one which had serious consequences, since why should an industrialist buy raw materials or machinery if he stood to get them free? This is not the way to create a climate favourable to investment.

On the 27th May Varvaressos returned to Athens and, after talks with Voulgaris, on 2nd June he took over as Supply Minister. On the 5th he published his programme. The *drachma* was to be de-valued (500 *drachmas* to the dollar). The Bank of Greece would buy gold sovereigns at the international market price. The losses suffered by small savers due to inflation would be compensated. The budget would be balanced and the rate of exchange stabilised by raising direct taxes and revising the whole taxation system. Wages would be raised from 50% to 83% above present levels. Civil servants' pay would also be raised and paid for by the new revenue. The price of foodstuffs would be reduced and controlled. Clothing would be rationed and the prices lowered. Distribution of UNRRA clothing supplies would be speeded up. The government would control the prices for home produce and the market control system would be reorganised. Agricultural and industrial productivity would be increased and communications would be improved. Profits from trade and industry would be taxed. The government would supervise the distribution of imported raw materials. Finally, anyone who actively obstructed this programme would be punished.[52]

Varvaressos' plan was received with general approbation. The price of the gold sovereign fell from 17,000 *drachmas* at the end of May to 1,500 by the middle of June. Price control began to take effect in Athens. The wage rises were made effective. Moreover Varvaressos made an effort to tax Occupation profits, which had been estimated at two billion *drachmas* and from which only sixty millions had been skimmed by taxation.[53] In mid-June he introduced a new tax from which he hoped to raise two billion *drachmas* a month. He ordained that trade and small crafts should be taxed monthly by a multiple of the rent in proportion to the space they occupied. Similar measures were to be taken for heavy industry, shipping, transport companies and banking, though here the tax was to be on the basis of capital. As few taxpayers had such sums available, Varvaressos hoped in this way to force them to sell their hoarded stock. If the shopkeepers closed down or refused to sell their stock in order to avoid paying tax, they would be imprisoned and the state would take over their shops.[54]

Though these measures were economically justified, they provoked violent opposition which in turn produced a peculiar alliance. Varvaressos' taxation measures hit not only the economic oligarchy but also many small craftsmen and traders. Whilst the former knew how to get themselves out of trouble, the latter were threatened with ruin. When Varvaressos went on to purge the public services of redundant personnel (and naturally Leftists were the first to be sacked), protest strikes broke out and shopkeepers threatened a sales strike.[55] For the moment, Varvaressos was able to keep this opposition in check and until the beginning of August the situation developed relatively smoothly. Revenue was satisfactory. But now there appeared the first signs of a new crisis. The textile manufacturers refused to process UNRRA cotton under government control, certain basic foodstuffs began to be in short supply, and tax revenues fell.[56] In addition there was trouble with the *parakratos* over recruitment to Varvaressos' control service and this forced him to compromises which implied a partial abandonment of his programme.[57] By the middle of August, it came to open conflict.

Further basic foodstuffs had disappeared from the market. Olive oil was available only on the black market at fantastic prices. *The Times* reported on the background as follows:

> 'Those who are mainly responsible for the scarcity of food in Athens today, and who then financed and inspired the Press campaign... were aiming not only at the Government's fall but particularly at preventing the Regent's visit to London... The main weapon used was the lack of olive oil, which has been bought up by big merchants but has been left in the hands of small producers thus making it difficult to seize. The same stratagem is used in regard to food generally. It is evident that the

extreme right-wing, working through the big industrialists, and the extreme left, who control the Trade Unions, together influence a large section of the population.'[58]

Varvaressos reacted to the disappearance of olive oil with the announcement that he would introduce a state monopoly which would function from the 15th September. But the concerted boycott of his measures went even further. Although he had reached an agreement with the textile manufacturers which was favourable to them, they still refused to start production and thus the 7,500 tons of cotton brought in at the beginning of July remained unused; whilst even the distribution of UNRRA clothing was obstructed by subordinate officials. Faced with this situation, Varvaressos took a decision of despair: on the 17th August he criticised the factory owners and shopkeepers for their lack of will to cooperate, announced drastic measures against hoarding and appealed to public opinion to support his programme; otherwise he would resign. He went on to paint a rosy picture of the future: the problem of relief from abroad had been solved; the US would give Greece a 250 million dollar credit; Greece would get all the goods she needed for reconstruction and this credit would exceed the total of what she had ever previously borrowed.[59]

The background to Varvaressos' announcement was as follows: At the beginning of July, on his way back from the San Francisco conference, the Greek Foreign Minister had had talks with President Truman and Under-Secretary of State Grew at the State Department and had voiced the Greek desire for additional economic assistance. Truman had promised this.[60] At the end of July, the Greek ambassador in Washington, Diamantopoulos, had made a further *démarche:* it would not be sufficient if Greece obtained the urgently-needed Export–Import Bank credit which would have to be repaid, what was needed was generous US economic aid.[61] Thereupon the Foreign Economic Administration conceded Greece a twenty million dollar short-term credit. But the State Department realised that this would not be sufficient and thought Diamantopoulos' suggestion worth considering.[62] How far this readiness to help was signalled to Greece is not known. At any rate, on the 20th August, Diamantopoulos applied to the Export–Import Bank for the 250 million dollars credit mentioned by Varvaressos and at the same time submitted a detailed list of the desired reconstruction supplies.[63] Questioned by MacVeagh, Varvaressos admitted that the credit requested was somewhat large and at the same time hinted that his announcement had been intended mainly to influence Greek public opinion.[64] Washington reacted with irritation and Byrnes let MacVeagh know that whilst moderate demands would receive a favourable hearing, there was no future for astronomic ones.[65]

Meanwhile in Athens opposition to Varvaressos was being drummed up. Both the right- and left-wing press attacked him violently and even the political centre's press only gave him lukewarm support. Disappearance of foodstuffs took on such proportions that Varvaressos was forced to appeal to the British and Americans to bring in oil and cheese from their stocks in Italy and the Middle East. Caccia reported: 'There are known to be large stocks of olive oil in Greece, and this request is a plain admission of his failure to ensure a distribution of local supplies.'[66] The British were prepared to respond to his plea, but the first consignments could not arrive before the end of September. This induced Varvaressos to take the decisive step: he resolved to resign in the hope that the chaos which would follow this resignation would bring his antagonists to their senses. Although the British and also Damaskinos tried to restrain him—at least until after the latter's return from London—on the 1st September Varvaressos resigned. On the 3rd he explained his reasons to the public in a radio broadcast, in which he damned the conscienceless economic oligarchy who had sabotaged his programme and spent millions on their propaganda campaign against him, even going to the length of corrupting officials.[67]

The reason for Varvaressos' failure was not his economic programme which, had it been realised, would certainly have made a decisive contribution to Greece's reconstruction. His main mistake was that he tried to force it through more or less on his own. His taxation programme must inevitably have led to conflict with the economic oligarchy and this, in turn, meant that he lacked adequate Cabinet support. Had he secured for himself the support of the masses—still represented by EAM—and had he, when forced to compromise, moved in that direction, he might have stood a chance. By making these enforced compromises with the economic oligarchy, he undermined his own position. They interpreted his concessions as weakness and stepped up their own boycott. The sufferers from this boycott were first and foremost the 'little people' and this resulted in the unnatural alliance between the Left and the Right which eventually brought about his fall. In the final instance, he was a victim of the *parakratos* against which from now on no Cabinet could prevail.

Voulgaris stated that the same economical policy would be continued after Varvaressos' resignation. He appointed as Economics Minister Panos Mavrikis, a Bank of Greece director and brother-in-law of Finance Minister Mantzavinos, and as Supply Minister Ioannis Paraskevopoulos, another Bank of Greece director. Mantzavinos, who was also a director at the central bank, remained at Finance. The three ministers immediately introduced a policy more acceptable to business. Their first measure was the lifting of price controls on those basic foodstuffs which had disappeared from the market, which promptly re-appeared though not, of course, at the previous controlled prices. Oil, which had cost 400 *drachmas* the *oka* (1.28 kg) under price control, now cost 700-800. On the black market it had cost 1,300 but even this reduced profit made it worth the traders' while to bring it back. At the same time the ministers negotiated new contracts with the industrialists for the processing of UNRRA raw materials. Simultaneously, too, the price of gold began to rise astronomically. The rise in food prices which by far exceeded the purchasing power of the workforce resulted in protest strikes by the trade unions.[68] The government's measures were contradictory. Paraskevopoulos tried to incite the industrialists to resume production by a series of further concessions. Meanwhile the government tried to unload responsibility for the economic chaos on to UNRRA.

On 13th September, Voulgaris turned to UNRRA with the request that it take over generalised control of the Greek economy and this put UNRRA in a dilemma: a refusal would expose it to the charge of having done nothing to prevent Greece's economic breakdown; acceptance to the charge of interference in the country's internal affairs. The British *chargé d'affaires*, Lascelles, considered UNRRA suitable for this task but was of the opinion that the decision should await the return of Damaskinos. The protest strikes were continuing and this prompted the Labour Minister to promulgate that trade union law which gave the government greater possibilities of intervention.[69]

By mid-September the economic situation had deteriorated still further. The price of gold was rising and so were food prices. UNRRA discovered huge discrepancies in the Greek Industrialists' Federation's statistics for the level of production, which was in point of fact 100% higher than was declared. Differences within the government were on the increase. Paraskevopoulos wanted to augment budgetary income by raising the sale prices of UNRRA goods. Finance Minister Mantzavinos wanted to deal with this problem provisionally by printing money.[70] At the end of September chaos reigned supreme. Basic food prices were rising steeply and this led to panic-buying by hoarders. Income from taxation was declining. And the government did nothing. On 2nd October Leeper felt himself obliged to intervene with Voulgaris, who accepted his criticisms and maintained that the problem could only be solved from abroad—by UNRRA and the Allies.[71]

The reason for what had happened was simple: the ministers responsible for the economy themselves came from the economic oligarchy and were not prepared to act against the interests of their class; whilst, even had they tried to do so, they would have suffered the same shipwreck as Varvaressos. Moreover, Varvaressos' announcement that Greece would get a 250 million dollar credit had put aside any thought of reconstruction through local initiative.

In the meantime, in Washington, the Export-Import Bank had received Greece's official application for the 250 million dollar credit. On 22nd September the Acting Secretary of State, Dean Acheson, informed MacVeagh of the Bank's decision. The application would not even be seriously examined: such an application would be beyond the Bank's potential, even if the recipient's solvency were absolutely above doubt. MacVeagh must make this clear to the Greek government and put a stop to any further publicity. The Bank was, however, prepared to put a credit of 25 million dollars at Greece's disposal, but its purpose must be specified; the Greek government should present such a programme.[72]

MacVeagh acted in accordance with these instructions. Nevertheless the impression remained that the 250 million dollar credit would be granted and that the 25 million dollars which the Export-Import Bank was prepared to make available was the first instalment. Even an official denial failed to register. Although the ministers knew that the credit would not materialise, the Greek bureaucracy seemed possessed by euphoria. MacVeagh reported:

'The British Embassy was informed by officials of the Ministry of Posts, Telegraphs and Telephones that certain telephone equipment ordered from the United Kingdom was no longer wanted, since the 250 million dollar loan from the United States would take care of all such needs.'[73]

The programme for the 25 million dollar credit was drawn up accordingly. It was not discussed either with the US Embassy or with UNRRA, so that it even cut across the UNRRA programme. MacVeagh commented:

'It is most unfortunate that the question of credit from the Export-Import Bank has been handled by the Greek government in a manner which can only be described as careless. Greece needs almost everything that can be obtained from abroad, but there is little evidence of any sense of responsibility in arriving at a proper balance of requirements within reasonable limits of cost. Many of the requests submitted to UNRRA are frankly extravagant, and the Eximbank list may well contain items of the same character.'[74]

The Greek government showed the same frivolous attitude in submitting the list of reparations claims against Germany, required by the State Department in mid-August for the 1st October. This was finally submitted in mid-October and demanded reparations to the tune of 10,449,506,903 dollars, a sum which in submitting the account to Acheson, Ambassador Diamantopoulos himself characterised as problematic.[75] At the same time he raised the question who should pay for Greek reconstruction and stated that UNRRA was not capable of this. Thus he let it be understood that the Greek government was not prepared to undertake the task of reconstruction itself. In other words, Diamantopoulos more or less repeated what Voulgaris had suggested on 14th September—the country's reconstruction should be carried out by foreigners. Whilst Voulgaris had still been prepared to consider UNRRA, Diamantopoulos made a direct demand on the Americans. Voulgaris' earlier suggestion had been transmitted by UNRRA to the US and Great Britain, and, in a letter of 29th September to Byrnes, Bevin had recommended that it be accepted. UNRRA would of course be accused of intervening in

Greek internal affairs but this would have to be taken into the bargain; the actual situation would be little changed. It would be essential to find a strong personality for head of UNRRA; he, Bevin, would have favoured an American, preferably Hoskins,[76] but Byrnes rejected this suggestion.[77] Eventually, at the beginning of October, UNRRA chairman Lehman decided to send one of his vice-chairmen, Commander Jackson, to Athens to make an analysis of the situation.

At this point the conclusions can be summarised as follows: the factor which determined the failure of Greek reconstruction was the breaking of the Greek people's will to renewal by British intervention. This intervention re-established the leadership of the pre-war regime and, along with the restoration of the old political oligarchy, the economic oligarchy likewise found its way back to the key positions in its own field. Every attempt to push through overdue reforms in the teeth of that clique had failed, whether it was undertaken by Greeks or by foreigners. Only the elimination of this clique could have brought about economic recovery and, against this, political considerations prevailed.

NOTES

1. See chapter 6, From Varkiza to the Fall of Plastiras, pp. 79–102.
2. Richter, *Griechenland zwischen Revolution und Konterrevolution*, pp. 248 ff.
3. Poulos, 'Greek Tragedy 1945', p. 452.
4. See p. 83.
5. MacVeagh to Secretary of State Edward R. Stettinius 12th March, 1945 (*FRUS 1945, VIII*, pp. 201 ff, p. 202 footnote 93).
6. MacVeagh to Stettinius 14th March, 1945 (*FRUS 1945, VIII*, pp. 202 ff).
7. *Ibid.*, p. 203.
8. National Liberation Front (EAM) Central Committee Memorandum 12th March, 1945 (R 5617/4/19).
9. Roosevelt to Churchill 21st March, 1945 (*FRUS 1945, VIII*, pp. 203 ff). Prime Minister's Personal Telegram Serial No. T 318/5 (R 6104/4/19).
10. Hayter's Minutes 22nd March, 1945 (R 6104/4/19).
11. Draft Minute to the Prime Minister from the Secretary of State, PM/45/146, 31st March, 1945 (R 6104/4/19).
12. Copy of Prime Minister's Minute, PM/45/146, 3rd April, 1945 (R 6104/4/19).
13. Churchill to Roosevelt 3rd April, 1945 (*FRUS 1945, VIII*, pp. 205 ff); Draft Message to President Roosevelt from the Prime Minister 3rd April, 1945 (R 6104/4/19).
14. Roosevelt to Churchill 8th April, 1945 (*FRUS 1945, VIII*, pp. 207 ff). The date, 8th April, comes from the relevant telegram in the Foreign Office archives (R 6678/4/19).
15. Prime Minister's Personal Minute Serial No. 314/5, 8th April, 1945 (R 6957/4/19).
16. Draft Minute to the Prime Minister from the Secretary of State and Draft Message to the President from the Prime Minister, both 11th April, 1945 (R 6957/4/19).
17. Prime Minister's Personal Minute Serial No. 337/5, 15th April, 1945 (R 6957/4/19).

18. See pp. vii–ix and Elisabeth Barker, 'Greece in the Framework of Anglo-Soviet Relations 1941-1947', *Greece: From Resistance to Civil War*, ed. Marion Sarafis, (Nottingham: Spokesman, 1980), pp. 15-31.
19. *FRUS 1945, VIII*, p. 218, footnote 31.
20. *Ibid.*
21. MacVeagh to Stettinius 18th July, 1945 (*FRUS 1945, VIII*, p. 226).
22. *Ibid.*, p. 228.
23. Details in MacVeagh's telegram to Stettinius 13th April, 1945 (*FRUS 1945, VIII*, pp. 209 ff). MacVeagh spoke of 'minor calibre'.
24. Leeper was not displeased with this development. Leeper to Foreign Office 21st April, 1945 (R 7165/4/19). He found Maben quite compliant.
25. *FRUS 1945, VIII*, p. 227.
26. *Ibid.*, pp. 211 ff.
27. See p. 80.
28. On the 18th June MacVeagh wrote: 'All matters in which UNRRA is interested are within its competence' (*FRUS 1945, VIII*, p. 225).
29. *Ibid.*, pp. 225 ff.
30. *Ibid.*, p. 217.
31. State Department to MacVeagh 11th May, 1945 (*FRUS 1945, VIII*, pp. 217 ff).
32. MacVeagh to State Department 14th May, 1945 (*ibid.*, pp. 218 ff).
33. MacVeagh to State Department 18th June, 1945 (*ibid.*, pp. 224-8).
34. State Department to MacVeagh 9th July, 1945 (*ibid.*, p. 229).
35. Bevin to Byrnes 29th September, 1945 (*ibid.*, pp. 238-40).
36. Poulos, 'Greek Tragedy 1945', p. 450.
37. McNeill, *The Greek Dilemma*, pp. 210 ff.
38. Poulos, *op. cit.*, p. 450.
39. McNeill, *op. cit.*, p. 205.
40. See pp. 81-2 *passim*. Greek *entrepreneurs* held enough gold to achieve enormous gains by speculation and therefore did not have to rely on ordinary gains from industrial production. *Tribune*, 30th November, 1945.
41. MacVeagh to State Department 24th May, 1945 (*FRUS 1945, VIII*, p. 221).
42. *Ibid.*
43. McNeill, *op. cit.*, pp. 212 ff. Poulos describes a characteristic episode. 'There is gaiety in Greece. Americans will probably see that gaiety soon in a March of Time film. They will see a luxurious night club with smartly dressed women and handsomely groomed men dining and dancing expensively. Outside the night club, in the night early in October when the March of Time unit was photographing the palace, a taxi driver was waiting for a party. 'Sure' he said bitterly, "'I served two years in jail in the thirties. I stole. I am going to steal again. The four people I am driving around tonight will spend in one hour in there three times what I make in one month. I have a family." Unskilled labourers, like the taxi driver, are making 75 cents a day. Skilled and white-collar workers get between $1.25 and $2 a day. . . A loaf of bread costs 50 cents, olive oil $1.40 a quart, meat 70 cents a pound, and sugar $2 a pound.' Poulos, *op. cit.*, p. 450.
44. *Ibid.*
45. See p. 83.
46. MacVeagh to State Department 24th March, 1945 (*FRUS 1945, VIII*, pp. 204 ff).
47. *Ibid.*, p. 216.
48. *Ibid.*, p. 214. The reason for the US rejection was a law of 1934 prohibiting loans to countries which had not fulfilled their past obligations. This law was

repealed on 31st July, 1945.
49. MacVeagh to State Department 21st April, 1945 (*ibid.*, p. 211).
50. Leeper to Foreign Office 21st May, 1945 (R 9322/4/19).
51. Leeper to Foreign Office 28th May, 1945 (R 9518/4/19).
52. Caccia to Foreign Office 11th June, 1945 (R 10344/4/19); MacVeagh to State Department 4th June, 1945 (*FRUS 1945, VIII*, p. 222).
53. Caccia to Foreign Office 22nd June, 1945 (R 10682/4/19).
54. Caccia to Foreign Office 25th June, 1945 (R 11161/4/19).
55. Caccia to Foreign Office 2nd July, 1945 (R 11552/4/19).
56. Caccia to Foreign Office 30th July, 1945 (R 13134/4/19); Caccia to Foreign Office 5th August, 1945 (R 13447/4/19); Caccia to Foreign Office 13th August 1945 (R 13927/4/19).
57. Thus Varvaressos had to accept the textile manufacturers' own assessments, which were sharply criticised by UNRRA because they were aimed at maximum profits. (*Ibid.*)
58. *The Times*, 3rd September, 1945.
59. Caccia to Foreign Office 20th August, 1945 (R 14320/4/19); *FRUS 1945, VIII*, pp. 232 ff.
60. *FRUS 1945, VIII*, pp. 228 ff., 230.
61. *Ibid.*, p. 231.
62. *Ibid.*, p. 232, footnote 57.
63. *Ibid.*, p. 234.
64. *Ibid.*, p. 235.
65. *Ibid.*
66. Caccia to Foreign Office 27th August, 1945 (R 14710/4/19).
67. Lascelles to Foreign Office 17th September, 1945 (R 15829/4/19); Stavrianos, *Greece: American Dilemma*, p. 159.
68. R 15829/4/19.
69. See pp. 136-7; Lascelles to Foreign Office 18th September, 1945 (R 16154/4/19).
70. Leeper to Foreign Office 25th September, 1945 (R 16632/4/19).
71. Leeper to Foreign Office 2nd October, 1945 (R 17396/4/19).
72. The short-term credit made available by the FEA (Foreign Economic Administration) had lapsed owing to the lack of any programme for its use. *FRUS 1945, VIII*, pp. 236 ff.
73. MacVeagh to State Department 2nd October, 1945 (*ibid.*, p. 243).
74. *Ibid.*, p. 244.
75. *Ibid.*, pp. 244 ff.
76. *Ibid.*, pp. 238-40.
77. *Ibid.*, pp. 242 ff.

FROM THE RETURN OF DAMASKINOS TO THE RESIGNATION OF VOULGARIS

Leeper's long absence and the change of government in Britain had clearly sharpened his insight in one direction. His hostility to the Left was unchanged but he now realised that the Greek Right, too, threatened the country's democratic evolution. On the 24th he sent London his first situation-analysis: the communists had become more militant but, on the other side, reactionaries in military and financial circles were opposing a moderate policy. The Voulgaris government did not enjoy the necessary confidence. It had no stamina, lacked imagination and had one foot in the counter-revolutionary camp. It had not purged the General Staff and had missed the opportunity to teach the industrialists a lesson. Therefore a change was needed, particularly in view of elections since the result of these would be considerably influenced by the government's policy. So he recommended that the present government should continue in office only until the election date was fixed. Then a new government should be formed which would hold the elections. He was for drastic measures but wanted first to discuss the question of personalities with Damaskinos.[1]

Leeper listed the following measures: the army must be rebuilt on a non-party basis; War Minister Merenditis must purge the Officers' Corps in close cooperation with the BMM under General Rawlins and new appointments must be made on military criteria only. The public service would continue to be controlled by the Greek Right and the ministers could not keep the mechanism under control: reform was essential and to this end he suggested the sending of a small Mission. The Greek Assistant-ministry for the Press was inefficient and deeply involved in party politics; the present assistant-minister, Dendramanis, was completely under the influence of Piniatoglou (publisher of *Ellinikon Aima*) and of the extreme Right and was apparently determined to exonerate himself from any 'charge' of being non-party. He had tried to get the Greek radio under his control and took no steps to restrain right-wing anti-Soviet propaganda. In the past, too, he had not supported Varvaressos' economic policy. Further points made by Leeper concerned economic policy measures and the proclamation of an amnesty.[2]

On the 22nd Damaskinos returned to Athens. The Athens press at once began to speculate about a possible change of government. To counteract this, on the 25th Damaskinos held a press conference. But before that he consulted the diplomatic representatives of Great Britain, the US and France. The Regent expounded to them a new idea: as many parties as possible should be urged to a joint effort to produce as democratic a parliament as possible in order to avert the communist danger. The best way would be if the party leaders could agree to a joint national programme. Of course, the existing differences between the parties would break out again after the elections but this—like the constitutional question—was a secondary issue. For the moment what mattered was to overcome the danger threatening democracy. In this he hoped for Allied support.[3]

Whilst MacVeagh and his French colleague, lacking instructions, took a reserved attitude to Damaskinos' proposal, Leeper was visibly displeased at the Regent's suggestion that he should use his influence on Theotokis, Kafandaris, Papandreou and Sofoulis. To MacVeagh he commented that Damaskinos had lost his grip on the situation, that he was developing autocratic tendencies and that sheer alarm at the communist danger was blinding him to the influence of the Greek Right over the government. He would try to correct this: to replace the government was inopportune prior to the elections but he would urge the Regent to change the Interior Minister and the Assistant-Minister for the Press and on the amnesty issue he hoped for MacVeagh's support. Finally, he suggested to MacVeagh that he should urge Voulgaris to make a declaration on the election date as soon as possible, which indeed the former did in a subsequent conversation. In general, MacVeagh formed the impression that, since the change of government in London, Leeper was becoming increasingly sensitive to the manoeuvres of the Greek Right.[4]

At the press conference on 25th September, Damaskinos appealed to the bourgeois parties to cooperate with the government so that the elections could be held as soon as possible. A change of government appeared to be excluded and, in the conversation between MacVeagh and Voulgaris, the latter expressed his conviction that he would remain in office until the elections which would in all probability be held on the 15th December. When MacVeagh drew his attention to reports that electoral booklets (the personal document entitling the elector to vote) were being illegally printed in large numbers, Voulgaris laughed and replied that it would not be a repetition of the 1935 situation when '1,000 men produced 100,000 votes'. He would make the possession of more than one electoral booklet a punishable offence.[5] On the 27th September EAM celebrated its fourth anniversary with a mass demonstration in the Athens Olympic stadium. On the 28th War Minister Merenditis resigned and on the same day Leeper urged Damaskinos to act on the amnesty issue.[6] On the 29th, on the occasion of a memorial service in the Athens cathedral in honour of the victims of the Bulgarian occupation, there was a counter-demonstration by the Right which reached a climax with the chanting of 'To Sofia, to Sofia'.[7]

Leeper formed the impression that, after Merenditis' resignation, a change of government was inevitable. In a conversation with Voulgaris on 29th September he gave the latter to understand that he no longer unreservedly supported him. Voulgaris himself realised that the governmental crisis must be brought to an end in one way or another and suggested that Damaskinos should summon the party leaders for talks to produce a solution: they should either form a coalition government or give their support to the present one. Leeper addressed himself to Damaskinos and recommended him to act quickly in accordance with Voulgaris' suggestion: if the party leaders could not agree he himself would have to find a suitable person such as Tsouderos.

To the Foreign Office Leeper added that he had already spoken with Tsouderos: the man had his faults but in comparison with the other party politicians these were insignificant. Tsouderos would pursue an economic policy similar to that of Varvaressos. He was in favour of a general amnesty excluding only about two hundred murderers (*sic*). The communists would accept this and in return they would not demand participation in the government. He, Leeper, could not say how the Regent would decide but in any case he would insist on a policy of reform.[8]

Next day the situation seemed more stable. Under pressure from Voulgaris, General Merenditis agreed to remain in the Cabinet for the time being. Damaskinos was pleased because he did not have to take an immediate decision. He found that there was no governmental crisis after all. Leeper however remained sceptical and, when he met Voulgaris on 1st October, urged him to take measures on the following: *amnesty:* by the end of the week there must be worthwhile results; *the army:* the process of de-politicising must be seriously tackled; *economic and financial policy:* these problems too must be speedily and energetically confronted; *press and radio:* existing problems to be solved with the British Press Attaché. On his side, Voulgaris reported on the preparations for elections: registration of electors was proceeding satisfactorily; but, at the request of the republican parties, he had prolonged the registration period by a further ten days and thus he would be able to announce the final election date in about two weeks' time. The date would be sometime in mid-January 1946. Leeper criticised this late date. Voulgaris replied that this was the last postponement. Finally Leeper told him that, from the 2nd October, he would start talks on the elections with the party leaders.[9]

Meanwhile, MacVeagh and his French colleague had received instructions to take action for the supervision of the elections in accordance with the London Three Power statement.[10] The next days were characterised by a plethora of talks between the Greek party leaders and the diplomatic representatives of the three Western powers. Whilst the French representative generally restricted himself to a listener's role, MacVeagh tried to bring the various party leaders to cooperate. Leeper, on the other hand, tried to achieve a union of the bourgeois parties on the basis of a common programme.

Sofoulis had no objection to a common programme but he was against an early election date. Communications with rural constituencies were wholly inadequate and, moreover, the existence of 'X' made it impossible to hold really free elections. Democratic politicians would be terrorised by 'X' men if they tried to speak in public in their constituencies. The present government was doing nothing against this, so an all-party government must be formed.[11] The Populist leaders (Theotokis, Tsaldaris, Mavromichalis and Stefanopoulos) stated that they too were working on such a programme, which would be agreed with Papandreou, Gonatas and Alexandris. But, until the election date was determined, they rejected any agreement with the other parties. Obviously, they were hoping to win the elections and therefore demanded the earliest possible date. The leader of the Agrarian Party, Alexandros Mylonas, rejected an early election date on the grounds of unsuitable conditions and in addition demanded that the elections be held on the proportional representation system. Georgios Kafandaris, leader of the Progressive Party, expressed himself similarly. EAM demanded the formation of an all-party government, revision of the electoral lists, postponement of the elections till the spring and the use of proportional representation; moreover persecution of the Left must cease and a general amnesty be proclaimed.[12] The situation is summarised as follows: the Right wanted the earliest possible date whilst the Liberals and the Left wanted postponement, otherwise they threatened to boycott the elections. MacVeagh and Leeper formed the impression that only when the election date was determined, would the parties end their tactical manoeuvring. They did not take too seriously the threat of the Centre and left-wing parties to boycott the elections.[13]

Under these conditions Leeper advised Damaskinos and Voulgaris to accept the challenge and fix the election date; whereupon, on 6th October, Voulgaris announced that the elections would be held on 20th January 1946: there were as yet no final figures but enough electors had registered to ensure that the result would represent the majority will of the Greek people. This announcement provoked varied reactions. The Right was jubilant. Sofoulis called a Liberal conference and, on 7th October, the following statement was issued to the press: the Liberals would not take part in the elections unless a new government were formed from moderate Centre forces; Sofoulis was in principle against a boycott but he was not prepared to participate in a wretched electoral comedy which would end in a national tragedy.

Kafandaris described the government's decision as a *coup d'état* which would lead to civil war and to the destruction of Greece. Mylonas declared that his party, too, would boycott the elections. Svolos severely criticised Voulgaris' action and Tsouderos demanded that the government decree be withdrawn. KKE spoke of a legalised *coup* against the people staged by collaborators, the Regent and Leeper.[14]

Apparently no one had expected such reactions. Leeper began to have second thoughts:

> 'How far reasons given by abstaining parties can in fact be justified I am not in a position to judge with any accuracy though there is enough substance in them to produce a case of sorts. On the other hand what really matters is [the] political consequence of having a Government here against which the whole Central Left would be in opposition. Elections held under such conditions would be a farce. In fact I would anticipate strikes and disorders which would make the holding of elections impossible.'

The Voulgaris government was in an impossible position; if Voulgaris tried to remain in office, there would be ministerial resignations; Damaskinos must form a new government without delay.[15]

Leeper sent a corresponding report to Damaskinos: in order to forestall possible criticism in the House of Commons, the Regent must let Tsouderos form a Left-Centre government; he was a republican and also had some understanding of economic and financial policy.[16] To MacVeagh Leeper said that the fundamental reason for the failure of the efforts to produce unity lay in the fact that the party politicians were exclusively preoccupied by the constitutional question and presumed that Great Britain wanted the monarchy restored. This impression must be removed, either by a suitable statement from the British government or by support for the republicans. The future government should include one or two non-communist Resistance politicians. This would lead to problems with the army and the National Guard which were royalist, but he did not believe the extreme Right would attempt a *coup d'état*.[17]

On the evening of the 7th Leeper visited Voulgaris and made it clear to him that he must resign. Voulgaris agreed and Leeper then informed Damaskinos of this and told him that Greece needed a 'Left-Centre' government, a government that in its composition and its policy must be incontrovertibly up-to-date, democratic and progressive. Damaskinos feared that this would lead to trouble from the Right. According to Leeper's report to the Foreign Office Damaskinos replied that he realised the danger today as fully as he did last autumn. Then the danger came from the extreme Left. Now it came principally from the Right. This new danger Leeper found less formidable because it had no external backing, certainly not in his own country. Then he told Damaskinos the policy he had suggested to MacVeagh: the British government would, by a suitable statement, administer a shrewd blow to the Right. Damaskinos found this a good suggestion and promised to play for time so that Leeper could coordinate the necessary tactics with London.[18]

Thus, on the 8th October, Leeper addressed himself to the Foreign

Office. After introductory remarks on his policy till then, he submitted his proposals: the Greek situation was dangerous and he therefore urgently recommended that this suggestion be accepted.

'I do not think the Greeks will get out of their present mess without a blunt and direct indication from His Majesty's Government of what they want in Greece. Diplomatic language will be wilfully misinterpreted by those whose interest it is to do so. We need here a breath of fresh air from England and I feel sure that if you provide it you will do immense good. . . I would not put it so strongly to you if I were not sure that my diagnosis was right and that remedy was the best available.'

Many Greeks too were of the opinion that a clarifying word from London would resolve the crisis.[19] Leeper enclosed the draft of a statement to be made by Bevin in the House of Commons.

'Position in Greece today is not satisfactory. There is acute party conflict. . . We have a direct interest in what is happening in Greece. . . Last month the three Allied Governments made joint recommendations to the Greek people. They advised them to go on with the elections and to postpone to a later date the vexed constitutional issue which has divided the nation for so many years. I am not sure whether that recommendation has been properly understood by the Greek people. Perhaps our language was too diplomatic. In what I say now I will be very blunt if you like undiplomatic. In the opinion of His Majesty's Government Greece cannot afford to divide on this constitutional issue. The welfare of the Greek people must come first. Greece is faced with urgent problems of reconstruction. They must receive priority. If the elections are held under the shadow of this constitutional issue the really urgent problems will not receive priority. I regret to say that the Royalist parties in Greece do not seem to have fully grasped the intention of the Allied Governments. They want an early election in order if they win to raise the constitutional issue with all its bitterness and disunity which that will cause. Let me say here and now that that was not the intention or the wish of the Allied Governments. It is certainly not the wish of His Majesty's Government.

'What then do His Majesty's Government wish to see in Greece? . . . We do not consider the early return of the King to be in the best interests of the country. . . What we want in Greece is a government between the two extremes of the Right and the Left, a democratic government composed of men with modern and progressive ideas who put the welfare of their people first, who will go forward to election of a fair and impartial character, who will uphold a proper democratic order in the State who without fear or favour will deal impartially with all disturbances of peace from whatever side they come and who will deal swiftly and adequately with the present serious economic and financial problems. This is what we want to see in Greece. This is what we are sure the Greek people also want. Such a Government will receive our full moral support and enable us to make more efficient the material help we are at present providing.'[20]

Leeper's reflections underlying this draft were fundamentally sound. He had seen through the royalists' plans, as developments after the 1946 elections would prove. He was right too in giving priority to reconstruction; and his aim for a Centre-Left government was likewise sensible. But he overlooked two important problems on whose solution his whole concept depended: where were the people from whom the Centre-Left coalition[21] could have been formed? We can take it that Leeper regarded Sofoulis' Liberals as the Centre. But what did he consider to be the Left? As he equated EAM with the Communist Party, there remained only the small left-liberal republican splinter parties, such as those of Mylonas, Kafandaris and Tsouderos, or the socialists grouped around Svolos and Tsirimokos. A government formed from these groups would have presented all the problems of a multi-party coalition and moreover would have had to rule in the teeth of opposition from the Right and the Left. In addition, its policy would have been determined in the main by the constitutional issue. Further, it would have been more than questionable whether such a government could have solved Greece's second problem, that of the *parakratos*—certainly, it could not have solved it by its own means. To break the power of the now firmly-established *parakratos* would have required massive British support and this would have necessitated a radical change in Britain's policy towards Greece. But London was not ready for that. Leeper's concept would only have had a chance of success if the Centre-Left government could have been formed on a broad basis, that is including the whole of the Left. To promote the country's reconstruction would have required certain radical social reforms which would have impinged on the business interests of the ruling oligarchy. In other words, such a government would have had to pursue a policy which could have been characterised as socialist. Whether the Liberals could have proved so altruistic as to sacrifice a great part of their own interests for the common good is more than questionable. What is certain is that the Labour government in London would have had to consent to this socialist policy, which it was not prepared to do.

There was willingness in London to engage in certain matters of detail, for example in regard to the release of detainees and the amnesty, but there was reluctance to get too far involved in Greek internal politics. Therefore the Foreign Office rejected, for instance, Leeper's suggestions for the sending of a Civil Service Mission. Reorganisation of the public service was a Greek affair and they themselves must know what needed to be done; 'What they seem to lack is a Minister of sufficient drive and determination to carry out the necessary measures'.[22] What this implied was that the Foreign Office had not understood the problem of the *para-*

kratos. Behind this reserved attitude on the part of the Foreign Office lay the fear of becoming responsible for all political issues.

'We need to be constantly on our guard against the danger of turning Greece into a second Egypt, and it is just this kind of proposal [a Civil Service Mission], reasonable enough when considered on its merits, which is likely to put us on this slippery path.'[23]

London's advice to Leeper concerning Greek economic policy was equally divorced from any relation to Greek reality.[24] These suggestions could certainly have been translated into practical politics in a well-organised West European state; in Greece they were simply not practicable, as Varvaressos' failure had shown. Leeper's suggestion to appoint Tsouderos as the new Prime Minister also raised doubts: it might cause difficulties in the House of Commons and Leeper was told to forget it.

'... Meanwhile you should know that a very bad impression would be created in this country if M. Tsouderos were to become Prime Minsiter ... Although Tsouderos no doubt holds genuinely republican views, his name is linked with the King of Greece and with the suppression of the left-wing mutinies in the Greek Armed Forces in 1943 and 1944. He is also regarded, however unjustly, as the man principally responsible for the failure of the Greek Government in Cairo to come to terms with the resistance movement in Greece. You should therefore warn the Regent that a new Government under Tsouderos could receive a bad reception here. The same objection would not apply if Tsouderos were given a post in the Government other than Prime Minister...'[25]

Eventually, on 9th October, the Foreign Office gave Leeper detailed instructions. It was the Regent's business to take the initiative for the formation of a new government. A statement of the sort drafted by Leeper could not be considered: the British government was neither ready to install a Greek government nor to lay down the policy such a government was to follow. The Greeks must be made to stand on their own feet; they must understand that Great Britain had no intention to govern Greece on their behalf. The Regent would know best what line would be most suitable at present. The British government was certainly not prepared to regulate internal Greek policy, but it was ready to remove particular misunderstandings. If the impression really prevailed in Greece that it was British policy to restore the king, then the government was ready to make a statement as soon as possible in order to clarify the British position; though this statement should only be made after the formation of a government in Greece. Leeper should make clear to the Regent and to the party leaders that the British government would oppose with force any attempt by the extreme Right to solve the crisis by a *coup*. As regards the elections, whilst a postponement of the elections until the spring was not seen as particularly advantageous, it would nevertheless not meet with opposition if they really could not be held earlier. If, when the Regent had formed a new government, the extreme Right tried to discredit it on the grounds that it was following a policy which contradicted British policy for Greece, then they would be dealt with peremptorily. The most important tasks for the new government would be the solution of the amnesty problem and of the country's economic crisis.[26]

On the same day (9th October) Damaskinos accepted Voulgaris' resignation and at once asked him to remain in charge of official business till the new government was formed. The instructions to Leeper made matters worse, as the Foreign Office itself was later to realise.[27] On the one hand Leeper was forbidden any intervention in the formation of the new government and on the other the Foreign Office had vetoed the suggested premier, Tsouderos. Clearly, the inner contradictions of British policy towards Greece[28] —the main characteristics of the wartime period—had become ingrained.

Lacking precise guidance, Damaskinos held to the line agreed in London and tried to build a broad coalition government. As Tsouderos was no longer available, on the 10th October he instructed Sofoulis to form a government charging him at the same time to secure Populist participation. On the 11th Sofoulis told Leeper that he had succeeded in securing Kafandaris, Tsouderos and Mylonas for his Cabinet and that Plastiras, Svolos and the communists would give his government their support, though they did not want to enter the Cabinet. However, as the Populists refused all cooperation, he asked Leeper to intervene with them since otherwise he could not fulfil the Regent's conditions. But if the Populists maintained their negative stand, would the British government accept a purely republican Cabinet? In conformity with his instructions, Leeper refused to intervene and stressed that the Regent had a free hand. Until the government was formed he would have no contact with any of the party leaders so as to avoid misunderstandings. Sofoulis thereupon said he would talk to the Populists himself but he was sure they would refuse as they had had orders from the king through Pipinellis and were under the impression that Great Britain wanted a Restoration.[29]

Sofoulis' predictions proved correct. The Populists refused to participate in a Sofoulis Cabinet and Damaskinos stuck by his terms. When further negotiations likewise failed, Sofoulis handed back his mandate on the 13th October. The Regent then instructed Voulgaris to form a new cabinet and, when he too failed, on the 15th October Tsouderos was mandated, with no better result. The Populists refused all participation and demanded a new service government. The Regent feared the outbreak of right-wing disturbances if he formed a purely republican government and therefore charged Anargyros Dimitrakopoulos (Minister for Public Works in the Voulgaris Cabinet) with the formation of a service government. But he likewise returned his mandate within a few hours.

Leeper saw that the crisis was approaching a climax. On the 16th October he addressed himself to the Foreign Office and asked for the lifting of the ban on intervention since otherwise there was the threat of a right-wing *coup*. In a talk with Damaskinos on the same day, he gave the latter to understand that, though London held to the principle of non-intervention, he would accept any government which had the Regent's agreement provided it could impose respect for law and order.[30] Damaskinos told Leeper that, since all his efforts to get the party leaders to cooperate had proved vain, he himself would take over the premiership.

On the 17th Damaskinos published his decision which was rejected by all the political parties except the extreme Right. Meanwhile, in London there had been a slight change of policy. On the same day, the 17th, the Minister of State, Philip Noel-Baker, had made a statement in the House of Commons clarifying the British attitude to the constitutional question: the British government was of the opinion that the future constitution of Greece was a question on which the Greeks themselves must decide and the impression that, if the future constitution were republican, there would be a reduction of British support was erroneous. In conclusion Noel-Baker reminded the House of the Three Power statement of September.[31]

In Athens the reactions to this statement were favourable, since all sides could interpret it at will. On the 18th Leeper visited Damaskinos and urged him to do something about the daily deteriorating economic and financial situation. Damaskinos objected that Leeper did not understand his position: he had not formed a new government, he had simply taken Voulgaris' place in the Cabinet. This Cabinet was a temporary one and a solution to the economic problem must await the resolution of the political crisis. If the British government did not soon make it clear to him what kind of government it wanted, he would form a right-wing Cabinet as this would have the majority of the population behind it and he after all was no revolutionary.[32]

Leeper reported this conversation to the Foreign Office. But London held fast to its non-intervention line. However, his warnings about the possibility of an extreme right-wing *coup* were taken seriously enough to prompt a further statement on Greek policy in parliament. On the 19th, the Labour MP Major Wilkes, drew the government's attention to the fact that for ten days Greece had been effectively without a government. He went on to ask that the British government do something about an amnesty. If the Populists did not want to participate in the government, a government should be formed without them. The elections should be postponed till the snows melted, in other words till May. Finally, the British government should send out a Civil Service Commission as soon as possible. Major Wilkes was answered by the Parliamentary Secretary to the

Foreign Office, Hector McNeil: the British government did not wish to intervene in the process of forming a Greek government, but it would oppose any attempt at a solution of the crisis by force, even using troops if necessary. In regard to the amnesty, McNeil implicitly acknowledged the violations of Varkiza and announced the sending of a British Legal Mission. As for the election date, that was a matter for the Greek government; should they decide for mid-May, this would be accepted.[33]

On 20th October Bevin told Leeper that, whilst he was still not prepared to instruct the Regent as to the composition of the future government, he rejected the formation of a Populist government or of a new service government under Populist control. 'The only reason for forming one would be the danger of royalist disturbances if a contrary decision is taken.' But, after yesterday's statement, he believed this danger to have been forestalled—the possible consequences must be clear even to the royalists. He agreed to the postponement of the elections till the spring, but this must be the last postponement. He had, in fact, supposed that Damaskinos would form a Centre-Left government; if the Populists did not wish to enter such a Cabinet, they could stay outside.[34]

In Athens, Major Wilkes' intervention and McNeil's reply provoked furious protests from the extreme Right. On the 21st October Leeper visited Damaskinos and told him of Bevin's message; but Damaskinos still hesitated. Obviously he shrank from a direct confrontation with the Populists and with the military-economic establishment. Moreover, he feared that a Centre-Left government could re-play the role of a Kerensky government.[35] His aim was to form a broadly-based bourgeois government and therefore he sought further potential Prime Ministers only from the ranks of the bourgeois parties. For some days there was talk of the Liberal, Georgios Exindaris. Then, when Sofoklis Venizelos returned from Egypt to Greece, he was mandated on the 30th October to form a new government. But he too failed.[36]

At the end of the month Leeper was telling London that the situation was serious. The Regent's prestige was diminishing daily and there was no leading personality in sight. He had so far held strictly to his instructions but developments were threatening to get beyond control. Conditions could be heading for a situation like that of last December, but in the opposite sense. He ended by asking for a free hand.[37]

On the 28th October Greece celebrated the fifth anniversary of the rejection of Italy's ultimatum of 1940. The official ceremonies, which glorified the dictator Metaxas, were boycotted by the Left and thus took on the character of a show of force by the extreme Right.[38] At the same time, left-wing demonstrations in the working class suburbs were forbidden. Meanwhile inflation and the budget deficit reached new heights.[39] In other words, Greece was hurtling at an ever-accelerating pace towards internal chaos. The Right controlled the state through the *parakratos* and, in the absence of a stable government, every day increased its influence. At the same time the Right began a new escalation of terror against the Left. In Patras right-wing extremists stormed the offices of the local EAM press and killed a printer. Left-wing protest demonstrations led to two more deaths. Faced with this untenable situation, Damaskinos finally decided to act: he nominated Panayotis Kanellopoulos as the new Prime Minister.

Before going on to trace the further evolution of events in Greece, it may be useful to add a few remarks on the policy of the Labour government which came to power on the 28th July 1945, since this was to have a great influence on further developments in Greece.

Since April 1945 (from the beginning of Leeper's 'High Commissionership'), the problem for British policy in Greece had lain, not in the fact of penetration of the Greek state apparatus in itself, but in how this should be consistently carried through. Churchill's imperialist intervention of December 1944 had overturned the stabilised balance of forces and thus had created a temporary vacuum which however was very quickly filled by the forces of the Right. Despite Churchill's militant anti-communism, it can hardly be supposed that he had aimed at starting the process which in fact took over. His aim was the restoration of the monarchy, in other words a return to the time when the Greek monarch was the unquestioned British pro-consul. But he did not realise—or perhaps did not want to realise—that this was a daydream belonging to the 19th rather than the 20th century, since in Greece too the advent of the ideologies had caused a polarisation of political life. If Greece was not to fall from one extreme to another, British policy should have been consistent in pursuing its intervention in order to hold Greece on a moderate democratic course.

Churchill had rejected a policy of in-depth penetration and thus had promoted the development of right-wing extremism. The opportunity for correction presented itself with the change to a Labour government. But the man who controlled Labour foreign policy, Foreign Minister Bevin, stated at his first appearance before the new House of Commons that the basis of Labour foreign policy would be that worked out by the wartime coalition government under Foreign Minister Eden.[40] There were indeed certain minor alterations, for example on the amnesty issue and in the priority of elections over plebiscite, but in principle nothing was changed. Bevin did not even react to unambiguously liberal suggestions from Leeper or from the Foreign Office staff.

The reasons would seem exceedingly complex. On the one hand, Bevin may not have wanted to contradict himself by changing his Greek policy, since in December 1944 he had strongly defended Churchill's policy at the Labour Party Conference. On the other, financial considerations may have restrained him from becoming more deeply involved, since Britain had an immense war debt to meet. Furthermore the period of barely two months at his disposal may not have been sufficient—in view of many other problems—to permit the necessary insight into Greek problems too. Nor had he, within the Foreign Office, staff who would have been ready to suggest alternatives—socialist alternatives. The only person in his entourage with expert knowledge of Greece was Minister of State Philip Noel-Baker with his large landed estate in Euboea. But for just that reason, he was not the best qualified Labour foreign policy adviser. Finally, one should not forget Bevin's strong anti-communist feelings: why should he intervene for the Greek Communists? In Parliament criticism of Bevin's policy towards Greece came from the ranks of his own party; the Tories on the other hand were greatly attracted by his Greek policy.

Yet in autumn 1945 it would have been an easy thing to initiate a change of policy. Agencies for control and intervention were present in the form of the various Missions and they would no doubt have taken suitable action if given clear instructions. Thus the lack of any will to change at the top of the Foreign Office became one of the causes of the continuing disastrous evolution in Greece.

NOTES

1. Leeper to Foreign Office 24th September, 1945 (R 16280/4/19).
2. Leeper to Foreign Office 28th September, 1945 (R 16628/4/19).
3. MacVeagh to State Department 25th September, 1945 (*FRUS 1945, VIII,* p. 162).
4. *Ibid.*, p. 163.
5. *Ibid.*
6. See p. 158, 164.
7. Leeper to Foreign Office 2nd October, 1945 (R 17133/4/19).
8. Leeper to Foreign Office 30th September, 1945 (R 16649/4/19).
9. Leeper to Foreign Office 1st October, 1945 (R 16720/4/19).
10. See p. 197.
11. Leeper to Foreign Office 4th October, 1945 (R 16948/4/19).
12. Leeper to Foreign Office 12th October, 1945 (R 17396/4/19).
13. MacVeagh to State Department 4th October, 1945 (*FRUS 1945, VIII,* p. 168).
14. *Ibid.*, p. 170.
15. Leeper to Foreign Office 8th October, 1945 (R 17083/4/19).
16. MacVeagh to State Department 7th October, 1945 (*FRUS 1945, VIII,* pp. 170 ff).
17. *Ibid.*, p. 171.
18. Leeper to Foreign Office 8th October, 1945 (R 17130/4/19).
19. Leeper to Foreign Office 8th October, 1945, no. 2062 (R 17131/4/19).
20. Leeper to Foreign Office 8th October, 1945, no. 2063 (R 17131/4/19).
21. MacVeagh reported to Washington that Leeper recommended—*expressis verbis*—a Left-Centre government. *FRUS 1945, VIII,* pp. 170 ff.
22. Foreign Office to Leeper 11th October, 1945 (R 16628/4/19). See also Laskey's Minutes 2nd October, 1945 (R 16720/4/19).
23. Hayter's Minutes 3rd October, 1945 (R 16720/4/19).
24. Foreign Office to Leeper 11th October, 1945 (R 16628/4/19).

25. Foreign Office to Leeper 8th October, 1945 (R 17083/4/19). The main argument was that Tsouderos' name was connected with the suppression of the troubles in the Greek armed forces-in-exile!
26. Foreign Office to Leeper 9th October, 1945 (R 17131/4/19).
27. Hayter's Minute 10th October, 1945 (R 17193/4/19).
28. Leeper, *op. cit.*, p. 3; Richter, *op. cit.*, pp. 186 *passim*, 221 *passim*.
29. Leeper to Foreign Office 11th October, 1945 (R 17309/4/19).
30. Leeper to Foreign Office 22nd October, 1945 (R 18327/4/19); *FRUS 1945*, VIII, p. 173.
31. See p. 197 Foreign Office to Leeper 17th October, 1945 (R 17131/4/19).
32. Leeper to Foreign Office 22nd October, 1945 (R 18327/4/19); *FRUS 1945*, VIII, p. 174.
33. *The Times*, 20th October, 1945.
34. Foreign Office to Leeper 20th October, 1945 (R 18452/4/19).
35. Leeper to Foreign Office 25th October, 1945 (R 18171/4/19).
36. Leeper commented: 'Venizelos is a man who is well intentioned rather than persistent, who tries to rise to an occasion but soon tires and will I suspect return with relief to his game of bridge of which he is a player of international note and distinction with a feeling that he has done his duty to his country.' Leeper to Foreign Office 31st October, 1945 (R 18452/4/19).
37. *Ibid.*
38. On Metaxas' OCHI (No!) of 28th October, 1940 see Compton Mackenzie, *Wind of Freedom: The History of the Invasion of Greece by the Axis Powers 1940-41* (London: Chatto and Windus, 1943), p. 64 and Richter, *op. cit.*, pp. 80 ff.
39. Leeper to Foreign Office 5th November, 1945 (R 18790/4/19).
40. C.M. Woodhouse, *British Foreign Policy since the Second World War*, (London: Hutchinson, 1961), p. 200.

THE EVOLUTION OF THE LEFT FROM VARKIZA UP TO OCTOBER 1945

On the 12th February 1945 George Siantos, Dimitrios Partsalidis and Ilias Tsirimokos had signed the Varkiza Agreement for EAM. Directly afterwards Siantos faced the international press: EAM had pursued two objectives—liberation of the country and the safeguarding of the people's liberties *(laïkon eleftherion)*. The first objective had been achieved with the German withdrawal. But the fight for the second objective continued. The December events had not been a revolution but a clash with those forces which regarded state power as their prerogative. EAM had not sought this clash; quite the contrary, it had done everything possible to ensure normal democratic evolution and for that reason had accepted the Lebanon Agreement and entered the government. By contrast, the other side had not fulfilled the obligations it had undertaken because these had threatened its monopoly of power. This had brought about the clash. KKE intended to be politically active as a party loyal to the constitution, within the limits set by that constitution. He was satisfied with the Varkiza Agreement, just as the people in its totality would be satisfied, except for those whose party-political interests were different. Now the task was to restore peace to the country as quickly as possible and to begin reconstruction.[1]

The EAM delegation left Varkiza the same day and reached Trikala, the Central Committee's headquarters, on the 14th via Thebes and Lamia.[2] Their arrival and the reaction of EAM's supporters to the announcement of the peace conditions has been graphically described by Dominique Eudes in a chapter entitled *Trauma*.[3] An account of that evening's Central Committee session published in EAM's evening paper, *Eleftheri Ellada,* of 15th February implies that the delegation's report on the Varkiza results aroused severe criticism. Siantos had to defend himself against the charge that, at Varkiza, he had surrendered unconditionally. He argued that the alternatives had been to conclude peace or to fight on. It had been EAM's firm resolve to put an end to the fighting and open the way for the country's peaceful development. At the time when the war against Germany was continuing it had been a matter of duty to end the armed conflict. But there had been no capitulation: the Varkiza peace treaty was a compromise. It gave the people the possibility of fighting for their interests by legal means and it gave EAM the right openly to pursue the realisation of its aims. The next task was to ratify the peace treaty;

later one could look again.[4]

At the session of the KKE Political Bureau on the same evening criticism was also heard. The former secretary of the Thessaly KKE and then editor of the party newspaper *Rizospastis,* Kostas Karagiorgis, with the support of the party theoretician Yannis Zevgos, attacked Siantos.[5] But it was reported that the criticism was unanimously rejected after an appeal to the critics to conform to party discipline. The party's appeal to Bolshevik solidarity *(bolsevistiki monolithikotita)* worked and the results of Varkiza were 'unanimously' approved.[6] In the same way Siantos achieved acceptance of the Varkiza terms from ELAS HQ where the GHQ capetan, Aris Velouchiotis, who with almost prophetic foresight predicted the future course of events,[7] put up a massive case for continuing the fight. He refused to sign the Order of the Day announcing the result of Varkiza to ELAS and ordering its demobilisation.[8] Siantos then put him under pressure, reminding him of his duty to conform to party discipline. Aris succumbed and together with the military commander of ELAS, General Stefanos Sarafis who also had reservations, they signed the last ELAS Order of the Day, the order for demobilisation. The reason why Aris backed down could have been twofold: despite his achievements during the Occupation, his position within the party was diminished by the 'repentance statement' *(dilosi)* which he had signed under the Metaxas dictatorship; also he may have feared that, if he refused, it might come to conflict with the party which would only help the British.[9]

But, in contrast to the party leadership, Aris was even now still concerned for the future of his comrades-in-arms. He submitted a memorandum suggesting that the most exposed and therefore endangered guerrillas should not return home but should go abroad, where they might perhaps get further military training and thus form a potential reserve in the case of renewed conflict. He himself would join this group.[10] Siantos, however, wanted Aris to go to Athens with the rest of the ELAS High Command. Sarafis who knew both that Aris was suffering from *trauma* as a result of the tortures he had endured under Metaxas and the *dilosi,* and that the British intended to declare him a war criminal, intervened for him and recommended that he be sent either to Albania or Yugoslavia.[11] Siantos agreed and Aris, with some of his closest followers, went to Albania to await developments. At an EAM rally on the 15th February, Siantos declared the armed struggle at an end and the start of a new struggle, for democracy and popular sovereignty. Everyone must join the pan-democratic front to overcome existing opposition and for an eventual victory.[12] To the subordinate party organisations Yannis Ioannidis gave the following radio message: it was the task of the party organisations to analyse the Varkiza Agreement and expound the reasons for its signing to the party members and to EAM and ELAS. The general political directives were: struggle for the complete restoration of democratic

EVOLUTION OF THE LEFT FROM VARKIZA TO OCTOBER 1945   237

liberties and for economic development; maintenance of the unity of EAM and creation of a broad pan-democratic front; enlightenment of the party and the people as to their chief duties under present circumstances. For the moment organisational problems were of decisive importance. Functioning must be ensured and so must vigilance on the part of the organisations and the technical apparatus. Measures were being taken to set up a party self-defence force *(ethnofylaki kommatikes dynameis)*. The basic pre-condition for fulfilling the party's obligations was contact with the masses. The open practice of terror by the Plastiras government must be subjected to daily exposure by the party organisations. To characterise the government as fascist would be inopportune for the time being. Under the responsible leadership of the district secretaries and with the co-operation of the capetans, the organisations should secrete a considerable quantity of arms. Guerilla assemblies should be held at which it should be explained why ELAS was being demobilised and why it was the duty of all ELAS members to return to the towns and villages. It should also be explained to them that an association of National Liberation Fighters 1941-1944 would be established which all ELAS members should join.[13]

If one compares this radio message with the final Order of the Day of ELAS GHQ, of 16th February 1945, for the demobilisation of ELAS,[14] the cynicism of the Political Bureau becomes apparent. The demobilisation of ELAS is here reduced to an organisational problem arbitrarily decided upon by the leadership. The former district secretary, Pavlos Nefeloudis, recalls with bitterness:

'The only right of the hundreds of thousands of party members during the Occupation was the right to work superhumanly, day and night, for the carrying out of the party line, for the liberation of the Greek people from fascist slavery, to sacrifice themselves, to fight and to get themselves killed. No discussion of the party line, no exposition or solution of party problems was ever. . . brought before the party members. The Lebanon Agreement and the Caserta Agreement were not even discussed within the party after the event. They simply announced that they had signed without ever publishing the texts. The policy pursued towards the British after the liberation, the decision for the December conflict—if there actually was such a decision—the Varkiza Agreement, were not seen as problems of policy concerning the party members, except in so far as concerned its execution and the consequences.'[15]

In other words, the behaviour of the KKE leadership described by Nefeloudis is an example of the well-known phenomenon of 'democratic centralism'—the leadership decided and the party members had to obey. In a consolidated Western European Communist Party, such as the French or the Italian, such a procedure could function without the internal cohesion of the party suffering. In the case of KKE the signing of the

Varkiza Agreement and the way in which it was imposed on the party led to a fundamental crisis.

Siantos had no alternative but to sign the agreement.[16] But the political objective of the KKE leadership of pursuing integration in the parliamentary system was unrealistic as there had never been a parliamentary system in Greece which would allow the KKE to participate. The whole illusory concept shows both the low theoretical level of KKE and its complete dependence on abstract revolutionary models 'made in Moscow' and schematically applied to Greek conditions.

As a result of the Comintern intervention of 1931, KKE's leadership had not only adopted the Comintern's revolutionary timetable but also the obligatory organisational methods including 'democratic centralism'. The introduction of this, with its iron party discipline, had worked well at that particular time: it put an end to the fighting fractions and the 2,000 party members registered in 1928 achieved a relative organisational cohesion.[17] But the theoretical level of the party hardly changed. The leading cadres, trained in the KUTV (Kommunisticheskii Universitet Trudyashchaya Vostoka, Communist University of the Workers of the East, 1921-1952), simply passed on what they had been taught. As a result of the world economic depression, the number of members had risen to 17,500 in 1935 but this relatively high figure should not delude one into thinking that more than a very few of them were true communists in the sense of being adherents of the teachings of Marx and Lenin. Most of them had come to KKE through opposition to the existing system, as a form of protest. This became clear directly the party was exposed to the persecutions of the fascist Metaxas dictatorship. By 1939 the number of members who, under massive pressure in the dictatorship's prisons, could not be brought to sign the notorious repentance statements (*dilosi*) fell to about 2,000. Of these about 700 were fortunate enough to escape from the prisons at the beginning of the Occupation.[18]

During the Occupation, membership figures rose mightily, so that, on liberation, the party claimed 400,000 enrolled members.[19] KKE had become a mass party. The most plausible explanation for this success may be the lack of any alternative to KKE. All the other parties, even the socialists, were patronage networks which had nothing, either politically or organisationally, to offer the masses, to fulfil their wish for common action against the invaders. The consequence was that KKE became a reservoir for many progressive forces. Meanwhile, the EAM popular movement and its subsidiary organisations proliferated and at the end of the Occupation numbered 1,500,000 members, recruited from all classes and strata of the population. To summarise, KKE became the fulcrum of a mass movement embracing the whole Greek people.

But this process of development into a mass popular movement had repercussions on KKE itself. At an increasing rate it evolved from a homogenous party of cadres into an extremely heterogenous mass party, in which were blended genuine communists, socialists, patriots with vague political aims and even opportunists and this was even more the case with EAM. The unifying factor was the general wish for liberation of the country from the occupying powers and the yearning for a socially just and democratic post-war society. The strongest bond was, however, a common object of hatred—the fascist conqueror. This was in itself a programme for conflict. Liberation would inevitably be followed by discussion within the popular movement of the form of post-war society which each of the different trends would seek to establish. This would not necessarily imply dissolution, provided that the debate proceeded democratically from discussions and decisions reached at the grassroots.

But just here lay the 'hereditary' weakness of EAM and KKE. The KKE leadership, which had had an important influence on the rise of this popular movement, tried not only to maintain the organisational principle of 'democratic centralism' within KKE but also to impose it on EAM. In other words, they did not comprehend the true character of the mass movement and tried to control a spontaneous mass rising bureaucratically, by the organisational principles suited to a homogenous cadre party. This resulted in the mistaken decisions of the Occupation period culminating in the Varkiza Agreement.

The tendency towards bureaucratic control of the revolution became apparent in the Ioannidis radio message to subordinate party agencies. It shows both the lack of psychological sensitivity and the political ignorance of the Political Bureau. The battle for Athens had indeed been lost, but the main body of the active ELAS units remained unaffected, whilst the EAM organisations still controlled large areas of the country. The Political Bureau's decision to carry on the fight for a better future by political means within the existing political system would have required a prior process of enlightenment at the grassroots. Without psychological preparation, the change from limitless power to submission before the restored bourgeois system inevitably led to the break-up of EAM and to a severe crisis within KKE. The way in which the Political Bureau ordered the demobilisation of ELAS and thereby bureaucratically liquidated the revolution shook the confidence of party members in the leadership to its foundations. The second-ranking leaders spoke of betrayal at the top;[20] whilst the membership was full of bitterness and distrust of the leadership.[21] Thousands left the party and EAM broke up with the withdrawal of the socialists. This gives the Varkiza Agreement another dimension. It can be seen as the starting point for the degeneration of KKE from a mass party to a cadre party of Stalinist character.

The decision of the Political Bureau to order concealment of part of the ELAS arms has been interpreted by historians such as Kousoulas[22] and Pavlopoulos[23] as meaning that already at the time of the signing of the

Varkiza Agreement, the KKE leadership was aiming at the next 'round' (the third) of armed conflict. As a proof they cite statements of Karagiorgis and Zachariadis from the years 1948-50.[24] But an analysis of this 'evidence' shows that Karagiorgis' criticism only referred to the way the decision was carried out; whilst Zachariadis' statements, which tried to re-interpret the Varkiza Agreement, only serve to conceal and obfuscate the real facts.[25]

It must be firmly stated that, when signing the Varkiza Agreement, the KKE leadership was not thinking of a 'third round'. The order to secrete a part of the arms—itself a habitual practice in Greece—was probably a precautionary measure so as to be able in case of need to arm the 'party self-defence force' referred to by Ioannidis.[26] It was a defensive measure and in no way a strategic decision in preparation for a 'third round'. To interpret the Varkiza Agreement as a tactical retreat to win time to re-group for a fresh attack does the strategic planning capabilities of the KKE leadership too much credit. Finally, the charge prevalent at the time that Siantos was a British agent who consciously led the Left to defeat, is quite simply absurd.[27] For the KKE leadership, the Varkiza Agreement meant the end of the armed conflict of December 1944 and the portal to integration in the existing system.

During the next weeks, the EAM and KKE leaderships fulfilled the obligations they had assumed at Varkiza. ELAS was demobilised and, with the exception of a few groups such as that of Aris Velouchiotis, the former guerillas accepted the leadership's decisions and returned to their homes. Their arms, with the few exceptions we have mentioned, were surrendered. Meanwhile the KKE leadership tried to justify the December events to their party members. In the February number of the Central Committee's theoretical journal, *Kommounistiki Epitheorisi (KOMEP)*, the Political Bureau members Chrysa Hajivasiliou and Vasilis Bartziotas (Fanis) took up the word from Karagiorgis. The Central Committee member and former National Unity Government minister, Miltiadis Porfyrogenis, wrote on the taking of hostages. The tenor of the articles was that the December events had been a regrettable misunderstanding, provoked by the Greek Right.[28] In the March number, the leading article demanded the application of the Yalta decisions in Greece, too, and this was followed by the texts of the Yalta and Varkiza Agreements. There was a long and detailed article by Bartziotas on organisational problems from the content of which one can draw conclusions as to the extent of the party's internal crisis. For example, Bartziotas demanded a purge of unreliable elements and systematic training in party discipline. He demanded that the subordinate party leadership carry out with exactitude the Central Committee's and Political Bureau's decisions, without adapting them in accordance with their own judgment. The leading party cadres must be 'engineers of souls', as Stalin had said. For subordinate party organisations to hold local plenums at which the political situation was discussed, was unacceptable. This was the business of the Central Committee alone. The 'enlightenment' branch must be considerably improved. To summarise: Bartziotas demanded the enforcement of 'democratic centralism' within the party, that is the transformation of a mass party into a rigorously-organised cadre party of Soviet type. At the same time, what he said showed that the KKE leadership was preparing the party for functioning legally within the system.[29]

To make clear to members the party's political line and to demonstrate to them that KKE was not alone in pursing integration, *KOMEP* published a speech of Maurice Thorez addressed to a session of the French Communist Party's Central Committee in January 1945.[30] The same purpose was served by an article on the relationship between the Chinese Communist Party and Chiang Kai-Shek, in the title of which the word *symfiliosi* (reconciliation) made its first programmatic appearance. Finally, in the 'Internal Affairs Retrospective', it was noted that KKE and EAM had fulfilled their obligations undertaken at Varkiza but that the other side had not. However, the criticism voiced in this article was fairly reserved. Instead attention was drawn to the memorandum submitted by EAM to the four embassies demanding the sending of an inter-allied commission to enquire into the situation in Greece and the formation of a representative government.[31] On 20th March, in an interview in *Rizospastis,* Siantos spoke in the same sense.[32]

But all this explanatory paperwork did not succeed in resolving the crisis amongst the KKE membership. On the contrary, as the National Guard's repressive measures extended to the whole of the country, criticism of the party leaders grew sharper. The ordinary members saw that, in contrast to their plight, the KKE leadership remained unmolested; as a result, they began to talk of betrayal. In Northern Greece, where National Guard repression was at its most brutal, many thousands of Slavo-Macedonians, former guerillas, disobeyed party orders to return to their homes and, on their own initiative, fled across the frontier into Yugoslavia.[33] The capetans close to Aris Velouchiotis began to talk of putting up a National Salvation Front against the party and of continuing the struggle.[34] On the 15th March the ELD Central Committee met, severely criticised the attitude of KKE during the Occupation and demanded the dissolution of EAM and its transformation into a mass organisation independent of the parties.[35] These alarming signs of disintegration of the left-wing camp in general and also of KKE itself prompted the KKE leadership to act. The Political Bureau called the Eleventh Central Committee Plenum for the beginning of April.

The importance attached by the leadership to the Eleventh Plenum is shown by the fact that not only Central Committee members but non-members too were invited.[36] The session began on the 5th April and ended on the 10th and was held in a house near the Larisa railway station in Athens. There were two topics: evolution of the party since the Tenth Plenum of January 1944 and the party's new organisational problems.

As with all KKE Central Committee sessions, source information about the Plenum is scarce. In 1945 KKE published only the notice of the Plenum, its programme and the decisions on the two topics; though the obligatory statement that all decisions had been taken unanimously was not lacking.[37] But an article by Zisis Zografos in *Neos Kosmos* of 1950 and also later articles by participants make possible a fairly complete reconstruction.[38]

The introductory report on the evolution of the party since the Tenth Plenum was given by Siantos. Its content is not known. But the subsequent discussion gave rise to heated debate within the Central Committee.[39] Kissavos even speaks of the 'chaos of the Eleventh Plenum'.[40] Lack of written sources makes it impossible to determine the composition of the various groups. There seem to have been three viewpoints: that of the Political Bureau, that of Karagiorgis and Zevgos and that of Markos Vafiadis. The Political Bureau's viewpoint, in addition to Siantos, was supported mainly by Chrysa Hajivasiliou, Partsalidis and Ioannidis. Chrysa's speech, for which there is most information, showed very clearly the Political Bureau's position and the line followed by the KKE leadership during the Occupation.

She made it clear that the policy of national unity against the invader and the national liberation struggle were not specifically a KKE policy but a policy followed by all the communist parties in the occupied countries. On this there was general agreement. It was only in the content and the goals of this struggle that there were differences. She energetically rejected the interpretation according to which the end of the national liberation struggle should have been the winning of power by KKE. The party had been right in not pursuing such a strategic aim. Certainly, the fight had been a fight for social change but not for the establishment of a People's Democracy. An evolution parallel to that in Yugoslavia had been impossible for geographic, economic and political reasons. The Greek problem was quite differently conditioned on grounds of both internal and external policy. The deciding factor was Great Britain. She went on to describe how a possible confrontation with the British had not only been in no way prepared but how the Political Bureau had inhibited all thought of this. The basic error had been the failure to search persistently for a compromise solution. There had been no clear political perspective. They had found themselves involved in the December events without knowing when or how to extricate themselves. The reason for this—she added by way of self-criticism—was the lack of a spirit of collectivity within the Political Bureau.[41]

Ioannidis confirmed Chrysa's criticism of the lack of perspective shown by the Political Bureau.[42] Finally, Partsalidis justified KKE's policy in not fighting for power on the basis of a letter from Zachariadis and assigned the main blame to Great Britain.[43]

From the above one can conclude: that the Political Bureau was of the opinion that the general KKE policy had been correct; that the basic error had lain in not pursuing a political compromise with Great Britain with sufficient consistency; and that a radically different line had not been possible. If events had led to the present unfortunate situation, this was due to foreign factors and to the human shortcomings of the KKE leadership. It is of interest that throughout this criticism and self-criticism by the Political Bureau Varkiza was not mentioned.

It was exactly here that the dissidents began their criticism. Zevgos, Karagiorgis and Markos stigmatised the Varkiza Agreement as a mistake. Karagiorgis, who was not present in person—he was in San Francisco reporting the UNO inaugural conference for *Rizospastis*—took his criticism one step further: he attacked the Political Bureau itself and demanded its replacement on account of Varkiza;[44] furthermore he made a fundamental criticism of the party's line during the Occupation.[45] According to Markos' report, the Political Bureau retreated in face of this weighty attack and declared itself ready to submit to the judgment of the Central Committee.[46] The result was that Zevgos withdrew his proposal to put the issue of Varkiza to a vote because he feared that, if the agreement were condemned as a mistake, the government could take this to imply repudiation. Markos who had condemned Varkiza for different reasons—he was of the opinion that the fight could have been carried on and he knew by personal experience the consequences of the disarming of ELAS—aligned himself with Zevgos. Thus there remained only Karagiorgis' criticism and, as he was not there to follow it up, the session proceeded according to programme.[47] Taken under these circumstances, the Eleventh Plenum's decisions were in the nature of a compromise. Though some mistakes were acknowledged, there was no in-depth analysis of the reasons for them.[48]

It was resolved that the Party's political line and tactics had been fundamentally correct; but that, in practical application, there had been serious defects, inefficiency, mistakes, and both left- and right-wing deviations which had complicated the struggle against fascism and for democratic renewal. The more serious mistakes of a right-wing character had been: the Lebanon Agreement, which had not corresponded to the true balance of forces and therefore had not sufficiently promoted and safeguarded the realisation of national unity and normal democratic development in the face of reactionary intrigues; and the Caserta Agreement which had been a consequence of the Lebanon Agreement. Support for Papandreou's economic policy had also been a right-wing deviation. Left-wing deviations of a political and military character had occurred during the December events. They had arisen from an incorrect assessment of the policy of the Churchill government, from under-estimation of the forces of reaction and an over-estimation of the movement's own resources and, finally, above all from inadequate political flexibility. These factors had prevented the party leadership from attaining a clear perspective on the evolution of the conflict and had led them to overlook favourable opportunities for the early conclusion of an agreement with the British, an agreement which would certainly have proved more favourable than Varkiza. The arrest of non-combatants (hostages) during December had been a serious political error which had permitted the reaction to start a slander campaign. In general the December events were interpreted as an act of resistance by the whole people against an attempted reactionary *coup d'état*. Finally, the Varkiza Agreement was seen as an important step in the fight against fascism and for normal democratic evolution.[49]

These resolutions show that the Political Bureau had won its case. Faced with the opposition within the Central Committee itself and from the ranks of the membership, the party leaders had admitted some of the more obvious mistakes. But this was done so cautiously that the leadership's authority remained unimpaired. This tactical withdrawal in the face of opposition proved successful: the Central Committee made no changes in the Political Bureau's composition.[50] Continuity of policy was guaranteed.

This, too, became apparent in that part of the resolution which dealt with foreign policy. KKE demanded Greece's independence and integrity, the safeguarding of the frontiers through peaceful solution of all differences with neighbours, and the fraternal cooperation of all Balkan peoples, and the application of the people's right to self-determination which would restore national integrity. Within the country all national minorities must be guaranteed equal rights. In its foreign policy, KKE demanded uniformly good relations with Great Britain, the Soviet Union, the USA and the country's Balkan neighbours. Any one-sided foreign policy orientation would be disastrous for national interests.[51] In other words, KKE stuck to its previous line. Opposition from the membership was countered with a second resolution on organisational problems, demanding the practical application of 'democratic centralism'.[52] Kissavos reports as follows on the way in which these resolutions of the Eleventh Plenum were brought home to party members.

> 'One day about a dozen cadres assembled in a house in the Agios Athanasios district of Larisa to hear this Plenum analysed. The analysis was presented by the No. 1 and No. 2 of the Thessaly Regional Bureau (Kosavras and Loules). When the former had finished, they asked those present to give their opinions. No one wanted to be the first to speak. This demonstrated—without any need of words—that all were dissatisfied on all the issues covered by the resolutions. The Secretary urged the comrades to express their opinions. Thereupon one or two

muttered grudgingly that they agreed or that they did not. Then he asked me. I replied that I had nothing to say. But he insisted on hearing my opinion. I replied: "I understand nothing from this resolution and see nothing fundamental regarding our future work".'[53]

In other words, KKE's crisis continued. This raises questions about the reasons for the leadership's behaviour.

The extent of the defeat should have demanded an investigation of the soundness of the Party's whole political line over the last years. But, since this line had not been evolved by the KKE leadership itself on the basis of an analysis of the Greek situation, but was rather a schematic adaptation of Soviet concepts to Greek conditions, any searching inquiry would have implied a criticism of the Soviet line and might have precipitated a conflict between the leaders of KKE and the Soviet leadership. Since this was unthinkable for the former, the line had to be certified as correct. Another basic issue should have been policy towards Great Britain since it was this that had eventually led to disaster. But here the fear was obviously one of renewed confrontation with the British and so the former line was adhered to. Moreover, a critical assessment of this policy would have been a *post factum* justification of the critics within their own ranks and particularly of Aris' actions. A detailed self-criticism which would have examined the leadership's other mistakes during the Occupation would have brought the Political Bureau's authority into question, intensified the crisis of confidence within the party and would probably have led to the replacement of the Political Bureau itself. As it was a self-evident truth for the Political Bureau that only they knew the correct road to socialism, they took the easiest way out and disciplined the Party by organisational measures. It is possible that Siantos, Zevgos and Chrysa Hajivasiliou might have been prepared to show more flexibility, but they could not prevail against Yannis Ioannidis, the *éminence grise* of orthodoxy. Partsalidis who had signed the Varkiza Agreement, Rousos who had condemned the Middle East 'mutiny' and had signed the Lebanon Agreement, and Bartziotas who was one of those mainly responsible for the defective organisation of the fighting in Athens, may well have feared that they would be held to account and therefore sided with Ioannidis. The other members were either not strong enough personalities to resist openly or were colourless *apparatchiks* conforming dextrously with the majority of the moment. Ioannidis' promise that existing problems would be discussed at the forthcoming Seventh Party Congress[54] may however have proved decisive. Thus the results of the Eleventh Plenum confirmed the victory of the former Akronafplia prisoners,[55] the victory for Stalinist orthodoxy within the Political Bureau.

But outside the Political Bureau this orthodoxy was not able to prevail to the same extent. Within the party it could indeed generally enforce its line, but amongst the former ELAS capetans it met with resistance; many of the well-known capetans refused to obey the party leadership's instructions to return to their homes and remained in the mountains.[56] The socialists, too, despite lengthy negotiations, refused to participate in KKE's suggested re-organisation of EAM. Instead the groups round Tsirimokos and Svolos united in ESSAK[57] and were joined by Askoutsis and Stratis. Thereafter, on 24th April, EAM was transformed from an Alliance of Parties and Organisations into a Coalition of Parties (Politikos synaspismos ton kommaton tou EAM). EEAM/ERGAS, EPON and the other subsidiary organisations of the old EAM lost their seats on the Central Committee. But each of the parties belonging to the new EAM[58] was to have one representative on the Central Committee, whose decisions would be put into practice by the existing party machines. The individual parties were to be independent and bound to EAM only by the common programme.[59]

Whilst at first sight this re-structuring would seem to give KKE a minority position, in fact its predominance was guaranteed because it was the only party in the coalition with a properly-functioning apparatus at its disposal and moreover some of the parties were communist-controlled 'front' parties. In other words, the EAM of the Occupation no longer existed.

At the same time there were rumours in Athens of an impending change in the KKE leadership. The trade unionist Vasilis Nefeloudis, who had played an important part in the Middle East troubles, was mentioned as a possible candidate, according to Leeper's report to the Foreign Office. But, as there was no hard news of Zachariadis' whereabouts, the contenders to succeed him hesitated to declare themselves.[60] But, as Leeper himself acknowledged, these were merely rumours; yet despite that he advised the Foreign Office to get the Americans to search for Zachariadis amongst the survivors of Dachau. Leeper's information did not come from the narrow circle of the KKE leadership—that was too well sealed off—but it could have emanated from the ranks of second-grade cadres. In Athens there are hardly any secrets. This must be regarded as another symptom of the crisis within KKE.

Discussion of a possible change in the leadership came to an abrupt end when, on 1st May 1945, *Rizospastis* published as a special edition a telegram from Karagiorgis, who was reporting the UN inauguration conference at San Francisco for the paper, under the title: 'Our heroic Party Leader, Comrade N. Zachariadis Free'.[61] American troops, liberating the Dachau concentration camp, had found Zachariadis amongst the survivors. The headlines of *Rizospastis* of 1st and 2nd May indicated that Zachariadis was still considered the legitimate party leader. But his return was delayed. On 16th May *Rizospastis* announced his imminent arrival. Actually, he returned to Athens on the 29th.

Despite all the joyful publicity, the fact that Zachariadis was alive was a cause of considerable anxiety to the KKE leadership. How would he take the existing situation? To 'tidy up the house' before his arrival, there now began a spate of hectic activity. An effort was made to close party ranks and to clear up relations with Great Britain. The Eleventh Plenum resolutions were discussed at rank-and-file meetings and, as *Rizospastis* reported, were 'unanimously' approved. But, as Markos was to say later,[62] all were united in repudiating Varkiza. On 23rd May Siantos, Partsalidis, Ioannidis and Kostas Despotopoulos (the former legal and diplomatic adviser to ELAS GHQ) met Woodhouse. In talks lasting four hours they tried to convince him of the need for a fresh start in relations between Great Britain and KKE: as communists, they had of course a special sympathy for the Soviet Union; but as Greek communists they had likewise a great sympathy for Britain. They asked Woodhouse to intervene for an improvement in relations. Woodhouse got the impression that the KKE leadership was in a state of great anxiety, almost of despair.[63] In other words—just as during the Occupation—the KKE leaders were trying to re-establish their respectability.

When Woodhouse reported the content of this conversation in London, the reaction was reserved. Hayter commented:

'. . . I think we might leave these discredited individuals to their own anxieties; if we want to get in touch with the Communists we could. . . [illegible] M. Zachariadis who is uncompromised by any participation in the December fighting.'[64]

Leeper was instructed accordingly.

On 28th May Markos Vafiadis addressed a letter to the Political Bureau. The introductory sentences are illuminating in regard to the atmosphere at the Eleventh Plenum. Markos wrote:

'I believe it is my duty to refer to certain views of mine on particular points which were, indeed, discussed at the Eleventh Plenum but which, in my opinion, were not made sufficiently clear since at the Plenum I was completely unprepared, neither knowing the subjects for discussion, nor having the time to think over them and draw conclusions. In other words, I was taken by surprise. But I admit that the atmosphere was not such as to afford me the opportunity for cool and objective consideration.'

Markos went on to deal with the problem of the winning of power. Neither the majority nor the minority of the Political Bureau had understood the issue aright. It was a fact that, from the beginning of the Occupation, the Party had not taken up a position on this issue. At that time this had corresponded fully to existing circumstances and had therefore been a correct position. But, like every other party, KKE had the winning of power as its strategic goal. The Party's tactics were, of course, determined by existing objective conditions, but needed to orientate themselves by this aim. A series of factors, arising during the Occupation, had created a new situation and had brought KKE close to its strategic goal, so that the original position had—at least after Lebanon—been superceded. The party had been confronted with the problem of winning power in the form of a workers' and peasants' government together with the other allied parties constituting EAM. Such a government would have solved the bourgeois-democratic problem and would have opened the way for further evolution. With the exception of Athens, the whole of Greece had been under the control of such a regime. But the Party had not realised this and had hesitated to install the same regime in Athens. This was the decisive mistake and in this context the decisive factor had been the attitude of the Party to Great Britain. At the Eleventh Plenum it became clear that the Party leadership was of the opinion that, so long as Great Britain took a hostile stand towards KKE, no other course was possible. This meant renunciation of any kind of change and was the worst sort of opportunism.[65]

In his analysis, Markos had pointed out exactly the two basic mistakes of KKE during the Occupation: the fear of Great Britain and slavish adherence to the revolutionary plan and Comintern instruction for Popular Front tactics. Markos' position is fundamentally the same as Tito's who, in the face of Soviet and British opposition, had dared to take Yugoslavia direct to socialism.[66] But Markos' letter to the Political Bureau was intended less as a show-down with the existing leadership than as an analysis of the situation to brief Zachariadis whose arrival was now imminently expected. He hoped Zachariadis would steer a new and different course. This hope was shared by the thousands of persecuted party members. 'Suddenly the errors of the past, the terror in the streets, seemed no more than temporary mishaps. Zachariadis would rewrite history.'[67] Zachariadis was awaited like a messiah. The explanation of this phenomenon lies in the almost mystic aura of his personality.

Nikolaos Zachariadis was born in 1903 in Adrianopol (now Edirne), the son of *petit bourgeois* parents. Because his father frequently changed his workplace, he grew up in several towns of the former Turkey (Skopje, Nicomedia-Ismit, Constantinople). His formal education consisted of primary school and a year of high school. From 1919 he worked in Constantinople as a docker and later as a sailor on the Black Sea route. In these years he made contact with local trade union organisations. In 1923 he joined the Turkish Communist Party. From 1923 until the beginning of 1924 he was in the Soviet Union where he got an initial training as a party cadre. In 1924 the Comintern sent him to Greece where, until 1929, he held various posts within the KKE youth movement OKNE and in the Party itself, his activity being punctuated by several short periods in prison. From 1929 to 1931 he studied at the Higher Party School KUTV in the Soviet Union. In 1931, in the process of a Comintern intervention, he was installed as secretary of the Political Bureau. In 1934, at the Fifth Party Congress, he was elected General-Secretary.[68] In 1936 he was arrested by Maniadakis' secret police and until 1941 was in prison in Corfu, whence he was collected by the Gestapo and taken to Dachau.

The Comintern's intervention put an end to factional fighting and in the next years membership rose by leaps and bounds. Both were seen by Zachariadis as personal successes and his entourage encouraged this belief. All party successes were attributed to him: in other words he began to cultivate what has now entered history under the name of personality cult. At the Sixth Party Congress in 1935 this was in full bloom. Pavlos Nefeloudis recalls:

> 'The Sixth Party Congress can be seen as the Party Congress which implanted and fostered personality cult in Greece. To all the defects which characterised the internal functioning of our party from its birth there was now added a new evil, the cult of one person, of the person of the leader... They began to weave the legend of the "omniscient" (panexypnos), the great theoretician, the heroic leader... It is he who has created the new party strategy for a bourgeois revolution based on deep study and scientific analysis of the Greek situation. He it is who inspired the Resolutions of the Sixth Party Congress for a united Peasant Party. He is the great conspirator, the phantom whom the Security Police cannot catch.'[69]

Personality cult reached its climax when Bartziotas proclaimed: 'The Party is Zachariadis and Zachariadis is the Party.'[70]

Even when Zachariadis was in prison, the leading cadres who were still at liberty went on cultivating this legend. Zachariadis became a mythical figure. During the Occupation, the party circulated an anthem glorifying the intransigent fighter: 'Prison cannot break him and his thoughts fly direct to the comrades who are fighting...'[71] In the end those who themselves had created the myth began to believe in his superhuman powers and expected that he would be able to turn back the pages of history.

The true Zachariadis was a somewhat less imposing figure. The much-trumpeted Marxist-Leninist equipment of the great theoretician emerges on closer study and analysis of his publications as second-hand knowledge.[72] Thanks to his several years of training at KUTV, he knew the party dogmas rather better than many of the leading cadres who had no acquaintance with foreign languages—there were hardly any translations of Marxist texts—and he could therefore shine by his greater learning. He used his organisational talent to concentrate control of the party in his own hands. He had powers of quick apprehension which enabled him to grasp the thoughts of others and then produce them as his own—a method which he even practised with orders from the Comintern.[73] Nefeloudis sums up his character thus:

> 'N.Z. suffered from over-developed egoism. He regarded himself as omniscient and infallible. Even when there was something he didn't

know, he would say with hindsight "I knew that. I foresaw it". He admitted no other opinion alongside his own. Colleagues who doubted the validity of his judgments or those who retained their own personalities and opinions he no longer regarded as colleagues but as enemies.'[74]

On the decisive issue of the Party's political line, Zachariadis originally (1934) upheld a position exactly opposite to that of the Comintern. He was of the opinion that KKE should aim directly at establishing the dictatorship of the proletariat. When he realised he could not hope to prevail, he changed course and took over the theory of the bourgeois-democratic character of revolution in Greece and gave it out as his own. But in fact he continued to hold that his own theory was the right one[75] and this factor was to be of decisive importance in the developments leading up to the Civil War. It is hardly necessary to suggest that he attached little importance to Marxist self-criticism. But of what avail would his autocratic ambitions have been without an entourage which gave them systematic support? Zachariadis surrounded himself with a cohort of yes-men who confirmed him in his chosen course. Moreover, he had a certain *charisma* which even influenced independently-thinking leading cadres such as Karagiorgis and Markos. But anyone who had a strong enough personality or anyone whose success seemed to call his claim to sole leadership in question sooner or later became the victim of a purge.

Even in prison he remained the uncontested party leader. In Corfu prison he had held what amounted to a court amongst the other imprisoned communists, in which hierarchy was strictly observed. The years in Dachau detached him from Greek realities. The fact that a popular movement had arisen in Greece without him and that KKE had become a mass party and that this had happened under the leadership of Siantos whom he had replaced as General-Secretary in 1931 may have given him feelings of envy and jealousy which were perhaps not the least of the reasons for his later denunciation of Siantos.

After these years of absence, instead of setting out to acquaint himself with the actual situation on the spot, he returned in the frame of mind that he would have done it all better himself. After his liberation from Dachau, he had stayed in Paris for a few weeks where he made his first public appearance as General-Secretary of KKE. He gave an interview to a representative of the Greek bourgeois press (the newspaper *Embros*) in which he rejected any Greek territorial claims on Northern Epirus or against Bulgaria.[76] This raised a storm of protest in Athens, because Foreign Minister Sofianopoulos had raised these claims at the UN Inaugural Conference. After a frustrated attempt to visit the Soviet Union[77] from Paris, he returned to Greece on 29th May 1945 in an RAF plane.

On the 30th *Rizospastis* reported the party leader's return as a major sensation and Zachariadis made use of the opportunity to modify his

Paris statement: the journalist had both misinformed and misunderstood him.[78] On the 31st the paper published a long article in which Zachariadis defined his view of political problems and also a report of the mass rally organised by the party for his return. To demonstrate to party members that, even in the hands of the Gestapo, Zachariadis had continued to fight for the aims of KKE, it also published the text of a letter he was said to have sent on the 18th June 1941 from the Gestapo prison in Vienna to the examining magistrate.

Examination of text and content both strongly suggest that this letter was a forgery, serving only to put Zachariadis in a favourable light[79] and to show the party rank-and-file how the great leader had continued to fight for the party, even in the concentration camp.[80] But the mere fact of his survival in itself is extraordinary because he was, with Thälmann (the German CP leader who was murdered) the only leader of a national Communist Party to fall into Gestapo hands. Many thousands of far less prominent CP members did not survive the concentration camps.[81]

On the 1st June there was a special session of the Political Bureau, presided over by Zachariadis. Despite contrary statements, it seems that it came to a confrontation between Zachariadis and the Political Bureau members over his Paris statement. Faced with a campaign by the press and the politicians against EAM and KKE, which they were slandering as anti-national, the Political Bureau no doubt recalled the negative effects of its former Macedonian policy and Zachariadis' action was criticised.[82] This resulted in a Political Bureau statement: in principle the Party was against any armed adventurism, but KKE, too, supported the solution of territorial claims, which had also been among the aims of resistance to the Occupation. As far as concerned Northern Epirus, the Party was against the immediate military occupation of Northern Epirus by the Greek army, which would implicate Greece in a dangerous adventure and would contravene Allied rulings to the effect that territorial changes should be settled peacefully at the Peace Conference. KKE had always proclaimed that there existed an unresolved Northern Epirus problem which should be freely settled by the people of the region themselves. But the KKE representatives on the EAM Central Committee stated additionally that, for the sake of democratic unity, KKE was ready to accept the following standpoint:

'If the majority [of the democratic forces] decides in favour of the immediate military occupation of Northern Epirus by the Greek army, KKE will formulate its reservations but will submit to the majority decision.'[83]

This tortuous statement—and indeed the whole episode—in no way profited KKE but rather damaged it significantly in the eyes of 'nationally-minded' citizens, at a time when practically everyone was 'nationally-minded'. Zachariadis' statement supplied the ammunition for a campaign slandering KKE as anti-national.

Many years later, in 1950, Zachariadis characterised the Northern Epirus statement as a serious, fundamental and capital error by which KKE had succumbed to bourgeois nationalism.[84] This criticism is to a certain extent justified, only Zachariadis forgot that his Paris statement had provided the occasion for that genuflection.

On the same day Zachariadis presented himself to the Press. After introductory statements on Greece's territorial claims which he answered in the sense of the Political Bureau resolution, he went on to speak of KKE's political goals and declared:

'KKE was never for social revolution, for a revolution in the form of society. KKE's effort has always been, and remains to-day, to draw the majority of the people to its side... KKE has never raised the question of seizing power against the will of the majority. Only certain Trotskyists, anarchists and fools have said they would seize power by force against the people's will. Moreover, it was made clear at the sixth Plenum in 1934 that the forthcoming revolution will be of bourgeois-democratic character. It will be brought about by the peasants, the workers, the lower middle-class, in brief by the majority of the working people.'

When a journalist objected that to-day there were only two alternatives: bourgeois democracy or dictatorship of the proletariat, Zachariadis continued:

'That is wrong. Look at the French government in which communists are participating. Is France a bourgeois democracy? Surely not. But it is also not a dictatorship of the proletariat. France is to-day a popular democracy. That is the new form of government. That is our goal too. We are working for such a popular democracy, not for dictatorship of the proletariat.'[85]

Quite apart from Zachariadis' assertion that a popular democracy had been established in France which was of course absurd and which was rightly criticised by Vukmanović,[86] the interview leads to some interesting conclusions. During his stay in Paris, Zachariadis had obviously made contact with the French Communist Party's leadership and had realised that the French CP had likewise rejected the direct route to socialism and by its participation in the government was trying to give a different quality to the bourgeois state, to make it more democratic and closer to the people. Similar concepts were put forward by the Italian Communist Party.[87] Basically, this was still an attempt to realise the decisions of the Seventh World Comintern Congress of 1934. It must, however, be added that when, in statements of this period, the term popular democracy is used, this should in no way be given the connotations which it later acquired through the establishment of 'People's Democracies' in Eastern Europe.

Thus, Zachariadis' statements do not contain anything new. Already before liberation, KKE and EAM had demanded *laokratia* which in its literal sense means rule by the people. The only thing that was new was that Zachariadis advanced *laokratia* as a third alternative form of government. His reference to the French situation was meant as a further signal that KKE was pursuing a line of integration in the bourgeois state. But conditions in Greece were, in at least one point, radically different from those in France and Italy: KKE was already a mass party and during the Occupation it had become, through EAM, the strongest political force in the country. Greece's situation resembled much more that of Yugoslavia and, accordingly, the voices advocating a 'Yugoslav solution' were politically much stronger. Zachariadis' statements therefore show that he had aligned himself with orthodoxy, with the majority in the Political Bureau; indeed that he had even gone a step further by treating the French line expressly as a model. In other words, we are again confronted with the schematic takeover of a model which had little relation to Greek reality.

Zacharaidis' statements had two objectives: on the one hand KKE's readiness for integration was signalled to the bourgeois parties and to the British; on the other hand a message was addressed to the dissidents within the KKE ranks who were given clearly to understand what was the party line.

On 4th June Zachariadis visited Leeper, accompanied by Porfyrogenis. Leeper opened the conversation by describing Britain's policy towards Greece: Great Britain wanted to assist Greece with the reconstruction of its economy and in establishing a situation in which elections could be held; Great Britain had intervened in December because KKE had tried to seize power.

'I liked to think [and here I shielded Porfyrogenis from my gaze with my hand] that if Zachariadis had been in Athens there would have been no fighting. In any case the British had shown that they were prepared to fight for their ideas of democracy which in our conception [the right conception] meant fair play for all. It was highly important that this word "democracy" was defined more accurately.'

Zachariadis assured Leeper that KKE stood for close cooperation between the three great Allies and for free elections; that it would make no difficulties and would give Varvaressos' economic programme a chance. He himself would work for pacification and would provoke no trouble between Great Britain and the Soviet Union. Finally, Zachariadis gave categorial assurances that KKE would not boycott the elections and would accept their result. Leeper reported his satisfaction with the interview.[88]

On 5th June Zachariadis published an article in which he took up a position on relations between Greece and Britain. He stated that these relations needed to be clarified. 'We must make it clear from the start that, on internal political issues, we differ fundamentally and radically.' The majority of the people are of the opinion—and here he quoted the *Times* correspondent—that British policy towards Greece aims to suppress the Left and support reaction. This impression had been intensified by the December events and by the behaviour of British troops in the provinces. In the House of Commons Eden had quoted incorrect figures for the trade union elections. There were British units in Lamia, where Sourlas had his headquarters, and they took no action against him in spite of their moral obligation arising from the Varkiza Agreement. Democratic citizens got the impression that official Britain tolerated this situation. Others thought the British were acting on purpose, so as to restore the monarchy; but this was going too far.

There was mutual mistrust. It looked as if official Britian believed that a republican-democratic or popular democratic Greece would undermine Britain's strategic interests in the Mediterranean and in Greece. Greek reactionaries did all they could to intensify this impression.

'Greece's foreign policy revolves and must revolve round two basic poles: the Balkan-European and the Mediterranean. Geographically, politically and economically, Greece belongs to the Balkans and in a wider sense to Europe. There can be no doubt of this and foreign trade, both export and import, orient Greece towards the Balkans and Europe as its commercial and economic hinterland. . . But geographically Greece also belongs to the maritime highway of the Mediterranean which constitutes one of the most important sea-links of the British Empire. This is a fact which in view of the balance of power in Europe and in the world in general we cannot ignore. If we ignore it, we shall find ourselves outside reality. Therefore the democratic Left must accept this so as to remove mistrust on this [the British] side.'

Mistrust on the Greek Left could likewise be removed if Great Britain ceased from intervening in internal Greek affairs.

'We shall settle our own internal problems, freely and democratically, as we ourselves wish and in accordance with the will of our people. And then, freely and without compulsion, on an equal footing and not on the basis of an overlord-and-vassal relationship, we shall discuss with Britain the questions arising in the Mediterranean from Greece's geographical situation; we shall come to an agreement with Britain so long as our national honour, independence and integrity are not violated.'

In Great Britain's interest too this was a long-term consideration.[89] Leeper found Zachariadis' statements very sensible.[90] In other words, Zachariadis took over the KKE leadership's anglophile policy of the Occupation period and thus made any form of social change in Greece dependent on Great Britain's consent. Markos' analysis of the end of May was not taken into account. But even the theory of the two poles was not exclusive to Zachariadis. The Italian CP took a similar line.[91] In general, it looks as though Vukmanović was right in seeing this as the application of Soviet instructions to the West European communist parties.[92]

So, at this time Zachariadis' policy did not differ greatly in principle from that of the Political Bureau during the Occupation; but in the methods of its execution fundamental differences soon became apparent. During the Occupation and up to the Eleventh Plenum, the fiction of the 'closed ranks' had certainly existed but, in point of fact, under Siantos' leadership there had been something resembling an attempt to ascertain opinions by discussion; there had even been groups representing different opinions. Even with Aris, Siantos had never completely severed contact and had tried to argue him into conformity. Briefly, until Zachariadis' return there had been within KKE definite—if not very strongly defined—elements of internal democracy. Criticism of the party leadership was possible, as the examples of the Eleventh Plenum and of Markos' letter had shown, without drawing down on the critics party penalties or in the last resort expulsion. There had indeed been mistakes, as we have shown, but these had not been as crass as they might have been had party orthodoxy been given full rein. The dissidents had proved a corrective.

Zachariadis' return put an end to this 'liberalism'. The principle of 'democratic centralism', the leadership principle, now ruled supreme. The first victim of this new style leadership was Aris Velouchiotis who was seen as sabotaging the two basic political objectives: integration and reconciliation with Great Britain. Where Siantos had tried to solve the problem by letting Aris go abroad, Zachariadis did not even give him the chance of submission. He refused to discuss Aris' case. When the latter's brother, Babis Klaras, tried to explain Aris' motives for rebellion, he was not received and, when he handed in an extensive memorandum setting out these motives, Zachariadis did not even take note of it.[93] His decision had been taken: Aris was to be made an example. Party members were to be shown that, from now on, the principle of iron party discipline held sway and the sacrifice of Aris would demonstrate to the British that KKE was serious in its pro-British line.

On 12th June, the following notice appeared on the second page of *Rizospastis*:

'KKE publicly condemns Aris Velouchiotis. Comrade Zachariadis has informed us that the KKE Central Committee, having discussed reports submitted by various party organisations, has decided to condemn publicly the traitorous and adventurist behaviour of Aris Velouchiotis (Thanasis Klaras or Mizerias). Velouchiotis continued his activities even after the conclusion of the Varkiza Agreement. This behaviour, which could only aid reaction by giving it a weapon to attack KKE for breach of the Varkiza Agreement and by justifying its crimes, allows of no delay in publicly condemning Aris Velouchiotis. As is known, during the Metaxas' period Velouchiotis was arrested and signed a repentance statement condemning KKE.'[94]

Without taking into account the fact that there had been no session of the Central Committee,[95] this condemnation of the ELAS GHQ capetan constitutes a classic example of Stalinist slander. Zachariadis' assertion that reports (probably negative) about Aris' traitorous activity had been received lacks any foundation. After Varkiza Aris had in no sense continued offensive guerrila action but on his journey into Albania and back had confined himself to defensive action when attacked by the National Guard. The assertion that Aris' post-Varkiza activities had provoked the excesses of the Greek Right is complete distortion of the facts. The reference to his repentance statement was the worst sort of attack on personal honour. It is true that he had signed such a statement when he had been unable to withstand Metaxas' torture methods but he had subsequently more than rehabilitated himself by his role in ELAS and had achieved a renown which far exceeded that of most KKE leaders. One cannot of course tell how far motives of envy and jealousy played a part in the condemnation of Aris but they cannot be altogether excluded.

Aris, too, had hoped that Zachariadis would bring with him a new policy. When, on the 16th June, he learned from the newspaper of his condemnation he killed himself.[96] Aris, the inspirer and first organiser of the National Resistance Army, was the first victim of Zachariadis. Others were to follow. A right-wing band found Aris' body, cut off the head and stuck it up in the main square at Trikala where Siantos had announced the results of the Varkiza negotiations to the waiting EAM–ELAS members. But even this was not enough.

On 15th June, Zachariadis issued an official Political Bureau decision which condemned Aris' 'treason' in even sharper terms.[97] The news of his suicide appeared on the 19th in a brief notice in *Rizospastis*. The death of the ELAS GHQ capetan did not even rate an obituary. Aris had become a non-person.

On 17th June, the Sunday edition of *Rizospastis* which for the first time had four pages, issued KKE's concept of a 'Programme of Popular Democracy' to be submitted to EAM for discussion. The introduction comprised an analysis of the situation: Greece was in thrall to a handful of big capitalists, black marketeers and banks, above all the Bank of Greece. This clique controlled the whole of the country's economic life. It had supported the monarchy and the fascist regime, collaborated with the Germans, enriched itself still further under the Occupation, was now trying to restore the pre-war regime and finally was responsible for the present situation. These exploiters had no interest in the normalisation of the country's life, the restoration of order and tranquillity and the reunification of the people, since discord and unrest were to their advantage.

It would be the task of the 'popular democratic' government, chosen by the people and ruling for the people, to put this clique out of business so that patriotic *entrepreneurs* and businessmen could get on with their work in the interests of the people and the nation. All collaborators must be punished, without exception. Power must proceed from the people alone. Civil liberties must be ensured. Then followed a definition of 'popular democracy'.

'Popular democracy is ruling power proceeding from the close alliance of workers, peasants, employees, craftsmen and intellectuals. It is a new type of democracy in which power rests in the hands of the people and which has put an end to the political suppression of the people by exploiters. Under popular democracy private property will not be abolished and private initiative will be encouraged though always in accordance with the general good. Popular democracy means that the people's interest, the people's progress comes first.'

This was followed in turn by a very detailed political programme covering the following points: employment, reconstruction, economic, agrarian and labour policy, promotion of craftsmen's, women's and youth problems, education and vocational training, armed forces, popular justice and local self-administration, foreign policy and national territorial claims.[98]

This programme contained no radical demands. Many of its elements had already appeared in the EAM programme. It was oriented to practicalities and, had it been realised, it could have brought about a complete renaissance of Greece from the grassroots upwards. Here, too, it is interesting to observe that, at almost exactly the same time, the Italian CP had evolved nearly identical concepts for the post-war Italian state.[99]

Meanwhile, the turmoil over Zachariadis' Northern Epirus statement had not subsided. The bourgeois press ran articles on Albanian excesses against the Greek minority in Northern Epirus (Southern Albania). Protests, petitions and resolutions were addressed to the Greek government by organisations at home and abroad. The right-wing press openly demanded that the Greek army invade Northern Epirus. This campaign provoked a strong reaction from Yugoslavia which denounced the persecution of the Slav minority in Greek Macedonia by the National Guard. Whether Zachariadis realised that, by the resolution of 1st June, KKE had put itself into the Greek right-wing camp and taken up a position against a fraternal party; or whether—as seems more probable—he was given a hint by Velichantsky, the Tass correspondent who was the highest-ranking Soviet representative in Greece, from whom even the Soviet Military Mission took orders,[100] the fact is that KKE tried to wriggle out of the statement, carefully covering their rear. The Political Bureau resolution of 15th June speaks of worsening relations with the northern neighbours.[101] In the popular democracy programme the right of self-determination is demanded for the people of Northern Epirus.[102] On 21st June *Rizospastis* went over to the offensive on a broad front. There was an afternoon special edition with a banner headline: 'Special edition. The reactionary Right again preparing anti-national adventures. Greek people, be on the alert!' Below this followed a statement from Zachariadis to the paper in which he called on the editor to publish a letter sent by a high-ranking army officer to Zachariadis himself.

This letter is an obvious forgery[103] but its content is nevertheless of great interest. The anonymous writer purports to be a member of IDEA and to have detailed knowledge of the plans of Generals Vendiris and Liosis: it is their aim to establish a dictatorship in Greece and arrest the whole Opposition. At the same time, the Greek army, under the supreme command of George II would invade Albania and occupy Northern Epirus; after this the monarchy would be officially restored. Though this story certainly sounds fantastic, its component parts had a foundation in reality. Invasion plans were actually being discussed in IDEA circles, not so much in connection with the army itself which at that time was organisationally incapable of such an exploit and also was too directly under British control to risk such an adventure, but rather by means of a volunteer corps as in 1912. Likewise, the suggestion that IDEA was preparing a *coup* and the Restoration of the king did not lack a factual background. Nor was Zachariadis' hint that certain British circles were behind all this without foundation. Only the weaving together of these elements was a fiction. On its own the whole story would have had little significance had not the Soviet radio taken it up and broadcast it in its programme for Greece, which raised it to the level of an international political event. The result was that, on the one hand IDEA had to give up its plans and on the other that KKE clarified its position in regard to Northern Epirus without having to admit that, at the beginning of June, it had taken up a mistaken position. At the same time Zachariadis challenged the state to take steps against him. But the final result was that the whole manoeuvre brought Greece on to the agenda of the forthcoming Potsdam Conference.

From another point of view as well Zachariadis' calculations bore fruit. Public Prosecutor Kollias brought an action against him and against the publishers of *Rizospastis* under a law of 1938 for 'spreading rumour'.[104] Kollias (later the junta's first Prime Minister) pursued his prosecution with such zeal and attracted so much attention that Caccia felt impelled to intervene. On 16th July he reported:

'The trial of Zachariadis. . . was to have taken place on the 14th July. As I had been advised that the trial might be concluded in a day and lead to a sentence of imprisonment for anything from one to two years, I asked the President of the Council whether he thought it wise to run this risk over an admittedly petty matter, on the eve of the Potsdam discussions and within a month of his release from confinement in Germany. Admiral Voulgaris said that he had no idea of what was impending in this case, but agreed that if a postponement could be arranged it would be all to the good. In the upshot Zachariadis failed to appear in court on the 14th July. His lawyers pleaded that their case was not ready and that the international situation made it inadvisable in any case to bring him to trial. The court agreed to postpone the proceedings indefinitely.'[105]

On the British side there had obviously been fears that Zachariadis could use his court appearance to present himself as complainant and this had prompted their intervention. As a result it was not until summer 1947, when he had already gone underground, that Zachariadis was sentenced *in absentia*.[106]

Thus the Northern Epirus problem ceased to exist for KKE, but the problem of its relations with Britain had not been finally resolved. That was achieved at the Central Committee's Twelfth Plenum.

The Twelfth Plenum was in session in Athens from the 25th to the 27th June 1945. It was the First Plenum since 1935 to be held under conditions of legality and under Zachariadis' leadership. There were two subjects for discussion: the present state of the party and preparations for the Seventh Party Congress. Zachariadis gave the introductory statement and concluding speech on the first subject.

He started by saying that KKE was at present in a transitional phase of the struggle. In order to understand correctly the problems and the duties facing KKE, it was necessary to analyse them in their historical perspective. In Greece, before the war, the exploiting class had not discharged its historic duty to establish a bourgeois republic, with the result that many semi-feudal elements had survived. The consequence of this continuing betrayal by the bourgeoisie could be seen in a weak, disunited, economically under-developed country which had not been able to mobilise the real power of the people against the occupying powers.[107]

Zachariadis went on to speak of the Resistance: it could be said without any doubt that the armed national liberation struggle had been the start of popular revolution in Greece since it had achieved the transition to bourgeois democracy. After the German withdrawal, even the problem of power had been solved for Greece since it had passed into the hands of EAM. He then asked rhetorically why things had gone wrong.

'Those who try to seek the causes in the minor errors and mistakes of the popular liberation movement are seeking in vain. Such mistakes are inevitable in so massive, broadly-based and unprecedented an effort. But these mistakes did not affect the fundamentally correct basis of the effort... from the beginning to the end of the Occupation EAM remained on the right road. There had been no mistakes. Not even the Lebanon Agreement was a mistake... What then was wrong?'[108]

Zachariadis found the error to lie in EAM's relationship with Britain and *vice versa*. The solution of this problem was influenced by two factors, by foreign capital and by Greece's geographical position. In 1934 at the Sixth Plenum, Greece had been described as a country half-way to capitalism, hence its dependence on foreign capital. This had been the main characteristic of Greek evolution since 1821 and at present this was more than ever the case.

He then repeated the analysis he had given in his article in *Rizospastis* of 5th June, but now he drew the conclusions.

'A realistic policy[109] for EAM and the PEEA should have moved between these two poles—the Balkan-European centred on the Soviet Union and the Mediterranean centred on England. A correct foreign policy would have been one which brought these two poles together through a Greek axis.'

Zachariadis went on to ask if EAM had pursued such a policy and came to the conclusion that, from the first moment, EAM had made serious efforts to come to an understanding with England and to cooperate. Naturally, there had been mistakes on the part of the EAM leadership but in general there had been an effort to help England overcome her difficulties in the Mediterranean. This had been a fundamentally correct policy.

But the decisive factors which had disturbed this relationship had been the slanders and intrigues of Greek reaction and the fact that the resulting cooperation with the British had not been based on sympathy but on a situation of political necessity. The British had relied more on Greek reactionaries than the interests of the British people demanded, despite the fact that in Greece they had collaborated with the Occupation powers. And all this in order to align themselves against EAM. There had been a disastrous error in British policy.

'British foreign policy failed to understand that, during the Occupation years and in the struggles of the war of liberation, the Greek people's mentality had radically changed. It did not realise that in these years other classes of society had come to power in Greece. . . England did not understand that these classes were not prepared to have their knuckles rapped as the old classes had been. . . England did not respect our people who had shed so much blood for her.'[110]

Thus, the December events had been unavoidable because the British had yielded to the demands of Greek reaction and had intervened by force. There had also been mistakes on the part of KKE which had not however affected the correctness of its basic line. Zachariadis mentioned the missed opportunity of Churchill's visit, the unorganised taking of hostages and certain excesses. In other words, he attributed the blame for defeat to factors outside the party: apart from a few minor errors, KKE had pursued a fundamentally correct line. In this way Zachariadis nullified even the tentative self-criticism of the Eleventh Plenum and justified the stand of the orthodox elements in the Political Bureau. The party leadership was once more infallible.

After this historical *resumé*, he turned to the present which was a transitional phase between the liberation struggle and the struggle for democracy and now it was essential to maintain unity of the movement. There must therefore be adaptation to the new circumstances. For this change KKE was ideologically ill-prepared and this had confused petty bourgeois elements like Velouchiotis and the party had had to react with resolution.

'Some comrades did not understand that Varkiza was a consequence of the December defeat which made necessary the transition from the lightly-armed guerilla war to mass political struggle. They wanted to keep their rifles and continue to fight on as outlaws *[kleftopolemos]*. But that was travelling today on yesterday's ticket. The party has criticised this attitude and will continue to do so.'

For the moment, normal democratic evolution had been interrupted and it must be re-established.[111] For this the country's economy must be got going again and the popular democracy programme must be realised. On both these points Zachariadis held forth at length.

He spoke next of fundamental problems. Recently there had been much talk of an immediate transition to socialism.

'In my opinion such a slogan is premature for Greece and therefore mistaken. It omits the stage of complete transformation into a bourgeois state; in other words it by-passes one stage of development.'

Such an attitude was sectarian. The necessary pre-conditions—the removal of semi-feudal elements from the countryside and independence of foreign capital—had not been achieved in Greece. First, the change to a national democracy must be accomplished. This was the conclusion to be drawn from a scientific socialist analysis.[112]

He went on to speak of the concepts of democracy and revolution. He described democracy as an historic category, an historical phenomenon undergoing changes to higher social forms. Then he distinguished revolution from armed rebellion. Revolution was unavoidable but need not necessarily be violent. Revolution was about power but the takeover of power could come about peacefully. KKE would never attempt to win power from a minority position because it knew that such an attempt would be bound to fail. But, when the moment came when the majority of the workers stood with KKE, then the party would organise the struggle for power.[113] So here too Zachariadis took the viewpoint of the Sixth Plenum of 1934.

The Plenum's resolutions were characteristic. To ensure the country's normal democratic evolution the following measures were necessary: application of the Yalta Agreement, formation of a representative government, purge of collaborators from the state apparatus and their sentencing, recognition of the Resistance movement, general amnesty as a pre-condition for free elections. If certain British circles would cease supporting reactionaries, a substantial improvement in the situation could be achieved in quite a short time.

It was the task of the party to go over to mass political struggle against the threatening fascist *coup* and for evolution to popular democracy. Massive popular self-defence *(aftoamyna)* should be organised against right-wing terrorism, with mass strikes and demonstrations as its weapons. A fascist *coup* must be prevented at all costs.[114] The foreign policy programme was based on the two-poles-theory. In regard to the party itself, the Plenum demanded vigilance against the dangers threatening it from the change in its social composition; also the raising of the ideological standards of members and cadres. The resolutions contained no word of allusion to the mistakes of the past.[115] Finally, it was announced that the Central Committee had resolved to reduce the membership of the Political Bureau. Its composition showed that the balance of forces within the Political Bureau had been one-sidedly altered to the disadvantage of the critics.[116]

The significance of the Twelfth Plenum therefore attaches to the organisational rather than the ideological sector. As Zachariadis stated in his concluding speech, only 18% of the party members were workers, in other words the vast majority were peasants[117] —a fact which disturbed him deeply since it called in question the leading role of the working class and the party and constituted a deviation from the correct line. In the published resolutions of the Twelfth Plenum this was only mentioned in passing. Bartziotas' collected material for the party history shows that the Central Committee had taken a much more far-reaching decision: the party organisations in the villages were to be dissolved and the members were to be transferred to the Agrarian Party of Greece (AKE), after which it was apparently planned to create a united revolutionary peasant party.[118] KKE should revert to a Leninist cadre party. By this decision—a further regression to the 1934 resolutions—Zachariadis speeded up the dissolution of the Left and of KKE. To conform with the orthodox concept of the party, he created the pre-conditions for the dissolution of KKE as a mass party.

Zachariadis' statements and the resolutions of the Twelfth Plenum were published in *Rizospastis* from 30th June to 3rd July. On 5th July, even before the rank-and-file membership had had time to study them, *Rizospastis* published a Political Bureau resolution referring to relations with Great Britain. It began by stating that the Military League (IDEA) and the fascist organisations were continuing their preparations for a *coup*. The government was informed of this but did nothing. Then came a sentence which struck an entirely new note and caused the paper's editor to ring the Political Bureau, to ask if there had not been an error in the wording.[119] The sentence read: 'All these manoeuvres are known likewise to the British authorities, political and military, to the Occupation *(katochi)* authorities.' There were no Greeks—it went on to say—who could have the least doubt that, when the British authorities so willed, the situation in Greece could change radically for the better within 24 hours. The Greek people were following the behaviour of the British authorities with disquiet since this encouraged fascist reaction towards a *coup*. The Political Bureau did not wish to believe the information according to which the Greek government and the Occupation authorities were ready to permit this. In this context the Political Bureau condemned the one-sided orientation towards England and demanded that KKE should be included in the all-party committee for foreign affairs.[120]

What did this change of wording mean? Was it meant to signal to KKE members a radical change of line towards confrontation with the British? Or was the Political Bureau perhaps acting under instructions from Moscow?

So soon before the Potsdam Conference, the latter would seem to be excluded. More likely the new wording was merely an element in the internal political campaign of all the democratic parties against right-wing terror and the penetration of the army by the Right, the campaign directed at that moment against the Voulgaris government.[121] The only difference from the protests of the bourgeois politicians was in the language and the target. Whilst the former's criticism was directed against Voulgaris and Damaskinos, KKE attacked the British. The use of the word *katochi* was meant to exert moral pressure on the British, to cause them to change course. But in principle nothing changed in KKE's policy towards Great Britain. The contrary suppositions of Zografos in 1950 are only justification from hindsight.[122] This Political Bureau resolution is in no way the start of the later 'Tommy go home' *(Na fygoun oi angloi)* policy.

This is also apparent in the Political Bureau resolution of the 19th July[123] which is much more moderate in its language and lacks any polemics against Great Britain. This resolution is another facet of the campaign against right-wing terrorism and for the formation of a representative government which occupied *Rizospastis* throughout July, a campaign which was to attract the attention of the Allies in session at Potsdam. How little KKE's basic attitude to Britain had changed became clear on 27th July when *Rizospastis* celebrated the Labour Party's election victory as a major sensation, with photographs of the Labour leaders on the front page. Partsalidis sent a telegram of good wishes to Attlee on behalf of EAM and *Rizospastis* congratulated the *Daily Herald* and the *Daily Worker* on this victory.[124]

On 29th July Zachariadis demanded the resignation of the Voulgaris government and the formation of a representative one.[125] As we have already seen, Zachariadis' hopes were doomed;[126] the Labour government took over the Greek policy of the Churchill government and Voulgaris remained in office. On 9th August Zachariadis protested against Attlee's policy in a statement to the *News Chronicle:* did Attlee really know what was going on in Greece? Did he know that the right-wing terror had even increased since he came to power? KKE for its part had done all it could—here Zachariadis referred to the condemnation of Aris Velouchiotis—to carry out the Varkiza Agreement. All that was wanted of Attlee was the formation of a representative government. Great Britain had the power to change the situation in Greece within 24 hours.[127] A further Political Bureau resolution of 15th August expressed the same standpoint.[128]

No doubt in order to counteract the tendency to disintegration and to give their persecuted members moral support, the EAM and KKE leaderships undertook a tour of Macedonia. Their first stop was at Kavalla on 20th August. In his speech there on the 21st, Zachariadis took issue with Bevin's House of Commons statement of the previous day. He described Bevin's statement as in contradiction to the will of the Greek people. An understanding could be reached with Great Britain but on a basis of equal rights.[129] In a leading article in *Rizospastis* of the 22nd, Petros Rousos expressed the same opinion. On the evening of the 21st Zachariadis arrived by steamer in Salonica to an enthusiastic mass welcome. On the same evening he gave an interview to the newspaper *Makedonia:* the object of his journey was the campaign for a representative government and for popular democracy. Bevin's statement was not in accord with the wishes of the Greek people. Elections organised by Voulgaris would have a fascist character. The attitude of the new British government had led to an intensification of right-wing terror. For this the British occupation authorities bore the responsibility since, if they wished, they could change the situation within 24 hours.[130] On the 24th Zachariadis spoke to an enormous mass demonstration.[131] Here he repeated his now habitual attacks on British policy, especially on that of Bevin and, as his audience responded with enthusiastic approbation, he intensified his polemics. If Bevin did not wish to take cognisance of the fascist chaos in Greece, this was because he was conciously ignoring the truth and had taken over Churchill's imperialist policy. Bevin was continuing to treat Greece as a colony and to treat the politicians as the Secret Service treated its agents. But he was deceiving himself, things had changed and Greeks were now masters in their own house.

'If the situation does not change soon and radically in the direction of normal democratic evolution, we will reply to the monarcho-fascists in the towns, in the mountains and in the villages with the same means with which they attack us. Hundreds of thousands of workers and peasants only restrain themselves to-day because they are well-disciplined. But what we to-day grit our teeth over and suppress will tomorrow become our duty and the responsibility for this will lie with

Messrs Bevin and Attlee because they are continuing their colonial intervention in Greece. . . Yet even now there is still hope. But self-control has its limits. If these limits are overstepped and the interests of Greece demand it, then the mountains and forests will once more resound with the call of "Forwards, ELAS, for Greece!' *[Embros ELAS ya tin Ellada]*. Such is the present situation. If Mr Bevin is not able to maintain order in Greece with his occupation troops, then he should withdraw them from our country. Then, despite the one-sided interpretation of the Varkiza Agreement applied against it, the Greek people will itself be able to restore order and tranquillity without any assistance.'[132]

After the meeting, which ended with chanted demands for the withdrawal of the British,[133] he gave an interview to the *Manchester Guardian* which the British Consul-General reported as follows:

'While still flushed with his eloquence and applause of supporters Zachariadis was visited by Mrs [Sylvia] Sprigge. . . to whom in the course of an hour's conversation in French he stated that the behaviour of the British in Greece was intolerable and that the Greek people were resolved to take up their defence vigorously. On being pressed Zachariadis said that they wanted the British to leave Greece. And can you foretell what will happen, asked Mrs Sprigge to which Zachariadis replied, "We do not foretell, we know and want it. We will have civil war." "Are you in favour of civil war?" "Only by civil war can we settle things" replied Zachariadis. "But do not be uneasy. After two months everything will be fine".'[134]

In the context of an open letter to Professor Harold Laski, Zachariadis issued a *démenti* on 28th August[135] but Sylvia Sprigge insisted that she had reported Zachariadis' words correctly. The Foreign Office was more than pleased by Zachariadis' emotional outburst.

'I think it is clear that M. Zachariadis has over-reached himself in this wild and irresponsible attack upon British policy and the conduct of British forces in Greece. In particular his admission to the *Manchester Guardian*. . . that civil war would be inevitable if British troops were withdrawn from Greece and that the Greek Communist Party would welcome such a development must have done the Communist cause great harm both in Greece and in this country. The News Department are making all they can of these telegrams. . .'[136]

Zachariadis' statements in Salonica and at the interview should by no means be taken as indications of a new line. They are spontaneous expressions of disgust, examples of a purely verbal radicalism resulting from the frustrations of the previous weeks. They do of course reflect pipe-dreams and stages of development in Zachariadis' thinking and they were also useful for keeping his followers up to the mark.

These outbursts provoked the Right to even greater brutality. On 28th

August the secretary of the wing of SKE which still belonged to EAM, Dr Ioannis Passalidis, was felled with a stone in Verroia and on the 30th, the former speaker of PEEA's National Council (parliamentary assembly in Free Mountain Greece), General Neokosmos Grigoriadis, was similarly injured in Kozani.[137] In both cases the gendarmerie and the National Guard intervened on the side of the assailants and beat up the assembled crowd so that eventually British troops had to restore order.[138]

But Zachariadis' speeches could not camouflage the continuing crisis in KKE and the fact that the party was going through a period of failure. The British too had cold-shouldered his offers of cooperation. On the issue of forming a representative government, KKE had isolated itself by its attacks on Plastiras and Sofoulis. Persecution of its members continued. ERGAS had indeed managed—as we have seen—to win the trade union elections but the government refused to recognise the results. The only sector in which KKE could show any success was in the organisation of strikes and mass demonstrations. Economic deterioration following Varvaressos' resignation provoked exceedingly successful mass strikes for improvement of workers' living standards. But, when KKE tried to transform these into political strikes against the government and the British, the previously solid strike front started to crumble away. The Political Bureau's resolution of 6th September reflects the deep frustration of the KKE leadership. Its content comprised the already familiar attacks on reaction, the government and the British; a new element was a massive attack on ELD-SKE. But the standard of faith in final victory was still held high.[139]

During September KKE was mainly occupied in preparing the Seventh Party Congress, organising the celebrations for the fourth anniversary of the foundation of EAM and with the Sixth Conference of the Athens party organisation. All over the country there were party activities in preparation for the Seventh Congress.

A highpoint was reached on 27th September with the mass demonstration in the Athens Olympic stadium to celebrate the fourth anniversary of EAM. Allegedly 200,000 participated[140] which showed yet again the enormous political potential of the National Liberation Front and how deeply it was rooted in the people. The Sixth Conference of the Athens party organisation (Kommounistiki Organosi Athinas, KOA) was in session on 28th and 29th September in the 'Kentrikon' Theatre with 193 delegates from Athens branches *(achtides)* participating. Zachariadis and Ioannidis were present representing the Political Bureau. The Order of the Day comprised two subjects: the Central Committee's *compte-rendu* for the period from the Sixth to the Seventh Party Congress, presented by Siantos; and the report on the Athens organisation's activities presented by its secretary Bartziotas, followed by elections. Siantos' report was identical with that which he was to give at the Seventh Party Congress (see p. 271).

Bartziotas' report was quite colourless and followed the line prescribed at the Twelfth Plenum. It was only when he examined some of the mistakes of KOA that he became more precise. Until December there had been no serious political errors, though there had certainly been two weaknesses: defective assimilation of new members and inadequate vigilance against penetration by enemies of the party. He mentioned the hostage-taking and the excesses. But the main error had been that the KOA leadership had fled Athens after the defeat and that the people had thus been left helpless at the mercy of reactionary propaganda for a whole month. The cause of this error must be sought in defective theoretical and ideological work and in organisation which was in need of improvement.[141]

Much more important were the speeches of Zachariadis and Ioannidis. Zachariadis interpreted the Twelfth Plenum resolution on the social composition of the party. The party's ultimate aim was a socialist, a communist society. This was also the aim of the working class. But, as this class was in the minority in Greece, it was not able to achieve the transition to socialism on its own; it needed allies which it could find within the EAM movement. But these allies had different class interests and therefore did not yet want the transition to socialism. Therefore the immediate aim was the establishment of popular democracy. But in the meantime KKE must not forget its ultimate aim and must therefore gather around itself those class-conscious forces which also included the intellectuals. Only the establishment of popular democracy, to which these allies would eventually achieve the right attitude, could open the way for transition to socialism.[142]

Ioannidis used a different emphasis. Reaction was terrorising the Left because it feared normality, since in a normal evolution KKE and EAM would have the majority of the population on their side. The Twelfth Plenum had called for massive self-defence *(aftoamyna)* on the part of the people. This should be put into practice by strikes and work stoppages. But what was of prime importance was to purge the party ranks of agents and provocateurs and to keep them purged. Although the party was legal, underground work must be developed. There might be difficult times ahead for which one must be prepared. The closing of the party's ranks was an order at the highest level. Then he went on to speak of ideological issues in connection with the alteration of the party's constitution planned for the Seventh Party Congress.

The Sixth Plenum of 1934 had demanded that the bourgeois democratic revolution should be achieved by the revolutionary democratic dictatorship of workers and peasants. But the character of the party does not change, no more than does the ultimate aim which is prescribed by Marxist theory. 'However, the problems of bourgeois democratic revolution, set by the Sixth Plenum, will be solved in the parliamentary way of popular democracy.' That was all the difference. Finally, Ioannidis demanded the greatest vigilance towards those who had signed repentance statements under the Metaxas dictatorship—and named Aris Velouchiotis as an example.[143]

Ioannidis' excursions into ideology constitute the second effort, after Zachariadis' return, to clarify the party's ideological position. At the Twelfth Plenum, as we have already shown, Zachariadis had stressed that the revolutionary transformation process could evolve peacefully. He had expressly referred to the decisions of the Sixth Plenum of 1934 and had rejected any direct transition to socialism, since this would 'omit the stage of complete transformation into a bourgeois state'. For a correct interpretation of what Ioannidis said, it may be useful to take a brief look at the decisions of that Sixth Plenum.

These decisions were based primarily on the proclamation of the Comintern Executive Committee of November 1931,[144] in which KKE was assigned the task of winning over the majority of the working class; and in the second place on the Comintern programme according to which there was a number of countries on the road towards capitalism in which, however, there still remained important semi-feudal elements. In these countries, before the socialist revolution could be carried through, the bourgeois revolution must first be completed.[145] In its decisions, the Sixth Plenum expressly referred to this by stating that Greece belonged exactly to this group of countries;[146] from which it drew the following decisive conclusion: 'In Greece the forthcoming workers' and peasants' revolution will be of bourgeois-democratic character with the tendency to develop quickly into proletarian socialist revolution.'[147]

This relatively clear statement was then immediately obscured by the description of the manner and evolution of the transformation process. Evidently elements of the Comintern programme were mixed up with KKE's own concepts in a way which shows that the authors of the resolution had no very clear idea what it was all about.

First, KKE must win over the majority of the working class and then draw to itself the broad masses of the population and the peasants. Next the problem of completing the bourgeois revolution must be solved. This would be achieved, first by taking over the large landed estates and distributing the land to the peasants, and second by freeing the country from the yoke of foreign capital and by winning independence from the imperialist powers. Further measures would include massive taxation of exploiters, separation of church and state, self-determination for national minorities, equal rights for Jews.

Finally, the road to socialist revolution was by nationalisation of the banks and monopolies and at this stage the leading role of the proletariat must be ensured:

'The hegemony of the proletariat in bourgeois-democratic revolution, won in the struggles leading to victorious revolution and safeguarded in the form of rule by soviets, with the active cooperation of the international proletariat, will ensure the rapid transition from bourgeois-democratic to socialist revolution. Government of workers' and peasants' soviets which in the first stage of the revolution will achieve the revolutionary-democratic dictatorship of the working class and the peasantry in the form of soviets, will become the government of the dictatorship of the proletariat.'[148]

In other words, KKE hoped to complete the bourgeois-democratic revolution by a radical-democratic system of government, a system of soviets somewhat resembling the workers', peasants' and soldiers' soviets in Russia in 1905 and 1917 or in Germany at the end of 1918. This means that in 1934 KKE rejected the parliamentary system and preferred the Leninist radical-democratic system of democracy by soviets.

Seen in the light of these extracts from the Sixth Plenum, Ioannidis' statement takes on a new dimension. The party allegedly still stood by the demands of the Sixth Plenum and held fast to its original aim. The fact that it pinned its hopes on the parliamentary road and had given up the original Leninist road via the rule of soviets, was played down as a tactical change although it constituted a break with the previous line. Nevertheless it is a fact that in 1945 KKE had given up a central component of Leninist revolutionary theory and was following the parliamentary road. It is perhaps useful to remind the reader once more that, for KKE in 1945, the term popular democracy did not have the meaning of dictatorship of the proletariat. This re-interpretation of the Sixth Plenum decisions was taken up by Partsalidis at the Seventh Party Congress and developed further.

Zachariadis' and Ioannidis' statements on organisational problems required of KOA that it put into practice the Twelfth Plenum's resolution on the social composition of the party, that it transform KOA from a heterogenous mass organisation back into a monolithic bolshevik cadre organisation, in which the working class would play its proper role of leadership. But even for an urban agglomeration like Athens this requirement was hard to fulfil. According to Bartziotas the proportion of workers among the party members was less than 50%.[149] Even this represented favourable circumstances for KOA, with ten urban branches *(achtides)* and only one rural one, Attica. The average worker participation throughout the country was about 18%.[150] As the composition of the KOA delegate conference showed, the Twelfth Plenum's appeal had already been heeded. The 193 delegates were divided as follows: workers 37.3%, employees 29.5%, students 14%, intellectuals 12.4%, professional people 4.1%, peasants 1%, school students 1%, housewives 0.7%.[151] Zachariadis' and Ioannidis' intervention intensified this process so that the newly elected KOA committee was composed as follows: out of twenty-three regular members, fifteen were workers (65.2%), five intellectuals (29.7%), two employees (8.7%) and one a student (4.4%):[152] that is the workers and intellectuals had an uncontested preponderance. There is however further conclusive statistical evidence in the texts of the Sixth KOA Conference which likewise permits interesting deductions.

Of the 193 delegates over 80% had joined KKE during the Occupation. On the new KOA Committee, however, this group was clearly under-represented with only just 30%.[153] The strongest group consisted of the cadres who had joined KKE during Zachariadis' reign as General-Secretary. This was true to an even greater degree of the membership of the party control committee[154] which was wholly in the hands of the old guard. Within KOA the victory of the Akronafpliots was assured. At least as regards its leadership, KOA had been re-bolshevised.

But the intervention of Zachariadis and Ioannidis at the KOA Conference was only the final step in a country-wide series of similar interventions as announced at the Twelfth Plenum,[155] of which Zachariadis' journeys to Macedonia and the Peloponnese were the most spectacular examples.

At the time of liberation KKE had allegedly had 400,000 enrolled members.[156] Even if one includes all KKE's front organisations, this figure seems to be much exaggerated. KKE has never published figures, but approximately 200,000 members may be nearer to reality. The basis for this assessment is a remark of Zachariadis at the KKE Panhellenic Organisation Conference in April 1946, when he set the party the task of achieving a 100,000 membership.[157] At the same conference, Ioannidis stated that, now the mass of peasants had left the party, workers were in the majority.[158] If one relates this to the 18% worker membership at the time of the Twelfth Plenum, the suggested 200,000 membership at liberation becomes a serviceable hypothesis for further consideration.

Thus, between October 1944 and April 1946, KKE lost approximately 100,000 members. Many of these losses can be attributed to the right-wing terror and to KKE's mistakes during and after December. But the great majority, certainly over 50,000, were victims of the re-bolshevisation which followed the Twelfth Plenum: they were transferred to AKE which, whilst in this way it gained members, at the same time lost many of its non-communists who did not wish to belong to an organisation subordinate to KKE. Under Zachariadis the orthodox KKE thus consciously dismembered the mass movement of the Occupation period which had consisted 60% of peasants.[159] It had again become an urban party. How 'effective' this intervention by the leadership at grassroots level had proved was demonstrated by the analysis of the social provenance of delegates to the Seventh Party Congress. The 223 delegates comprised one hundred and nineteen workers, eight self-employed, twenty-two peasants, twenty-six employees, twenty-nine members of the traditional and technical professions, eight intellectuals and eleven students.[160] Analysis of the duration of party membership shows that the Congress was in the main controlled by cadres who had belonged to the party since before 1936.[161] The Central Committee elected at this Congress was almost identical in its social composition with the KOA Committee: workers 64%, intellectuals 24%, employees 12%. But in one point the Central Committee differed radically: not one of its members belonged to the generation of the Occupation.[162] The Central Committee was firmly in the hands of the Akronafpliots, of the old guard controlled by Ioannidis,[163] those old cadres who during the first bolshevisation phase, after the Comintern's intervention, had been adjudged worthy to remain in the party.

The Congress was in session from Tuesday 1st to Saturday 6th October in the Titania cinema in Panepistimiou Street in Athens. The programme covered six topics: 1) The Central Committee's *compte-rendu* (Siantos); 2) The present situation of KKE and the problems of popular democracy (Zachariadis); 3) The agrarian problem (Stringos); 4) KKE's programme (Partsalidis); 5) KKE's constitution (Ioannidis); 6) Elections for the new Central Committee and for the party control committee.[164]

At the Eleventh Plenum the Political Bureau had reassured its dissidents that, at the Seventh Party Congress, the mistakes of the past would be submitted to a fundamental and comprehensive analysis.[165] But in Siantos' introductory statement, though the well-known mistakes were admitted and indeed a few more as well, in general he took the standpoint of the Twelfth Plenum that, yes, there had been mistakes but the party's general line had been correct; and in the whole report there was no attempt to examine the causes of these mistakes.[166]

From Siantos' concluding speech one can assume that, despite the Political Bureau's influence on the selection of delegates, it had not proved possible to stifle all criticism. For example, Siantos had to defend himself against some of the Macedonian comrades (Tzimas, Markos?) who asked why the party had organised struggle in the towns in 1941 instead of starting guerilla warfare in the mountains.[167] Nevertheless, Siantos' report was 'unanimously' approved.[168]

Zachariadis, too, maintained the Twelfth Plenum line in his report, though he presented a somewhat rosier picture. The phase of transition from armed struggle to mass political struggle had been concluded and KKE was again in working order. He cited, amongst other examples, ERGAS' successes in the trade union elections. The party had been able to draw to itself the majority of the working population. Referring to the terror he threatened that, if there were not soon a radical change, the people would reply by the same means.[169] But all this was little more then rhetoric. In regard to Britain he repeated the essence of his two-poles-theory, albeit with the reservation that, if Britain was not able to put an end to the one-sided civil war of the Right against the Left, the British troops should be immediately withdrawn. This would open the way to the formation of a representative government and to a normal democratic evolution.[170]

He then went on to speak of the programme for popular democracy. Popular democracy would solve the problem of bourgeois democratic transition and would prepare the way for the transition to socialism by a series of economic measures. He named the nationalisation of certain major industries and the development of heavy industry. In other words, he supplemented the concept of popular democracy with concepts drawn from Soviet models. Finally, he examined internal party problems.

He criticised the low ideological level. The social composition of the party membership had indeed improved, but much remained to be done. There was no place in the party for members who had signed a repentance statement *(dilosi)*. In his conclusion he quoted a remark of the independent left-wing liberal General Othonaios:

'If the plans of Damaskinos, the government and the Military League are realised and the king returns, then a peaceful solution will no longer be possible and every honourable man will be forced to take to the mountains.'[171]

But he drew in his horns at once: the popular-democracy programme—unity, order, tranquillity, work, reconstruction, culture—would save the people from this. In his concluding speech, too, Zachariadis contributed nothing new.

But the importance of these expositions and of that of Leonidas Stringos on the agrarian problem was surpassed by the reports of Partsalidis and Ioannidis on the programme and the KKE constitution. Until the Seventh Party Congress KKE had never had a programme. Up to the Sixth Plenum of 1934 there had not even been an attempt to draw up such a thing; then one simply adhered to the Comintern analysis. At the Sixth Congress in 1935 the party constitution had at last been formulated but the Congress had not got round to working out a programme.[172] So Partsalidis' draft is the first attempt by KKE to base its policy on programmatic foundations.

However, from the beginning of his introductory statement Partsalidis made it clear that his draft was no more than discussion material on a few basic points of the future programme; the programme itself would have to be worked out and would only be presented at the Eighth Party Congress. In the meantime this would be a task for the party's theoreticians.[173] At the Eighth Party Congress (1961) Partsalidis again presented a new draft programme, which the Congress adopted and thus, forty-three years after its foundation, KKE at last acquired a programme.[174]

Partsalidis' draft for the Seventh Party Congress was published in the September number of the Central Committee's theoretical journal, *Kommounistiki Epitheorisi*.[175] The historical introduction to the programme followed in the main Zachariadis' thesis on the history of KKE,[176] in its turn a schematic transfer of the abstract Comintern revolutionary model to Greek conditions. Partsalidis then referred to the Comintern theories of 1934 which he expressly recognised as correct. Though the country's economy had demonstrated considerable growth since 1934, its basic structure had in no way changed. Power, too, had remained in the hands of the same classes which collaborated with foreign capital and were still trying to continue this. Therefore the direction indicated by the Sixth Plenum of 1934 was still the right one.[177] The EAM movement had, however, introduced some important changes. By uniting the people around itself, by instituting PEEA and the National Council, it had realised the transition to bourgeois democracy in the political sector. But foreign intervention had interrupted the natural evolution—normal democratic development—and thus the original problem was to be solved in a new form. The solution to this problem could only come from EAM which alone was interested in bourgeois-democratic change.[178]

The establishment of a communist society was indeed KKE's ultimate aim, but first the stage of socialism must be achieved and to this popular democracy would open the way. 'As our party emphasised at the Twelfth Plenum, the Second World War created certain conditions making possible a peaceful transition to socialism.'[179] Here he named the destruction of the fascist power machine and the rise of a new state with a new type of democracy, popular democracy. This would ensure a peaceful transition. But in Greece this evolution had been interrupted by foreign intervention. The attempt to restore the pre-war regime naturally reduced the chances of a peaceful transition, for a normal democratic evolution.

'Only the struggle of the Greek people—with the guaranteed solidarity of democratic Europe—for a change in British policy and for the application of the Yalta principles to Greece could still give hope for a normal restoration of democratic order. Otherwise, come what may, the Greek people is constrained and resolved to impose respect for its sovereign desires by all means at its disposal.'[180]

Partsalidis then proceeded to speak of the programme for popular democracy and of the party itself. Here too he introduced some new elements. In the economic sector, the building of heavy industry was particularly important. In foreign policy, a popular democracy must lean more towards the socialist states; good relations with the Soviet Union were of particular importance. With Great Britain cooperation must be on the basis of equal rights.[181] As concerned EAM, the errors of the Occupation period, the attempt to steam-roller natural allies, must not be repeated.[182] Finally, Partsalidis warned against further relapses into a Greater Greece ideology *(Megali Idea)*.

It seems that in the subsequent discussion the question of peaceful transition must have been a central point and that this had the support of the majority. This prompted Zachariadis to intervene: 'Here the following must be made clear at once: we are dealing with the *possibility* of a peaceful transition, not with the certainty. Any hypothesis based on the latter would be completely erroneous and could lead to serious mistakes, mistakes with disastrous consequences for KKE and for the whole movement.'[183] This was only a possibility because of the foreign factor. It would be a serious error were the party to prepare the people for peaceful transition alone.

'We must emphasise the possibility of such a development, but at the same time we must show who is hindering this, why we are not heading for a peaceful transition though that is what most people want, and we must prepare the people for the eventuality that the transition— provided that is what the majority wants—will have to be forced by all the means the people has at its disposal, even by crushing— should this prove necessary—the resistance of the monarcho-fascist, plutocratic minority. Therefore to-day we must be cautious about such formulations.'[184]

He said that contemporary popular democracy exactly represented the bourgeois-democratic transition which is the first stage in the transition to socialism and therefore corresponds exactly to the demands of the Sixth Plenum. There was however a difference: the bourgeois-democratic transition would not be achieved by the bourgeois class which had betrayed its historic task, but by the workers and peasants. This fact made popular democracy into the transitional stage to socialism. In the first transition, the bourgeois-democratic one, all classes and strata except the present capitalist exploiters would participate; but in the transition to socialism only the workers, the poorer peasants, the lower middle classes and the urban middle class bourgeoisie would take part. The change in social composition was the whole problem of the transition; and here the foreign factor had to be taken into careful account.[185] But Zachariadis did not go into details as to how this should be done.

In his concluding speech, Partsalidis declared his adherence to this viewpoint. It was entirely correct that, on the question of a peaceful transition there must be no illusions. 'We must stress that the situation demands of us that we prepare ourselves to push through the people's will by all means and, if necessary, even by force of arms.'[186] Certainly, in these considerations of strategy the foreign factor must be taken into account. But Partsalidis, too, did not go into detail on this.

Three points from the draft programme deserve particular attention: 1) the concept of popular democracy; 2) the nature of the transition to socialism; 3) relations with Great Britain.

If one compares what the draft programme had to say about popular democracy with the original statements of 17th June, a fundamental change becomes apparent. The June programme resembled very closely the popular rule programme of the original EAM. The demands put forward in this programme were reformist and pragmatic. Politically, the main emphasis had been on the people's anti-fascist unity. But at the same time integration in the parliamentary system was an aim, as demonstrated by Zachariadis' express reference to the French model. Popular democracy was raised to the level of a third constitutional alternative.[187] This was now no longer the case. Popular democracy had taken on a new quality. As is shown by the repeated references to the need to build a heavy industry, the concept of popular democracy was being oriented towards the East European model of Soviet origin. The growing influence of the orthodox within the KKE leadership during the past months was bearing its first fruits: KKE was again orienting itself more clearly towards Moscow. Under Zachariadis, the KKE leadership had observed how, in the Balkan countries whose social and economic structure closely resembled that of Greece, popular democracies of a different sort were being established and so in the course of the past months they had changed their model. The only difficulty now was to make this change convincing to the members. This was undertaken at the Seventh Party Congress where it was made clear to them that the previous political goal, the establishment of a bourgeois-democratic republic, had already really been achieved during the Occupation period, though it had suffered a slight setback by the December events; but in general the party was on the right road. Instead of submitting the actual situation—especially the problem of power—to a sober analysis, KKE was practising dialectic acrobatics to orient its members to an objective from which the necessary pre-condition, the presence of Soviet troops, was lacking; and this despite the fact that the actual balance of power in the Mediterranean area remained unchanged. Zachariadis' two-poles-theory had been much more realistic. All this shows the low theoretical equipment and lack of insight of the KKE leadership. Just as in the past, they were again applying foreign models and concepts about the road to socialism to Greece. But not even in this were they consistent. As Zachariadis' and Partsalidis' statements on the character of the transition to socialism show, they were wavering between different concepts and wanted to keep all options open for themselves. Their foreign policy concepts were even further removed from reality. Here the second step preceded the first. The demand for a closer *rapprochement* with the Soviet Union and for dealing with Great Britain on a basis of equal rights recalled vividly the policy of the Occupation period: the possibility of a clash with Great Britain was simply repressed. The programme's concepts were based on illusions and wish-fulfilment and led only to a muddled orientation confusing to the members. It will be shown that the resulting policy of 'not only, but also' led KKE to a new disaster. The decisive error of the Seventh Party Congress is the complete lack of any self-criticism. The KKE leadership was not prepared for a rigorous analysis of past mistakes, to practise self-criticism and to learn from the past in order to gain a clearer perspective on future developments.

In contrast to this confusion in the ideological sector, the KKE leadership had clear ideas about party re-organisation. To this end Ioannidis submitted to the Congress a draft for a party constitution twice the length of the previously valid constitution of 1935, which regulated party life in the minutest detail in forty-eight articles (against sixteen in 1935).[188] The introductory statement no longer referred to the Comintern and did not mention the dictatorship of the proletariat. Instead, it specified the struggle to establish popular democracy. The demand for iron discipline and prohibition of groups and factions were new elements. The duties and the rights—especially the former—were much more explicit. Another new element was an obligatory probation period for all party members. Means of imposing discipline had also been considerably refined. Where in the 1935 constitution, the chapter on party structure had begun with the base organisation, the cell, this was now reversed and the rights of the leadership were worked out in much greater detail. The constitution ended with a long article on party penalties, not present in the 1935 constitution. In general, the constitution was significantly more bureaucratic and more centralising. So-called democratic centralism was given an organisational structure. Ioannidis' report reflected his satisfaction—the party had at last found its way to a monolithic closing of the ranks.[189] The constitution was 'unanimously' adopted by the Congress.[190]

The content of Party Congress resolutions in general corresponded to the respective reports. Greetings were sent by the Communist Parties of Britain, Czechoslovakia, France and Italy. But the Soviet Union took no notice of the Congress. At the afternoon session on the 6th October, as well as the Central Committee, a newly created party agency was elected: the Central Control Committee *(kentriki epitropi elenchou)*. According to Article 23 of the constitution, it had the following functions: control of the execution of Central Committee resolutions by the party and assignment of responsibility for breaches of the constitution and of party discipline.[191] With this committee, the KKE leadership created for itself an instrument by which it could in the last instance exercise sovereign control over the party. This concluded the process of re-bolshevisation. Its composition was probably similar to that of the KOA Control Committee—only the most 'tried' comrades of whose orthodoxy there could be no doubt.

A second important election had slipped through almost unnoticed on the first day of the Congress. In addition to the usual Congress praesidium, the delegates had elected a team to study military issues.[192] Its title can be found in the memoirs of Kissavos: Panhellenic Military Committee; likewise the fact that this committee met twice, once shortly after the Seventh Party Congress and once more after the Second Plenum.[193] Its members came from all over the country and its leadership was in the hands of Zachariadis, supported by Ioannidis and Ektoras (Major Theodoros Makridis).[194]

Its functions were uncertain but Kissavos reports:

'After the Seventh Party Congress, the Panhellenic Military Committee elected at the congress went into session. Various issues were raised and opinions were interchanged. I put the following problem: what will happen if we come to an armed clash in the event of a probable renewed intervention by the British? Ioannidis answered approximately as follows: "There are now other protectors ["uncles"] as well".'[195]

On the supposition that at the great debates and settling of accounts within KKE (at the Third Party Conference in 1950 and the Sixth Plenum in 1956) every event relevant to the origin of the armed struggle came up for discussion, then the fact that the Panhellenic Military Committee was not mentioned must lead to the conclusion that it had played no part in the origins of the civil war. Thus, its election and establishment would in no way imply that Zachariadis had decided for armed conflict. Yet on the other hand we have the fact of its existence and that it concerned itself with the possibility of such an armed conflict. After weighing up all possible interpretations, the following may be a reasonably plausible explanation. During the summer of 1945, persecuted party members—in particular those who had served in ELAS—were becoming increasingly aggressive and ready to confront right-wing terror with the same means, that is by force of arms. Kissavos' recollections suggest the former capetans were discussing the possibility of armed action. The Military Committee could have been formed in order to bring them under control. How little Zachariadis was really interested in this line is proved by the fact that the committee never met again. It may have been a kind of tranquilliser for the more militant elements within KKE. As long as the slightest chance of a normal evolution remained, Zachariadis clung to his former line. Thus, Ioannidis' answer becomes a lame excuse. At the same time, however, Zachariadis kept the option for a military solution open, as can be concluded from a remark of Petros Rousos in his introduction to the published Seventh Party Congress proceedings: it was the party's duty to defend itself against the right-wing terror *by every means*.[196] So the result here too was a policy of 'not only, but also'.

On the 7th October the newly-elected Central Committee met in its First Plenum and elected the new Political Bureau. The full members were: Nikos Zachariadis, Giorgios Siantos, Yannis Ioannidis, Chrysa Hajivasiliou, Mitsos Partsalidis, Vasilis Bartziotas, Tasos Petritis (pseudonym of Stergios Anastasiadis). Alternate members were: Leonidas Stringos, Yannis Zevgos and Petros Rousos. At first sight it looks as though nothing much had changed. As before there are the two wings, the pragmatists and the orthodox, the doves and the hawks, who counterbalanced each other. But in fact there was one great difference from the past—the personality of Zachariadis with his claim to absolute leadership to which even the Political Bureau members had to bow. He decided on the line and the whole party had to follow. Critics had to reckon with the party's repressive measures. But Zachariadis himself was at that time by no means certain what course to take and this resulted in a wavering line. There was no clear perspective and Zachariadis' decisions were often taken *ad hoc*. The Seventh Party Congress therefore produced no clear political line but, on the contrary, led to a continuously wavering course and that at a time when the KKE leadership was faced with the most serious decisions and when a clear perspective and a consistent policy were more necessary than ever before.

NOTES

1. Siantos' statement to the representatives of the press. *Episima Keimena V*, pp. 350-2.
2. Sarafis, *op. cit.*, p. 523.
3. Eudes, *op. cit.*, pp. 230-2.
4. *Episima Keimena V*, pp. 353 ff.
5. Kostas Karagiorgis, *Apo ti Varkiza os ton emfylio polemo*, Vol. I, 1945, (Athens: Dialogos, 1977), pp. 21, 42; Eudes, *op. cit.*, pp. 231-2; Pavlos Nefeloudis, *Stis piges tis kakodaimonias: Ta vathytera aitia tis diaspasis tou KKE 1918-1968*, 4th ed., (Athens: Gutenberg, 1974), p. 252. The reference to Karagiorgis' criticism comes from a letter he wrote to Zachariadis in 1948. Unfortunately this letter was not fully reproduced in the book referred to above. The full text which throws an interesting light on the attitude of Karagiorgis to ELAS and to the EAM and KKE line during the Occupation can be found in: Polyvios Arkadinos, *I esoteriki krisi tou KKE (1946-1955)*, Vol. 3, *Kostas Karagiorgis i 'Liaskovas', (Gyftodimos)*, (Athens, 1955), pp. 45-56. Pavlos Nefeloudis was a KKE district secretary (Peristeri) during the Occupation. Eudes' information probably derives from Andreas Tzimas.
6. Thus Karagiorgis in a letter addressed to the Central Committee on 6th June, 1950, published in the Central Committee's theoretical organ *Neos Kosmos*, August 1950, under the title 'I antikommatiki likvidaristiki platforma tou Kosta Gyftodimou (Karagiorgi)', reprinted in Karagiorgis, *op. cit.*, p. 42.
7. In contrast to Siantos who hoped that the Varkiza Agreement would open the way to legal political activity for EAM and KKE, Aris saw Varkiza as the door to outlawry and persecution. See letter from his brother Babis D. Klaras to Zachariadis in June 1945, reprinted in Kostis Papakongos, *Grammata ya ton Ari*, (Athens: Papazisis, 1976), pp. 145-183.
8. Sarafis, *op. cit.*, pp. 523-4.
9. Papakongos, *op. cit.*, p. 178; Woodhouse, *The Struggle for Greece*, p. 138. According to Marion Sarafis, it was considerations of the need to preserve unity that persuaded Sarafis to sign.
10. Papakongos, *op. cit.*, p. 177.
11. Sarafis, *op. cit.*, p. LXIII. On the intention to declare Aris a war criminal see Stefanos Sarafis, *Meta ti Varkiza*, (Athens: Epikairotita, 1979), p. 16.
12. *Episima Keimena V*, pp. 355 ff.
13. Political Bureau radio message of 15th February, 1945, *ibid.*, p. 357.

14. See footnote 8.
15. Nefeloudis, *op. cit.*, p. 254.
16. See chapter 5.
17. Solaro, *op. cit.*, p. 77.
18. *Ibid.*, p. 124.
19. *Ibid.*, p. 161; Nikos Zachariadis, 'Eisigisi stin 3i syndiaskepsi tou KKE', in Nikos Zachariadis, Syllogi ergon, (n.p.: KKE Central Committee, 1953, p. 551. At the Eleventh Plenum Bartziotas maintained that KKE had 406,224 members. Petros Rousos, *I megali pentaetia 1940-1945. I Ethniki Antistasi kai o rolos tou KKE*, Vol. II (Athens: Synchroni Epochi, 1978), p. 390.
20. Woodhouse, *The Struggle for Greece*, p. 138, on the basis of Lagdas' biography of Aris Velouchiotis.
21. Nefeloudis, *op. cit.*, p. 256.
22. Kousoulas, *Revolution and Defeat*, pp. 224 ff.
23. Athanasios Pavlopoulos, *Istoria tou kommounismou en Elladi*, (Athens: Geografiki Ypiresia Stratou, 1971), p. 81.
24. In his letter of 1948, Karagiorgis wrote to Zachariadis: 'It is unfortunate that the leadership's important decision to conceal arms was not accompanied by a technical decision that all who did this should go abroad...' Arkadinos, *op. cit.*, Vol. 3, *Kostas Karagiorgis*, p. 50; Kousoulas, *Revolution and Defeat*, p. 221; Pavlopoulos, *op. cit.*, pp. 81 ff. The instructions of the Salonica EAM Committee to local EAM members of 15th January, describing the armistice as 'temporary', further cited by Kousoulas, is likewise no proof since these instructions refer to the period before the Varkiza Agreement, when a renewed conflict was still quite possible.
25. So too Woodhouse, *The Struggle for Greece*, p. 138.
26. This view was confirmed by Partsalidis. According to him, the main reason was fear of the collaborators. Dimitrios Partsalidis, *Dipli apokatastasi tis Ethinikis Antistasis*, (Athens: Themelio, 1978), p. 183.
27. At the Third Party Conference in 1950 Zachariadis posthumously 'exposed' Siantos as an agent. See *Neos Kosmos*, (February 1951), pp. 60-4, 'Stoicheia pano stin prodotiki drasi tou G. Siantou'. In 1967 the party officially rehabilitated him, but this did not hinder the old Stalinist Vlandas from repeating these defamations recently. Dimitrios Vlandas, *I prodomeni epanastasi 1941-44*, (Athens: Evangelios, 1977), pp. 380 ff. Periklis Rodakis writing in the newly-issued popular historical journal *Tote* analyses Zachariadis' alleged 'evidence' for this charge and demonstrates its inadequacy, 'Giorgis Siantos itan prodotis'; (George Siantos, was he a traitor?), *Tote. . .* 5, (1983), pp. 12-27.
28. Kostas Karagiorgis, 'To elliniko provlima ston pankosmio stivo', *KOMEP*, (February 1945), pp. 4-8; Chrysa Hajivasiliou, 'Palia provlimata se kainourya fasi', *ibid.*, pp. 2 ff.; Fanis [Vasilis Bartziotas], 'Agonas 33 imeron', *ibid.*, pp. 11 ff.; Miltiadis Porfyrogenis, 'Oi omiroi', *ibid.*, pp. 13 ff.
29. Vasilis Bartziotas, 'Ta organotika provlimata tou KKE', *KOMEP*, (March 1945), pp. 24-9.
30. Maurice Thorez, 'I ethniki apostoli tou gallikou Kommounistikou Kommatos', *ibid.*, pp. 30-4.
31. Dimitrios Karandonis, 'Episkopisi tis politikis katastasis', *ibid.*, pp. 44-6.
32. *Episima Keimena V*, pp. 358-66.
33. Woodhouse, *The Struggle for Greece*, p. 140.
34. Papakongas, *Grammata*, pp. 108 ff.
35. ELD, *Theseis*, p. 51.
36. *Episima Keimena V*, p. 367. Thus, many regional party secretaries and EAM

leaders. Nefeloudis, *op. cit.*, p. 256. Rousos, *I megali pentaetia*, Vol. II, p. 390 reports forty participants and thirty-seven speakers.
37. The relevant texts can be found in *KOMEP*, (April-May 1945), pp. 1-10 and *ibid.*, (June 1945), pp. 6-7; republished in *Episima Keimena V*, pp. 368-83.
38. Zisis Zografos, 'Merika zitimata tis politikis mas grammis', *Neos Kosmos*, (September 1950), pp. 641-60; Yannis Ioannidis, 'Logos' [Speech at the Third Party Conference], *Neos Kosmos*, (November-December 1950), pp. 828-31; Nefeloudis, *op. cit.*, pp. 256-9; Blanas-Kissavos, *op. cit.*, pp. 65-7; Markos Vafiadis, 'O Markos Vafiadis apanta sto Mitso Partsalidi ya tin "synantisi me ton Stalin", ti Varkiza kai tin "katangelia" Zachariadi', *ANTI* 53, (4th September 1976), pp. 30-5; Vlandas, *op. cit.*, p. 386.
39. Nefeloudis, *op. cit.*, p. 256; Rousos, *op. cit.*, p. 390 where he writes of 'various critical voices'.
40. Blanas-Kissavos, *op. cit.*, p. 66.
41. Zografos, 'Merika zitimata', pp. 642 ff. With the reference to Yugoslavia Chrysa was making a point against Zevgos who had recommended a policy similar to Tito's. Rousos, *op. cit.*, p. 390.
42. Zografos, 'Merika zitimata', p. 644. At the beginning of his exposition, he acknowledged that KKE was in a state of crisis but at the end of the Plenum he retracted this. Rousos, *op. cit.*, p. 391.
43. *Ibid.*; for Zachariadis' third open letter see *Episima Keimena V*, pp. 31 ff.
44. Markos Vafiadis, 'O Markos Vafiadis apanta', p. 32. As Rousos reports, Karagiorgis had submitted his criticism to the praesidium in writing, Rousos, *op. cit.*, p. 391.
45. See the already oft-quoted Karagiorgis texts in Arkadinos, *op. cit.*, Vol. 3), pp. 45-56. The critical remarks contained in these texts are not necessarily identical in detail with the document submitted to the Eleventh Plenum, which is why they are not directly quoted here. As Zografos writes, *op. cit.*, p. 643, Karagiorgis submitted his criticism in the form of a memorandum to the praesidium of the Eleventh Plenum.
46. Markos Vafiadis, *op. cit.*, p. 32.
47. *Ibid.* Vlandas' assertion that he had exposed the Political Bureau members as traitors is not worthy of credence. Vlandas, *op. cit.*, p. 386.
48. Nefeloudis, *op. cit.*, p. 257.
49. *Episima Keimena V*, pp. 372 ff, 375.
50. The composition of the Political Bureau was as follows: George Siantos, Yannis Ioannidis, Dimitrios Partsalidis, Vasilis Bartziotas, Yannis Zevgos, Stergios Anastasiadis, Nikos Ploumbidis, Chrysa Hajivasiliou, Leonidas Stringos, Petros Rousos. *Ibid.*, p. 367.
51. *Ibid.*, pp. 378 ff.
52. *Ibid.*, pp. 380-3.
53. Blanas-Kissavos, *op. cit.*, p. 65.
54. Nefeloudis, *op. cit.*, p. 256.
55. Yannis Petsopoulos, *Ta pragmatika aitia tis diagrafis mou apo to KKE*, (Athens, 1946), p. 231. On the Akronafplia group: Yannis Manousakas, *Akronafplia: Thrylos kai pragmatikotita*, (Athens: Kapopoulos, 1975); and the same author, *Chroniko apo tin Antistasi (meta tin Akronafplia)*, (Athens: Kapopoulos, 1976). Akronafplia was the ill-famed prison where most of the communist leaders were held during the Metaxas dictatorship. This division within the Political Bureau gains confirmation from the later denunciation of Siantos, Zevgos and Chrysa Hajivasiliou by Zachariadis.
56. Eudes' version, *op. cit.*, p. 234 ff., of Aris' odyssey during this period should be taken with reservations. *cf.* Sarafis, *op. cit.*, p. LXI.

57. ESSAK (Epitropi Synergasias Sosialistikon Agrotikon Kommaton) comprised the following parties: ELD-SKE (Svolos and Tsirimokos), Kalomoiris' group from ESKE which seceded from EAM, and AAK (Anexartiton Agrotikon Komma, Independent Agrarian Party) of A. Voyatzis.
58. The following parties belonged to the EAM coalition: KKE; AKE (Agrotiko Komma Elladas, Gavriilidis); DRK (Dimokratiko Rizospatiko Komma, Democratic Radical Party, M. Kyrkos and A. Loulis); DE (Dimokratiki Enosi, Republican Union, M. Proïmakis and S. Kritikas); a part of SKE (I. Passalidis, G. Oikonomou and G. Georgalas). In addition a number of well-known Leftists and left-liberal personalities (such as General N. Grigoriadis and S. Hajibeis) co-operated with the new EAM. Readers are reminded that in Greek the word *dimokratikos* means both republican and democratic.
59. *Eleftheri Ellada*, 25th April, 1945.
60. Leeper to Foreign Office 27th April, 1945 (R 7515/4/19).
61. Eudes, *op. cit.*, p. 236 wrongly dates this 11th April, 1945.
62. Interview with Markos Vafiadis in 1976: 'Apostoli sta Ouralia', *Epikaira*, 16th December, 1976, pp. 74 ff.
63. Leeper to Foreign Office 24th May, 1945 (R 9144/4/19).
64. *Ibid.*
65. Letter from Markos Vafiadis to the Political Bureau of 28th May 1945: 'I alithia ya tin esokommatiki pali', *Neos Kosmos*, (November 1956), pp. 57 ff.
66. Richter, *op. cit.*, p. 322; Fitzroy Maclean, *Eastern Approaches*, (London: Cape, 1949), pp. 402-3; 526-7.
67. Eudes, *op. cit.*, p. 246. According to Rousos, Karagiorgis, too, wrote a critical letter to the Political Bureau. Rousos, *op. cit.*, p. 390.
68. The biographical data are based on an article by Karagiorgis: 'Merika viografica stoichia tou Nikou Zachariadi', *KOMEP*, (November 1946), pp. 606-9.
69. Nefeloudis, *op. cit.*, p. 107.
70. Zisis Zografos, 'Provlimata schetika me to esokommatiko mas kathestos', *Neos Kosmos*, (December 1956), p. 48.
71. Reprinted in *Kokkino Asteri*, (9th July, 1976), p. 20.
72. Nefeloudis, *op. cit.*, p. 109. Up to the Second World War, Zachariadis had only produced two substantial written works. One dealt with the poet Palamas and the other with the history of KKE. Nikos Zachariadis, 'Theseis ya tin istoria tou KKE', in: Nikos Zachariadis, *Epilogi Keimenon*, (Athens: Poreia, 1974), pp. 9-45. The latter is a very superficial summary presentation of KKE history without any deeper analysis.
73. Nefeloudis, *op. cit.*, p. 107.
74. *Ibid.*, pp. 110 ff.
75. *Ibid.*, pp. 111 ff. Based on Vasilis Nefeloudis' book *Achtina IX: Anamniseis 1930-1940*, (Athens: Olkos, 1974).
76. Eudes, *op. cit.*, p. 246; Zografos, 'Provlimata schetika me to esokommatiko mas kathestos', p. 51.
77. Information given by Dimitris Partsalidis to the author in 1976.
78. *Rizospastis*, 30th May, 1945; Zografos, 'Merika zitimata tis politikis mas grammis', p. 647.
79. For the text of Zachariadis' letter see *Epilogi Ergon*, (Athens: Protoporos, 1974), pp. 21 ff. Even the publishers of *Episima Keimena V*, who belong to KKE/Interior (Euro-communist), regarded this letter as genuine and reprinted it. *Episima Keimena V*, pp. 56 ff. In translation the text reads as follows:
'To the Examining Magistrate,
As I am not satisfied with the way the hearing is conducted, with the interpreter, I am submitting the following statement which I regard as alone having

validity.

First of all, I protest against my transfer to Germany, which I regard as illegal, and I demand my immediate return to my native country.

As regards the questions you put to me on personal and organisational matters concerning KKE, I have nothing to answer.

As regards the political line of KKE, I must state the following: The fundamental and central element in KKE's political line is absolute and irreconcibable opposition to and struggle against fascist (national socialist) theory, policy and *praxis*. KKE has fought and fights against national socialist violence and occupation of Greece and for the restoration of national independence and integrity. KKE has always fought every attempt to subjugate the country's independence through foreign capital, to whatever foreign power it belonged. KKE recognises no territorial changes brought about by the German occupation of Greece; nor will it recognise any future changes of this sort. KKE will continue to fight with all means to obstruct such changes, for the liberation of the country from foreign occupation and for its integrity.

KKE regards as a basic element of its policy, defence of the Soviet Union from all external threats, such as those which have lately become obvious.

I request that the translation of this statement of mine be supplied to me. Vienna, Gestapo prison, 18th June 1941.

N. Zachariadis, Secretary of the Central Committee of KKE and member of the Comintern Executive.'

Quite apart from the tone of this letter, which would have provoked a strong reaction from the Gestapo, but which we will leave unquestioned, the text contains internal errors. Zachariadis speaks of territorial changes when, at the time he is supposed to have written, there had been no territorial changes in the sense of annexations, only the division of the country into Occupation zones. His reference to defending the Soviet Union against a German threat is likewise an anachronism. At that time the Hitler–Stalin pact still held and the attack on the Soviet Union, as is known, began on 22nd June 1941. Furthermore the denunciation of national socialism does not fit the period of the Hitler–Stalin pact. Finally, there is the question: how did Zachariadis, after nearly three years in a concentration camp, still have the text of a letter of 1941 in his possession. In the author's opinion the above-listed suspect elements suggest the conclusion that this letter is a forgery. But the question of who forged it remains open.

80. In his biographical study, Karagiorgis suggested that in Dachau Zachariadis had organised not only the Greek but also the German Communists into resistance groups. Karagiorgis, *op. cit.*, p. 609.

81. Zachariadis evidently survived the concentration camp in good form. The photographs published by *Rizospastis* after his return by no means show the well-known image of a half-starved concentration camp inmate. Leeper reported on 5th June: 'I began by asking him about his experiences in Dachau which he described as one of the best concentration camps. He bore no marks of suffering and looked very fit.' Leeper to Foreign Office 5th June, 1945 (R 9722/4/19). Zachariadis must therefore at least have understood how not to attract attention in Dachau. We have reliable information that, after de-stalinisation, the Soviet leadership investigated Zachariadis' record in Dachau, but nothing is known of the result. The author has tried hard to find a former inmate of Dachau who remembers Zachariadis. At last he found one who told him: 'It always amazed me that Zachariadis lived there totally unmolested among his compatriots.'

82. Zografos, 'Merika zitimata tis politikis mas grammis', p. 647.

83. *Rizospastis*, 2nd June, 1945; *Deka chronia agones 1935-1945*, (Athens: KKE Central Committee, 1945), pp. 252 ff. Elisabeth Barker gives valuable informa-

tion on Zachariadis' motives. 'However, as Zachariadis explained when I interviewed him in 1946, this was a tactical move to appease the non-communist groups allied with the communists in EAM; the Party's real policy was that the northern frontier questions should be settled on the basis of self-determination.' *Op. cit.*, p. 29.
84. Nikos Zachariadis, *Deka chronia palis*, p. 25.
85. *Rizospastis*, 2nd June, 1945, p. 2.
86. Vukmanović, *op. cit.*, p. 68.
87. Helga Koppel, *Partito Communista Italiano: Die Entwicklung der Italienischen KP zur Massenpartei*, (Berlin: Verlag für das Studium der Arbeiterbewegung, 1976), p. 63, where, in a proclamation of the CPI, we read: '. . . the democracy we mean. . . must be a popular democracy, basing its support on the masses with the working-class as its vanguard and secure leadership. . .'
88. Leeper to Foreign Office 5th June, 1945 (R 9722/8001/19).
89. *Rizospastis*, 5th June, 1945.
90. Leeper to Foreign Office 5th June, 1945 (R 9736/8001/19).
91. Koppel, *op. cit.*, p. 69.
92. Vukmanović, *op. cit., passim*.
93. For the text of Babis Klaras' letter see Papakongos, *op. cit.*, pp. 145-83.
94. *Rizospastis*, 12th June 1945. Rousos holds that Aris had already been expelled from the party by the Eleventh Plenum, Rousos, *op. cit.*, p. 391.
95. Zachariadis arrived on 29th May. On 1st June there was a meeting of the Political Bureau. (As it had a large membership, another meeting would have not have passed unnoticed.) The Central Committee met from 25th to 27th June for the Twelfth Plenum. It is not even certain whether the Political Bureau met before the denunciation. *Rizospastis* mentions a Political Bureau session on the 15th June.
96. Doubts as to Aris' suicide (Richter, *op. cit.*, p. 567) have since been cleared up. The most recent reports and publications remove the last doubts. Rizos D. Bokotas, *Etsi chathike o Aris*, (Athens: Kodros, 1976); Yannis G. Hajipanayotis (Capetan Thomas), *I politiki diathiki tou Ari Velouchioti*, (Athens: Dorikos, 1976).
97. *Rizospastis*, 16th June, 1945.
98. *Ibid.*, 17th June, 1945.
99. Koppel, *op. cit.*, p. 77.
100. Caccia to Foreign Office 27th June, 1945 (R 11022/4/19).
101. *Rizospastis*, 16th June, 1945.
102. *Ibid.*, 17th June, 1945.
103. Even Zisis Zografos admits this in an article in *Neos Kosmos* where he more than once speaks of the 'alleged' letter from the high-ranking officer. Zografos, 'Merika zitimata tis politikis mas grammis', p. 647.
104. Caccia to Foreign Office 2nd July, 1945 (R 11552/4/19); *Rizospastis*, 28th June, 1945.
105. Caccia to Foreign Office 16th July, 1945 (R 12399/4/19).
106. Woodhouse, *Apple of Discord*, p. 242.
107. *Apofasi tis 12is olomeleias tis Kentrikis Epitropis tou KKE*, (Athens: O Rigas, 1945), pp. 12 ff.
108. *Ibid.*, p. 19.
109. *Ibid.*, pp. 20 ff.
110. *Ibid.*, p. 23.
111. *Ibid.*, p. 27.
112. *Ibid.*, p. 37. Without naming the precise reference, Kousoulas claims that, at the Twelfth Plenum, Zachariadis stated that the bourgeois-democratic phase had

been completed and that the forthcoming revolution would be a socialist one. Kousoulas, *Revolution and Defeat*, p. 223. This has apparently been taken over by Eudes and Solaro: Eudes, *op. cit.*, p. 249; Solaro, *op. cit.*, p. 177. Despite intensive search the author has been unable to find any such passage in the Twelfth Plenum texts, and its content does not coincide with Zachariadis' ideological theorising.
113. *Ibid.*, pp. 41 ff.
114. *Ibid.*, pp. 5 ff.
115. *Ibid.*, pp. 9 ff.
116. *Ibid.*, p. 3. The members were: Nikos Zachariadis, George Siantos, Yannis Ioannidis, Mitsos Partsalidis, Vasilis Bartziotas and Chrysa Hajivasiliou. Yannis Zevgos, Stergios Anastasiadis, Nikos Ploumbidis, Leonidas Stringos and Petros Rousos were no longer members of the Political Bureau. Stringos however was instructed to prepare a report on the agrarian problem for the Seventh Party Congress.
117. *Ibid.*, p. 62.
118. *Voithima ya tin Istoria tou KKE*, (Athens: Ekdoseis tou Laou, 1975), p. 22. This edition is a reprint of the first edition of 1952. It is confirmed by the old Stalinist Gousias. Giorgios Vontitsos-Gousias, *Oi aities ya tis ittes, ti diaspasi tou KKE kai tis ellinikis Aristeras*, Vol. 1, (Athens: Na Ypiretoume to Lao, 1977), p. 129.
119. Zografos, 'Merika zitimata tis politikis mas grammis', p. 654.
120. *Rizospastis*, 5th July, 1945. So far the British had been described as allies.
121. See p. 177.
122. Zografos, *op. cit.*, p. 654, where Zografos says that the two-poles-theory applied only to the Occupation period.
123. See p. 178; *Rizospastis*, 20th July, 1945.
124. *Rizospastis*, 27th July, 1945.
125. *Ibid.*, 29th July, 1945.
126. See p. 179.
127. *Rizospastis*, 10th August, 1945.
128. *Ibid.*, 16th August, 1945.
129. *Ibid.*, 22nd August, 1945.
130. Consul-General Rapp to British Embassy in Athens 23rd August, 1945 (R 14318/8001/19).
131. *The Manchester Guardian* reported 50,000–100,000 present, 28th August 1945. *Rizospastis* reported 120,000.
132. Consul-General Rapp to British Embassy in Athens 25th August, 1945 (R 14411/8001/19) and 28th August, 1945 (R 14520/8001/19); also *The Manchester Guardian* and *Rizospastis*, 28th August, 1945. 'Embros ELAS' was the ELAS anthem.
133. Consul-General Rapp to British Embassy in Athens 3rd September, 1945 (R 14865/4/19). After Zachariadis the following spoke: General Neokosmos Grigoriadis, Kostas Gavriilidis, Mitsos Partsalidis, Michaïl Kyrkos and G. Marangos.
134. Consul-General Rapp to British Embassy in Athens 27th August, 1945 (R 14520/8001/19) and *The Manchester Guardian*, 28th August, 1945.
135. *Rizospastis*, 28th August, 1945.
136. Laskey's Minutes 31st August, 1945 (R 14520/8001/19).
137. Caccia to Foreign Office 10th September, 1945 (R 15349/4/19).
138. Consul-General Rapp to British Embassy in Athens 3rd September, 1945 (R 14864/4/19).
139. *Rizospastis*, 8th September, 1945.

140. *ANTI,* 17th June, 1978, p. 28.
141. *I 6i syndiaskepsi tis kommounistikis organosis Athinas 28-29 Septemvri 1945,* (Athens: KOA Editions, 1945), pp. 13 ff.
142. *Ibid.,* pp. 84-93.
143. *Ibid.,* pp. 93-8.
144. Text in *Episima Keimena III, 1929-1933* (n.p.: Politikes kai logotechnikes ekodoseis, 1966), pp. 294-306.
145. Comintern programme, Greek edition of 1932, quoted from *Episima Keimena IV,* p. 19.
146. *Ibid.*
147. *Ibid.,* p. 23.
148. *Ibid.,* p. 25. Kousoulas' version contains several omissions, not marked, which eventually lead to distortion of the meaning; *op. cit.,* p. 89. In his recently published study, George Alexander bases his whole analysis of KKE's policy of the wartime and post-war period on some effusions by Zachariadis of 1935, which were mere interpretative adaptations of the 1931 Comintern proclamation and the Sixth Plenum resolution of 1934. Though he seems to know the latter, he did not refer to them in his text, George M. Alexander, *The Prelude to the Truman Doctrine: British Policy in Greece 1944-1947,* (Oxford: Clarendon Press, 1982), p. 8.
149. *Pros tin 6i syndiaskepsi tis kommounistikis organosis Athinas: Logodosia tis Epitropis Polis tis KOA apo tin 5i Syndiaskepsi (Aprilis 1944) mechri simera,* (Athens: KOA Ekdosi, 1945), p. 18. That the term 'worker' should be understood in its widest possible sense is suggested by the fact that even in 1962 workers represented only approximately 40 per cent of the economically active section of the Greek population. *Concise Statistical Yearbook of Greece 1962,* (Athens: National Statistical Service of Greece, 1963), p. 57.
150. See footnote 117 to this chapter.
151. *I 6i syndiaskepsi tis KOA,* p. 107.
152. *Ibid.* The alternate members *(anapliromatika)* consisted of one worker, five intellectuals, two employees and two students.
153. Length of party membership of the delegates:

Duration	No. of members	Percentage
over 20 years (before 1925)	7	3.6%
20-15 years (1925-30)	3	1.6%
15-9 years (1930-6)	23	11.9%
4-2 years (1941-3)	160	82.9%

Length of party membership of the new committee members:

Duration	Regular members No.	%	Anapliromatika No.	%
over 20 years (before 1925)	3	13%		
20-15 years (1925-30)	2	8.6%		
15-9 years (1930-6)	11	48%	2	20%
4-2 years (1941-3)	7	30.4%	8	80%

154. Of the five members of the party control committee two had joined the party before 1930, three between 1930 and 1936.
155. *Apofasi tis 12is olomeleias,* p. 3; Partsalidis toured Epirus: Vontitsos-Gousias, *op. cit.,* p. 181.
156. See p. 238 and footnote 19 to this chapter.
157. *I panelladiki organotiki syskepsi (15-17 Aprili 1946),* (Athens: KKE Central Committee, 1946), p. 9. Zachariadis spoke of the intake of new members and recommended extreme caution and a limit of 100,000 members. His formulation suggests the conclusion that KKE's membership must have stood just below this figure.

158. *Ibid.*, p. 17. This assessment also correlates well with Burks' assessment. R.V. Burks, 'Statistical Profile of the Greek Communist', *Journal of Modern History* 17, (1955), p. 155. Burks' assessments are for the year 1952. For the removal of the peasant members from KKE see p. 262.
159. Like EAM, the KKE of the Occupation period may well have included all strata of the population, as also stated by Burks, *op. cit.*, p. 158.
160. *To 7o synedrio tou KKE*, Vol. I, *Apofaseis-Psifismata-Chairetistiria*, (Athens: KKE Central Committee, 1945), p. 11.
161. *Ibid.*, p. 12. Sixty-three delegates had been party members from before 1930, seventy-five from before 1940 and eighty-five had joined since 1940.
162. *Ibid.*, 12 per cent joined before 1920, 80 per cent before 1930 and 8 per cent before 1936.
163. Nefeloudis, *op. cit.*, p. 263.
164. *To 7o synedrio*, Vol. I, p. 13.
165. See p. 245; footnote 54.
166. *To 7o synedrio tou KKE*, Vol. II. *Eisigisi kai telikos logos tou Giorgi Siantou*, (Athens: KKE Central Committee, 1945), pp. 3-28.
167. *Ibid.*, p. 31.
168. *To 7o synedrio*, Vol. I, p. 17; Eudes, *op. cit.*, p. 253, names Tzimas and Karagiorgis.
169. *To 7o synedrio tou KKE*, Vol. III, *Eisigisi kai telikos logos tou s. N. Zachariadi*, (Athens: KKE Central Committee, 1945), p. 18.
170. *Ibid.*, pp. 20 ff.
171. *Ibid.*, p. 63.
172. *Episima Keimena IV*, p. 281.
173. *To 70 synedrio*, Vol. V. *Eisigisi kai telikos logos tou s. D. Partsalidi, logos tou s. N. Zachariadi, eisigisi kai telikos logos tou s. Y. Ioannidi*, (Athens: KKE Central Committee, 1945), p. 3; Kousoulas, *Revolution and Defeat*, p. 228, speaks of a party programme of 1935 but without citing any source.
174. *To 80 synedrio tou KKE. Eisigiseis, omilies, chairetistiria, apofaseis:* (n.p.: Politikes kai logotechnikes ekdoseis, 1961), pp. 171-207.
175. 'Proschedio programmatos tou KKR', *KOMEP*, (September 1945), pp. 1-9.
176. See footnote 72 of this chapter.
177. 'Proschedio programmatos', p. 3.
178. *To 7o synedrio*, Vol. V, p. 7.
179. *Ibid.*, p. 8.
180. 'Proschedio programmatos', p. 5. In his letter Partsalidis omitted to refer to this.
181. *Ibid.*, p. 7.
182. *To 7o synedrio*, Vol. V, p. 13.
183. *Ibid.*, p. 16.
184. *Ibid.*
185. *Ibid.*, pp. 19 ff.
186. *Ibid.*, p. 28.
187. See p. 252.
188. The constitution of 1935 can be found in *Episima Keimena IV*, pp. 312-18. The constitution of 1945 is reprinted in *To 7o synedrio*, Vol. I, pp. 51-61.
189. *To 7o synedrio*, Vol. V, pp. 30-44.
190. *To 7o synedrio*, Vol. I, p. 33.
191. *Ibid.*, p. 57.
192. *Ibid.*, p. 10.
193. Blanas-Kissavos, *op. cit.*, p. 75.
194. *Ibid.*, p. 62.

195. *Ibid.*, p. 71.
196. *To 7o synedrio*, Vol. I, p. 8.

KANELLOPOULOS' CABINET

The appointment of Panayotis Kanellopoulos as Prime Minister on 1st November 1945 took even Leeper by surprise since, at the age of 43, Kanellopoulos belonged to the younger generation of politicians.[1] He came from Patras where he had been born in 1902. In the early '20s he had studied in Munich and Heidelberg, where he was promoted *doctor jurisprudentiae,* and then returned to Greece. Later he had held various public posts and had at the same time pursued an academic career. In 1933 he was appointed to the Chair of Sociology at Athens University. In 1935 he resigned and founded the National Unity Party (Ethnikon Enotikon Komma) but had no success in the 1936 elections. During the Metaxas dictatorship he showed himself an upright democrat and was therefore exiled. He served at the front in the Albanian campaign as a simple private, a volunteer. Immediately after the Occupation he declared himself in favour of armed resistance to the occupying powers. To this end he established an underground organisation which, until his flight to the Middle East in 1942, cooperated with EAM. From May 1942 to March 1943 he was Defence Minister and Vice-Premier in the Tsouderos Cabinet. Although he was a convinced republican, during his successful stint as Defence Minister he had held himself aloof from the party political quarrels and intrigues within the Officers' Corps of the armed forces in exile. In March 1943, as a result of the first stirrings of unrest in these forces provoked by monarchist officers of SAN, he resigned. He was a fervent patriot and believed that politics should be conducted on ethical principles. As a Liberal, he was opposed to the use of violence in politics and for this reason took a stand against the Left at the Lebanon Conference. He had held ministries in both the Papandreou governments. As a typical intellectual he was somewhat unworldly and at the same time a strong sense of loyalty to friends made him easy to influence. He rejected the old-school politicians but did not know how to construct a political party base of his own. In contrast to George Papandreou, he was no demagogue. It was just these weaknesses which brought about his appointment.

William Hardy McNeill described Kanellopoulos' Cabinet as follows:
'This Government had perhaps the ablest collection of brains of any of the post-war Governments of Greece. But it lacked any vestige of popular support. Kanellopoulos was neither fish nor fowl; neither

definitely a royalist nor definitely a republican. He preferred a republic on theoretical reasons, but was not convinced that republican government was well suited to Greece under the extraordinary difficulties of the time. He asserted that he would become either one or the other, obedient to the verdict of the people. Such an avoidance of key issues in Greek politics won him no political friends. Both republicans and royalists declined to support his Government, so that good intentions and a high-minded program came to nothing.'[2]

McNeill's statement on the quality of the Cabinet must only be accepted with reservations. There is no doubt that it fits Kanellopoulos himself and that he had managed to recruit a number of distinguished technocrats and experts from the universities[3] who, in politically settled times, could certainly have achieved much. But these did not hold the key posts in Kanellopoulos' Cabinet and perhaps they were no longer what Kanellopoulos had imagined them to be. The developments of the past twelve months had taken their toll. The four key ministries (Defence, Security, Interior and Finance) were in the hands of the Right. The Army Minister was a formerly Liberal general, Spyridon Georgoulis, made commander-in-chief of the National Guard in 1944 and now in command of a division—not at that time exactly a certificate of liberal attitudes. Security was in the hands of General Pavsanias Katsotas. At the time of Kanellopoulos' Middle East activities Katsotas had commanded the First Brigade of the Greek armed forces-in-exile and in 1944, after liberation, he had been military commander of Athens and Piraeus and during the December events had commanded the National Guard in that area—again not exactly a good omen for liberal control of the security forces. The Interior Minister was the brother of the EKKA Resistance group leader, Dimitrios Psarros, who was killed by ELAS, and he too could not be accused of a liberal attitude to the Left. Finally, the key Finance Ministry was in the hands of Professor Grigorios Kasimatis. He too belonged to the younger generation of Greek politicians (born 1906) and, like Kanellopoulos, had studied abroad (law, political sciences and national economy in Paris). Until 1936 he had made his career as a barrister and, unlike Kanellopoulos, had continued to make his career under the Metaxas dictatorship when he was appointed to the Chair of Civil Law and Social Sciences at the Panteios Institute. In 1936 he had been Assistant-Minister for Economics in the Demertzis–Metaxas Cabinet. In the Voulgaris and Damaskinos Cabinets he had successively held the Ministries of Economics and Welfare. Politicaly, he could be assigned to the right-wing of the Liberal Party. Thus, as can be seen from the manning of these key ministries, the Kanellopoulos Cabinet would not bring about any radical changes. Yet in another respect too continuity was guaranteed.

The key man in the Cabinet was Konstantinos Tsatsos, whose wife Ioanna was a sister of Seferiadis (better known under his pen-name

Seferis) and whose brother Themistoklis belonged to George Papandreou's intimate entourage. All three were united by a longstanding friendship with Kanellopoulos and his appointment therefore had the following implications: Damaskinos would continue to control the government's policy through Tsatsos who was to be Assistant-Minister for Press and Information in the new Cabinet—an office burdened with the odium attaching to a propaganda ministry since the Metaxas period when it was held by the fascist Nikoloudis. The lateral connection with Papandreou, who in the last weeks had been drifting steadily towards the Right, would ensure that the government was subject to Populist influence. The importance of Tsatsos' role is shown by the fact that he played a leading part in the selection of the future ministers.[4]

In other words, general continuity of previous policy on the decisive issues of internal security and finance was ensured. Kanellopoulos would not introduce any new policy of opening towards the Left and the economic interests of the oligarchy would remain untouched.

On these topics Kanellopoulos thought quite differently. Just as during his time in Cairo, he wanted to leave the constitutional question open. His priority was the country's reconstruction and the revival of its economy. Of the backstairs manoeuvring he had no inkling. Leeper commented:

'Kanellopoulos himself is an honest and earnest man whose long and eloquent discourses convince himself more than his listeners. I speak from experience. I am sure that at this moment he is filled with a high sense of public duty and that his motives are purer than those who decry him, but today we are living in a hard world in which words and motives have to be translated very quickly into definite action. I find it difficult to see Kanellopoulos giving the translation that the times require.'[5]

Kanellopoulos' appointment provoked a hymn of hate from the right-wing Greek press, but this was silenced by his inaugural statement. It was realised that he was the first Prime Minister since liberation who was not telling fairy tales about the country's economy.[6]

His inaugural statement of 2nd November was a proof of his goodwill and idealism but at the same time also a proof of the illusions from which he was suffering: the most important task was to find a solution to the economic problem; the Greek people's morale must be raised to overcome their near panic about the future; law and order must be restored by the use of democratic justice towards all and by combatting every tendency to violence from whomsoever it might proceed; collaborators must be punished; the problem of the election date would be settled by agreement between the political parties and in accordance with the international situation; the date and electoral system would be settled by the Cabinet in discussions with the parties.[7]

In fact the economic situation had deteriorated catastrophically. The Voulgaris government had done nothing to get this rapidly deteriorating situation under control. The *drachma* continued to depreciate in value and, at the beginning of October, the prices of basic foodstuffs rose by 23% in one week.[8] After Voulgaris' resignation there had ceased to be any government economic or financial policy. On 18th October, when Leeper urged Damaskinos to do something, the latter told him that economic and financial measures could be taken only after the government crisis had been solved.[9] Meanwhile the banknote presses were working at high speed and the budget deficit grew at a corresponding rate.[10] At the end of October this was the situation: the country's October revenue of 6.3 billion *drachmas* faced an expenditure of 13.1 billion (increasing the total budget deficit to 37.2 billion). By 31st October the circulation of banknotes had risen to 62.2 billion *drachmas* and 50,000 *drachmas* were being paid for one golden sovereign.[11] Food prices continued to escalate until, at the beginning of November, they reached a level three times higher than that of the 30th June,[12] and many foodstuffs once more disappeared completely from the market. Naturally, wages did not keep pace with this rate of inflation so that those who had work were scarcely better off than the majority of the population who had none.

Thus, the basic problem for Kanellopoulos' government was to get a grip on the economic and financial situation. At his congratulatory visit on 4th November, Leeper made this crystal clear to him. Kanellopoulos assured him that his Cabinet consisted of young, dynamic personalities, keen to act and to take decisions, rather than to sit in their offices and sign documents.[13] Leeper however was not convinced and on the same day told Tsatsos, when the latter visited him, that Kasimatis was certainly not such a strong personality. Tsatsos countered this, saying an effort was afoot to make Tsouderos Governor of the Bank of Greece, in other words coordinator for economic and financial policy.[14]

Not only Leeper was alarmed at the economic situation. At the beginning of October UNRRA chairman Lehman had sent one of his representatives, Commander Jackson, to Athens to carry out an on-the-spot situation analysis.[15] On the 24th October he had arrived in Athens with his British colleague, Gale, and had started talks with the Greek government, with the US, British and Canadian ambassadors and also with the local UNRRA representatives. On the 27th he summarised his impressions for Lehman: between 1st April and 30th September UNRRA had brought in 1.2 million tons of vital supplies and thus it had been possible to keep the Greek population alive; there had also been some successes in the agrarian, transport, health and welfare sectors.

> 'However, it has not been possible to achieve much in the major field of reviving Greek industry owing to initial late arrival of raw materials, the attitude of most factory owners and incompetence and lack of will on

the part of the Government. It is true that if UNRRA ceased importing supplies into Greece now, the basic economic condition of the country would be little better than it would have been if we had not come here.'

Economic breakdown was approaching; and the economic situation was closely connected with the political one. The previous governments had suffered shipwreck for two reasons:

'a) The absence of a competent and effective administrative machine; b) the decisive influence on these Governments of a number of people, usually behind the scenes, whose main object is to make money quickly at the expense of the country.'

An improvement in the situation could only be attained if these factors were eliminated. Damaskinos was indeed trying to form a new government to counter this situation but a pre-condition for its success was that he should be supported by one of the Western allies. As the present Greek government did nothing, UNRRA had become the only competent authority on economic questions, whose advice was sought on even the simplest matters.[16]

Jackson went on to analyse various possible solutions. UNRRA could withdraw from Greece; this would lead to chaos and would have repercussions on the Western Allies who would then have to intervene. UNRRA could—as had been repeatedly suggested from the Greek side—take Greek economic policy under its control. But this would implicate UNRRA in day-to-day Greek politics and was therefore likewise to be rejected. He recommended that the Western Allies should establish some sort of Advisory Mission in Greece which would advise the Greek government on administrative and economic reconstruction and would supervise its implementation of the advice. Only if a new administration could be built up under Western Allied leadership, would Greece have a chance to get on her feet again. UNRRA would not participate in this Advisory Mission, but its very existence would be a kind of guarantee that the Greek government would take the measures necessary for UNRRA to operate successfully.

As an immediate measure the Allies should prompt the Regent to form a 'middle of the road' government. If Lehman agreed with his suggestions, would he please make the relevant representations to the US government. His British colleague, Gale, would do the same at the Foreign Office. He himself realised that such a step exceeded UNRRA's actual mission, 'nevertheless we believe that the policy we are advocating is the only one which can prevent an economic collapse in Greece which will destroy all the work which UNRRA has done in and for Greece and probably affect the general future of UNRRA'.[17]

Gale and Jackson concluded with an urgent appeal to Lehman to enter into immediate negotiations with the governments of the US, Great Britain and Canada.

'The situation here demands some allied intervention, both to save Greece and to save UNRRA. We believe that economic intervention now will be necessary if military intervention later on is to be avoided, but UNRRA itself cannot be the authority to intervene. . . Action must be taken in the next 4 or 5 weeks if the internal situation in Greece is not to deteriorate beyond the point at which a fresh collapse can be prevented.'[18]

We do not know how far these recommendations by Gale and Jackson influenced Damaskinos' decision to appoint Kanellopoulos Prime Minister. Certainly they must have played a role as did the talks going on simultaneously in Athens between the Supreme Allied Commander Mediterranean, Lt.-General Sir William Morgan, and the Chief of the Imperial General Staff, Field-Marshall Lord Alanbrooke.[19]

After his return to Caserta, Morgan relayed his impressions in a telegram to the Chiefs-of-Staff and the Foreign Office: Greece's economic and financial situation needed drastic reforms and a strong government was required to put these through, but this was not in sight. From a military standpoint, Greece was in a dangerous position. Building up of the armed forces and the gendarmerie was indeed making excellent progress under the British Missions, but Allied troops would have to remain in Greece for a considerable time. If the Fourth Indian Division were to be withdrawn in spring 1946 and were not replaced by Allied troops, this could encourage Yugoslavia, Bulgaria and Albania to provoke further frontier incidents which could end in an armed intervention by these countries in Greece.[20]

Morgan went on to make recommendations: the Greek government had recently been informed that, from 1st January 1946, it would have to bear the cost of the Greek army (about £12 million) alone. This he did not think right. Then he made a sensational suggestion.

'British effort to assist the Greeks to reestablish their state on a sound basis is grievously handicapped by being an individual instead of an Allied effort. American participation on an equal basis would not only lighten our load but would give added prestige and confidence for the future.'

The US had already agreed to action of this sort in Venezia Giulia where—in contrast to Greece—they had no economic interests. Moreover the bulk of the UNRRA expenditure came from the USA and its personnel consisted very largely of US citizens. The British troops must remain in Greece at least until the end of 1946, and the Greek army must continue to be financially supported since otherwise it would not, even by this date, be in a condition to carry out its tasks. He therefore recommended that the British government address itself in these terms to the US government, so that a long-term Allied Greek policy could be determined and financial support of the Greek armed forces continued.[21]

In conversation with the US ambassador to Italy, Alexander C. Kirk, Morgan went into this line of thought more deeply and added that Great Britain could no longer bear this financial burden alone; he hoped that the US would take over a part of it; if the US was not prepared to play a more active role in Greece, Britain would be forced to withdraw. He would urge Attlee to talk over the matter with Truman.[22] On 4th November Morgan informed Kirk of the content of his telegram to London and the latter, for his part, reported it to Washington.[23] Reactions in London and Washington differed. Secretary of State Byrnes asked Ambassador MacVeagh for his opinion on Jackson's report: he was worried about the lack of willingness—or the inability—of Greek politicians to cooperate in the interest of their country.

'Impression gaining ground abroad that selfishness and cupidity are blinding them to all broader issues and that perhaps Greece [is] incapable of running herself and solving immediate economic problems. Under these circumstances [it] may be impossible to obtain additional funds for UNRRA's work in Greece. In such event there is no other machinery for further support from outside. At least no US assistance [is] possible by any other method. Although US [is] prepared [to] give sympathetic consideration [to] Greek request for loans these must be made on sound economic basis.'

In the present insecure situation a loan was not very probable. The Greek politicians should be made aware of this. But, in view of the situation, the UNRRA suggestions were receiving consideration in the State Department.[24] In other words this meant the US government was not prepared to deviate from its previous policy of non-intervention in Greek affairs.

In London, Morgan's suggestions were met with mild resignation. Hayter commented:

'One had been trying in vain for a long time to win over the Americans to support British policy in Greece. But the State Department reaction has always been: "Greece is *your* headache".'

It would not be possible to get them to send advisers; anything more than activities in connection with UNRRA and supervision of the elections could probably not be expected. The Greeks should be encouraged to continue trying for a loan. Financial support for the Greek armed forces had been discussed with the Treasury *ad nauseam* and eventually it had been accepted that the Greeks must bear the costs themselves. Another effort could perhaps be made at Cabinet level. The Foreign Office favoured the continued presence of British troops but any hope of US troops was evidently quite without prospect.[25] Morgan's telegram, Gale's statements and finally Leeper's reports on the programme and demands of the new Finance Minister Kasimatis prompted Bevin to propose to the Cabinet the immediate despatch of the Foreign Under-Secretary, Hector

McNeil, to Greece and this was agreed and announced in the press on 7th November.[26]

Kasimatis' programme had two key points: the fight against inflation and an increase in revenue to bring about a balanced budget. He had realised that the inflation stemmed primarily from the rolling of the banknote presses but that it was at least equally encouraged by psychological factors of which the flight from the *drachma* into gold was the outward sign. To stop the speculation in gold he intended to use the same method as Hitler's Special Plenipotentiary for the South-East, Neubacher, had used during the inflation of the Occupation period: he would sell gold and, by establishing a free market in it, reduce its price. For this he wanted to use the Bank of Greece's gold reserves to the extent of 385,000 sovereigns. But, as this would not be enough, he hoped for a British loan of 650,000 sovereigns (approximately 6 million dollars). With this he hoped to cure the Greek gold neurosis and at the same time to give the *drachma* back its value since the sale of gold would cover about 75% of the money in circulation. As a parallel measure he suggested unrestricted currency dealings and a devaluation of the *drachma* which would boost Greek exports.[27]

To combat the budget deficit, he wanted to increase the tobacco tax, to tax war-profiteering and luxury goods, to sell enemy property and to raise the selling price of UNRRA supplies. A loan for private industry was also of importance: above all, the psychological factor would be decisive. A loan—even of relatively small dimensions—from the Export-Import Bank would change the psychological climate.[28]

When Kasimatis developed these ideas in a meeting with the US and British economic experts, he encountered massive opposition from Sir Quintin Hill. He rejected Kasimatis' gold project on instructions from the British Treasury. The priority was to balance the budget, which would convince Greek public opinion that inflation had been brought under control. A devaluation of the *drachma* could not be considered for the present as this would lead to disaster. Hill's views were supported by the UNRRA representatives. When Kasimatis asked if this was final, Hill conceded that he could address himself to the British Treasury on the whole issue.[29] On the other hand, the US Embassy representative considered Kasimatis' project practicable.

In the next days, Kasimatis continued his efforts to put his project through: on the morning of 6th November he submitted a somewhat modified version which emphasised measures to balance the budget to Rankin, the US Embassy's economic adviser. But he continued to regard the gold project as the pre-condition for successful stabilisation. This, together with the budgetary measures, and a loan from the Export-Import Bank would produce a fundamental change in the situation.[30]

While Kasimatis was talking with Rankin, Kanellopoulos visited

MacVeagh to win him over to Kasimatis' programme and to this end he gave assurances that he would try to get all parties with the exception of the Communists to support his programme. On the question of the electoral system he had found a compromise between the majority system and proportional representation which had already been accepted by the Populists, Papandreou, Plastiras and Venizelos. He intended to pursue a 'middle of the road' policy by disbanding 'X' and prohibiting young people—up to about 18—from belonging to political organisations.[31]

On the same evening Kasimatis had further talks with Hill and the UNRRA representatives. By exerting heavy pressure, Hill persuaded Kasimatis to forego devaluation and the gold project for the time being. On the other hand both Hill and the UNRRA representatives approved his proposals for improving revenue.[32] By these measures the budget would be practically balanced.

On 9th November Hill told Kasimatis of the British Treasury's final decision: since the Greek government itself had currency at its disposal, there could be no question of a British loan; sovereigns could not be made available since the Greek gold market should be reduced, not stimulated; the most important pre-condition for stability was internal reform and on this Britain was prepared to help.[33]

Thereupon Kanellopoulos broadcast the following programme—which had the approval of all the advisers. Taxes and the prices of UNRRA supplies were to be raised. To encourage merchants to import goods which were essential to the state, currency would be made available without bureaucratic formalities; though the prices and use of the imported goods would be controlled by the government. Currency would be made available at the official rates of exchange plus a surcharge. Loans would be available for industrial development and for internal trade. The government would try to raise loans from the Allies for reconstruction. UNRRA supplies would be more promptly distributed. An effective system of price control would be organised.[34]

This programme was merely a declaration of intent for an efficient administration. The immediate measures for its implementation did not exist. The raising of the excise tax and the prices of UNRRA supplies hit the poorest section of the population. Taxation of the well-to-do would be as ineffective as it had always been. In other words, this programme could only retard the general downhill progress; it could not reverse it. This was already proved by the fact that the banknote circulation still continued to increase (by 2.8 billion *drachmas* to 65 billion on 8th November) and the budget deficit grew (by 2.4 billion to a total of 39.6 billion on 6th November).[35]

Damaskinos himself seemed to have no great confidence in the Greek government's prospects and suggested to Gale that either the US and Britain should intervene to restore economic order or UNRRA should appoint advisers who would control the Greek economy through 'dummy' ministers. He himself was ready to nominate these.[36]

Meanwhile the Foreign Office had been going ahead with detailed preparations for Under-Secretary McNeil's visit. Bevin had himself participated in working out the programme that McNeil was to set before the Greek government. This programme consisted of an economic and a political section.

In the introduction to the economic section it was stated that the British government was prepared to supply advisers for the following sectors: army, finance, railways, roads, distribution and supplies. These advisers should be assigned to the corresponding ministries. They would have no direct authority but in general their advice should be regarded as binding. There was also willingness to advise Greece on its import programme but attention must be paid that the imports be such as would crank up the Greek economy. UNRRA must be supported. Inflation should be fought by a lottery which would absorb superfluous purchasing power and at the same time provide a further source of revenue for the state. This had given good results in Cyprus, Iraq and Palestine.

The Greeks, for their part, should purge the army, give every facility to the Legal Mission which was to investigate prisons, pass empowering legislation for the take-over of industries where necessary and for compulsion to get roads in order, and institute a system of state control of retail trade. A long-term plan must be developed for the Greek railways. The electoral lists should be checked for reliability in cooperation with the international Observers' Commission; and a final election date should be determined.[37] Armed with this programme, Under-Secretary Hector McNeil flew to Athens on 12th November, accompanied by William Hayter, head of the Foreign Office Southern Department, and the Labour MP Captain Francis Noel-Baker.

Meanwhile, MacVeagh's commentary on Jackson's telegram had reached Washington on 7th November. In this he distanced himself from Jackson's radical demands and recommended, instead of establishing an Advisory Mission, the sending of a small high-quality US delegation by the Export-Import Bank to examine the best method for a loan. Such a step would be much more effective than the present system of permanent economic tutelage. Nor was UNRRA leadership in Greece without responsibility for the calamity. He therefore recommended the sending of a top man equipped with the necessary authority to get the Greek Supply Ministry to distribute UNRRA goods more efficiently.[38]

This telegram and those which had preceded it as well as Attlee's forthcoming visit to the US, when it was possible that he might raise the Greek problem, prompted Henderson, the director of the Office of Near Eastern and African Affairs at the State Department, to address a memorandum to Secretary of State Byrnes on 10th November. In this he set out the US position. Participation in military responsibility was ruled out on considerations of principle. But the situation in Greece was sufficiently critical to justify the taking of some positive steps since Greece could not be left to its fate. He therefore recommended that, in agreement with the British government and perhaps with that of France, it should be made clear to the Greeks that further assistance would be given only after the Greek government had taken certain definite measures. Here he named price-and wage-control, devaluation of the *drachma,* exchange-rate control, better distribution of UNRRA supplies, stringent taxation, cutting of state expenditure, administrative re-organisation, stimulation of agrarian and industrial productivity, import controls and promotion of exports.

'Since the beginning of 1945. . . no Greek Government, whether for reasons of its political representation or other causes, has been able to enforce the rigid kind of economic measures which are essential to Greek recovery. . . It appears, therefore, that some measure of responsibility and firmness must come from outside Greece and it is thought that making known the existence of this source of pressure might provide the present Government with an added bulwark in embarking on the essential economic program which will inevitably be unpalatable to influential groups in Greece.'

In agreement with Britain, a suitable Note should be sent to the Greek government.[39]

Byrnes took up Henderson's suggestions and put them before President Truman. Kanellopoulos' government should be supported and the Note should comprise the following three points: the US government expected of the Greek government that it would carry through a programme of economic stabilisation. The effectiveness of this programme would influence the degree of future US economic assistance. The US government was prepared to send economic advisers if the Greek government wished this. All practical steps to carry through these suggestions should, of course, be coordinated with the British.[40] President Truman agreed. But, before the necessary negotiations could be started with the British, things began to move in Athens.

McNeil's forthcoming visit had raised tense expectations on all sides of the political spectrum. This was all the more significant since British policy had lost greatly in esteem during the past weeks. After the Seventh Party Congress, the Left had initiated an undisguised anti-British press campaign, culminating in the publication of a series of compromising telegrams from Woodhouse and other liaison officers (Barnes, Hammond etc.) to HQ Middle East during the winter 1943-44.[41] For its part, the Greek Right was furious because the Allies had, a few days previously, recognised Enver Hoxha's government in Albania and thus frustrated their claim to Northern Epirus. From the Liberals to the Left there were hopes that the visit would clear up the question of the electoral registers.

In general, public opinion expected the visit to result in generous economic assistance which would drastically improve the existing situation. Briefly, everyone hoped that McNeil would cut through the Gordian Knot of present problems.

McNeil arrived in Athens on 12th November. On the morning of the 13th he paid a courtesy visit to Damaskinos. Then he had talks with the staff of the British Embassy and with the financial adviser to the US Embassy. In the afternoon he had a first exchange of views with Kanellopoulos. The actual negotiations began on the 14th.

The first talk between McNeil, Leeper and Kanellopoulos was a sort of *tour d'horizon* of Greek problems. But from the beginning it was clear that this was not to be an exchange of opinions. McNeil lectured on possible solutions, basing himself constantly on Bevin's mandate, hardly taking any notice of Kanellopoulos' counter-arguments. Nevertheless he was careful not to reveal the full implications of the projected Economic Mission.

His first topic was the elections and he asked that the Greek government should cooperate as closely as possible with the Allied Mission and—if the latter found it necessary—even promulgate laws for its support. Kanellopoulos then introduced the subject of Greek armed forces financing and stated that, if the government took over, the costs would double the budget. He gave figures which were at once contradicted by Leeper and McNeil. Finally, it was decided to shelve this problem and leave it to be discussed by the experts. McNeil now turned to economic problems and hinted that the economic chaos could result in the countries which provided UNRRA's resources cutting off their payments. Bevin insisted that the Greek government should get better cooperation from bankers and industrialists. Distribution of supplies must be made more effective by improvement of the transport situation. Britain was prepared to provide experts. Kanellopoulos said he would gladly accept technical advisers and agreed that the transport problem must be solved. But he went on to criticise UNRRA. It had only delivered half of the planned supplies and that was why the previous governments' reconstruction programme had failed. Furthermore there was the black market in gold. When McNeil asked why the black marketeers were not arrested, Kanellopoulos replied that he did not expect much result from this. Like taxation, this would not change the general psychological climate, as had been shown by Varvaressos' failure. These would be final measures. It was much more important to get the producers to bring their wares on to the market and the pre-condition for this was the improvement of transport facilities and reasonable, guaranteed prices. McNeil passed over Kanellopoulos' arguments and dug in his heels for police action against black marketeers. Kanellopoulos rejected this: measures would indeed be taken against them but what would be decisive was increased supplies and a rise in production.

Varvaressos' policy had been one-sided; the problem must be comprehensively dealt with.

McNeil turned to the problem of industry and requested that the Greek government take steps towards possible nationalisation of industries, should the industrialists again boycott or sabotage the government's programme. Kanellopoulos agreed in principle but objected that, for various reasons, the Greek administration might not be up to this. McNeil offered advisers for this too, which Kanellopoulos readily accepted. Then McNeil asked him if he would be prepared to enforce these advisers' suggestions in every case. Kanellopoulos answered in the affirmative. Finally, McNeil went into a number of particular problems such as distribution, taxes, lotteries and wages. Kanellopoulos re-affirmed the importance of assistance from abroad and then raised the question of Allied recognition of Albania. McNeil brushed this aside: Britain too had its problems and amongst these recognition of Albania was a very minor one. Kanellopoulos protested that, for Greece, this problem was of top-ranking psychological importance and could even affect the reconstruction programme. At the end of the conversation McNeil promised to give Kanellopoulos his suggestions in writing.[42]

On the evening of the 14th Kanellopoulos received a memorandum in which the above discussion topics were listed and supplemented by a few further points. The memorandum ended as follows:

'His Majesty's Government are willing to send an economic mission upon whom the Greek Government would rely in carrying out the task of economic reconstruction. . . So long as the Mission is there, His Majesty's Government would expect the Greek Government to assume whatever powers are needed to implement and operate the programme which the Mission devises. Indeed His Majesty's Government would be unwilling to despatch such a Mission until an undertaking of this nature had been given by the Greek Government.'[43]

In other words, McNeil demanded that Kanellopoulos surrender the sovereignty of the Greek state and make complete submission to British policy.

MacVeagh commented as follows on this plan. In the short run it would strengthen the Greek government and produce some positive results for the economy, but in the long run its effects would be more than dubious.

'Greek people accustomed [to] foreign advisers. . . detest dictation [in] any form, particularly from outside. Drastic measures adopted at foreign instigation to enforce foreign program [are] only too likely [to] stir nationwide resentment against "mandate" (as plan [is] described privately by British official). . . British contemplate [to] control Greek economic life to even greater extent than Germans attempted during occupation when rationing took place and similar control far less drastic than in Britain today.'

McNeil regarded the Greek business world as mainly responsible for the disaster but he, MacVeagh, believed: 'Current economic troubles due at least as much to impractical advice from UNRRA and British sources as to failure [of] Greek business [to] cooperate.' He recommended the State Department to steer clear of the Economic Mission.[44]

At talks on the morning of 15th November in the British Embassy the Greek government was represented by both Kanellopoulos and Kasimatis.[45] To the British Kanellopoulos submitted two proposals: the elections to be conducted on a mixed system[46] and the plebiscite to be postponed until 1948. For the latter he recommended a British and US official statement from which it could be inferred this was the wish of these governments. McNeil stated that he had no objection to the mixed electoral system but that it was important to him that the Greek government be willing to associate itself publicly with a possible Allied statement on the postponement. Kanellopoulos answered in the affirmative.[47]

Then the talks turned to economic problems. Kasimatis emphasised that the economic problem could not be looked at in isolation; it was inextricably connected with the country's political problems. He went on to develop his position. The budget must be divided into a normal budget including all regular state expenditure and an extraordinary budget for social and economic reconstruction. The regular budget would be covered by the regular revenue (taxation), though the possibilities even for this were viewed with extreme scepticism by Greek experts. However Greece was quite unable to provide the financial resources needed for reconstruction. During the Occupation, Greece had been so thoroughly plundered by the Germans that she had no ready resources at her disposal. Reconstruction could only be achieved through foreign aid. One possible form of aid was a loan.

To counter Allied mistrust, Kasimatis produced a new concept. An Organisation for Reconstruction should be created—possibly a kind of bank consortium under government supervision. In this way he intended to unite the advantages of private enterprise and state control. This organisation could coordinate not only official assistance from the Allies but the efforts of other relief organisations and would follow the advice of the Allied governments involved. To McNeil's questions, Kasimatis replied that he hoped for participation by the US, Britain and Canada in this organisation, which must remain outside the sphere of government and party politics. Furthermore he hoped that such an organisation would restore the Greek people's confidence in the future. To this end, however, it was essential that one of the Allied governments make a loan available immediately, a kind of advance payment to the organisation. This would have a considerable psychological effect. Without such a credit concession, the present government would fail.

Kasimatis turned next to particular problems. He went into the financing of the Greek armed forces. These costs could double government expenditure. The only possibility would be to use some of Greece's currency reserves for the purpose. But, if this became known to the public, the results would be extremely unpleasant. In this connection he referred to the British demand that Greece should take over the expenses of the British Military Mission to the tune of 11 billion *drachmas*. To raise such a sum was utterly impossible.

He had nothing against the sending of technical advisers. This would be useful and would not make a bad impression on public opinion. But as to the suggestion about enforcement of their views, the Greek people had a highly-developed sense of its freedom and had enjoyed the right to vote since 1848. McNeil's proposals would meet with systematic opposition and more especially could give EAM a propaganda field-day. On the other hand, the government was ready to avail itself of every form of expert advice, though he rejected the idea of observers in each ministry. The Economic Mission should consist of people who knew Greek conditions and, if possible, had been in the country since liberation. It should have a purely advisory function and be attached to the Embassy. It would be psychologically effective if there were also US advisers. The main task of this Mission should thus be to set up the reconstruction organisation to which he had already referred. But he stressed that the sending of technical advisers alone—however useful it might be in itself—could only have negative psychological results. The Greek people expected material aid and that without delay.[48] McNeil closed the session, saying that Kasimatis' statements required consideration.

Comparison of the two standpoints shows their fundamental incompatability. Bevin and McNeil based themselves on premises which did not hold for Greece. Their conception presumed a balanced budget, rationing and price control—such as functioned in Britain—for Greece, where the organisational apparatus simply did not exist. For example, Bevin's and McNeil's suggestion to solve the clothing problem by importing and establishing a Dutch clog factory was quite outside Greek reality. The problem was not one of lack of factories but of lack of raw materials. Provision of leather would have been enough to activate Greek shoe production and would at the same time have provided work for thousands of small and medium-sized businesses. It is true that the industrialists had sabotaged the reconstruction programme, but Bevin's and McNeil's solution—the undifferentiated application of British nationalisation concepts—was the least suitable method for bringing the boycotters to their senses. The real problem was the inadequate supply of raw materials. Up to summer 1945 UNRRA had by-and-large restricted its imports to food supplies and this only to an extent sufficient to avert famine. There had never been a surplus which could have brought about price reductions. It was only from summer 1945 that raw materials were brought in in substantial quantities but still these were insufficient to stimulate industrialists to produce.

Basically, Neubacher's formulation for a similar situation during the Occupation period still held good:

'This mechanical application in Greece of a prescription [state compulsion] which had proved itself under quite different economic, administrative and psychological conditions would have destroyed the great advantages which this country will always possess namely the individual's extraordinary initiative and capacity to make a way for himself.'[49]

What was needed was not compulsion and control, but encouragement of private enterprise. For this, however, another precondition was required—freedom from fear of the future.[50] All sections of the population were possessed by this fear: the Right feared the communist neighbouring states; the Left feared persecution by the Right; the industrialists feared possible losses on investment; the government leadership feared to find itself without allies; the population feared that UNRRA could cease its activity.

These are the fundamental psychological reasons of which Kanellopoulos and Kasimatis were speaking. The gold project would have broken through the vicious circle of fear and a long-term loan from the Allies would have given a perspective for the future. Bevin's and McNeil's suspicions that in the future, too, a considerable proportion of the aid would be improperly used were, of course, justified; but an end to fear of the future would have given a chance to change circumstances in Greece. Thus far, Kanellopoulos' and Kasimatis' ideas were by no means useless, and the suggestion to create a Reconstruction Organisation might well have reduced 'wastage' to a minimum. On the other hand, the British concept which combined Labour theories of compulsory nationalisation with elements of colonial control offered no alternative. This became clear when, at a reception on the evening of 15th November, McNeil made a speech in which he let it be understood that Britain could be reckoned on only for moral and not for financial support. The next day the price of the gold sovereign rose to 63,000 *drachmas*,[51] and by the 19th it had reached 75,000.[52]

On the 16th November, Kasimatis defined his ideas still further. It was essential for the creation of the Reconstruction Organisation that Britain should publicly declare its support. Britain must approve a loan and must guarantee that potential profits from exports would not be taken out of the country to Britain. McNeil, however, rejected any form of participation in such an organisation.[53] Thus, an *impasse* had been reached: McNeil refused to accept the Greek government's proposals, whilst Kanellopoulos and Kasimatis were not prepared to accept the British plan for a mandate.

To find a way out, Kanellopoulos and Kasimatis turned on the 17th November to MacVeagh. They complained of the unreasonable British demands and explained that, as a transitional government, they had no right to take so far-reaching a step. The British proposal was unacceptable. MacVeagh advised them to stick to their guns. Reporting to the State Department, he added: 'Consequently pending consideration strictly advisory joint mission if this proposed by Greeks and accepted [by] British would urge immediate action. . .'[54] But, before Washington could answer, there were new developments in Athens.

Damaskinos, without consulting Kanellopoulos, now approached Leeper saying that the country's economic situation was deteriorating so rapidly that he had decided to call together the political leaders and appeal to them to form a strong all-party government; the plebiscite should be postponed in order to unite all the country's forces for reconstruction.[55] He asked the consent of the British government. Thereupon McNeil and Leeper addressed themselves to Bevin for instructions. On the 18th Bevin replied. He wanted a firm and comprehensive programme and a Greek government pledged to carry it out and with the necessary strength to do so. He hoped that the Regent would form such a government immediately. Any Greek government which made a sincere and determined attempt to carry through the programme would be assured of his full support and would be given all the economic assistance in British power. But he was not prepared to touch the plebiscite issue except as part of the programme as a whole. If such a government could be formed speedily he would state in the forthcoming Foreign Affairs debate that it had the full support of the British government. McNeil must, of course, insist that the new government accept the general programme.[56]

McNeil and Leeper told Damaskinos of Bevin's reply and, on the evening of 19th November, they visited Damaskinos in his official residence for a final discussion. The head of the Regent's political bureau, Seferiadis (Seferis), opened the conversation by reading out the 'formula' which had in the meantime been agreed between the British Embassy and the Regent for the talks with the party leaders. The Regent would analyse the difficulties of Greece's present situation and state that, having considered this situation, he had thought it useful to seek the British government's opinion. This had given an opportunity to examine the whole Greek problem and the following conclusions had been reached.

'(a) A political coalition Government should be formed on the broadest possible basis.
(b) An economic reconstruction programme should be adopted and applied, by which under proper control and with the active participation of British experts, rail and road communications would be restored, industrial and agricultural production developed, goods fairly distributed and taxes equitably levied.

(c) The plebiscite should be postponed till the end of March 1948 in order that the nation should be united for reconstruction.
(d) Elections should be held as soon as it was found, in consultation with the Inter-Allied Supervision Commission, that conditions were adequate and at any rate not later than in March 1946.'[57]

McNeil made it clear that the March date was the latest for the elections. Damaskinos agreed and went on to deal with the electoral system. He favoured a mixed system as simple proportional representation would bring too many communists into parliament. Leeper agreed, adding that it would be the new government's task to negotiate this with the parties; on the British side there were no objections. McNeil stated that, if difficulties arose, the Electoral Mission should function as an arbiter and he hoped that the Regent would support them in this. Damaskinos agreed.

Conversation then turned to the reconstruction problem. Leeper warned Damaskinos that, at the forthcoming conference with the party leaders, he should on no account go into details. These would be discussed by McNeil and himself with the future Prime Minister. Damaskinos wanted to know what Britain could offer in addition to advisers. McNeil's answer was: 'Let us have a Government which will perform an act of faith in accepting the taxation proposals and the proposed advisers, and I will promise to the Regent and his ministers at any rate a minimum of material help.' He would go back and say to the Secretary of State, 'These people are being involved. They have suffered and we will strain ourselves to get what the Regent's advisers think necessary to get reconstruction under way.' Shortly afterwards Bevin would make a suitable statement. Damaskinos should not insist on figures but should have trust. He would tell Bevin: 'These people cannot make bricks without straw.' The questions of US participation, Italian and German reparations and the problem of financing the Greek armed forces should be left pending for the present. He would indeed bestir himself energetically; but these details should be negotiated with the responsible ministers.

Next, Damaskinos spoke of the composition of the future government. He hoped it would be an all-party government but he feared it would be a purely Liberal Cabinet. Leeper expressed himself optimistic: the republicans would certainly participate in the government and he would work on the Populists. Damaskinos mentioned Papandreou. Leeper expressed doubts. Damaskinos remained sceptical: such a government would have Communist support and this he rejected.

Leeper went on to add that time was pressing; he should act that very night. Damaskinos did not accept. In Leeper's words:

'He had an obligation; for reasons of decency he must tell the present Prime Minister in confidence first what he was going to do. If he was to call for the party leaders he would appear to the Prime Minister to be acting behind the scenes. The Regent was certain that the present Prime

Minister would consent to the proposed course of action, because he was an upright and honest man.'

Leeper objected: it would be better 'not to give the Prime Minister too much time before the proposed other meeting. He also knew the Prime Minister very well and would agree with the Regent's opinion of him but the Prime Minister was not a strong man and was very talkative'. Thereupon McNeil, too, pointed out to Damaskinos that time was pressing, since Bevin would shortly make a statement on Foreign Affairs and by then the names, at least of the new Prime Minister and Finance Minister, must be settled. After some hesitation Damaskinos agreed and asked whether there was any possibility of a Three Power statement on postponement of the plebiscite till 1948. McNeil replied that for this there was not sufficient time before Bevin's statement. Damaskinos now stated that, to the forthcoming conference, he would invite all former prime ministers and the leaders of all parties which had at some time formed a government. This would exclude EAM and KKE from the negotiations. Leeper opposed this, saying it would be better to summon all the parties. EAM was of great importance. Damaskinos wanted to know if Leeper would agree if—should the question arise—EAM were to be included in the government. Leeper replied that this would be the business of the future Prime Minister. McNeil stated that EAM should only be included on condition that it unambiguously repudiated the December events and those who had committed crimes. In this way the argument about the allegedly innocent detainees would come to an end.

Finally, Damaskinos informed his interlocutors that the new Prime Minister would be Sofoulis. Leeper repeated his request that the new Prime Minister should visit the British Embassy immediately on nomination. Damaskinos agreed, but pointed out that the new government would be a political government. Leeper riposted that it was for that very reason one had to talk to Sofoulis.[58]

McNeil and Leeper then stressed that Damaskinos must make it clear to the politicians that this programme had Bevin's approval and that, according to his opinion, it represented the only possible solution for the Greek problem. Its acceptance would have the support of the British government, but Bevin would only accept a government which actually put this programme into action.[59]

The same night Damaskinos summoned Kanellopoulos and told him of the result of the negotiations. At the end of a long session, Kanellopoulos stated that he would not stand in the way of this solution and would announce his resignation on the morning of the 20th.

Meanwhile, on the afternoon of the 19th McNeil had concluded his talks with the party leaders.[60] Stamatis Mercouris had made a particular impression on him. The latter had pointed out that the electoral lists were unacceptable. In many parts of the country the administration had not yet been functioning during the registration period. When this period had been extended, forgeries had occurred. In the meantime a French journalist had produced proof of how easy it was to get hold of voting documents.[61] Moreover, an Athens court had declared ninety electoral lists invalid.[62]

McNeil's talks were accompanied by unpleasant 'noises off'. On Sunday, 18th November, the Right organised a mass demonstration in Constitution Square to protest against the Allied recognition of Albania, at which chauvinistic and anti-British slogans could be heard. A few days earlier the trial of the Chief of Security Police under the Occupation, General Lambou, had come to an end. Of the nineteen accused only two received death sentences. Lambou had defended himself on the grounds that he had not collaborated, he had only defended the state against the communists. At the same time there were rumours circulating in Athens that McNeil was blackmailing the Greek government and that the army was preparing a *coup*.

On the morning of the 20th, as had been agreed, Kanellopoulos announced his resignation and Damaskinos summoned the party leaders and former Prime Ministers and informed them of his programme. They asked for time to think this over and Damaskinos agreed. Then, on the evening of the same day, they reassembled. Only the Populists rejected the programme. Despite this, Damaskinos charged Sofoulis, as Greece's senior statesman, with the task of forming a government on the broadest possible basis. Later that evening, on Damaskinos' suggestion, Sofoulis and Tsouderos visited McNeil and Leeper. Sofoulis spoke of his ministerial list and gave assurances that the next morning he would have his Cabinet ready for swearing-in. Tsouderos made an appointment with McNeil, likewise for the next morning, to discuss his proposals with him.[63]

During the morning of the 21st Sofoulis made contact with the party leaders. Tsouderos accepted the post of Vice-Premier and coordinator of the reconstruction programme and promised to win over personalities of the Centre-Left for the new government. Kafandaris, too, declared himself willing to accept a Cabinet post. The Populists refused any participation in government responsibilities. When Sofoulis addressed himself to Papandreou and Kanellopoulos, he found that they had made a *volte face*, obviously under the influence of Konstantinos Tsatsos. The evening before they had approved the new programme unreservedly; now they refused to participate in the government and in this they had the support of Sofoklis Venizelos. Late in the morning Sofoulis presented the following provisional Cabinet list to Damaskinos:

Themistoklis Sofoulis	Prime Minister	Liberal
Georgios Kafandaris	1st Vice-Premier	Progressive
Emmanouil Tsouderos	2nd Vice-Premier	Liberal
Ioannis Sofianopoulos	Foreign Minister	

KANELLOPOULOS' CABINET

Konstantinos Rendis	Interior	Liberal
Alexandros Mylonas	Finance	Agrarian
Theodoros Manetas (General)	War	Liberal
Georgios Vorazanis	Economy	Liberal
Theodoros Chavinis (General)	Public Works	Liberal
A. Iasonidis	Welfare	Liberal
Chrysos Evelpidis	Agriculture	Agrarian
Stamatis Mercouris	Public Order	Progressive
Georgios Kartalis	Supply	EKKA–Eleftheria
Alexandros Merenditis (General)	Governor-General (N. Greece)	
Georgios Athanasiadis-Novas	Education	Progressive
Dimitrios Machas	Transport	

Meanwhile, however, a protest telegram from King George II had arrived from England. Damaskinos sent for Leeper and blamed Sofoulis for not carrying out his mandate since he had failed to win Papandreou, Kanellopoulos or Venizelos for his Cabinet. He himself would rather resign than swear in such a one-sided Cabinet. When Leeper tried to calm him and suggested that he talk to Sofoulis, he refused even to receive the latter; Leeper should talk to Sofoulis. Leeper thereupon said that he was more interested in the implementation of the programme than in personalities; but if he ascertained that anyone who accepted the programme had been excluded from participation in the government, then he would intervene.

Shortly afterwards Sofoulis visited Leeper and informed him about the situation and about his vain endeavours to win Kanellopoulos and Papandreou for his government. Venizelos wanted to take over leadership of the Liberals and therefore was not prepared to enter his Cabinet. Leeper sent a message to Damaskinos asking him to receive Sofoulis, Papandreou, Kanellopoulos and Venizelos and arrange an agreement so that the government could be sworn in without further delay. But Damaskinos refused to receive anyone and went off to his villa outside Athens. In the late afternoon he summoned Kanellopoulos, as the still serving Prime Minister, and handed him his own resignation statement, so that it could be telegraphed to the king. Kanellopoulos betook himself to Leeper and they tried to work out together what to do. Finally, they decided that Kanellopoulos should go back to Damaskinos' villa accompanied by Leeper and McNeil, so that together they could talk him into swearing in the new Cabinet, and that he should wait to resign until this had been achieved. For a whole evening the three worked on Damaskinos and finally, at 2 a.m., persuaded him to return with them to Athens and to swear in the rump Cabinet at 2.45 a.m.

On the background to Damaskinos' curious behaviour, Leeper reported as follows:

'In the early months after the civil war, he acted with enlightened decision and took advice in the right quarter. Since my return to Athens two months ago, I have noticed a big change. I have found him obstinate, suspicious and lacking in decision. My own influence with him, which at one time was considerable, has grown steadily less. He has allowed his mind to be constantly poisoned by Constantine Tsatsos, a renegade Liberal who has fallen out with all parties of the Left and has even warned the Regent against my associations with many men from the moderate Left camp. This was the Regent's frame of mind when the crisis broke. He made up his mind or let others make it up for him, that he was being deceived by Sophoulis and by the British and that Papandreou who has for some months been consorting with the royalists was playing a noble part in this ignoble political scene and was an essential member of the new Government... He is in an exhausted state nervously and has behaved like a suspicious and mulishly obstinate Greek peasant.'[64]

After the swearing-in, McNeil and Leeper continued their conversation with Damaskinos and finally at 4.30 a.m.—with stick and carrot—got him to postpone his actual resignation for a short time. He drew up a new resignation statement which he gave to McNeil who promised that, on returning to London, he would hand it to the king.[65] However, enough of all this had leaked to provoke a variety of public reactions. On the day of Kanellopoulos' resignation, the sovereign fell to 52,000 *drachmas*, only to bound up again the next day to 64,000.[66] The right-wing press started furious attacks on Sofoulis and declared his government unconstitutional: the postponement of the plebiscite was closely connected with the British lack of will to support Greece's territorial claims; but if the king returned, they would be obliged to support them; the whole trouble could be traced to pressure from the left-wing of the Labour Party which was composed of crypto-communists. The Left, however, was pleased with the change. KKE made an official statement of support for the new government; but Damaskinos must go.[67]

As late as the morning of the 22nd Damaskinos continued to demand that Papandreou must be included in the new Cabinet, although he knew that, in that case, Sofoulis and the other ministers would resign. Even when Papandreou declared publicly that he had no claim on any Cabinet post and would support the government, the Regent maintained his stand. Leeper was so angry at his behaviour that he stated that, in future, political intervention by the Regent would no longer be tolerated.[68] But no sooner did Papandreou learn of Damaskinos' intention to resign than he again changed his mind and even prompted Kanellopoulos and Venizelos to take up an intransigent position. Obviously this was a concerted action by the Heidelberg *alumni* grouped around Konstantinos Tsatsos. On the evening of the same day, with Woodhouse as go-between, the former EDES leader

Napoleon Zervas visited McNeil at the head of a Populist delegation and told him that Stefanopoulos was ready to enter the government on condition that Sofoulis was replaced within 24 hours.[69] It is difficult not to suspect some connection between these two manoeuvres.

Three lines of political activity occupied the next few days: Leeper's and McNeil's efforts to keep Damaskinos in office, negotiations between McNeil and the government on the reconstruction programme, and completion of the Sofoulis Cabinet list.

On the morning of the 22nd Tsouderos in his capacity as reconstruction coordinator, Finance Minister Mylonas and Supply Minister Kartalis visited McNeil and Leeper. Just as at the previous day's conversation with Tsouderos, both sides were satisfied. The Greek ministers gave their word of honour that the British experts' advice would be accepted and that, as soon as the latter had taken a decision together with their Greek colleagues, this would be carried out. The Greek reconstruction programme consisted of two parts: an immediate programme of road, railway and harbour reconstruction must be carried through and then a long-term programme must be worked out with the British experts for which they would recommend a loan from the Export-Import Bank. McNeil promised he would again bring up the financing of the armed forces in London.[70] In other words, he had backed down on his original mandate programme. Obviously he had realised it could not be enforced and did not want to burden the new government with such a millstone.

On the afternoon of the 22nd the new Cabinet met for its first session. Tsouderos, Mylonas and Kartalis reported on their talks with McNeil. An appeal was then addressed to Damaskinos to refrain from resignation. A statement was issued calling on the people to maintain discipline and get down to work; there was now a sure hope that the Allies would support reconstruction.[71] With the exception of the Populists, Greek public opinion reacted favourably. The Populists however were furious. They held the British responsible for the whole process which had robbed them of power. Tsaldaris stated that Greece would never forgive this humiliation and tutelage by a foreign power. Slogans were chalked up proclaiming: 'We will not barter our country's sovereignty for food tins.' Meanwhile the negotiations with Papandreou continued. Damaskinos demanded that he be made War Minister and Kanellopoulos Navy Minister. This would have meant that the country's armed forces would come under the control of a man 'who is considered—rightly or wrongly—as the political brain of SAN, the secret reactionary military league',[72] as *The Times* described him. Sofoulis rejected this excessive demand but Damaskinos stuck by it. This prompted the Populists to encourage the king to take a hard line and to send protest telegrams to the Allied governments. At the same time 'X' and SAN were alerted to be ready for any eventuality.[73] This led in turn to a further hardening of the Regent's stand, with the result that

McNeil and Leeper found themselves obliged to have recourse to Bevin.

Thereupon, on 23rd November, Bevin sent a message to Damaskinos urging him to continue in office: McNeil brought the Regent this message when he took his leave before flying back to London. Damaskinos, however, would not yield but merely promised to think the matter over.[74] Later in the same afternoon the crisis once more became acute, when one-sided and distorted reports of Bevin's House of Commons speech reached Athens and made Damaskinos believe that he had been tricked by McNeil. It was only with difficulty that Leeper could restrain him from issuing a premature statement. The Populists were delighted to be able to announce that Sofoulis' government lacked Bevin's support. Leeper addressed himself once more to Bevin asking for immediate instructions,[75] since there was a danger the government might fall.

Bevin reacted at once and on the morning of the 24th summoned the Greek Ambassador to the Foreign Office. He expressed his astonishment that, after his House of Commons speech,[76] the Regent could still contemplate resignation. This could only derive from misunderstood press reports. The Greek ambassador should let Damaskinos know that he, Bevin, was of the opinion that the Regent owed it to him personally—at such a critical moment—to do his duty. He had given him unreserved support in the House of Commons. Resignation could cost Greece both British and US sympathies. He hoped that, as a patriot, the Regent would remain at his post and support the government's reconstruction programme.[77]

Meanwhile in Athens the Right carried on with their efforts to make Damaskinos resign and to overthrow the government. By the use of bribery they organised a Press strike for 24th November, with the result that *Rizospastis* was the only paper to appear.[78] At the same time the Right began to speculate in gold against the *drachma* so as to undermine the government's economic measures. There was also unrest in the Officers' Corps.[79] Since the Right could not block diplomatic channels, the real content of Bevin's speech and his message to Damaskinos reached Athens during the day and this calmed the situation. Leeper, too, made contact with Sofoulis and advised him to make further efforts to broaden his government. Sofoulis explained that he was still working on Kanellopoulos but that Papandreou was working against him; perhaps Leeper might be able to influence Kanellopoulos. Leeper promised to try. In addition, Sofoulis told him that within the Populist Party there were forces opposed to the leadership's hard line. Leeper recommended the inclusion of Petimezas and Peltekis (from the Non-EAM Resistance) in the Cabinet, to which Sofoulis readily agreed.[80]

Finally, on the morning of the 25th, Leeper called on Damaskinos and by means of a heavily emotional appeal got him to say that, if MacVeagh would associate himself with this appeal, he would withdraw his resignation. After some difficulty, Leeper ran MacVeagh to ground in hospital at the bedside of his wife who had been taken seriously ill. MacVeagh grasped the situation at once and, although he had no instructions from Washington, declared himself willing to urge Damaskinos to remain in office. He went straight to Damaskinos and told him that, as a friend of Greece, he was appealing to him not to resign. Having thus saved face, Damaskinos issued a *communiqué* in which he stated that, in response to urgent appeals from Bevin and the two Allied ambassadors, he had decided to remain in office.[81] London and Washington were satisfied. With this obstacle removed, Damaskinos swore in the remaining members of the Sofoulis Cabinet on 26th November.[82]

George II had been kept in the dark about the developments leading to the formation of the Sofoulis government and about the plans for postponing the plebiscite. The British government's viewpoint was that the proper negotiating partner was Damaskinos.[83] Thus, the king first learnt of the new government and of the proposed plebiscite postponement from the newspapers of the 20th November. On the 21st he issued the following protest statement to the Press.

'The postponement of the plebiscite for 3 years, accompanied by the formation of a one-party Government, creates a completely new situation. When Greece was liberated I agreed, at the suggestion of my Government and on the advice of the British Government to return to my country only after the freely expressed consent of the Greek people. For this reason I entrusted to the Archbishop-Regent the exercise of my royal duties for the time of emergency resulting from the civil war. The Varkiza agreement specifically laid down that the plebiscite would be held before the end of 1945 and that it would precede the elections. In September, however, it was decided the elections should precede the plebiscite, which was to be held at a future unspecified date. Now it is unilaterally decided that the plebiscite should once again be postponed for 3 years, and in the meantime a Government has been formed made up exclusively of Republicans. This solution is no more applicable than the proposal that elections should precede the plebiscite because since the Greek people are to be called upon to go to the polls sooner or later, it is obvious that the question of the régime, either explicitly or implicitly, will automatically be put before the electorate. Such a solution is also harmful to the economic and political recovery of the country, as it would lead to the perpetuation of a state of uncertainty that would aggravate the present political tension and prevent economic rehabilitation. The lack of stable government for some months now, through the succession of temporary administrations which speedily lose control of the situation, has shown beyond all doubt that the imperative collaboration among the Greek people cannot be achieved unless recourse is taken, honestly and frankly, to the will of the Greek people. Finally, this solution, and especially the manner in which it has been linked with the continuation of financial assistance, constitutes an insult to the Greek people, who have, no less than any other people, the right to express their opinion regarding their régime and Government. The postponement of the plebiscite for 3 years would amount to the stifling of the sentiment of the Greek people which, as is known to all, is being expressed clearly in my favour at every opportunity. So far as I am concerned, the repudiation of every decision that has so far been taken compels me to regulate my future attitude without any reservation other than the interests of my people and the respect of its sovereign will.'[84]

This statement implied no less than that improvement in Greece's economic situation could only be achieved through the return of George II. How far this gave the signal for the Populists' exchange-rate sabotage cannot be known. George II had only one aim—his own return to the throne. The consideration that this would surely lead to a revival of civil strife was of no interest to him. Nothing in his attitude had changed since the December events: for his own personal advantage he was ready to throw Greece into a new civil war.

He found support from his traditional friends, the Tories. In the House of Commons Foreign Affairs debate on 22nd November, Eden asked awkward questions: did not postponement of the plebiscite contravene the Varkiza Agreement and its acceptance by Britain? Was it true that the postponement had been connected with financial support for Greece?[85]

Bevin justified his policy in the speech to which we have already referred: it had so far been his policy to intervene as little as possible in the internal affairs of Greece; but the present critical economic situation had made intervention unavoidable. He repelled Eden's attacks; but when he was attacked by Churchill, he expressed himself more definitely.

'Since that time [December 1944] up to the time the Regent of Greece came here, I have tried to give effect to the Varkiza agreement and have never put forward the Labour Party's statement [the Party Conference statement of December 1944] at all. But did I get a Government? It is not for me to suggest who prevented me from getting a Government in order that I could get an election. But I candidly confess that I do not think I have had a square deal. I think that here have been influences going from this country to Greece, which have prevented me. . .'

Nevertheless, he had refused to nominate a government himself. It was only when he had been warned that, if the plebiscite were enforced civil war would break out, that he had agreed to postponement. 'I have no objection to monarchy. . . as an institution, but let it be a constitutional monarchy and not a party monarchy.' When Churchill interrupted him and wanted to know how there could be a plebiscite without an alternative, Bevin replied:

'It is between the two opinions that the decision would be, but these two opinions ought not to be influenced by economic disaster. When the head of a State is to be elected, a country ought to be in such a tranquil state, and as prosperous as possible, that judgement, and not prejudice and starvation, should be the guide. I have by this decision tried to get Greece on to a basis where the question of the monarchy could be decided on its merits, without any influence at all either way...'[86]

Churchill was not satisfied with this explanation and therefore, on 27th November, he wrote to Bevin criticising his Greek policy up to that date. The interchange of sequence between elections and plebiscite had been a mistake. Anyway, what would happen if the royalists won the elections and demanded an earlier date for the plebiscite? It would then be difficult to prevent this. On the other hand, it was clear why the communists and the other parties of the Left rejected an early plebiscite: they feared that it would result in the king's return. Churchill went on to appeal to Bevin's anti-communism and continued: 'I doubt whether these deep impressions [from the communist "atrocities"] will fade, and I consider it would be very dangerous and also wrong for Great Britain to interfere heavily, using the economic weapon, in order to bring about a Communist–Left-Wing triumph in Greece. I could not myself remain silent in the face of a policy of that kind...'[87] He concluded with the hope for a meeting with Bevin.

Churchill's line of argument showed that his position remained the old one. Bevin detailed Sir Orme Sargent to prepare a draft reply. This letter was, in fact, never sent: Bevin preferred the meeting. But its contents give a certain insight into Bevin's thought processes. After long explanations of previous developments, the draft arrived at the basic problem: the election result could indeed lead to an earlier date for the plebiscite. He would, however, use his influence to ensure that this did not occur as long as there was still a danger of civil war. His policy was oriented towards the interests of Greece and not towards those of the king. The latter had, in point of fact, behaved very 'foolishly' on this occasion, as his statement demonstrated. A postponement of the plebiscite was in the king's interest too since only this would give him a chance to rule as a constitutional monarch. If he returned prematurely, the Populists would prevent this. 'It seems to me therefore that if the Royalists win the election in March and then force an immediate plebiscite, a Royalist dictatorship would probably follow within a month or two.' Finally, the Labour Foreign Minister gave assurances that he was not pursuing any party policy towards the king.[88] In other words, though Bevin was fully aware of the part played by George II both in the past and at the present juncture, he held by his policy. When, on 17th December, Sargent informed Leeper of the interchange of opinion between Bevin and Churchill, he named only two eventualities in which the plebiscite should be postponed: economic difficulties or the possibility of unrest.[89]

On 3rd December, George II called on Bevin and handed him a long memorandum in which he justified his own previous policy and complained bitterly of the injustice which had been done him. His whole line of argument showed that he was living in a world of illusion, surrounded by countless imaginary enemies, to a degree that bordered on the pathological. For example, he maintained that, after his return in 1935, he had been able to unite all political circles behind his rule and that this was what he was aiming at now. He forgot to add that this 'unification' occurred under the fascist Metaxas dictatorship. The appointment of Plastiras as Prime Minister had poisoned the atmosphere, but one should have been forewarned of this. After all, Plastiras had been involved in the execution of the six ministers and had established a dictatorship in 1922-3.[90] All the fanatical republicans had congregated around him and this had caused conservative mistrust which had brought about a new cleavage within the nation.

'Immediately after the civil war the two main sections of public opinion in Greece—Venizelists and Monarchists—had forgotten their differences through common fear of communism. *That* was the moment when the political and the régime question should have been solved through the cooperation of the parties and early elections. . . an almost unique opportunity was thrown away.'

The king wasted not a single word on his own dictatorial past. Nor did he realise that the feud between Venizelists and Populists had taken on a different dimension.

His programme was to hold elections as soon as possible under a system which would produce a strong majority. Only this could overcome internal disunity. But first, of course, a new government was needed. It was not permissible that a government of extreme republicans should hold the elections. Either a service government or a moderate political government must be formed. The present situation could only provoke civil war. Despite the Regency, he himself was the supreme head of the Greek state and a great proportion of the nation looked to him. 'It's to me personally that you addressed yourselves during the worst periods of the war; it is I personally who shouldered the heavy responsibility of continuing the war when Germany joined Italy in her attack against my country.' In view of this fact it was not right that he was constantly ignored. He had lost confidence in the Regent but continued to tolerate him so as not to cause complications. But the problem of the plebiscite must be solved—a three years' postponement was a hostile act towards himself. He demanded an assurance from Bevin that the plebiscite would be held directly a normal democratic government, elected by the people, was in existence.

In the appendix to this memorandum George II denounced the members of the present government: Tsouderos was responsible for the troubles in the Middle East because he had tolerated EAM; General Manetas was a revolutionary (in 1916, 1922 and 1933) and, instead of purging the army of undesirable elements, he was trying to get rid of officers whose political opinions differed from his own; Sofianopoulos was a left-wing extremist who had made far-reaching concessions to the communists at Varkiza and who took a highly suspect attitude towards the Soviet Union; Kafandaris was a particularly mischievous anti-monarchist; Rendis, too, was a revolutionary and so was Mercouris; the author Kazantzakis (Minister without portfolio) he called 'the Rosenberg' [chief Nazi ideologist] of EAM—he had written a pro-Japanese and anti-American book; Evelpidis was a tool of Zevgos; General Chavinis had been a member of the revolutionary tribunal which condemned the six ministers and was a revolutionary (1916, 1922, 1933, 1935); Peltekis had enriched himself illegitimately; Georgakis (Assistant-Minister, Governor-General of Ionian Islands) was a collaborator. In brief, George II sought to blacken the whole Cabinet in the eyes of Bevin.[91]

But it was not only in the Greek Cabinet that the king unmasked 'enemies'. During his conversation with Bevin he said that, in the past, Leeper had done everything in his power to prevent his return to Greece at the head of his army. The Foreign Office and Eden in particular had never liked him. Postponement of the plebiscite was traceable with certainty to Leeper's initiative. Directly he himself had heard of McNeil's visit, he had had premonitions. Bevin eventually got him to give his retrospective approval to the elections coming first; but on the plebiscite George II could not be moved. Bevin promised him to think the matter over.[92]

On 10th December, McNeil reacted to the king's effusions. If the elections produced a royalist majority, George II would be assured of a speedy return. The result would be either a massive suppression of free speech and freedom of assembly, etc., or within a short time renewed civil war. 'The most rigorous suppression will not avert it but will only postpone it.' If the Left won the elections, the same would happen, but that was anyway less probable.

'The only possibility of avoiding civil war, it seems to me, would be to produce a body of Centre thought, committed. . . to remedy the economic chaos of Greece rather than concentrate on securing party advantages.'

This had been the object in forming the Sofoulis government. McNeil went on to rebut the king's accusations.

'The King's note suggests that we should have a Government of neutral experts. Surely that was the shape of the Voulgaris government which came down. The other suggestion is that we should have a Government of "politicians known for their moderate views". "Moderate" about what? Who are they? Where have they been over the last eighteen months if we don't know them and if they have not been tried out? Throughout his paper he argues that this is a one-party Government and that out of the Left. Sofianopoulos is the one man who could be labelled "Left". In my opinion he is dangerous and must be watched but I doubt if he really is a crypto-communist. I think he is just a nasty opportunist who can be tripped up and disgraced. Kafandaris is an old, rather sad and negative man. I ought also to add that in the covering "Who's Who" the King seems to be most unfair about the Resistance people brought in. Georgakis is a young man about whom I made particular enquiries, mainly because I disliked his appearance. I was assured that during the occupation he displayed great courage and saved many Greeks by his bold appearance in the court on their behalf.'[93]

In other words: if the Sofoulis government failed, the Right would take over and George II would return; his return would lead to increased suppression of opposition and thus would speed up the onset of civil war. Rarely has any historical process been more precisely forecast.

NOTES

1. Leeper to Foreign Office 3rd November, 1945 (R 18698/4/19). Details of his political record in Richter, *op. cit.*, pp. 177 ff.
2. McNeill, *The Greek Dilemma,* p. 219.
3. The new Cabinet was as follows:
   Panayotis Kanellopoulos: Prime Minister, Foreign and Navy Minister.
   General Spyridon Georgoulis: Army Minister.
   Professor Grigorios Kasimatis: Finance Minister and temporarily Agriculture and Economics Minister.
   Charalambos Psarros: Minister of the Interior.
   General Pavsanias Katsotas: Internal Security Minister.
   Georgios Oikonomopoulos: Justice Minister.
   Dimitrios Katavolos: Labour Minister and Minister of Economics from 7th October (Katavolos was a former Interior Ministry Director under Voulgaris and a close friend of Damaskinos).
   Admiral Konstantinos Alexandris: Merchant Marine Minister (in 1943-4 he had been in command of the Greek Navy).
   Professor Ioannis Theodorakopoulos: Minister of Education (a friend of Kanellopoulos from their student days in Heidelberg).
   Konstantinos Kallias: Minister of Posts and Communications, and Welfare (a friend from Kanellopoulos' own party).
   Epaminondas Kypriadis: Agriculture Minister from 5th November.
   Vasilios Voilas: Health Minister (as in the Voulgaris and Damaskinos Cabinets).
   Konstantinos Tsatsos: Assistant-Minister for Press and Information.
   Panayotis Papaligouras: Supply Minister.
   Giorgios V. Mangakis: Minister to the Prime Minister.
   Provatas, *op. cit.*, pp. 587 ff.
4. R 18698/4/19.
5. *Ibid.* For the relations between Papandreou, Tsatsos and Damaskinos see also

FRUS 1945, VIII, p. 181.
6. Panayotis Kanellopoulos, *Ta chronia tou megalou polemou 1939-1944: Istoriki anadromi kai keimena,* 2nd ed., (Athens, 1974), p. 79.
7. *The Times,* 3rd November, 1945.
8. On 6th October the price of a gold sovereign was 35,500 *drachmas.* The price of bread rose in one week from 150 to 235 *drachmas,* meat from 520 to 750, sugar from 2,200 to 3,000, fish from 290 to 360 (price per *oka,* approx. 1 kg). Leeper to Foreign Office 12th October, 1945 (R 17396/4/19).
9. Leeper to Foreign Office 22nd October, 1945 (R 18327/4/19).
10. Banknote circulation: July 4.8 billion, August 6.8 billion, September 8.2 billion, 23rd October 10.7 billion, on which date the total circulation amounted to 59.5 billion *drachmas.* Budget deficit: July 2 billion, August 4 billion, September 5.4 billion, on 23rd October another 4.3 billion, so that the total deficit amounted to 34.7 billion. The price of gold rose to 40,000 *drachmas* for a sovereign. Leeper to Foreign Office 30th October, 1945 (R 18790/4/19). The illusions from which the ministers responsible were suffering can be gauged from a remark of Finance Minister Mantzavinos on 19th October when he assessed the total 1945 budget deficit at 6 billion. Leeper to Foreign Office 22nd October, 1945 (R 18327/4/19).
11. Leeper to Foreign Office 16th November, 1945 (R 19662/4/19). In October UNRRA supplies to the value of 2 billion *drachmas* were sold; 1.7 billion of this was absorbed by the administrative and distributing authorities, so that the state received the residue of 3 million as revenue. By the 6th November the budget deficit had risen by another 2.4 billion to 39.6 billion. During the same period the banknote circulation rose by another 2.8 billion so that the total circulation amounted to 65 billion.
12. Leeper to Foreign Office 22nd November, 1945 (R 20169/4/19).
13. Leeper to Foreign Office 4th November, 1945 (R 18726/4/19).
14. *Ibid.*
15. See p. 216.
16. Jackson to Lehman 27th October, 1945 (*FRUS 1945, VIII,* pp. 246 ff.
17. *Ibid.,* pp. 247-50.
18. *Ibid.,* p. 251.
19. General Morgan arrived on 25th October and Field-Marshal Lord Alanbrooke on 27th October. *The Times,* 26 and 29th October, 1945.
20. Resident Minister for the Central Mediterranean to Foreign Office 4th November, 1945 (R 18735/4/19). Kirk's report shows that Morgan even talked of a 'Red Tide' which was menacing Greece (*FRUS 1945, VIII,* p. 252).
21. R 18735/4/19.
22. *FRUS 1945, VIII,* p. 252.
23. *Ibid.,* pp. 253 ff.
24. Byrnes to MacVeagh 2nd November, 1945 (*FRUS 1945, VIII,* pp. 252 ff).
25. Hayter's Minutes 6th November, 1945 (R 18735/4/19).
26. *The Times,* 7th November, 1945.
27. *FRUS 1945, VIII,* p. 255.
28. *Ibid.,* pp. 256 ff.
29. *Ibid.,* p. 256.
30. *Ibid.,* p. 259.
31. *Ibid.,* pp. 259 ff.
32. *Ibid.,* pp. 260 ff.
33. Leeper to Foreign Office 16th November, 1945 (R 19662/4/19).
34. *Ibid.; FRUS 1945, VIII,* p. 261.
35. R 19662/4/19.

36. *FRUS 1945, VIII,* p. 263.
37. Draft Cabinet Paper (R 18732/4/19).
38. MacVeagh to State Department 5th November, 1945 (*FRUS 1945, VIII,* pp. 257 ff).
39. Henderson's Memorandum to Byrnes 10th November, 1945 (*ibid.,* pp. 263 ff). And quite recently: Terry H. Anderson, *The United States, Great Britain and the Cold War,* (London: Columbia, 1981), p. 149.
40. Byrnes' Memorandum to Truman 10th November, 1945 (*FRUS 1945, VIII,* pp. 266 ff).
41. *Rizospastis,* 11th-15th November, 1945. 'On the 11th November Rizospastis began a series of much advertised revelations of "Tory intrigues" against ELAS during the occupation, in the form of secret telegrams from British Mission officers to Cairo, the text of which has somehow got into the hands of this newspaper's correspondent in the United States.' Leeper to Foreign Office 16th November, 1945 (R 19662/4/19).
42. Record of a Conversation between the Prime Minister, Mr. McNeil and His Majesty's Ambassador on 14th November, 1945 (R 19823/4/19).
43. Text of the memorandum in R 19826/4/19.
44. MacVeagh to State Department 16th November, 1945 (*FRUS 1945, VIII,* pp. 268 ff).
45. On the British side the following were present: McNeil, Leeper, Noel-Baker, Lascelles, Hayter, Davidson, Hill, David Balfour. Davidson represented the Treasury.
46. A combination of the majority and proportional representation systems.
47. Leeper (McNeil) to Foreign Office 15th November, 1945 (R 20769/4/19). McNeil recommended the acceptance of this suggestion.
48. Record of Meeting with Greek Ministers. Held at British Embassy at 11 a.m., Thursday, 15th November, 1945 (R 19825/4/19); Record of a Conversation. Held at His Majesty's Embassy, Athens, on Thursday, 15th November, 1945 at 11 o'clock (R 19830/4/19).
49. Herrmann Neubacher, *Sonderauftrag Südost 1940-1945,* (Göttingen: Musterschmid, 1956), p. 76.
50. Thus MacVeagh in a Memorandum to Byrnes 15th November, 1945 (*FRUS 1945, VIII,* p. 286).
51. *Ibid.,* p. 271.
52. Leeper to Foreign Office 22nd November, 1945 (R 20169/4/19).
53. *Ibid.*
54. MacVeagh to State Department 17th November, 1945 (*FRUS 1945, VIII,* pp. 270 ff).
55. Leeper to Foreign Office 29th November, 1945 (R 20613/4/19).
56. Bevin to McNeil 18th November, 1945 (R 19555/4/19).
57. Discussion held at the Palace of the Regency on 19th November, 1945, at 6 o'clock (R 20281/4/19); Leeper to Foreign Office 29th November, 1945 (R 20613/4/19). Present were: Damaskinos, McNeil, Leeper, Seferiadis and Balfour.
58. R 20281/4/19.
59. R 20613/4/19.
60. McNeil saw the following: Sofoulis, Venizelos, Rendis, Varvoutis, Melas, Tsaldaris, Mavromichalis, Stefanopoulos, Partsalidis, Gavriilidis, Oikonomou, Loulis, Kritikas, Tsirimokos, Papandreou, Tsouderos, Sofianopoulos, Kafandaris, Exindaris, Mylonas and Mercouris.
61. R 20169/4/19. The journalist Outrillo had reported this to his newspaper and the Greek authorities promptly instituted criminal proceedings against him for

deception.
62. *Ibid.*
63. What follows is based on two reports by Leeper: Leeper (McNeil) to Foreign Office 22nd November, 1945 (R 19793/4/19); Leeper to Foreign Office 29th November, 1945 (R 20613/4/19).
64. R 19793/4/19.
65. Leeper (McNeil) to Foreign Office 22nd November, 1945 (R 19794/4/19).
66. *Ibid.*
67. R 20613/4/19.
68. R 19793/4/19.
69. McNeil's Memorandum to Bevin 10th December, 1945 (R 20769/4/19).
70. Leeper (McNeil) to Foreign Office 22nd November, 1945 (R 19794/4/19).
71. *The Times,* 23rd November, 1945. On the 21st McNeil had made the following demands of Tsouderos: 'a) The budget must be balanced. b) Vigorous action should be taken against gold speculators and tax evaders. c) His Majesty's Government would be prepared to send a mission comprising a limited number of experts. . . He had no authority to promise a loan, but. . . His Majesty's Government would be prepared to provide a limited amount of reconstruction material' (R 20613/4/19).
72. *Ibid.*
73. *Ibid.*
74. R 20613/4/19.
75. Leeper to Foreign Office 24th November, 1945 (R 19884/4/19).
76. *Hansard,* No. 416, 22nd November, 1945.
77. Bevin to Leeper 24th November, 1945 (R 19893/4/19).
78. Leeper to Foreign Office 24th November, 1945 (R 19917/4/19).
79. Leeper to Foreign Office 7th December, 1945 (R 21125/4/19).
80. R 19917/4/19.
81. Leeper to Foreign Office 25th November, 1945 (R 19927/4/19); MacVeagh to State Department 26th November, 1945 (*FRUS 1945, VIII,* p. 183), where the text of the *communiqué* can be found.
82. Provatas, *op. cit.,* p. 593 lists the following:

Nikolaos Manousis	Labour	Liberal
Iraklis Petimezas	Press	non-EAM Resistance
Ioannis Peltekis	Merchant Marine	non-EAM Resistance
G. Bourdaras	Post	Progressive
Petros Evripaios	Air Transport	Progressive
Evstathios Malamidas	Health	Liberal
Nikolaos Kazantzakis [the author]	Without portfolio	Independent Socialist
Georgios Mavros	Cabinet Office	Liberal

83. *Hansard,* No. 416, 22nd November, 1945, col. 839. Minister of State Philip Noel-Baker.
84. *The Times,* 22nd November, 1945.
85. *Hansard,* No. 416, 22nd November, 1945, cols. 618 ff.
86. *Ibid.,* cols. 767-74.
87. Churchill to Bevin 27th November, 1945 (R 20543/4/19).
88. Bevin to Churchill (draft letter) (*ibid.*).
89. Sargent to Leeper 17th December, 1945 (*ibid.*).
90. Here George II refers to the following events. When in 1922 the Greek army was beaten by the Turks, King Constantine I, who was afraid of a possible military *coup* gave an order dissolving the army. Thereupon Plastiras (then a colonel) set up a revolutionary committee which managed to re-organise the army, thus saving Greece from a further Turkish advance. This committee

forced Constantine to abdicate in favour of his son George II and sent the politicians and generals who were considered guilty of the catastrophe to a revolutionary tribunal. Six of them were found guilty of the disaster and shot. Probably the only case in known history where the political leaders were made to bear their responsibility.

91. George II to Bevin 3rd December, 1945 (R 20769/4/19).
92. The King of Greece. Bevin's notes of a conversation 5th December, 1945 (R 20745/4/19).
93. McNeil's Memorandum to Bevin 10th December, 1945 (R 20769/4/19).

THE SOFOULIS GOVERNMENT

The government which started its career under these auspices in no way confirmed George II's gloomy forebodings. His description of it as a one-party government was absurd unless, of course, one defines parties as he did by their attitude to the constitutional issue. Only in such a sense was his description accurate: the Sofoulis government was a wholly republican government. In fact the Cabinet was recruited from three of the traditional parties: the Liberals, the Progressive Party and the Agrarian Party. In addition, there was the so-called *Eleftheria* Group[1] centred on George Kartalis as well as a number of prominent non-party personalities. Politically, the Sofoulis Cabinet represented all bourgeois trends from the Right-Centre to left-wing Liberals, excluding the conservatives and the extreme Right. Sofoulis had succeeded in winning all the important figures of the traditional republican camp for his cabinet and, what was more important, in Kartalis he had won one of the most important representatives of the non-EAM Resistance. His cabinet brought together not only names of high political standing but also men of technocratic accomplishment. Tsouderos was an extremely able financier and could get his projects through. Kartalis proved himself to be the best Supply Minister with whom UNRRA had ever cooperated. As Foreign Minister Sofianopoulos could offer the prospect of better relations with the Soviet Union. The Sofoulis Cabinet was the best that could be imagined for Greece at that time. Moreover, in contrast to the previous governments, it had the majority of public opinion behind it and could even count on support from the Left. So a fresh start was a possibility.[2]

But the problems confronting it were still the same. The most urgent task was to overcome the economic crisis. The second problem urgently demanding solution was the imposition of government authority in all spheres of public life. This latter task involved finding a solution to the following: putting down the *parakratos;* control of the army, gendarmerie and administration; ending the White Terror; emptying the congested prisons; general amnesty; independence for the trade unions; establishment of law and order; preparation for elections. Only if the Sofoulis government proved able to accomplish these two basic tasks, could the underlying problem of the Greek people's fear of the future be overcome, thus providing the necessary conditions for truly free elections and a stable normality. Only success in this could prevent what was otherwise the certainty of a third civil war. Despite all these premises for success the Sofoulis government failed.

The armed forces
The first edict of the Sofoulis government was most promising. On 23rd November the Cabinet issued the following order: every member of the armed forces and the gendarmerie, whether officer or other ranks, who was involved in political activity or belonged to a political organisation would be disciplined or discharged.[3] Then came a decree annulling the law which regulated the bearing of arms by civilians.[4] But when War Minister Manetas started to purge the armed forces of former collaborators and fascists, with resulting unrest in the Officers' Corps, he was stopped by the head of the British Military Mission, General Rawlins. Leeper's report to the Foreign Office contains the following characteristic passage.

> 'There is some unrest among the officers, who fear that the new Government will carry out many changes in appointments in order to ensure that the Republicans are in control. It is felt that such changes, far from neutralising any Right-wing political tendencies which may be latent in the corps of officers, would only serve to bring back acute political rivalries into an army which is beginning to forget them under the influence of professional zeal stimulated by the work of the British Military Mission. Anxiety in the army is growing to such an extent that official reassurances to it on the part of the Government may soon be imperative.'[5]

In other words, because the army leadership which was controlled by SAN/IDEA was worried that it could lose its exclusive control through transfers and new appointments, it intervened with the British authorities and told them that Manetas' measures were endangering the reconstruction already achieved. Because this army reconstruction had been almost the only successful British activity and the British Military Mission saw the failures of their colleagues in the civilian sector and feared that intervention by the political authority could cause unrest in their territory and lead to chaos similar to that in the civilian sector, the Mission blocked Manetas' plan. What is not clear is whether the BMM was aware of the true character of the Greek armed forces. It may be assumed with reasonable probability that the British military did not see through the situation.[6] They were conservative by disposition, though in party political terms neutral, politically inexperienced but anti-communist; and only interested in creating an army which functioned efficiently from a military standpoint. It must have been easy for the Greek officers to camouflage the true character of the Greek Officers' Corps and convince their British colleagues that every change in personnel would be grist to the communist mill. But, in case of doubt, there were in the BMM a few people who *did* know. Colonel Sheppard reports that in every British Mission or local post in

THE SOFOULIS GOVERNMENT 325

Greece there were members of a special Foreign Office service (the SIS?) who took care that the 'right' decisions were taken.[7] And these members of this service pursued their own independent policy which was not even controlled by the British Foreign Minister. In brief, the British Military Mission took a blocking stance and all that Manetas and Sofoulis achieved was the removal of the Chief of the General Staff, General Vendiris. Even he was not retired, but was transferred to another high command post as Military Governor of Macedonia and Thrace.[8]

From Leeper's report to the Foreign Office one might conclude that apparently Sofoulis, too, rejected an army purge and was satisfied so long as the officers abstained from day-to-day politicking.[9] But in fact things were quite different. After the British had successfully blocked any intervention in questions of forces and gendarmerie personnel, at the beginning of December Sofoulis and Kafandaris addressed themselves to the advance team of the American section of the Election Supervision Commission which had in the meantime arrived in Athens under the leadership of ambassador Henry F. Grady.

On 4th December Grady reported to Washington:

'Premier and Kaphandaris repeatedly but unsuccessfully attempted by devious verbal maneuvers to force Allied mission into position of undertaking to press British military and police missions to allow Government a "free hand" in making personnel changes in army and gendarmerie. . . They claimed "five or six changes" in high command of army and gendarmerie would suffice but that Government's hands are tied by Voulgaris Agreement with British military and police missions whereby such changes must be concurred in by those missions.'[10]

Grady, however, refused to intervene because he suspected Sofoulis of only seeking to remain in power. Thus, in the first weeks of its existence, the Sofoulis government had already failed in one of its most important tasks. How could fair elections be held and the White Terror be ended if the gendarmerie remained under the control of the extreme Right? And how could Sofoulis get the *parakratos* under control if he was not even allowed to control his own army? Sofoulis might have taken a harder line and given publicity to these problems. But as EAM and KKE had announced that one of their principal conditions for supporting the government was a purge of the armed forces and the gendarmerie, it would have been easy for the Right to make propaganda equating his government with the communists, especially as there was a tendency to equate all forms of republicanism with KKE.[11] As Sofoulis was no friend of the communists, did not want their support and did not wish to expose himself to slanders from the Right, he drew back, but not completely. Officially, he accepted the British demands, but privately he told his minister that he should nevertheless carry out changes of personnel behind the backs of the British.[12] Obviously, he was playing for time and hoped that, in the next few months, he would still be able to prevail—a hope which was to prove illusory.

On 12th December, the Supreme Allied Commander Mediterranean, General Morgan, visited Athens. During his conversation with Sofoulis he urged the latter to issue a statement on the army to reassure the officers. On the 14th Sofoulis responded to Morgan's wish: he affirmed that no officer would lose his post on account of his political convictions, provided he kept them to himself. No personnel changes were contemplated except those necessitated by alterations in the command system; the government's only wish was that the army should become a law-abiding agent of the state and keep out of politics. But, despite this statement, army leadership circles were not satisfied; they feared that War Minister Manetas would nevertheless attempt to carry out changes of personnel.[13]

These fears were not wholly groundless. General Manetas feared that, when the command reorganisation was completed, he—or rather the Greek government—would lose all influence on the manning of the Officers' Corps, since in the projected Higher Military Council the British Military Mission would have legal claim to a seat and a voice. He therefore delayed signing the reorganisation decree and circumvented a possible British veto by taking two measures without either consulting or even informing them: he promulgated a new retirement pension scheme, very attractive for senior officers; and he initiated a series of promotions. Both produced strong opposition. The army leadership's negative attitude to the Sofoulis government was re-enforced and the BMM considered that Manetas had exceeded his competence—he was not cooperating to the extent that could have been expected of him. At the same time there were attacks from the Left which strongly condemned continued discrimination against ELAS members entering the Military Academy and preference for former members of the Security Battalions when filling officers' posts.[14] Finally, at the end of December, the reorganisation decree was signed. But Manetas had made enemies not only of his own army leadership but also of the BMM. Nevertheless he continued his endeavour to democratise the army.

At the second session of the Higher Military Council, on 14th January 1946, it came to an open clash between General Rawlins and War Minister Manetas. Manetas proposed that Colonel Kallergis, who had been arrested in connection with the Middle East disturbances in the armed forces-in-exile in spring 1944, should be brought back into the army. In addition he submitted to the Council a draft law providing for a revision of List B (of officers who were not to be used again in active posts). By this measure Manetas first and foremost hoped to reintegrate into the army republican officers purged by Kondylis after the failed rising of 1935.[15] Rawlins rejected both proposals for reasons of principle but could not prevail against the Greek members of the Council, with the result that the matter had to be referred to Sofoulis,[16] since in a case of deadlock he had the final decision. Sofoulis delayed his decision and, at the beginning of February, tried to get a change of British policy through his new Foreign Minister, Rendis (Sofianopoulos had been removed from this post shortly before). On 9th February Rendis made his complaint to Bevin that the British Missions were preventing the removal of right-wing extremists from the army and the gendarmerie, although these latter openly sympathised with the terrorist organisations of the Right—even if they did not actually collaborate with them. This made the restoration of law and order practically impossible. Bevin stressed that he wanted a politically neutral army and police and promised to take up the matter himself.[17]

On the same day he telegraphed to Leeper: he was indeed against removing anyone from the army or the gendarmerie on account of his political convictions, but it was not suitable that right-wing members of these forces should disregard orders from the Greek government; Leeper should investigate this matter with Rawlins and Wickham; the best course would be to make examples of a few individuals by dismissal.[18] Meanwhile, news of the deadlock had reached the Greek press and both left- and right-wing papers condemned the British intervention. On 11th February, Leeper sent his answer: in the past months he had frequently discussed this problem with Rawlins and Wickham. Rendis' assumptions were quite groundless. As regards the gendarmerie it was true that their sympathies were mainly with the Right, but this was natural in view of communist misdeeds in the winter of 1944. The latter were at present still far more dangerous than their right-wing opponents.

'Gendarmes know that whereas the Right Wing extremists will fight them when driven into a corner but are not fundamentally hostile, Communists are their permanent enemies and are out gunning for them all the time. They also know they can only cope successfully with the lawbreakers in so far as the population though being on their side is ready to supply force, and that for the most part the population is in fact not willing to cooperate against the Right.'

Moreover, the gendarmerie expected the Right to emerge victorious from the forthcoming elections and it was only human that

'they... think in terms of their prospects under the country's future administrators. Even the present interim government has shown a marked political bias in regard to gendarmerie transfers also the police mission's attempts to check this, and gendarmes have consequently no reason to suppose that under an elected government they will be adequately protected by the mission against political interference'.

Regarding the obstruction of changes to personnel, the situation was just the opposite of that depicted by Rendis: the 'highly unsatisfactory' Minister for Public Security, Mercouris, had of late completely ignored the British Mission. He was undertaking personnel changes without consulting, or even informing, Wickham. He himself had spoken to Sofoulis about removing Mercouris. In general, it could be said that 'if purges were effected merely on the score of political leanings, the great majority of the whole gendarmerie force would have to be purged and could not be replaced without a long period of chaos'.[19]

This inclination to trivialise Greek right-wing influence in the gendarmerie, police and armed forces could be found at all levels of the British hierarchy. On 22nd February Hayter drew up a memorandum for Bevin in which he explained that it was British policy to render Greece's armed forces politically neutral and to put an end to the hitherto existing 'spoils system'. That naturally meant institutionalising the *status quo* in the army and the gendarmerie. The contention that this would lead to a preponderance of the Right was incorrect and exaggerated. After all, a considerable proportion of the senior officers had been appointed by Plastiras. Noel-Baker obviously realised how little this line of reasoning corresponded to fact when he added the following marginal note: 'Including some strong and extreme Royalists'. Hayter went on to say that Rawlins and Wickham had reported that gendarmerie and army officers themselves disliked the 'spoils system' and, if this were got rid of, would serve the government of the day with loyalty. This was why they had opposed any kind of purge. On the other hand, they had always recommended that officers who neglected their duty should be deprived of their posts. Noel-Baker's comment was revealing: 'This is of course almost impossible to prove in cases when it matters most.' However, despite his realisation that all was not well with the Greek army and gendarmerie, Minister of State Noel-Baker took no further action.[20]

In Athens meanwhile the arguments between the British missions and the relevant Greek ministers continued. On 20th February Mercouris succumbed to the British pressure on Sofoulis by submitting his resignation and Sofoulis took over the Ministry for Public Security. General Manetas proved to be of sterner stuff. Although Sofoulis was in principle ready to accept the British viewpoint, he refused to remove Manetas from his Cabinet and Manetas himself showed no inclination to resign. He held to his own standpoint that he could make appointments without first getting approval from the British Mission.[21] At the third session of the Higher Military Council on 22nd and 33rd February, it came to an open clash. Manetas refused to recognise the principle that General Rawlins' opinion should normally be accepted and that, when agreement could not be reached, no decision should be taken without consulting the Prime Minister. Furthermore, Manetas and the Greek army representatives on the Higher Military Council did not recognise any right of the BMM to cooperate on promotions and appointments. The cause of the clash was General Rawlins' decision to appoint Major-General Spyridon Georgoulis Deputy Chief of the General Staff.[22] When the Greek members of the

Higher Military Council resolutely refused to agree to this, Generals Morgan, Scobie and Rawlins visited Sofoulis. Sofoulis accepted the appointment and instructed Manetas to summon a further session at which Georgoulis' appointment must be confirmed. Sofoulis then immediately summoned the Chief of the General Staff, Lieutenant-General Georgios Dromazos, and gave him the same instructions. At the decisive session on 26th February, Dromazos was absent and the Higher Military Council took the desired decision; though in the public *communiqué* it was made clear that this decision had been taken under pressure from Rawlins. Dromazos himself submitted his resignation and, when this was refused, he took leave of absence 'for health reasons'. On principle, he rejected intervention in his sphere of responsibility.[23] On 7th April, Georgoulis' appointment was made official.

However, in two other matters Manetas had more success. First, he refused to discuss the manning of the seven Greek divisional commands within the Higher Military Council or to accept the candidates proposed by the BMM; secondly, the Greek members accepted Manetas' suggested revision of List B, despite BMM opposition.[24]

In the middle of March 1946 he still made a last effort to bring republican officers into the army in advance of the elections. General Rawlins had gone to London for a few days and the Selection Boards were not in functioning order since many of their members had been detailed for tasks in preparation for the elections. Manetas made use of the favourable opportunity to submit a long list of republican appointments to Damaskinos for signature. The latter was ready to sign and could only be stopped at the last minute by a threat from the British Embassy that, if he did so, the BMM would be withdrawn.[25]

On this the Labour MP Lyall Wilkes was to write in January 1947:
'Questions in the House... reveal the staggering fact that after one and a half year's work by the BMM 228 former members of the German armed Quisling Security Battalions now hold active service commissions in the Greek army whilst (as evidence of impartiality?) 191 ex-members of ELAS also hold commissions. These figures cannot be accepted without reserve, as there are good grounds for believing that the number of ex-collaborators now holding commissions is considerably higher than the figure of 228. Indeed, excluding ex-members of the Evzones Battalions and the Volunteer Battalion, Karditza, which acted as German Security Forces during the Occupation, the number has been listed by the Left (with names and units provided) at around 1,000. But even if one takes the Foreign Office figures Greece remains the one country in Europe outside Spain whose Army contains in positions of authority a greater number of ex-Nazis and collaborators than those identified with the Resistance. And if the 228 are actually members of the S.B.s, how many more officers must have been at best acquiescent

during the Occupation?'[26]

This final desperate effort—even at the last minute—to improve somewhat the balance of forces in the army in favour of the republicans (not, be it noted, of the Left), failed—as had so many previous efforts—after opposition from the British Embassy. It was to be the last attempt for many years to make some change in the composition of the Officers' Corps and to democratise it. From now on the army leadership, controlled by IDEA, would be able to rule supreme and unhindered and to build up the army into a rigorously anti-communist organisation in whose ranks even liberal officers could only be accommodated under grave suspicion. The election victory of the Right initiated a new process: it introduced a purge of all democratic elements from the army.

Election date and electoral lists

The second important problem to confront the Sofoulis government during its first days in office was that of the election date and the electoral register. There were long drawn-out negotiations between the Allies over the setting up of a commission to supervise the elections and on 27th November 1945, the advance team of this commission arrived in Athens. As well as Ambassador Grady, the US sent the Assistant Chief of the State Department's Divsion of Near Eastern Affairs, Foy D. Kohler, and Major-General Harry J. Maloney. France was represented by General Arnaud Laparre and Great Britain by the Labour Party official, R.T. Windle.[27] Immediately upon arrival the team paid a courtesy visit to Damaskinos and then held a series of talks with Sofoulis, Kafandaris, Sofianopoulos, Rendis and Mercouris. The representatives of the Greek government drew the team's attention to the fact that terror still reigned in the provinces, that the armed forces and the gendarmerie were royalist-directed, that the electoral registers needed revision, that measures against plural voting were needed and that—at least in the towns—there was need of a population census.

It was obvious that the government was trying to get help from the team to increase its freedom of action and to free itself, at least partially, from the British embrace. We have shown how the government's plans for staffing the army and the gendarmerie had suffered shipwreck. But even in the sphere which directly concerned the commission, they had no success. In forming his government Sofoulis had undertaken the obligation to hold the elections at the latest in March 1946. However, on taking up office, he had realised that the problems were more serious than he had originally imagined. So now he tried to bring the team to a point where they themselves would demand a further postmonement: a demand from which even the British could not have extricated themselves. (The same result could have been obtained had the team demanded a purge of the armed forces and the gendarmerie.) But the team took the stand that these were internal Greek matters in which it must not intervene: these were problems for the Greek government to solve. When Sofoulis realised that he could not count on the team's support, he tried at least to unload responsibility for what he considered the premature election date on to the team: he would leave the determination of the election date to them. But even here he failed. They declared this too was wholly a matter for the Greek government; their task was confined to supervision of the elections. Grady formed the impression that the Greek government showed a 'disheartening lack [of] resolute determined leadership' and was trying to use the team for its own ends.'[28]

Grady's remarks show two things: first, how scantily at least the US members of the team were informed about the true situation. Sofoulis' attempts to get a 'free hand' and to postpone the elections were not the result of lack of resolution but were prompted by anxiety about the country's future. Secondly, the advance team of the future AMFOGE (Allied Mission for the Observation of the Greek Elections) regarded their task in exactly the same way as the later British Legal Mission, as a non-political action, a kind of technical supervision of the election process. They did not realise that the preparations for the elections—and not only the purely formal arrangements—had great political significance.

When the AMFOGE team failed to show itself open to Sofoulis' objections and reservations, he reacted in a characteristic way. On the evening of 3rd December 1945, without consulting his Cabinet, he announced that the elections would be held on 31st March 1946—even if the skies fell.[29] But this reaction of anger and refractory frustration did not prevent him from agreeing with Kafandaris next day that the Greek ambassadors in London, Paris and Washington should inform the three Foreign Ministries as follows: the Greek government had bowed to the pressing recommendations of AMFOGE and had accepted the 31st March as election date; the attention of the Allied governments must be drawn to the fact that Greece's internal situation had not altered and that revision of the electoral lists had not yet begun. 'As it is not certain that the essential conditions for fair balloting could exist by that date, the fixing of a definite time is extremely inadvisable, for without a genuine popular vote the internal troubles could be aggravated.' It would therefore be necessary to postpone the elections till April. 'Thus a greater opportunity would be afforded for the purification of the public services, of the election lists, enlightenment of the people and the instilment in their conscience of the feeling that they are really free to vote as they please.' In making these recommendations, the Greek government was not pursuing any party-political goals. 'It simply believes that this postponement would strengthen somewhat the hope of a more general expression of public sentiment and would give to the Government greater opportunity to make the necessary changes in some main places of the public services, presently under the control of the extreme right wing.'[30]

Meantime, Grady and Kohler had learnt of this telegram and protested to Sofianopoulos about the behaviour of Kafandaris. The AMFOGE team's only task was to ascertain the election date, not to determine it. The date was exclusively the business of the Greek government, with only one condition: that, if it came too late, it was possible that the US observers could no longer be kept available. Should there be an agreement between the Greek government and the British as to the date, that would be a bilateral affair and would not concern the US and French governments. Sofianopoulos apologised for what had happened and gave assurances that he would instruct the Greek ambassadors to set matters straight. Kohler then pointed out to Sofianopoulos that the US observers would be available till the end of April at the latest. The period up to 31st March should suffice for preparing the elections; a further fifteen or twenty days' postponement would be absurd. Moreover, after Sofoulis' categorical statement, further postponement would irritate public opinion. Sofianopoulos said they would stick to the 31st March and he would instruct the Greek ambassadors accordingly.[31]

On 8th November the AMFOGE team received representatives of the parties outside the government to hear their opinions on the election problem. KKE and EAM maintained that the electoral lists had been falsified. A thoroughgoing revision under conditions of order and tranquillity was an essential condition for their participation in the elections. They also demanded a proportional representation system. Papandreou, who represented himself and his party as republican-socialist, maintained that the electoral lists were as good as could be expected and public order satisfactory. He pointed to the existing freedom of the press and stated that he supported the earliest possible election date and the majority system. The Populists certified the electoral lists as excellent; terrorism was exercised by the communists and, if only the government would take energetic action, tranquillity could prevail within five days. They regarded the majority system as urgently necessary. They would accept any election result and never resort to force. Kanellopoulos was of the opinion the electoral lists were the best in Greek history. Terrorism was non-existent. Existing psychological pressure on the electors would be dissipated by the presence of the observers. A few personnel changes in the gendarmerie were, of course, necessary. He preferred a mixed electoral system. ELD-SKE said that elections would only become possible when order and tranquillity had returned and when suitable preparations had been made, which could not be before May. The local authorities were tolerating the royalist terror, if they were not actually supporting it. They would decide in accordance with subsequent developments whether they would advise their members to register and to vote. They were for proportional representation. Their position resembled that of EAM with whom, however, they were not associated. Finally, the right-wing group under Gonatas and Zervas expressed the same opinions as the Populists.[32] The AMFOGE team was satisfied with these results: the election date had been determined and they could begin their preparations. As regards the remaining problems, they took the view that their solution was the business of the Greek government. On 9th December they left Greece.

Washington took an identical view. On the evening of 7th December, Sofianopoulos had instructed the Greek ambassadors in Washington and Paris to inform the two Foreign Ministries that the election date had been determined in conformity with British demands and not with those of the AMFOGE team; but they were at the same time to hint at a possible postponement.[33] Thereupon, on 10th December, the Greek ambassador in Washington, Symeon Diamantopoulos, sent a Note in this sense to the State Department. In his reply, Byrnes pointed out to Diamantopoulos that determination of the election date was purely a matter for the Greek government; though postponement to an indefinite date in the future would make the sending of US observers problematical.[34]

For Washington this ended the matter: it would of course participate in supervising the elections but it wanted nothing to do with the undemocratic conditions in Greece—that was a matter for the British to break their heads over. Thus, the tentative effort of the Sofoulis government to win for itself a somewhat wider freedom of political action by American help, came to nothing. The last chance to overcome the *parakratos* was frustrated by the British veto and by US lack of interest. Elections held against this background would indeed formally meet AMFOGE criteria but the real condition for free and fair elections—freedom from fear—was by no means guaranteed. The only results of the negotiations were that agreement was reached on the formal arrangements under which AMFOGE would operate and the time limit for registering on the electoral lists was extended from 12th December 1945 to 14th January 1946, to be further extended on 15th January to the 10th February.[35]

The amnesty question

A further problem which urgently demanded a solution was the problem of emptying the over-congested prisons, in other words the question of an amnesty. Although the release programme started in September had been continued until the beginning of November—according to the Ministry of Justice during this period more than 6,000 detainees had been released—the number in prison on 1st November was 18,058 (against 16,700 in mid-September). Of these 15,006 were pre-trial prisoners. The new arrests therefore far exceeded the releases, though the figures supplied had admittedly been rounded down. The tendency to treat collaborators with leniency and to use the full rigour of the law only against former Resistance members was still making itself felt. Out of 2,773 prisoners sentenced judicially, only 279 were former collaborators and of the 15,006 pre-trial prisoners, only 2,132 awaited a possible charge of collaboration. As the total number of sentenced collaborators in prison had also been reduced during this period, it can be concluded that many of the sentences had been light ones and had already been served. Leeper reported that he was persisting in his efforts to make the Greek authorities speed up the trials but that they just as persistently told him that they were awaiting the arrival of the British Legal Mission. Leeper therefore urgently requested the Foreign Office to send it out.[36]

Shortly after he took office, Justice Minister Rendis reported on the situation as follows:

'According to information assembled by the Ministry for Justice, the total number detained in prison amounts to 17,984. Of this number 2,388 are serving judicially imposed sentences; 15,596 are preventively detained [pre-trial prisoners]. The number of files concerning crimes at present under investigation amounts to 18,401. We still lack, however, information for seventeen provinces and 48,956 individuals are wanted as members of EAM-ELAS. . . [But here, too, necessary information is lacking for fourteen provinces.] The total number of wanted individuals, including those preventively detained, exceeds, according to our reckoning, 80,000.'[37]

These figures were, if anything, too low an estimate. One must also add approximately 150,000 people in hiding in the mountains for fear of persecution.[38]

After the departure of the AMFOGE team the Greek Cabinet went on to deal with the amnesty question. It was at once apparent that there were three viewpoints. Sofianopoulos and Tsouderos held that all prisoners under investigation for offences during the Occupation should be released and only people accused of murder during the December events should be charged. Rendis, Kafandaris and Sofoulis wanted no distinction made between the Occupation and the December events and insisted that every-one accused of murder should stand trial. Finally, Kartalis and the other former Resistance members wanted to exempt and release all those who had killed collaborators or members of the Occupation forces at the prompting of Greek and British authorities including the BBC and to prosecute only those who had committed murders for party-political reasons. In a talk with Tsouderos, Leeper agreed with Kartalis' opinion and recommended the introduction of a suitable clause in the projected Amnesty Law, excluding punishments of genuine acts of resistance. The British government hoped that the new law would release from prison all those who were not guilty of murder. If there were to be resignations over the amnesty question—Kartalis had hinted at the possibility of this— that would have repercussions on the financial situation. Tsouderos promised to act in this sense and expressed himself similarly to Sofianopoulos: what was needed was a consensus amongst the members of the Greek government; Kartalis' proposal had his consent and constituted a generous amnesty; he could not see why Sofianopoulos was thinking of resigning; Kartalis' suggestion was acceptable; if he and others resigned, this would certainly have a negative effect on forthcoming negotiations with the British Economic Mission. Under this pressure, Sofianopoulos retreated and, when Leeper gave him to understand that reconciliation, too, would have its limits, he declared himself willing to support Kartalis proposal.[39] But in this way Leeper had prevented the only consistent solution; that of Sofianopoulos which—failing a general amnesty—would have had the best chance of clearing the country's internal atmosphere.

The past had already shown that any other solution would prove unworkable and this became clear on 13th December 1945, the day when Justice Minister Rendis issued a statement in which he reinterpreted Kartalis' proposal in two directions. Since the Security Battalionists had acted under the orders of the collaborationist government, they would have immunity for their actions. But those who had murdered members of the Security Battalions without the relevant instructions from the Greek government-in-exile for each individual case would be brought to trial. Kartalis went at once to Leeper and told him that after this infamous statement neither he nor any other former Resistance member could remain in the Cabinet unless Sofoulis repudiated Rendis' statement and removed him from his post. On the morning of 14th December, a furious Sofianopoulos presented himself to Leeper, stated that his own original suggestion constituted the sole solution, and demanded that Leeper should put this through with Sofoulis. During the ensuing conversation between Sofoulis and Leeper, the latter expressed his indignation: Rendis' statement would make a very negative impression in Britain, especially as the British had openly condemned the Security Battalions. He hoped Sofoulis would repudiate Rendis. In view of the situation, it might be best if Sofianopoulos' proposal were to be adopted and a general amnesty be declared for the Occupation period.

Sofoulis replied that he would, of course, disavow Rendis' statement, get Kartalis' proposal accepted and replace Rendis by Georgios Mavros. But he would have to reject Sofianopoulos' demand for a general amnesty as public opinion rejected this. He hoped however that Sofianopoulos would remain in the Cabinet. Leeper agreed to this and recommended him to act in such a way as not to provoke ministerial resignations. When Sofoulis had left, Sofianopoulos arrived and urged Leeper to insist with Sofoulis on a general amnesty. Without this there would be trouble with EAM. Leeper refused, sheltering behind his lack of instructions from London. London had never proposed a general amnesty and it was for the Greek government to decide about this. Sofoulis was not at the moment ready for this but would certainly get more used to the idea after a time. Sofianopoulos left in a state of complete frustration. Leeper justified his line to the Foreign Office saying he hoped that he had steered the right course, though he had in fact had no instructions.[40] But it would have been easy for Leeper to push through a general amnesty had he so wished; the past had shown that. However, Leeper only wanted an emptying of the congested prisons; for him a fresh start with a general amnesty did not come into consideration. Furthermore, EAM and KKE were at that time agitating for a general amnesty and on 7th December they organised a mass demonstration together with ELD-SKE at which this was the demand; it would be unthinkable for a British ambassador to adopt a demand of the Left as his own.

On the evening of 14th December, Sofoulis held a press conference, at which he stated that Rendis had been misunderstood by the journalists, who had mis-reported his statement. Naturally, members of the Security Battalions and of similar collaborationist groups would be brought to trial.[41] Finally, on the morning of the 15th the Greek Cabinet united on the following formula: all crimes committed between 27th April 1941 and 12th February 1945, with the exception of murder (though not of moral responsibility for murder) and of various other serious crimes connected with politics and with Resistance, would be amnestied. But even this did not put an end to discussion and the relevant law was not signed until 21st December.[42]

The Right abruptly rejected the draft law which was promulgated on 15th December. The Left argued that it allowed of varying interpretations and would not change the actual situation. Liberal circles were shocked at the relevation that 80,000 were on the wanted list. A change in the situation could only have been achieved by a general amnesty, or at least by an amnesty going as far as Sofianopoulos had demanded. This was to be further confirmed by the results of the British Legal Mission's investigations.

The members of this Mission were nominated by Bevin at the end of November 1945, when he had assigned them five tasks. They were:

'(a) to consider whether the procedure for arrest and preliminary hearing are satisfactory and whether there are adequate safeguards against arbitrary arrest; (b) to consider whether the measures already taken by the Greek Government to speed up the examination of cases awaiting trial are satisfactory and sufficient; (c) to consider whether Greek methods of investigation are adequate and equitable; (d) to consider whether prison conditions in Greece are reasonably satisfactory, after taking into account the differences which must be expected to exist between prison conditions in this country and in Greece, and the added difficulties with which the Greek Government is faced owing to the war and the enemy occupation; (e) where necessary to make proposals for improving matters in regard to (a), (b), (c) and (d)'.[43]

These were the tasks as published in the British Legal Mission's report. But in the original version of the instructions there is a further point which rigidly circumscribed the Mission's sphere of activity in advance, limiting it to the purely legal aspect and prohibiting the drawing of political conclusions. Bevin had written:

'It will not be part of the Mission's task to decide whether a general amnesty should be granted. The Greek Government's reason for declining to grant such an amnesty is that it would not be tolerated by Greek public opinion and that it would lead to acts of private vengeance. It will evidently be impossible for the Mission to reach a conclusive opinion on this point.'[44]

The British Legal Mission was in Greece from 28th November till 19th December. It held talks with the judiciary, defence counsel, British experts and members of the British Police Mission. It examined the relevant legislation and how it was applied, visited trials and prisons and received delegations from EAM and from other organisations. In brief, it did not take its task lightly and the conclusions it drew constitute—within its terms of reference—the most objective picture of the conditions then prevailing in the Greek judicial and criminal prosecution apparatus.

In conformity with its instructions, the first subject of the Mission's investigations was the Greek procedure for arrest. After a thorough analysis of the entire system, the British jurists came to the conclusion that, in theory, Greek procedure was unobjectionable and that, under normal conditions, there was indeed adequate security against arbitrary arrest, but that the civil war of December 1944 had led to mass arrests of actual or alleged members of EAM. The Report mentions the figure of 50,000 arrests. In these cases there had been no previous inquiry into the grounds for arrest which had simply been carried out on the basis of informers' statements. The legal justification for arrests without warrant had been martial law, which had been lifted in Athens and Piraeus on 14th February but had continued in force in the rest of Greece until 25th August. The arrests had not only affected those accused of crimes during the civil war but also had been carried out for deeds during the Occupation period.[45] In this way people who, during the Occupation, had sat in judgment on collaborators or who had executed them by the sentence of a Popular Court were now accused of murder.[46] Others who had collected taxes for the PEEA were now accused of robbery and looting. The examining magistrates who had been appointed to investigate these arrests had been overwhelmed by this deluge and special committees were set up to safeguard against improper arrests. During the course of these investigations, up to April 1945, 29,000 detainees had been released. The Legal Mission had the impression that at present—that is in December 1945—no one whose case had not been investigated remained in detention.[47]

Then the Report expressly stated that the Greek courts had systematically ignored the Varkiza Agreement (which since its publication constituted valid law) and Law 119 of 14th February 1945 which supplemented it.[48] According to both the above, all breaches of the law from 3rd December 1944 to 14th February 1945, with the exception of those unconnected with the civil war, were amnestied. For the rest, according to Article 4 of Law 119, persons accused of breaches of the law not covered by the amnesty should not remain in prison longer than six months; if within that time they had not been sentenced, they must be released and any further attempt at prosecution would be illegal. The Mission stated:

'It is clear to us that the provisions of Law 119 in this respect have not been implemented and successive Greek Governments have taken no steps to ensure that the terms of Article 4 thereof were enforced. Only one of the several persons with whom we discussed the matter in Greece did otherwise than admit these facts. The provisions of Article 4 could be avoided by preferring an additional charge against a person already detained, accusing him of an offence committed before the 3rd December, 1944, and thus outside the period dealt with by Law 119. The various deputations from Left-wing organisations which we received in Greece roundly asserted that such a course had been adopted and we are not prepared to say that such allegations are unfounded. In other cases the provisions of Article 4 have simply been ignored...'[49]

When the Mission asked representatives of the Left why they had not filed a complaint against this openly illegal practice, the latter explained that this was useless since the judges would find a way to circumvent Article 4. One method was to charge the defendant with other crimes committed before 3rd December 1944. The British jurists did not find this argument convincing since they had opposite information from their Greek bourgeois colleagues.[50] Basing themselves on their experience of British justice, it was incomprehensible to them that in Greece even judges were prepared to bend the law out of hatred for the Left and that, from every standpoint, the Greek judicial system must be characterised as class justice. Nevertheless, with typical British understatement, they observed that, had Article 4 of Law 119 really been applied, a considerable number of pre-trial prisoners would have been released a long time previously.

The Report then dealt with a number of special cases of individual detainees, allegedly imprisoned on false charges. The first case was that of a former judge from one of EAM's Popular Justice courts. He was charged with murder because, during the Occupation, he had sentenced collaborators to death. The Mission's examination of the indictment showed that the charges were based on hearsay evidence.

'If it were not for the fact that one witness had given direct evidence of having been stripped and beaten on the orders of the accused the evidence against him would have been entirely hearsay, and on English conceptions of justice would have been insufficient to justify his detention. In view, however, of the direct evidence above referred to, it was impossible to say that the accused had no case to answer.'[51]

The second case was that of an EAM member accused of the murder of a Security Battalionist. The accused denied murder but admitted that he had participated in the investigations which led to the arrest and execution of the man. The examining magistrate was of the opinion that, in this case where patriotic motives obviously came into play, a charge should not be brought and the accused should be released. The public prosecutor had rejected this on the grounds that it was not legal for the accused to have taken the law into his own hands; also, that he must prove that his victim had really been a member of the Security Battalions. The examining magistrate accepted the prosecutor's opinion and the accused remained in prison.[52]

So too, in the other cases investigated by the British Legal Mission there was always one point or other which at least legalistically justified detention. Here the Mission did not take into account the fact that for anyone who had lived in Greece during the Occupation and in Athens and Piraeus during the December events it would have been almost impossible not to become in some sense guilty according to the letter of the law. This held good as much for former Resistance members as for those who had in some way collaborated with the enemy. But apparently this was beyond the imagination of British jurists who themselves had not been confronted with any of these agonising problems. They employed criteria which were totally unrealistic in what had been an occupied country, not comprehending that, on these criteria, each one of the one and a half million former EAM members could have been brought before a court, and that the only solution was to call a total halt to the accusation process by an amnesty. But at the same time they themselves understood that the justifiable bringing of a charge 'is not the same thing as saying that such evidence would always be reliable. That question could be decided only at the trial'.[53]

The British jurists went on to criticise the admission of heresay evidence in Greek judicial procedure and the category of 'moral responsibility' under which many, themselves not implicated in any crime, could be charged and sentenced in the same way as actual murderers. In their conclusions the British jurists implicitly assumed that trials based on charges of this sort would be fair and that the accused would have a chance of obtaining a just verdict.

Dealing with the second point in its programme the Report analysed the reasons why, despite all the measures introduced in August and

September to reduce the number of detainees, the figures had nevertheless steadily risen. The examining magistrates had only recently begun to function again on a normal basis and therefore many charges could only now be subjected to investigation. Moreover, during examination of civil war cases, an increasing number of people were being implicated.[54]

On point 3 of the programme (adequacy and equity of methods), the Report noted that the EAM Central Committee had presented the British Mission with a detailed memorandum making these points.

'(1) That executions of traitors carried out after trials and under the authority of P.E.E.A. . . . during the occupation were being treated as crimes, and the persons concerned in such executions tried as murderers, if they were followers of E.A.M. but not if they were followers of Right-wing organisations. This was being done notwithstanding that such executions were being urged upon the Greeks by the Allies, and by the Greek Government abroad.

(2) That the requisitioning of supplies for E.L.A.S. during the occupation was now being treated as a crime, and the persons concerned were being tried for theft.

(3) That persons who left the Gendarmerie during the occupation to join E.L.A.S. were being prosecuted and sentenced for desertion from the Gendarmerie.

(4) Vague and ridiculous charges had been brought against followers of E.A.M. such as stealing unknown objects from an unknown person on an unknown date.

(5) That there had been prosecutions for murder in which the alleged victims had appeared in Court during the trial, whereupon a new and different charge was preferred against the accused upon which he was found guilty and sentenced.

(6) That special legislation enacted for the trial of collaborators had been improperly invoked against followers of E.A.M.

(7) That the benefit of Law 119 had been improperly withheld: and in particular that the Athens Court of Appeal had held that the taking of hostages during the Civil War is an offence altogether outside the provisions of Law 119. Accordingly most of the charges against followers of E.A.M. include one of taking hostages.

(8) That most of the examining judges were royalist.

(9) That Law 755 of 1917 dealing with illegal gatherings and originally passed to deal *ad hoc* with an emergency in that year, had been invoked to punish innocent gatherings in private houses.

(10) That judges with democratic sympathies were suspended after the Civil War; whereas none of those who assisted the enemy during the occupation had been removed.'[55]

The British jurists had to acknowledge that EAM's criticisms were justified in regard to Points (1)–(3) and (7). Failure to apply Law 119 was an open breach of the law. But these complaints were connected with the civil war and 'the fact that the Civil War has produced a reaction in Greece. . . does not of itself involve that when such charges come to be tried they will not be fairly tried'.[56] They had attended trials and, although, as they themselves acknowledged, they had no acquaintance with Greek, they had formed the impression that proceedings were properly conducted and that the judges were unbiased. The idea that special 'visitors' show-trials' might have been mounted for the Legal Mission does not seem to have occurred to these honest British lawyers and this despite the fact that both in Salonica and in Piraeus they had endeavoured in vain to witness a trial. One cannot help asking whether a similar Mission to Bulgaria or Romania would have been quite so credulous.

The Legal Mission's Report makes no attempt to examine the EAM Central Committee's charge that many of the judges had continued to hold their positions during the Occupation—and under Metaxas; although just at that time the Sofoulis government was trying, in face of noisy protest from the Right, to relieve some of the Metaxas period judges of their posts by a lowering of the retirement age and by bringing back judges removed in connection with the December events.[57] Given the anti-communist attitude of the Sofoulis Cabinet, the latter could hardly have been communists. The British jurists contented themselves with the assurances of two Greek lawyers that, with few exceptions, the Greek judges would try cases with objectivity.[58] They also considered this problem less important because the sentences were imposed not by the judge but by the jury. Here the Report gave the following explanation: the public prosecutor attached to each court drew up an annual list of possible jurors. These were people either holding particular posts, or with particular professional or property qualifications. The Report mentioned: Cabinet ministers, parliamentary deputies, ambassadors, university graduates, professors and teachers, notaries and those holding other diplomas, officers, shopkeepers, landed proprietors and people with a certain level of income.[59] In other words, the juries were recruited from the anti-communist upper social classes and the fears of the British Legal Mission that people from these circles 'would not all be sympathetic with EAM'[60] seem almost comical. The judgments passed by these courts were unambiguously judgments passed by one class upon another. The further point that the courts used the purist language *(katharevousa)*, incomprehensible to anyone without secondary education, is almost superfluous.

Examination of the Legal Mission's final point, prison conditions, produced unqualified condemnation. Conditions in the Greek prisons were far from being even remotely satisfactory. The prisons were dangerously over-crowded. Before the war the average prison population had been 8,000; now it was approximately 18,000. During the civil war sixteen prisons had been wholly destroyed and another fifteen damaged.

Many of the 'replacement' prisons were virtual ruins and in many there were no beds and the prisoners had to sleep on the concrete floors. There were hardly any sick-bays, not even for infectious diseases. Medical care was inadequate and dental care non-existent. Some of the prisons were breeding-grounds for vermin. The prisoners had nothing to do. The only glorious exception was the Zeliotis prison in which the more eminent former collaborators were housed.

'This prison consists of eleven rooms in a block of flats in Athens in which a total of twenty-seven such persons as aforesaid are detained. These persons enjoy considerable personal comforts, and such amenities as wireless sets and electric heaters. We were unable to ascertain any valid reason for such discrimination in their treatment.'[61]

The Report devoted a special section to the problem of the collaborators in general. The relevant laws were so vaguely formulated that a few legal acrobatics had on occasion sufficed to get former ELAS members condemned for collaboration. Therefore a revision of all sentences for collaboration was urgently needed.[62] However, the Report made no mention of the fact that the majority of collaborators got off scot free and that despite an open scandal which had arisen during the period of the Mission's investigations. When Austria was occupied, British army units had detained 192 men of the notorious Poulos Security Battalions, who had withdrawn with the Germans and had got as far as Austria, and had sent them back to Greece for trial. On their arrival 162 had been set free because there were no arrest warrants in their names. The Greek Minister for Justice expressed his regret: he had been the victim of a misunderstanding.[63] Woodhouse has succinctly encapsulated the situation thus:

'During 1945 membership of the resistance movement had come to be regarded as a political crime, and collaboration with the Germans against Communism a political virtue. Whatever the rights and wrongs the plain fact was that an ex-guerrilla was as likely as not to be found in gaol, and an ex-member of the Security Battalions as likely as not to be found in the uniformed services.'[64]

The Legal Mission concluded its report with a number of recommendations for improving the situation. Judicial processes should be speeded up and for this purpose the number of courts should be tripled by establishing special tribunals, each consisting of two lawyers and a professional judge from the judiciary. To avoid any further avalanche of arrests, a law should be promulgated to prevent further detentions. This was all the more important

'since there is evidence that the Gendarmerie is at present being exclusively recruited from persons professing Anti-Communist political beliefs; and if this is so, there is an ever present danger that as soon as prisons are cleared to any extent they will be filled up again with persons professing opposite political beliefs'.

In addition, prosecutions which could not proceed because the witnesses did not turn up should be abandoned and the accused be set free. Conditions in the Greek prisons must be drastically improved. The practice of sentencing defendants accused of a criminal offence under the special Constitutional Law for collaborators must be discontinued. The hope was expressed that the Sofoulis government's new amnesty law would bring about a change.[65]

In general, the Legal Mission's suggestions were well-meaning and sensible and, if they had been properly applied in a Western European country, they would have brought about the desired results. But for Greece they were an unsuitable prescription since they treated only the symtoms and not the real causes of the trouble. The causes of the malaise afflicting Greek justice lay in persons and not in institutions. With few exceptions, the judges had served under Metaxas and he had purged the judiciary of all liberal elements. The Greek government could pass as many liberal laws as it wished; the judiciary simply did not apply them. Even Leeper was sceptical and doubted whether the new amnesty law would not—like previous efforts—be rendered null and void by renewed obstruction from the judges.[66] It speaks for the moral integrity of the British jurists that for them such an attitude on the part of their Greek colleagues was unimaginable, but it is also a proof that they were unfitted for their task. The only solution to offer any promise of success would have been a general amnesty. Bevin's briefing meant that the British jurists could not recommend this and thus the whole of the Legal Mission's investigation was rendered useless. The Report distracted attention from the undemocratic character of Greek justice and rather served to confirm the Greek judiciary in their former habits.

Leeper's suspicions were only too well justified. The law 'on the de-congestion of the over-crowded prisons'[67] signed by Damaskinos on 21st December 1945, from which the Greek ministers hoped for a drastic reduction in the prison population, was only very conservatively applied. By 27th December, in Athens and Piraeus, only 185 detainees accused of 'moral responsibility' had been released. This provoked renewed protests from the Left who again complained of the inadequacy of the measures. On the 27th, the former members of PEEA issued a joint statement to the effect that it was they—and not the detainees—who bore the responsibility for any use of force during the Occupation; the latter had merely acted under their orders; either they themselves should be arrested as those really responsible and be brought to trial, or a general amnesty should be issued.[68] This statement, however, was ignored by the judiciary. There was no sense in arresting the PEEA leadership since this could have produced protests abroad. The purpose was to strike at the following of the Left and thus separate the rank-and-file from the leadership. By 5th

January 1946 the number of releases had risen to 503. By the middle of January about 10 per cent (1,700) of the detainees had been released.

Dilatory as the Greek judiciary was in taking measures to release the detained EAM members, it was just as tardy in bringing collaborators to justice. The release of the Poulos Battalionists had created such a scandal that the courts felt themselves obliged to issue arrest warrants for them. But this was done only at the beginning of January 1946 which gave the wanted men time to disappear[69] and thus the arrest warrants proved ineffective. On 23rd December the Third Collaboration Court acquitted the second-in-command of the notorious Tripolis Security Battalion (Papadongonas), Lt.-Colonel K. Kostopoulos.[70] After all, he had fought against the communists and, according to his own testimony, had killed several hundred of them.

By 1st February, the figure for releases had risen to approximately 3,000. On the 9th, in a conversation with Foreign Minister Rendis, Bevin pressed for a further speeding up of the releases. He hoped that, before the elections, the number of political detainees could be reduced to 2,000-3,000. Rendis doubted that this would be possible and gave 5,000 as a more probable figure. There were recurring cases in which the judges and prosecutors did not apply current legislation correctly or in the spirit in which it was intended. He would, however, send a telegram to the Justice Minister and advise him to speed up the procedure.[71]

But in Athens officialdom did not act with undue haste and by mid-March only another 500 had been released. For this period the British Police Mission produced the following statistics for the prison population:[72]

19th December 1945	19,000
1st January 1946	17,000
1st February 1946	15,000
1st March 1946	14,500

Up to the election date, approximately 3,800 detainees had been released and by mid-April this figure had risen to 4,800, so that there were still more than 14,000 detained. This figure was to remain for many years the minimum level of the Greek prison population. The advent of the Populists to power would unleash a new wave of arrests which put all previous round-ups in the shade.[73]

If one compares the attitude of Greek ministers and the British authorities to the amnesty question with their attitude to democratisation of the army and gendarmerie, one notices fundamental differences. On the army and gendarmerie question it had come to open conflict between the British and the Greeks and, on the Greek side, several ministers had resolutely committed themselves. On the amnesty question the British had been extremely restrained and, with the exception of Sofianopoulos, no Greek minister had taken a strong stand for a comprehensive amnesty.

This difference in attitudes raises a question, the answer to which must be sought in the social cohesion of the Sofoulis government. With the exception of the 'left-winger' Sofianopoulos and the emotional socialist Kazantzakis, the Sofoulis Cabinet consisted of liberal republicans of various shades. The conservatives grouped around Sofoulis, the left-Liberals around Kartalis. Their aim was the estalishment of a Liberal—but in no sense a left-wing—republic. Thus, in the disagreement about the armed forces, they were not concerned with democratisation in any wide sense, for example by re-integrating former ELAS officers, but simply with changing the balance in the leadership of the time to their own advantage. In their view at least, the disagreement was a revival of the old feud of the 20s and 30s between Venizelists and royalists. In this they overlooked the qualitative change which had taken place in the intervening years: the disagreement was no longer about whether royalists or republicans should control the army and the gendarmerie but about whether these forces should come under the control of the extreme Right, with its pro-fascist and totalitarian tendencies. However, one cannot absolutely equate the extreme Right with the Populists. The British, too, had not recognised this problem. It was their policy to make the armed forces effective, politically neutral—and anti-communist. Their rejection of Manetas' measures sprang from exactly the same motivation as his, though with opposite goals. They wanted to prevent the army and gendarmerie from becoming involved again in traditional party conflict and thus, without noticing it, they promoted the Right. By blocking Manetas' measures, they did in fact prevent the continuation of the party-political quarrel within the bourgeois camp about control of the armed forces; but at the same time they initiated the process which would make the armed forces autonomous.

The class character of the Sofoulis government became most clearly apparent over the amnesty question. Only the 'left-winger' Sofianopoulos really pressed for a comprehensive amnesty. For the rest of the ministers —even for the former members of the bourgeois (so-called 'Golden') Resistance[74]—this did not come into consideration. By reason of their liberal attitudes and for practical reasons, Sofoulis and his colleagues wanted to correct certain erroneous trends and all too crass anomalies which they had discovered, but they were too much influenced by their class solidarity to pursue a fundamentally different policy, a policy of reconciliation. On the other hand, the British—by reason of their anti-communism—were likewise not prepared to insist on a general amnesty, which they could well have done. But their 'reserved' attitude in this matter undermined the real aim of British policy at that time which was to create an effective political Centre. A Centre policy could only prove effective if Greece's basic problem, the people's fear of the future, could be overcome and the forces of moderation be strengthened again. One of the pre-conditions for this would have been a restoration of confidence in justice and it was just at this point that the British failed. Thus the problem of British policy at this time was its lack of consistency. On the one side the British authorities intervened massively; on the other hardly at all. The result was that, instead of achieving normality, Greece moved even farther into an anomolous situation. Had British policy aimed at an electoral victory for the extreme Right—which it did not—it could not have prompted this more effectively than it did by its inconsistencies.

The Trade Unions

Since mid-September 1945, chaos had reigned in the trade union leadership. Labour Minister Zakkas' attempts to intervene were disrupted by the government crisis in October. By 22nd October, the situation was again calm enough for Zakkas to go into action. He now promulgated the law which extended the time limit for government intervention in trade union affairs by another fourteen days and which also provided for supervision of the elections by magistrates.[75] On the basis of this law, on 23rd October, he issued a decree appointing the new provisional GCL Executive.[76] According to Zakkas' plan of early October, the Secretariat would consist of the leaders of the four groups, each functioning as General-Secretary for four weeks. These four Secretaries, together with eleven elected representatives of the Athens and Piraeus Trades Council, would constitute the provisional GCL Executive. The eleven would be elected at a meeting of all legally-elected members of the Executives of individual unions belonging to the Athens and Piraeus Trades Councils and this meeting would itself be chaired by a magistrate. Each group would submit a list of thirteen names. The electors would vote for the list of their choice with the right to delete three names. No group could elect more than five members and each would be able to elect at least one, provided that it had obtained a basic one hundred votes. The provisional Executives of Trades Councils, the Federations and the individual unions, as also the electoral control commissions, would be re-organised accordingly and fresh elections would be held within fifty days in all cases where the validity of the previous elections were challenged. Once these elections were concluded, the Panhellenic Trade Union Congress should be called by 18th March 1946 at the latest.[77] In other words, the government decree represented fairly accurately Zakkas' original plan, except that the measures unambiguously directed against ERGAS had been omitted. Despite this, Zakkas hoped that it would serve to restrain ERGAS' influence.

On 26th October the Secretariat met for its first session. Stratis was elected General-Secretary. On the same day the Labour Ministry ordained that Greece should be represented at the International Labour Conference by the four Secretaries with the addition of Mastroyannakos (ERGAS),

Kritsas (Kalomoiris group) and Theopoulos (Makris group). As five of these belonged to EEAM, Makris raised furious objections: the Minister's ordinance was undemocratic and anti-trade union. Makris intended to go to Paris himself and there to denounce the government's intervention. He demanded that his faction be represented in the same strength as the 'communist bloc'. When this was denied him he decided to stay in Athens. A further action of the GCL Secretariat redoubled his anger. At the end of October Kalomoiris, Stratis and Theos decided that the provisional Executives of the main provincial Trades Councils should be reconstructed as soon as possible according to the following system of distribution: four representatives of ERGAS and two each of Kalomoiris, Stratis and Makris. Makris who, in this way, would have lost all influence, rejected this and thereafter boycotted the Secretariat.[78]

On 1st November the GCL delegation left for Paris, having nominated Kouzentzis (Kalomoiris), Laskaris (Stratis) and Nefeloudis (Theos) to replace them during their absence. Laskaris became the acting General-Secretary. In accordance with the decree and with the Secretariat's decision, the acting Secretariat began to reconstruct the union Executives.

On the basis of the above distribution system, they nominated a similar Executive for the Athens Trades Council. As Makris refused all co-operation, two seats were left vacant for his group. The Labour Ministry approved the eight nominations but took no steps to make available the office still kept closed by the police, so that the newly-nominated Executive had to take it over on its own initiative. In Piraeus there were still the two rival Executives and the Trades Council remained closed. Morever, since an objection had been entered against the legality of the August elections, the Secretariat left things for the moment as they were. When, at the beginning of December, the court invalidated the August election results, a new provisional Executive was nominated in accordance with the distribution system. In Patras the acting Secretariat succeeded in nominating a new eight-member Executive, but the previous Executive, on which the Makris group held the majority, refused to resign in which it had the support of the prefect of Patras. By mid-December nothing had changed, although the new Labour Minister, Manousis, twice telegraphed the prefect, telling him to respect the GCL Secretariat's decision. In Salonica an Executive comprising all four groups had been established in September but, since all Salonica unions belonged *de facto* to ERGAS, the provisional Executive dissolved itself. The Secretariat now tried to install a new Executive which, according to the distribution formula, would represent all trends. Likewise in Volos all attempts at change had failed because, there too, the ERGAS leadership had mass grassroots support. Nevertheless, the Secretariat instructed the Trades Council Executive to reconstitute itself on the basis of the distribution formula. In many smaller provincial towns, however, the Executives could not be reconstituted because the local Trades Councils' offices were in the hands of the police.[79]

Meanwhile, in Paris, the GCL delegation had succeeded in winning support from the WFTU (World Federation of Trade Unions). The General-Secretary of the WFTU, Louis Saillant, agreed to be present at the delegate meeting which would elect the eleven members of the new provisional GCL Executive. On 2nd December, Saillant arrived in Athens accompanied by Victor Feather representing the TUC and A. Verret (in charge of the General-Secretariat office). But no preparations had been made for the delegate meeting because the Labour Ministry was not functioning owing to the change of government and thus could not send a representative. For this reason Saillant summoned Theos, Stratis, Kalomoiris and Makris to a conference and, within the space of a few hours, succeeded in getting an agreement obliging them.

'1. to accept and respect the results of the elections undertaken in order to reconstruct the unity of the Greek Confederation of Labour;
2. to reconstitute each one of the organisations constituting the Greek General Confederation of Labour on the basis of a democratic regime ensuring free representation, free discussion, freely agreed discipline, and the responsibility of the leaders of the trade union movement to their meetings and congresses;
3. to work for the adoption, at a national congress of the Greek trade unions, to be organised on 1 March 1946 by the leaders chosen at the forthcoming elections, of the rules of the Greek General Confederation of Labour, in accordance with the main, fundamental trade union principles contained in the Charter of the WFTU;
4. as an immediate measure, to withdraw without delay any protest which might have been formulated against the provisions of Decision No. 24,792 of the Greek Ministry of Labour in order to make it possible to appoint the leaders of the Greek General Confederation of Labour; and
5. to undertake to submit to the decisions of a delegation consisting of four representatives of the WFTU, whose duty it would be to consider and settle any detailed protest which might exist concerning individual elections for certain local trade unions.'[80]

Directly Saillant departed, preparations for the delegate meeting began. A control commission was set up, consisting of a magistrate, three Labour Ministry officials and a representative of each of the four trade union trends. The four trends drew up their lists of candidates and even Makris told his followers to participate in the meeting and to vote. As the proposed date (16th December) fell beyond the time limit ordained by Decision 24,792, the goverment promulgated a new law on 8th December[81] extending the time limit by a further fifteen days and confirming again the Labour Minister's right to appoint a new GCL leadership based on the elections. He had the additional right to issue instructions prescribing how these elections and the ensuing distribution of seats should be conducted; finally the control commission would be in *quorum* provided the presiding magistrate and five of the other members were present and, in case of parity, the chairman would have the casting vote.

The control commission decided that only delegates from Athens and Piraeus should take part in the elections since provincial elections could not be exempt from question. Even for Athens and Piraeus only those unions would be admitted at whose elections a magistrate had been present. The result was that out of 260 Athens unions only 177 were admitted and out of 140 Piraeus unions only 90. It was further decided that all members of properly elected trade union Executives in Athens and Piraeus were entitled to vote, a system which gave undue voting power to small unions with large committees, mainly non-ERGAS unions and especially those of Makris. Makris was nevertheless dissatisfied and maintained that the commission's decision was incorrect and that in Athens and Piraeus only fifty union elections had been properly conducted.

Of the 2,860 entitled to vote, 2,146 presented themselves on 16th December. The meeting was well-organised and the voting was impeccable. The counting too, on 18th December, was correctly conducted. The results were astounding. ERGAS had 1,531 votes, Makris 456, Stratis 105 and Kalomoiris 54. In conformity with Decision 24,792[82] seat distribution was as follows: ERGAS five, Makris three, Stratis one, Kalomoiris none. The ERGAS representatives were: S. Mastroyannakos (a non-communist from Dr Passalidis' socialist group), Ch. Machairopoulos (KKE, chairman of the Athens Trades Council), G. Dimitriou (KKE, chairman of the Piraeus Trades Council), D. Mariolis and V. Nefeloudis (the latter expelled from KKE after the Seventh Congress), Makris' group was represented by S. Stavropoulos, P. Matorikos and N. Polydoropoulos. Stratis' group elected G. Laskaris. There was to be a fresh election for the remaining two seats.[83] Since ERGAS had already achieved its maximum permitted representation, at this later election it must either refrain from voting or support the candidates of another group. This further vote was held on 21st January and ERGAS instructed its Athens voters to vote for Kalomoiris' candidates and its Piraeus voters to vote for Stratis'. With the inclusion of the four Secretaries (Kalomoiris, Makris, Stratis and Theos) the composition of the elected GCL Executive was as follows: ERGAS six, Makris four, Stratis three, Kalomoiris two.[84]

Thus the newly elected GCL Executive consisted in the majority of the same personalities who had controlled the GCL from liberation until the events of December 1944, a fact which demonstrated once more who were the true representatives of the organised Greek working class. It also showed that Kalomoiris' group was more of the type of a clientele-network and that Stratis too—who was close to ELD-SKE—had hardly any following and would have done better not to have split off from the successors of EEAM. Finally, Makris' vote should be taken as an indication of the massive intervention in his favour. The British Labour Attaché, Hill, described the two main trends as follows:

'The reformist (Makris) is definitely anti-communist and is probably backed (and subsidised) from time to time by royalist politicians, but is not a coherent political or social entity. It is the respectable residue of the Hadjidimitriou group emerged after the eclipse of the EAM-Confederation. . . ERGAS in some respects corresponds in the Trade Union world to EAM in the political world, but is more successful. It is KKE's means of trying to control the Trade Union Movement. . . It attracts support by its virile policies and leadership but most of the workers who "vote ERGAS" are in no sense Communist.'[85]

On 23rd December an effort was made to replace the provisionally reconstituted Executive of the Athens Trades Council by a properly elected one and a delegate conference had been announced for that date. Makris, who for a short time after Saillant's visit had been cooperative, now returned to the boycott line he had pursued since August and refused to participate because, according to him, the delegate conference was not representative. His reason was that the election would not be carried out on the proportional representation system. The other three groups ran on a joint ticket and, by a private agreement between the leaders, the seats were to be shared on the following basis: ERGAS seven, Stratis three, Kalomoiris three. But ERGAS went back on this. The final voting gave nine seats to ERGAS and two each to the Stratis and Kalomoiris groups.[86]

By the end of December the GCL Executive could state that in many provincial towns committees had been nominated on the prescribed 4:2:2:2 formula and in a number of others properly-conducted elections had been held producing suitable Executives.[87] Makris opposed not only the leaderships but also the holding of elections. This was particularly evident in Salonica where a provisional Executive had been formed on the accepted formula. Makris' local representative pursued the same tactics as his leader by trying to block the election. When he failed to secure the majority on the control commission, he withdrew from the local GCL branch and founded a competing organisation which hardly attracted any support. Elections were held in the individual unions in January. The local Stratis representative testified that these were fair. ERGAS won control of the majority of union Executives. On 20th February the Salonica Trades Council delegate conference assembled to elect the Trades Council's Executive. Makris' followers boycotted the conference. The result was a committee consisting mainly of communists.[88]

In Levadia the situation was much clearer. There there were fifteen trade unions totalling 1,350 members. All the unions belonged to ERGAS. In September 1945 elections had been held for the Executives of the individual unions and of the Trades Council. Here neither Stratis nor Kalomoiris, nor indeed Makris, had any followers. In Lamia the situation was the same. Of thirty-eight delegates to the Trades Council conference two belonged to the Makris group, but even these voted the ERGAS ticket. In Larisa, Kozani and Verroia likewise, ERGAS had the majority. In other words, in the provincial towns there was at that time only one trade union organisation. In view of the small membership (Lamia 1,800–2,000, Larisa 4,000, Kozani 1,500, Verria 2,300) a splintering into fractions would have been grotesque and the local trade unions were right in refusing to bring this about artificially. But this did not prevent Makris from complaining about it to the WFTU.[89]

By the end of February the elections for delegates to the Eighth Panhellenic Trade Union Congress had been concluded in almost all the individual unions and Trades Councils. The British Labour Attaché, Hill, made the following assessment:

'Makris took the view that there had been wholesale irregularities in the trade union elections which had preceded the Congress. As ERGAS had won sweeping successes and Makris could muster very few delegates, this accusation was natural. There certainly were irregularities, but it is very difficult to estimate the extent to which, if at all, ERGAS secured its lead by intimidation and corruption. It seems fair to say that in all circumstances it need not have resorted and possibly did not resort, to such expedients. After all it had very little effective opposition.'[90]

In other words, the elections of delegates to the Eighth Trade Union Congress were as correctly conducted as the existing situation would permit. In view of this it is astonishing that the ILO Report on the situation in the Greek trade unions only published a Greek Labour Ministry memorandum of August 1946 on these elections, in other words from the period after the Right came to power, which presents the case exclusively from the Makris standpoint.[91]

On 20th February, according to the agreement with Saillant, the British WFTU representative, George Bagnall, arrived in Athens.[92] The French representative, Lunet, arrived two days later. They at once started talks with the representatives of the various trade union groups and, faced with Makris' boycott threats, they declared that any group which turned its back on the Congress would be refused recognition by the WFTU. Nevertheless Bagnall and Lunet tried to avoid a final break with Makris and they succeeded in bringing the other group leaders to accept in advance a formula according to which each group would have a seat and a voice on the future Executive Committee. But this did not satisfy Makris. He stated that, despite all the irregularities in the elections, he was ready to participate in the Congress on condition it was regarded as an organisational and re-unification Congress and that the Executive which it elected would have only provisional status. The WFTU representatives and the representatives of the other groups rejected this demand. The Congress would indeed be a kind of preliminary for another Congress to be held within six months, but it must have the authority to elect a sovereign Executive with which the WFTU could deal. Makris refused, took his organisation out of the GCL and set up his own confederation, EREP (Ethniki Reformistiki Ergatiki Parataxi, National Reformist Workers' Front). At the same time he submitted a fresh complaint to the Council of State against Decision No. 24,792 which he denounced as unconstitutional,[93] despite his previous signature to the Saillant agreement. The WFTU delegation did not let this worry them (the Soviet representative Veshnikoff had arrived on 27th February) and decided that the Congress should take place even without the participation of the Makris group. Thus, on 1st March, 1,790 delegates representing 1,352 individual unions, fifty Trades Councils and eight Federations assembled in Congress. The WFTU delegation, Assistant Labour Minister Zakkas and the British Labour Attaché were all present at the opening session which was chaired by Stratis as acting General-Secretary. Makris and his followers stayed away and denounced the Congress on posters which were to be seen all over Athens: 'Down with the meeting of Bulgars, ELAS capetans and OPLA executioners which is masquerading as Eighth Panhellenic Congress of Labour.'[94]

The first days were taken up by the speeches of the various trade union leaders, all of them swearing by unity and denouncing Makris' behaviour. At the same time it became apparent that the Congress had a marked political character and that trade union matters took second place. In general, there was considerable unity between the participating groups. On 5th March there was an incident. On the first day the Congress platform had received a telegram from the Naousa Trades Council complaining that the police had prevented their delegates from travelling. The WFTU delegates addressed themselves to Zakkas asking him to regulate the matter. When, on the 5th, a further telegram arrived making the same complaint, they protested sharply to Zakkas. Bagnall reported this to the Congress, using fairly strong language. When, on the 6th, his report was published in an even stronger tone in *Rizospastis*, the British Labour Attaché felt obliged to draw Bagnall's attention to the possibly disastrous consequences of his act. Bagnall retreated and issued a *démenti* in which he considerably watered down what he had said.[95] Hill's ticking off had the further consequence that Bagnall began to distance himself from his two colleagues.

On the last day of the Congress he made a speech defending British policy.

'He then proceeded to tell the Congress bluntly that they were preventing unity in industrial field by organising trade unions according to political concepts; that if they wished to link up with the World Organisation they must cease their quarrellings amongst themselves; and that they should show more tolerance and less bigotry. They were now on trial. There had been irregularities in elections but it was now the duty of Congress to take measures against abuses. Makris should have attended Congress to air his grievances there but hope of complete unity in industrial field should not be abandoned. Energy expended in internal strife should be devoted to bread and butter questions.'[96]

Bagnall distanced himself in the same way when, on 9th March, the WFTU delegation met the press at the Athens Trades Council. Lunet and Veshnikoff explained what had happened as follows:

'Elections have been held in whole of Greece for Delegates to Congress. In general those elections indicated spirit of majority of Greek workers. There were of course, very small irregularities but these could not bring validity of elections for delegates into question. We have discovered a few interferences which I and Veshnikoff characterised as terrorist. For example ousting of trade union executives. Bagnall is of opinion word "terrorism" is rather a forceful term. In his opinion what we call "terrorism" would be more aptly described as police interference with law. From what has been confirmed up to date however there did exist interferences which obstructed free practice of trade union regulations.'[97]

Bagnall's behaviour began more and more to resemble that of Citrine.

During the second half of the Congress the delegates turned their attention to actual trade union affairs. They nodded through certain additions to the GCL constitution which the newly elected Executive was going to submit to the Athens Appeal Court for approval. This was done and on 7th May 1946 the Court approved the changes.[98] In addition, the delegates elected a new GCL Executive and other committees. The new Executive was as follows: D. Paparigas, G. Dimitriou, S. Mastroyannakos, K. Theos, N. Arabatsis, D. Stratis and I. Kalomoiris.[99] The communist Paparigas became General-Secretary. Two places were kept for the Makris group. On 8th March the WFTU delegation held a press conference and issued a statement to the effect that they had attended the Congress and sat with its *praesidium* as official representatives of the WFTU and could state that:

'The composition and conduct of the Eighth Congress of the Greek General Confederation of Labour, held at Athens from 1 to 7 March have been entirely in accordance with the laws in force and with the rules of the Greek General Confederation of Labour, and according to its directives given by the World Federation of Trade Unions.

'Consequently, the decisions of this Congress were such as to express the will of the working class in Greece, and the Executive of the Greek Confederation of Labour elected by the Congress is considered to be the only legal Executive.'[100]

The WFTU delegation observed:

'We have noticed failure of Makris' party to participate. We realise that real reason for this was he had no influence over working class masses. We noted absolute regularity of Congress. We were moved by admiration when we saw that delegates had come from everywhere in many instances with great difficulty and without money. Many were eating only once a day. The principle aims of the Congress were that unity of trade union movement may be realised and then organised, that an orientation and method of work should be given to general confederation that democratic election should be held for executives of Supreme Trade Union Organisation with sovereign rights and that new C.O. *[sic]* should be prepared. We think all these aims were achieved. We think up to time when this Congress took place stability and democracy did not exist. We are also of opinion Government handling of trade union movement was not successful. We consider that now that the movement is regularised it will become independent of State interference. Congress unanimously voted in favour of joining World Federation of Trade Unions. This gives Greek trade union movement rights and puts it under obligations. It also means that the various parties in confederation will no longer exist.'[101]

On 10th March there was a mass demonstration in the Athens football stadium, called by EAM, at which the results of the Congress were to be made known. Well over 100,000 (according to *Rizospastis* of 12th March up to 400,000) took part. After introductory speeches by the GCL leaders, the WFTU delegates spoke. Whilst Lunet and Veshnikoff restricted themselves to commonplaces, Bagnall revealed a paternalistic attitude: yelling slogans was not enough; now was the time for unremitting hard work. When he began to speak of British policy, the crowd reacted with such irritation that he had to break off his speech. At the end the demonstrators passed a resolution, demanding wage rises in proportion to the enormously increased cost of living, increase of pensions, laws for the protection of labour, equal pay for women, repeal of illiberal laws and the speeding up of reconstruction. Since this could only be achieved under democracy, it was the workers' task to fight for trade union freedom, the purging of fascist elements from the state apparatus, national independence and the conditions for free elections. This meant political equality, dissolution of the armed bands and a general amnesty.[102]

Thus the trade union situation had at last been stabilised. The GCL had a new elected Executive on which the communists were indeed strongly represented but without a majority. Makris had counted himself out with the result that many of his followers went over to ERGAS. ERGAS itself was not a communist organisation, more a kind of coalition of the various left-wing trade union trends, as Mastroyannakos expressed it. According to Kalomoiris less than 25 per cent of ERGAS members were communists.[103] ERGAS was, indeed, a creation of KKE, but not its creature. The Labour Minister, too, had taken into account the new situation and promulgated a law which considerably restricted the influence of execugive and judiciary on internal developments within the GCL. The GCL would now go through a period of consolidation which would finally be stabilised at the Ninth Congress. Thus, in this sector at least, KKE's efforts to achieve integration were apparently crowned with success.

But appearances were deceptive. Makris had by no means given up his struggle for control of the GCL. The day after the Congress closed, he submitted a further complaint to the Council of State, demanding annulment of the decisions and elections of the Eighth Congress. His chess move in appealing to the Council of State proved extremely adroit. Had he intended to challenge elections to the Congress, he would have had to do this before an ordinary court and the burden of proof would have been on him, that is he would have had to show in which trade unions the elections had not been properly conducted. This would have been difficult, the case would have dragged out over a long period of time and the outcome would have been very doubtful. Therefore he challenged the Labour Ministry's laws and instructions of 23rd October and 28th December as in breach of Article 11 of the Constitution, alleging that the Ministry had over-extended its legislative competence which it had also misused. If the Council of State condemned the Ministry's action then the elections would be automatically invalidated and the new GCL leadership would be illegal.[104] Makris also knew that the political attitude of the Council of State was such that it would more probably decide for him than would a subordinate court which would be more subject to pressure from the Ministry. Finally, in order to ensure his bid for power politically, Makris presented himself as a candidate for the Populists at the forthcoming elections.

Makris' calculations proved sound: when power passed to the Populists, the Council of State accepted his appeal and thus the GCL was thrown back to the situation in which the Citrine Agreement had left it.[105] But the Council of State's ruling provoked strong reactions in TUC circles. The 1945 TUC Congress had passed a resolution expressing the profound concern of the delegates at the renewed state intervention in the internal affairs of the GCL and had instructed the General Council to send a deputation to the British Secretary of State for Foreign Affairs, to submit the TUC's views on this subject.[106] From the records of the 1946 Congress we see that the General Council presented itself three times to Bevin.[107] Though, at the first meeting on 30th October 1945, Bevin had promised to convey the misgivings of the Congress to the Greek government and 'to inform them of the great concern felt within the British Trade Union Movement at the reported development of the position in Greece',[108] he apparently did nothing. Quite the contrary: when, at the ILO Conference in Montreal in September–October 1946, Makris' representatives presented themselves as the true representatives of the GCL, the chief British government delegate 'actually voted for the retention of the bogus Greek delegates' against all the efforts of the TUC delegate (Sir Joseph Hallsworth) to prevent their recognition.[109] The speaker (A.F. Papworth) then referred to a declaration of the WFTU Executive Bureau of September 1946 which was very outspoken in its condemnation of the trade union situation in Greece and he continued:

'The General Council have no wish or desire to embarrass the Labour Government. We have taken notice of Mr. Bevin's intimation to the deputation from the General Council that he is doing everything he can to aid the Trade Union Movement to help to create a stabilised position, but at the same time we would wish Mr. Bevin never to give cause for suspicion. . . When Mr. Bevin describes the Greek trade union affairs as far from satisfactory even before the decision of the Council of State was known the General Council were reminded that, unsatisfactory as they were, at least, by the joint efforts of the Council of the TUC and the WFTU for the first time in twelve years the general executive of the workers of Greece had been elected—I say "elected", mark you, not appointed. That surely was an improvement on anything there had been in Greece for the last twelve years. . .'[110]

Renewed pressure from the TUC induced Bevin to take some action later in 1946 but by then it was too late.[111] Makris and his right-wing friends were firmly entrenched for many years to come. The Declaration of the Executive Bureau of the World Federation of Trade Unions, Washington, September, 1946, amply demonstrates the lost opportunities.

'The Executive Bureau. . . holds the opinion that trade union liberties have been seriously infringed and that the Greek Federation of Labour is prevented from functioning democratically. The Executive Bureau condemns the action of the reactionary government of Greece in suppressing the democratic liberties of the workers freely to exercise their trade union rights. The WFTU Executive Bureau has decided:

1. That the Bureau of the Greek Federation of Labour elected March 1, 1946 is the only representative body of the country's trade unions. No other bureau or committee can have the confidence of the World Trade Union Movement.
2. To demand of the Greek Government that trade union liberties be restored in Greece and in particular that a new Trade Union Congress be held, with the aim of restoring the democratic functioning of trade unions, on the basis of proportional representation of all trade union tendencies and opinions, excluding none.
3. That the Bureau elected March 1, 1946 be authorised to convene this new Congress. One position on the Bureau, which shall act as

the organiser of the Congress, shall be reserved for the National Reformed Trade Union Movement if this Movement wishes to associate itself in the calling of the Congress.
4. To take all the necessary steps to ensure that Greek workers have the right to organise freely in trade unions and trade union federations...'[112]

Greek economic development up to spring 1946
Before turning to the elections and to the closely-related problem of the maintenance of law and order, we must first take a look at Greece's further economic development since this was a contributory factor in determining the general political climate and, thus, the election result.

On 21st and 22nd November McNeil and Tsouderos, Mylonas and Kartalis had agreed in rough outline on an economic programme.[113] On the 26th Tsouderos and Kartalis had talks with leading industrialists at which the latter undertook to step up production. On the 27th Tsouderos expressed the hope that he would succeed in bringing down the price of the black market sovereign to 40,000 *drachmas* but after this a readjustment of the official exchange rate would be necessary.[114] On the 29th Mylonas told Hill that the *drachma* would have to be devalued but that it was not clear whether balancing the budget or stabilising prices should have priority. A rise in taxation was out of the question as this would put too great a strain on the Greek economy.[115] What this demonstrated was that, while ministers were trying to do something, they were simultaneously trying to work out what could be done. On the 29th this process of clarification reached its conclusion.

On that day Tsouderos sent similar letters to Leeper and MacVeagh in which he noted that the exchange rate of the *drachma* to the sovereign was still rising (65,000 on 28th November). If this continued it could lead to serious difficulties. One method of preventing this would be a public statement by the Allies that they would support Greek exports by loans. This must be independent of the reconstruction materials promised by McNeil. Without some such assurance the Greek government's reconstruction programme would be endangered by a further speed-up of inflation. Only if he could include this assurance and other concrete measures in the announcement of his reconstruction programme and only if this could happen soon, would the psychological climate change and the population take heart again. As accompanying measures he suggested the following: Great Britain should put at the Greek government's free disposal the sterling equivalent of the advance *drachma* payments accruing from the costs of the British armed forces stationed in Greece (up to now they had been reckoned against Greek debts from the wartime period). The Allies should make an advance on future reparations from Germany and Italy. For this purpose Greece should receive some of the gold which the Allies had confiscated in Germany. In other words, just like the previous Kanellopoulos government, Tsouderos was trying to raise Allied loans because he had come to the conclusion that this was the essential pre-condition for an improvement in the situation.

Leeper's reaction was typical: Tsouderos' letter would make a bad impression in London as it did not include any suggestions for action on the part of the Greek government. MacVeagh, on the other hand, encouraged Tsouderos to make his ideas known to the State Department through the Greek ambassador in Washington.[116]

On 2nd December Tsouderos protested against Leeper's criticism. His suggestions were in complete conformity with the programme agreed with McNeil. But the reconstruction programme would misfire unless it was accompanied by an announcement of Allied support. He had drafted laws to strengthen the government's control over banks and industry and to restrict the traffic in gold. For the moment, until the experts arrived, stabilisation of prices and wages had priority over the budget.[117]

In London, after McNeil's return, a start had been made with assembling the commission of experts. When Tsouderos' letter of the 29th November arrived, Bevin took this as a pretext to address himself to the Americans. In a memorandum of 3rd December he suggested to the US that they participate in the advisory mission, which would have no executive powers but a purely consultative function.[118] In a further memorandum of 5th December, the Foreign Office took up a position on Tsouderos' letter: its opinion was that foreign loans were not of immediate use to Greece but discussion in the Greek press had taken on such proportions that most Greeks believed that a loan was the *sine qua non* for reconstruction.

> 'An early announcement that Greece will be granted a foreign loan might therefore contribute to the restoration of confidence provided that it were coupled with strong measures on the part of the Greek Government. His Majesty's Government are, however, not in a position to grant a loan...'[119]

Tsouderos' suggestions were impracticable; but, since it was necessary to restore confidence in the future in Greece, the Foreign Office suggested that the US and Great Britain issue a joint statement. A suggested text for such a statement was attached to the memorandum, expressing the following train of thought. During the last nine months Greece had received UNRRA supplies to the value of 300 million dollars. This far exceeded its imports for a corresponding period before the war and was amply sufficient to get reconstruction going. Moreover, the Greek government had adequate currency reserves. UNRRA aid was the practical proof that the Allies were supporting Greece. It was now for the Greeks to support this aid by their own measures. The US and Great Britain were, however, prepared to give favourable consideration to the problem of how the necessary goods could continue to reach Greece once UNRRA had ceased to function. This held good, too, for the assistance programmes which were outside the UNRRA framework. Greece was therefore in an exceptionally favourable position.[120]

The State Department reacted with marked reserve to both suggestions—participation in the commission of experts and the loan—since already on 1st December MacVeagh had warned them against participating: the British were still flirting with the idea of direct control of Greek administration.[121] On 7th December the Greek ambassador handed Tsouderos' letter to Under-Secretary of State Acheson and pressed for a prompt decision.[122] But the State Department remained dilatory.

Meanwhile, in Athens, the government had promulgated two stringent laws (on the 5th and 7th respectively) intended to control credits and the gold and currency market. Both laws proved unavailing—it could hardly have been otherwise. By 7th December the budget deficit had risen to 47.4 billion *drachmas*, in other words a further 9.5 billion within one week. Banknotes in circulation on that date totalled 80.5 billion. The sovereign appeared stabilised at 70,000 *drachmas* and the cost-of-living index fluctuated at around 4,950 (from 100 in October 1940).[123] From then until mid-December, however, the situation deteriorated rapidly. By the 14th the budget deficit was 52.8 billion; banknote circulation had risen to 84.5 billion and the value of the sovereign to 95,000 *drachmas* —though it fell back again on the 15th to 91,000 *drachmas*—and this despite the fact that since 1st December the Bank of Greece had secretly begun selling 20,000 sovereigns in order to bring down the price. By the 15th December the cost-of-living index had risen to 6,060.[124]

On the 13th the advance guard of the British Economic Mission, the transport and supply expert Sir Vivian Board, and the financial expert, Edward Grove, arrived in Athens. Mylonas presented them with a memorandum on the situation in which he more or less suggested that Greece would have to declare bankruptcy if there were no help from abroad: he was indeed trying to bridge the budget deficit, but inflation and the ensuing rise in state expenditure kept widening the gap. To MacVeagh he made it clear that, if something did not happen quickly, it would come to a serious political crisis. The speculation in gold was a sign of lack of public confidence. This could only be restored by psychological expedients and these were the pre-condition for all further steps leading to stability. Then Mylonas repeated Tsouderos' requests of 30th November that, if there were no gold available, dollars should be placed at the Greek government's disposal. MacVeagh urgently recommended to the State Department that, if nothing else could be done, they should at least announce immediately that the 25 million dollar Export–Import Bank loan was ready. A statement by the US government that it would support Greece until her difficulties had been overcome would be extremely useful.[125]

MacVeagh regarded the situation as so serious that, on 15th December, he drew up a long memorandum and sent it to the State Department. In this memorandum his analysis was as follows. The opinion—put forward by the British—that the Greeks had not made proper use of the extensive UNRRA assistance was incorrect. The UNRRA relief supplies had in fact only filled the gap between what was available and the minimum necessities for life. War damage, the losses through the civil war and, above all, an almost unprecedented drought in summer 1945[126] had reduced agricultural production by more than a half of its pre-war productivity. Until summer 1945 UNRRA had done nothing to stimulate Greek industry and thereafter little had been accomplished. In the face of these facts it would be very unfair to expect any improvement before the 1946 harvest. UNRRA aid would be necessary for survival and now there was talk of this aid running out at the end of 1946. There had been signs that agricultural production would do better in 1946, however industrial reconstruction was proceeding very slowly. But that was not the fault of the Greeks.

'With the best will in the world Greece cannot expect to bring total agricultural and industrial production back to pre-war levels in less than three or four years, not to mention the difficulties of replacing the country's merchant marine and reviving its tourist traffic and export trade, all of which are essential to restore the balance of payments. How are imports of food and other absolute necessities to be paid for during the interim period after UNRRA leaves? To the Greek mind there is only one answer: foreign financial assistance.'

Greeks were completely obsessed with fear of the future.

'Therefore, it is scarcely to be wondered at if they are hesitant to take a long-term view utilizing what liquid capital remains to them in efforts to expand production. A small bag of gold, jewelry, or foreign currency, held in readiness for sudden flight, would be worth far more than a large factory under conditions which many Greeks and others regard as by no means unlikely. The Greek also realizes that the traditional safeguards of military alliances or pacts of mutual assistance are of doubtful value, even in the improbable event that the United States and Great Britain would extend such guarantees under present circumstances.'

For the Greeks the security guaranteed by the UN was not enough; they wanted substantial proof of these guarantees and direct financial support would be such a proof. UNRRA aid did not imply direct political support.

'Its contribution towards Freedom from Fear is no way comparable to that of direct loans, investments or the extension of commercial credits by the United States and Britain, which would be taken as the best evidence of intention to support the Government in power and to preserve Greece as a sovereign state based upon a free society.'

Here the psychological factor would be decisive, as had been shown by the efforts of Varvaressos and Kasimatis. The British demands for a balanced budget, nationalisation, etc. were non-starters in the presence of this all-pervasive fear.

From 1941 to 1947 Greece would have cost the US approximately 400 million dollars in Lend-Lease, UNRRA and private assistance. The greater part of this would have been absorbed by relief programmes and war expenses. But until now hardly anything had been spent on reconstruction. MacVeagh concluded:

'A comparatively few millions applied in this manner might easily have more far-reaching effects than much larger contributions through UNRRA. The proposed Export-Import Bank credit of $25 million is a step in the right direction; there remains to be found a longer term approach which, while not dissipating American money or neglecting American business interests, would advance Greece towards the attainment of all four Freedoms.'[127]

Meanwhile, the Greek government had been promulgating laws and introducing measures to get the economic crisis under control. But, just as before, these proved ineffective because they could be circumvented. On 20th December the budget deficit stood at 56.2 billion *drachmas* and the price of the sovereign had gone beyond the 100,000 *drachma* limit. This prompted the Greek government to turn again to London and Washington and to press for speedy financial help.[128] The Foreign Office told the Greek ambassador that it had to await the report of the two experts but that, otherwise, responsibility for restoring economic and financial stability lay with the Greek government. At the same time, however, it notified the British Embassy in Washington: a decision was urgently needed from the US government on the questions of a US loan to Greece and of participation in the Economic Mission; the Embassy should work for a quick reply as a matter of urgency.[129]

But Washington took its time. On 17th December the State Department told MacVeagh that on the question of experts, it would follow his suggestions; that is, it was ready to send experts but it would not participate in a Joint Mission with the British. In addition a statement was being prepared for publication directly the Export-Import Bank had taken its final decision on the 25 million dollar credit. This was held up at the moment as two newly appointed members of the Bank's board had not yet received their confirmation from the Senate.[130] On the 20th December Acheson presented the draft statement to Truman for his approval.

The text followed the British suggestions closely. Attention was drawn to the assistance already supplied by the US through ML and UNRRA and through the 25 million dollar credit. It was of course necessary that the Greek government itself should now take rigorous measures. Further

American help would to a great extent depend on the effectiveness of these measures. The US was prepared to send its own experts to Greece. The Greek government's difficulties were appreciated but it was hoped that a firm attitude would overcome these. Truman did not agree with the tone of the message and requested that it be revised.[131] This again delayed the decision.

In Athens meanwhile, the talks between the British experts and the Greek government had produced results. Grove confirmed Tsouderos' opinion that the present *drachma* could no longer be saved: the country's real currency was the sovereign. Laws and police measures against the gold market were to no avail; confidence would have to be restored. He would suggest to the Treasury in London that one million gold sovereigns out of Greece's foreign assets should be put at the disposal of the Bank of Greece. The sale of this gold would in fact introduce a new currency. Furthermore, a loan of 5 million pounds sterling should be made available to Greece for the purchase of basic materials and war debts to the value of 20 million should be remitted, whilst further relief measures should be prepared. At the same time the Greeks should be assured that, even after the ending of the UNRRA programme, the Western Allies would not let Greece starve. To respond as effectively as possible to these suggested measures, the Greek government should establish a Finance Committee which would have the sole responsibility for the revenue and expenditure of the state. On this committee a British adviser should have the key role.

Board put the view that Greece should engage experts from foreign private enterprises as advisers on prices and costs. A foreign coordinator should be called in for each branch of industry, to act as intermediary between the government and that industry under the supervision of one of the British Economic Mission officials. In all this, of course, the Greek government's face must be saved.[132] In other words, both the experts' suggestions resembled closely the ideas of Finance Minister Kasimatis, rejected in November by McNeil.

On 19th December Finance Minister Mylonas again addressed himself to MacVeagh and, in view of the further deterioration of the situation, pressed for a speedy decision. (On 19th December the sovereign had risen to 120,000 *drachmas*, to reach 140,000 on the 23rd;[133] the cost-of-living index rose to 8,973.) On 21st December Board and Grove returned to London to report. On the same day Tsouderos and Kartalis visited Leeper. They told him that, in the face of galloping inflation, the disappearance of foodstuffs from the market and the growing number of strikes, it was becoming difficult for the government to remain in office. It was absolutely necessary that they should go to London, to take part in the British government's talks with the experts. Leeper allowed himself to be convinced that this would be psychologically advantageous and telegraphed accordingly to London on the 22nd. At the same time he suggested that

Secretary of State Byrnes, who was on his return journey from the Foreign Ministers' Conference in Moscow, should be invited to make a stopover in London to participate in these talks. MacVeagh approved of this suggestion. Apparently Leeper was very worried that the threat of resignation was meant seriously.[134] Therefore he protested sharply when the Foreign Office wanted to restrict the invitation to Tsouderos.[135] London relented and Kartalis, too, was invited.

On 23rd December the British Embassy was unofficially informed of the US position.[136] The 25 million dollar credit would be approved on 2nd January. Under special circumstances further loans might be considered. Halifax's report to the Foreign Office indicates that the Embassy had also received a copy of the draft statement and had been told that the US would not participate in the Economic Mission. But there was to be no public statement until 2nd January.[137] London welcomed the US decision and undertook to make no statement before that date. It was important that the US and Great Britain should agree on their policies towards Greece. Halifax should make an effort to get a US representative sent to London for the forthcoming talks with Tsouderos and Kartalis.[138] But in Washington there had still been no official decision and the State Department authorised officials of the US embassy in London to participate as observers in the talks, but without giving them any precise instructions.[139] The US Finance Department also sent a representative with the same unofficial status.

Meanwhile in Athens the situation had deteriorated rapidly. By 29th December the price of the sovereign had risen to 180,000 *drachmas* and the cost-of-living index climbed from 8,973 on 21st December to 13,374 on the 29th. An ordinary restaurant meal cost $50, a dozen eggs $17 and a pound of cheese $11. Meat, fish and olive oil had disappeared from the market. The budget deficit had grown to 66.4 billion *drachmas*.[140]

Kartalis and Tsouderos got ready for their journey which was postponed owing to bad weather. Leeper made use of this opportunity to remind the Foreign Office again of the importance of the talks.

'These discussions, although of a financial character, are essentially political and I trust the political considerations will be given priority. I have told the two ministers concerned that you will have many home truths to say about Greeks helping themselves if we are to help them but I would ask you particularly in the course of the discussions which I hope will be brutally frank to bear in mind that a narrow financial view of Greek problems can wreck our Greek policy, whereas a wide and realistic view may bring us big results.'[141]

But in reply the Foreign Office warned Leeper that the Greeks should not expect any concrete measures. There was no intention to be pettyminded but the problems must first be examined and there must be agreement with the Americans.

'We cannot be dictated to by visiting Greek Ministers who insist on coming here before we are ready for them because they hope to take back with them an immediate cut-and-dried scheme which will get them out of all their troubles.'[142]

On the 31st Tsouderos and Kartalis flew to London accompanied by the UNRRA representative Maben and talks began on 1st January. By the 3rd they had seen Hector McNeil, Sir Orme Sargent and D.S. Laskey from the Foreign Office and also Sir David Waley, Principal Assistant-Secretary to the Treasury. On the 4th Maben held a press conference at which he stated that the situation in Greece was serious. In remote districts people were living on bread and water. In general, only between 4 or 5 per cent of the population had enough to eat, the rest were undernourished. Children fared particularly badly. The figures for tuberculosis were fifteen times higher than in Britain. Greeks were meant to get 2,100 calories daily (against 2,850 in Britain) but two-thirds of the population had to get by with 1,700; 60 per cent of foodstuffs came from UNRRA. Of the seven million Greeks, two million suffered from malaria. The economic situation was catastrophic.[143]

From the first day of the talks it became obvious that London was totally unprepared. In conversation with Sir Orme, Tsouderos and Kartalis put the following position: Greece was facing two problems: financial chaos and the problem of reconstruction. But these two problems were one and could not be approached independently. Therefore a long-term reconstruction plan was needed. Only on the basis of such a plan would it be possible to solve the financial problem (stabilisation of the currency and balancing of the budget). Previous experience had shown that every effort to solve the problems separately had failed. Sir Orme said that the Greek ministers should have patience: the whole problem was just then being analysed in the light of Grove's and Board's reports. At the same time Sir Orme advised Bevin to suggest to the Greeks that they themselves bore the main responsibility and that any British aid programme could cover at the most two years; after that they would have to stand on their own feet.[144]

On 2nd January Tsouderos and Kartalis delivered their ideas in the form of a memorandum to the Foreign Office and to the US Embassy in London. They emphasised that the reconstruction programme must have priority over the currency stabilisation programme. (The British were of the contrary opinion.) But such a reconstruction programme exceeded Greece's financial possibilities. As the hope of financial gains from German reparations had come to nothing, the only remaining chance was foreign loans since increased taxation would call increased productivity into question. Financial assistance was the essential pre-condition for currency stabilisation and for reconstructing industry and would also have a psychologically stabilising influence on the Greek population. In order to get this help, Greece was ready to put her economy under foreign control.[145] The creation of a currency commission was under consideration.

The talks dragged out over the next few days. The Greeks held to their demand for long-term financial assistance, which the British continued to reject. All they were prepared to do was to participate in the currency commission and provide five million pounds sterling for stabilisstion. The Americans, too, reacted with marked reserve. They were ready to send experts for this commission but categorically rejected any ensuing responsibility on the part of the US. Financial participation in currency stabilisation was turned down out of hand; for the present the 25 million dollar loan from the Export–Import Bank must suffice.[146]

In Athens Leeper and MacVeagh had followed the London talks with growing anxiety. By 10th January the budget deficit had risen to 75.2 billion; on the other hand the cost-of-living index had remained relatively stable at 18,498. The sale of gold by the Bank of Greece had knocked the price of the sovereign back to 170,000 *drachmas* but gold reserves would soon be exhausted. Public attention was fixed on the London negotiations which were being followed with great expectation and excitement. In this situation it was not surprising that, when the 25 million dollar loan was finally announced, this had hardly any impact. It had been too much discussed in advance[147] and Greek public opinion had been hoping for more. At the same time there was a wave of strikes throughout the country involving the public services and almost all sectors of industry. Faced with this, MacVeagh and Leeper felt they had to act. On the 11th January they sent a joint telegram to Bevin and Byrnes, the latter being just then in London for the UN session.

They declared themselves seriously worried by the state of the London talks. The Greek problem was not a financial problem which could be solved by orthodox financial measures: it was a political problem.

'Under such conditions it is our firm and considered opinion which is supported by the advisers of both Embassies that the financial and economic proposals shortly to be put forward to the Greek Ministers in London do not sufficiently meet the realities of the Greek question. We have to deal with a public in a highly nervous condition convinced that it cannot find economic recovery without long term financial aid from outside whether this is true or not (and we ourselves believe it to be true on all the evidence available to us) the belief is so widely and strongly held that it has become a fact which dictates the policy of any Greek Government. No Greek Government could survive which failed to secure satisfaction in this respect.

'Rightly or wrongly the Greeks believe that they put up a finer resistance against the enemy in 1940 than any other small country and that the magnitude of their sufferings during the war has not been understood. This sense of being insufficiently appreciated as allies is very widespread and is only aggravated by admonitions to them to do more for themselves. On the other hand it can be eradicated by a generous long term policy on the part of our two Governments.

'If we fail to deal with the Greek Problem with imagination and understanding at this moment it is our view that the present democratic government will certainly fall and probably be succeeded by a regime of the extreme right which in turn could scarcely fail to produce in due course a Communist dictatorship. We are faced with a highly inflammable situation. . . where fear for the future grips the whole public.

'We believe that our Governments have an opportunity right at this moment to give hope and encouragement to this people, to put them on their feet again and get them to work by a broad generous and statesmanlike approach, by wiping out debts which cannot and will not be paid by giving a definite guarantee that whatever material or financial assistance is in fact found to be necessary will be made available. The response to such a policy would be immediate and would produce more practical results than anything else. What Greece needs is a plan (1) which gives her the reassurance of continued economic existence after the present year; and (2) which prevents the Greek vices of extravagance and incompetence from wrecking the plan.

'The moment is extremely critical. If we permit detailed discussions to hold up broad lines of positive action we may find that the economic structure here has collapsed before we have finished the argument. We suggest therefore. . . to the British and American Secretaries of State. . . that they should lift the discussions with the Greek Ministers on to a higher plane, giving them the necessary assurances that their people will be enabled to live and that necessary financial assistance will be provided for the stabilization of the currency though guarantees of sound financial administration will be required at the same time. We suggest as time presses here that a statement incorporating these assurances should be coupled with the announcement that the dicussions in London are at an end and that any British and American experts and advisers who are to assist Greece should immediately be sent to Athens to work out details.

'We consider that this is a matter of extreme urgency and that if our advice is accepted the situation can almost certainly be saved and that relief and gratitude will give an immediate impetus to work and hope. Otherwise we feel it is our duty to warn you that Greece will not only be a source of grave political trouble for some time to come, but will also in all probability be condemned to bloodshed and famine.'[148]

Thus, MacVeagh and Leeper had accurately diagnosed the nature of the Greek problem. Had their proposals been accepted, this could really have brought about a fundamental change in the Greek situation. But the US government was not at that time prepared to grant direct financial assistance and therefore did not even condescend to acknowledge MacVeagh's suggestions.[149] London did indeed adopt some part of the proposals but was neither able nor willing to undertake long-term financial obligations. The outcome was that the London talks resulted in measures which individually were perfectly sound, but which taken together were not such as to cure the Greek troubles since they only tinkered with symptoms and did not go to the root of the disease.

The London talks dragged on. They only livened up when, on 15th January, some of the intended measures were indiscreetly leaked to the Athens press and thus one important measure, the devaluation of the *drachma* was endangered. On 20th January the negotiations had been virtually completed and the text of an agreement was formulated.

The details of the agreement were as follows: the British government would suggest to Parliament a loan of 10 million pounds sterling to Greece, to stabilise the Greek currency. This sum should be more than sufficient to cover present circulation. The present *drachma* would be withdrawn and replaced by a new currency 100 per cent covered by this loan. Further cover to the extent of 25 million pounds sterling was provided for by other measures. Cover for the currency would be deposited in a special account for the Bank of Greece at the Bank of England and invested by mutual agreement.

The British government would remit repayment of Greece's war credit of 46 million pounds sterling. Of this credit the Bank of Greece still had 19 million pounds, which would therefore remain at its disposal. This could be used as cover for the Greek currency and for purchasing goods. Great Britain would make available to Greece supplies to the value of 500,000 pounds, which would also include clothing, though there was still a shortage of this in Britain. Furthermore a number of coastal steamers would be made available to revive Greek internal shipping and to speed up the distribution of UNRRA supplies and the country's agricultural and industrial produce. The British government would sell Greece construction equipment from military (Pioneer Corps) stock at favourable prices so that this could be used for restoring land communications. An effort would be made to provide tyres and spare parts for the 4,000 lorries brought to Greece by ML and also to supply other repair materials the lack of which had up to now delayed reconstruction.

Britain would send advisers for all economic, financial and industrial matters under the leadership of General Clark; and in addition advisers would be made available to the various ministries. As regards bilateral problems of exchange, these would be regulated in such a way that Greece would not suffer any additional currency burdens in 1946. The Greeks had stressed the need for a long-term reconstruction plan (five years) and had explained that for this further foreign loans would be required. The British government did not question this need and suggested that the

Greeks should apply to the Bretton Woods Reconstruction Bank.

On its side the Greek government promised a speedy currency reform. To cover the new currency, Greece would deposit with the Bank of England 15 million pounds from the remaining war credit of 19 million, as well as the new 10 million pound loan. It would draft the necessary legislation for the currency commission, which would have the following members: the Greek Co-ordination Minister as chairman, the Finance Minister, the Governor of the Bank of Greece and one British and one American representative. With the exception of measures against the flight of capital, the new Greek currency would be subject to no restrictions. The Greek government would draw up a programme for reducing the budget deficit as soon as possible. For this it would be necessary to raise taxation and throttle expenditure. Wages would be adapted to the new currency and then kept stable. For goods in short supply a price control system would have to be established. In collaboration with UNRRA the price of UNRRA supplies would be raised and the number of those entitled to free supplies would be reduced. The Greek government would take every possible measure to stimulate industrial and agricultural production in order to raise the standard of living and also income from taxation.[150]

A first impression of this agreement suggests that the British had acted with real generosity.[151] But a closer analysis shows that Kartalis and Tsouderos were quite right in not returning at once and in waiting till they had a concrete list of what was to be supplied and a time schedule. Otherwise the agreement would have been 'hot air'.[152] In fact the Greeks had only obtained an effective credit of 4 million pounds sterling for the purchase of reconstruction materials, the coastal steamers and the Pioneer Corps materials, as the 10 million were needed for currency cover. In other words, the agreement of January 1946 in no way came up to the expectations with which Tsouderos and Kartalis had arrived in London and could not in any case produce a change in the psychological atmosphere in Greece. Moreover, the announcement of the London results coincided exactly with the Soviet attack in the UN Security Council and thus forfeited much of its effect on publication. Consequently the agreement was of little significance for Greece. After further gold sales, the price of the sovereign fell to 130,000 *drachmas* by March.[153] The cost-of-living index had also fallen, to 15,500 *drachmas* by the end of February. Despite increased income, the budget deficit rose to 98.9 billion by the end of January and banknote circulation rose from 101.8 billion on 31st December 1945 to 135.8 billion on 31st January 1946. In general therefore there was little change in the critical situation. The agreement of January 1946 decelerated Greece's economic and financial decline; but nothing changed for the people. Rather, their conditions became worse, since from 1st March UNRRA was obliged to reduce its ration of foodstuffs. The result was that one of the most important conditions for free elections—freedom from need—was non-existent. Thus the economic crisis became one of the deciding factors in Greek internal policy. The efforts of the Sofoulis government to restore the country to economic health failed because of the Americans' lack of readiness to afford Greece generous financial support (the British, on account of their own critical situation, could do little more). Had the US given the Sofoulis government in 1946 a fraction of what a year later they gave the Tsaldaris government which was controlled by the extreme Right, the course of events in Greece would certainly have developed differently. The story of how Greece came to civil war is thus also a story of missed opportunities, since the aid later so amply provided was to be used only for prosecuting this war.

Law and Order
The Sofoulis government had begun its life under favourable auspices. Towards the end of the previous Cabinet's lifetime, the Left had put forward the demand for a representative government in which it would itself participate. When the Sofoulis Cabinet was formed, it withdrew this demand and announced that it would support—or more properly tolerate—the new government. In this the Left was acting on the presupposition that the Sofoulis Cabinet would try to remedy certain ills which the new ministers had themselves criticised and promised to alter before they assumed responsibility. Basically, it was a matter of the following demands: 1) A general amnesty should be announced for all political prisoners and the former Resistance should be officially recognised (this had to wait for another thirty-seven years until summer 1982). 2) New electoral lists should be drawn up on the basis of a general population census. 3) The armed forces, the police, the judiciary and public administration should all be subjected to a purge. These were consistent with demands put forward by the Liberals themselves. If they were fulfilled, the Left was even prepared to tolerate and support unpopular measures in the economic sector which would help the country's recovery, provided that these did not fall entirely on the shoulders of the working population. The Left hoped the Sofoulis government would put an end to the White Terror and begin the return to normality.[154]

The Sofoulis Cabinet failed on the first and third counts and the Left did not restrict itself to appeals and verbal protests. In December, EAM sent a delegation to London under the leadership of Partsalidis to draw official attention to these problems. In the middle of the month this delegation told Hector McNeil that the Left had ceased to support the Sofoulis government since it had in no respect fulfilled their expectations of it. No amnesty had been issued; there were still 18,000 detainees in the prisons, over 50,000 were still sought by the police and more than

200,000 were in hiding to avoid arrest or persecution by the Right. Before they took office, the Liberals had declared that the only way to get correct electoral lists was to compile them anew. Now the government was of the opinion that the existing lists could be corrected and completed. As regards the requested purge, practically nothing had been done. Faced with this obvious failure on the part of the government, EAM had withdrawn its support and now demanded a broadly-based government in which it too would be represented. There was still time to create the conditions for free elections within the prescribed time limit and thus to open the way to a normal democratic evolution and to the country's economic reconstruction. Should McNeil's November intervention prove to have been only a superficial measure, then the present situation would continue to deteriorate still further and finally nullify all the British efforts to help Greece. Economic recovery would only be possible if political stability were first guaranteed. Partsalidis went on to refer to the two-poles-theory and gave McNeil to understand that the Left in every way respected Great Britain's position in regard to Greece. Therefore, a change in the situation would be in British interests as well.[155]

But the Foreign Office was not interested in these explanations and cold-shouldered the EAM delegation. EAM's change of attitude was seen as a tactical political manoeuvre and the demand for a re-compiling of the electoral lists was rejected unexamined on the grounds that it would take too much time.[156] Generally speaking, there was a tendency to shrug off complaints from the Left as propaganda manoeuvres to be met with counter-propaganda. Unfortunately, there were too few 'good' correspondents in Greece. 'More sympathetic' reporting was 'certainly needed'. This had been 'most strongly' impressed upon *The Times* whose editor was considering Leeper's suggestion that a 'suitable' diplomatic correspondent should visit Greece. Similar pressure was exerted on the BBC which was therefore contemplating 'moves of their overseas men' and promised 'to keep the representations' of the Foreign Office about Greece 'well in mind'. Finally, as regards misinformed members of the House of Commons, a 'rather more robust' line would be taken in answering them;[157] after all, the situation in Greece had improved substantially in recent months.

In view of the Foreign Office attitude, it cannot be wondered at that, in Athens, Leeper did nothing to encourage the Sofoulis government in its original intention of re-compiling the electoral lists, since even Windle of the AMFOGE Mission was of the opinion that they were quite satisfactory. The result was that Sofoulis contented himself with a further extension of the time limit for enrolment and with ordering a revision of the existing lists.[158] But Sofoulis' inconsistent policies did not only provoke opposition from the Left. His cautious measures for de-congesting the prisons and his transfers within the army called forth an indignant protest from the Right. Simultaneously with EAM's withdrawal of support from the government, the Right initiated a press campaign against Sofoulis, whose government was said to be unconstitutional and dictatorial, to be dissolving the state, betraying Greece to the communists, trying to postpone the elections, wrecking the army, planning to release all murderers, etc.—Damaskinos should intervene to save the state.[159] Similar cautious measures to counteract the influence of the extreme Right led the right-wing parties to close ranks. On 12th December thirteen leaders of these parties sent a joint memorandum to Damaskinos in which they repeated the gist of the press accusations and demanded that he intervene.[160] All that was remarkable about this was that the Populists, too, allied themselves publicly with these denunciations. By mid-December the attacks were gaining impetus. The Left concentrated its attack on the government on the amnesty issue and the Right

'continued to rail against any measures which they felt to menace in the slightest their carefully built up hold over the State machinery, protesting in particular at the government's measures on the retiring age of judges, officers and diplomats and against alleged intentions of the Minister of Education to purge the university...'[161]

At this point right-wing opposition became more sharply defined. Tsaldaris told Leeper the Populists had not agreed to postponement of the plebiscite till 1948 and therefore, if they won the elections, they would hold it within a few months. Only when Leeper objected would Tsaldaris concede that his party would first consult the British. At the same time he gave Leeper to understand that he would like to be on better terms with the British and that he regretted the attacks on them in the Populist press in connection with the formation of the new government. He also hinted that he thought a further change of government possible and this Leeper rejected sharply.[162] But all that did not hinder Tsaldaris from continuing his attacks on the government. On 19th December he publicly declared that the Sofoulis government was a dictatorship and that, as in 1936, Sofoulis himself had come to a secret agreement with the communists. Parallel with this, preparations were set in train for an eventual fall of the government by making contact with Venizelos.[163]

On 19th December, after long hesitation, Venizelos had taken over leadership of the Liberals from Sofoulis. Whether his disapproval of Sofoulis' policy was due to his own conservatism or to opportunism, the fact was that he tried to steer the Liberals rightwards. He summoned a general meeting of Liberals for the 10th January, to discuss the party's political line. On 29th December he had issued a statement, addressed effectively to the Populists, signalling to them that he was ready for extensive cooperation. The Populists took a favourable attitude to this and the possibility of a Venizelos–Tsaldaris government began to dawn on the horizon. This approach was facilitated by the (groundless) fear on the Right of an opening by the Sofoulis government towards the Left, provoked by the simultaneous presence in London of Tsouderos and Kartalis, Sofianopoulos (for the UN Plenary Session) and the EAM delegation. Suspicion of Sofianopoulos went so far that there was a request to Sofoulis to appoint Populist 'watch-dogs' to his entourage which Sofoulis—under pressure from Sofianopoulos—refused. The hysterical denunciations of Sofianopoulos received further nourishment when, on 28th December a telegram from Stalin replying to a New Year message from Sofianopoulos arrived in Athens, to be followed on 30th December by the new Soviet ambassador, Admiral Rodionov. Up to then only EAM had been honoured with such greetings missives.[164]

On 4th January 1946 Venizelos' Populist contacts bore fruit in an agreement: the elections should be held at the latest on 31st March and should be conducted on the majority system. They should be held by a government enjoying their complete confidence—which they themselves were prepared to form. Such a government should consist of three representatives each from the two parties who would be ministers without portfolio and of non-party experts who would hold the ministries. The two parties would cooperate in the elections and afterwards in the formation of a coalition government. On the constitutional issue each party would retain its freedom of action but under an obligation to settle the problem through a plebiscite and not through a *coup*. Other parties could adhere to this agreement.[165]

Apparently, Venizelos and Tsaldaris were acting on a secret understanding with Damaskinos.[166] In the following days they were able to bring Papandreou, Kanellopoulos and Zervas into the agreement. On 9th January 1946 Venizelos made the agreement public and at the same time sent Zervas to Leeper to get his opinion. Zervas showed Leeper the text of the agreement and explained that a broadly-based government was needed. Sofoulis would naturally remain Prime Minister. Leeper met these proposals with a sharp rejection. His efforts had always aimed at the greatest possible unity but he could not countenance a change of government at this point. Continual changes would shatter British and US confidence in Greece. If Venizelos and his allies now accepted the programme blessed by the British government in November, the implementation of which was the task of the Sofoulis government, then the only correct policy was to support this government. To form an all-party government excluding the communists would only deepen the conflict. Were such a government to be formed after the elections that would be a different matter, since it would then represent the people's will. Zervas accepted Leeper's dismissal without argument and only added that Venizelos himself would visit Leeper during the day, which however did not happen. Apparently, he had been discouraged by Zervas' report.[167]

On the evening of the same day Leeper went to see Damaskinos. He got the impression that the latter took a benevolent view of these developments, with the result that he felt obliged to give the Regent to understand that he should keep off and leave Sofoulis to clear up the matter. Damaskinos explained that the agreement would have support from many sides and also from industrial circles. He was shortly expecting Venizelos: what answer should he give him? Leeper made it crystal clear to him that he must tell Venizelos that this was not the right moment for a change of government and that the whole situation should be left to Sofoulis to sort out. Damaskinos hesitatingly complied.[168]

Leeper's total rejection brought about a tactical retreat by Papandreou the very same day. He sent Themistoklis Tsatsos to Leeper with instructions to distance himself from the agreement's demands and, simultaneously, to tell Leeper that he, Papandreou, regarded it as important to realign himself with the British viewpoint. Leeper responded without enthusiasm.[169]

Sofoulis reacted adroitly. He stated that he knew nothing of the negotiations, that Venizelos had no right to speak for the Liberals and that the agreement was unacceptable and could lead to the fall of the government. Probably to gain more space for manoeuvre, on the evening of 12th January, he expressed himself with even greater clarity in an interview with Geoffrey Hoare of the *News Chronicle*. He described the agreement as an intrigue by the Right, the only purpose of which was to exploit the people's longing for national unity in order to secure its own return to power. At the forthcoming elections there would be three blocks: the Right, the Centre and the Left. None of these would secure a majority so that, after the elections, there would have to be a coalition. As leader of the Liberals, he himself would like a coalition between the Liberals and the Left. For the moment, however, he did not intend to take any EAM members into his government as this would only strengthen the Right. 'Leaders of KKE have no brains and no policy', he said. 'If they continue to make trouble now, cooperation between us after the election will become impossible. They should tolerate my government, and enable me to hold free elections.'

Sofoulis went on to speak of the electoral lists and owned that they were not 'immaculate'; but the government would try to get them revised. He also hoped to have purged the Security forces in time for the elections. 'We faced a terrible legacy of a sinful period which lasted ten years... The period was continued by Voulgaris. It is impossible to purge the entire administration in a moment... Most of the trouble today comes from the Right... and we must do everything in our power to dissolve the 'X'ites, who are nothing more than the private army of the king. When the gendarmerie see what our attitude is I think they will change their tactics.'

Finally, Sofoulis promised a far-reaching amnesty.[170]

On Sunday, 13th January, the Right staged a mass demonstration in the Athens football stadium and announced the creation of a National Front. The speakers were: Papandreou, Kanellopoulos, Zervas, Gonatas, Venizelos, Mavromichalis and Tsaldaris. Attendance was about 40,000. The most impressive speaker was Papandreou which discomforted the Populists because in this way the National Front threatened to escape from their control.[171] On 15th January almost the entire Athens press reprinted Sofoulis' interview. The Left reacted to his offer at once: on the 16th the EAM Central Committee told EAM members to enrol on the electoral lists, though at the same time they stated that this did not necessarily mean that they would participate in the elections. This would depend on how far the government lived up to its promises to revise the lists and purge the security forces.[172] At the same time the Left called all democrats to a mass demonstration on Sunday, 20th January.

On the same day (the 16th), Sofoulis had a talk with Leeper. He said that Venizelos had no following to speak of, and that the Liberal Party would publicly repudiate him. In addition, the National Front had now split into two camps. Papandreou and Kanellopoulos were only cooperating on their own terms since the majority of Liberals had not decided in favour of the new organisation. The whole matter had been a manoeuvre by the Right in order to weaken the Centre. He was not considering a one-sided opening of his government towards the Right: until the elections it must steer a middle course.[173] Meanwhile the right-wing leadership had to acknowledge that the new organisation in practice consisted of themselves. Moreover, Papandreou had made it clear to them that an agreement with the Liberals would only be of value if it were supported by Sofoulis. To try to win the Prime Minister to their cause, a delegation consisting of Theotokis, Papandreou and Alexandris visited him on the 18th.

They demanded a statement from Sofoulis that the elections would after all be held on 31st March, that they would be held on the majority system and that the bourgeois parties would present a united list to the voters. Sofoulis pointed out to them that the relevant decree for the election date had already been signed by Damaskinos; whilst, as regards the system, no final decision had yet been taken and he was ready to discuss it again with Papandreou. As for national unity, he was himself in favour of it but not in the form suggested by the Right.[174] In other words, Sofoulis rejected the Right's demands and held to his predetermined policy. Venizelos, too, who visited him the same day, got a similar reply.

At the same time Sofoulis tried to carry out his promise to take action against right-wing excesses. Since mid-December, the country's internal security had progressively deteriorated. Up to then the Left had only occasionally offered active resistance to the White Terror and had generally restricted itself to verbal protest, thus giving the Right and its gendarmerie collaborators a free hand. The protests of the Left were not taken too seriously, either by the Greek government or by the British authorities, since the victims of the excesses were communists. Moreover, there were no official reports of these cases—hardly surprising, since the gendarmerie were responsible for such reporting. But in December the picture began to change. Individual resistance to right-wing repression began to be replaced by collective action, the first results of KKE's self-defence (*aftoamyna*) policy, though individual violence and private vendettas continued on both sides.

There were regional differences. In North Greece, where the Left had the deepest popular roots, collective action was at its most successful. Strikes were accompanied by mass demonstrations which the gendarmerie took as provocations. Even Leeper, wrote of 'ugly clashes between the security forces and crowds sympathetic to the strikers'.[175]

However, this harder left-wing policy was not restricted to defensive action against the security forces: resistance to right-wing repression began to take the offensive. Where before there had only been small groups who had opposed the armed bands, now larger units appeared prepared for active clashes with these right-wing bands. In a considerable number of former EAM-ELAS strongholds the right-wing commune chairmen, nominated by the previous government to replace elected EAM chairmen, were forced to flee. But in general, the Left held to the *aftoamyna* concept of unarmed resistance. Use of arms against political opponents remained largely a right-wing preserve.[176]

In Central Greece conditions were less favourable. The countryside continued to be terrorised by Sourlas' armed bands.[177] The security forces had so far let him be and, for this reason, on 17th January the Minister for Public Order, Merkouris, felt obliged to go to Larisa himself to supervise the gendarmerie action against the 'wanted' bandit.[178] The towns were to a large extent controlled by 'X' whose hatred for the Left went so far that they attempted—unsuccessfully—to blow up Chalcis cathedral because the local bishop was said to sympathise with EAM.[179] At the beginning of January the Left extended its self-defence to Central Greece. On the 13th there was a public meeting just outside Volos, addressed by Zachariadis. At the end those present formed a procession, headed by a band. Shortly before they entered the town they were halted by gendarmes who demanded that the procession dissolve. The demonstrators, by now in a state of exuberance, refused and tried to disarm some of the gendarmes. Thereupon the gendarmes—in defiance of express orders—fired warning shots which provoked the crowd to fire back. There was soon a shooting battle which resulted in four dead and twenty-six wounded.[180] At the same time there were similar episodes in Lamia. In general, it could be said that in Central Greece, too, these cases were on the increase and Leeper was quite right when he reported to London that the increase was due to a harder attitude on the part of the Left. In fact, the Left was no longer ready to accept passively the right-wing and gendarmerie repression.[181]

In Athens and Piraeus there was daily friction between Left and Right, involving the police. Here the initiative was wholly with the Right which missed no opportunity to provoke the Left. In the Peloponnese the situation was even worse. EAM had never been strong there and the White Terror was all-pervasive. Local right-wingers indiscriminately persecuted any left-winger they could lay their hands on. The alleged justification was the mass executions of Security Battalionists in October 1944.[182] Political persecution overlapped with private vendettas. Often former EAM members, returning home after release from prison, were slaughtered by the local Right immediately on arrival, so that many preferred not to return at all. Murders were practically a daily occurrence. On 16th January armed men, probably of the Left, stopped a bus outside Sparta and shot a prominent local 'X' leader, his bodyguard and his six year old son. On the 18th, 'X' members in Kalamata took their revenge: they threw a handgrenade into a café frequented by the Left. Two were killed and several injured. The gendarmerie thereupon arrested a few suspects. On the 19th the dead were buried and EAM organised a demonstration which the local 'X' regarded as provocation to more highly-organised action. On the night of the 19th–20th they erected roadblocks around Kalamata in order to search the buses for communists.[183] Two days earlier, on the 17th, the KKE leader Zevgos, travelling to a meeting at Corinth, had been beaten up by 'X' members on the open road and before the eyes of the gendarmerie. The Corinth episode prompted Sofoulis to suspend the local gendarmerie commander from his post and to order an investigation.

The 20th January was marked by two contradictory events. In Athens there was a mass demonstration of the Left in the football stadium with, according to *Rizospastis,* half a million participants. The main speaker was the republican General Othonaios.[184] The meeting acclaimed a resolution demanding that the Left be included in the government. About the same time that this resolution was handed to Sofoulis, he received a letter from Grivas threatening that, if the government were unable to protect the lives of 'nationally-minded' citizens, 'X' would undertake the task itself. Sofoulis reacted decisively to this provocation and ordered the police and gendarmerie to close down the 'X' offices in Athens and in the rest of the country; at the same time he instituted legal proceedings against Grivas for threatening the government.[185]

At Kalamata, in the Peloponnese, events took their course. The 'X' units, about 1,000 strong, occupied all roads into the town the whole night through. When, by mid-day on the 20th, they had had no success with their manhunt, their leader, a certain Manganas, ordered them to march into Kalamata. At about 5 p.m. two columns armed with revolvers and machine pistols and wearing combat fatigues reached the gendarmerie station, overpowered the guard and freed thirty-two detained 'X' members. The remaining gendarmes contented themselves with holding the prison and the Public Prosecutor's office. The consequence was that in the rest of the town Manganas had a free hand. He had it combed for left-wingers and took more than eighty (according to another report one hundred and fifty) as hostages. Meanwhile the gendarmerie had managed to request reinforcements which set out at once. But Manganas did not let that worry him and continued to occupy Kalamata till mid-day on the 21st, after which he made a leisurely withdrawal. During this period, the mayor and the bishop had tried in vain to negotiate release of the hostages. Instead Manganas had the hostages herded into a village near Kalamata where, in October 1944, fifty villagers belonging to the Security Battalions had been killed by ELAS. At about 2 p.m. the head of the British Police Mission in Tripolis (Noble) and the Tripolis gendarmerie commander arrived in Kalamata. Noble's personal intervention persuaded Manganas to release his hostages, but only after fourteen people had died, shot by 'X'.[186] Martial law was declared in the provinces of Messenia and Laconia and the government put a price on Manganas' head. Sofoulis ordered the gendarmerie to arrest as many of the insurgents as possible and bring them before a court-martial. At the same time he instructed the Prosecutor-General to examine whether 'X' could not be altogether banned.[187] In talks with Papandreou and the Populists he tried to get the backing necessary to cover his rear. Whilst Papandreou agreed, the Populists rejected any such stand although Sofoulis assured them he would proceed against the left-wing para-military bands as well.[188] Sofoulis was apparently determined to take a hard line against the Right. But this readiness to act was stifled at birth by the Soviet complaint in the UN. The resulting internal querulousness so pre-occupied Sofoulis that he could no longer give priority to following up the Kalamata case. The result was that hardly any of the 'X' members who had participated in the attack on the town were arrested or sentenced. Manganas could continue in his evil ways and the gendarmerie units transferred to the Peloponnese to arrest him and his followers showed singularly little zeal so that the impression was created of a secret understanding with the insurgents.[189]

However, the Kalamata affair was of the greatest significance as it showed for the first time the extent of right-wing control over the country. So far the Right had restricted themselves to terrorising the Left. At Kalamata, for the first time, they had dared to challenge the authority of the state and the state had put up a very poor defence. And this was only the tip of the iceberg. According to a British Military Security report

(MI3) of March 1946, the strength of 'X' was as follows: in the Peloponnese 13,000 members of whom about 25 per cent belonged to armed 'X' groups; in Macedonia and Thrace (excluding Salonica) 9,000 members; in Central Greece approximately 20,000; the Athens and Piraeus 'X' units amounted to 4,000 of whom about two-thirds were armed and the Salonica units (1,000) were almost all armed. The total strength of 'X' was approximately 50,000 of whom 25,000 were armed. Grivas' figures of August 1945 giving 'X' 350,000 members must therefore be interpreted as including members of other right-wing organisations. One must also bear in mind that 'X' had successfully penetrated all the armed forces.[190] In other words, by this time the Greek Right had built up a respectable military potential which was able to compete successfully with the armed forces of the state. What was even more important was that this active arm of the *parakratos* was in a position to exert its control over large tracts of the country and thus to influence directly the forthcoming elections. In contrast to the Left, which at that time restricted itself to the unarmed *aftoamyna* resistance policy and whose few armed groups in Macedonia remained defensive, the armed right-wing bands were an ever-present and aggressive factor in the power struggle.[191] The White Terror continued to flourish.

Whilst the British Embassy had previously shown a tendency to make light of the excesses of the Right, this tendency was strengthened after the Soviet intervention. On 24th January Leeper telegraphed to London:

'As a result of Kalamata affair there may be a good deal of exaggerated talk about reign of terror in Greece. Incidentally I see no reason for the occurrence partly because there is so much more freedom here than elsewhere in the Balkans. The Communist press in spite of its open revolutionary and anti-British propaganda is quite free, the Communist leaders are able to travel about the country and make speeches, even if Zevgos got a bit man-handled the other day in Corinth, open air demonstrations have been permitted in Athens and other centres. In a mountainous and thinly populated country like Greece banditry on a certain scale is not surprising under present economic and political conditions but I imagine that banditry exists over large areas of post-war Europe. Greece is singled out by foreign press for special condemnation because foreign correspondents are free to go where they will and report what they like without any restriction. I see no valid ground for contention put forward by the Communists that State of law and order is so bad as to make early elections a farce and I suggest that our own press should be careful not to fall into this trap.'[192]

The motives behind Leeper's cynicism are transparent. This was a direct result of the Soviet intervention. Without this intervention, there would have been a chance that the Kalamata episode might have prompted a change of British policy on the issue of the *parakratos* and the White

Terror. But because the Soviets seized on just this point, it followed automatically that British policy took the opposite position and denied the existence of a White Terror. Thus the Soviet *démarche* at the UN Security Council took on decisive importance for Greece's internal evolution. Yet neither the Russians nor the British were primarily concerned with Greece.[193]

NOTES

1. See p. 127, footnote 11.
2. Leften S. Stavrianos, 'Vacuum in Greece', *New Republic*, 113, (24th December, 1945), p. 265. 'The new Government is much more representative of the Greek public opinion than its predecessors. It has the support of the centrist elements and of those slightly to the left of center. It does not include representatives of the leftist EAM, and this constitutes its greatest weakness.'
3. *The Times*, 24th November, 1945.
4. Leeper to Foreign Office 7th December, 1945 (R 21125/4/19).
5. *Ibid*.
6. General Rawlins regarded the reports on the extent and influence of 'X' and SAN as exaggerated. He believed that the majority of the senior officers were republicans because they had been appointed under Plastiras. He overlooked the fact that all of them were fanatical anti-communists and that, out of fear of the Communists, many of them had made their peace with the king. According to Rawlins about 60 per cent of the junior officers were royalists. Laskey's Minutes 30th October, 1945 (R 21142/4/19).
7. Sheppard, *Britain in Greece*, p. 14.
8. R 21125/4/19. How far British intervention in army matters extended is shown by a report from Leeper to the effect that Sofoulis intended to promulgate four laws: 'which have been worked out in detail by the previous two Governments in close collaboration with the British Military Mission. These provide for (a) the amalgamation of the Greek General Staff and the War Ministry as one department of State, and the setting up of (b) a Supreme National Defence Council, (c) a Higher Military Council similar in its functions to the British Army Council, and (d) two Selection Boards. When this has been done, retirements, promotions and appointments will be made on a regular professional basis by the competent military authorities without political or governmental interference. . .' Leeper to Foreign Office 14th December, 1945 (R 29/1/19).
9. R 21125/4/19.
10. MacVeagh (Grady) to State Department 4th December, 1945 (*FRUS 1945, VIII*, p. 185).
11. Woodhouse, *Apple of Discord*, p. 257.
12. *Ibid*.
13. Leeper to Foreign Office 21st December, 1945 (R 155/1/19).
14. Leeper to Foreign Office 29th December, 1945 (R 465/1/19); Leeper to Foreign Office 4th January, 1946 (R 466/1/19).
15. In 1935 more than 1,100 officers out of a corps of barely 5,000 were purged from the army. Grigorios Dafnis, *I Ellas metaxy dyo polemon, 1923-1940* Vol. II, (Athens: Ikaros, 1955), pp. 359 ff.
16. Leeper to Foreign Office 24th January, 1946 (R 1735/1/19).
17. Bevin to Leeper 9th February, 1946 (R 1906/1/19).
18. *Ibid*.
19. Leeper to Foreign Office 11th February, 1946 (R 2233/1/19).

20. Minutes of 22nd February 1946 (R 3491/1/19). Noel-Baker's attitude is even clearer from a letter of 25th December 1945 to Major Wilkes in which he wrote: 'In the first place. . . it is not part of the job either of the Military or of the Police Mission to secure the dismissal of Greek collaborators. Proper legal machinery has long been in existence for investigating all charges of collaboration, and it is not for the Police or the Military Mission to take action themselves. The point on which there is some risk of their coming into conflict with the Government is that of political appointments and dismissals.' (R 21444/4/19).
21. Leeper to Foreign Office 27th February, 1946 (R 3553/1/19).
22. On Spyridon Georgoulis see p. 290.
23. Leeper to Foreign Office 9th March, 1946 (R 4201/1/19).
24. *Ibid.*
25. Norton to Foreign Office 3rd April, 1946 (R 5409/1/19).
26. Lyall Wilkes, 'British Missions and Greek Quislings', p. 88.
27. *Report of the Allied Mission to observe the Greek Elections, Athens, 10th April 1946, Greece No. 3,* (London: HMSO, Cmd. 6812, 1946); from here on quoted as *AMFOGE Report.*
28. MacVeagh (Grady) to State Department 4th December, 1945 (*FRUS 1945, VIII*, pp. 185 ff).
29. *Ibid.,* p. 186.
30. Greek Embassy to State Department 6th December, 1945 (*FRUS 1945, VII,* pp. 186 ff).
31. MacVeagh (Grady) to State Department 7th December, 1945 (*FRUS 1945, VIII,* pp. 187 ff).
32. *Ibid.,* pp. 189 ff. Zervas, whose EDES organisation had started in 1941 as a liberal republican movement but had become royalist under British influence, underwent a further metamorphosis towards the Right culminating in his becoming Security Minister during the civil war. The majority of his former underground organisation joined him in this move to the right. Dissenting voices, such as that of the left-wing Liberal Komninos Pyromaglou, attracted his persecution and Pyromaglou even had to go abroad.
33. *Ibid.,* p. 190.
34. *Ibid.,* pp. 192 ff.
35. *AMFOGE Report,* pp. 4 ff.
36. Leeper to Foreign Office 26th November, 1945 (R 19943/4/19). See also p. 165.
37. *Eleftheria,* 11th December, 1945. Text translated from the French version in *La verité sur la Grèce,* p. 15. Cf. R 155/1/19.
38. *The Times,* 12th January, 1946.
39. Leeper to Foreign Office 11th December, 1945 (R 20809/4/19).
40. Leeper to Foreign Office 14th December, 1945 (R 20944/4/19).
41. *Ibid.*
42. R 155/1/19.
43. *Report of the British Legal Mission,* p. 3.
44. Foreign Office instructions to the British Legal Mission 25th November, 1945 (R 19920/4/19).
45. The author knows a former ELAS member who, during Liberation, shot a Security Battalionist who was resisting arrest by an ELAS unit. He was sentenced for murder and served twenty years in prison. In 1980 the publisher met in Greece a former ELAS man, now working as a gardener, who had served twenty-five years after a false conviction for murder on the testimony of a 'professional widow' and 'professional witnesses' who were known in all the

THE SOFOULIS GOVERNMENT 381

courts of the region.
46. See pp. 160 ff.
47. *Report of the British Legal Mission*, pp. 10 ff.
48. Anangastikos Nomos No. 119, *Efimeris tis Kyverniseos*, Law Sheet No. 31, 14th February, 1945.
49. *Report of the British Legal Mission*, pp. 11 ff.
50. *Ibid.*, p. 12.
51. *Ibid.*, p. 13.
52. *Ibid.*
53. *Ibid.*, p. 15.
54. *Ibid.*, pp. 15-8.
55. *Ibid.*, pp. 21-2.
56. *Ibid.*, p. 22.
57. R 155/1/19.
58. On this subject, Georgios Mavros made the following comment at the end of April 1946: 'The situation today is much worse than it was in November. The State machine is in the hands of the Right. Justice cannot work. Ninety per cent of the judges belong to the extreme Right. They are so fanatical that, without regard to evidence, they will always return a verdict for the Right against the Left. As regards the amnesty, three quarters of the prisoners would have been released under the de-congestion laws passed by the Sofoulis Government, if the judges had exercised their judicial functions properly. In some cases I found that twenty to thirty people had been charged for the same murder. Under the de-congestion law, if within a hundred days from December 31, 1945, people accused of murder had not been charged, they had to be released. March 31, 1946 was therefore the target date for the release. On December 21, 1945, there were 18,000 prisoners not yet charged, but only 3,400 were released under the law. Applications to the Public Prosecutor are futile because of the fanaticism of the judges.' Dodds, Solley, Tiffany, *Tragedy in Greece*, p. 49.
59. *Report of the British Legal Mission*, p. 19.
60. *Ibid.*, p. 23; Dodds, *op. cit.*, pp. 49 ff. 'The Court of Appeal would draw up a list of persons with the required property qualifications, who were legally entitled to serve on juries. Workers and peasants were specifically excluded by the new law. From the small number of persons eligible a limited list was to be drawn up for each area each year. We were told by the chairman of the Special Court of Patras, somewhat naively, that he himself had taken part in drawing up the original list and he made sure that the persons on the list were 'respectable' people, financiers, industrialists and the like.'
61. *Report of the British Legal Mission*, p. 24.
62. *Ibid.*, pp. 27-30.
63. R 155/1/19.
64. Woodhouse, *Apple of Discord*, pp. 256 ff.
65. *Report of the British Legal Mission*, pp. 26 ff., 30 ff.
66. Leeper to Foreign Office 29th December, 1945 (R 465/1/19).
67. *Efimeris tis Kyverniseos* Vol. I, Law Sheet No. 311, 21st December, 1945, pp. 1566 ff. For English translation see *Report of the British Legal Mission*, pp. 32 ff.
68. Leeper to Foreign Office 4th January, 1946 (R 466/1/19).
69. Leeper to Foreign Office 11th January, 1946 (R 868/1/19).
70. Kostopoulos appeared at his trial in army uniform, as he was once again a Greek army officer. Letter from the Labour MP Lyall Wilkes to McNeil 23rd January, 1945 (R 1335/1/19).
71. Bevin to Leeper 9th February, 1946 (R 1906/1/19).

72. Norton to Foreign Office 21st March, 1946 (R 4702/1/19). The difference between Greek and British figures shows conclusively how poorly the Greek government was informed on the activities of its subordinates.
73. See footnote 58 to this chapter.
74. The term 'Golden' Resistance describes Peltekis' group which received a massive sum in sovereigns to organise a spy-ring in Athens, thus arousing suspicion that the participants had enriched themselves. See Woodhouse, *Something Ventured,* p. 60.
75. Anangastikos Nomos No. 620, *Efimeris tis Kyverniseos* Vol. I, Law Sheet No. 256, 22nd October, 1945, p. 1307.
76. Decree No. 24,792, *Efimeris tis Kyverniseos* Vol. II, Law Sheet No. 153, 23rd October, 1945.
77. International Labour Office, *Labour Problems in Greece. Report of the Mission of the International Labour Office to Greece (October–November 1947),* (Geneva: I.L.O., 1949), p. 233.
78. General Labour Memo (Greece) No. 12 (R 20571/4/19); Leeper to Foreign Office 21st November, 1945 (R 19692/4/19).
79. Leeper to Foreign Office 18th December, 1945 (R 21126/4/19 and R 19692/4/19).
80. ILO, *Labour Problems in Greece,* p. 228. Both Makris and Theos had raised objections to Decision 24,792. For the original French text see General Labour Memo (Greece) No. 19, 9th January, 1946 (R 2262/130/19).
81. *Efimeris tis Kyverniseos* Vol. I, Law Sheet No. 296, 8th December, 1945, pp. 1498 ff.
82. See p. 346.
83. Leeper to Foreign Office 20th December, 1945 (R 21221/4/19 and R 2262/130/19).
84. Leeper to Foreign Office 25th January, 1946 (R 1394/1/19).
85. R 262/130/19.
86. *Ibid.*
87. Provisional Executives were nominated in the following towns: Almyros, Amaliada, Corinth, Drama, Edessa, Katerini, Komotini, Kozani, Larisa, Lesvos, Patras, Pyrgos, Salonica, Verria, Volos, Xanthi, Yithion.
Elections had been held in the following: Agrinio, Athens, Chalkis, Chania, Corfu, Egion, Elefsis, Kalamata, Karditsa, Kavalla, Kefalonia, Lamia, Levadia, Loutraki, Missolonghi, Preveza, Sparta, Trikala, Yannina, Zante. R 2262/130/19. The information is incomplete.
88. General Labour Memo (Greece) No. 22. Trade Union Developments in Provincial Towns from 4th March, 1946 (R 4591/130/19).
89. *Ibid.*
90. Labour Situation, May 24th (No. 15) (R 8097/130/19).
91. ILO, *Labour Problems in Greece,* p. 235; Jecchinis, *op. cit.,* p. 94 takes the same line.
92. In mid-January Leeper had recommended that a 'suitable' trade union representative be sent and had suggested Tewson (R 1374/1/19).
93. R 8097/130/19.
94. Leeper to Foreign Office 4th March, 1946 (R 3438/130/19).
95. Leeper to Foreign Office 7th March, 1946 (R 3617/130/19).
96. Lascelles to Foreign Office 9th March, 1946 (R 3743/130/19).
97. Lascelles to Foreign Office 12th March, 1946 (R 3872/130/19). Bagnall replied with the following statement: 'British delegate Bagnall cannot agree for following reasons. Up to date statements made the *[sic]* allegations only. Without doubting honesty of persons who have made them they cannot be accepted as

facts until they have been investigated. Documents submitted by complainants have not even been read by Delegation as they have not been translated. In opinion of British Delegate representations made to Minister of Labour would be more aptly described as protests against interference with law by police and against repressing rather than terrorism.' Lascelles to Foreign Office 9th March, 1946 (R 3744/130/19).
98. ILO, *Labour Problems in Greece*, p. 236.
99. *Rizospastis*, 8th March, 1946.
100. ILO, *Labour Problems in Greece*, p. 236.
101. R 3872/130/19.
102. Lascelles to Foreign Office 12th March, 1946 (R 3873/130/19).
103. Norton to Foreign Office 20th March, 1946 (R 4452/130/19).
104. ILO, *Labour Problems in Greece*, p. 237.
105. *Ibid.*, pp. 237 ff.; Jecchinis, *op. cit.*, pp. 100 ff.; *Greek Trade Unions in Chains*, ed. League for Democracy in Greece, London, 1947.
106. *TUC Report*, 1945, p. 419.
107. *TUC Report*, 1946, p. 434.
108. *Ibid.*, p. 154.
109. *Ibid.*, Supplements, p. 254.
110. *TUC Report*, 1946, p. 435.
111. Jecchinis, *op. cit.*, pp. 102 ff.
112. Declaration of the Executive Bureau of the World Federation of Trade Unions, Washington, September 1946 (*TUC Report*, 1946, Supplements, p. 261). Jecchinis does not mention this declaration.
113. See p. 311.
114. Leeper to Foreign Office 27th November, 1945 (R 20032/4/19).
115. Leeper to Foreign Office 7th December, 1945 (R 21125/4/19).
116. R 21125/4/19; MacVeagh to State Department 1st December, 1945 (*FRUS 1945, VIII*, pp. 274 ff). Text of the letter in *ibid.*, pp. 281 ff.
117. R 21125/4/19.
118. British Embassy to State Department 3rd December, 1945 (*FRUS 1945, VIII*, pp. 276 ff).
119. British Embassy to State Department 5th December, 1945 (*FRUS 1945, VIII*, p. 278).
120. *Ibid.*, Annex A, p. 280.
121. MacVeagh to State Department 1st December, 1945 (*FRUS 1945, VIII*, pp. 275 ff). MacVeagh remarked: 'In this connection British Ambassador assures me no intention giving British advisers administrative responsibility in Greek Ministries but presence such advisers in Greek Govt. offices with aggressive British backing likely amount to same thing and certain to be so interpreted by local opinion.' For details of what occurred within the US government see Michael Mark Amen, *American Foreign Policy in Greece 1944-1949: Economic, Military and Institutional Aspects*, (Frankfurt, Bern, Las Vegas: Peter Lang, 1978), pp. 61-70, 83 ff.
122. *FRUS 1945, VIII*, pp. 280 ff.
123. Leeper to Foreign Office 14th December, 1945 (R 29/1/19).
124. Leeper to Foreign Office 21st December, 1945 (R 155/1/19).
125. R 155/1/19; *FRUS 1945, VIII*, p. 284.
126. Before the war, annual wheat production stood at 800,000 tons. The 1945 harvest brought in 350,000 tons. In autumn 1945, with UNRRA assistance, 90 per cent of the pre-war wheat acreage was sown, so that a 700,000 tons crop was expected for 1946. *The Times*, 16th January, 1946.
127. MacVeagh to State Department 15th December, 1945 (*FRUS 1945, VIII*,

pp. 284-8).
128. The Greek Embassy to the State Department 18th December, 1945 (*FRUS 1945, VIII*, p. 269); Foreign Office to Washington 19th December, 1945 (R 20990/4/19).
129. R 20990/4/19.
130. Acheson to MacVeagh 17th December, 1945 (*FRUS 1945, VIII*, p. 288).
131. *Ibid.*, pp. 290-2.
132. MacVeagh to State Department 20th December, 1945 (*Ibid.*, pp. 293 ff).
133. *Ibid.*; Leeper to Foreign Office 29th December, 1945 (R 465/1/19).
134. MacVeagh to State Department 22nd December, 1945 (*FRUS 1945, VIII*, pp. 296 ff).
135. Leeper to Foreign Office 23rd December, 1945 (R 21403/4/19). 'I do beg you to take my advice on this as I feel sure that I am right and that you will gain by having Kartalis in London. He is far and away [the] most determined man in the Government and a short visit to London would clear up the air more than anything else. If you refuse to have him with Tsouderos he will certainly resign as he insists that he will only take responsibility for the very unpopular measures he has to take if he is allowed to have it out with you in London. If you reach agreement with him he is more likely to stick to it than any Greek I know.'
136. This represented a private initiative by an official of the State Department (*FRUS 1945, VIII*, pp. 29 ff., note 57).
137. Halifax to Foreign Office 23rd December, 1945 (R 21406/4/19).
138. Foreign Office to Halifax 24th December, 1945 (R 21406/4/19).
139. *FRUS 1945, VIII*, pp. 296 ff.
140. Leeper to Foreign Office 4th January, 1946 (R 466/1/19); MacVeagh to State Department 1st January, 1946 (*FRUS 1945, VIII*, p. 298). On 31st December the budget deficit had reached 71 billion. Banknote circulation had risen to 101.8 billion.
141. Leeper to Foreign Office 28th December, 1945 (R 21543/4/19).
142. Foreign Office to Leeper 30th December, 1945 (R 21543/4/19).
143. *The Times*, 5th January, 1946.
144. Memorandum to Bevin from Sir Orme Sargent 1st January, 1946 (R 138/1/19).
145. Acheson to MacVeagh 8th January, 1945 (*FRUS 1946, VII*, p. 88).
146. *FRUS 1946, VII*, pp. 89 ff.
147. Leeper to Foreign Office 19th January, 1946 (R 1375/1/19).
148. MacVeagh to Byrnes 11th January, 1946 (*FRUS 1946, VII*, pp. 91 ff).
149. *Ibid.*, p. 92, note 16.
150. Foreign Office to Leeper 20th January, 1946 (R 821/1/19); *FRUS 1946, VII*, pp. 100-104.
151. Thus Loy Henderson in a letter to Acheson (*FRUS 1946, VII*, p. 104). And quite recently Anderson, *op. cit.*, p. 149.
152. *FRUS 1946, VII*, p. 102.
153. As Woodhouse writes, *Apple of Discord*, p. 256, the Bank of England had made gold available for this.
154. Memorandum to Mr Hector McNeil from EAM Delegation 17th December, 1945 (R 21484/4/19).
155. *Ibid.*
156. Laskey's Minutes 30th December, 1945 (R 21484/4/19).
157. Minutes by Laskey and other Foreign Office staff members 30th December, 1945-16th January, 1946 (R 21142/4/19).
158. Leeper to Foreign Office 14th December, 1945 (R 29/1/19) and 7th December, 1945 (R 21125/4/19): 'The Government appears more and more persuaded that no drastic revision of the rolls is necessary.'

159. R 29/1/19.
160. Leeper to Foreign Office 18th December, 1945 (R 134/1/19). This memorandum was signed by P. Mavromichalis, S. Stefanopoulos, K. Tsaldaris (Populists); S. Gonatas (National Liberals); A. Alexandris (Reformists); N. Zervas (National Party); A. Sakellariou (Panhellenic Party); A. Hajikyriakos (Patriotic Party); P.I. Argyropoulos (National Reconstruction Party), as well as by less well-known political personalities. Particularly shocking was the denunciation of Sofianopoulos as an anarcho-communist. Papandreou did not participate as this step was an indirect attack on British policy and, moreover, he was not sure whether the future did not lie with a republic. Thereupon both left- and right-wing press called him a weather-vane. Kanellopoulos, likewise, did not sign as he had in the meantime openly declared himself for a republic.
161. Leeper to Foreign Office 21st December, 1945 (R 155/1/19).
162. Leeper to Foreign Office 19th December, 1945 (R 21167/4/19). See also Leeper to Sir Orme Sargent 27th December, 1945 (R 330/1/19).
163. Leeper to Foreign Office 29th December, 1945 (R 465/1/19). Tsaldaris alluded to the notorious Sofoulis-Sklavainas agreement of April 1936. See Dafnis, *op. cit.,* II, pp. 416-8.
164. Leeper to Foreign Office 4th January, 1946 (R 466/1/19).
165. Leeper to Foreign Office 10th January, 1946 (R 554/1/19).
166. *New York Times,* 11th January, 1946.
167. Leeper to Foreign Office 10th January, 1946 (R 553/1/19).
168. *Ibid.*
169. Leeper to Foreign Office 10th January, 1946 (R 579/1/19).
170. *News Chronicle,* 14th January, 1946.
171. Leeper to Foreign Office 24th January, 1946 (R 1735/1/19).
172. *News Chronicle,* 17th January, 1946.
173. Leeper to Foreign Office 17th January, 1946 (R 867/1/19).
174. Leeper to Foreign Office 22nd January, 1946 (R 1109/1/19).
175. Leeper to Foreign Office 26th January, 1946 (R 1396/1/19).
176. *Ibid.*
177. See p. 151.
178. Leeper to Foreign Office 24th January, 1946 (R 1735/1/19).
179. R 1396/1/19.
180. Leeper to Foreign Office 29th January, 1946 (R 1523/1/19).
181. *Ibid.*
182. Lars Baerentzen, 'The Liberation of the Peloponnese, September 1944', in: John O. Iatrides, ed., *Greece in the 1940s: A Nation in Crisis,* (Hanover: University Press of New England, 1981), pp. 131-141.
183. Leeper to Foreign Office 23rd January, 1946 (R 1195/1/19).
184. For the text of this speech see A. Othonaios, *Treis logoi dia tin dimokratian,* (Athens, 1946), reprint (Athens: Ellinika Themata, 1976). Leeper to Foreign Office 22nd January, 1946 (R 1137/1/19).
185. Leeper to Foreign Office 2nd February, 1946 (R 2196/1/19).
186. Leeper to Foreign Office 23rd January, 1946 (R 1195/1/19); Leeper to Foreign Office 22nd January, 1946 (R 1116/1/19).
187. Leeper to Foreign Office 24th January, 1946 (R 1209/1/19).
188. Leeper to Foreign Office 24th January, 1946 (R 1210/1/19).
189. There were even reports of fraternisation. Leeper to Foreign Office 22nd February, 1946 (R 2984/1/19). All in all seven members of Manganas' band were arrested. A few dozen gendarmes were given disciplinary transfers for fraternising. At the beginning of February Manganas attacked another village and took twenty hostages of whom three were clubbed to death. Leeper to

Foreign Office 15th February, 1946 (R 2713/1/19).
190. C.-in-C. Middle East to War Office 28th March, 1946 (R 5126/1/19). Just how precise this information was can be judged from the figure of 30,000 for the potential armed strength of the Left, a figure closely corresponding to the later strength of the Greek Democratic Army in the 1947-9 civil war.
191. Leeper to Foreign Office 6th March, 1946 (R 3555/1/19).
192. Leeper to Foreign Office 24th January, 1946 (R 1252/1/19).
193. On this see D.F. Fleming, *The Cold War and its origin 1917-1960* Vol. I, (London: Allen and Unwin, 1961), pp. 340 ff.; Stephen Xydis, *Greece and the Great Powers 1944-1947: Prelude to the 'Truman Doctrine'*, (Thessaloniki: Institute for Balkan Studies, 1963), pp. 163 ff.; Joyce and Gabriel Kolko, *The Limits of Power: The World and United States Foreign Policy 1945-1954*, (New York: Harper and Row, 1972), pp. 218 ff.

GREECE AT THE UN SECURITY COUNCIL

On 21st January 1946, Andrei Gromyko, acting head of the Soviet Union's delegation to the United Nations, addressed a document to the Security Council in which he made the following points.

'The presence of British troops in Greece after the end of the war is not called for now, even in the interest of protecting the communications of the British troops stationed in the defeated countries. On the other hand, the presence of British troops in Greece has been turned into a means of bringing pressure to bear upon the political situation inside that country, pressure which has not infrequently been used by reactionary elements against the democratic forces of the country. Such a situation, signifying interference in the internal affairs of Greece with the aid of the armed forces of a foreign Power, has given rise to extreme tension fraught with the possibility of serious consequences both for the Greek people and for the maintenance of peace and security.'

The Soviet delegation asked that the Security Council discuss this problem.[1]

Simultaneously, a detailed Tass report making the same points appeared in all Soviet newspapers.[2] On 22nd January the Soviet press published a sensational report of the Kalamata episode.[3]

The Soviet move in the Security Council was primarily a high-level diplomatic riposte to a corresponding Western manoeuvre in connection with Iran. Since the sources of these developments within the UN are reasonably good it is possible to reconstruct the course of the diplomatic and political manoeuvring in the Security Council. But sources for the effects of the Soviet *démarche* on British and Greek policy are far less satisfactory. It is always just when the Foreign Office documents concern a critical point in British relations with Greece that they are missing from the Public Record Office. Thus, for the first days after 21st January 1946, the telegrams to and from Athens are almost all missing from the file. Since the archives of the Greek Foreign Ministry have been—at least officially—inaccessible, reconstruction of the actual developments is extremely difficult and can only be attempted with great caution.

Directly the Soviet document arrived in the Foreign Office it was clear that, when the time came for confrontation in the Security Council, a Greek representative must be present to support the British case. At the second Security Council session on 25th January a decision was therefore taken that the Greek representative should participate in discussion but without the right to vote.[4] For the Foreign Office it was obvious who should represent Greece: Foreign Minister John Sofianopoulos, who had been in London since 7th January for the UN General Assembly meeting. Foreign Office motives are transparent: on the one hand it would be maintained before the Security Council from the Greek side that British troops were stationed in Greece at the wish of the Greek government; whilst at the same time the fact that British policy would be defended by the 'Russophile' Sofianopoulos would have a powerful political impact in Greece. There were even hopes that it would lose the Left a great number of votes in the forthcoming elections.[5] There was also the consideration that Sofianopoulos was the only Greek politician who enjoyed a measure of respect in the Soviet Union. Therefore the Foreign Office tried to harness Sofianopoulos in the interests of British policy and to use his prestige as an alibi.

But this was just what Sofianopoulos was not prepared to allow. He was of the opinion that a small country like Greece should not become a pretext for friction between the Great Powers but, on the contrary, should do all it could to preserve their unity. Moreover, as his biographer reports, he held that

'the Russian complaint exactly described the situation existing in Greece: the British military authorities were assisting reaction by every means and the British ambassador was in fact the supreme leader of our country who appointed and dismissed governments by his own sole decision. But the interests of the Greek people. . . required that British troops be removed from Greece since only thus could there be any hope of averting the outbreak of civil war. If the British withdrew, the Right would be more ready to compromise and would itself make efforts for internal tranquillity; whereas now, with the foreigners covering its rear, it was promoting evolution towards a 'Third Round'[6] in the belief that thus the Left could be completely annihilated. British withdrawal would also prevent the restoration [of the monarchy] because it would allow the country's democratic forces to develop unimpeded and because it would facilitate internal pacification. The bourgeois system was no longer threatened by the communists, who at that time were disarmed, but by the British themselves and the royalists who, by their terrorism, were pressing matters towards a new conflict during which the question of survival or abolition of the bourgeois system would inevitably arise once more'.[7]

A British withdrawal would certainly not have been followed by Soviet invasion because of the 'spheres of influence' agreement of October 1944 which the Soviets continued to regard as valid and to respect. But a British withdrawal would have altered the balance within Greece in favour of the democratic forces and, in all probability, would have prevented the civil war. Sofianopoulos', sensible views were the result of calm and sober analysis, unswayed by irrational responses and conditioned, above all, by considerations of what was best for Greece, a policy which brought him into conflict with all existing influences in Greece and thus deprived him of any support. The Foreign Office wanted him to appear before the Security Council as the apologist for British policy. From its own motives the Greek government, too, expected him to justify British policy, and the Left hoped that he would support the Soviet criticism. By his policy Sofianopoulos fell between all these stools and thus became the victim of the divergent forces and their intrigues. But in the final resort the Soviet leadership must bear the responsibility for his fall and thus a share in the responsibility for the developments which led Greece to civil war.

As soon as Sofianopoulos received a copy of the Soviet document on 22nd January, he informed the Greek government and asked for directions. At the same time he sent Ambassador Agnidis to the Foreign Office to talk to Sir Orme Sargent. Agnidis told Sir Orme that, the moment Sofianopoulos heard this news, he had decided that he had better return to Greece at once. The reason he gave was, first and foremost, the number of ministers absent at the time from Athens. He would like to know the British government's opinion on the matter. Sir Orme said that the matter required careful consideration and Sofianopoulos should discuss it with Bevin before taking a final decision. Agnidis then spoke on a personal and unofficial basis, reported as follows by Sir Orme.

'The Ambassador said that there might be some advantage in M. Sofianopoulos's returning to Athens. In his absence the Ambassador would become head of the Greek delegation and would represent Greece in any discussions at the Security Council. He felt sure that he would be able to do so in a manner which supports our view.'

Sir Orme got the impression that the Greek delegation was considerably disturbed by the Soviet *démarche*,

'for M. Aghnidis, contrary to his normal practice, interlarded his remarks with irrelevant complaints about our allowing the Royalists to continue to hold key positions in the Army and the Gendarmerie, and about our failing to enforce a general amnesty in Greece, since, according to him, the recent law on the subject had proved quite ineffective'.

Sir Orme expressed his hope that the Greek delegation would keep calm and would not panic.

'If they contemplated appeasing the Soviet Government by making sudden concessions on the matters he had mentioned, this was completely futile, besides being bad tactics. H.M. Government saw no need to appease the Soviet Government, and were quite prepared to justify their policy in Greece, which could stand the most thorough investigation. The Soviet Government's present move was typical of their usual technique; when they were being criticised in one quarter they took the offensive by criticising their critics in another quarter. In any case, the Soviet Government's appeal to the Security Council was directed not against the actions of the Greek Government but against the actions of H.M. Government.'[8]

In general, the Foreign Office got the impression that Sofianopoulos was not willing to defend the presence of British troops in Greece against the Russians.[9] Therefore Bevin decided to discuss this matter with Sofianopoulos himself and to persuade him to stay on, since his sudden return to Athens could only cause panic there. At the same time the Foreign Office gave Leeper detailed information on what had happened and suggested that he see Sofoulis and Damaskinos, to calm them and to make sure that Sofoulis gave Sofianopoulos the right instructions. Thereupon Leeper visited Sofoulis on 23rd January and later reported his conversation to London.

'Mr. Sofoulis said he would telegraph at once to M. Sofianopoulos telling him to stay at his post and back His Majesty's Government in any way that might be required. He would not hear of his returning to Athens which would merely create panic.'

Then came an ominous sentence.

'He could telegraph without revealing source of his information as Sofianopoulos, before he left Athens, had suggested the possibility of returning before the end of Assembly';

in other words, Sofoulis did not want to admit to Sofianopoulos that his information derived from the British. However Leeper did not content himself with informing Sofoulis about the actions of Sofianopoulos but began to intrigue against him.

'I suggested that Sofianopoulos wanted to escape the position of having to back the British against Russia and that if he were allowed to return he would stay and clamour for general amnesty in order to appease the Russians. Sofoulis smiled and said he would not be given this opportunity. Sofoulis said he fully understood the Russian position and had complete confidence in His Majesty's Government. He was not in the least perturbed by the Russian move. The Communists alone desired British troops to go. Every Government since the liberation had welcomed their presence.'[10]

Leeper went on to visit Damaskinos.

Lack of sources makes it impossible to say with certainty whether, in his first telegram to the Greek government, Sofianopoulos had mentioned his intention of returning to Athens or whether the information came from Leeper alone. But from Sofoulis' reply to Sofianopoulos reprinted by Patatzis,[11] which makes no mention of it, we must conclude that the information stemmed from British channels. However this may have been, the whole matter somehow percolated through to the press which 'went to town' on it, thus helping to undermine Sofianopoulos' position.[12]

The Athens evening press of 22nd January had carried sensational reports of the Soviet document. The left-wing press, which had launched massive protests from the day after the Kalamata episode, welcomed the Soviet intervention and began an intensive and wide-ranging anti-British campaign. The right-wing press denounced the 'Slav threat' and saw the left-wing attacks as proof of their servility to Moscow. The Liberal press let itself be carried away by this, with the result that the socialist paper *Machi*, which represented the Svolos faction, was the only moderate and sober voice from the press.[13]

A similar polarisation took place among the politicians. From the Right to the Centre there was agreement that this threat could only be averted by unconditional obedience to Great Britain. The outward sign of this attitude was the unanimous decision of the Foreign Policy Committee welcoming the presence of British troops in Greece and stating that they were there by the wish of the Greek government and presented no threat to the country's independence.[14] The text was sent to Sofianopoulos in London on 23rd January, for him to transmit to the Security Council. The main motive for this decision was apparently the bourgeois politicians' fear of Slavs and communists. But absence of the more liberal ministers also contributed. Had Tsouderos and Kartalis been in Athens, there would have been a chance that the decision might have favoured Sofianopoulos; though personal antipathies towards him likewise played a considerable role.

On the Left, the Russian intervention was seen as some sort of encouragement for a harder line. On 23rd January an EAM delegation, led by Siantos, visited Leeper to protest against British passivity in the Kalamata affair and to demand, quite openly, the withdrawal of British troops whose presence only encouraged the Right in its terrorism.[15] The KKE Political Bureau had already published an exhaustive critical analysis of the situation on 21st January.

According to this, the Kalamata episode, as well as events in Laconia, Volos, Thebes and Corinth, showed that the Right was trying to get power into its hands through civil war. The main responsibility for this development lay with the British occupation authorities who had systematically supported the monarcho-fascists. The British Police Mission had frustrated any purge of the security forces and had allowed them to arm the 'X' bands. The Secret Service was financing and directing the 'X' organisation. This made the British government responsible for the over 1,300 murders since Varkiza and this situation had been made even worse by the hesitant attitude of the Greek government. Instead of complaining that the British were preventing them from taking radical measures, they should resign. A government should be formed which included the Left. The government should arrest all 'X' and SAN leaders and disband their organisations.

Officers of the armed forces who belonged to 'X' or were former members of the Security Battalions should likewise be arrested. A volunteer force should be formed from former Resistance members to rid the country of the right-wing bandits. The government should appeal to the people for support against the insurgents of the Right. The situation was extremely critical and the most important premise for avoiding civil war was ending the British occupation.[16]

The radical wording of this statement was an outcome of the Kalamata episode. In substance, the protests were justified. However, the Soviet intervention gave them a new perspective: they became part of the foreign 'aggression' against Greece. Without the Soviet intervention, the Kalamata episode could well have caused a change of policy. The Soviet intervention was a provocation to the nationalist pride of the bourgeois camp and, since it was seen as an interference in Greece's internal affairs, there was no longer any question of yielding to the justified demands of the Left, as this would have been equivalent to submission to the Soviets. The result was partition of the country into two camps: one pro-British and one anti-British, the latter being immediately denounced by the Right as pro-Soviet. In such circumstances it is not surprising that Sofianopoulos' attempt to steer a moderate course was doomed to failure.

When Sofianopoulos had received Sofoulis' instructions that he should give total support to British policy, on 23rd January he addressed himself again to the Cabinet in Athens and suggested that the Greek government should make the following statement: the government had taken note of the Soviet document; it was in favour of the peaceful resolution of conflicts between the Great Powers; as regards the restoration of normality in Greece, the Greek government considered this is be an internal Greek affair and therefore, on the basis of Paragraph 7 of Article 2 of the United Nations Charter, declined to have this matter discussed either in the Security Council or the General Assembly; for the same reason it regarded itself as incompetent to put its viewpoint to the Security Council.[17] The Greek government's reply of 24th January showed that Athens saw the matter quite differently. But Sofianopoulos held to his opinion and telegraphed to Athens that he still regarded his own suggestion as correct and that only thus could Greece preserve its independence and free itself from the undesirable and unprofitable quarrel between the Great Powers. If his views were not accepted, he would see himself obliged to return to Athens for discussions.[18] Replying on 25th January, Sofoulis told him that the government irrevocably insisted on the transmission of the Foreign Policy Committee's decision and that he, Sofianopoulos, must stay on in London and put Greece's case in accordance with the government's wish.[19]

In the meantime, on 24th January, Sofianopoulos had worked out a compromise suggestion to put to the Security Council which had the approval of the other members of the Greek UN delegation, Exindaris,

Varvaressos and Agnidis. The crucial passage states:

'The Greek Government state that the British forces, whose continued presence in Greece is due to the initiative of successive Greek Governments and accords with the latter's wishes, are collaborating with the Greek authorities with a view to the gradual restoration of order and the securing of a free expression of the people's will and that this holds true until such time as the purposes have been fulfilled.'[20]

But even this compromise proposal, in which the main difference from the Greek government position consisted only in the time limit for the presence of British troops, found no favour in Athens. So, on 26th January, Sofianopoulos sent Agnidis once more to the Foreign Office, to see Sir Alexander Cadogan and tell him that he would not appear before the Security Council but would return to Greece at once and leave it to Agnidis to carry out the Greek government's instructions. Even should he remain in London Agnidis would have to represent Greece before the Security Council. He did not tell Cadogan of the Greek government's order for him to remain in London. In view of this situation, Cadogan thought it preferable for Sofianopoulos to return to Athens.[21] Sofoulis' behaviour was indeed somewhat strange. Minister of State Noel-Baker commented as follows in mid-February:

'It may be true that Sofianopoulos kept the Prime Minister "most inadequately informed", but is it not a strange proceeding for a Prime Minister to telegraph a formula to his Foreign Minister for use in a supremely important international debate without hearing the Foreign Minister's view or giving him an opportunity to agree or disagree?'[22]

The explanation is to be sought in the prevailing Slavophobia and in the personal animosity of the bourgeois politicians towards Sofianopoulos, but above all in the fact that Leeper (if he did not actually encourage them) did nothing to bring Sofoulis and the Regent into a calmer state of mind. Leeper himself was personally hostile to Sofianopoulos, whom he regarded as an enemy of Great Britain, an opinion shared by many of the Foreign Office staff. On 27th January Leeper reported to London that, with the exception of the communists, all the Greek parties supported the British Government's line.

'The reluctance of Sophianopoulos to obey the orders of his Government and to support His Majesty's Government at Security Council has aroused contempt and indignation and, even if [he] finally obeys the orders of his Government I should be surprised if he were kept in the Government after his return. The Regent said to me that he was ashamed that a Greek Minister of Foreign Affairs should not welcome the opportunity of supporting the country which had done so much for Greece instead of trying to shirk his duty.'[23]

A word from Leeper would have been sufficient to consolidate Sofianopoulos' position. But as he expressed no such opinion, the Greek politicians took his silence for consent and got on with the undermining of Sofianopoulos. At the end of his telegram Leeper added a few very significant remarks which showed the depth of his own involvement.

'When Sophoulis formed his Government in November the inclusion of Sophianopoulos was unlikely. At first there was to be question of making him Minister of Public Order. When Sophoulis asked me about this I suggested there would be less criticism if he returned to the Ministry of Foreign Affairs and Sophoulis agreed. Presence of Sophianopoulos in the Government was useful in the early stages as it helped to keep EAM quiet at a difficult period. Now the EAM are attacking the Government violently and are conducting vigorous anti-British propaganda Sophianopoulos ceases to be an asset to the Government. I think that Sophoulis is fully aware of this though he has not discussed it with me. Demands are already being made by various party leaders that Sophianopoulos should be made to resign.'[24]

The Southern Department agreed in principle with Leeper but Laskey pointed out the unfavourable repercussions it would have in Labour circles if Sofianopoulos were allowed to fall, since he was regarded as a socialist. Another Foreign Office commentator, Williams, was much more incisive: he blamed Sofianopoulos for sabotaging his government's policy; likewise he was no friend of Great Britain and 'I contemplate his resignation with some satisfaction'.[25] Meanwhile, in constant contact with the Foreign Office, Sofianopoulos had prepared a statement in which he announced his departure and once more clarified his stand on the compromise formula. The Foreign Office was completely satisfied and, on 28th January, instructed Leeper to intervene with Sofoulis not to dismiss him from his ministerial post.[26] Although this telegram was marked 'urgent' on its despatch, this mark was no longer present on its arrival in Athens, so that it was put aside and was only de-coded later.

Thus, when he visited Sofoulis on the morning of 29th January, Leeper knew nothing of this instruction and therefore let things take their course. Sofoulis told him he had been informed by Agnidis that Sofianopoulos had left London by plane, despite his orders to remain there. He had thereupon at once transferred the leadership of the Greek UN delegation to Agnidis and Exindaris. Sofianopoulos' behaviour had aroused 'disgust' and 'indignation' and he could no longer remain in his Cabinet.

'He [Sofoulis] felt that there must have been a secret understanding between him [Sofianopoulos] and the Russians and that he had promised the latter not to support the British case at the Security Council. In his telegrams he had not spoken of resignation and Sophoulis feared that he intended to make mischief on his return to Athens by agitating for the overthrow of the present government in favour of a new government under himself, with participation of EAM. Such plans would have no chance of success.'

He therefore intended to suggest to the Regent that Rendis be nominated Foreign Minister.[27]

Sofoulis now went to Damaskinos and, in the space of a few hours, Sofianopoulos had been dismissed by the Regent and Rendis sworn in as Foreign Minister. Sofianopoulos learned of this from reporters when his plane made a stopover at Rome.[28] The Foreign Office was displeased with Sofoulis' hasty action[29] and, on the 30th, Leeper visited Sofoulis again to inform him of the contents of the Foreign Office telegram which had been de-coded too late. But Sofoulis did not let himself be deflected: Sofianopoulos had to go; with the exception of Svolos and the communists, all the politicians were against him; had he not reacted so briskly, the government would have fallen; public opinion had decided that, with Sofianopoulos, Greece's case was in unsure hands. Leeper subscribed to Sofoulis' viewpoint.[30]

Leeper had not restricted himself to intriguing against Sofianopoulos but had directed his enmity against all those who supported him. For example, he had opposed a demand by Labour MPs for the re-instatement of Alexandros Svolos in his Chair of Constitutional Law because the latter had taken a critical line in *Machi* towards the presence of British troops in Greece.[31] For Leeper anyone who was against British policy was an enemy.

On his return, Sofianopoulos held a press conference and replied to Sofoulis' accusations. It was incorrect that he had left London without informing the Greek government. Between him and the Cabinet there had arisen an unbridgeable difference of opinion and he was not a government employee to have to give unquestioning obedience. Greece must not become an apple of discord between the Great Powers but must become a meeting-point, since only thus could she hope for fulfilment of her national claims. He went on to describe what he had done, how he had tried to prevent the debate on Greece. In London, all the delegation members had been in agreement with his actions. He had also shown Tsouderos his telegrams to Athens. Since the Soviet document was submitted, he had had no contact with the Russians. As regards the presence of British troops in Greece, the elections could only be held when law and order prevailed in the country. Thereafter there would be no further need for their presence.[32] In an article for the *News Chronicle* he added that one of the essential pre-conditions for free elections was the announcement of a comprehensive amnesty. The law for the de-congestion of prisons had proved wholly inadequate. Furthermore, there must be an end to terrorism and the administrative apparatus must be purged of all fascist and reactionary elements who were nothing more than survivors from the period of dictatorship and Occupation.[33]

Sofoulis replied to Sofianopoulos' attacks with a somewhat vague denial. London was not very pleased with the new Foreign Minister whom it quite unjustifiably suspected of alcoholism.[34] Political circles in Athens were happy to have got rid of the dangerous 'leftist' Sofianopoulos and continued their efforts to ensure British support. The Greek government was particularly disturbed by the prospect that the British might possibly withdraw their troops after the elections since this might bring about a change in the balance of political forces within the country. To forestall such a development, which had also been foreseen by Sofianopoulos, and to bring the need for the continuing presence of British troops into the open, Sofoulis and Damaskinos began to stress the communist peril to Leeper, saying that bands had stepped up their activity in Western Macedonia and that there had been warnings of serious trouble to come. Sofoulis suspected that Tito was behind it. Leeper—who thought the communists capable of anything—accepted this calculated information uncritically and drew the following conclusion for the Foreign Office: 'It appears that communists are preparing operations in order to start an armed revolt as soon as the British troops withdraw.'[35] Unfortunately, it is not possible to ascertain how seriously his warning was taken in the Foreign Office, though in general the whole affair was subsequently summarised as a 'deplorable episode'.[36] For the ministerial leadership, the affair was a political and diplomatic dispute with the Soviet Union in which Greece was only by chance involved. It was the personal tragedy of Sofianopoulos that this far-sighted and consistent politician fell from office over such a matter. In him Greece lost the only post-war Foreign Minister who was able (according to his biographer Patatzis) to steer an independent course between the Right who wanted to make Greece a satellite of Great Britain and the Left who wanted to make her a satellite of the Soviet Union.[37] Although, by his attitude, Sofianopoulos had alienated the Right and also the extreme Left and was, for the time being, isolated, he was to continue in the future—and even during the civil war— his efforts to find an equitable settlement. Unfortunately, this was to prove unavailing. During the Cold War a settlement was not desired.[38]

The dispute between Bevin and Vyshinsky in the Security Council began on the 1st and ended on the 6th February. From the start it was apparent that it was not about Greece but about issues of power politics between the USSR and Great Britain. Greece was the chance cause of the quarrel. It nevertheless had repercussions within Greece. The Right, which identified itself with Great Britain, felt confirmed in its line and the Left began to cherish delusions about support from the Soviet Union. This despite the fact that it was obvious, during the whole of the Security Council debate, that the 'spheres of influence' principle held good under all circumstances. The whole matter was thus a kind of political cabaret show for world public opinion.

On 1st February, Vyshinsky opened the debate with a very superficial background survey of Soviet interest in Greek developments during 1945.

Then he cited selected extracts from the Western press to show that White Terror reigned in Greece. Finally he stated that there was no further justification for the presence of British troops. The original wartime justification for their presence had lapsed. He likewise rejected the argument that they were taking care of law and order.

'There is no order in Greece, and thus far the presence of British troops has not established such order. On the contrary, the presence of British troops, since it is used by reactionary elements against progressive elements, has resulted in intensifying the political struggle, a struggle which is directed in the interests of a small part of the population, the pro-fascist elements, against the democratic majority of the population . . . What is happening in Greece at present has nothing to do with order, and only the most vivid imagination would construe the events taking place in Greece as any kind of order even in a relative sense of that word. . .'

At the end he drew his conclusion.

'The presence of British troops in Greece is not dictated by any necessity and, unfortunately, only leads to dangerous internal difficulties.'

For this reason the Soviet UN delegation demanded the immediate withdrawal of British troops from Greece.[39]

Here it must again be emphasised that Vyshinsky's demand was simply a counter-demand to the Iranian one for the withdrawal of Soviet troops from North Iran which the Russians held to have been inspired by Bevin. The assumption that Vyshinsky had demanded the withdrawal of British troops in order to open the way to power for KKE is quite outside reality.[40] Greece belonged to the British 'sphere of influence' and the Soviets respected this. Therefore, the proofs which were supposed to back up the Soviet complaint were poorly researched and only went to prove once more how little the Russians were interested in Greece's internal situation. Although the British clearly saw through the Soviet manoeuvre,[41] Bevin reacted much more sharply than could have been expected and, in contrast to Vyshinsky, he went into the details of the Greek situation. It may be that his motives for this were in the last resort connected with British internal politics. By sharply refuting Soviet criticism of his policy towards Greece, he may also have hoped to silence the critics within his own camp or at least to bring them into a dangerous proximity to Soviet policy. But a side-effect of these tactics was that British policy towards Greece lost much of its ability to manoeuvre and took on certain obligations which had to be fulfilled if Vyshinsky's attack was not to be proved justified after the event.

Bevin's reply opened provocatively. 'I think the speech we have just listened to. . . points not to the necessity of withdrawing British troops, but to the imperative necessity of putting more there.' He went on to speak of Soviet policy towards Greece. At Yalta Stalin had expressed his complete confidence in Britain's Greek policy. Thereafter, disputes about Greece had always arisen whenever the British mentioned Romania, Bulgaria or Poland. He gave details and showed that there was a 'curious' coincidence between Soviet criticisms and attacks by the British Communist Party on British policy towards Greece. Then he spoke of the historical background to the presence of British troops in Greece and hinted that Stalin had originally been in agreement with this (this hint clearly referred to the 'percentage agreement' of October 1944). Afterwards it had come to civil war, for which the Greek Communists were mainly responsible because they had tried to seize power from a minority position. For this Bevin cited the Citrine Report as an 'objective' proof. Every subsequent Greek government had had to confront the problem that the communists were still trying to win power.

'We could have done as was done in Roumania by Mr. Vyshinski. We had the power. Greece would no doubt have responded. We could have put in a minority government, but we did not do that. We have not set up governments in Greece. We have asked Greece to find her own government. We knew that governments would rise and fall; we knew there would be difficulty. We believed that democracy must come from the bottom, not from the top.'

Eventually, it had been possible to get Greece on the right road again; then Zachariadis began to speak of civil war. Bevin quoted at length from Zachariadis' interview with the *Manchester Guardian* correspondent.[42]

Bevin refuted the individual issues raised by Vyshinsky and showed them to be undifferentiated generalities. The British troops were in Greece at the wish of the Greek government. It was British policy to take care of law and order and to enable free elections to be held. The British troops would be withdrawn at the earliest possible moment. Then he went over to the counter-offensive:

'I have difficulty in believing—and I am in the habit of being fairly frank—that this is brought forward because of what we are doing in Greece. I cannot help feeling that there is a deeper reason for it than that, which can be known only to the Soviet Government. It is difficult to understand why this propaganda and incitement, with regard to a country that is trying to re-establish itself is going all over the world day by day.'

He went on to ask the Security Council to give a clear answer to the question whether the British government was endangering world peace with its Greek policy. The real danger to world peace proceeded from Moscow propaganda and the related propaganda of the communist parties. He asked the Security Council to give an unambiguous decision.[43]

Agnidis' statement, which followed immediately, was essentially restricted to confirming that the British troops were in Greece at the wish of the Greek government and that neither the British civilian nor their military authorities had ever in any way interfered with Greece's internal affairs. After this, the Security Council adjourned until Monday, 4th February.[44] The US delegation was pleased with Bevin's hard-line reaction, particularly with his plain speaking. The US representative, Stettinius, hoped that the matter could be settled without a formal decision but simply by a statement from the President of the Security Council. In other words, Stettinius was trying to bring about a settlement which would save face on both sides.[45] For this purpose, on Sunday, 3rd February, he made unofficial contact with both Bevin and Vyshinsky. But both sides took up entrenched positions.[46]

So on Monday, 4th February, the dispute continued. Vyshinsky rejected Bevin's charge that the whole affair was a diplomatic counter-attack by the Soviet Union and went on to deal with the latter's opinion that the Greek communists were responsible for the whole Greek entanglement. He cast doubt on the objectivity of the Citrine Report and cited statements in the House of Commons by Seymour Cocks which differed radically from the conclusions of the Citrine Report. Then he came to Bevin's thesis that all this was Soviet propaganda. That was well-known tactics.

'When we speak of the inhuman terroristic regime in Greece, this is treated as "Moscow propaganda". When we say that the presence of British troops in Greece is being made use of by reactionary elements and adventurers against the interests of the Greek people themselves and of all the United Nations, including Great Britain, this is also declared to be "Moscow propaganda".'

As proof that it was not propaganda he quoted several statements of Seymour Cocks, Maurice Edelman, Major Lyall Wilkes and Arthur Greenwood in the House of Commons and elsewhere. Finally, he asked Bevin if Sofianopoulos' statement in the *News Chronicle* was also Moscow propaganda. The presence of British troops in Greece was causing a critical situation and he therefore demanded their immediate withdrawal.[47]

Bevin's reply included a number of corrections to Vyshinsky's statements and reduced the value of his proofs (the Cocks' quotations, etc.) by characterising them as outsiders' opinions. But he avoided going into the problems they raised and, instead, returned to his original demand: Great Britain had been accused before the Security Council of endangering world peace by the sending of troops to Greece. He demanded a clear answer.

'I did make a mention of propaganda. I am sure Mr. Vyshinski will not deny that the continuous reference to Greece is very unsettling, and he is setting one section of the community against the other. But he says, as I understand it, that the British troops there are protecting the Right. I give the lie direct to that. We have protected all the people whenever the Greek Government has called upon us to do it, or whenever we have discovered a danger to public order.'

Then he argued that Sourlas was not in control of the countryside in Thessaly. Vyshinsky was misusing Greece in order to achieve certain diplomatic aims of the Soviet Union. The whole matter had been handled with downright criminal irresponsibility, without thought of possible repercussions. He wound up by once more demanding a clear answer to the question whether Great Britain had threatened world peace by its Greek policy.[48]

Bevin's tactics in reducing the Soviet complaint to this one question proved to be extremely astute. He knew that, if it came to a vote in the Security Council, the Soviet Union could not muster a majority. On the other hand, such a result would serve as both a *post factum* and a future justification of British policy in Greece. The other Western Security Council members were doubtless not in agreement with all the details of this policy; but, if it were called in question, Western solidarity would tell. Though in their content Vyshinsky's attacks were sound and justified, their generalised formulation gave Bevin the opportunity for a checkmate. The reason for this formulation lay in the Security Council Statutes. The Security Council could only concern itself with the internal affairs of a country if these caused a threat to peace. Whilst, by presenting the case in this way, Vyshinsky tried to bring Greece's internal situation to debate and distract attention from his real aim, the diplomatic counter-attack against the Iranian complaint, Bevin held to the wording of the Statutes and demanded the acquittal of Great Britain. That this confrontation ended in a solution which saved the face of both parties was due to the skill with which the other Security Council members handled it.

Agnidis, who also spoke again, scented the danger conjured up by Bevin's hard line and tried to moderate it with the result that, in some ways, he took a line resembling that which Sofianopoulos had wanted to take. He admitted that in Greece things were not too good, but there was no danger of war from Greece. The Greek people wanted to live in peace with all the Allies and Greece should be given the chance to get on her feet again. At present Greece was in a difficult situation but the government was doing all it could to improve matters. The idea that the situation was continuously deteriorating was an exaggeration. There was much talk of democracy and the country was on the eve of elections, the results of which were completely open. 'But, in our view, democracy means that whichever party wins, the other party should have the right to live, to live in peace and not be molested.' Agnidis minimised the vendettas and the bands, explaining them as some sort of romantic phenomenon and stressed that for the country, as a sovereign nation, the basic issue was that 'our friends could at least leave unhampered the natural forces in Greece, so that the natural forces themselves will display the answer democratically or politically at the appropriate time'. In regard to Bevin's demand, he appealed to Security Council members' sense of proportion—a few bandits did not constitute a threat to world peace.[49]

In the subsequent Security Council debate Stettinius stated that, in accordance with US opinion, the presence of British troops in Greece did not constitute a threat to world peace, though the situation in Greece was anything but happy. Therefore, in conformity with Security Council procedure, no vote should be taken; the statements of the three governments should be noted and the whole matter should be regarded as concluded. The French representative, Bidault, likewise took the view that the British troops in Greece did not endanger world peace but added the critical comment that the Yalta Declaration on the establishment of representative governments in the liberated countries had not been fully adhered to by any side. The Chinese and Australian representatives supported the US proposal. The Polish representative said that Bevin s question about whether British policy in Greece threatened world peace, had to be answered negatively, but he demanded a statement from the British that they would withdraw their troops as soon as possible. When Vyshinsky saw that the majority of Security Council members denied that Britain was endangering peace, he began to beat a retreat. He agreed that no formal decision should be taken but he, too, demanded a statement from Bevin that the British troops would be withdrawn as soon as possible. Bevin, who had been prepared to accept Stettinius' proposal, categorically rejected Vyshinsky's demand. This resulted in two draft resolutions, one Polish and one Egyptian. The Polish resolution found only Soviet support. The Egyptian resolution was blocked by the threat of a Soviet veto, so that the Security Council adjourned till the next day.[50]

On 5th February the session had hardly begun when it was interrupted for five minutes to give the members a chance to resolve their differences in private conversation. According to an American source, in what was described as a two hours' interruption, but in fact was a session *in camera*, there was again a sharp dispute between Bevin and Vyshinsky. The latter suggested to Bevin a trade-off: if Bevin did not insist on a statement that the Security Council had found no evidence of a threat to peace through the presence of British troops in Greece, he would not insist on the statement about withdrawal. When Bevin forcefully pointed out that the Soviet document constituted an attack on the British people, Vyshinsky took evasive action, saying that the Soviet Union had not suggested that the *presence* of the British troops endangered peace but that the danger came from the *resulting situation*. Then he suggested that an enquiry commission be sent which Bevin rejected out of hand. As both sides were now regressing to the previous interchange of charge and counter-charge and tempers were escalating, Stettinius intervened with a compromise proposal designed to satisfy both. Bevin and Vyshinsky agreed to submit this to their governments. Thereupon, the official session was resumed and at once adjourned.

The text of Stettinius' compromise proposal was as follows:

'I feel we should take note of the declaration made before the Security Council by the Representatives of the Soviet Union, the United Kingdom and Greece and also of the views expressed by the Representatives of the following members of the Security Council—the United States, France, China, Australia, Poland, Egypt and the Netherlands—in regard to the question of the presence of British troops in Greece, as recorded in the proceedings of the Council, and consider the matter closed.'

Bevin was in such a rage that he was ready to risk the dissolution of the UN in order to get a clean bill for his country.[51]

On the morning of the 6th Bevin told Stettinius that he himself agreed to the text but that Attlee was still hesitant; the final decision would be taken at a Cabinet meeting. The Australian representative, Norman Makin, at that time Chairman of the Security Council, told Stettinius that his government had instructed him not to agree to any statement which did not fully justify Great Britain.[52] At its evening session, when the Security Council dealt with the matter again, Makin tried to put through a statement in this sense, expressly stating that, according to the chairman's impression, the majority of the Security Council members were of the opinion that the presence of British troops in Greece represented no threat to international peace. Vyshinsky at once intervened and, for his part, submitted a draft statement identical in wording with that of Stettinius. After a little more to-ing and fro-ing, this text was eventually agreed.[53]

Thus the Greek problem officially disappeared from the Security Council Order of the Day, but that was far from meaning that it had ceased to exist. As would be seen in summer 1946, the Security Council debate of February was to be only the first in a long series of United Nations debates which would drag on into the 1950s. What Sofianopoulos had wanted to avoid had now begun: Greece had become a focus of dispute between the Great Powers. Stettinius' compromise settlement had been a temporary face-saving solution but it barely concealed the continuing resentment on both sides at the humiliation suffered. The Russians neither forgot Bevin's public attacks, nor the fact that he had isolated them over their complaint within the UN; much less did they forget that Greece had been the cause of their diplomatic defeat. From now on, in all matters concerning Greece, they were on a collision course. On the other hand, the British—who had also suffered a partial defeat—saw no reason to be more flexible than heretofore since every concession on security matters or on postponement of the election date would have been a *post factum* acknowledgement of the justice of the Soviet charges. Thus, here too the consequence was an entrenchment of positions. But the consequences for Greece herself were far more serious: the Security Council debate polarised public opinion still further: on one side the Anglophile Right; on the other the Russophile Left. The moderate Centre remained impaled between them.

NOTES

1. *UN Security Council. Official Records,* First Year: First Series, Supplement No. 1, (London, 1946), pp. 73 ff., Annex 3.
2. Roberts (Moscow) to Foreign Office 22nd January, 1946 (R 1139/1/19).
3. Roberts (Moscow) to Foreign Office 23rd January, 1946 (R 1207/1/19).
4. *UN Security Council. Official Records,* First Year: First Series, Supplement No. 1, p. 72.
5. Thus Noel-Baker on 16th February, 1946 (R 1626/1/19).
6. Patatzis refers to the civil war 1947-1949. The 'Second Round' was the December 1944 conflict and the fighting between ELAS and EDES in the mountains in autumn-winter 1943-4 is regarded by some as a 'First Round'.
7. Patatzis, *op. cit.,* p. 245.
8. Foreign Office to Leeper 22nd January, 1946 (R 1147/148/19).
9. Hayter's Minutes 20th February, 1946 (R 1626/1/19).
10. Leeper to Foreign Office 23rd January, 1946 (R 1191/1/19).
11. Patatzis, *op. cit.,* pp. 244 ff. Nor does Sofoulis' statement to the press on Sofianopoulos' resignation clear this up. Leeper to Foreign Office 31st January, 1946 (R 1656/1/19).
12. Leeper to Foreign Office 2nd February, 1946 (R 2196/1/19).
13. *Ibid.*
14. *UN Security Council. Official Records,* First Year: First Series, Supplement No. 1, pp. 74 ff. This decision was signed by Kafandaris, Melas, Theotokis, Venizelos, Gonatas, Sofoulis, Rendis, Papandreou, Politis, Mylonas, Plastiras, Alexandris, Maximos, Kanellopoulos, Voulgaris and Dragoumis.
15. A summary of this conversation will be found in Leeper to Foreign Office 23rd January, 1946 (R 1186/1/19) and the complete text in R 1916/1/19.
16. Leeper to Foreign Office 23rd January, 1946 (R 1187/1/19).
17. Patatzis, *op. cit.,* pp. 246 ff.
18. *Ibid.,* p. 247.
19. *Ibid.,* pp. 247 ff.
20. Hayter's Minutes 20th February, 1946 (R 1626/1/19).
21. *Ibid.*
22. *Ibid.;* Noel-Baker's Minutes 16th February, 1946.
23. Leeper to Foreign Office 27th January, 1946 (R 1374/1/19).
24. *Ibid.*
25. Laskey's and Williams' Minutes 28th and 29th January, 1946 (R 1374/1/19).
26. Minutes (R 1626/1/19).
27. Leeper to Foreign Office 29th January, 1946 (R 1558/1/19).
28. Patatzis, *op. cit.,* p. 248.
29. Foreign Office to Leeper 31st January, 1946 (R 1558/1/19).
30. Leeper to Foreign Office 30th January, 1946 (R 1626/1/19).
31. Leeper to Foreign Office 29th January, 1946 (R 1517/1/19).
32. Leeper to Foreign Office 31st January, 1946 (R 1656/1/19).
33. John Sofianopoulos, 'Why I left UN and returned to Athens', *News Chronicle,* 4th February, 1946.
34. Foreign Office to Leeper 1st February, 1946 (R 1753/1/19); Leeper to Foreign

Office 2nd February, 1946 (R 1763/1/19).
35. Leeper to Foreign Office 2nd February, 1946 (R 1796/1/19).
36. The shared opinion of Hayter and Noel-Baker (R 1626/1/19).
37. Patatzis, *op. cit.*, p. 249.
38. Joannis Sofianopoulos, 'Le problème Grec', pp. 389-96; also 'How to End the Greek Tragedy', *Nation*, 167, (25th December, 1948), pp. 715-8; and 'Greece: prescription for Peace', *Nation*, 2nd July, 1949, pp. 5-7. A speech delivered at a meeting in London on 6th October 1946, organised by the League for Democracy in Greece, the National Council for Civil Liberties and the London Trades Council, was reprinted as a pamphlet by the LDG under the title *How to save Greece* by John Sofianopoulos (LDG archives in Byzantine and Modern Greek Studies Department, King's College, University of London).
39. *UN Security Council. Official Records*, First Year: First Series, Supplement No. 1, pp. 78 ff.
40. This is Edgar Puryear's interpretation in his thesis *Communist Negotiating Techniques: A Case Study of the United Nations Security Council Commission of Investigation concerning the Greek frontier incidents*, (Princeton, 1959), p. 5. 'It is important to analyse what the Soviet motives were... The first point was the fact that the British forces in Greece were an obstacle to the Greek Communists' attempt to overthrow the legal Greek Government. Therefore, if these troops could in some way be removed, the Greek Communist Party might be able to take control of Greece. One possible way in which the Communists might be able to bring this about was by bringing pressure on Great Britain to remove her forces through the United Nations. Thus this Russian move to exert pressure through the medium of the world platform furnished by this newly created international body.' Against this, Xydis' interpretation is much closer to reality, despite the fact that it is somewhat coloured by his estimate of Sofianopoulos' conduct. S. Xydis, *Greece and the Great Powers*, pp. 163 ff.
41. On 22nd January Sir Orme Sargent formulated it thus to Agnidis: 'The Soviet Government's present move was typical of their usual technique; when they were being criticised in one quarter they took the offensive by criticising their critics in another quarter. In any case, the Soviet Government's appeal to the Security Council was directed not against the actions of the Greek Government but against the actions of H.M. Government.' (Foreign Office to Leeper 22nd January, 1946 (R 1147/1/19).
42. See p. 245, footnote 134.
43. *UN Security Council. Official Records*, First Year: First Series, Supplement No. 1, pp. 79-88.
44. *Ibid.*, pp. 88-90.
45. *FRUS 1946, VII*, p. 105.
46. Memorandum of Conversation, by the Political Adviser to the US Delegation at the UN (Bohlen) 3rd February, 1946 (*ibid.*, pp. 160 ff).
47. *UN Security Council. Official Records*, First Year: First Series, Supplement No. 1, pp. 91-100.
48. *Ibid.*, pp. 100-7.
49. *Ibid.*, pp. 108-10.
50. *Ibid.*, pp. 111-132.
51. Record of Secret Session which took place during the Meeting of the Security Council, Tuesday, Februray 5, 1946, from 9.10 p.m. until 11 p.m. (*FRUS 1946, VII*, pp. 108-12).
52. *Ibid.*, p. 114.
53. *UN Security Council. Official Records*, First Year: First Series, Supplement No. 1, pp. 165-73.

ELECTION PREPARATIONS

It was under these unfavourable auspices that the final phase of election preparations began. On 19th January, Damaskinos had signed the law naming 31st March 1946 as the election date and at the same time authorising the parliament resulting from these elections to alter articles of the Constitution, with the exception of those defining the form of the regime. But he refused to sign a second law which would have extended the registration period for electors, on the grounds that such an extension could lead to a postponement of the election date.[1] Thus, for the time being, the issue of the election date was cleared up, but the problem of the electoral system remained unsolved.

Whilst in London it was held that elections should be on the proportional representation system which had been used for the last free general elections in Greece, in January 1936 voices could be heard both within Greece and outside in favour of the majority system. Already on 15th January South Africa's representative in London had addressed himself to Bevin, demanding the majority system: in view of Greece's strategic situation and its importance for British Commonwealth lines of communication, the future Greek parliament must be controlled by a strong majority of Centre and right-wing parties, which could only be ensured by the majority system.[2]

In Athens at the beginning of February differences of opinion on this question became apparent between Sofoulis and Damaskinos. Sofoulis was for proportional representation and Damaskinos for the majority system. On 1st February Damaskinos presented his views to Leeper in a detailed memorandum: if proportional representation were used, the alliance between Venizelos and the Populists would break up. The extreme Right would then base its election programme on the constitutional issue' and the Left would give its support to the republican cause. This would result in a weakening of the Centre and a strengthening of the Right. The parliament produced by such elections would probably give the following picture: 150 extreme Right, 100 extreme Left, 50 Centre and other republicans. As a consequence it would be impossible to form a government, as neither the Centre nor the Left would nor could enter a coalition with the Right. This would wreck the whole reconstruction and normalisation programme. And, even should it come to a coalition between the Centre and the Right, the presence of 100 communists in parliament would render the government's work impossible. National questions (territorial claims) could not be solved.

'It can, on the contrary, be considered as certain that foreign interests and foreign influences directly contradictory to Greek interests would find ready advocates among the representatives of the Extreme Left, both in Parliament and in the various committees in which they would of necessity participate.'

The Left, protected by its parliamentary immunity, would preach revolution and the consequence would be internal unrest and tension with the Allies. The Right would feel itself provoked by this and it might lead to the establishment of a dictatorship. Even a dissolution of parliament would not solve the problem, since fresh elections on a proportional representation system would produce no change. This led to the imperative conclusion that the elections should be held on the majority system.

The majority system would strengthen the Patriotic Front of Venizelos and the Populists and would mean that the constitutional question would not become an election issue. A government resulting from this alliance would be stable and have sufficient authority to push through the reconstruction and normalisation programme. Then followed a passage characteristic of Damaskinos' thinking.

'Such a coalition would fully apply the principle of equality of all Parties before the law [he meant the Liberals and the Populists], with the result that administration would be improved, public respect for the state would be restored and the purge of public life would be carried out without excesses and prejudices; and once the political manners of Greece were restored to normal health and the conditions of life were improved with the progress of the Reconstruction Programme, there is reason to hope that a large number of citizens who have been carried off by the resounding slogans of the extreme Left would return to the national outlook.'

In other words, Damaskinos was trying to re-unite the bourgeois camp under the leadership of the Right.

The one 'regrettable' aspect of the majority system, he continued, was that the Left would boycott the elections. But a clause could be introduced into the relevant law giving the minority a 10 per cent representation in parliament, so that the Left would have approximately thirty deputies or more.

'It would, at all events, be preferable to face the ephemeral displeasure of a few theorists of the proportional system at home and abroad, and part of European public opinion, rather than to have to face a chamber with such a strong representation of the Autonomists of Northern Greece,[3] who would not hesitate much, as experience proves, to adopt quite openly all the anti-Greek schemes of our neighbours.'

Finally, Damaskinos appealed urgently to Leeper to accept his recommendations.[4]

On 3rd February Leeper spoke with Sofoulis on the same subject. The latter explained that there was tension between himself and Damaskinos on the question of the electoral system. The reason was simple. Damaskinos wanted to ingratiate himself with the Right so that, if the Right won, he should not lose his archbishopric. The Right was still supporting Chrysanthos, the archbishop appointed by Metaxas (for whom Damaskinos had substituted himself with German assistance). By this manoeuvre he hoped to neutralise his rival. Leeper promised to support Sofoulis, even against Damaskinos.[5]

In a further conversation on 6th February Sofoulis spelt out to Leeper that he preferred the proportional representation system and had no fear of a sizeable communist presence in parliament. It was better to have a running battle with them in parliament than to have to fight their underground tactics. The majority system together with nomination of joint candidates by Liberals and Populists would obliterate these parties' real differences and would reduce the political contest to a confrontation between communists and anti-communists, in which case the anti-communists would be dominated by the royalists. The Left, however, had unmasked itself sufficiently by its association with the Soviet *démarche* at the Security Council and could hope for no great success at the elections. But to make the most of this development, it would be necessary to postpone the elections.

Although Sofoulis had fixed the election for 31st March, he regarded the date as 'disastrous' because order was not yet re-established. He was alluding to the more violent examples of *aftoamyna* in Northern Greece. He intended to set up rural self-defence units to fight banditry. But that needed time. Premature elections would deepen the political split in the country, increase unrest and hinder the carrying out of the economic programme. A two months' postponement would be in every way advantageous and would lead to a parliament whose composition would approximate to British hopes.

If this postponement were agreed, he would try to broaden his government by taking into his Cabinet members of the moderate Right such as Papandreou, Kanellopoulos and some progressive Populists. But he would not take in even moderate left-wingers. He intended to dismiss troublemakers like Kafandaris and his followers, but hoped that he could keep Kartalis. His Cabinet would remain a Centre Cabinet but the Centre-Right would participate. He knew of course that, in the last resort, postponement of the election date was the business of the Regent and himself but, since their hands were tied by the McNeil agreement, he wanted to know whether the British Government would be against his proposals.[6]

Leeper transmitted these suggestions to London, warmly recommending their acceptance. Postponement of the elections together with the proposed government reshuffle was the only way to strengthen the forces of the Centre. Such a government could deal with the right- and left-wing bands and likewise put through the economic programme.[7]

London reacted immediately. On 7th February Leeper was told that Damaskinos' suggestions were unacceptable; as regards Sofoulis' suggestions, these would be answered immediately.[8] On 8th February Bevin himself telegraphed: the majority system was excluded; the Cabinet had decided that proportional representation should be used, as in 1936. Any alteration would give the impression of manipulation. Postponement of the elections was also excluded and would be seen as a breach of trust. The Greek government and the Regent had issued the necessary law and he, Bevin, had committed himself in the Security Council to this date. A postponement would undermine his entire position.

'It would at once be suspected that the object of the postponement was to prolong the period for which British troops are to remain in Greece. You should make it plain once and for all that I am not and shall never be prepared to give favourable consideration or support to any such proposal and that I hope that matter will not be raised again.'

For the same reasons a government reshuffle could not be considered.

'You should let the Regent and the Prime Minister know that it is my strong opinion that there should be no change before the elections, and that the present Government should remain in power and concentrate on pushing through the elections in time and on working for the economic rehabilitation of the country in accordance with our agreement.'[9]

Already on the 7th, London's unexpectedly strong reaction caused Leeper to retreat: the initiative for Sofoulis' proposals did not emanate from him. He had only concurred with Sofoulis that the Soviet Security Council *démarche* had brought about a *rapprochement* between the Centre-Right and the Liberals and Sofoulis had spun out the resulting possibilities.[10] Bevin's detailed instructions of the 8th reduced Leeper once more to an efficient executant of Foreign Office policy. On the 9th he visited Damaskinos and Sofoulis to inform them of Bevin's views. Damaskinos welcomed the adherence to the election date but was less pleased with Bevin's opinion in favour of proportional representation. Leeper had the impression that he still supported the majority system but would nevertheless accept proportional representation. For his part Damaskinos complained of the uncooperative attitude of the Greek Cabinet.[11]

In contrast to Damaskinos, Sofoulis accepted Bevin's views immediately —on principle—but at the same time he gave Leeper to understand that, by the election date, the law and order situation would not be satisfactory. He would authorise Rendis to discuss the problem directly with Bevin. In principle, he was himself still in favour of 31st March as election date.

Leeper then said that, on the law and order question, the main obstacle was the personality of the Minister for Public Order, Mercouris. Wickham had reason to have no confidence in him. Sofoulis agreed and said he would probably take over this ministry himself. In conclusion Leeper recommended better cooperation with the Regent, which Sofoulis promised albeit with some reservations.[12] One of the main arguments advanced by Leeper against Damaskinos' doubts about proportional representation had been handed him by EAM. On 16th January EAM had summoned its members to enrol on the electoral register, emphasising at the same time that this did not exclude the possibility of a boycott. On 8th February the left-wing press published a joint decision by the EAM Central Committee and the Left-Liberals. The Left would not take part in the elections unless the following conditions were fulfilled: 1) formation of a representative democratic government with EAM participation; 2) dissolution and disarming of the terrorist organisations and restoration of law and order; 3) a general amnesty for all former Resistance members; 4) a general revision of the electoral register; 5) a purge of the army, the security forces and the public service, at least of those who had served in the Security Battalions. Leeper knew that these conditions would never be fulfilled and therefore took it as more or less certain that EAM would stick by its election boycott. But in this way one was rid of the worry that there might be a hundred communists sitting in the new parliament and, thus, Damaskinos' chief objection to proportional representation went by the board.[13]

Meanwhile, on 9th February, Foreign Minister Rendis visited Bevin and assured him that the Greek government would hold to the appointed election date, which the latter welcomed. Bevin then went on to speak of the problem of emptying the prisons and urged Rendis to speed this up.[14] Rendis promised to speak in this sense to the Justice Minister and then attacked the problem of law and order, complaining of the unwillingness of the British Missions to cooperate with the Greek government on the problem of purging the security forces of right-wing extremists. Bevin promised to help.[15] Rendis mentioned the tension between the government and Damaskinos: the latter was hindering the revision of the electoral register and was still promoting the majority system. On this too Bevin promised help and stressed that, in the meantime, the Regent must have been informed of his viewpoint. He, Bevin, thought it would be much better for the Communists to be represented in parliament in proportion to their real strength, than for them to burrow underground. Rendis agreed. Finally, Bevin gave Rendis to understand that the formation of a new government before the elections was excluded, though this did not mean that some individuals could not be replaced. Concluding remarks to the effect that the British government would make an effort to get US economic aid for Greece brought the conversation to an end.[16]

Meanwhile, Leeper brushed Rendis' arguments aside:[17] the situation was exactly the opposite; Kafandaris (Mercouris' protector) was to blame for everything.[18] This was not the least of Sofoulis' reasons for suggesting a government reshuffle. For Leeper the law and order problem reduced itself to the problem of one man's personality and this appeared to satisfy the Foreign Office.

Bevin's objection to the majority system prompted Damaskinos to a final effort to push through his own ideas. On 10th February he handed Leeper a document addressed directly to Bevin. Leeper warned him that, though the document and the memorandum of 1st February would be read carefully in London, it was improbable that they would result in a change in British policy. But Damaskinos insisted it be transmitted, even though it was now clear that this would be a mere formality.[19] One of the reasons for Damaskinos' tough stance was the massive pressure being brought to bear upon him by Venizelos and Tsaldaris. On 16th February he had received a memorandum signed by both with the demand that the government introduce the majority system or resign.[20]

Damaskinos' document was transmitted to London with some delay. On 25th February Bevin telegraphed to Leeper that an official reply would follow shortly and repeated the already-known grounds for rejection.[21] On the 28th Leeper replied that he had informed Damaskinos of Bevin's attitude, that Damaskinos had thereupon ceased his resistance and had signed the law on the electoral system. This law was almost exactly identical with the electoral law of 1936.[22] Bevin's written reply was dated 9th March and contained no really new arguments: Bevin thought it better for the Communists to be represented in parliament, since they would cause trouble whatever happened. But, if proportional representation were used and the Communists participated in the elections, the number of their deputies would then be in exact proportion to their following and would thus make it difficult for them to justify the use of force. If the majority system were used, then there would be the danger that, even if the Communists participated in the elections, the Right would win such a majority that it would not respect the rights of the minority. 'Since the strength of the extreme Left is by no means negligible, this would greatly increase the danger of civil war or of the imposition of a dictatorship.' These were the reasons which had made him espouse the cause of proportional representation, though he himself preferred a majority system.[23] With this the problem could be regarded as closed.

In contrast to Damaskinos who yielded very quickly as soon as he felt the force of London's resistance to his proposals, Sofoulis—once he had been informed by Rendis of the latter's conversation with Bevin—undertook a further effort to persuade Bevin to postpone the election date. As this document is one of the most important for the period it will be quoted at some length. In this memorandum Sofoulis said that he had received Bevin's message and that he agreed that the elections should be held at the earliest possible moment. But he regarded it as his duty to make Bevin aware of the real state of affairs in Greece. Bevin was expecting that elections would express the genuine will of the Greek people.

'Unfortunately I am compelled to state that under conditions of today (i.e. under the influence of the terroristic methods now being employed, in Western Macedonia by the extreme Left and in Southern Greece by the extreme Right) the hoped-for popular verdict will be the product of psychological pressure and violence exerted principally by the armed X organisation.

'When I undertook to form a Govermment I gave the people of Greece a categorical promise that I would restore order and maintain it against any form of violence from whatever quarter it might threaten, left or right; and if this promise has not in fact been fulfilled this is due not to a lack of good will or courage but to opposition on the part of the State's organs of security, which have either passively acquiesced in, or openly abetted, the disturbance of public order.

'Unfortunately I inherited, as the legacy of a misguided regime of ten years, a one-sided situation, a royalist situation which has been intensified mainly through the actions of previous Governments that took office since the Liberation of the country. The whole machinery of state, the public prosecutor's office, the security services and even, to a great extent, the ranks of the army are in the hands of the extreme monarchist right. Consequently, if elections are held on the 31st March, under the conditions at present ruling, they will take the form of a savage clash between two armed groups fighting under the battle-cries of monarchy or communism. The Democratic Centre, that is, the Liberal parties comprising the law-abiding elements of the middle class, will be crushed between the two extremes and thereby will sustain an overwhelming defeat. The victor will be whichever of the groups disposes of the greater material strength. But, in any event, the result cannot be a genuine expression of the popular will. On the contrary it will be the outcome of violence and fraud and passions roused in bitter antagonism. Whichever group prevails, the consequence will be disaster and destruction for Greece.'

The reconstruction programme would be ruined. If the Right won, it would hold the plebiscite as soon as possible.

'Such an action would provoke a fresh outbreak of civil war, perhaps more terrible than that of December 1944.

'In the light of this situation and of the grievous consequences that may flow there from, it may perhaps be felt that the Government's resignation is indicated. Such a course would at any rate have the advantage of assuring the future position and influence of the Liberal party and the democratic centre generally. Nevertheless I am conscious that my resignation would in present circumstances produce political chaos, amid which the perils that are foreseen in the post-election period would be hastened and intensified. Moreover, I have grounds for hoping, or rather I am convinced, that all dangers may be averted and public order and full equality of rights be firmly established if I am granted an extention of two or three months beyond the 31st March. . .'

He intended to form a new gendarmerie unit of men from Macedonia and Crete and this would be led by officers who had hitherto been on the B List.

'Previous Governments have carried out successive revisions of the army lists. . . As a result, all democratic elements have been placed in List B, that is on the reserve. During the period that the army and gendarmerie were being re-organised under the orders of the special Mission, it was not an easy matter to revise List B. Now, however, with a view to meeting an imperative need, the Government have promoted a law permitting the temporary employment from List B of the gendarmerie of such persons as are considered suitable for the task of maintaining public order.'

This new unit, about 3,000 in strength, would be posted to Western Macedonia and South Greece. 'This force will constitute the principal instrument for restoring order and maintaining security.' Sofoulis ended with an emotional appeal to Bevin to grant the postponement of the election date.[24]

Rendis sent Sofoulis' message, with a covering letter, to the Foreign Office on 15th February and asked for a meeting with Bevin. But, as the latter was pre-occupied with UN Security Council matters, he delegated Sir Orme Sargent to receive Rendis on the 16th. On the 15th Hayter of the Southern Department spoke about this to Sir Orme Sargent and McNeil, neither of whom had seen Sofoulis' message, and they came to the conclusion that, despite Sofoulis' doubts, the pre-determined election date should be upheld. It was true that law and order in Greece left much to be desired but this would not be changed in two months. In their view the unrest was a product of the previous postponement of the elections; this was itself a reason for speeding them up. Moreover, a report had come in from the British representative on AMFOGE (Windle), according to which the electoral lists were in good shape, and, in the opinion of AMFOGE, there were no grounds for postponement. As for the alleged right-wing sympathies of the gendarmerie, Bevin had already telegraphed to Athens about this.[25]

On the 16th, as arranged, Rendis visited Sir Orme who told him that Bevin had given careful consideration to Sofoulis' message but that he remained of the opinion that the elections should be held on 31st March. As justification Sir Orme cited the points enumerated in Hayter's Minutes and added that Bevin had moreover several times publicly committed himself to this date. If a two months' postponement were conceded, this could easily become a postponement till November, as for instance had been demanded by the newspaper *Eleftheria*. Rendis conceded that, in such a case, the Sofoulis government could not remain so long in office. When Sir Orme asked him whether Sofoulis' desire for an election postponement derived from the influence of Kafandaris or Sofianopoulos, Rendis rebutted this: Sofoulis' motives derived from the continual excesses of the Right and the weakness of the gendarmerie. Finally Sir Orme promised that the Foreign Office would give Wickham renewed instructions to do everything possible to strengthen and purge the gendarmerie before the elections.[26]

About the same time, Leeper learned of Sofoulis' message and of the fact that Rendis had had talks with the Foreign Office. He found it improper that Sofoulis had mentioned the possibility of his resignation without informing him in advance and he requested another interview. Sofoulis therefore called on Leeper on the morning of the 17th and told him of the content of his message to Bevin. Leeper had two comments: 1) that Soufoulis' picture of what might possibly occur was too black, and 2) that there was no prospect of Bevin changing his mind about the election date. Leeper did concede that there were difficulties, but these were there to be overcome. Restoration of law and order would more probably be delayed by any postponement of the election date, which would undermine public confidence and also encourage illegal activity. If Sofoulis' suspicions about the gendarmerie were really justified, then something must be done at once. He himself naturally relied on the reports from Sir Charles Wickham in whom he had complete confidence; unfortunately, however, Mercouris did not consult Sir Charles but went behind his back. Mercouris had now been in office three months and could have worked out a plan to reform the gendarmerie with Sir Charles long ago, instead of secretly carrying out transfers and reporting to the government without consulting Sir Charles. If things were really so bad, said Leeper, he should himself have been informed. It was quite clear that Mercouris had failed and must be replaced.

'The fact that he was supported by Kaphandaris who so far as I could see had done nothing but obstruct the Prime Minister left me cold. I would if I were the Prime Minister rather face resignation of Kaphandaris and his satellite Minister than see public order deteriorate under an incompetent and unreliable Minister. There was little chance of getting the gendarmerie to play straight if they were convinced that their Minister played crooked.'

He therefore suggested the following:

'(a) No further tinkering with the elections.

(b) The Prime Minister himself to take over the Ministry of Public

Order and call [an] immediate conference at which Sir Charles Wickham and I would be present.

(c) The Prime Minister to indicate at what places he would desire British troops to be present at the time of the elections in order to reassure the public.'

Sofoulis accepted these suggestions and Leeper went on:

'There must be no question even in his own mind of his resigning. I would regard this as a dereliction of duty.'

The only alternative was a government of the Populists and Venizelos with the latter as puppet-premier. This would give the Communists the excuse to declare a General Strike, to wreck the economic programme and to boycott the elections. All this, together with the world-market wheat shortage which would shortly make itself felt in Greece, would bring about chaos. For the Foreign Office, Leeper added the following sentence to his report:

'The object of the meeting was to give him [Sofoulis] a pep talk and I think the pep worked itself into his veins. To be Prime Minister of Greece at any time seems to a foreigner a thankless task, but to be Prime Minister here in 1946 at the age of 85 is a task and an ambition which can only be expressed in an official telegram by a group of (undecypherable).'[27]

Sofoulis left Leeper after promising to remain in office. Shortly afterwards Leeper was visited by Kartalis who assured him that his conversation with Sofoulis had worked wonders. He was of the opinion that the elections must either be carried out now or must be postponed to November. As the latter was impossible, the previously-determined date should be adhered to.[28]

Far more than the security reasons alleged to Bevin, it was the probable election prospects of his own party which influenced Sofoulis. He feared that the Right would emerge from the elections as the strongest party and that his own party would suffer severe losses. As he did not want to form a coalition with the Right after the elections, it was necessary for him to gain time to win the voters back to the Centre. Meanwhile, he hoped to win over some of the moderate leaders of the Right, such as Papandreou and Kanellopoulos, for the Centre cause. In this he was deluded: Papandreou was counting on profiting from this situation. He knew that he was the only presentable right-wing politician and that, through his good relations with the Centre, he could act as a mediator. He therefore believed that he might be the future premier of a Centre-Right coalition.[29]

Sofoulis' arguments for postponing the elections on security grounds were justified in view of the conditions but, since he was only using this as a pretext to make party political capital for himself, his position was greatly weakened as everyone saw through these tactics and therefore did not take his threats of resignation seriously. Had Sofoulis really wanted to postpone the elections for the reasons alleged, this disavowal by the British would have left him no alternative but to resign.

Leeper knew this and therefore kept to his hard line; on the other hand his attitude to the security problem can only be characterised as frivolous:
'There is no reasonable chance of dissolving the disturbers of the peace on the Right and the Left before the 31st March. Perfect conditions for perfect elections in an imperfect part of an imperfect Europe cannot prevail by the 31st March. Nevertheless the results of the elections under such conditions will in my view reflect, as closely as it can be obtained, the real attitude of public opinion. Our object is to establish the facts. If Greek public opinion moves further to the Right than is convenient to His Majesty's Government, I have little doubt that the Government which emerges will be more than anxious to adapt itself to the requirements of His Majesty's Government.'[30]

The Foreign Office approved Leeper's actions. Bevin himself noted: 'I approve your langauge.'[31] Then he told Leeper of the conversation between Rendis and Sir Orme and expressed his appreciation of Leeper's initiative. It was obvious that the Greek gendarmerie could not be trusted to act impartially and he regarded it as essential that this should be corrected before the elections. He was really disappointed that this was still the case.

On 19th February Leeper and Sofoulis met once more. Sofoulis told Leeper of the report sent him by Rendis and declared that he now accepted the 31st March as election date. Leeper asked him whether he had yet taken any action in regard to Mercouris. Sofoulis said he would take over the Public Order Ministry himself next day no matter what objections Kafandaris might raise.[32] On 20th February, he kept his promise. Mercouris was transferred to the Ministry for Public Works and Sofoulis took his place as Minister for Public Order. At the same time both ELD and EAM announced that, if the elections were not postponed, they would not participate. The newspaper *Eleftheria* also demanded postponement, blaming the British for pressing the early date. Leeper got the impression that even Sofoulis still did not support the early date wholeheartedly and that he could only be kept on course by constant British pressure.[33] On 23rd February Leeper sent the Foreign Office an optimistic report on the general security situation in which he wrote that, since the Kalamata affair, the excesses had fallen off. The present degree of unrest was 'normal' and could not be altered by a postponement of the election date.[34]

Meanwhile the party leaders continued to intrigue. The British refusal to agree to the majority system removed one of the premises of the agreement between Venizelos and the Populists. The result was a new constellation: 1) the Populists and their satellites; 2) the Centre-Right around Papandreou, Kanellopoulos and Venizelos; 3) the Sofoulis Liberals and their associated groups; 4) the Left around EAM and KKE. Leeper assessed their potential voting strength as follows: 1) 35-40 per cent; 2) 10-15 per cent; 3) 15-20 per cent; 4) 25-35 per cent.[35]

After it had become clear in mid-February that proportional representation had been chosen, Venizelos announced the founding of a new party, the Venizelist Liberals, which he presented as the legitimate heir of the old Liberal Party. At the same time he made it known that he had formed an election alliance with Papandreou and Kanellopoulos and that section of the Democratic Union (the former party of Papanastasiou) which did not belong to EAM.[36] A joint list of candidates and a joint republican election programme would be drawn up. The Populists reacted with irritation to this 'affront'. Since, with the exception of Kanellopoulos, the republicanism of the other Centre-Right representatives was more than doubtful and they would try to win votes mainly from the traditionally royalist voting constituency of the Populists, this caused the latter to take a harder line: for them the elections would be an advance referendum on the constitutional issue.[37] On the Left, too, there were signs of a movement for unity. EAM was trying to start an All-Greek Republican Movement under General Othonaios. An organisational framework was growing up to reinforce polarisation. The government observed these developments with growing unease, since this threatened to deprive the Centre of its voting base. Defeatism began to spread and even a few ministers began to talk of abstention. Kafandaris went so far as to sponsor a newspaper article making a demand for postponement if not for abstention. In conversations with the ministers Leeper tried several times to recall them to their moral duty, but without great effect.[38]

On 28th February Sofoulis visited Leeper and complained of Kafandaris' manoeuvre but refused to break with him. He was still holding to the pre-determined election date and intended to send Bevin a message to this effect. But he would also warn him that if EAM boycotted the elections, the Right would carry off an overwhelming victory which would at once have the worst result for Anglo-Greek relations. The Right had no social programme, no experience of governing and had no presentable leader at its disposal.

'But this lack of leadership did not prevent them from being dangerously cohesive on one question namely the need for the immediate return of the King and this chiefly through their hatred and fear of communism. To bring the King back at an early date would however inevitably plunge the country in civil war. If on the other hand EAM/KKE took part in the elections the result would be an equilibrium between the extreme Right and the extreme Left which would leave the initiative and leadership in the hands of the Centre.'

Leeper agreed that, whilst it was certainly not desirable that the Left should boycott the elections, it would not have such serious consequences if Sofoulis would himself make an effort and win back that section of the Right which traditionally belonged in the Liberal camp. This group had turned away from the Liberals because they feared collaboration between them and the Left. From talks with Papandreou, who was the leader of this new group, he knew that the latter was ready to enter a Sofoulis Cabinet provided Kafandaris was not a member. Sofoulis was not in principle against this but had reservations about Venizelos. Leeper agreed but brought Sofoulis to the point of promising not to let the line to Papandreou be cut off, and assured him of his support. Sofoulis asked Leeper to make his influence on the *Eleftheria* group felt, particularly Kartalis, to make him see reason: his 'flirtation' with EAM over election postponement must be ended. In conclusion Sofoulis demanded that the Liberals should retain their party's name, even in the event of an election alliance with Papandreou's group. Leeper agreed to this.[39]

In reporting this conversation to the Foreign Office, Leeper added the following comments. The Centre was suffering from its isolation and from defeatism. The influence of Papandreou's group was growing daily. The voters were turning either to the Left or to the parties to the right of the government.

'This tendency is fatal to what I conceive to be the fundamental policy of His Majesty's Government viz. to support the moderate elements in the Greek population. Short-sighted and foolish as many of the Right undoubtedly are, I think that Sofoulis fails to distinguish clearly enough between the several groups of which it is composed...'[40]

On the same day, 28th February, Damaskinos signed the law prescribing proportional representation. On 2nd March a delegation representing EAM, SKE/ELD, the Left-Liberals and the Union of Left Republicans (Sofianopoulos) visited Sofoulis and told him that, if the election date were postponed for two months and the interval used for revising the electoral lists and for the restoration of law and order, they would be prepared to participate in the elections.[41] Sofoulis was alarmed and at once sent a personal message to Bevin:

The statement from the Left created a serious situation. Although he himself continued to adhere to the agreed policy, he wanted to make Bevin aware of the consequences of an election boycott by the Left.

'By participation, those elements would constitute, in the matter of terroristic methods, a balance to the extreme Right, that is to the members of the 'X' organisation; and in this way the acts of violence of either group would be neutralised, since both possess approximately equal means of enforcing their will.'

A boycott by the Left would lead to control of the state by the Right.

'Relying on the armed "X" organisations which will be reinforced by almost the whole of the police and gendarmerie, the latter group will lead the electors in the countryside like cattle to the polling-booths, with the slogan: "He [the King] is coming". The result of the elections, being the product of violence, will be false and precisely similar to the notorious plebiscite of 1935.[42] The consequence will be the immediate formation of an exclusively right-wing Government and, probably the immediate recall of the King: provocation to the extreme left and opportunity for a fresh attempt at forcibly seizing power.'

This danger could only be avoided if the Left took part in the elections so that a balance of forces resulted. In spite of this situation, he was holding to the agreed course.

'My sole purpose in reporting the above matters to you is to keep you informed of the situation so that you may not be unprepared for, or disappointed by, results that we anticipate as inevitable in view of the decision taken by the extreme Left to abstain from the elections.'[43]

At the Foreign Office Hayter interpreted this message as no more than a tactical manoeuvre: Sofoulis was trying to wash his hands of responsibility for any undesirable result of the elections. His message contained no constructive suggestions and did not really require a reply, but his remarks about the police and 'X' should not be left unanswered and he should be given a lesson.[44] Hayter's comments show that, even in the Foreign Office, there was no clear view and things were being left, almost fatalistically, to run their course. British policy towards Greece restricted itself to insisting on the pre-determined election date. This had been clear from the middle of February.

On 21st February Hayter had analysed the possible election results in a detailed memorandum. He had come to the conclusion that probably the Right would win. The government to be formed after this victory would indeed subscribe to a pro-British line but would pursue a policy which would not be in accord with British wishes. It would at once take up the issue of restoring the monarchy and embark on a repressive internal policy which would nullify the little that had been achieved on the amnesty question. In foreign policy such a government would also take an extreme line. Moreover, since the Greek Left would probably boycott the elections, such a government would be met with implacable enmity by the British Left. But the British government bore a heavy measure of responsibility for determining the election date and could hardly afford not to recognise the results, even if these were contrary to its expectations. It would be obliged to support even a government of this sort.

'We can do, of course, our best to guide and advise such a Government, but we shall have to recognise that Greek internal politics are in the last resort a matter to be decided by the elected Greek Government and not by H.M.G., and that we cannot allow such internal politics to affect our own policy of supporting Greek independence.'

The only alternative would be to postpone the elections and continue to support the present government economically and financially so that it could win over the electors. However this was impracticable.

'But we should realise that by committing ourselves to March elections we have also committed ourselves to supporting whatever Government emerges from them, and that it will almost certainly be a Government whose internal politics we shall not like.'[45]

One asks oneself whether Hayter would have been quite so ready to accept such an election result if a left-wing victory had been probable.

Sir Orme Sargent doubted a right-wing victory in view of proportional representation: the result would be a three-way split in the Greek electorate, producing a weak government which would therefore lean heavily on Great Britain. Should the Right win the elections, they too would orient themselves according to British wishes because they would be under threat from a communist opposition supported by Russia. Difficulties in supporting such a government would be found rather within Britain itself. The repressive internal policy foreseen by Hayter would come to the fore only when the British troops were withdrawn. Then Britain could wash her hands in all innocence.[46]

McNeil agreed with Hayter: the Centre had failed.

'I too, therefore, have found myself wondering what we should do about the emerging Government between the period when they take over and when the banked-up civil war overtakes them. I conclude that we would offer to retain our Missions and our goodwill if they pursued a semi-liberal policy about courts, prisons, gendarmerie etc. and prepare to get out our troops by this autumn at the latest.'[47]

So the Foreign Office had more or less resigned itself to a victory of the Greek Right and acknowledged that the policy pursued up to now for the creation of a strong Centre had failed. Instead of making an effort for a last minute change of course, it refused to face reality and surrendered itself to illusions that the elections might perhaps produce a different result. But, since there was no danger that the future right-wing Greek government would pursue a foreign policy damaging to British interests, the Foreign Office was ready to accept the ugly accompanying phenomena of its internal policy. This line of thought emerges very clearly from a draft telegram compiled from the above-quoted opinions of its staff for sending as a political brief to the new British ambassador in Athens, Sir Clifford Norton (Leeper had left Athens on 9th March). Although on Bevin's orders this telegram was eventually not sent, its content makes it a key document for British policy towards Greece.

'. . .2. The decision of the Left Wing Parties to abstain from the elections suggests that a victory by the Right must be seriously considered. It would certainly be most unsatisfactory that the Right should come to power in Greece as the result of an election which is not seriously contested. But since the decision of the other Parties to abstain is clearly due for the most part to a belief that the majority of the electorate is not on their side, it can reasonably be claimed that elections held without them would nevertheless give a fair indication of the real wishes of the Greek people. H.M.G., by initiating the proposal for the Allied Observer Mission and in other ways open to them, have done everything in their power to see that the elections are as fair as possible, and there is every reason to believe that, by Balkan standards at any rate, the elections will permit a free expression of the popular will.

3. In view of their responsibilities in the matter, H.M.G. will have no choice but to accept the results of the elections, however unpalatable they may be. The principal interest of H.M.G. in Greece is that she should remain independent and should not be under the control of another power. Greek internal politics are in the last resort a matter to be decided by the elected Greek Government, not by H.M.G. So long as there was no elected Greek Government, and so long as British forces in Greece were obliged to assume responsibilities in connexion with the preservation of law and order, a certain amount of intervention by H.M.G. in Greek domestic affairs was more or less inevitable. This period is rapidly drawing to a close, and the time will shortly come when our intervention should cease, together with the reasons for it.

4. Nevertheless, public opinion both at home and abroad has grown accustomed to the idea that H.M.G. have some special responsibility for the actions and conduct of the Greek Government. And it will no doubt continue to be the case that Greece will depend on Great Britain for considerable help and advice, and that this will ensure to H.M.G. in return a certain influence over the policy of the Greek Government. I believe that our policy should be to offer the new Greek Government a continuance of our present support, including the retention of the Service, Police and Economic Missions, on the condition that *they* agree to press on with the economic programme laid down in my exchange of letters with M. Tsouderos, to maintain parliamentary institutions and constitutional liberties, and to refrain from raising the issue of the Monarchy until the time agreed last year (i.e. March 1948). If the new Greek Government agree to a policy on these lines, H.M.G. for their part will be prepared to give them their wholehearted support. . .'[48]

This means that the Foreign Office was ready to go on supporting the future Greek government on condition that it did not establish a dictatorship or step up repression—though, as the future would show, these were somewhat elastic concepts. But in general this document can be interpreted as a confession of the failure of British policy in Greece; only the actual fact of failure was not acknowledged and no words were wasted on British responsibility for that. Everyone was to blame except the architects of the policy, and the disastrous consequences were ignored.

In this connection Leeper, analysing his three years as ambassador, makes a much more honourable showing, even if he saw no cause for self-criticism. His final report, dated 22nd February, differs from those which had gone before in its somewhat more detached perspective. This is particularly noticeable in his character sketches of Greek politicians which show that he had fully realised their inadequacies. More important, however, are his forecasts for the post-election period.

'I cannot see how Greece, even under an elected Government, can win through without a serious clash between the Right and the Left. Too much blood has been shed and there is too much hatred for the two sides to live together peacefully or for anybody to mediate between them. One side or the other must come out on top and the other side very much under. In January 1945 the civil war came to a quick settlement and was not pursued to the bitter end owing to British intervention. . . But once the British Army has been withdrawn, passions will not easily be restrained. . . If an elected Greek Government then takes the law in its own hands acting on the motto *Salus populi suprema lex* will Anglo-Greek relations suffer. If they do, how far will British interests suffer in the Mediterranean?'[49]

The answer to this question and a suggested solution to the Greek problem were proferred by Leeper himself in a letter of 27th February to Sir Orme Sargent. In his introductory words he said that his final report addressed to the Southern Department, in which he analysed the Greek political situation, gave only a symptomatic, superficial picture of the position; the underlying problems were much more disturbing. There were two basic questions: '1. Is an independent Greece possible? and 2. If not, how can Greece be kept on our side of the fence?'

No state could be truly independent if it were not financially independent. Even before the Second World War and under considerably more propitious conditions, Greece had not been able to keep herself financially above water. Since the end of the war, she had been totally dependent on foreign aid. The elections would now provide a pretext for reducing British support, should that be desired. 'We can say that the period of post-war tutelage is over and that our responsibilities are at an end.' But the elections would not bring about any improvement in conditions, rather the post-election situation would become more acute. UNRRA assistance would be reduced and at the end of the year it would be terminated. Great Britain would no longer bear the costs of the Greek army and Greece would not be in a position to take these over, at least not to the extent the British thought necessary. Moreover, the voices demanding withdrawal of the British troops were becoming louder.

'Are we today facing realities in Greece? I think not. We have made an economic agreement and have sent a mission to see that the Greeks carry out their part of it by balancing their budget. But they can only do so by reducing their armed forces and gendarmerie far below the safety line. If they don't make the reduction, they collapse through bankruptcy. If they do make it, and we then withdraw our troops, they have no chance of keeping order in the country and therefore no chance of balancing their budget. Thus whichever way you look at it the financial argument defeats itself.

'The plain fact, which His Majesty's Government have shown no signs of recognising so far, is that Greece in the conditions of the post-war world is not, and cannot be, a really independent state. Whether she can ever become one is a moot point; but it is obvious that it will take many years before conditions again become as favourable as they were in the pre-war period during which. . . she could only get along by defaulting on foreign bonds.

'As an independent Greece is an impossibility for many years to come, one of two things must happen to her, depending on our decision: either she must be kept as a satellite in our own orbit, at the cost to us of military in lieu of financial and economic assistance; or she must inevitably gravitate into the Russian orbit for lack of such assistance from us. The first alternative means for us not merely the military cost, but also the political difficulties which the continuance of our tutelage would involve. Against this, however, we must put the facts that it preserves for us a vital link in our system of Imperial communications and defence, and that it imposed on a country which has deserved well of us a tutelage which need be neither irksome nor permanent. The other alternative means the permanent loss to us of the vital link, and the permanent loss to Greece of her independence. It condemns our first fighting ally for good and all to the bondage of the Kremlin; and it brings Russia down to Cape Matapan and Crete. Just how much do we care?

'The final decision is one we shall have to take very soon. And let us not delude ourselves, in a private correspondence, with the all too common idea that there is a third possibility, namely, that we can somehow "get Greece to stand on her own feet" in the course of the present year and thereafter sit back and watch her remaining on our side of the fence. It simply cannot be done. Quite apart from all the psychological difficulties of restoring Greek morale and the will to work, the purely factual calculations of every expert who has studied the problem on the spot have proved, as conclusively as anything can be proved, that in the financial and economic sphere Greece could not make herself *viable* even if she were to acquire tomorrow a perfect government enjoying widespread popular support and taking our own advice promptly on every single point in her programme. These calculations have never been rebutted, nor yet seriously and factually disputed: they have simply been officially ignored; and the Treasury people who have ignored them have made it pretty plain that in their heart of hearts they accept them but consider that we should cut our losses. Well, that is one of the two alternatives; but it seems to me to be one that ignores our own vital interests, including financial interests in the widest sense. Can we, in the last analysis, *afford* to let Russia control the whole of the Balkans and—at one short remove—Turkey also?

'If, as I sincerely hope, the reply of His Majesty's Government as a whole is that we cannot, and that we must consequently go on with the job, I see in theory three ways of doing so:
1. merely to go on keeping British troops in Greece indefinitely, on a sufficient scale to ensure her external and internal security, and with or without the help of Greek forces for which we should have to pay in so far as they were above the very low maximum which Greece herself can afford;
2. to attempt to run Greece more or less on the Cromer model;
3. to allow an elected Greek government to apply (after a plebiscite) for membership of the British Commonwealth.

'Method (1), though superfically the least drastic of the three, has all the disadvantages of a compromise. It looks fishy and makes it hard to explain to our own people and foreign critics what we are really at. It does not give us anything like enough control to enable us to terminate within measurable time what must inevitably be described as a transition phase of protection and tutelage.

'Method (2) is franker and would give us the control we needed to make the transitional phase a fairly short one; after which we could retire with the job done and grimace to those who had talked (as many certainly would) of "disguised imperialism" and "the thin end of the wedge". Unfortunately criticism on these lines prove *[sic]* too strong for us: the Cromer technique, though still what is really required in Greece today, is, I assume, impossible for reasons of general international psychology in the world of 1946.

'There remains method (3). I fully realise the difficulties, but I know of no other solution. Here again, of course, there would be many accusations to face of "disguised imperialist expansion" and the like. But they can be refuted. Nobody of good faith can deny that the Dominions (unlike the component republics of the Soviet Union) are voluntary members of the group to which they belong and have not only the theoretical right, but also the practical possibility, of seceding from the Commonwealth whenever they choose. Objections could no doubt be raised to the incorporation of a very foreign, very Mediterranean element from the other end of Europe in a predominantly Anglo-Saxon group. But France, to whom we offered Commonwealth status not long ago without any great outcry on the score of "imperialism", is nearly as foreign racially and in outlook as Greece; and are we not hoping that before long the utterly foreign peoples of India will enjoy that status?

'The request would of course have to be demonstrably genuine as regards the great majority of the Greek population, but I believe there would be no difficulty about that. Excluding the hard core of EAM/ KKE the idea would, I consider, arouse unmistakably genuine enthusiasm here if it ever came to be mooted. What all non-EAM Greeks want more than anything else is a reasonable degree of liberty within a framework of security. Except in a few restricted Right-wing cliques, there is no enthusiasm for George II as an individual, and of course nobody regards him as a Greek. Most of the Greeks who now want him back would very much rather have King George VI than King George II. And most of the non-EAM remainder would, I am convinced, willingly sacrifice their republican principles for the acquisition of Dominion status under a genuinely constitutional monarch. Incidentally, the Cyprus problem would solve itself.

'Of course there are. . . difficulties. Our own lack of imagination is one. Another is our fear of what Russia might say and do. As regards what she might say, I have yet to learn of a post-war action by His Majesty's Government that Moscow has publicly approved, and I have heard of many entirely blameless ones which Moscow has stridently condemned. Why should we take into consideration the criticisms of people who regard all non-communists as potential or actual fascists? As regards what she might do, is it irrelevant that she has already expanded her "Empire" by swallowing (manifestly against their will) of the Baltic States, and has not been deterred by the creation of U.N.O. from starting on the same digestive process in Persia? Have we any real reason to believe that she is at present being restrained by our "correct behaviour" in Greece from absorbing the other Balkan States by her well-known technique of bogus plebiscites? If she has not yet done so, it seems to me that that is because, at a time when the conduct of her troops has made her intensely unpopular, she feels that the mouthful would be embarrassingly large. It is the technique of the Russians (who taught the Nazis their stuff) to take the initiative and brazen it out. On the rare occasions when the same technique is tried out on themselves, they take it lying down, since force is the only thing they either admire or understand. . . a Greek plebiscite on the Commonwealth issue would, unlike the ones in the Baltic States, reveal what the people really wanted. It would, however, be a display of resolution on our part to hold our own and cope with a vital Imperial problem. The alternative of letting Greece go would be clear indication that we had lost the will to maintain our position in the world. Have we lost it?'[50]

The Foreign Office reaction to this declaration by Leeper of the bankruptcy of British policy for Greece shows once more its complete helplessness and lack of ideas. Hayter rejected Leeper's suggestion.

'None of Sir R. Leeper's three prospects will do. . . Dominions are independent and self-supporting states, and Sir R. Leeper's whole argument is to prove that Greece can be neither. What he perhaps means is that Greece should become a part of the Empire and that we should assume responsibility for controlling and defending her. But this would turn Greece not into a Dominion but into a Crown Colony, which would be more indefensible internationally and would be quite unacceptable to the Greeks themselves. Several Greeks when I was in Athens, notably General Zervas, talked about Greece entering the British Empire. What they clearly meant was that they should govern the country themselves and that we should pay for it and defend it. But this is not Dominion status. . .'

Warner was of the opinion that even a state which was not economically self-supporting could achieve Dominion status. This would at least solve the problem of the troops and likewise the constitutional problem would be liquidated by the appointment of a British Governor-General. But he was afraid that British and US public opinion would not accept this; and moreover it would not solve the financial problem. Noel-Baker dismissed Leeper's idea out of hand. McNeil's bitter comment was conclusive:

'I still think that colonial treatment whether by us or by some trusteeship group is the only method which offers any hope of nursing Greece towards solvency and political stability. "Dominion status" is meantime impossible because as Mr. Hayter infers Greece is a backward, extravagant and irresponsible country whose vanities are made greater and whose difficulties are therefore accentuated because for both us and the USSR Greece has strategic importance.'[51]

McNeil's commentary was the final blow to Leeper's last attempt to prompt the Foreign Office—via Sir Orme Sargent—to a reconsideration of British policy towards Greece. From the Southern Department minutes— Sir Orme himself refrained from expressing any opinion—it becomes apparent that they were at their wits' end. They held inexorably to their chosen course, repeating their habitual formulas, hiding themselves behind information which was often tainted, one-sidedly optimistic, or propaganda-motivated, hoping—against better knowledge—that the catastrophe would not happen. As we noted earlier, they were still washing their hands of responsibility. They did not notice that in the final analysis they had become victims of their own propaganda terminology. By phrasing their instructions in this spirit, they blocked the only source, the British Embassy in Athens, which could have corrected the existing picture. Thus, they became trapped in a vicious circle. Another important factor in the one-sidedly rosy reporting from Athens may also have been Leeper's impending transfer to the British Embassy in Argentina. In the past he had several times taken initiatives for a new policy towards Greece and each time he had come into collision with the political leadership of the Foreign Office. Why should he, shortly before his departure, expose himself to another such confrontation? This would have implied an open acknowledgement that his activities over the last years had been a failure, which would certainly not have improved the prospects for his further career. Therefore, to the last day of his sojourn in Athens, he held—in his official correspondence with the Foreign Office—to his chosen line of adaptation to the instructions of his superiors. Basically, he was acting on the motto *après moi le déluge.*

In the whole matter, the only one who made a different assessment was Minister of State Noel-Baker. He did not accept the Foreign Office mandarins' one-sided condemnation of Svolos and Sofianopoulos and also did not share their optimism on the amnesty issue. He knew that many of the senior officers appointed by Plastiras had in the meantime become extreme royalists and that Rendis' reports were wholly justified. He realised that Bevin's instructions to suspend politically-involved officers from active service were spoken to the wind because it was just in those cases which mattered most that it was almost impossible to prove party involvement. Noel-Baker, too, did nothing to bring about a change of policy but contented himself with writing sarcastic marginal comments.[52]

A change of British policy for Greece was simply not under discussion. The tenacity of the Foreign Office apparatus proved stronger than the forces demanding a change. It is therefore hardly surprising that Bevin's reply of 7th March to Sofoulis' message of the 2nd was formulated in terms of the previous policy.

Bevin regretted that the Left would not participate in the elections but this could only mean that they had a poor estimate of their electoral prospects. He did not think that abstention by the Left would justify depriving the Greek people of the right to a free choice of government. Before the elections were held no one could know anything about the real wishes of the Greek people and it was therefore British policy to hold the elections as soon as possible. As regards Sofoulis' statement about 'X' and the gendarmerie, he was extremely surprised at this. Nothing of the sort had emerged from the reports submitted to him and he firmly believed that Sofoulis, as Minister for Public Order and with the help of Sir Charles Wickham, could prevent collaboration between the security forces and the illegal armed bands.

'In any case I cannot see how the X organisation can compel the electors in the countryside to vote in a manner contrary to their convictions provided a reasonably secret ballot is secured. It seems to me that the right course for Greece would have been that all Parties should participate in the elections in a peaceful manner, so that the Greek people on March 31st may be assured of the opportunity of expressing its will in conditions of tranquillity and order. If Greece is to win respect of her Allies and particularly United States' and public opinion here, it is essential for the Greek Government to show determination to deal with this matter effectively. It will establish her credit in the eyes of her friends more than anything else.'[53]

Meanwhile in Athens party-political manoeuvring continued. On 2nd March Papandreou informed Leeper of a new plan. In order to reduce to the minimum the negative results of a right-wing victory, he suggested an immediate agreement between the Populists, his own group and Sofoulis' Liberals. Sofoulis would remain in office until the elections. The parties would fight the elections separately but, irrespective of the result, they should now agree on the formation of a coalition government. The plebiscite would be temporarily postponed and only held after discussions with the British government. Directly the new parliament assembled, the coalition government would submit to it a law introducing a modified majority electoral system. If the Left was represented in parliament and if they proved obstructive, parliament would be dissolved and fresh elections held. If the Left were not in parliament, then fresh elections would be held only when the reconstruction programme was concluded. This plan had the support of Damaskinos and of some of the moderate Populists who themselves were afraid of the more radical elements in their own ranks. Sofoulis would be the future premier as the Populists would not accept Papandreou. Leeper welcomed this initiative because it would encourage *rapprochement* in the bourgeois camp and increase the chances for a peaceful evolution.[54] London was satisfied and expressed the hope that, after the elections, right-wing excesses would cease.[55]

On 3rd March Sofoulis told Leeper of his message to Bevin. Leeper urged him to take a less pessimistic view of the situation. On the 4th Sofoulis began to lose control of developments. In a broadcast on that day the Press Minister, Iraklis Petimezas, recommended the summoning of an all-party conference including both extreme Left and extreme Right and the inclusion of representatives of all the big parties in the government. If this were not done, the elections would be biased and security conditions would be inadequate. Sofoulis sharply condemned this statement, demanded Petimezas' resignation, and, when he did not comply, sacked him on the 5th.[56] On the 6th Tsouderos wrote a letter to Sofoulis saying that, whilst the latter's decision to go through with the elections was an honourable and courageous gesture, there were nevertheless important reasons which spoke for postponement. The boycott by the Left would create a situation far removed from normality and just for this reason it was necessary to ensure the country's reconstruction during the next months. On these grounds he would not take part in the elections and he put his ministerial post at Sofoulis' disposal.[57] On the same day Trade Minister Ioannis Peltekis told Reuter that if the Left did not participate in the elections there would be a renewal of civil war and this civil war would not be restricted to Athens but would spread over the whole of Greece. Throughout the country the hatred between the two extremes was building up to a climax. An all-party conference should be summoned, with representatives of the Allies in attendance, to reach agreement with the Left.

'Unless all the major parties are represented in the new Greek Government. . . the bitter internal disagreement which divide[s] the Greek people will be solved once again by hand grenades and dictatorship instead of by Parliamentary debates. The absence of Communists from the new Chamber will perpetuate civil war.'[58]

To Peltekis too, Sofoulis reacted with firmness, demanding his resignation; Tsouderos, on the contrary, he begged to remain in office to which the latter agreed from a sense of duty.[59]

On the 9th Leeper left Athens. On the 8th he had sent his last analysis to the Foreign Office. In contrast to his official final report of mid-February, there were no half-tones and no attempt to explore the causes leading to the present situation. The Centre had failed; the Left was a tool of Russian imperialism and the Right was the only guarantee of a pro-British foreign policy in Greece. He therefore recommended unreserved recognition of the future government.[60] Then he preferred suggestions on how to treat this government. The real problem of the forthcoming Populist victory was not only that their leaders were very second-rate but also that they were controlled by forces outside their party such as 'X'. 'It is the latter which will push them into provoking dangerous conflict in the country by trying to bring the King back at an early date.' To escape this very real danger, he recommended that his successor should make it clear to the Populist leaders as soon as possible that the British government disapproved of any such attempt at the present time. The constitutional problem could only be resolved when normality had been established and the reconstruction programme was nearing completion. Such a warning would bring the more reasonable Populists to their senses. It must, of course, be done before the elections. It was perfectly possible to keep the Right under control; but a strong hand would be needed and they must be clearly given to understand that only if they behaved properly could they reckon on British support.[61]

In arguing thus, Leeper completely overlooked the fact that this control machinery would hardly operate after a right-wing electoral victory. As would soon become apparent, the Right had no interest in promoting Greece's economic recovery since its clientele—more especially the forces in the background (big money and the wire-pullers of the *parakratos*)— were wholly uninterested in the restoration of conditions of order. They were interested only in power; and, moreover, they knew that the British government had no alternative. Leeper's hope that his successor could continue to control the Greek government in the way he had done heretofore was an illusion.

At midday on the 9th, after Leeper's departure, Lascelles, who was temporarily replacing him, visited Sofoulis and handed him Bevin's answer of 7th March. Sofoulis said that he was not surprised by the contents but that Bevin's expectations concerning a secret ballot were based on false premises. He would nevertheless adhere to the pre-determined election date, although he foresaw his own electoral defeat. He hoped that something could still be done about the partisan attitude of the gendarmerie. Perhaps exemplary punishment in a few well-attested cases of this and of insubordination would bring the gendarmerie to act with more restraint. The Governor-General of Northern Greece had reported to him that the gendarmerie commander at Verroia had adorned his command post with 'X' emblems and obstinately refused to remove them. The Governor-General was therefore threatening resignation. Lascelles thought that this could be a case for making an example. Sofoulis agreed and went on to tell him that he had heard from the Governor-General of Epirus that right-wing terror would make free elections in his area impossible, though he had produced no proof of this. Lascelles emphasised how important it was to have concrete proofs.

'He [Sofoulis] had evidently been misled, for example in [an] alleged case of fraternisation with Manganas. His own source had given a completely different version to us and we had checked independently and found the story to be untrue. He replied that the facts were well-established: his source had told him he must be allowed to put out a watered down version of episode because otherwise his life would be in danger. (I suspect this of being merely a face saving retreat).'[62]

Anyone who knows Greek political life will be unlikely to doubt Sofoulis' version.

In his next telegram Lascelles registered his opinion on Petimezas' dismissal and on the cases of Tsouderos and Peltekis. A resignation landslide was threatening: Kafandaris and Mercouris (certainly undesirable elements whose departure he would have welcomed earlier); the Mylonas group; the *Eleftheria* group around Kartalis (who in the last days had been most stupidly flirting with EAM and had only been restrained from resigning by Leeper); and finally Tsouderos. If these ministers resigned, it would mean the end of the Sofoulis Cabinet since the greater majority of his party was also in rebellion against him and was demanding that he postpone the elections. In that case the only solution would be the formation of a caretaker government: an all-party government, as demanded by Petimezas, was excluded, since the Left was making exorbitant demands and the Right—in view of their certain electoral victory—would not consider entering such a government. A one-sided opening of the government to admit the Left would bring the Right to 'boiling point'. The inclusion of representatives of the Papandreou-Kanellopoulos-Venizelos group would be taken as provocation by the Left and would have negative reverberations abroad. Furthermore, a change of government implied not only a change of Cabinet members but also a change of many subordinate officials who, moreover, were directly employed on preparations for the elections. The Left was unlikely to revise its boycott decision. In addition, the replacement of Leeper and Scobie was being interpreted as a sign of British weakness. They would probably go on to an attempt to sabotage the elections by strikes. This would provoke the Right to intensify its reprisals and repressive measures which could even go so far as a *putsch*.

> 'I can see no way out, and hope that this gloomy picture will prove to have been overdrawn though I do not think it is. Apart from incompatability with the declared policy of His Majesty's Government and the very serious risk of the Right kicking over the traces, a postponement would only defer the evil hour. Present Government are far too demoralised to have any hope of improving conditions if given a month or longer. Moreover, they could not go even half way to meet the Left's demands, prefixed [sic] by gaol clearance during that period, without driving the Right to open violence. Only precaution I can suggest is for His Majesty's Government to draw all possible attention now in advance to implications of an eventual attempt at physical sabotage of elections by EAM/KKE. I realise, however, that this would not be easy to put across.'

It was therefore a question of the survival of the Sofoulis government. Sofoulis was a tired old man. He did indeed keep loyally to his promise but he would surely be happy if the force of events would prevent him from having to carry it out. His ministers had always been undisciplined; now they were demoralised by the certainty of forthcoming defeat and of renewed bloodshed.[63]

The Regent took a highly critical view of Sofoulis whom he believed was only pretending to hold to the election date while in practice still toying with the thought of postponement. The undesirable elements in the government were trying in every way to sabotage the election date. He would not allow this to happen. As soon as he was clear on the matter, he would dismiss the present government and replace it with an interim one, even if he himself had to be premier. In this case, he would address himself to the leadership of the army and the security forces and demand that they maintain order and tranquillity. The communists might perhaps obstruct the 31st March elections but this would mean at most a delay, not a postponement. Lascelles warned Damaskinos that the British government did not want a change of government before the elections if this was not absolutely unavoidable. Even if a substantially better government could be found, the change would appear suspect to world public opinion.

Damaskinos agreed and assured Lascelles that he regarded the certain victory of the Right with no particular pleasure. They had no leader, were narrow-minded and could only be brought by 'massive persuasion' to steer a moderate course. Anyway, he intended to resign after the elections. Lascelles ended by asking the Foreign Office for instructions.[64]

On the evening of the same day (9th March), Kafandaris addressed himself to the press. He and his party would not participate in the elections. The 31st March had been agreed upon on the premises that the state would have been purged of the extremist partisans of the Right and that resolution of the constitutional problem would be postponed for two years. Neither premise had been adhered to.

> 'The British are to blame not as the Russians contended at UNO for the intervention but on the contrary for *not* intervening to prevent their justified suppression of the December revolution from producing a state of reactionary terrorism. They impeded [a] purge which the present Government would otherwise have carried out by demanding exhaustive enquiries whenever changes were suggested. The Royalists are openly putting forward [the] constitutional issue at the elections with the result that serious trouble is likely. Under these circumstances the elections will only be a parody and he [Kafandaris] cannot face lending them a semblance of legality by his participation.'[65]

This was published in the Athens press on the morning of 10th March together with statements by Kartalis and Mylonas. Kartalis demanded a Cabinet meeting on the election problem at which all ministers should give their opinion so that the government could reach a united standpoint and the situation be clarified. Mylonas considered that the Left's boycott made the elections one-sided and he therefore demanded a postponement. In the face of pressure from both extremes, peasant voters could not at present make a free decision. Postponement would also help towards economic reconstruction. If the elections were not postponed, he would resign. In addition the press hinted that Kafandaris and his four party members were contemplating resignation and that Kartalis, with Pappas and Georgakis, would also resign if Sofoulis did not accept their demands. A total of ten to twelve ministerial resignations were expected.[66]

Simultaneously, Kafandaris (Vice-premier), Bourdaras (Communications), Mercouris (formerly Public Order) and Evripaios (Air Traffic) submitted their resignations. Kafandaris told the journalists that the conditions for free elections did not exist. To a certain extent Great Britain was responsible:

> 'British policy. . . instead of guiding the development of the situation until some degree of normalcy had been established in the country,

chose, by using the pretext of non-intervention in Greek affairs, to ignore what was happening and to leave the country in the full control of the Right. Now Greece is being led to an electoral fiasco involving great dangers for the country.'[67]

Sofoulis—as he told Lascelles—did not let these resignations disturb him. Desertion by Kafandaris and his followers did no real harm since in the past this gorup had only caused trouble. Kartalis, too, was not irreplaceable: he had told him that his demand was childish and unacceptable. Anyway he had only been taken into the government because the British wanted a representative of the Resistance in the Cabinet. Kartalis had no right to demand a revision of the original government decision; after all he, too, had signed it together with the rest.

Lascelles agreed with Sofoulis, at least in regard to Kafandaris; but Kartalis was a key man in the reconstruction programme which would be endangered and its evolution complicated by his resignation. Sofoulis brushed this objection aside: better people could be found amongst his Liberals who remained loyal to him; only if Tsouderos resigned would there be danger. Kartalis had come to an agreement with the communists and it would be better if he vanished from the scene. The sound Liberal core would carry on with the programme. But Lascelles doubted that Kartalis could be so easily replaced.[68]

After Sofoulis had rejected Kartalis' demand and, on 11th March, had made a defiant statement to the effect that he was ready to accept the resignation of any minister who wanted to resign, Kartalis (Supply Minister), Pappas (Assistant-Minister for Supply) and Georgakis (Governor-General of the Ionian islands) submitted their resignations, to be followed on the 12th by Finance Minister Mylonas. Sofoulis was unimpressed. He stated that the posts left vacant would be taken over by the ministers remaining in office and that the elections would be held on 31st March. The Foreign Office, too, was unshaken by the mass resignation of Greek ministers. On 11th March Bevin brought the question of an eventual postponement to the attention of the British Cabinet and found unanimous approval for his rejection of any postponement. On the 13th he informed Lascelles and, to make his stand completely clear, he added a version of the draft telegram of the 12th,[69] slightly modified to suit the new circumstances. About the same time one of Kafandaris' ministerial colleagues leaked Bevin's reply to Sofoulis to the Athens press. *I Machi* (ELD) commented bitterly:

'One would seek in vain to find less opposition in Bevin than in Churchill towards the Greek Left. . . Is this the sort of solidarity the Labour Party shows towards the Left parties in Europe. . .?'[70]

In a later comment it complained

'the Greek workers, who suffered the terror inflicted by fascists and traitors, expected a different tone from this Labour man. They did not expect this "Socialist" Minister to believe that the Left was abstaining because they "did not enjoy popular support".'[71]

But the opinion that the elections should be postponed was not confined to Greek left-wing circles. The League for Democracy in Greece (founded on 28th October 1945, the anniversary of the Italian attack on Greece) succeeded in collecting eighty signatures of members of the House of Commons to a resolution including the following recommendations:

'(1) If the election is to be honest the Cabinet in charge of it must represent the democratic forces in the country, and we suggest that it should include members chosen by the Resistance organisations. This will imply no special support of the EAM but merely a recognition of the political balance in Greece.

(2) An immediate and far more thorough purge of collaborators is needed in the Civil and Military organisations.

(3) The political amnesty must be genuinely carried out, the gaols emptied of political prisoners and those now hiding in the mountains included in the amnesty. The Government should make it clear that it no longer counts against a man that he was a member of the Resistance, but rather that he is respected for it.

(4) The electoral register should be revised and fair facilities given to all electors.'[72]

Even the conservative London *Times* considered a postponement to be indicated.[73]

On 14th March the left-wing parties sent a joint telegram to Bevin signed by Sofianopoulos, Partsalidis, Gavriilidis, Kyrkos, Oikonomou, Kritikas, Svolos and Hajibeïs. This telegram set out the reasons for the Left's election boycott. But they were prepared to participate in the elections if an all-party government was formed, a general amnesty declared, the public services, army and security forces purged, the electoral registers revised and the elections postponed for two months.[74] On 19th March a telegram from the New Zealand Prime Minister, Mr Frazer, reached London, expressing strong doubts about the British government's line. In view of the situation

'it would appear at this distance that insistence by His Majesty's Government in the United Kingdom on this date [31 March] may put the United Kingdom Government in the position where they are out of sympathy with the majority of the Greek people. No doubt such a situation would give the opposition in Greece, which appears not inconsiderable, as well as the Soviet Government, an opportunity—and with some apparent justification—for attacking the policy of His Majesty's Government'.

He wanted to know whether the majority of the Greek people agreed that the elections should not be postponed.

'It is too late to have the whole matter reconsidered, or is the United

Kingdom Government still satisfied as to the correctness and the wisdom of its decision? I feel it would be a great disservice to the British Commonwealth if our critics could exploit any rigid insistence upon the holding of the elections on 31st March as being contrary to the will of the Greek people and in face of their overt opposition.'[75]

Bevin did not let himself be deflected by this intervention. On 20th March he stated that it had always been and still was British policy that the elections in Greece should be held as early as possible. Speaking at the Labour Party Conference, on December 13th 1944, he had said that first of all, as soon as tranquillity and order were established, there was to be a general election and the only thing the British government stipulated was that, if their name was to be associated with it, the Greek government must take all precautions to ensure that the general election was fair and above board and that there was no rigging. After that a plebiscite on the question of monarchy or republic was to be taken.

The Varkiza Agreement had reversed the order of elections and plebiscite. EAM had thereupon changed position and pressed that elections should be held first as he (Bevin) had suggested in his speech. Though the royalists were against this, in the end it was generally agreed to hold the elections first. During the Regent's visit to London a statement had been issued by the three Western Allied governments expressing the hope that elections would be held in 1945. When the Sofoulis government took office in November it was part of its mandate that the elections would be held not later than March 1946. The Sofoulis government fully accepted this and so at the time did all other parties. The Greek government then fixed the date of the elections as 31st March and after some hesitation EAM and the communists instructed their followers to register for the elections which they had now done.

He went on to state that the government did not think that a two months' postponement would improve the state of security in Greece, and to give details of the arrangements made for observing the elections. He wound up as follows:

'The right thing for the Greek people, and indeed the duty of the parties and the press, is to use all their power and influence to get an overwhelming poll on March 31st. Greece, for the first time for years, will then express her democratic and independent opinion as to the Government she desires and deserves.'[76]

In this whole matter the US had shown itself far more reserved. On 11th March Rankin, the US *chargé d'affaires* in Athens (MacVeagh was on leave), by agreement with Ambassador Grady (the State Department's Special Envoy) had advised against direct intervention, which would only intensify the impression that the election date was being forced on the Greek government; but a hint that, for organisational and financial reasons, AMFOGE could not be kept waiting too long would be useful.[77]

Thereupon, on 19th March, Secretary of State Byrnes stated that, whilst elections at the earliest opportunity would be welcomed, determination of the date was a matter for the Greek government alone.[78] This statement satisfied neither his staff in Athens nor those in London. Grady told Byrnes that in Athens this was being interpreted to mean that the US was not unsympathetic to a postponement and he asked for instructions what to do if it actually came to this.[79] Bevin addressed himself to the US *chargé d'affaires* in London: he welcomed the fact that the US took the same standpoint that the elections should not be postponed; but, unfortunately, Byrnes' statement was ambiguous and susceptible of misinterpretation. He had instructed the British ambassador in Washington, Halifax, to make representations to the State Department about this.[80] Accordingly, on 20th March, Halifax submitted a memorandum to the State Department in which Bevin expressed the hope that the US government would instruct its *chargé d'affaires* in Athens to make representations to the Greek government urging them to stick to the pre-determined election date.[81]

But Byrnes was not ready to move from his attitude of reserve. On 21st March he instructed Rankin that—provided he and Grady saw no objections—they should hand Sofoulis Byrnes' statement of 19th March, telling him by word of mouth that, whilst fixing the election date was the business of the Greek government, the US government nevertheless hoped that a postponement could be avoided. Byrnes added some further arguments for sticking to the date but he left the final decision to the Greek government.[82]

Halifax reported to London that there were two motives for the US government's reserve. On the one hand they did not want to endanger their Persian policy by openly siding with the British government on the Greek question and thus exposing themselves to Russian criticism. On the other hand, they did not want to provoke criticism from American liberals. Moreover, the State Department was of the opinion that British pressure was sufficient. The Near East Division of the State Department was of more or less the same opinion as the Southern Department, but there was political resistance at the highest level for the above-mentioned reasons.[83]

Bevin was not at all pleased with this US reaction. In his reply telegram of 22nd March to Halifax he said he found Byrnes' statement wholly inadequate but that he hoped his instructions of 21st March to Rankin would have the desired effect.[84] Had Bevin known the contents of Byrnes' telegram of 22nd March to Grady, he probably would not have awaited developments so calmly. In this strictly confidential telegram, Byrnes said that, whilst he hoped it would not come to a postponement, if it did, the State Department intended getting the President's consent for the US AMFOGE contingent to stay on until 1st June. This plan, however, had to be kept top secret.[85] On 23rd March the AMFOGE leadership informed the three Allied governments that the agitation for postponement had failed and that the elections would be held as planned on 31st March.[86]

Bevin's statement of 20th March was published in the Athens press on the 21st in the form of summaries or extracts. *Eleftheria*, however, made a decisive change which the newly-arrived British Ambassador, Clifford Norton, reported as follows:

> '*Eleftheria* which is still generally regarded as an organ of the Greek Government has published only a summarised version of the statement and this summary asserted *inter alia* that agreement to hold elections by the end of March this year *and the plebiscite in March 1948* was "ratified by the Three Great Powers" as well as being accepted by "all parties in Greece". This appears to be a distortion of the passage in your statement which recalls that British, United States and French Governments published last September a joint statement "expressing the hope that *elections* would be held in 1945".'

Moreover Norton was afraid that the Populists would make play with the inaccuracy contained in *Eleftheria*'s version of Bevin's statement. He continued:

> 'As regards the assertion... that not only the holding of elections this March but also the postponement of the plebiscite until March 1948 were fully accepted by "all other parties" at the relevant time I must point out that the Populist Party... definitely rejected His Majesty's Government programme (of which two years' postponement of the plebiscite formed an essential part)... In their propaganda the Populists have consistently maintained that if they come to power after the elections they will be in no way committed as regards the date of the plebiscite...'

Their participation in the elections did not imply that they had changed their mind.[87]

On the same day Norton had his first talk with Sofoulis. After a general review of the situation, Sofoulis said that the boycott by the Left would hold since the time limit for participation had run out at midnight. He would nevertheless carry through the elections even if there were to be further difficulties. He agreed with Bevin except that he doubted that the general law and order situation really permitted free elections. Norton said that it was the wish of the British government that, after the elections, a coalition government should be formed on the broadest possible basis. Sofoulis doubted the possibility of this since, immediately after the elections, the Right would demand a solution of the constitutional problem.[88]

When the British government forced Sofoulis to announce the 31st March as election date, it should have made some effort to assist him in creating the necessary pre-condition for genuinely free elections—freedom from fear. We have seen how this effort was neglected; but then came a chance—the Kalamata affair. But for the Soviet intervention at the Security Council, this spectacular case of right-wing terror might well have proved the incentive for a change of course. A drastic reaction would probably have changed the climate; but Bevin's policy in the Security Council made this impossible. *The Observer*'s commentator wrote:

'In London it may have seemed that Mr. Bevin had a resounding triumph during the Greek debate in UNO. Here in Athens, one can only suspect that he was badly out-manoeuvred. The Russians waved the red flag, and he charged, to find himself—where? Committed to an early election held in dubious conditions whose results can only bring us trouble.'[89]

In the Foreign Office this was understood though not openly admitted; the result was the *après moi le déluge*-mentality. Thus after the Security Council debate British policy towards Greece immobilised itself. The only side from which—theoretically—a new initiative could come was the Greek government. However, within a week, eight ministers and four assistant-ministers resigned while a couple of others remained in the Cabinet only conditionally, thus reducing it to a mere shadow whose political bankruptcy was evident. Under normal conditions such a state of affairs would have led to the resignation of the Prime Minister and to the formation of a new government, so that it is difficult to understand why Sofoulis soldiered on to the bitter end. Had he resigned together with his Cabinet ministers, he might have brought about a new start. What was necessary was not a postponement for two months but a new government including the Left, a postponement of six months and a new policy to tackle drastically such problems as general amnesty and a high-level forces purge. Certainly, this would have meant disavowal of and conflict with Bevin, but what could he have done to hinder it? Sofoulis had nothing to lose but apparently he was too demoralised and too entrenched in the mentality of Greek policy makers (what does the protecting power want?) to take this step which, for him, would have been almost a revolution. So he, too, like the Foreign Office, began to let things take their course. The elections thus became the curtain-raiser to the tragedy of civil war.

NOTES

1. Leeper to Foreign Office 24th January, 1946 (R 1735/1/19).
2. South African Representative to Bevin 15th January, 1946 (R 1583/1/19).
3. See pp. 34 and 396. Damaskinos apparently fell back on the anti-communist propaganda of the 1920s and 1930s. This, however, was only the beginning of a whole campaign which reached its climax during the civil war.
4. Translation of Memorandum addressed by the Regent of Greece to H.M. Ambassador on the Question of the Electoral System 1st February, 1946

(R 2918/1/19).
5. Leeper to Foreign Office 4th February, 1946 (R 1830/1/19). On Damaskinos' relations with the Germans see Woodhouse, *Apple of Discord*, pp. 29, 38, 123; *The Struggle for Greece*, p. 22.
6. Leeper to Foreign Office 6th February, 1946 (R 1905/1/19).
7. Leeper to Foreign Office 6th February, 1946 (R 1906/1/19).
8. Leeper to Foreign Office 7th February, 1946 (R 1906/1/19).
9. Foreign Office to Leeper 8th February, 1946 (R 1905/1/19).
10. Leeper to Foreign Office 7th February, 1946 (R 1979/1/19).
11. Leeper to Foreign Office 10th February, 1946 (R 2192/1/19).
12. *Ibid.*
13. Leeper to Foreign Office 10th February, 1946 (R 2150/1/19).
14. See p. 344.
15. See p. 327.
16. Foreign Office to Leeper 9th February, 1946 (R 1906/1/19).
17. See p. 328.
18. Leeper to Foreign Office 11th February, 1946 (R 2233/1/19).
19. Leeper to Foreign Office 11th February, 1946 (R 2246/1/19). Text of the document in R 2918/1/19. This text is identical with that sent by Damaskinos to Leeper on 1st February.
20. R 3527/1/19.
21. Foreign Office to Leeper 25th February, 1946 (R 2904/1/19).
22. Leeper to Foreign Office 28th February, 1946 (R 3279/1/19).
23. Bevin to Damaskinos 9th March, 1946 (R 3279/1/19).
24. Greek Embassy to Foreign Office 15th February, 1946 (R 2633/1/19).
25. Hayter's Minutes 15th February, 1946 (R 2633/1/19).
26. Notes of Conversation by Sir Orme Sargent 16th February, 1946 (R 2634/1/19).
27. Leeper to Foreign Office 17th February, 1946 (R 2520/1/19).
28. Leeper to Foreign Office 18th February, 1946 (R 2598/1/19).
29. Leeper to Foreign Office 15th February, 1946 (R 2628/1/19).
30. *Ibid.*
31. Foreign Office to Leeper 18th February, 1946 (R 2633/1/19).
32. Foreign Office to Leeper 19th February, 1946 (R 2666/1/19).
33. Leeper to Foreign Office 21st February, 1946 (R 2771/1/19).
34. Leeper to Foreign Office 23rd February, 1946 (R 2930/1/19).
35. Leeper to Foreign Office 23rd February, 1946 (R 3288/1/19).
36. Before the Metaxas dictatorship the Greek party system had known two major parties: the Liberals of Eleftherios Venizelos and the Populists. After the death of Eleftherios Venizelos, Themistoklis Sofoulis inherited the Liberal leadership. Eleftherios' son Sofoklis, who showed only a sporadic interest in politics, was here obviously trying to oust Sofoulis though he had nothing to offer but his name. The two major parties each had two or three smaller splinter parties orbiting around them. In the Venizelist camp the most important were the Democratic Union of A. Papanastasiou, the Progressive Party of Kafandaris and the Agrarian Party of A. Mylonas. Their right-wing counterparts were the parties of I. Metaxas, I. Rallis and G. Stratos as well as the Macedonian Union of G. Gotzamanis. The latter, however, were scarcely more than patronage networks of their leaders who only gained weight when they combined with factions of the Populist Party (as in the 1936 elections with Theotokis and Tourkovasilis).
37. Leeper to Foreign Office 27th February, 1946 (R 3553/1/19).
38. Leeper to Foreign Office 27th February, 1946 (R 3193/1/19).
39. Leeper to Foreign Office 28th February, 1946 (R 3315/1/19).

ELECTION PREPARATIONS 439

40. *Ibid.*
41. Lascelles to Foreign Office 9th March, 1946 (R 4201/1/19).
42. The way this plebiscite was rigged was an open scandal even at that time when rigged elections were a common occurrence in Europe. The republicans abstained but nevertheless '97.8%' voted for the monarchy.
43. Message from the Prime Minister of Greece to the Secretary of State for Foreign Affairs 2nd March, 1946 (R 3462/1/19).
44. Hayter's Minutes 5th March, 1946 (R 3462/1/19).
45. Hayter's Minutes 21st February, 1946 (R 3032/1/19).
46. Sargent's Minutes 21st February, 1946 (*ibid.*).
47. McNeil's Minutes 1st March, 1946 (*ibid.*).
48. Draft telegram 12th March, 1946 (*ibid.*).
49. Leeper to Bevin 22nd February, 1946 (R 3338/1/19). This report was received on 2nd March, 1946 and printed for submission to members of the Cabinet.
50. Leeper's letter to Sir Orme Sargent 27th February, 1946 (R 3496/1/19). In a conversation with the US *chargé d'affaires* in Athens, Leeper openly acknowledged the failure of his policy (*FRUS 1946, VII*, p. 116).
51. Hayter's Minutes of 8th March, Warner's of 11th March, Noel-Baker's of 12th March, McNeil's of 29th March (R 3496/1/19).
52. Bevin to Leeper 7th March, 1946 (R 3383/1/19).
53. Draft-answer to Major Wilkes MP, end of February, 1946 (R 3491/1/19).
54. Leeper to Foreign Office 3rd March, 1946 (R 3347/1/19).
55. Foreign Office to Leeper 7th March, 1946 (R 3347/1/19). Bevin telegraphed: 'I agree with you that any attempt to prevent the Right from exploiting an election victory is to be encouraged. . . once elections are held we shall hope for stable Government and this business of the Extreme Right or others resorting to extra-constitutional methods will be finished with.'
56. Leeper to Foreign Office 7th March, 1946 (R 3635/1/19); *The Times*, 6th March, 1946.
57. *The Times*, 7th March, 1946. Text of the letter in R 4293/1/19.
58. *Glasgow Herald*, 7th March, 1946; *The Times*, 7th March, 1946; Leeper to Foreign Office 7th March, 1946 (R 3367/1/19).
59. Lascelles to Foreign Office 8th March, 1946 (R 3670/1/19).
60. Leeper to Foreign Office 8th March, 1946 (R 3765/1/19).
61. Leeper to Foreign Office 9th March, 1946 (R 3741/1/19).
62. Lascelles to Foreign Office 9th March, 1946 (R 3742/1/19).
63. Lascelles to Foreign Office 9th March, 1946 (R 3746/1/19).
64. Lascelles to Foreign Office 9th March, 1946 (R 3748/1/19).
65. Lascelles to Foreign Office 10th March, 1946 (R 3749/1/19).
66. Lascelles to Foreign Office 10th March, 1946 (R 3750/1/19).
67. *The Times*, 11th March, 1946.
68. Lascelles to Foreign Office 10th March, 1946 (R 3731/1/19).
69. See p. 418, note 44. Foreign Office to Lascelles 13th March, 1946 (R 3748/1/19).
70. *I Machi*, 12th March, 1946; cited from *Greek News: The Journal of the League for Democracy in Greece* 1:2 (March/April 1946), p. 3.
71. *Ibid.*, 1:3 (May 1946), p. 3.
72. *Ibid.*, 1:2 (March/April 1946), p. 2. The Chairman of the League was Compton Mackenzie; Vice-Chairmen F. Seymour Cocks MP, Lord Faringdon, Benn W. Levy MP, Wilfred Roberts MP. Another seven members of the House of Commons and two from the House of Lords were on the Executive Committee.
73. *The Times*, 8th March, 1946. The same view was expressed by *The Observer* and *News Chronicle*; Stavrianos, *Greece*, p. 168.

74. Text of the telegram in R 4373/1/19.
75. New Zealand Government telegram to British Government 19th March, 1946 (R 4451/1/19).
76. Foreign Office to Norton 20th March, 1946 (R 4527/1/19).
77. Rankin to State Department 11th March, 1946 (*FRUS 1946, VII*, p. 120).
78. Byrnes to Rankin 19th March, 1946 (*FRUS 1946, VII*, p. 121).
79. Rankin to Byrnes 20th March, 1946 (*ibid.*, pp. 123 ff).
80. Bevin to US *chargé d'Affaires* 20th March, 1946 (R 4396/1/19).
81. British Embassy to State Department. Aide Memoir 20th March, 1946 (*FRUS 1946, VII*, pp. 124 ff).
82. Byrnes to Rankin 21st March, 1946 (*ibid.*, p. 126).
83. Halifax to Foreign Office 21st March, 1946 (R 4458/1/19).
84. Bevin to Halifax 22nd March, 1946 (R 4458/1/19).
85. Byrnes to Rankin (Grady) 22nd March, 1946 (*FRUS 1946, VII*, pp. 126 ff).
86. *Ibid.*, p. 127. Norton to Foreign Office 23rd March, 1946 (R 4606/1/19).
87. Norton to Foreign Office 21st March, 1946 (R 4498/1/19).
88. Norton to Foreign Office 21st March, 1946 (R 4542/1/19).
89. Hugh Massingham, 'Greece: After the polls', *The Observer,* 7th April, 1946.

THE ELECTIONS

The last days before the elections passed without any striking events. Sofoulis' campaign could be seen as an effort to go down with honour, all the more so as he wholly lacked press support. (The press from Centre to Left demanded abstention.) At the same time he tried—even at the last moment—to secure certain material advantages for his party followers by issuing ministerial decrees. This prompted Tsaldaris to threaten that, after the elections, he would annul them all. There had been a renewed attempt to appoint republican officers but that was prevented by British objections. Tsaldaris, on the contrary, adopted the dignified pose of an already-designated Prime Minister; though his party's election propaganda was less reserved, less dignified. Their posters denounced the Left as lackeys and toadies of pan-slavism; Papandreou's 'social democracy' was approximated to communism; photographs were circulated showing Kanellopoulos in the company of Aris Velouchiotis (during the liberation of the Peloponnese); leaflets recalled the 'good old times' when the Populists governed and food prices were much lower. The abstaining parties in the main contented themselves with the omnipresent slogan *Apochi* (abstention). KKE propaganda concentrated so heavily on Papandreou as to give the impression that the party desired a victory of the Right. The election campaign was interrupted by Greek Independence Day (25th March). In general, the last phase of the campaign was characterised by a certain lack of reality. Everybody knew the Right was going to win. Evidence of this was that public discussion concentrated far more on post-election problems than on the elections themselves. The law and order situation would have struck a superficial observer as satisfactory. There were no major episodes and the small local incidents appeared negligible. Even for experienced international correspondents it was difficult to assess the situation accurately. Sefton Delmer could detect no sign of oppression;[1] nor could the *Manchester Guardian* correspondent find anything sinister.[2] Dudley Barker came to the conclusion that the supposition that terror reigned in Greece was erroneous: 'Widely circulated stories of excesses, intimidation and fake registers, even prophecies of a new civil war, are largely false, or at least, wildly exaggerated'. There were indeed attempts at intimidation in the countryside but, in the end, no one could prevent the voter in the polling booth from voting for the party he trusted,[3] and in the final resort AMFOGE was there to ensure genuine elections.[4] Vernon Bartlett saw nothing for it but to go through with the elections, but prophesied a deep-seated crisis resulting from a one-sided parliament.[5] Christopher Buckley wrote:

'That the elections will be conducted with the nice courtesies associated with Western Parliamentary democracy no one would pretend. That they will be markedly unfair and corrupt by Balkan standards in these things is neither proven nor probable. Eastern Macedonia is not West Kensington, and much of the misunderstandings of the present Greek situation is due to those who suppose that it is or can be.'[6]

These British correspondents drew their information mainly from British and official Greek sources.

If one compares these optimistic pictures with the material collected in the EAM Black Book which derives in the main from extracts from the Greek bourgeois press and from first-hand reports from grassroots EAM committees, one would hardly think they were describing the same country at the same time and during the same events. On the one hand a relatively optimistic assessment of the situation; on the other a sinister impression of omnipresent White Terror of which the Black Book cites seven full pages of examples. In accordance with the analysis up to this point, the Black Book's version seems far nearer to the truth than those press correspondents' reports. They had come to Greece only shortly before the elections, mostly spoke no Greek and had no intimate knowledge of Greek conditions. They based themselves primarily in Athens and their English-speaking informants seldom belonged to the circles from which the Left recruited its followers. When the Left spoke of an 'election terror', this was in the same degree both true and false. It was false in so far as, since the arrival of AMFOGE, there had been hardly any further spectacular right-wing acts of terrorism such as that of Manganas at Kalamata (though Manganas himself was still at liberty). However, it was not these spectacular cases which were decisive but the total sum of minor excesses and acts of terrorism since Varkiza which had created a climate of fear that decisively influenced the election result. During the preceding twelve months the *parakratos* had created such an atmosphere of terror that it was in no way necessary to maintain this by further spectacular action during the last weeks before the elections. The election result was assured at the very latest from the moment when Sofoulis failed to break the power of the *parakratos*.

Even AMFOGE recognised that the Left's complaint that the Right was terrorising their voters was to a certain degree justified.

'The Mission finds that there is some substance to these charges. It is convinced that there was everywhere in Greece considerable antagonism to the extreme Left-wing adherents and that in some localities, particularly in the agricultural regions of the Peloponnesus, in Thessaly and northwest Greece, most markedly in the neighbourhoods of Larissa,

Volos, Missolonghi, Arta, Agrinion, and in the mountain regions south and west of Yannina, there was fear of EAM and a bitterness against it and the former members of its disbanded armed force (ELAS) which led to a determination of the part of its opponents that it should be excluded from influence in the Government of the country. In the larger cities and towns the charges of intimidation were not so grave nor so generally made, and the Mission is not convinced that there was any serious intimidation outside of the areas specifically mentioned above and a few scattered localities elsewhere.

'In a few localities along the border of Albania, Bulgaria and Yugoslavia, intimidation was exercised against the Rightest adherents by extremist bands of the Left.

'Thus intimidation by both sides was to some extent exhibited in acts of violence which occurred in the early months of the year and tended to diminish as the elections approached. The more important part of the intimidation was intangible and very difficult to prove. It took the form of village ostracism, persecution in the way of attacks upon houses, the humiliation of women, threatening gestures and messages, depredation upon flocks of sheep, gardens and vineyards, assaults along lonely trails, and all sorts of minor incidents.'[7]

Thus far the AMFOGE report depicted the realities of the situation. But, when it went on to analyse the background to this intimidation, it confined itself to the terminology promulgated by Churchill more than a year earlier: EAM had been an organisation completely under communist control; towards the end of the Occupation it had fought against various right-wing organisations including 'X'—there was no word of the true character of 'X' which was practically a collaborationist organisation. After Liberation ELAS had marched on Athens (sic) in order to seize power by force; British troops which had landed in Greece to expel the Germans (sic) had therefore had to intervene. In Athens and in some provincial towns there had been heavy fighting. The present enmity between the two parties was the result of the fear and bitterness which had developed before and during the time of the civil war.

In other words, the Allied observers had a completely one-sided picture of the developments which had led up to their mission to Greece. How had this come about? One of the most experienced correspondents, Constantine Poulos, who was thoroughly acquainted with Greek conditions, reported as follows:

'When the creation of AMFOGE was announced in Washington, it was said that the observers would be assembled in Italy for "indoctrination in inspecting elections". The activity has been going on in the small town of Bagnoli near Naples, during the last two weeks. But "indoctrination" was not limited to "training in election inspection". There were lectures by persons who have already gone on record, either officially or privately, as being against the Greek Left. There were persons lecturing who have officially supported British policy in Greece during the past few years and who are anxious to have the elections "prove" that the Greek Left is a small, unimportant minority... British efforts to influence the American observers are also obvious in the appointment of Col. C.M. Woodhouse as liaison officer with the American Mission.'[8]

It was the British who took responsibility for information on recent Greek History (1940–46).[9]

Moreover, the great majority of AMFOGE members (1,038 out of 1,155) were officers. This raised two questions about all the activities of the Mission, beyond mere observation of the election process. First, it can be assumed that, even without the one-sided 'indoctrination', professional officers would not have too much sympathy for the Left. Second, in comparison with most officers' experience of brutality and terror during the Second World War, the hardly spectacular Greek terrorism of the pre-election period may have appeared wholly negligible. Destruction of vines might seem almost ridiculous compared to other devastation, though for the peasant affected it could endanger survival. As observers, beyond the explicit task of supervising the election process, the officers at least were hardly competent since they were simply not in a position to assess the weight and influence of repression on the conduct of elections. Perhaps the sensitivity of the mission's members might have been heightened had they been told that not only communists were victims of right-wing persecution, but this they were evidently not told. The Mission arrived in Greece with a blinkered attitude to the situation.

On their arrival in Greece, this subtle process of influence continued. Poulos reports:

'Young American officers and soldiers working for AMFOGE have been besieged by English-speaking Greeks, men, women and girls, nearly all of whom are members of Royalist and Right wing groups. The Americans are being invited to fancy parties at wealthy homes where they are treated royally and at the same time fed with propaganda against the Greek Left. The effects are already evident.'[10]

Of course, this did not go so far as to make the mission members ready to tolerate open electoral falsification, but it was sufficient to prevent them from taking opposition complaints quite seriously. Mission members who did not agree with the pre-determined line, for example the American professor Jerzy Neyman, were sent home.[11]

The next problem facing the mission was the problem of interpreters, since hardly any of the members spoke Greek. The mission certainly realised that the selection of interpreters had political implications.

'Naturally it was not possible to obtain so great a number (224) of intelligent English-speaking Greeks who had no political views or sympathies of their own. It can be stated, however, that extremists of both Left and Right, and also German collaborators, were ruled out, although efforts were made by some politically-minded groups in Athens to pack the body of interpreters...'[12]

Despite this, the majority of interpreters probably came from the upper class and were unlikely to have been distinguished by any great sympathy for the Left. The social provenance of the interpreters gained in significance from the fact that hardly one of the leaders of the Greek Left, let alone their followers, spoke English.

The Mission had taken as its task, not only to supervise the electoral process itself, but to arrive at a valid assessment of the electoral registers, of the voters registered, of participation in voting, etc. For this they had prepared a carefully worked-out system for statistic-taking and control on the basis of questionnaires. In a Western European country, with a functioning bureaucracy and administration, this would certainly have produced accurate results; but in Greece it could not produce any such incontrovertible evidence since the data on which AMFOGE's calculations were to be based were either wholly lacking or were grounded in arbitrary assessments.

A few examples will suffice to make this clear. AMFOGE based its calculations on a total Greek population of 7.5 million. But that was a more or less arbitrary figure since the last population statistics dated from 1940 and had given a total of 7.3 million. But this figure, too, was hypothetical since the last census had been taken in 1928. Pre-war Greek governments had presumed that the population was increasing at the rate of just 100,000 annually. The AMFOGE figure was obviously based on a halved rate of increase for the war years. The next more or less reliable figure comes from the year 1951 when, on the basis of a not very accurate population census, the total was assessed at 7.65 million.[13] But as these figures come from the post-civil war period, after the heavy loss of life, they cannot be relevant for 1946.

The next important figure for the 31st March elections is the total of those entitled to vote. Only men over 21 had this right. The Greek government stated that the electoral registers contained the names of approximately 2.2 million voters. AMFOGE correctly characterised this assessment as unreliable since the lists contained the names of many dead. The last reasonably correct assessment of voters dated from 1928. From 1928 to 1935 the lists had been brought up to date annually. AMFOGE reported:

'In many places the revisions were never incorporated in the original registers; moreover, additions and substractions were often included in the same list, giving rise to misunderstandings and charges of irregularities in registration.'[14]

After Metaxas' *coup d'état*, revision of the lists had been suspended. During the Occupation many lists were destroyed or lost. From June 1945 to February 1946 the lists had been revised and in part compiled anew. Nevertheless, after checking the lists, the AMFOGE experts came to the conclusion that only 70 per cent of the names were in order, 13 per cent were obviously false and 17 per cent doubtful. They assessed the number of men over 21 at approximately 2 million (27.9 per cent of 7.5 million) of whom they regarded 97.89 per cent as entitled to vote, in other words 1,989,000. They assessed the number of those actually registered as 1.85 million, that is at 93 per cent of those entitled to vote. They assessed the number of unregistered voters at 139,000. A few comparative figures will show how questionable it is to assess the number of those entitled to vote by manipulating statistics.

For the elections of 5th March 1950 the Greek government fixed the population total at approximately 7.4 million—and this after the losses of the civil war and the inclusion of the inhabitants of the Dodecanese. Numbers of registered voters were not given. For the election of 9th September 1951 the government reckoned again on a population of 7.4 million (despite the census), giving the number of registered voters as 2.25 million. For the elections of 16th November 1952 the population 'remained the same' (7.4 million) but the registered voters' numbers decreased to 2.12 million. Since 1952 women have had the right to vote but as their registration in the women's electoral rolls had not been completed, they voted for the first time in 1956. For the elections of 19th February 1956, the numbers were: total population 7.4 million, registered male voters 2.2 million (female 1.9 million). At the elections of 11th May 1958, with the same (assumed) population total of 7.4 million, there were still 2.6 million registered male voters (female 2.3 million).[15]

Those comparisons show two things: first, that the continuous complaints of the Left and of the other opposition parties that the electoral registers were incorrect were absolutely justified, in so far as AMFOGE's conclusions concerned the already revised lists. Second, AMFOGE's estimates of the total of those entitled to vote and of those actually registered seem to be far too low. At least, in comparison with above data for later years, they appear very arbitrary and doubtful. Moreover, in the whole of the AMFOGE Report there is no single mention of the fact that over 100,000 persons were reckoned to be living as outlaws.

AMFOGE's estimates resulted in the percentage of those who did not participate being assessed at 40.1 per cent, based on 1,106,510 votes actually cast. When the report was drawn up the results from six electoral constituencies were still missing, which raised the total of votes to 1,121,696[16] and so exceeded AMFOGE's estimated maximum of 1,114,000 possible votes. Thus, AMFOGE's assumption that approximately 60 per cent of the electorate voted becomes as questionable as its assumptions about those entitled to vote: it is simply not verifiable.

Even more questionable than these assumptions is the assessment of the reasons for non-participation of that 40.3 per cent (which included the results of the above mentioned six constituencies), *i.e.* the 743,000 electors who did not participate:[17]

	Percentage of Electorate
Claim to have participated in boycott	9.3
Denied having voted, though listed on protocol book	0.4
Not in the neighbourbood on election day (moved, army, unknown)	17.9
Ill or otherwise physically unable to reach polls	5.7
Gave other reasons (business, etc.)	2.5
Unfairly prevented from voting	0.6
No reason given	3.9

On these results the AMFOGE report stated:

'It was found by inquiries pursued by the technical sampling method that 9.3 per cent of the valid registrants assert that they took part in the boycott. It seems reasonable, however, to assume that an additional number of persons who did not vote because "they were not in the neighbourhood on election day" would have reached the polls if they had strongly desired to do so. Taking this class into consideration, it is estimated that the proportion of qualified voters who abstained for "party" reasons is about 15 per cent, and certainly between 10 and 20 per cent. The Mission is convinced that these figures are approximately correct.'[18]

Numerically this means that only 280,000 electors boycotted the elections for political reasons and that 463,000 abstained for other reasons and that, had there been no boycott, the opposition would have secured between 20 and 25 per cent of the seats.

This result, achieved by taking a sample opinion poll, seems to the author even more dubious than the rest of AMFOGE's estimates. It is still to-day an established fact that when political opinion polls are taken in Greece, those polled do not say what they really think. Either the interviewer receives the answer he is thought to want, or the answer avoids the issue. But the essential condition for an opinion poll is just that those polled should give their real opinion; though for this the political climate must be free of repression. Such a climate did not exist in Greece in 1946. This deprives the AMFOGE estimates, based on 1,345 electors interviewed, of any validity. Any elector who did not vote exposed himself to the suspicion that he had boycotted the elections from political motives, therefore that he sympathised with the Left and might even be a communist—something which would undoubtedly have unpleasant consequences for him. This in itself is a reason why the number of those who did not vote through lack of interest was probably not very great. Anyone who abstained for other than political motives would have had to have very convincing reasons beyond all political suspicion. This group must therefore have been virtually restricted to those who were literally unable to go to the polls. Moreover, at least at the polling stations in the small rural districts, the gendarmerie observed the electors' behaviour closely. Many who boycotted the elections for political motives could not summon the courage to admit this openly to an AMFOGE interpreter and ticked the most innocuous answer on the questionnaire. The number of those who boycotted the election for political reasons must have been considerably higher than assumed by AMFOGE.

There is another statistic in the AMFOGE report which is exceedingly dubious. AMFOGE assessed the extent of illegal voting as follows:

'Not more than 2 per cent of the votes were cast illegally in the names of dead or unidentified persons... The irregularities observed were few and by their nature would have had little, if any, effect on the returns for these places.'[19]

The total, in AMFOGE's estimation, was a maximum of 22,000 illegal votes.[20] This figure must be correlated with the 30 per cent false or dubious entries in the electoral registers, which after all represented an approximate total of 600,000 potential votes. Both figures are projections based on AMFOGE's technical sampling method (the number of potentially illegal votes is based on 2,365 names). whilst the estimate of actual illegal votes was based on those 1,345 interviews, not on factually attested cases. Furthermore, the AMFOGE sampling method could only detect one form of illegal voting, that by unidentified persons. Multiple voting with or without the electoral booklet could not be detected, especially when the local authorities were accomplices. Multiple voting could only have been prevented by chemical identification, for instance by marking the thumbs of those who had voted. This had been suggested before the elections but was rejected on not wholly plausible grounds.[21] In general, AMFOGE's estimate that of a potential 600,000 illegal votes only 22,000 actually were cast seems too good to be true. It is not clear how many of the approximately 1.1 million votes cast really belonged in the category of illegal votes and how much this could have raised the percentage of actual abstention.

The AMFOGE Report says nothing of the many other ways in which the election result could be influenced, though these were entirely relevant. As AMFOGE reported, in each polling booth a judge or other official of the Justice Ministry acted as supervisor—persons to whom AMFOGE accorded a blanket certificate of moral integrity even when they had administered the laws in favour of the Axis Occupation during the war years. Obviously the Report of the British Legal Mission was unknown to them. This functionary was assisted by representatives only of those parties participating in the elections; abstaining parties were not represented. On entering the polling booth, the voter had to identify himself and he then received a complete set of the candidate lists of the participating parties. In the solitude of a voting compartment—or, if this did not exist, behind a curtain—he would select the list of the party of his choice, put a cross against the name of his preferred candidate, put the list into the envelope he had been given and, after leaving the voting compartment, throw this into the ballot box. At first sight this seems a procedure ideally suited to guarantee a secret ballot. But Bevin's assumption that, in the solitude of the voting compartment, the voter would have a free choice was nullified in a variety of ways. At polling stations in sparsely-populated rural districts the local opposition followers were well known and there could be no secret ballot. Anyone who abstained or voted differently from the village majority exposed himself to reprisals. Another example shows that, even in Athens, secrecy was not fully guaranteed. On the day after the elections public servants were obliged to show their superiors their rejected candidate lists. In short, manipulation of this sort, going as far as the sale of votes, was customary until the 1960s. Factory workers and others were regularly forced by their employers to exchange their booklets for payment or otherwise be sacked. Peasants had their pitiful debts paid in return for voting for the local deputy. How far this influenced the election result cannot of course be proved by statistics.

Thus, the only reliable account in the AMFOGE report is that of the election day itself.

'The election day weather was ideal everywhere in Greece. The day was sunny, the air mild, the sky almost cloudless and there was little or no wind. Except in a few mountain villages, representing a negligible number of voters, the quiet and order were unbroken. The observers of the Mission almost everywhere reported little gatherings of people near the polling places or groups strolling on the streets and roads, but scarcely any public demonstration of political feeling. The conduct of the election in the voting places was rarely anything but regular and lawful. Disputes or complaints by party watchers at the polls were few. The counting of the ballots which followed after sunset was also almost universally quiet and proper, and there were no celebrations or party demonstrations of any size when the results began to appear. It may be said in general that the Greek election of the 31st March ranks well as respects peace, order and regularity of proceedings on election day when compared with earlier national polls and that, as respects public decorum, law obedience and orderly ballotting it can stand comparison with conditions which prevail in France, Great Britain, and the United States on election days.'[22]

Jean Meynaud's commentary on this report hits the nail on the head. 'Taking into account the composition and functioning methods of the Mission, it would be very naive to see in this certificate of good democratic conduct anything beyond an attempt to buttress the international status of a government entirely subservient to the Anglo-Saxon powers.'[23]

The official election result confirmed the expected victory of the Right. The Liberal Centre of Sofoulis and Mylonas—the latter having at the last minute decided to participate—had only just managed to secure 15 per cent of the votes. The moderate Right of Papandreou, Venizelos and Kanellopoulos took a republican stand but likewise made a weak showing with 20 per cent. It was a clear victory for the Right. This, and the fact that in the resulting parliament there would be no real opposition, signified a disaster for Greece. The commentator of the left-Labour journal *Tribune* was obviously aware of the underlying problems and their consequences when he made the following analysis under the headline 'Sowing the Wind'.

'That the majority of the Greek people do not want a Communist dictatorship is clear from their attitude since the liberation as well as from the election results. . . But while the people of Europe make it clear, wherever they have the opportunity to do so, that they did not fight Nazi enslavement in order to be put into the Communist straitjacket, they have been even more emphatic in their determination once and for all to rid themselves of the pre-war past, which, in the majority of the countries concerned, came to be identified with ultra-reactionary and inefficient regimes, semifascist kings, corrupt officials and intolerable extremes of wealth and poverty.'[24]

The commentator went on to point out that British policy in Egypt and Persia was following exactly the same line. But it was just this policy which was driving the progressive forces into the arms of the communists. 'Is that what Mr. Bevin wants?' Doubtless this was not Bevin's intention but it was the inevitable consequence of his policy. Bevin had been right that a mere postponement of the elections would not have been a solution. Postponement with a simultaneous re-building of the government to include both Left and Right, with the Centre in the role of arbiter, would probably have strengthened the latter. At first, the Right would probably have refused to cooperate, but British pressure could have brought them to it. That the Left was ready to take a constructive line had been proved in the past. In this way it might have been possible to rein in the extremists on both sides and to find an open road to compromise. Elections held against the background of such a government would probably have produced a much greater vote for the moderate Centre, since most of the population only sided with the extremes for lack of alternatives. Such a policy would, of course, have required direction and generous help from abroad.

The elections of 31st March and the victory of the Right handed the Greek state over to the forces of the *parakratos* which prevented any peaceful solution and initiated that escalation of violence which culminated in civil war. At the same time Great Britain lost her previous power of control. The Right had gained the majority in internationally-recognised 'fair' elections and the resulting government could therefore maintain, with full authority, that they were Greece's legitimate rulers. Even had the British government sought an alternative, after the elections this no longer existed. The Greek Right realised that and thus acquired a free hand which none of the previous governments had possessed. They knew the British could not drop them. Bevin had become the prisoner of his own policy. He had not even the possibility of remaining neutral in the forthcoming civil war since Greece belonged to the British 'sphere of influence'. And when Great Britain was financially exhausted, the US was ready to take over and support the 'legitimate' Greek government in the civil war it had provoked, and that to the bitter end.

TABLE OF ELECTION RESULTS

Parties	Names of Party Leaders	Valid Votes	% of Votes Cast	Seats	% of Seats	Electoral Districts	Number of Candidates
1.0 **United Nationalists' Front, composed of:**							
1.1 Populists (Laikon Komma)	Konstantinos Tsaldaris, Ioannis Theotokis, Petros Mavromichalis	610,995	55.12	206	58.2	38	354
1.2 Liberal Nationalist Party (Komma Ethnikon Fileleftheron)	Stylianos Gonatas			156			
1.3 Reformist Party (Metarythmistikon Komma)	Apostolos Alexandris			34			
1.4 National Panhellenic Party (Panellinion Komma)	Alexandros Sallellariou			5			
1.5 Patriotic Union (Patriotiki Enosi)							
1.6 Royalist Party (Komma Vasilofronon)							
1.7 Re-construction Party (Komma Anasynkrotiseos)							
1.8 Social-Radical Union (Koinoniki Rizospastiki Enosi)							
1.9 Embros Group				11 (in election alliance)			
2.0 **National Political Union** (Ethniki Politiki Enosi)		213,721	19.28	(68)	19.26	37	340
2.1 Venizelist Liberal Party (Komma Venizelikon Fileleftheron)	Sofoklis Venizelos			31			

Parties	Names of Party Leaders	Valid Votes	% of Votes Cast	Seats	% of Seats	Electoral Districts	Number of Candidates
2.2 Social-democratic Party (Dimokratiko Sosialistiko Komma)	George Papandreou			27			
2.3 National Unionist Party (Ethnikon Enotikon Komma)	Panayotis Kanellopoulos			7			
2.4 Republican Union (Dimokratiki Enosi)				3 (in election alliance)			
3.0 Liberal Party (Komma Fileleftheron)	Themistoklis Sofoulis	159,525	14.39	48	13.56	34	287
4.0 Greek National Party (Ethnikon Komma Ellados)	Napoleon Zervas	66,027	5.96	20	5.65	20	190
5.0 Union of Nationalists		32,538	2.94	9	2.54	5	40
5.1 Natinalist Party (Komma Ethnikofronon)	Theodoros Tourkovasilis			9			
5.2 Populist Agrarian Party (Laikon Agrotikon Komma)	Georgios Pamboukas						
6.0 Union of Agrarian Parties (Enosi Agrotikon Kommaton)		7,447	0.67	1	0.28	5	40
6.1 Greek Agrarian Party (Agrotikon Komma Ellados)	Alexandros Mylonas			1			
6.2 Democratic Agrarian Party (Agrotikon Dimokratikon Komma)							

453

Parties	Names of Party Leaders	Valid Votes	% of Votes Cast	Seats	% of Seats	Electoral Districts	Number of Candidates
6.4 Agrarian Groups of the Peasants' & Workers' Party (Agrotikai Omadai tou Agrotikoụ uni Ergatikoụ Kommatos)							
7.0 'X'-followers' National Resistance Party (Komma Chiton Ethnikis Antistaseos)	Konstantinos Efstathopoulos	1,848	0.17			2	15
8.0 Urban & Rural Property Owners' Party (Astikon kai Agrotikon Komma Idioktisias)	Achillefs Antonopoulos	1,114	0.10			2	22
9.0 Front of Christian Orthodox Greeks (Christianiki Orthodoxos Parataxi Ellinon)		298	0.03			2	14
10.0 Patriotic Reservists' Party (Patriotikon Komma Efedron)		63	0.01			1	2
11.0 Party of National Unity (Komma Ethnikis Enoseos)	Dimitrios Papapolyzos	15				1	1
12.0 Greek Social Party (Koinonikon Komma Ellados)		13				1	1
13.0 Independents		12,036	1.08	2	0.56		25

Parties	Names of Party Leaders	Valid Votes	% of Votes Cast	Seats	% of Seats	Electoral Districts	Number of Candidates
14.0 Unattached candidates		2,833	0.25				209

TOTALS

Votes cast	1,121,696	
Valid votes	1,108,473	
Non-valid votes	13,223	
No of electoral districts	38	No. of seats 354
Electoral system	Hagenbach-Bischoff Proportional Representation	

(adapted from Meynaud, *op. cit.*, p. 494 and Appeals to the Electorate, pp. 3 ff.)

NOTES

1. *Daily Express*, 15th March, 1946.
2. *Manchester Guardian*, 26th and 27th March, 1946.
3. *Daily Herald*, 25th March, 1946.
4. *Ibid.*, 27th March, 1946.
5. *News Chronicle*, 27th March, 1946.
6. *Daily Telegraph*, 27th March, 1946.
7. *AMFOGE Report*, p. 20.
8. Constantine Poulos, 'The American Observers', *Greek News*, 1:3 (May 1946), p. 3. Woodhouse was replaced on 9th March, see *AMFOGE Report*, p. 13. Woodhouse was in fact appointed one of the three Secretaries-General of AMFOGE with a French and an American colleague. Woodhouse, *Something Ventured*, p. 102.
9. *AMFOGE Report*, p. 24.
10. Poulos, *op. cit.*, p. 3. On this problem see also the report of the former UNRRA Public Relations Director, Allen D. Fields, 'Kolonaki and the Others', *Nation*, 164 (29th March, 1947), pp. 358 ff. 'In Greece there are in the main just two kinds of people. The Kolonaki—meaning the people of the hill—and the others. You could identify people quickly and easily that way. Is he Kolonaki? We'll get to know many more Kolonaki than "others". They'll be our interpreters, and our friends, and when we go out to dinner it will be on Kolonaki Hill. We're small-d—democrats—certainly. But the Kolonaki will be better dressed—neater—cleaner—and they'll talk more English than the "others". They'll make better aides; they know how to get things done. It would be crazy and inefficient as hell not to use them. We can handle them, and they're more fun to be with.'
11. *Greek News*, 1:3, (May 1946), p. 1; *Facts on Greece 1949*, (New York: American Council for a Democratic Greece, 1949), p. 1. According to this, three members of the US contingent either resigned or were dismissed.
12. *AMFOGE Report*, p. 7.
13. See *Synoptiki statistiki epitirisis tis Ellados 1954*, (Athens, 1955), p. 1, footnote 8; *Synoptiki statistiki epitirisis tis Ellados 1966*, (Athens, 1967), p. 9. Approximately 120,000 inhabitants of the Dodecanese, returned to Greece in 1947, must be subtracted from the figure quoted.
14. *AMFOGE Report*, p. 9.
15. *Appeals to the electorate in Greece since the end of the Second World War*, (Athens: Ministry to the Prime Minister's Office, 1961), pp. 15, 26, 28, 32, 37. According to the statistical yearbook for 1966, the respective population figures were: 1951 7.6 million (including the 120,000 inhabitants of the Dodecanese); 1956 8 million and 1958 8.17 million. Even from these figures it is obvious that little reliance can be placed on Greek statistics. This has been the case until recently, with the result that OECD has refused to take over statistical data from Greece which it has not verified itself.
16. *AMFOGE Report*, p. 29; *Appeals to the electorate*, p. 3.
17. *Ibid.*, p. 28.
18. *Ibid.*, p. 22.
19. *Ibid.*, p. 29.
20. *Ibid.*, p. 28.
21. *Ibid.*, pp. 11 ff.
22. *Ibid.*, pp. 18 ff.
23. Meynaud, *op. cit.*, p. 80.
24. *Tribune*, 5th April, 1946.

FROM THE SEVENTH PARTY CONGRESS TO THE SECOND PLENUM, OCTOBER 1945-FEBRUARY 1946

The evolution of KKE during the four months from the Seventh Party Congress of October 1945 to the Second Plenum of the Central Committee in February 1946 is not characterised by striking events or decisive changes of policy, but rather by uncertainty and continuous vacillations, in themselves reactions to specific events which were outside the party's control. The initiative had passed completely to the other side.

The end of the Seventh Party Congress and of the First Plenum of the new Central Committee coincided almost exactly with the resignation of the Voulgaris government. Whether the KKE leadership was pre-occupied with working out the consequences of the Party Congress and was therefore not ready to act, or whether they cherished hopes of possible participation should an all-party government be formed, they proceeded with the greatest caution. On 11th October signals were made to Sofoulis that the party was prepared to support a government formed by him but that there was no wish for participation in his Cabinet.[1] When Sofoulis did not succeed and three further attempts by other politicians likewise failed, Zachariadis took up the issue himself: Greece urgently needed a government of the political parties in order to return to political normality; only thus could the road to free elections be opened; if the British had left Greece a long time ago there would not be the presently prevailing chaos.[2]

When, in the middle of October, rumours of a forthcoming right-wing *putsch* began to multiply, so that even the Foreign Office found itself obliged to issue a public warning to the Greek Right,[3] the Political Bureau took the following decision. KKE would take any *coup d'état* by the Right as a signal for mass struggle by the whole people and by every means, in the towns, in the villagers and in the mountains. In such a case democratic citizens would have the elementary democratic duty to meet the use of arms with the same means.[4] Despite its sharp formulation, this decision was merely sabre-rattling: to interpret it as the decision for civil war would be completely mistaken. It was simply a sign of the self-confidence newly acquired at the Seventh Party Congress and signalled that KKE was taking a more militant line.[5] To make sure that party members did not regard the Political Bureau's decision as an empty threat, and at the same time to deprive them of the illusion that a peaceful evolution was assured, the Sunday edition of *Rizospastis* published on 21st October

Zachariadis' statements to the Seventh Party Congress about the possibility of a peaceful transition to socialism.[6]

After the British warning had averted the immediate danger of a *putsch* and Damaskinos' assumption of the premiership had reduced the temperature of the governmental crisis, *Rizospastis* adopted a more moderate tone and returned to its ordinary reporting.[7]

On 23rd October it gave big headlines to French Communist Party successes in the French elections. In the context of the paper's habitual reporting and complaints of White Terror, it published quotations from the British press to the effect that, unless such actions ceased, elections would not even be possible in spring 1946.[8] In other articles KKE presented itself as *the* national force: whilst others had simply enjoyed themselves during the Occupation, only they had fought. The 'NO' of 28th October 1940 had not been the 'No' of the Metaxas regime but the 'No' of the people to fascism as such. In a leading article on 27th October 1945, Petros Rousos repeated KKE's demand: formation of a government of the political parties, general amnesty for all former Resistance members, dissolution of SAN and 'X' and free, unobstructed elections. Finally, on 28th October 1945, *Rizospastis* published Zachariadis' letters of 1940 and 1941[9] and described how imprisoned comrades had been ready to go to the front as volunteers, which the regime had not permitted. In short, *Rizospastis* was trying to stress the national character of KKE.

Meanwhile the government crisis had led to an intensification of right-wing excesses with the result that KKE followers, especially in the villages, were exposed to massive persecution so that many of them took refuge in the mountains. This prompted the KKE leadership to take the position, formulated in the November number of *KOMEP*,[10] that Greece was in the throes of the deepest economic, political and moral crisis of her history. The Greek plutocratic oligarchy and the British occupation forces were to blame for this. A *coup d'état* by the Right was threatening. For its part, the Seventh Party Congress had laid down the following line: organisation of the popular masses for the struggle for bread, work and freedom, mass self-defence *(aftoamyna)* against White Terror, establishment of a pan-democratic front for normal democratic evolution and free elections, every sort of preparation to enable the people to answer the Black Front and SAN with their own weapons, whether by violent *coup* or by a legal takeover of power; demand for British withdrawal; realisation of these aims within EAM as the most suitable organisation.

At the present the party was confronting the following problems. KKE had the majority of the population with it and, internationally, the establishment of the Peoples' Democracies rendered conditions more favourable than ever before. But there was one fundamental obstacle to Greece's normal democratic evolution, namely British policy. There were two ways in which this obstacle could be overcome. There could be agreement with the British on a basis of equal rights and KKE had the duty to exhaust all its resources in the pursuit of this goal. But there were limits—the interests of Greece and her people—which could not be betrayed and should the British not be ready for agreement, renewed preparation for the hardest and most decisive of struggles would become a duty.

Party members and the people must prepare ideologically, politically, organisationally, militarily and technologically for these struggles which were being forced on KKE by the uncompromising attitude of Great Britain. This was the basic duty of every worker and every honest democrat. The article went on to repeat the guidelines of the Seventh Party Congress, but with a few important alterations. In the villages and the mountains, the citizens and the persecuted, whose lives are in danger from armed monarcho-fascist terrorism, offer armed resistance.' The party was taking all the organisational and technical measures which would enable it to continue its political activities even under the most difficult conditions of fascist terror. KKE was taking all those practical measures which would enable it, first to counter any monarcho-fascist attempt to set up an openly fascist regime with armed defence by the people and beyond that to lead the people in struggle against internal and foreign reaction for their economic and political independence, for freedom and for popular democracy.

At first sight this article could be taken as a declaration of civil war. But closer analysis shows its content to be a well-balanced mixture of threats, offers of cooperation to the British and tranquillisers for its own members. The threat was directed as much against the Greek Right as against the British as the decisive factor. But this was an empty threat, since at that time it lacked all material basis. It must be seen in connection with the offer of cooperation: it should be made unmistakably clear to the British that KKE was, as always, ready for integration but not for submission. The decision that KKE members in the villages and those living as outlaws in the mountains should offer armed resistance to armed terrorism by the Right may well have been, in the first instance, a concession to the persecuted rank-and-file in the countryside. The KKE leadership had apparently realised that, in those regions where the party could not organise passive self-defence *(aftoamyna)* on a mass scale, party members could no longer be expected to bear the terror with patience, an eventuality which must result either in the destruction of the local party base or in uncontrolled, spontaneous action. In general, the *KOMEP* article is no more than a sign of the party's new-won self-confidence after the Seventh Party Congress and at the same time a call to members to close ranks and look to the future. A similar note was struck in a series of articles published in *Rizospastis* and *KOMEP* on the first anniversary of the December 1944 events; *KOMEP*'s re-publishing of the Political Bureau's thesis of 8th November 1945 portrayed the December 1944 incidents as the climax of the National Liberation struggle during the Second World War.[11]

This thesis was the answer of EAM/ELAS to the attempt by the reactionary Greek oligarchy and the Churchill government to prevent normal democratic evolution and the popular-democratic re-birth of Greece. The British were therefore to blame; the December events were an act of national resistance by the people for independence and democracy against exploiters from home and abroad; and KKE identified itself unreservedly with the struggle of the people of Athens and Piraeus. The Varkiza Agreement had been a necessary compromise intended to ensure democratic evolution. But British occupation policy, with its one-sided support for the Right, had brought matters to the present crisis. The military defeat, however, should be attributed to British armed intervention alone: it in no way implied a political defeat and could certainly not be attributed to any political or military superiority on the part of Greek reaction. The present chaos was a *post factum* justification of the December fighting. This was followed by lengthy explanations of the present-day situation and, in conclusion, a discussion of present relations with Great Britain.

The Greek people had nothing against the British people. Despite the armed British intervention, the Greek people regarded cooperation with Great Britain and with the Soviet Union as the corner stone of Greek foreign policy; though of course on the basis of equal rights, national independence and mutual understanding. Any other policy would widen the gulf and lead eventually to dangerous international developments. The party appealed to the British working class to bring its influence to bear on the responsible British politicians, to find a way to democratic agreement on a basis of equality. 'So long as the British authorities in Greece do not restore order and so long as they encourage monarcho-fascist terror, the immediate withdrawal of British troops will be absolutely necessary, so that the people can itself restore this order.' The party welcomed the founding of the League for Democracy in Greece whose aim was, likewise, equal cooperation of both peoples and their governments. Only those who threatened the freedom and independence of Greece were regarded as enemies by KKE.

In addition, the discussion paper stated that, though there had been mistakes in the past, these had been revealed and recognised at the Twelfth Plenum and, since then, measures had been introduced to rectify them. Now the party must be prepared, politically, organisationally and practically, for a new period of hard struggles. The paper ended as follows:

'Long live December—the continuation and indivisible part of the National Resistance struggle, the call to arms for freedom and independence of the Greek people and for popular democracy.'

Thus the KKE leadership closed—for the time being—the chapter which questioned past mistakes. At the same time its public acknowledgement of the December events gave the Greek Right to understand that there would be no shrinking from confrontation. But, since that would have implied conflict with the British, the withdrawal of British troops was demanded. However, since there was no question of this at least for the moment, KKE was trying to find a way to produce a change in British policy. The past had shown that this could not be achieved through Foreign Office channels. So a new idea was developed: an attempt to bring about a change in policy towards Greece by direct contact with personalities and groups in Britain itself. Basically, this was a new edition of the 'campaign for respectability' of the Second World War period, but by a different route. Moreover it shows that KKE was still prepared for compromise, on condition that it was allowed to integrate itself in the existing political system on a basis of parity. The following facts will show that this readiness to compromise was not merely rhetoric, but a practical policy.

At the end of October 1945 an EPON delegation, led by Professor Georgalas, attended the World Youth Congress in London and used this opportunity to make contact with left-wing Labour MPs and trade union leaders, from whom there was a rather positive response.[12] No doubt from the same motives KKE bridled its criticisms of the Kanellopoulos Cabinet. In a *Rizospastis* leading article Karagiorgis confined himself to describing it as 'a tragic operetta' and, in Volos, Siantos stated that only the formation of a democratic government could bring the country back to normality.[13] When articles appeared in the British press mentioning Hector McNeil's forthcoming journey to Athens, *Rizospastis* welcomed this on the assumption that it was the result of Labour MPs' criticism of conditions in Greece and would bring about an alteration in British policy.[14]

Two days after McNeil's arrival in Athens, *Rizospastis* published a Political Bureau resolution on the situation in Greece. For this to improve, a complete change in British policy was needed, especially as regards the methods employed by Churchill, Leeper and Scobie. Continual interference in Greek internal affairs must cease, likewise the British military occupation. A democratic government must be formed, SAN must be dissolved, the National Resistance recognised, a general amnesty proclaimed and conditions of democracy introduced into the armed forces, the police, the gendarmerie and also the state apparatus. The electoral registers must be compiled anew on the basis of a population census and elections should be held on the proportional representation system. KKE would give such a programme its full support.[15]

The day before McNeil's arrival, *Rizospastis* had begun a series on Tory intrigues in Greece, including compromising telegrams from Woodhouse and other British liaison officers in autumn 1943.[16]

After McNeil's arrival, *Rizospastis* pointed to the seriousness of the situation. On the 14th November its front-page carried an enormous map of Greece, with figures for the left-wingers murdered or injured since Varkiza entered for each province. The headline read:

'780 names of murdered Greek patriots, 5,677 injured, 28,450 tortured, 70,528 arrests. The brutes who collaborated with Schimana[17] acquitted. The patriots who co-operated with the Allies sentenced to death. The number of prisoners rising. Censorship a year after Liberation. The Government directing the Terror. This article is dedicated to Mr. Rex Leeper.'

On 16th November McNeil received an EAM delegation consisting of D. Partsalidis, K. Gavriilidis, G. Oikonomou, A. Loulis and S. Kritikas, who submitted to him concrete evidence of the White Terror, the government's responsibility and the corrupt state of the electoral registers. Together with this they submitted a detailed memorandum on the situation.[18]

When, on 20th November, the Kanellopoulos Cabinet finally announced its resignation and Sofoulis was instructed to form a government, Greek left-wing and Liberal circles interpreted this, not as a simple change of government, but as a radical change in the situation. At Athens University and in the Averoff Prison there were delirious demonstrations of joy.[19] The Right refused to recognise the new government; when there was even a protest telegram from George II and Damaskinos threatened resignation, excitement rose to boiling-point.[20] Rumours of preparations for a right-wing *putsch* were circulating.[21] In this situation *Rizospastis* called on its readers to exercise the greatest vigilance. The EAM Central Committee issued a statement assuring Sofoulis of EAM's full support. EAM was even prepared to support all the government's economic measures provided they helped towards reconstruction and did not impose a one-sided burden on the working class. The conditions were a general amnesty for political prisoners, official recognition of the Resistance Movement, redrawing of the electoral registers on the basis of a general population census and a purge of the armed forces, the police, the judiciary and the state apparatus. Only thus could the government acquire real authority.[22]

On 22nd November the KKE Political Bureau met and passed a similar resolution, with an additional demand for the deposition of Damaskinos as Regent, which would promote the restoration of normal internal conditions and tranquillity. The Political Bureau ordered all party organisations to regulate their activities in the spirit of this resolution.[23]

The KKE leadership interpreted the change of government as a completely fresh start. Their demands were moderate and in complete conformity with earlier demands by those Liberal politicians who were now in the Cabinet. Had the Sofoulis government succeeded in translating these demands into practical policy, KKE would probably have returned wholeheartedly to its integration policy and would have played a role within the Greek political system similar to that of the French and Italian Communist Parties in their own countries. But it is Greece's tragedy that the KKE and EAM leaderships' assessment of the situation was incorrect. British policy had not changed and the Sofoulis government was too weak to push through its own programme in the face of internal and external opposition.

Just how firmly KKE and EAM believed in a change in British policy is demonstrated by the very different tone of *Rizospastis* during the following weeks. A clear line was drawn between Labour and Tory policy and fresh 'proofs' of a change were continually discovered.

At the end of November EAM sent Dimitris Partsalidis, Alkiviadis Loulis and General Neokosmos Grigoriadis on a 'goodwill' public relations visit to England, where they were joined by the EPON chairman, Professor Georgalas, and by the EAM journalist Nikos Karvounis. This was about the time that the British Legal Mission arrived in Athens. The KKE leadership waited impatiently for the Sofoulis government to introduce its promised reforms; in particular they were hoping for the proclamation of an amnesty. As the weeks rolled on and practically nothing happened, the Left became increasingly frustrated.

On 8th December, Zachariadis put this frustration into words: the government was following the same line as its predecessors; for this the British were to blame and therefore they must go.[24] When, on 10th December, it became clear that there would be no general amnesty, *Rizospastis* took on a more aggressive tone: the government's proposal[25] was a provocation to the people; Zachariadis stated that, in view of the increasing right-wing terror, especially in Macedonia and Thrace, it was the party's duty to intensify 'mass popular self-defence' *(maziki laïki aftoamyna)*.[26] On the 11th the EAM parties declared that they could no longer support the Sofoulis government because it had betrayed its democratic mission. In three weeks the government had taken no single measure to transfer even a part of the economic burden to the rich. The EAM parties would continue to reject registration on the corrupt electoral rolls and participation in farcical elections. EAM had done everything in its power to make possible a normal, democratic evolution. It was the government which had not kept its promises. Therefore EAM demanded the formation of a representative government in which it too would be represented. EAM further demanded recognition of the National Resistance, a general political amnesty and a programme of bread, work, freedom, democracy and independence. This resolution was transmitted to the EAM delegation in London.[27]

In the same issue of *Rizospastis* in which this resolution appeared there was a report of a successful self-defence action in a village in Thessaly and it was pointed out that self-defence against attack was in conformity with Article 99 of the Penal Code.

The EAM resolution of 11th December in no way signified a fundamental change in left-wing policy. It merely signalled a return to a harder line. The articles on self-defence were sabre-rattling, largely without substance. KKE was in the midst of a reorganisation process initiated at the Twelfth Plenum and Seventh Party Congress, which had apparently raised considerable organisational problems—especially in the villages—and prompted the Political Bureau to pass an organisational resolution on the 16th December.[28] In other words, even if the KKE leadership had decided on a radical change of line involving the use of force, this would have been quite impracticable in view of its internal disorganisation.

Against this background, Kousoulas' theory that KKE had at this point already decided in favour of armed struggle—in agreement with the Soviet Union—appears purely speculative.[29] Nor is O'Ballance's hypothesis much more credible, especially as he cites no supporting sources:

'Although the Greek Communists regard February 12th, 1946 as the official opening of the "third round", the birth of the "Greek Democratic Army", the successor to ELAS, can be more accurately quoted as being December 15th, 1945. It came into being as the result of a Politburo level meeting at Petrich, in Bulgaria, which was attended by members of the Central Committee of the KKE, and representatives of the Yugoslav and Bulgarian General Staffs. At this meeting the decision was made to reorganise an insurgent army to fight against the Greek Government. Yugoslavia promised massive material aid, and it was hoped that the Soviet Union would help materially too.'[30]

Even Woodhouse doubts the authenticity of this report:

'December 1945, the month in which the Yugoslav, Bulgarian and Greek Communists were reported to have met at Petrich, was also the month in which the Greek and Yugoslav Governments agreed to establish diplomatic relations, and in which Admiral Rodionov arrived in Athens as Soviet Ambassador. It is unlikely that at such a moment either the Yugoslavs or the Bulgarians were encouraging the KKE to subversive action. The Bulgarians, with Dimitrov again in power, would have known that Stalin wanted no such action. They had no resources to offer in support of the KKE; and in the circumstances of 1945, they knew that they must lose any competition with the Yugoslavs for the control of Aegean Macedonia if it were to be detached from Greece. The Yugoslavs, though less subservient to Moscow, had no more reason to incite the KKE to subversive action.'[31]

Had this conference actually taken place, certainly neither Zachariadis nor the other KKE leaders would have forgotten to mention it in their anti-Yugoslav tirades after the defeat of 1949.[32]

The actual internal and external political developments of the next two months also tell against this hypothesis.

In its foreign policy KKE continued its previous 'respectability campaign'. The EAM delegation to Britain was briefed in accordance with the resolution of 11th December and in conversations with McNeil and Noel-Baker pressed home the new line. On 17th December they submitted the following memorandum to McNeil: the Sofoulis government had resulted from McNeil's visit and a thoroughgoing analysis of the background to the dangerous political and economic instability in Greece. The new government had been welcomed by the majority of the population, 'as a significant start towards a final settlement of Greek internal problems through recognition of the will of the people!' The memorandum described the developments which had led up to the EAM resolution of 11th December.[33] Here, we will simply note the concluding passage which is interesting in its relation to KKE policy, and stated that EAM wanted free elections at the earliest possible opportunity; the government had chosen 31st March as the election date; therefore conditions for free elections must be created immediately; the government was obviously not able to deliver these, only a government with EAM participation would be able to withstand right-wing pressure.

'Free elections can still be held within the limit already fixed and Greece would then be able to enter on the path of normal democratic development and economic recovery, with the assistance of her great Allies, especially Great Britain.

'Through securing the above-mentioned prerequisites for free elections in the shortest possible time, political normality will be attained. On the contrary, should the change brought about by the British Under-Secretary for Foreign Affairs' recent visit to Athens degenerate into a mere superficial reshuffle, the present situation will deteriorate still more, leading to ruin and frustration the efforts made by the British government to help Greece in a decisive start towards recovery.

'No economic recovery is possible without previously securing political stability. The Greek people realise that the work of reconstruction and the general rehabilitation must not be delayed any longer. They realise that this work will mainly depend upon themselves. To be enabled to start on it, Greece hopefully expects the assistance of Great Britain.

'The EAM Coalition looks forward to a stable understanding between the Greek and the British democratic peoples linked together by long tradition. Greece, being situated in the Eastern Mediterranean, between the Straits and the Suez Canal, has also common interests with Britain in that part of the European Continent. The EAM Coalition believes that these interests, backed by ancient and friendly relations between two freedom-loving nations, can be served in the best possible way by an understanding based on equality and mutual respect, both in the political and economic field.

'The EAM Coalition believes that the establishment of equally friendly relations with all great Allied powers and with the Balkan neighbours of Greece, will contribute towards securing peace in that part of Europe and will render Greece a factor of constructive collaboration in a better post-war world.'[34]

In other words, the EAM delegation gave McNeil to understand that EAM acknowledged British interests in the Eastern Mediterranean and was prepared to be cooperative, that such cooperation was indeed in British interests. But the Foreign Office did not understand this offer—or did not want to understand it—as is shown by the attitude taken by the Southern Department which did not even allude to it.[35] For the Foreign Office, participation by the Left in government could not even be a subject for discussion.

The EAM delegation stayed in England till the beginning of January and had further talks with Labour MPs and with trade union representatives, as well as other public personalities. But their good-will mission brought only meagre results, as was noted in the League for Democracy in Greece's bulletin, *Greek News:* 'They went away disappointed with the Government's attitude, but hopeful that, when public opinion asserts itself, as it will, there may be a change.'[36]

On 3rd January the EAM delegation left London for Paris where, at a press conference on the 10th, Loulis described the situation in Greece. Georgalas stated that, under present conditions, free elections were not possible and, to the question in what way France could help, he replied that a delegation of French deputies should come to Greece, get a general view of the situation and produce a report to enlighten world public opinion. On the 16th, the EAM delegation spoke at a public meeting and Georgalas repeated his request which was confirmed by a resolution of the meeting.[37] Originally the delegation had planned to continue their tour to the US but, for some reason, whether or not because they did not receive visas, they went instead to Moscow, where they arrived on 21st January, the day on which Gromyko submitted his document to the UN Security Council.

But first a recapitulation of developments in Athens. *Rizospastis* followed up the EAM resolution of the 11th December with optimistic daily reports of the EAM delegation's successes. Though it had withdrawn its support from the government, KKE's public criticisms remained muted until on the 15th December the paper's tone became sharper after publication of the draft law on amnesty had shown this to be no more than a half-measure for emptying the overcrowded prisons.[38] On the 16th it published an article by Petros Rousos in which he severely criticised the draft law. On the 18th EAM telegraphed a memorandum to the Moscow Foreign Ministers' Conference, describing the situation in Greece, demanding the formation of a representative government in conformity with the Yalta Declaration, and calling for the withdrawal of British troops.[39]

Though there was no reply to this, *Rizospastis* noted with satisfaction that a critical article on the Greek situation had appeared in the Soviet journal *New Times*.[40] At the same time *Rizospastis* appealed to all former Resistance members and all democrats to attend a public meeting in the Athens football stadium on Sunday, 23rd December, to demand recognition of the National Resistance and a general amnesty.

The meeting itself demonstrated that EAM was still well able to move the masses. *Rizoapastis* reported 200,000 present. In addition to EAM, ELD/SKE and ESSAK participated. The speakers were S. Hajibeïs, M. Kyrkos, I. Tsirimokos and G. Siantos. Nikos Kazantzakis was present 'unofficially' representing the government. All the speakers unanimously demanded recognition of the Resistance, general amnesty and the formation of a representative government.[41]

During the following weeks, until the middle of January, KKE's line was confused and vacillating. *Rizospastis* welcomed Stalin's greetings telegrams to Sofianopoulos and EAM and reported in detail on the constructive results of the Moscow Foreign Ministers' Conference.[42] On the 30th December there was another mass meeting, in the bicycle-racing stadium in Piraeus, at which a resolution for general amnesty and the formation of a representative government was acclaimed.[43] On the same day Zachariadis spoke at the Plenum of the Macedonia and Thrace provincial committee. He demanded inclusion of EAM in the government, since only this could put an end to internal chaos and open a way out of the foreign policy *cul-de-sac*. An understanding must be reached with Yugoslavia, Bulgaria and Albania; and the British troops must be withdrawn at once.[44] Siantos said the same in an article in *KOMEP* where he analysed the reasons why the Sofoulis government had not brought about any change in the situation and found the answer in its class character. A change could be brought about only by the formation of a representative government with EAM participation. This was at present the only way out of the prevailing chaos and the deep-seated political, economic and moral crisis.[45]

Up to 10th January *Rizospastis* concentrated on reporting strikes against the rapidly-rising cost of living.[46] On the 10th Zachariadis condemned the agreement between Venizelos and the Populists and announced that, despite this, EAM would enter the government and free elctions would be held. Siantos demanded the establishment of a Pan-Democratic Front.[47] On 11th January, Zachariadis stated that any right-wing *coup* would be crushed by every means and that British policy was responsible for the increasingly critical situation.[48] On the 13th he spoke at a public meeting outside Volos which ended in a clash with the gendarmerie resulting in four left-wing dead and twenty injured.[49] The brutal behaviour of the gendarmerie stung Zachariadis to a sharp reply at a further mass meeting on the 14th: Greece was the only country in Europe where chaos ruled and collaborators were in power; the army was in fascist hands; a wave of right-wing terror was rolling over the land. Only the inclusion of EAM in the government could bring about a change. The British were responsible for this situation. KKE absolutely rejected the manoeuvrings of British imperialism. In conclusion Zachariadis repeated the party's habitual demands and called on the people for massive self-defence.[50]

On the very same day the *News Chronicle* published an interview with Sofoulis in which the latter made far-reaching overtures to the Left. He advocated cooperation between the Liberals and the Left, though he said that at the moment he did not want EAM representatives in his Cabinet because this would provoke the Right. But, if the KKE leadership would tolerate his government for the time being, cooperation would be possible after the elections. He should be given the chance to hold free elections. He knew that the electoral registers were not beyond question, but he would try to get them revised. He wanted to purge the security services and to dissolve 'X' which was nothing more than a private army of the king. Furthermore, he was planning a far-reaching amnesty.[51] On the 15th, the *News Chronicle* interview was reprinted by almost all the Athens press and the EAM Central Committee reacted at once. On the 16th *Rizospastis* published their resolution calling on EAM members to register on the electoral rolls, though at the same time it was stated that this still did not mean participation in the elections. That was made dependent on how far the government kept its promises to revise the registers and to purge the security forces.[52] Apparently the Left still hoped that a representative government might be formed. In a leading article on the same day, Zachariadis called for the creation of a Pan-Democratic Front to counter the Right's so-called National Front and a KKE delegation, consisting of Siantos, Bartziotas and Porfyrogenis, visited Sofoulis. They protested against rumours circulated by the police that KKE was going about the job of preparing revolution. Sofoulis conceded that this was a slander campaign and promised to take action against those responsible.[53] This was followed on the 17th by an official denial from the Political Bureau and a call to all readers to attend a public meeting of the democratic rally movement in the Athens football stadium on Sunday, the 20th.[54]

On the 18th *Rizospastis* published a Political Bureau resolution sharply rebutting a remark of McNeil's of 10th January to the effect that KKE was still pursuing revolutionary goals and calling on all democrats to participate in the meeting on the 20th. Alongside this resolution, the paper reported the onslaught by 'X' members on Yannis Zevgos and the EAM Central Committee member Manolis Proïmakis in Corinth.[55] On the 19th an EAM Central Committee delegation protested to Damaskinos and Kafandaris against the heightening of violence and demanded inclusion of EAM in the government and demotion of the responsible police officer in

Corinth. Sofoulis thereupon suspended the gendarmerie commander and ordered an investigation.[56]

The 20th January witnessed two contradictory events: the mass meeting of the democratic rally movement was, according to *Rizospastis'* figures, the biggest demonstration yet seen in Athens. The paper spoke of half a million participants, with the republican General Alexandros Othonaios[57] as main speaker. At the end of the meeting a resolution was acclaimed, demanding: an end to the White Terror, a purge of all fascists, collaborators and anti-democratic elements from the whole of the state apparatus, the judiciary, the army and the security forces, revision of the electoral registers, the holding of free elections and the formation of a representative government. This resolution was presented to Damaskinos and Sofoulis and to the ambassadors of the Big Four.[58] There was likewise a public meeting in Salonica with 150,000 participants. About the same time Sofoulis received a letter from 'X' chief Grivas, threatening to take security matters into his own hands. Sofoulis reacted sharply and ordered the police to close down the 'X' premises throughout Greece. Simultaneously he had Grivas charged with threatening the state.[59] Meanwhile news had reached Athens of the Kalamata incident.

On 21st January, prompted by this episode in which 'X' took over in Kalamata,[60] the Political Bureau issued the following resolution: the monarcho-fascist *coup* in Kalamata, together with the murders of democratic citizens in Laconia, Volos and Thebes and the incident at Corinth showed that the Right feared normality and was resorting to civil war methods. It was no coincidence that this occurred just when EAM had recommended its followers to register on the electoral rolls. The Right obviously saw that it had no chance at the elections and was therefore resorting to the method of *coups*. This present *coup* could accurately be said to put Greece into a state of civil war. The British occupation authorities bore the main responsibility for this situation, since they had systematically supported the monarcho-fascists. The British Police Mission had permitted the security forces to be filled with 'X' members and collaborators. The government had not even the right to replace a single gendarme. The Right derived its weapons directly or indirectly from the British; for example the Athens and Piraeus police had received new arms without the older type being called in and these had been passed on to 'X'. If the British so wished, they could put an end to right-wing terror within 24 hours. Thus, the British were responsible for the more than 1,300 murders since Varkiza. Grivas was financed and directed by the Secret Service.

The whole situation was made still worse by the dilatory behaviour of the government. The only measures it had taken had been directed against the Left. It was simply unacceptable that a Greek politician should say that the British don't let us do anything since, at the first interference by the British, a self-respecting government should resign. In face of this critical situation, only by uniting all democrats could Greece be saved from the danger of a monarcho-fascist take-over. The Political Bureau challenged the government to take EAM into the Cabinet. With a general strike organised by the trade unions and with the help of democratic elements in the army and the security forces, it would be possible to crush any right-wing *coup*. The leaders of SAN and 'X' must be arrested at once and their organisations disbanded. All officers and men of the army and the security forces who were known to belong to 'X' or to have been collaborators must be disarmed and detained. A volunteer corps should be formed from democrats who had belonged to the Resistance, to clear the country of the right-wing bands. The government should call on the people for support in crushing the right-wing putschists. KKE would support with all its powers every energetic government measure against the insurgents of the Right. Since December 1944 the situation had never been so critical. Never had the need for tranquillity and order and for the elimination of monarcho-fascism—which was sowing civil war— been so essential to survival. However, the pre-condition for this was the end of the British regime of occupation.[61]

If one disregards the unrealistic suggestion for a volunteer corps, these demands are thoroughly moderate and sensible. Withdrawal of the British troops who, in the last resort, were the main obstacle to normalisation, was at that time demanded not only be KKE and EAM but also, for example, by the left-wing Liberal Foreign Minister, Sofianopoulos. He was of the opinion that only withdrawal of the British could prevent the threatening civil war, since in this case the Right would be forced to pursue a conciliatory and more yielding line; whereas, with British cover, they could continue with their policy of complete annihilation of the Left which would inevitably lead to the 'third round'. Withdrawal of the British would moreover prevent the restoration of the monarchy since, after they were gone, the country's democratic forces would be able to develop unhindered which would lead to internal pacification. Sofiano- poulos saw no danger of a communist takeover since the communists were unarmed. The threat of danger to the bourgeois system came far more from right-wing terrorism which was driving the country to a new conflict during which the liberal bourgeois system would be destroyed.[62] For the same reasons ELD/SKE also demanded British withdrawal.

But the Soviet intervention at the Security Council changed the situation at a stroke.[63] Without it, Kalamata might have led to press reports about conditions in Greece which would have affected public opinion and prompted questions in the House of Commons. Bevin might have realised that the one-sided reports from the British Embassy in Athens and the analyses produced in the Southern Department had little connection with the real situation in Greece and thus might have changed his policy. But the Soviet intervention reduced Kalamata to a secondary issue and in the last resort prevented a potential liberalisation and led to a deterioration of the internal situation in Greece.

It also had internal effects on KKE. *Rizospastis* of Tuesday, 22nd January was—unusually—a four-page issue, a luxury normally restricted to Sundays. The reportage centred on two other topics: Kalamata and the mass meeting of 20th January. There was only a brief mention of the Soviet *démarche* on the back page: the paper obviously had no detailed information. On the following days too, up to 2nd February, *Rizospastis'* reportage was fairly reserved. Apparently the KKE leadership was not clear on the implications of this initiative. On 23rd January, a leading article gave the background to the present state of anarchy, once more emphasising British responsibility. On the other hand it was noted that, on the previous day, the British Communist Party had demanded the withdrawal of British troops and that the EAM delegation had arrived in Moscow. The paper's London correspondent, (the late Theodore Doganis) reported on British reactions to the Soviet *démarche,* but in general the reports and articles were still emphasising Kalamata. On 24th January an article by Zachariadis blamed the British for not even desiring order and tranquillity in Greece, since only its absence could justify their troops continued presence. At present Greece was not an independent country: independence could be achieved only through a representative government and British withdrawal. A further article dealt with the economic negotiations between the British and the Greek governments in London and made the British responsible for the economic chaos. *Rizospastis* also published the EAM Central Committee's telegram of 23rd January, demanding withdrawal of the British occupation troops, safeguarding of national independence, formation of a representative government and the holding of free elections. On the same day there was a comment pointing out that the Soviet intervention had no relation to the Persian question. Finally, the paper published a call to workers from the GCL, to react against the fascist bandits by massive self-defence.

On 25th January, *Rizospastis* reported the Right's preparations for a *putsch* and on the 26th it suggested that right-wing terrorist organisations had hit-lists of left-wing leaders. In a leading article Karagiorgis condemned the British–Greek economic agreement: Greece was getting a loan from Britain from what were her own resources. On the 27th there followed an urgent call to all democratic citizens to register on the electoral rolls. On the 29th (the 28th was a Monday and there are no Monday morning papers in Athens) *Rizospastis* published an EAM Central Committee resolution of the 26th demanding immediate withdrawal of British troops and the formation of a representative government.

Finally, in the February number of *KOMEP* there was a leading article clarifying the KKE leadership's present position.

'At the end of January two roads lie open to Greece: a) the road of internal and external slavery, anarchy and chaos, the road of the Black Front leadership and of the corrupt leaders of the democratic Centre; and b) the road of order, freedom, independence and renewal for Greece under the leadership of the Pan-Democratic Front and, in the final resort, the people's massive self-defence, by inclusion of EAM in the government and the immediate withdrawal of the British from Greece. Greece's honour, independence and future are at stake; no time should be lost; as during the period of the Occupation, anyone who wants to call himself a Greek and a democrat must take careful thought where he stands.'[64]

It was not until 2nd February that *Rizospastis* came out with a sensational report of Vyshinsky's demand for immediate British withdrawal and added that Bevin was repeating Churchill's policy. At the same time the Political Bureau stated that the assumption of the Foreign Policy Council that all parties welcomed the presence of British troops was false at least in regard to KKE. On the 3rd the paper published an EAM Central Committee telegram to the Security Council, requesting the sending of an investigation team; likewise a statement by Zachariadis in which he accused Bevin of using forged documents. There was nothing left for the Greek people but to close ranks once more and fight with resolution for their national honour, for freedom and for independence. Along with this went a renewed call to all party members to register on the electoral rolls. In addition there was a report of a demonstration outside the British Consulate in New York, demanding British withdrawal.

On the 5th *Rizospastis* appeared with the banner headline 'Vyshinsky blasted Bevin in the Security Council with British testimony. . . Vyshinsky: The Greek communists have no need of a defender. EAM is a broad national and popular movement.' Below this came long extracts from Vyshinsky's and Bevin's speeches. The paper commented bitterly on Agnidis' statement that he knew nothing of right-wing terror in Greece. On the 7th *Rizospastis* interpreted the compromise which concluded the Security Council debate as a success for the Soviet Union.

That same day the EAM Central Committee passed a resolution of significance for the future: the parties forming the EAM coalition and the representative of the Left-Liberals (Hajibeïs), having analysed the present situation, had come to the following conclusion. The country's present deep economic, political and moral crisis was a consequence of British armed intervention. This intervention had produced the present regime which, with Damaskinos as leader, was under the control of the royalists, fascists and collaborators. This regime had only one goal: to serve Britain's Greek policy and to safeguard the privileges of the plutocratic oligarchy. Before they took over government authority, the parties of the so-called democratic Centre had recognised the existence of the right-wing terror and had declared that, under these conditions, free elections were impossible. Hardly had they come to power, but they forgot this and the dominance of right-wing terror was intensified. In view of these circumstances, the EAM Central Committee had come to the conclusion that there would be participation in the elections only if the following conditions were fulfilled:

1) the formation of a representative, democratic government, with the EAM parties represented in due proportion;

2) an end to the terror, with actual disbanding and disarming of the terrorist organisations, restoration of order and equality before the law throughout the country;

3) a general political amnesty for National Resistance fighters;

4) a thoroughgoing and guaranteed clean-up of the electoral registers;

5) a purge of all who had served in the Security Battalions or had openly collaborated with the enemy, from the army and the security forces;

6) if these conditions were not fulfilled, the EAM parties would boycott the elections, since in this case they would be a farce but with a tragic ending for the country.[65]

Considered against the background of a full year of White Terror it must be acknowledged that these EAM demands constitute a moderate list. Despite more than 1,000 political murders, more than 6,000 injured and countless arrests, EAM did not demand penal prosecution of right-wingers. Its aims was integration in the parliamentary system on acceptable conditions. The inclusion in the government of some EAM representatives—not necessarily communists—and above all the fulfillment of the above demands would, in fact, have totally changed the political climate within the country. But this would have necessitated a radical change of British policy and, after the Soviet intervention at the Security Council, this was more than ever impossible of achievement.[66] Furthermore, the boycott threat proved a blunt weapon. Leeper who feared that, if the Left participated, they would win approximately a third of the seats, was much attracted by this boycott threat.[67] Unfortunately, the Left did not realise that and maintained this position even when it became obvious that, despite the boycott—later joined by other parties as well—the British would insist that the elections be held. For this the KKE leadership bears a decisive responsibility.

After the conclusion of the Security Council debate, the KKE leaders had shrouded themselves in silence. On 8th February *Rizospastis* had published the EAM statement. On the 9th it reported that elections would be held next day in the Soviet Union for the Supreme Soviet. On the 10th there was a sensational report of a speech by Stalin on the 9th, with a banner headline: 'Marshal Stalin's speech. Unmistakable reference to the atom bomb. The war proved the superiority of the Soviet system.' On

12th February, the anniversary of Varkiza, the first part of Stalin's speech appeared *verbatim* and the rest followed on the 13th, enabling the readers to see that Stalin's speech was much more moderate than the headlined version, based on a French correspondent's report, had suggested. Obviously, *Rizospastis* had been just as much a victim of wish-fulfillment as anti-communist writers of their fears.[68] In fact the speech contained nothing war-like unless one were set on interpreting it in this way.[69] Nevertheless, this speech took on a disproportionate significance. The US Secretary for the Navy, Forrestal, regarded it as the 'Declaration of World War III'.[70] There is no possibility of demonstrating what effect the speech had on the KKE leadership in matters of detail but it cannot have left the Central Committee members who assembled on 12th February for the Second Plenum wholly uninfluenced.

NOTES

1. See p. 229.
2. *Rizospastis*, 16th October, 1945.
3. R 20623/4/19.
4. *Rizospastis*, 18th October, 1945.
5. Woodhouse, *Struggle for Greece*, p. 164 also cites this statement but without setting it in its historical context. Nevertheless he too regards it as verbal radicalism.
6. *Rizospastis*, 21st October, 1945.
7. See p. 230.
8. *Rizospastis*, 23rd October, 1945.
9. Woodhouse, *Struggle for Greece*, pp. 16 ff.
10. 'To kentriko provlima', *KOMEP* (November 1945), pp. 1-3.
11. 'O Dekemvris stathmos kai nea afetiria tou agona ya tin anexartisia kai ti dimokratia', *KOMEP* (December 1945), pp. 1-6; Bartziotas, 'O pallaikos charaktiras tou Dekemvri', *ibid.*, pp. 7-10; Chrysa Hajivasiliou, 'Oi ellinides sto Dekemvri', *ibid.*, pp. 12-13; Petros Rousos, 'O ellinikos Dekemvris kai i diethnis thesi tou', *ibid.*, pp. 14-15; also articles by P. Simos and L. Apostolou. There were also a couple of articles in *Rizospastis* between the end of November and mid-December.
12. Woodhouse, *Struggle for Greece*, p. 143; *Rizospastis*, 6th November 1945.
13. *Rizospastis*, 3rd November, 1945.
14. *Ibid.*, 7th November, 1945.
15. Political Bureau resolution of 9th November, 1945 in *ibid.*, 10th November, 1945.
16. *Ibid.*, 11th November 1945; see also p. 299.
17. The senior SS and Police Commander in Occupied Greece.
18. *Rizospastis*, 17th November, 1945.
19. Leeper to Foreign Office 29th November, 1945 (R 20613/1/19).
20. See p. 309.
21. R 20623/4/19.
22. *Rizospastis*, 22nd November, 1945.
23. *Ibid.*, 23rd November, 1945.
24. *Ibid.*, 8th December, 1945.

25. See pp. 334-5.
26. *Rizospastis*, 11th December, 1945.
27. *Ibid.*, 12th December, 1945.
28. 'Ta trechonta organotika provlimata tou KKE: Apofasi tou PG tis KE tou KKE', *Rizospastis*, 16th December, 1945 and *To KKE apto 1931 os to 1952*, KKE Central Committee, 1953, (n.p.: pp. 132-141.
29. Kousoulas, *Revolution and Defeat*, pp. 229 ff.
30. Edgar O'Ballance, *The Greek Civil War 1944-1949*, (London/New York: Faber/ Praeger, 1966), p. 121. This report's credibility is not increased by its repetition by Eudes, *op. cit.*, p. 258. Eudes, likewise, does not name his source and this suggests that he took over the 'information' uncritically from O'Ballance. Solaro, *op. cit.*, p. 181, is then in turn relying on Eudes but ante-dates this alleged conference to October 1945.
31. Woodhouse, *Struggle for Greece*, p. 160, also p. 155.
32. In the propaganda pamphlet *La trahison de Tito envers la Grèce démocratique* (place and date of publication unspecified) containing anti-Yugoslav articles by N. Zachariadis, K. Karagiorgis, Z. Zografos, P. Mavromatis, M. Porfyrogenis and P. Rousos, there is no mention of this.
33. See p. 333 ff.
34. EAM Delegation Memorandum of 17th December, 1945 (R 21484/4/19).
35. Laskey's Minutes of 30th December, 1945 (*ibid.*).
36. *Greek News* Vol. 1, No. 1, February 1946, p. 2.
37. British Embassy, Paris, to D. Laskey 19th January, 1946 (R 1198/1/19).
38. See pp. 343-4.
39. *Rizospastis*, 19th December, 1945.
40. *Ibid.*, 20th December, 1945.
41. *Ibid.*, 24th December, 1945.
42. *Ibid.*, 28th, 29th, 30th December, 1945.
43. *Ibid.*, 1st January, 1946.
44. *Ibid.*
45. Giorgos Siantos, 'I simasia tis politikis metavolis tis 21.11.45', *KOMEP*, (January 1946), p. 15.
46. See p. 363.
47. *Rizospastis*, 11th January, 1946.
48. *Ibid.*, 12th January, 1946.
49. For details see p. 375; *Rizospastis*, 15th January, 1946.
50. *Rizospastis*, 15th January, 1946.
51. See p. 373.
52. *Rizospastis*, 16th January, 1946.
53. *Ibid.*, 17th January, 1946.
54. *Ibid.*
55. See p. 376.
56. *Ibid.*; *Rizospastis*, 20th January, 1946.
57. Text of this speech in *Rizospastis*, 27th January, 1946 and in A. Othonaios, *op. cit.*, pp. 3-6. General Othonaios had been prominent in the liberal republican movement since 1916. In 1922 he presided over the court-martial which tried ministers and the Chief-of-Staff responsible for the Asia Minor catastrophe, see Dafnis, *op. cit.*, pp. 10-20. At the Lebanon Conference he was suggested and agreed on as commander-in-chief of the Greek armed forces, though not actually appointed. In November 1944 he was made Chief-of-Staff (instead of Vendiris) only to resign a few days later after a disagreement with Lt.-General Scobie. Richter, *op. cit.*, pp. 504 ff.
58. *Rizospastis*, 22nd January, 1946.

59. See p. 376.
60. See pp. 376-7.
61. *Rizospastis*, 22nd January, 1946.
62. See p. 388 ff.
63. See chapter: Greece at the UN Security Council, pp. 387 ff.
64. 'Oi dyo dromoi', *KOMEP*, (February 1946), p. 51.
65. *Rizospastis*, 8th February, 1946.
66. See pp. 402-3.
67. See p. 409.
68. The Defence Minister in the second New Democracy Government 1977-81, Evangelos Averoff-Tositas, interprets this speech as some sort of declaration of Cold War. E. Averoff-Tossizza, *By Fire and Axe: The Communist Party and the Civil War in Greece, 1944-49*, (New York: Caratzas, 1978), pp. 161-2.
69. Fleming, *op. cit.*, p. 348; Joyce and Gabriel Kolko, *op. cit.*, pp. 54 ff.
70. Walter Millis, (ed.), *The Forrestal Diaries*, (New York: Viking Press), p. 134.

THE SECOND KKE CENTRAL COMMITTEE PLENUM, 12th–15th FEBRUARY 1946

The only direct sources for the Second Plenum are the introductory statement by Zachariadis, published in *Rizospastis*, and the resolutions published in the March number of *KOMEP*.[1] Beyond these there are a number of indirect sources such as articles in KKE journals and official publications, party documents and reminiscences of former protagonists which appeared over a considerable period of time.

From the indirect sources the first important mention, a pointer influencing all subsequent assessments, came in March 1947, in a memorandum from Zachariadis to Stalin: 'The Plenum reached decisions which resulted in the organisation of the Democratic Army of Greece.'[2] This formulation must be taken into account in assessing all subsequent statements concerning the Second Plenum's resolutions.

The next important group of statements likewise comes from Zachariadis, from the time of the Third Party Conference after the civil war,[3] as well as from shortly afterwards, that is from 1950 to 1953. These published statements read very much like an *apologia* and should therefore be used only with caution. The same holds good for the two official accounts of party history from the same period.[4]

In contrast to these, publications from the years 1956 and 1957 are most informative. These appeared after the Twentieth Congress of the Communist Party of the Soviet Union when KKE, too, went through the process of de-stalinisation before, during and after the Seventh Plenum in March 1957.[5] About a year later, however, outspoken self-criticism came to an end and from the Eighth Party Congress (1961) on there is again an official interpretation which even survived the split in KKE in 1968 and became a part of the 'official' KKE's orthodox line. This holds good even for the memoirs of former protagonists who—though they were expelled—managed to remain close to the party.[6]

Finally we have two further groups of statements in the 1960s and 1970s, which have one thing in common: they come from quarters outside the official party. The first group came from Zachariadis and his closest henchmen.[7] Their accounts must be assessed with the greatest caution since they are defence pleas and alibis for the past. Assessment is further complicated by the fact that each author's present ideological position must be taken into account. The second group comes mainly from former leading cadres who are now members of KKE/Interior (Euro-communist) or independent Leftists.[8] Their memoirs and articles are characterised by an effort to take a more critical view of the past. Though their accounts are notably open and informative, they too are not completely unprejudiced, whether deliberately or because of psychological difficulty in confessing publicly the mistakes and errors of the past.

Secondary accounts of the Second Plenum are equally controversial. The hard-line anti-communist authors such as Kousoulas (1965), O'Ballance (1966), Pavlopoulos (1971) and Averoff (1973) take it as axiomatic that the KKE leadership took the decision for civil war during the Second Plenum (O'Ballance with the qualifications stated on p. 464). Their thesis is based exclusively on Zachariadis' statements between 1950 and 1953.[9] Authors close to KKE such as Foivos Grigoriadis (n.d.), Eudes (1970) and Solaro (1973) give a somewhat different picture, but not even they make full use of all available sources and they come to some rather contradictory conclusions.[10] The first whose conclusions closely approximated to the facts was Woodhouse (1976), though he, too, did not utilise the material from the Sixth and Seventh Plenums, apparently because he had no access to *Neos Kosmos* for 1956 and 1957.[11] The investigation by Ole L. Smith in 1977 worked over the greater part of this secondary literature and made use of sources reprinted in a KKE/Interior publication.[12] But he, too, did not have the Sixth and Seventh Plenum material available, so that his conclusions likewise are not entirely valid.

At the Second Plenum Zachariadis delivered the introductory statement,[13] which coincides generally in content with the Plenum's resolution. Zachariadis began his speech with the Varkiza Agreement. Several times he stated with emphasis that the signing of the agreement had been a sound political act *(sosti politiki praxi)*, since it had opened the way to political normality. At the end of his speech he raised the double-edged question whether developments would proceed peacefully or not *(omala tha pame i anomala;)* and stated that the Twelfth Plenum and Seventh Party Congress had examined this question: through the struggles of the Resistance the pre-conditions had been created for a basically peaceable transition to the building of popular democracy. The armed British intervention had interrupted this evolution. In order for it to continue, that extraneous obstacle must be removed. How could the factor of British power be neutralised? By organisation, mobilisation and struggle on the part of the whole people. One things was certain: so long as the people did not voluntarily submit, were British power never so great, it could not for ever succeed in obstructing the establishment of popular democracy. And there could be no submission by the people. So the struggle must be organised. The British must be given no respite. They must be unmasked and exposed in Greece, in Britain, throughout Europe and the rest of the world. The party's mass political bastions must be strengthened and extended and suitable conditions for the forthcoming struggle must be created. A fundamental element of this policy was to avoid the snares set by the enemy, whilst at the same time as much damage as possible must be inflicted on him. Naturally, there must be no illusions that, out of sheer kind-heartedness and well-meaning intentions towards Greece, the British would give up their interests there or that this could come about without a struggle. But the stronger the party, the easier this struggle and the sooner the enemy could be forced to respect the rights of people and country. It must not be forgotten that in the general democratic atmosphere of the present day, the situation in Britain itself, in Europe and in the world at large was working in favour of the party, provided of course that this external factor was seen as a auxiliary and provided that the party, too, was campaigning. This struggle was forced on the party by the British and that led to the conclusion that the British occupation, political intervention and the bloodlust of Britain's Greek agents would continue and would make normal evolution more difficult. But the party would coolly and resolutely exhaust all the means at its disposal without for a moment forgetting the primary national interest: a free, democratic and independent Greece.

What all this meant was that Zachariadis was avoiding a direct answer to the question he himself had put. On the one hand he let it be understood that, whilst he felt equal to a show-down with the Greek Right alone, he also realised that this must lead to renewed confrontation with the British and that must be avoided. Apparently, he hoped for a speedy British withdrawal, probably in connection with the Soviet *démarche* in the Security Council. Until then he wanted to hold the party's forces together and, if possible, strengthen them. Despite this, he evidently still believed in the possibility of normal evolution.

The analysis included in the resolutions of the Second Plenum (as reported in the March 1946 *KOMEP*) was routine stuff. (Section 1.) In Greece there was neither democracy nor national independence, nor freedom; the country was ruled by monarcho-fascists and collaborators who had come to power through British armed intervention; at the same time Greece had been reduced to political, military and economic dependence on British imperialist occupation policy—Greece had become a British colony.

The government of the democratic Centre had once more betrayed democracy and had bartered national freedom and independence. To-day neo-fascism and a foreign—British—occupation ruled over Greece. For the Greek people there was therefore only *one* way: to struggle in even greater unity, with discipline and resolution, with all the forces of the people *(pallaïka)* and of all democrats *(pandimokratika)* for bread, life, freedom, democracy and national independence. Greeks would either live as slaves of home-bred fascists, of exploiters and of the occupation, or struggle as free men, overcome, and establish an independent, free and democratic

Greece. The KKE Central Committee proclaimed it the mission of the people to achieve democracy and national independence and for this it must struggle with all its might, in unity with all popular forces and as resolutely as in the years 1940-1945.[14]

Up to this point the content and also the language of the Central Committee Resolution hardly differ from the *KOMEP* leading article of 1st February,[15] save for a slightly more explicit reference to the wartime Occupation. The Resolution then went on to deal with the elections.

Section 2. In view of recent developments, it had become clear that the Right feared the restoration of normal democratic evolution and free elections and was therefore increasingly bent on violent solutions, on a *coup d'état*. Under such conditions, free elections were excluded. The elections now in preparation were a sleight of hand, a 'legal' *coup* and an attempt to deceive world public opinion as to the real situation, and the sending of observers did not alter this. The observers would merely be misused to legalise the electoral *coup*. The people would not fall into this trap. The Central Committee fully approved the EAM Resolution of 7th February (the text of which was given at this point).

Section 3. The Central Committee charged the KKE representatives on the EAM Central Committee with the task of promoting the following proposals:

   a. EAM would continue to have the overriding duty to struggle for democratic evolution and to unite all democratic forces immediately in a Pan-Democratic National Front. EAM must therefore support the initiative of the democratic organisations of Athens and Piraeus in calling a panhellenic, pan-democratic congress.
   b. EAM and the Pan-Democratic National Front must cooperate with all progressive, democratic forces in Britain, Europe and the rest of the world and organise the vindication and defence of Greek democracy and independence at the international level.
   c. EAM must, on the one hand, continue to work for agreement with Great Britain on a basis of equal rights; but, at the same time, enlighten the world on the main reason for the disastrous situation in Greece which lay in official British policy, with the result that an improvement could only be achieved by immediate withdrawal of the British occupation troops, without which free elctions would be impossible.
   d. At the same time EAM must make it clear beyond all doubt that it would resolutely oppose any *coup d'état* and must at once take all organisational and practical measures which would permit the people to fend off the murderous terror and to bring to naught the fascist plans of their exploiters. The first step in this direction would be for the people to call a halt to the present terrorism of the right-wing bandits and agents of the state by mass self-defence, using the

same means as their murderers were using. It was the duty of every Greek citizen and of their popular-democratic organisations to struggle by every means and to be ready for any sacrifice to defend freedom, democracy and national independence. Our enemies, too, must be answered with the same firm, decisive measures.
e. EAM must support the democratic forces within the army, the police, the gendarmerie and the state apparatus.
f. EAM must also make an effort to win over former enemies and opponents, provided these were ready to stop murdering. At present there were in Greece only two camps, the camp of national betrayal and the camp of national independence. KKE would do everything in its power to assist the success of any attempt at reconciliation from whatever quarter it might come.

Even this extract contains no radically new elements. It is a synthesis of the policy promoted in *KOMEP*'s article 'To kentriko provlima'[16] published at the beginning of November and of the same journal's thesis of 8th November on the December Events.[17] The only difference was that the first *KOMEP* article was in the form of a leading article—though its formulation sounds more like a Political Bureau resolution; whilst that of 8th November determined how the December Events should be described. What now emerged from these directives was the official party line. But in content there was no change: integration still remained the aim. The means for achieving this aim were the establishment of a Popular Front, the 'respectability' campaign and self-defence *(aftoamyna)*. The only new element was that self-defence could now be directed against the agents of the state. In other words, the KKE Central Committee charged its representatives on the EAM Central Committee with the task of bringing EAM into line with KKE policy as determined early in November.

Section 4 appears as part of the resolution but, instead of a text, there is a line of dots.

Section 5 deals with the results of the British–Greek economic negotiations of January and draws the conclusion that these had worsened rather than improved the people's living conditions. Therefore a struggle for trade union unity must develop.

In Section 6 the Central Committee sharply rebutted the Right's charge of supporting autonomist movements in Macedonia: KKE regarded Greece's present frontiers as sacred and inviolate; there was no 'Slav peril' from the north, but there should be cooperation with the northern neighbours on a basis of friendship and good-neighbourliness. Section 7 concerned Cyprus. The Central Committee supported the struggle of AKEL (Anorthotiko Komma Ergazomenou Laou, the Cyprus CP) and demanded the union *(enosis)* of Cyprus with the motherland.

The following sections dealt with internal party problems. Section 8 demanded the practical application of the Political Bureau resolutions of

15th December on reorganisation. Section 9 demanded that, at all levels from the base upward to the top leadership, the party should take the necessary organisational measures to be able to offer resistance even under the most difficult conditions. Section 10 dealt with relations between KKE and the socialists and trotskyists and Section 11 with women's problems.

But to return to the ominously missing Section 4—in accordance with the internal structure of the Central Committee resolution, it should have set the political tasks for KKE itself. But neither in *Rizospastis* nor in *KOMEP* of the period, nor in later KKE publications was the text of this section ever published. It continued to figure as No. 4 with that row of dots. This sinister *lacuna* later gave rise to speculation. Interpretations and hypotheses all pointed—with hindsight—in one and the same direction: the unpublished Section 4 contained the Central Committee's decision for civil war! And this theory has been supported equally by Left and Right.

But the phenomenon has another very simple explanation. All these assumptions are based on statements by Zachariadis in the years following the civil war (1950-53). All the other KKE accounts faithfully followed Zachariadis' wording which had only one aim: to conceal what had actually happened behind a veil of generalities. Right-wing authors have gladly followed Zachariadis because his position fitted ideally with their concepts of conspiratorial communism. Since the new Central Committee journal, *Neos Kosmos*,[18] was not available in the West, and thus the 1956 and 1957 statements of former participants in the Second Plenum remained unknown, this interpretation continued to hold good until recently. (For example, this led Katsoulis, in his 1978 history of KKE, to conclude that Section 4 had dealt with the organisation of armed struggle.[19])

However, had Section 4 really contained the decision for civil war, this would have been kept secret and would not have been directly pointed out to opponents, to the Security Police and the General Staff in this way. Such culpable frivolity—if not downright stupidity—should not be attributed even to Zachariadis despite his personality cult megalomania, especially since he could in no way be sure that amongst the Central Committee members there was not an agent of the enemy. Even the explanation that it was intended as a further threat to the government pre-supposes Zachariadis capable of highly complicated political manoeuvring, an ability that he simply did not possess. For that purpose the self-defence policy was sufficient threat.

The explanation for the non-publication of Section 4, both then and later, must be much simpler, much more purely formal—no decision was taken: the issues to be dealt with under Section 4 remained open. According to the internal structure of the Central Committee resolution, Section 4 should have dealt with KKE's political tasks, which raises the question what tasks came up for discussion. From the statements of Markos Vafiadis,[20] Leonidas Stringos,[21] Petros Rousos[22] and Panayotis Mavromatis[23] at the Seventh Central Committee Plenum of 1957 and from the so-called 'platform' of Markos of November 1948,[24] the memoirs of Vontitsos Gousias[25] and Partsalidis,[26] the topics were participation in the elections and the question of armed actions by the *aftoamyna* (self-defence).

On the first, there were two contrasting opinions: Thanasis Hajis, former General-Secretary of EAM and at that time a leading cadre of the party's Macedonian organisation, Markos Vafiadis, Chrysa Hajivasiliou and George Siantos[27] thought that KKE should participate in the elections. In 1976, Markos wrote of the dicussion as follows:

'At the Second Plenum Zachariadis, speaking for the Political Bureau, raised the question of abstention and that in a very decisive manner. Thanasis Hajis, the then Secretary of the Salonica party organisation and member of the Macedonian KKE Bureau's secretariat, spoke first and expressed the opinion that abstention did not correspond to the realities of the situation, that it was absolutely necessary that we participate and that, in the present situation 130–150 seats—though probably not more—could be won, etc. Since further speeches were swinging the feeling against abstention, Zachariadis closed the discussion on the grounds that: "Partsalidis, who will shortly return from Moscow, will bring us the views of the Communist Party of the Soviet Union." Therefore it was decided to remit this problem to the Political Bureau, on the clear understanding that the latter would take into account the opinion of the Soviet comrades which Partsalidis would transmit.'[28]

Thus a decision on abstention was postponed, or rather transferred to the Political Bureau, which gave Zachariadis the final decision.

Markos had already given the Seventh Plenum of 1956 further details of Zachariadis' tactics and aims.

'The impression exists that the decision not to participate in the elections was taken at the Second Plenum. That is not correct. In this instance the truth is that Zachariadis extracted from the Plenum the following decision: "The Political Bureau will decide whether we participate in the elections or not." Thus the Plenum was deprived of the right and the opportunity to discuss the most important problem of that time. The behaviour of Zachariadis at the Plenum was typical. Every opinion different from his own which the Central Committee comrades dared to utter he opposed rudely and in a manner not in accordance with party spirit *(anti-kommatiko)*. For instance, he said: "So-and-so doesn't know what's happening; he's become estranged from the masses; he is speaking heedlessly." These attacks under cover of the office and authority of party General-Secretary, were accompanied by boasting and pseudo-militancy, for example: "A lot of things can happen in this country but it will never again experience fascism and dictatorship." To what purpose was Zachariadis behaving like this? Was it perhaps a question of lack of perspective and an erroneous estimate of the actual facts? No, comrades, it is Zachariadis' purpose to lure the party more easily into abstention and at the same time to a *putschist* position of armed rising as he calls it.'[29]

Regarding the second topic, the question of armed action by the *aftoamyna*, one must discriminate carefully between discussion of this topic at the Plenum and at the subsequent session of the party's so-called Panhellenic Party Military Committee.

It was in the 1947 memorandum to Stalin that Zachariadis first said that the Second Plenum had taken the decision for civil war.[30] With this he had given the directive for future usage, with which he was obliged at all costs to remain consistent since he had committed himself towards Stalin. The result was increasingly explicit insistence on this interpretation until the de-stalinisation of 1957.[31] At the Seventh Plenum in 1957, Zachariadis for the first time began to edge away from this position.

'Comrades, what did the Second Plenum do? The Second Plenum assembled precisely one year after Varkiza. . . What happened at the Second Plenum, comrades? . . . after discussion in which the following opinions were expressed—one side saying we should keep to the peaceful way—the other, our military men, saying we should simply take up arms—the Plenum decided for further development [for dialogue], for progressive development of the movement with support for the Groups of the Persecuted, for a progressive transition to partisan warfare, to armed resistance. The basic point of this policy, comrades, was to strengthen the movement, the grassroots, through the policy of reconciliation *[symfiliosi]* and unity, through development of the people's struggle and the growth of popular resistance, with the creation of mass self-defence in the towns and the promotion of groups in the mountains. . . If to-day Vlandas maintains that there was no plan, he is outside reality. There was no military plan; we took a political decision. Thus we made no military plan of action; that was worked out later. . .'[32]

It is obvious how desperately Zachariadis was trying to save as much as possible of his original version and how in this effort he was mingling the Second Plenum with the session of the Panhellenic Military Committee. Against this there is a series of remarks showing that the Second Plenum, as such, did not deal with this issue at all.

Markos, for example, stated categorically at the Seventh Plenum that the Second Plenum, as a body, had not discussed the matter of civil insurrection. The question of armed action was only discussed in a parallel secret session with a few provincial secretaries and ELAS capetans participating;[33] by which he obviously meant the session of the Panhellenic Military Committee. Markos' version is confirmed by the following statement by the former *Rizospastis* and *Eleftheri Ellada* correspondent in Paris, later the Provisional Democratic government's 'ambassador' in Warsaw, Vasos Georgiou, who stated in 1978: 'Contrary to all that has been written, the Second Plenum of February 1946 took no sort of decision for the start of civil war.'[34]

Further testimony points in the same direction. At the Seventh Plenum, Mavromatis stated that the Second Plenum had only taken a very general decision to orient the party towards armed struggle,[35] by which he obviously meant armed self-defence. In his memoirs Gousias writes that the Second Plenum only decided to reply to right-wing terror with the same means, which again must be understood as a reference to armed self-defence.[36] Vlandas' comments are much more outspoken. In his memoirs he says:

'Who took the decision for the second armed struggle? Today no one can any longer doubt—the Second KKE Central Committee Plenum of February 1946 did not take that decision. Of the surviving members of the Political Bureau of that date (Partsalidis, Stringos, Bartziotas) not one has said that such a decision was taken, not even by the Political Bureau. In his last interview, Partsalidis said that even the Political Bureau took no decision for armed struggle. That is correct.'[37]

In an interview Partsalidis recalled:

'At the time of the Second Plenum, the probability of a conflict was indeed growing. But it was not at that time decided to measure our strength in battle. However, political conditions did give rise to a first discussion as to what form a possible armed conflict could take.'[38]

The former editor of *Dimokratikos Stratos* and later news editor of Eleftheri Ellada (radio station of the KKE leadership in Eastern European exile 1951–55, afterwards renamed I Foni tis Alitheias), Leftheris Eleftheriou, now a Central Committee member of the Euro-communist KKE/Interior, replied to an interviewer in the same sense, though his answer is somewhat involved.

'Zachariadis, in common with the party as a whole, did not come to any clear decision for a resolution on armed struggle at the Second Plenum in February 1946. And the military and political conference held after the Second Plenum [session of the Panhellenic Military Committee] . . . only very briefly considered the possibilities for armed struggle, in fact rejected the suggestion of a rising in the towns and left the question open.'[39]

A further statement in the same sense comes from Michalis Tsantis, Central Committee member and Party Secretary for Epirus at the time of the Second Plenum.

'The Second Plenum did not decide for armed conflict and, above all, not for civil war. The Second Plenum was facing a one-sided civil war

dating from 1943 and decided on military preparations in case we would be forced to take armed counter-measures.'[40]
Here, as we shall show, the terms 'armed/military preparations' refer in the main to armed self-defence.

Vlandas provides a further important argument.

'Did Zachariadis perhaps take such a decision on his own? In no way. Armed struggle in Greece would inevitably have had international repercussions. Could such a decision have been taken without securing Stalin's consent? In no way.'[41]

Similarly the party would not have taken such a decision without Moscow's blessing.

These accounts lead to the conclusion that no fundamental decision was taken on the *aftoamyna* beyond the previous formula—to meet right-wing terror with the same means, *i.e.* by limited armed self-defence. All the later assurances by Zachariadis and his apologists serve only to conceal that in fact no decision was taken, the party continued on its former line, leaving the initiative to its opponents and drifted into unplanned civil war without even wanting this. Likewise the formula used up to now by Zachariadis' critics, the generalised preparation and orienting of the party towards armed conflict, should be regarded with caution and be seen only in the light of the decision for limited armed self-defence. Even the sternest critics of Zachariadis have hitherto found it hard to admit that precisely no decision was taken and no military preparations made. Section 4 of the Central Committee's resolution could, therefore, at most have contained the demand for limited self-defence, if even that.

In contrast to the Second Plenum, the subsequent session of the Panhellenic Military Committee did concern itself with military matters. The following participated: Zachariadis and Ioannidis representing the Political Bureau and former ELAS staff officer Thodoros Makridis; secretaries and military experts from the party's provincial organisations, for example Markos Vafiadis as military adviser to the Macedonian KKE Bureau.[42] The issues and decisions can be established in outline from the memoirs of Gousias[43] and Blanas-Kissavos[44] and from Markos' testimony.[45] From these it seems that Zachariadis spoke first on the decisions of the Second Plenum and stressed that it was the party's first duty to follow the reconciliation policy *(symfiliosi)*; but that, in view of the existing situation, armed conflict could not be excluded and therefore the party must prepare for it. Then he apparently sounded the opinions of the meeting on the possible *form* this conflict might take. The then provincial secretary for Epirus, Tsantis, reports:

'The conference was very short and had no result. From the start there was a disagreement which affected the whole discussion. The disagreement was as follows: when the question of military preparations came up, there was a request for clarification of the form of armed conflict if, indeed, we had to have recourse to it. Two opinions were formulated: one by Thodoros Makridis, who maintained that there ought to be an armed rising of people and army in the towns, because that was where the movement had its main forces; whilst guerrilla warfare needs long preparation and gives the opponent opportunity to take better countermeasures.

'The other opinion came from Markos, who recommended the creation of a guerrilla army on the basis of the Groups of the Persecuted (ODEK), at that time in process of formation. Neither of these opinions was discussed. . . Zachariadis would not allow discussion but only offered—an escape clause. He said: "Let that be! Let each organisation take its measures according to conditions in that district. . ." Zachariadis took no position.'[46]

Tsantis' account is borne out by Markos' statement to the Seventh Plenum in which he notes that the actual suggestion for risings in the towns came from Zachariadis. He reports that there was also a further act of Zachariadis, hardly known within the party. At the military and political conference which took place during the second Plenum, Zachariadis took a stand for armed rising and an immediate seizure of power in the larger towns, in other words he suggested a sort of *coup d'état* in the form of earlier military *pronunciamentos*. But he met with opposition and questions were asked, such as: how will the party carry out this *putsch* and with what forces? How can the *putsch* be brought off without previous organisation of the party's forces? How did he see the *putsch* in the light of the presence of British intervention troops? Moreover the party must first win over the working class and the mass of the population for such an action. Zachariadis then changed his tune and wound up the conference quickly, after it had only lasted a few minutes. To shelve the issue, it was assigned to the subordinate party organisations, for them to examine the means available and the existing possibilities.[47]

From these sources one can reach no clear conclusion as to who actually developed the idea of a rising in the towns, Makridis or Zachariadis. Markos' statement was made to the Seventh Plenum, where all the mistakes of the past were attributed to Zachariadis. Tsantis' statements date from 1980 and he owns that he himself at that time shared Makridis' view. Makridis was the Political Bureau's military adviser and one may conclude that he expressed opinions which he knew were not opposed in principle by either Zachariadis or Ioannidis. One can therefore presume a certain identity of views, so that in the last resort it is irrelevant who proposed them. In 1980 Makridis refused to give details on this and restricted himself to polemics against Markos' interpretation: preparations for guerrilla war needed too much time and time was on the side of the enemy; if there was to be armed conflict, this must be in 1946 and in the towns.[48]

When Zachariadis realised that obviously the majority of those present were against Makridis' idea and when, furthermore, it was clear to him that this must involve renewed confrontation with the British,[49] he retreated. When, after the meeting, Makridis again urged him to action, he was once more evasive, saying that the great Soviet-Hungarian economist, Varga, foresaw a world economic crisis similar to that of 1930, the consequences of which would compel the British to withdraw.[50]

The achievements of the Panhellenic Military Committee were scanty in the extreme. The more far-reaching assertions of Gousias[51] and Bartziotas[52] only serve to conceal the actual state of affairs: what Zachariadis ordered was simply a stocktaking of party forces. Thus, according to Markos, the Macedonian and Thracian Provincial Bureau reported a few weeks later that it would be able to field 25,000 armed men.[53] How obscurely even this directive was formulated is shown by Gousias' memoirs where he says that Siantos was never even informed of it.[54] This is confirmed by the categorical statement of Blanas-Kissavos, who says there was no overall plan for the organisation and leadership of armed struggle, indeed that this was not even discussed.[55]

> 'Neither the Political Bureau of the KKE Central Committee, nor the Party's Panhellenic Military Committee ever undertook [*i.e.* during the whole of this time up to the Third Plenum of 1947] the working out or setting up of a plan in preparation for armed action against enemy forces throughout the whole of Greece.'[56]

Markos again provides a further indication when he reports Zachariadis' reaction as stocktaking of the forces began: 'Stop it! The whole business was only a bluff to force the government to give way.'[57] Improbable as this testimony may sound, it was nevertheless amply confirmed by subsequent developments. Up to summer 1946 absolutely nothing was done to build up guerilla groups and Zachariadis even expressly forbade the Groups of the Persecuted (ODEK) to arm themselves; the few groups which did so, did it on their own initiative.[58]

These internal contradictions in Zachariadis' policy are still to-day inexplicable, even to former leading cadres. Blanas-Kissavos speaks of double-dealing and card tricks, characterising Zachariadis' actions as a right-wing, opportunist and adventurist deviation.[59] Thus he does not go beyond the Seventh Plenum of 1957 which likewise sought the reasons for Zachariadis' mistaken policy solely in his character, and found them in the personality cult. Neither in 1957 nor later did authors close to KKE (with the exception of Nefeloudis) try to examine the problem fundamentally and to clarify what policy Zachariadis was really following, in other words what were his ideological concepts at that time. But only in this way can it be possible to analyse his political line and make its implications transparent.

To recapitulate, within KKE there were two main camps, both with their representatives on the Central Committee and in the Political Bureau.

The majority of the membership and of the Central Committee wanted integration into the system and participation in the elections. In the Political Bureau, this line was represented by Siantos, Chrysa Hajivasiliou and Partsalidis against a majority for the Zachariadis line. Through Partsalidis there was a line to EAM which held to much the same course and on this issue it was not KKE which influenced EAM, rather the reverse. Just because Partsalidis and Siantos had close contact with the broad non-communist grassroots through the EAM leadership, they knew that the great majority of their following was not interested in violent action, and therefore they supported an integration policy. Certainly the representatives of this policy threatened an election boycott, but this was a pre-election political manoeuvre to secure better conditions which would make it possible for the Left to participate with success. In principle, they wanted to participate in the elections. Possibly, without Zachariadis' influence, they would—in the last resort and despite the failure of their demands—have participated on grounds of practical politics and would have accepted, like the Communist Parties of France and Italy, integration into the system as long-term opposition parties. It was their hope that one day they would win the majority to their side in an election—which given their numerous following was by no means excluded—and that they would be able to bring about a transition to socialism without the use of force but by peaceful evolution.

The second camp's position could be called revolutionary and here two sub-groups must be distinguished. The first of these consisted mainly of leading cadres from Northern Greece, many of them former ELAS capetans who had not accepted the defeat in December 1944 and had never come to terms psychologically with the Varkiza capitulation. They took as their premises the successes of ELAS during the Occupation and Tito's successes. It was their following which suffered the most from the right-wing terror and this strengthened their militancy. Their goal was the revival of the partisan war. How far this group was already influenced by Mao's ideas cannot be ascertained for certain but neither can it be excluded. Their main spokesman was Markos Vafiadis. But, unlike the 'evolutionaries', they were not represented on the Political Bureau.

Widely as these two positions differed, they still had something in common. Both were based in the realities of their living conditions and could have been pursued with at least a medium-term prospect of success. For the integrationists, participation in the elections would have certainly produced a hundred deputies of the Left whose mere presence in parliament would have set limits to the repressive measures of the Right; though a takeover of power by an election victory was for the time being an illusion. The result would have been a long period in opposition. For the advocates of partisan warfare, an immediate start would probably have led quickly to the mustering of a guerrilla army at least as strong as ELAS.

But military successes would have called forth intervention by the British, possibly ending in a second Varkiza, but with better conditions. For international, geopolitical reasons (the 'spheres of influence' agreement), prospects for a victory, such as Mao and Tito had achieved, did not exist in Greece.

The second 'revolutionary' sub-group consisted of Zachariadis and his immediate entourage. He rejected both participation in the elections and partisan warfare. For him the first would have been a right-wing and the second a left-wing deviation from Leninist principles. His later critics at the Seventh Plenum, for their part, charged him both with adventurism and left-wing deviation. The fact is that Zachariadis was far more bound by Leninist–Stalinist ideology than were his critics of 1957 and the two contending groups of 1946. During and after the years of Occupation, Siantos, Partsalidis, Markos and many other leading party cadres had realised that political actuality does not always correspond to theory and had become realists, pragmatists. On the other hand Zachariadis had spent the years 1936–45 in prisons and concentration camps, and his devotion to theory therefore remained intact. He continued to think in undiluted Leninist–Stalinist categories as he had been taught at the Comintern's cadre school (KUTV) and applied them schematically to Greek conditions.

Since his return he had tried to bring KKE back into the paths of orthodoxy. He had taken his first decisive step at the Seventh Party Congress, when he abandoned the hitherto prevailing line of the Sixth Plenum of 1934, stating that the process of bourgeois-democratic transformation had been largely concluded during the Occupation and that popular democracy was now the goal. During the next months his repeated expressions of opinion that Greece was going through the deepest crisis of her history can be taken to indicate that he thought Greece was on the way to revolution. On the manner of transition, Partsalidis had stressed the possibility of a peaceful process; Zachariadis on the other hand had emphasised the need to prepare for revolutionary transformation.[60] Facing the immediate development of a revolutionary situation, it would— in Zachariadis' eyes—naturally have been wrong to take part in the elections, since these could only help to stabilise the regime. In this context, the plans for a *putsch* take on a new dimension. Zachariadis apparently believed that revolution was at hand and could be achieved directly the British factor was eliminated. True, there are no direct statements on this subject by Zachariadis from the time of the Second Plenum; whilst his long disquisitions of 1952, trying to 'prove' explicitly that a revolutionary situation had existed and buttressing this with long citations from Lenin and Stalin amount only to *post factum* arguments and are therefore of restricted significance.[61] But what has been quoted up to now shows the extent of Zachariadis' ideological purblindness and his loss of contact with reality.

From another angle too his advocacy of a *putsch* is very significant. It shows that Zachariadis still held to the Comintern ideas of the 1920s which had had such catastrophic results in China (in the Shanghai rebellion of 1926-27). The concept of seizing power in the towns meant a return to orthodox theory. Zachariadis had learned nothing from the experiences of his own party during the Occupation, from the experiences of Tito and Mao; instead he held to the abstract revolutionary model of the KUTV school. If, from summer 1946, he increasingly inclined towards Markos' line, this was not from conviction but under the compulsion of events and in the hope that he might in this way succeed in bringing about a revolutionary situation in the towns. Then, at the end of 1947, he had to acknowledge that this attempt had failed.

Zachariadis' abstract theories of revolution were shared by only very few of his immediate entourage (Vlandas, Gousias, Ioannidis, Bartziotas). In the Central Committee the majority was for participation in the elections; nor did the concept of a rising find a majority in the Panhellenic Military Committee. When he saw that control was slipping from him and that there was a likelihood of the party taking a revisionist line, he curtailed the Second Plenum in order to prevent this. Superficially, this tacking course between the two factions might give the impression that Zachariadis was playing a double game, possibly a cunning twofold strategy. In fact, it was merely his attempt to prevent deviation from the course determined by him. The result was the inconsistent policy which led the party stumbling into civil war without any clear idea of where it was going.

The degree of ideological confusion became obvious during the election campaign, when KKE propaganda was directed much more against Papandreou's moderate Right than against the extreme Right. The *Manchester Guardian* correspondent apparently got the impression from talks with KKE members that KKE's main interest was in producing as right-wing a government as possible: such a government would hold a plebiscite, bring back the king and then revolution would follow.[62] Zachariadis apparently hoped that a right-wing victory would render the situation so acute as to provide the conditions for a qualitative leap, for the revolution. In principle it is the same policy as that followed by the German Communist Party before 1933 when it considered the social democrats as a greater evil than Hitler and his Nazis. In Greece this was to have similarly catastrophic results.

NOTES

1. Nikos Zachariadis, 'I simerini oikonomiki kai politiki katastasi stin Ellada kai ta provlimata tou dimokratikou kinimatos kai agona', *Rizospastis*, 24th February, 1946. (Woodhouse, *Struggle for Greece*, p. 169 wrongly dates this 17th February.) On the 17th *Rizospastis* published the Second Plenum Resolu-

tions. 'Apofasi tis 2is olom. tis K.E. tou K.K.E.: I katastasi stin Ellada: Ta provlimata tou kimokratikou agona kai ta kathikonta tou KKE', *KOMEP,* (March 1946), pp. 105-11 and *Rizospastis,* 17th February, 1946. Quotations are from *KOMEP.* Resolution reprinted in 40 chronia tou KKE 1918-1958 (n.p.: Politikes kai Logotechnikes Ekdoseis, 1958), pp. 544-52 and in To KKE apto 1939 os to 1952, pp. 142-54.

2. 'To ypomnima tou Zachariadi ston Stalin', *I Avghi,* Athens, 14th December, 1980, p. 3. As will be shown this statement is incorrect. But Zachariadis had to pretend in this way, even to Stalin, since otherwise he would have had to admit that KKE stumbled into the civil war without any clear perspective.

3. Nikos Zachariadis, 'Deka chronia palis: Symperasmata, didagmata, kathikonta. (pros ti syndiaskepsi tou KKE), *Neos Kosmos,* (August 1950), pp. 397-433 and (September 1950), pp. 509 ff. This article was subsequently published as a book under the same title. Quotations are from the book.

   Nikos Zachariadis, 'Kainouryia katastasi, kainouryia kathikonta: Oi diapistoseis, i grammi kai oi apofaseis tis 6is olomeleias tis Kentrikis Epitropis tou KKE, 9 tou Ochtovri 1949', in *Epilogi Ergon,* pp. 99-136. This book contains extracts from the collected works in Nikos Zachariadis, *Syllogi Ergon,* (n.p.: KKE Central Committee, 1953), where this article is on pp. 437-76. Quotation is from the *Epilogi Ergon.*

   Nikos Zachariadis, *Ta provlimata kathodigisis sto KKE* (n.p.: KKE Central Committee, 1952, reprinted Athens, Poreia, 1978).

4. *Chroniko tou agona (1878-1951). Dokoumenta kai ylika apo tin istoria tou laïkou mas kinimatos,* KKE Central Committee, 1952, reprinted Athens, *Na ypiretoume to lao,* 1975, p. 60. *Voithima ya tin istoria tou KKE,* (n.p.: KKE Central Committee, 1953), reprinted (Athens: Ekdoseis tou laou, 1975), pp. 233 ff. Both titles were published by Vasilis Bartziotas.

5. Because of the large number of relevant articles, they will not be listed here but each one will be referred to where cited.

6. Vasilis Bartziotas, *O agonas tou Dimokratikou Stratou Elladas,* (Athens: Synchroni Epochi, 1981).

7. Nikos Zachariadis, 'Provlimata tis krisis tou KKE', 1963, reprinted in *Kokkino Asteri* No. 9, (July 1976), pp. 15-62. Dimitrios Vlandas, *1950-1967: Tragodia tou KKE,* (Athens, 1976); Dimitrios Vlandas, *Emfylios Polemos 1945-1949* Vol. I, (Athens, 1979); Vol. II, (Athens: Gramni, 1981).
   Giorgios Vontitsos-Gousias, *op. cit.*

8. Giorgis Blanas-Kissavos, *Emfylios Polemos. 1946-1949. Mitsos (Dimitrios) Partsalidis, Dipli Apokatastasi.* To this group belong likewise two statements by Markos Vafiadis, 'Apostoli sta Ouralia', and 'O Markos Vafiadis apanta; also the statements by Tsantis, Makridis and Partsalidis in the Athens daily newspaper *I Avghi* (date references where cited).

9. Kousoulas, *op. cit.,* pp. 231 ff.; O'Ballance, *op. cit.,* p. 122; Athanasios Pavlopoulos, *op. cit.,* p. 97; Averoff-Tossizza, *op. cit.,* pp. 171-2. Another example of a historian who, as late as 1982, fell victim to Zachariadis' 1950 statements is George Alexander, *op. cit.,* p. 182 ff.

10. Foivos Grigoriadis, *op. cit.,* Vol. 2, p. 625; Eudes, *op. cit.,* p. 258; Solaro, *op. cit.,* pp. 181 ff.

11. Woodhouse, *Struggle for Greece,* pp. 169 ff. His main sources are Zachariadis and Vlandas. Woodhouse had apparently been able to see the then still unpublished manuscript of Vlandas' book on the civil war.

12. Ole L. Smith, 'On the beginning of the Greek Civil War', *Scandinavian Studies in Modern Greek* No. 1, (1977), pp. 15-31; Panos Dimitriou, (ed.), *I Diaspasi tou KKE,* 2 vols. (Athens, 1975).

13. Nikos Zachariadis, 'I simerini oikonomiki kai politiki katastasi', *Rizospastis*, 24th February, 1946.
14. 'Apofasi tis 2is olomeleias', pp. 105 ff.
15. See pp. 472-3.
16. See p. 458, footnote 10.
17. See pp. 459-60, footnote 11.
18. The KKE Central Committee's theoretical organ was renamed several times. Until November 1947 it was *Kommounistiki Epitheorisi*; in 1948-9 this was followed by *Dimofratikos Stratos*. After the civil war defeat in 1949, there appeared—somewhere in Eastern Europe—*Neos Kosmos* (autumn 1949-summer 1974). After the downfall of the Junta in 1974 and the legislation of KKE, the new journal returned to the old name *Kommounistiki Epitheorisi*. This *KOMEP* must not be confused with the journal of the same name issued from 1969-74 by KKE/Interior, to be replaced in the latter year by *Kommounistiki Theoria kai Politiki (KOMTHEP)*.

    Neos Kosmos from 1951 is available to researchers in KKE's Kentron Marxistikon Erevnon in Athens. The 1949 volume (an outsize journal, almost resembling a newspaper) and the 1950 volume are missing and so are the two volumes of *Dimokratikos Stratos*, one number of which is available in the League for Democracy in Greece archives in the Dept. of Byzantine and Modern Greek Studies, King's College, University of London.
19. Giorgios D. Katsoulis, *op. cit.*, Vol. 6, p. 99. The same holds for Pavlos Neteloudis, *op. cit.*, p. 272.
20. Markos Vafiadis, 'Omilia pano sto proto thema tis imerisias diataxis', *Neos Kosmos*, (April-May 1957), pp. 45-72.
21. Leonidas Stringos, 'Omilia pano sto proto thema tis imerisias diataxis', *ibid.*, pp. 82-8.
22. Petros Rousos, 'Omilia pano sto proto thema tis imerisias diataxis', *ibid.*, pp. 89-97.
23. Panayotis Mavromatis, 'Omilia pano sto proto thema tis imerisias diataxis', *ibid.*, pp. 98-104.
24. 'I opportunistiki platforma tou Markou Vafiadi', *Neos Kosmos*, August 1950, pp. 476-80.
25. Vontitsos-Gousias, *Oi aities*, Vol. I, p. 133.
26. Partsalidis, *Dipli apokatastasi*, p. 196.
27. Partsalidis, *op. cit.*, p. 196; Markos Vafiadis, 'O Markos Vafiadis apanta', p. 33. The former military commander of ELAS, Stefanos Sarafis, was likewise opposed to abstention. In a conversation with Zachariadis, he criticised this policy and warned him against an ensuing civil war. Sarafis thought that participation in the elections might prevent this; Sarafis, *op. cit.*, p. lxxix. According to Marion Sarafis he certainly had no idea that the possibility of civil war had been discussed at the Second Plenum.
28. Markos Vafiadis, 'O Markos Vafiadis apanta', p. 33. Markos' version is confirmed by Leonidas Stringos. 'The Second Plenum took no decision on abstention from the elections but left the final decision to the Political Bureau, although many voices were heard at the Second Plenum against abstention. It was Zachariadis who pushed abstention through!' Stringos, 'Omilia', p. 85.
29. Markos Vafiadis, 'Omilia pano sto proto thema', p. 49.
30. See p. 477, footnote 2.
31. For an example, see *Voithima*, by Bartziotas, p. 260. For further specimens from Zachariadis see footnote 3 to this chapter.
32. These remarks by Zachariadis are derived from the shorthand minutes of the Seventh Plenum.. In parts the text is difficult to follow. Dimitriou, *op. cit.*, Vol. I, pp. 92 ff.

33. Markos Vafiadis, 'Omilia pano sto proto thema', p. 50.
34. Vasos Georgiou, 'Poioi kai pos mas odigisan ston Emfylio', *Eleftherotypia*, 23rd December, 1978.
35. Mavromatis, 'Omilia pano sto proto thema'.
36. Vontitsos-Gousias, *Oi aities* Vol. I, p. 134.
37. Vlandas, *Emfylios Polemos* Vol. II, p. 424, also Vol. I, p. 43.
43. Vontitsos-Gousias, O
39. *Ibid.*, 27th January, 1980.
40. *Ibid.*, 10th February and 2nd March, 1980.
41. Vlandas, *Emfylios Polemos* Vol. II, p. 424.
42. *I Avghi*, 10th February, 1980, in Tsantis' statement.
43. Vontitsos-Gousias, *Oi aities* Vol. I, pp. 134 ff.
44. Blanas-Kissavos, *op. cit.*, pp. 73 ff.
45. 'I opportunistiki platforma', p. 476; Markos Vafiadis, 'Omilia pano sto proto thema', p. 50.
46. *I Avghi*, 10th February, 1980. Makridis confirms the accuracy of this account, *ibid.*, 2nd March, 1980.
47. Markos Vafiadis, 'Omilia pano sto proto thema', pp. 47, 50. Eudes' version (*op. cit.*, p. 259) 'Markos wrote later "It was more a question of a putsch than of a revolution. It was an adventure which would have ended with not only the putsch but also the people's movement being smashed" (2)' is not to be found in the Seventh Plenum material to which his accompanying footnote 2 refers. Apparently this is a case of 'broad-minded' interpretation of sources.
48. *I Avghi*, 2nd March, 1980.
49. *Ibid.*, 4th March, 1980.
50. *Ibid.*, 2nd March, 1948.
51. Vontitsos-Gousias, *Oi aities* Vol. I, p. 134. According to this author, Zachariadis said that armed self-defence was only the beginning. When the *aftoamyna* groups had acquired strength, they would go over to the offensive and eventually march on the towns.
52. Bartziotas, *O agonas*, p. 31.
53. Markos Vafiadis, 'Omilia pano sto proto thema', p. 50.
54. Vontitsos-Gousias, *Oi aities* Vol. II, p. 134. Gousias alleges that Zachariadis concealed it from Siantos because he was a traitor. Siantos died on 20th May 1947 and the party mourned him extensively in its press and organised a most solemn funeral. However, in 1950, at the Third Party Conference, Zachariadis and his closest henchmen (Vlandas, Gousias, Ioannidis, Bartziotas) 'unmasked' Siantos as an agent and provocateur, but the alleged proofs were totally unconvincing. Together with Siantos, Zachariadis denounced Chrysa Hajivasiliou (who was then dying) and Karagiorgis. Karagiorgis was attacked but not denounced until 1951. The attacks against Siantos and the others were accompanied by a revival of the campaign against Markos. The whole deplorable affair served only one purpose: to distract the attention of KKE's members from Zachariadis' own mistakes and to put the blame on the previous leadership. In 1957, after de-stalinisation, all charges against Siantos and the others were silently dropped and the victims of Zachariadis' smear campaign were officially rehabilitated, but not before Karagiorgis had died in detention. See p. 240, footnote 27.
55. Blanas-Kissavos, *op. cit.*, p. 75.
56. *Ibid.*, p. 59.
57. Markos Vafiadis, 'Omilia', p. 50. So too Mavromatis, 'Omilia', p. 102. This was confirmed by Kikitsas in an interview published in *I Avghi*, 3rd February, 1980. 'When the Macedonian Party Bureau declared that it was in a position to

send 20,000 armed fighters to the mountains within two weeks, Zachariadis replied: "Stop it! This is a bluff to bring the government to yield".'
58. Markos Vafiadis, 'Omilia', p. 528. 'Even up to March 1946, the party leadership in its circulars forbade these fighters to arm themselves in their own defence. Various groups, who did arm themselves, did this on their own initiative.' This was confirmed by Tsantis in *I Avghi*, 10th February 1980, and by the so-called Secret Letter of the Central Committee to KKE members in 1956 in Dimitriou, *op. cit.*, Vol. I, pp. 52 ff. and Fokos Vetas, 'Pano stis apofaseis tis 6is plateias olomeleias', *Neos Kosmos*, September 1956, p. 16.
59. Blanas-Kissavos, *op. cit.*, pp. 73 ff.; Ole Smith, *op. cit.*, p. 28 does not take into account the election abstention factor and thus reaches a similarly mistaken conclusion, speaking of a double strategy: 'increased partisan activity *and* parliamentary legal work'.
60. See p. 274.
61. Zachariadis, *Provlimata kathodigisis*, pp. 81-90; Nefeloudis, *op. cit.*, pp. 273-9 examines these arguments thoroughly, but without recognising their true character as justifications after the event.
62. *The Manchester Guardian*, 26th March, 1946.

FROM THE SECOND PLENUM TO THE ELECTIONS AND LITOCHORO

According to *KOMEP*, Partsalidis returned from the Soviet Union on 17th February 1946,[1] though it is not clear whether he returned alone or with Alkiviadis Loulis and Neokosmos Grigoriadis. Throughout February, however, *Rizospastis* made no mention of his return.

The EAM delegation had arrived in Moscow on 21st January.[2] But their hosts were obviously embarrassed that they arrived on the very day Gromyko handed in his letter to the Security Council *praesidium*. However, the delegation was allowed to hold a press conference on the 22nd,[3] though the Soviet press took no notice and devoted the next day's papers to the Kalamata affair.[4] It cannot be ascertained how long the delegation stayed in Moscow but what is certain is that, during the Security Council debate (1st–6th February), they were in Leningrad on a public relations visit.[5] Apparently, the Soviet authorities did not want to identify themselves unduly with EAM. In general, it would seem that the delegation was not too heartily welcomed.[6]

It is very probable that the serious talks took place after the delegation's return to Moscow from Leningrad. Two sets of talks must be distinguished: those involving the whole delegation and the private talks with Partsalidis, the first KKE representative to visit Moscow since 1935.[7] The EAM delegation's mission was to inform ruling circles in the European capitals about conditions in Greece and to mobilise international public opinion in support of EAM's policy.[8] In Moscow they were received by the then Under-Secretary of State in the Foreign Ministry, Lavrentiev, who was responsible for the Balkans. During these talks, Partsalidis gave Lavrentiev to understand that on behalf of KKE's Political Bureau, he wanted contact with the Foreign Affairs department of the CPSU's Central Committee. This he had agreed with Ioannidis before his departure.[9]

Thereupon Partsalidis was received by a Greek-speaking cadre from this department called Petrov, to whom he expounded the problem of election abstention. He asked for advice from the CPSU. Then he addressed another topic:

> 'During the conversation, I stressed that, in view of the continually intensifying persecution of the movement, it was KKE's opinion that it would in the long run be very difficult to avoid armed counter-measures. I told him we hoped that, now wartime obstacles no longer existed, we would get full international support to neutralise imperialist inter-

vention in Greece and that it was natural that we would like to know how the CPSU leadership saw this problem. Comrade Petrov promised that he would pass on what I had said; and the next time we met he told me that Molotov had stated unequivocally that KKE should participate in the elections. In the meantime, however, we should certainly support the self-defence *(aftoamyna)* movement of the persecuted. After the elections we should make up our minds according to how the situation developed, whether we would put our main emphasis on political struggle or on armed action.'[10]

In other words, Partsalidis was not received by either Stalin or Molotov, but neither did he—as Zachariadis later alleged[11]—discuss KKE's problems with some subordinate official, but with the CPSU Central Committee's responsible representative, whilst the advice to participate in the elections came from Molotov himself. However, the Soviet reply does seem to have had more the character of a recommendation[12] than of a directive; at least it seems to have been susceptible of misinterpretation since subsequent developments would otherwise be inexplicable.

After Partsalidis' return there was a meeting of the Political Bureau at which he reported on the attitude he had found in the Soviet Union.

'When I arrived and told the Party Central Committee's Political Bureau about the CPSU's advice, I had to submit to an unprecedentedly fierce attack from Zachariadis. "There is no longer any Comintern! You will have to convince the Party" he said. At that time no one in the Political Bureau took a stand against him. Neither Siantos nor Chrysa.'

But as Partsalidis stuck to his words and therefore there was a danger that the EAM Central Committee might draw different conclusions and reach a different decision, Zachariadis charged Siantos to accompany Partsalidis to the Central Committee session and keep him to the line determined by the Political Bureau.[13]

Zachariadis' reluctance to accept the Soviet leadership's advice has raised serious questions. Nefeloudis thinks it possible that Zachariadis had received further instructions direct from Stalin and mentions this in connection with an alleged meeting between Stalin and Zachariadis in the Crimea, said to have occurred before the Second Plenum.[14] The occurrence of such a secret meeting can in fact be proved, but *after* the Second Plenum, at the beginning of April 1946.[15] Knowledge of this was restricted to a very narrow circle of leading KKE functionaries. Nefeloudis' information is obviously based on rumour circulating within KKE. Moreover, at this time Zachariadis was constantly in the public eye and *Rizospastis* carried daily reports of his movements and activities. He could not possibly have disappeared unnoticed.

Nefeloudis' story is significant from another angle. It shows that even KKE cadres could not imagine that Zachariadis was pursuing an independent policy and developing his own initiatives. But Zachariadis' behaviour can only be explained in this way. He saw the immediate prospect of a revolutionary situation. To follow Soviet advice would, in his eyes, have meant passing up this unique opportunity and this he was not prepared to do. Moreover, the Soviet advice did not come from Stalin in person and Zachariadis may well have rejected the idea of taking advice from a functionary who stood below himself in the party hierarchy—he was, after all, a CP General-Secretary. In the days of the Comintern he would almost certainly have accepted such advice because at that time he was himself a member of the decision-making hierarchy: now he would only be prepared to take advice from someone of equal rank.

Zachariadis' statement of 1956 to Gousias may have held good—with a few deletions—for 1946 as well.

'One does not accept opinions or suggestions from a subordinate. [Partsalidis] should have had discussions with the CPSU leadership and an interchange of opinions, and only after that ought he to have listened to advice.'

There follows a very revealing remark:

'as regards the relations with other parties, Partsalidis held the opinion, which he developed [in his post-civil war exile] in Tashkent, that a Greek general should stand at attention before the lowest-ranking Russian soldier. Therefore the opinion of any chance Russian citizen is a directive'.[16]

In other words it would not have been consistent with Zachariadis' self-esteem and sense of personal worth to have accepted the 'advice' of a Soviet Central Committee functionary and on account of that to have surrendered his own policy. How far this trait of individualistic chauvinism had already coloured his thinking in 1946 cannot be ascertained but it seems to be consistent with his personality cult.

Within the Political Bureau Zachariadis managed to keep secret the content of the message brought by Partsalidis from the Soviet Union. The result was that the party membership got the impression that the Soviet leadership approved the abstention policy.[17] Markos remembers:

'Apart from the Political Bureau, the rest of the Central Committee and the party as a whole had the impression that the Soviets, too, were for abstention. It has often been stressed that abstention played a decisive part in our further evolution, that it was one of our mistakes and this mistake can be laid exclusively to Zachariadis' account, whilst all his fellow-travellers washed their hands of any responsibility. Partsalidis never spoke of his own quite special responsibility in agreeing to abstention and he capitulated to Zachariadis at one of the most critical and decisive moments for our movement, instead of insisting that the problem be brought before the party's Central Committee. Thus, both he and Zachariadis deceived the Central Committee and the party. But Partsalidis has his arguments: he says that the others were to blame;

that Siantos was to blame (though it is questionable whether Siantos would have dared to say anything in the Political Bureau, even about other problems, since they regarded him as suspect and had in practice isolated him), that Chrysa was to blame because she did not speak out!'[18]

This was to prove decisive for future developments.

Markos' charges were in fact justified. Had the Central Committee been summoned and told the advice of the Soviet leadership, the majority would certainly have decided for participation in the elections. After all, at the Second Plenum, the majority had been for it. Partsalidis' excuses in his memoirs are implausible and are simply intended to distract attention from his failure.[19] If Partsalidis made a fatal blunder, then it was at this moment when, as General-Secretary of EAM, he certainly had the opportunity to call a halt to Zachariadis' mistaken policy. A word from him in the EAM Central Committee or to the KKE Central Committee members who were for participation in the elections would have been sufficient to change the course of Greek history. Such a stand would, of course, have meant that Partsalidis would have had to be ready to risk confrontation leading a fraction, if not a rebellion, which might well have led to an open split in the party and in any case would have been an offence against fundamental Leninist principles. In 1968, when KKE split over the 'fraternal' occupation of Czechoslovakia and he became one of the leaders of the Euro-communist KKE/Interior, Partsalidis was in fact prepared for this, but in 1946 he was evidently incapable of taking such a step. By submitting to Zachariadis' leadership, he strengthened the latter's position and helped him to establish his claim to absolute rule within the party, to which he himself was to fall a victim after the end of the civil war.[20] But despite all his self-criticism in his final years, Partsalidis still could not face the decisive fact of his own guilt. Until his death in 1980 he remained silent about this aspect of his responsibility.[21]

Despite his brusque rejection of the Soviet leadership's advice, Zachariadis apparently did not dare to dismiss it completely. He developed an idea, which he must have been conscious offered no prospect of success but which provided him with the perfect alibi and would help him to overcome the resistance of still doubting members of the Political Bureau. He suggested a purely symbolic participation in the elections, by putting up only one candidate in each electoral district. Simultaneously there would be an announcement that, as of now, the election results would not be recognised.[22] Partsalidis and Siantos were charged with putting this suggestion to the EAM Central Committee. They did and the EAM Central Committee rejected it.

On 21st February, *Rizospastis* published a report on EAM's position, to the effect that EAM still held by the Resolution of 7th February. At the same time it was denied that EAM had received any advice from abroad—

that would never be accepted. Evidently, rumours of this sort were circulating in connection with Partsalidis' return.[23] The next day there followed a KKE Political Bureau resolution: in view of the existing situation, KKE would not participate in the elections; KKE supported the EAM Central Committee demands of 7th February; with good will on the British side, the situation could within a very short time be so altered that truly free elections could be held.[24] At the same time it was noted that *The Times* and the *News Chronicle* had both demanded postponement.

The same day saw the start of negotiations between EAM, Sofianopoulos, SKE/ELD and the Left-Liberals for joint action.[25] On 25th February, Zachariadis welcomed these unifying tendencies.[26] On the 27th, Karagiorgis advocated the creation of a Pan-Democratic Front in a leading article.[27] On 2nd March, a delegation consisting of representatives of EAM, SKE/ELD, the Left-Liberals and Sofianopoulos' party visited Sofoulis and told him that, if the election date were postponed for two months and the intervening time used to revise the registers and restore law and order, they would be prepared to participate.[28] On the 5th, *Rizospastis* gave maximum publicity to a statement signed by J. Sofianopoulos, D. Partsalidis, K. Gavriilidis, M. Kyrkos, S. Kritikas, G. Oikonomou, I. Tsirimokos, S. Hajibeïs and others, formulating the following demands: 1) Formation of a new, democratic government with National Resistance participation; 2) Postponement of the elections for two months; 3) A purge of the state apparatus, the army and the security forces; 4) A general amnesty; 5) Revision of the electoral registers. If these conditions were fulfilled, they would participate in the elections.[29] At the same time it was noted that the British had used administrative means to prevent the visit of the French deputies invited by the EAM delegation; on the other hand Petimezas' initiative for an all-party conference was greeted with satisfaction.[30] On the 7th *Rizospastis* reported the statements of Tsouderos and Peltekis.[31]

On the same day Zachariadis appeared in print again: no doubt in response to Papandreou's coalition manoeuvre.[32] He used a leading article to suggest to the Sofoulis Liberals that the parties of the Left were prepared to enter an election coalition and give them 50 per cent of any seats they might win. The only condition was postponement for two months so that the electoral registers could be revised. Thus, the present government could go on governing.[33] For Sunday, 10th March, the final day of the Eighth Trade Union Congress, EAM summoned a mass meeting in the Athens football stadium. Like previous such demonstrations, this too was a great success, with well over 100,000 participants (*Rizospastis* even made it 400,000).[34] On the same day Kafandaris' five ministers resigned and on the 11th and 12th there followed other resignations.[35] On 12th March, *Rizospastis* announced a joint mass rally of EAM, SKE/ELD, the Left-Liberals and Sofianopoulos' party and on the 13th it reported that

Zachariadis and Porfyrogenis would shortly leave for the Czechoslovak CP's Eighth Party Congress.

KKE's Political Bureau met on the 14th, approved the course taken so far and repeated Zachariadis' offer of the 7th. On the same day EAM and the parties cooperating with it sent identical telegrams to the governments of the Big Four, demanding the formation of a government with sufficient freedom of action to proclaim a general amnesty, purge the state apparatus and revise the electoral registers.[36] The Congress of the Pan-Democratic Union took place on the 15th, with the participation of 250 representaties of EAM and its allies plus other democratic groups from all over Greece. The first speaker was General Othonaios,[37] followed by Admiral Yannikostas and General Kallidopoulos. Then Sofianopoulos spoke and the high point of his speech was the following:

'I own that, had I known that the government would take the glorious weapons with which our people fought in the National Resistance and which ELAS handed over after the Varkiza Agreement, to give them to the followers of 'X', I at least would not have committed such a sacriligious act by putting my signature to the Agreement.'[38]

After Sofianopoulos, Svolos and Partsalidis spoke, as well as a series of less well-known personalities. Svolos' speech reached its climax with the appeal: 'Democrats of all Greece, unite!'

The congress lasted until the 19th March. On the final day this heretofore loose association of parties and groups was given an organisational structure, constituting itself the Panhellenic Federation of Democratic Associations (Panellinios Omospondia Dimokratikon Syllogon), with General Othonaios as chairman. At the same time a resolution was passed in general conformity with the Left parties' statement of 5th March.[39]

In all these efforts for the building of a Democratic Front KKE hardly appeared—or only indirectly, through EAM. The reasons for this reserve are not entirely clear. Probably, Zachariadis was satisfied with the way things were going and therefore kept himself in the background; also he may have been busy preparing his journey to the Czechoslovak Party Congress which would at the same time be a meeting of the most important party leaders. According to Foivos Grigoriadis, Zachariadis left Piraeus for Salonica by steamer on 20th March.[40] According to the same author, that day also saw a further development. About midday on the 20th, the two Left-Liberal leaders, General Neokosmos Grigoriadis and Stamatis Hajibeïs were together in their party's office and in low spirits. Both had from the beginning rejected the policy of election abstention but had then yielded to the majority in EAM, though continuing to regard abstention as mistaken. Suddenly there came a telephone call from the KKE Central Committee which Hajibeïs took. Siantos and Ioannidis wanted to speak to him or to Grigoriadis at once; one or other of them should come to the Central Committee immediately. Grigoriadis was not keen as he thought there was no longer any point. So Hajibeïs went on his own and returned shortly afterwards in a completely altered frame of mind. Thereupon there ensued the following dialogue:

'Neokosmos, perhaps we are saved. Who knows, this may be our salvation.'

'What do you mean?'

'Listen, what the Old Man [Siantos, nicknamed *O Yeros*] told me— No, what both of them told me. We should demand of the government a simple extension of the time-limit, not a postponement of the elections: only the time-limit for submitting lists of candidates need be extended. Then we should put up Left-Liberal candidates all over the country. The whole Left will support us. It's a compromise solution. Do you get it?'

'Stamatis, the bird has flown; they won't accept this extension.'

'We must try everything humanly possible. Think from what a disaster we would be saving the country.'

'Of course we must do everything possible, but it is useless. I repeat: the bird has flown.'

'You can't know that, so don't say it. Maybe they know something which made them adopt our opinion. Who knows—perhaps they have had a hint. Perhaps that is why Zachariadis has gone off: it was he who was always for the hard-line solution. Perhaps his journey to Prague is only a pretext, perhaps he went to have a good time. . . They told me he would be away a whole month. That means he won't be back till after the elections. That means Siantos will cope with the election business. Do you get it?'

Like all who worked with KKE, the two Left-Liberals had a real affection and respect for Siantos and by always showing this they, at the same time, demonstrated their equally strong antipathy to Zachariadis. Grigoriadis, in particular, used often to say to Siantos: 'We old-timers can always agree.' So it was on this occasion. The news that Siantos was in charge revived him, as it had previously revivied Hajibeïs. He agreed:

'You're right. Something's going on. We must do all we can. Working with Giorgi [Siantos] is one thing; with that egomaniac Zachariadis it's something quite different. Let's try to get an appointment with Sofoulis as soon as possible.'[41]

They succeeded after much difficulty in making contact with Sofoulis' assistant-minister, Yerasimos Lychnos. Hajibeïs saw him at 6 p.m. Lychnos showed great interest and promised a speedy answer. But this never came because, on the same day, Bevin decided that a postponement of the elections was excluded.[42] The time-limit for submitting lists of candidates closed at midnight and Sofoulis informed the new British ambassador, Norton, that the elections would be held on 31st March.[43] Grigoriadis' report, so far as it concerns the Left-Liberals, is above question; after all it was first-hand information—General Neokosmos Grigoriadis was his father. But his assumption that this initiative on the part of Siantos and Ioannidis was undertaken without the knowledge or against the will of Zachariadis is pure hypothesis. Ioannidis was at that time Zachariadis' right-hand man.[44]

It is much more probable that this dramatic story was no more than another manoeuvre by Zachariadis to give himself an alibi and was intended as a kind of tranquilliser for the Siantos–Partsalidis–Hajivasiliou faction in the Political Bureau, though it must of course be accepted that Siantos was acting in good faith. Moreover, it is highly unlikely that, a few hours after Zachariadis' departure, Siantos could have taken such an initiative against the will of the Zachariadis' faction in the Political Bureau which had the majority. That would have been tantamount to rebellion. On the contrary, this initiative was a chess move planned to the last detail and known, in its content at least, to the Political Bureau;[45] though its real aim may have been known only to Zachariadis and Ioannidis.

On 21st March *Rizospastis* started its abstention campaign at full blast. In a leading article, Karagiorgis damned Bevin's decision as a *firman* of the Foreign Office. Another article said that the only answer to Bevin's ruling was abstention.[46] On Sunday, 24th, the paper carried a fiery message from the EAM Central Committee in which the abstention campaign was compared to the 1821 Independence War. The same day saw a mass meeting in Piraeus with, according to *Rizospastis,* 500,000 participants. Partsalidis and Sofianopoulos called on all democrats to abstain, Partsalidis attacking Papandreou in particular.[47] In the days up to the 31st *Rizospastis* constantly intensified its abstention propaganda. On the 30th its front-page was taken up by an enormous photograph of a mass meeting of the previous day, set at an angle with the word 'Abstention' *(apochi)* over-printed. Finally, on election Sunday, *Rizospastis'* banner headline read: 'Democrats Abstain!'

Election boycotts have been almost traditional in Greece. In 1923 the Populists boycotted the elections and in 1935 the republicans and Liberals carried out two boycotts, of the elections of 9th June and of the plebiscite of 3rd November. There had also been boycotts in 1911 and 1916. In 1923 and 1935 the result had been that the leaders of the boycotting parties had found themselves excluded from a share in power for a period of time and had been subject to various restrictions. But, for all the enmity between republicans (Venizelists) and royalists (Anti-Venizelists), these repressive measures had on the one hand been limited to the leading personalities of the competing parties (which were in reality patronage networks) and to their immediate followers (for example the officers); whilst, on the other, persecution had only very rarely sunk to the level of physical extermination. Basically, these had been contests within the bourgeois camp and, since the participants knew that the tide could turn again, they acted with restraint and soon readmitted their opponents to a share in political power.

In 1946 circumstances were completely different. Only to a very restricted extent were these elections a contest within the bourgeois camp. Basically, they were a struggle between Left and Right in which the Right, at least, was determined on the total annihilation of its adversary. Developments since the December events and Varkiza had given ample proof of that. When Kafandaris, Kartalis and Tsouderos boycotted the elections, they were acting within the traditional framework and they knew that their existence and that of their following was not threatened. The same held good to a certain extent, for the non-communist Left. But KKE must have known that, after a right-wing election victory, the persecution of their members would intensify beyond bounds, since the restraints imposed by the previous moderate governments on the Right would then be lifted.

At the outset, KKE's policy of threatening to boycott the elections was fully justified in so far as they could hope to win an improvement of the conditions under which these would be held. But when it became clear that their threats were achieving no result, the KKE leadership should have tried to change course and participate in the elections, albeit under protest. However, by that time they had become the prisoners of their own policy. As more and more parties and groups joined the abstention front and even the left-wing Liberal forces joined in the boycott, they could no longer retreat. Zachariadis was responsible for thus manoeuvring KKE, EAM and the rest of the non-communist Left into a political blind alley. There can be no doubt that, had the KKE leadership changed its policy when it became clear that the boycott threat was not working, the rest of the Left would have followed this altered course. Together the whole Left could certainly have won a third of the parliamentary seats. Probably, too, the parties and groups around Kafandaris, Tsouderos and Kartalis would then have participated in the elections, although under protest at the conditions under which they were being conducted. As a consequence, the resulting parliament would not have been under the one-sided control of the Right. True, the Right would then most probably have entered parliament as relatively the strongest faction, but the non-extremist democratic forces would have had the majority. A government formed on this basis would have had the authority and probably also the will to break the strength of the *parakratos*. At the very least, the Left together with the Centre could have prevented the carrying through of extremely illiberal laws and measures. But, because KKE stuck to its boycott policy, the initiative passed to the Right. This development could have been foreseen but Zachariadis, blinded by ideological delusions, hoped that events would take the course he expected and lead to a revolutionary situation.

The chronological account must be interrupted at this point to consider an event which occurred on the same date as the elections—the attack by a guerrilla band on the village of Litochoro, on the eastern slopes of Mt. Olympus, during the night of 30th-31st March. As this attack was later interpreted as the beginning of the Civil War, it may be useful to take a closer look at the circumstances. According to a telegram sent by the gendarmerie commander at Katerini and published in a few Athens newspapers, it appears that on the evening of 30th March a guerrilla group attacked the Litochoro gendarmerie post which was occupied by a few gendarmes and National Guardsmen who were to take care of order and tranquillity on election day. The building was set alight and there were some dead and wounded. The guerrilla band then withdrew to Mt. Olympus.[48]

When *Rizospastis* learned of this it reacted angrily: on 1st April it reported the event on the basis of the official government *communiqué* and went so far as to charge the government with falsification. The headline read: 'Government authorities and bandits stage an alleged communist attack.' In the article itself the purist *(katharevousa)* form of the name, Litochorion, was used. Apparently *Rizospastis* had no idea what had actually happened. On the 3rd it corrected its first accounts: now the Litochoro episode had been provoked by the gendarmerie and the village inhabitants had simply defended themselves; *Rizospastis* obviously considered it a case of *aftoamyna*. On the 9th Litochoro was mentioned again when *Rizospastis* reported that, when elections had finally taken place there on the 7th, 51.5 per cent of the voters had abstained.[49] The May 1946 number of *KOMEP* published a speech Zachariadis delivered to a party meeting in Salonica on 12th April, after his return from Czechoslovakia. There he said:

'The events which happened at Litochoro are known. During the ten to fifteen days before the events, four democratic citizens were murdered in that area and dozens *(dekades)* tortured. Naturally people took to the mountains and because they went there many times without arms and without results, this time they took arms to defend themselves and that is what they did. The events which took place at Litochoro are a message to monarcho-fascism and to the British. Where murderous action exults unhindered, where government agents or venal gangsters carry out executions, the peasants take to the mountains and then the murderers raise hell about EAMO-Bulgarian bandits and start mopping-up operations.'[50]

Zachariadis went on to add other, similar cases where persecuted peasants had defended themselves. For him, obviously, the Litochoro affair was a case of armed self-defence and nothing more. Thereafter, the episode relapsed into oblivion.

The next time Litochoro was mentioned was in *Exormisi* on 28th October 1947.[51] That article was published on the first anniversary of the estalishment of the Democratic Army of Greece's GHQ and was intended to prove that the party had been following a consistent line since the Second Plenum. According to it, the attack on Litochoro was the beginning of the new guerrilla war. The article starts with a description of developments from Varkiza to the elections and goes on to say that, in Spring 1946, a group of former ELAS men had taken cover in the Olympus massif. Most of them were from the village of Litochoro. Their leader was Capetan Tzavellas (Pappou). On 26th March they were joined by two former ELAS leaders, Panos and Ypsilantis. A decision had been taken that from now on they would defend both themselves and the democratic people more actively. The little group of persecuted fighters had then resolved to undertake an armed action which should be a warning to the monarcho-fascists. Litochoro was chosen as the scene because there the right-wing terrorists had been particularly rampant. Therefore during the night of the 30th-31st March thirty-three people's fighters had attacked Litochoro. The enemy had suffered heavy casualties and the guerrillas had taken prisoners and considerable booty in arms.[52] A year later, in November 1948, there followed another article in the theoretical journal of the KKE Central Committee, *Dimokratikos Stratos*.[53]

In the first article it was still implicitly admitted that the attack on Litochoro had been a spontaneous action and to be understood only as a symbolic start. But the article in *Dimokratikos Stratos* now identifies it as the real start. A myth had been created which was to have a long life. At the Third Party Congress in 1950 Litochoro was the beginning of the civil war and Bartziotas leaves no doubt of this in his two party histories.[54]

Even after the 'de-stalinisation' of KKE this myth was still being embellished. In his four-volume work on the civil war published in the mid-1960s, Foivos Grigoriadis maintains that the attack on Litochoro was carried out by order of Zachariadis. On 21st March, when Zachariadis passed through Salonica on his way to the Czechoslovak Party Congress in Prague, he had told the Macedonian party leadership that he wanted a spectacular action, a blow *(vrotima)* which would make even the obdurate understand the meaning of the election boycott. After his departure the local party leadership had determined the details and Markos himself had selected the village of Litochoro in the Olympus foothills. Ypsilantis and Panos were then sent to Olympus to organise the attack and arrived there on the 25th.[55] The only blot on this story is that Grigoriadis cites no sources for his assumption.

His story was taken over by Eudes and by him further embroidered: the former commander of the tenth ELAS division, Giorgos Kikitsas, had been involved in planning the attack. But Eudes, too, does not give any source.[56] Comparison of the two versions shows that, as concerns Zachariadis' orders, Eudes' version derives from that of Grigoriadis; but his assumption that Kikitsas, too, took part in the planning would seem to be purely speculative.[57] Grigoriadis, on the other hand, used the fact that Zachariadis had been in Salonica shortly before Litochoro to draw somewhat daring conclusions. Evidently, he could not imagine that the guerrilla group on Mt. Olympus might have developed its own initiative and therefore he, too, preferred the above hypothesis.

The guerrilla group which attacked Litochoro evidently consisted of persecuted former ELAS men—perhaps 'wanted' for trial—who had taken refuge on Mt. Olympus and had so far remained passive. The two new arrivals may have belonged to that category of the persecuted, of whom Markos reported that they took up arms on their own initiative and went over to active self-defence *(aftoamyna)*.[58]

But there are other facts which tell against Grigoriadis' version. As we have already noted, Markos reported at the Seventh Plenum that in March 1946 the party leadership had issued a circular expressly forbidding the arming of the self-defence groups.

'After the Second Plenum a member of the Political Bureau [Ioannidis, Stringos?] came to Salonica and later Zachariadis came himself. Abstention at the elections had already been decided and we were moving towards armed conflict. The Macedonia Party Bureau stated that its party organisation was in a position to arm and make ready 25,000 fighters in the villages and most important towns and to start arming the Groups of the Persecuted and military organisation of the popular forces. Both party secretaries [Zachariadis, Ioannidis, the organising secretary?] obstinately refused to give the order for arming these groups.'[59]

This is confirmed by Vasos Georgiou who states with crystal clarity:

'The attack on Litochoro, which the Right take as the beginning of the Third Round, occurred without any preparation or plan, without any corroborating resolution, even from the Political Bureau.'[60]

Our hypothesis that the attack on Litochoro was an isolated initiative taken by a local group of the persecuted has recently been corroborated by Markos himself. In an interview with the *Ta Nea* journalist, Dimitris Gousidis, he said:

'Litochoro does not actually mark the beginning of the Civil War. There, in the Katerini area, a seat of reaction had been created and EAM/ELAS cadres were being killed. We decided that one of our armed groups should dissolve this gang. Panos, Ypsilantis and other cadres undertook to carry out this task. The relevant order was given by me through Kikitsas. On his way abroad, Zachariadis stopped there by chance and we discussed the issue with him. Zachariadis readily consented: "Go ahead" he said. When our armed group reached the area, the gang was no longer there and on its own it decided to attack the gendarmerie station at Litochoro. For us this event was not the beginning of the Civil War. . .'[61]

There is also the following consideration: when Zachariadis arrived in

Salonica on 21st March, he was on his way to the Czechoslovak CP Congress in Prague, where he would meet the leaders of the other European CPs and representatives of the CPSU and would discuss the future policy of KKE. It is hardly probable that, before these conversations, he would have prejudiced the outcome by an action like that at Litochoro.

Just as with the question whether the Second Plenum took the decision for civil war, here too the assumptions of the 'cold warriors' of Right and Left coincide. For Kousoulas[62]—just as for Bartziotas[63]—the attack on Litochoro constitutes the start of the 'Third Round', the beginning of the civil war. Ole Smith comments as follows:

'The difference between the official Party history and Kousoulas is not very great; in fact Kousoulas based his account on the official Party documents from the Seventh Plenum (1950) and the Third Party Conference. The ironical circumstance is, however, that this agreement between a Rightist historian and the KKE is not due to the fact that both parties analyse correctly, but that the KKE had been forced into a position where its tenets could be used against the Party itself. The official Party history of 1952 is in fact a one-sided defense of Zachariadis and his party. . . To Kousoulas the attack on Litochoron is proof of the civil war as Communist aggression, to Zachariadis and the Party leadership the attack is proof of a consistent course and a resolutely applied Party line.'[64]

In other words, Kousoulas gladly took over Zachariadis' *post factum* justification: that Litochoro had been a planned action. If this had really been the case, it would—as Woodhouse says—have attracted more attention at the time.

'Foreign observers writing during and after the civil war ignored Litokhoro. It passed unmentioned in the works of McNeill (1947), Voigt (1949), Leeper (1950), Chandler (1959) and O'Ballance (1966). The best American source [Spencer?] mentioned Litokhoro, but by implication did not regard it as a deliberate initiation of civil war. If it had been so intended, a supporting campaign of propaganda would have been launched by the Communist press; but there was none.'[65]

Woodhouse himself did not mention it in *Apple of Discord* (1948).

Until 1980 all that was known of Zachariadis' journey was that he travelled to Prague, via Belgrade, took part in the Czechoslovak CP's Party Congress, was in Belgrade again on 2nd April and returned to Salonica on the 9th.[66] In his memoirs (1978) Partsalidis writes that in Prague Zachariadis was told the opinions of the Italian and French CPs on the situation in Greece. Both Palmiro Togliatti and Maurice Thorez were opposed to the election boycott and held the view that an armed rising would be senseless.[67] Only Tito, when Zachariadis discussed the Greek problem with him on his return through Belgrade, promised support in an armed struggle.[68] The CPSU leadership had been sceptical about armed struggle from the start.[69] In other words, their position remained, as they had told Partsalidis, that KKE should give the main weight to legal forms of struggle or to armed conflict according to how circumstances developed.[70]

In January 1980 Leftheris Eleftheriou revealed a secret closely guarded for twenty years and supplied hitherto unknown details about Zachariadis' journey to Prague.[71] His report was based on conversations he had with Zachariadis in Moscow in 1956, after the latter's demotion from the post of Secretary-General. Although there can be no question as to Eleftheriou's personal integrity and his intention to tell the truth, it must be borne in mind: 1) that more than twenty-five years had passed since these conversations and therefore some points of detail are imprecise; and 2) that Zachariadis might not have told the whole truth, even to Eleftheriou, since at that time grave charges were being brought against him. But here is what Eleftheriou reported.

On his arrival in Belgrade at the end of March, Zachariadis had had a first meeting with Tito and they had discussed the situation in Greece. Here Eleftheriou is obviously wrong since, according to *Rizospastis,* Tito left for Prague on 20th March, when Zachariadis was still in Salonica, and returned only on 1st April.[72] On 2nd April, after his return from Prague to Belgrade, Zachariadis flew to Moscow.

'He said that at that time he met Stalin, Zhdanov and Molotov and told them his views about armed struggle. During this conversation Molotov repeated his criticism of the 1946 election boycott. There were the three of them: Stalin, Zhdanov and Molotov. That is how Zachariadis told it. To Molotov's repeated criticism of the election boycott, Zachariadis answered with his known views. During the course of this conversation, N. Zachariadis and the Soviet leaders agreed on the prospects for armed struggle. But the Soviet leaders told Zachariadis: "You will make the final detailed arrangements with Tito." Tito was at that time the leading personality in the Balkans. . . They agreed that we could go over to armed struggle. But now as to the objectives: from Zachariadis' narrative it is not clear whether his conversation with Stalin took place directly after this conversation with the three CPSU leaders. But it is a fact that there was also a private conversation with Stalin, which took place in the Crimea, at which—as Zachariadis said— Stalin even spoke of the tactics of armed struggle: "You will advance gradually from the villages to the towns in order to avoid the untimely armed intervention of the British *and your aim will be a compromise".* '[73]

If we disregard the obvious discrepancies (for example, that Zachariadis first met Stalin, Molotov and Zhdanov in Moscow and then once more Stalin, by himself, in the Crimea and that Tito should determine the details—obviously a defensive argument on the part of Zachariadis), then we are left with the following probahilities: in the first days of April 1946 Zachariadis had talks with the Soviet leadership on KKE's future policy; he was criticised for his abstention policy and certainly did not receive the green light for a civil war with the aim of seizing power, but only for an intensification of guerrilla action. The aim of such action would be to reach a further compromise, a new edition of Varkiza. The main weight would continue to be on political struggle. Stalin had no objection to sporadic guerrilla fighting, provided it under no circumstances led to direct confrontation between the Soviet Union and Great Britain, and above all the USA.[74] At the same time fighting of this sort in Greece would distract attention from Stalin's own plans in Eastern Europe, for example in Poland and Czechoslovakia.

In contrast to Stalin, Tito did not shirk confrontation. It is not wholly clear when Zachariadis met Tito, before or after his visit to the Soviet Union. In any case, Tito seems to have advocated the policy of armed struggle. Eleftheriou reports:

'According to what Zachariadis told me, Tito came out clearly for armed struggle. Not only was he for it, but he supplied a model strategy for armed struggle. And it is no coincidence that, both in its political concepts and in its organisation, the Democratic Army followed the prototype of the Yugoslav Partisan army.'[75]

Eleftheriou's report is surely correct and is strongly confirmed by Partsalidis. Tito had promised full support.[76]

Zachariadis had arrived in Belgrade on 2nd April, where he at once made a press statement on the Greek elections: the Greek problem could be summarised in a single point—the British occupation must end so that order and tranquillity could return to the country.[77] On 9th April he was back in Salonica and on the 12th he spoke at a party meeting there. His topic was: 'The situation in South-east Europe and the position of Greece'.[78] In the first part of his speech he praised the socialist achievements in the countries of South-east Europe and then went on to speak of Greece. There were two Greeces: the Greece of the National Resistance and popular democracy and the monarcho-fascist Greece. Here he said:

'Our country is a projection and a part of South-east Europe, forming a geographical and economic unit with it. From South-east Europe we can get everything which we lack and which we need, not only in industrial and agricultural goods but in technical economic aid, too...'

The unnatural separation from the natural hinterland had led to Greece's dependence on foreign capital. The present deep economic, political, social and moral crisis was a direct consequence of this. The British intervention of December 1944 was responsible for this evil situation as it had interrupted the country's normal evolution; the British occupation had followed on the German one. The elections of 31st March had made the situation still worse by deepening the cleft between the people and their leaders.

He went on to examine the elections and asked where the country was going. The party's attitude was clear: the elections must be invalidated; a government of broad democratic unity must be formed to lead Greece to normality through the free expression of the people's will. In this the Right could play no part. It had terrorised the population both before and during the elections. In Macedonia the position was particularly bad. No wonder that a little while ago some had taken to the mountains and, if things went on like this, hundreds would soon follow them. A moment would come when the people would decide that they could no longer let themselves be slaughtered like chickens and then they would take to arms. If the policy of the British and their disciples did not change radically, it would inevitably come to this.

Zachariadis dealt next with the situation of the Slavo-Macedonian minority which was suffering particularly under the persecutions. Members of NOF (Narodni Osvobodilački Front, People's Liberation Front, the Slavo-Macedonian EAM) were singled out as targets for attack. Zachariadis gave some examples which in the light of experience of the region sound convincing. In the courts of Kastoria there were about 600 indictments pending against more than 4,000 Slavo-Macedonians; 156 peasants of one village were charged with autonomist activities (Ohrana); several girls were sentenced because they had sung Slavo-Macedonian songs at a wedding. Further prosecutions were based on banditry and alignment with Tito.

'Of course', Zachariadis said, 'if the Slavo-Macedonians can't endure the terror and the murders any more, than the persecutors talk of "bandits" and of "autonomists" and start their "cleansing" operations again.'

He wound up his speech with a vision of the future: this future belonged to popular democracy alone; apart from this there was nothing for Greece but the ruin of her people and the death of the nation. But popular democracy could only win through to victory by hard struggles and it was for these struggles the party must be prepared.

In other words, he retracted the two-poles-theory[79] of summer 1945; but his remarks, in so far as they referred to future conflict, scarcely went beyond radical rhetoric—a verbal concession to the militant attitude of the Macedonian comrades. How little Zachariadis was prepared to alter his former line can be seen from a characteristic incident related by Markos and Kikitsas.[80]

A group of forty professional (former ELAS) officers, all party members, who at that time were under the Salonica army command[81] and were organised in the Macedonia-Thrace Anti-Fascist Front, requested a meeting with Zachariadis, at which they asked him whether they ought not to go to the mountains, to support and lead the armed Groups of the Persecuted (ODEK) which were already there. Zachariadis' reply was unambiguous: 'The party has taken no decision for guerrilla warfare.'[82] When the officers pointed out that they had reliable information that the War Ministry would summon them to Athens, to 'isolate' them, he answered: 'The party has taken no decision for guerrilla warfare, so go where your military superiors tell you to go.' Kikitsas comments bitterly:

'Naturally, the War Ministry ordered these officers and many hundreds more to Athens and isolated them in camps on uninhabited islands, or in prisons and some were condemned to death and executed.'

Finally, Zachariadis told the officers they must wait for instructions from the party. In this context there seems to have been a further conversation with Colonel Yannis Mousterakis, who had served during the Occupation as Chief-of-Staff to the PEEA's Defence Secretariat and later in command of the first ELAS Division. Markos reports that Mousterakis demanded of Zachariadis that he, Mousterakis, and Markos should go at once to the mountains to take over leadership of the guerrilla struggle. Zachariadis abruptly rejected this: the appearance of known ELAS cadres and members of the KKE Central Committee in the mountains would be taken as a challenge and would be made the pretext for provocations against the party and against EAM; the party was fighting for reconciliation *(symfiliosi)* and for its right to function legally.[83] When Zachariadis had thus restrained the militant Macedonian comrades, he returned to Athens. On 15th April he gave an interview to *Rizospastis* in which he stressed the need for self-defence *(aftoamyna)*.[84]

NOTES

1. *KOMEP*, March 1946, p. 152.
2. See p. 466.
3. *Rizospastis*, 23rd January, 1946.
4. See p. 387.
5. *Rizospastis*, 6th February, 1946, reported that the delegation returned to Moscow from Leningrad on the 5th.
6. Eudes, *op. cit.*, p. 260.
7. Partsalidis in an interview with G. Matzouranis in *I Avghi*, 24th February, 1980.
8. *Ibid.*
9. *Ibid.*
10. In his memoirs Partsalidis writes: 'During the EAM delegation's visit to Moscow early in 1946, I had the opportunity to explain the views of our party leadership on the situation in Greece to the comrades of our fraternal party's Central Committee's department for Foreign Affairs. I stressed that, in view of the continuing murders of our National Resistance fighters, it seemed very difficult to avoid armed conflict. We hoped that wartime obstacles to full development of support of our people no longer existed. The CPSU's leadership gave us this advice: participate in the elections now; later we can see *[meta vlepontas kai kanontas]*; according to how the situation develops at a particular time, you can put the main weight now on legal forms of struggle, now on armed action.' Partsalidis, *Dipli apokatastasi*, p. 199. And on p. 195 'In Moscow the comrades

of the Central Committee's department of Foreign Affairs transmitted to me the advice of the CPSU leadership that we should participate in the elections.' In conversation with A. Hajopoulos, Partsalidis added further details. 'The advice of the Soviet Party that we should participate in the elections was correct. In Moscow I had a meeting with people from the Central Committee's department for Foreign Affairs and with the official responsible for the Balkans. The latter told me the advice of the Soviet Party's Central Committee.' Achilefs Hajopoulos, *Oi prostates 1943-1949*, (Athens: Papazisis, 1977), pp. 175 ff. Vasos Georgiou, however, gives a different version: 'When the KKE leadership asked the CPSU if we should participate in the elections, the answer was: that is your affair, but they would regard it as reasonable and correct if we participated. In no case did they advise us to start a civil war.' Georgiou, *Eleftherotypia*, 23rd December, 1979.

11. Vontitsos-Gousias, *Oi aities* Vol. II, p. 243. According to Gousias, Zachariadis confided to him after the Seventh Plenum as follows: 'Partsalidis is telling disgraceful lies when he says we had advice from the fraternal parties to participate in the elections. There were no such suggestions and you will remember that when, at the Seventh Plenum, we asked him for proofs, he said that when he was leaving Moscow by train some minor Soviet official—in the moment of leave-taking—told him we should participate in the elections. Partsalidis told us that the Soviet official told him the following: take part in the elections and, according to how the situation develops, put the main weight now on armed action and now on legal methods of struggle.'

12. Markos Vafiadis, 'Apostoli sta Ouralia', pp. 39 ff., said: 'Amongst the questions they put to the Soviet comrades there was also the problem of the elections. They asked what was their opinion in regard to the elections, since Zachariadis and other members of the Political Bureau favoured abstention. Here Stalin told them that it would be the right thing to participate in the elections. He gave them the advice they wanted but he did not put them under obligation to follow it. But that was the one thing they didn't do.'

13. Partsalidis, *Dipli apokatastasi*, p. 196. In conversation with Hajopoulos, he added: 'Under Zachariadis' leadership the Political Bureau declared: We are not changing our position. We shall not participate in the elections.' Hajopoulos, *op. cit.*, p. 176; *I Avghi*, 24th February, 1980.

14. Nefeloudis, *Stis piges tis kakodaimonias*, pp. 270, 281; followed by Solon Grigoriadis, *O Emfylios Polemos: I Ellada tou 1945-1949* Vol. I, (Athens: Tytranis, 1979), pp. 47 ff.

15. Partsalidis in *I Avghi*, 24th February, 1980; Leftheris Eleftheriou in *I Avghi*, 27th January, 1980 for the details. Vlandas, *Emfylios Polemos* Vol. II, p. 424, says it was in the first half of March.

16. Vontitsos-Gousias, *Oi aities* Vol. II, p. 243.

17. Markos Vafiadis, 'Apostoli sta Ouralia', p. 40. 'Partsalidis said this to Zachariadis [in Greece] and they kept it secret. After Partsalidis returned and because he said nothing, we believed that the Soviets actually held the same view—abstention—I only learned of this for the first time in 1948, when I was in the mountains, when we were quarrelling and had differences of opinion. . . with Zachariadis and the leadership. . . That was when—very much later—I heard about the advice.'

18. Markos Vafiadis, 'O Markos Vafiadis apanta', p. 33.

19. He alleged that he could not have foreseen the serious consequences of abstention and that a discussion in the Central Committee would have achieved no result. Partsalidis, *Dipli apokatastasi*, pp. 196 ff.

20. Partsalidis was born in Pontus (on the Black Sea) in 1904. After the Asia Minor

disaster he came to Salonica in 1924, where he became a member of OKNE (KKE Youth). In 1932, though in prison, he was elected deputy for Kavalla, to be re-elected in 1936. In 1934 Kavalla had elected him as mayor. He had been a member of the KKE Central Committee since 1931 and of the Political Bureau since 1934. In 1938 Metaxas' police arrested him and jailed him in Corfu whence, in 1941, they handed him over to the German authorities who transferred him to the Haidari concentration camp. In early 1944 he escaped to the mountains where he became Secretary-General of EAM in July of that year, in succession to Thanasis Hajis. In 1947 he was exiled to Ikaria whence he escaped in 1948 to join the Democratic Army. In April 1949 he became Prime Minister of the Provisional Democratic Government. After the defeat of the Democratic Army, he did not accept Zachariadis' defence at the Sixth Plenum of October 1949 that the reason for the defeat was Tito's treachery and he attacked him at the Seventh Plenum in July 1950 and criticised the whole line of the Party since the Occupation. However, at the Third Party Conference in October 1950, Zachariadis denounced Partsalidis' position as revisionist, opportunist, fractional and calculated to cause a split and he was expelled from the Party. For the following six years he lived as a private individual in Romania. In 1956 he was re-admitted to the Party and in 1957 re-elected to the Political Bureau. During the Twelfth Plenum of 1968, when the Party split on the issue of Czechoslovakia, he broke with the then leadership and became a member of the Central Committee of the Euro-communist KKE/Interior. He died in Athens in 1980.
21. Markos Vafiadis, 'O Markos Vafiadis apanta', p. 33.
22. Partsalidis, *Dipli apokatastasi*, p. 196; Vontitsos-Gousias, *Oi aities* Vol. II, p. 244.
23. *Rizospastis*, 21st February, 1946.
24. *Ibid.*, 22nd February, 1946.
25. *Ibid.*, 23rd February, 1946.
26. *Ibid.*, 26th February, 1946.
27. *Ibid.*, 27th February, 1946.
28. *Ibid.*, 3rd March, 1946. See p. 417.
29. *Ibid.*, 5th March, 1946.
30. *Ibid.*, see also pp. 427-8.
31. *Ibid.*, 7th March, 1946. See also p. 427.
32. See p. 427.
33. Zachariadis, 'Brosta ston kindyno tis dimokratias', *Rizospastis*, 7th March, 1946.
34. *Rizospastis*, 12th March, 1946.
35. See pp. 429-31.
36. *Rizospastis*, 15th March, 1946. See also p. 433.
37. Text of his speech in Othonaios, *Treis Logoi*, pp. 7-10.
38. *Rizospastis*, 16th March, 1946.
39. *Ibid.*, 21st March, 1946.
40. Foivos Grigoriadis, *op. cit.*, Vol. III, p. 659.
41. *Ibid.*, p. 661.
42. See p. 434.
43. See p. 436.
44. The same holds good for Eudes' version, *op. cit.*, pp. 261-2. Eudes' narrative is obviously based on Grigoriadis' report, though he does not name his source. Markos also mentions this incident, Markos Vafiadis, 'Apostoli sta Ouralia', p. 38.
45. There is a reference, too, in Partsalidis' memoirs, *Dipli Apokatastasi*, p. 196.

46. *Rizospastis*, 22nd March, 1946.
47. *Ibid.*, 26th March, 1946.
48. Grigoriadis, *op. cit.*, Vol. III, p. 669.
49. *Rizospastis*, 1st and 3rd April, 1946.
50. Zachariadis, 'I katastasi sti Notoanatoliki Evropi kai i thesi tis Elladas', *KOMEP*, (May 1946), p. 211.
51. Woodhouse, *Struggle for Greece*, p. 170.
52. Grigoriadis, *op. cit.*, Vol. III, pp. 668 ff.
53. 'Chroniko: Apo to Litochoro os to Grammo kai to Vitsi. O dromos pros ti niki', *Dimokratikos Stratos*, (November 1948), pp. 482-7.
54. *Voithima*, p. 236; *Chroniko tou Agona*, p. 60.
55. Grigoriadis, *op. cit.*, Vol. III, pp. 666 ff.
56. Eudes, *op. cit.*, p. 262 writes: 'After imposing the election boycott he dispatched an order to the KKE organisation in Macedonia telling it to make an armed attack on a target of its choice the day before the elections were scheduled to take place.

    Markos and Kikitsas, of the Macedonian Committee, chose the town of Litochoron as their objective. It had close historical connections with the Klephtic resistance and three EAM officials had been disembowelled there in the course of the last few weeks.' Eudes embroiders his account of the attack itself with another feature for which there exists not the slightest proof: 'When British armoured vehicles approached the town Ypsilantis ordered his men to retreat.' Litochoro is a village and there were no British in the vicinity.
57. The next time Eudes mentions Litochoro his account is even more distorted. On p. 265 he narrates the following: 'At the beginning of May *[sic]* Zachariadis visited Salonika. The people's leader Markos Vafiadis, the kapetanios now destined to lead the armed struggle, told the General Secretary that the Macedonian organization could "arm and train 25,000 fighters in the villages and major towns within two months", and asked for authority to "arm the self-defence groups which are in the mountains already".(1)

    Zachariadis replied' "You are not informed on all the Central Committee's decisions. What we did at Litochoron was a bluff intended to force the government to make concessions".(1)' The reference (1) which Eudes gives for both quotations is an alleged letter from Markos to the Central Committee dated October 1957, but he does not say where this letter can be found. Despite intensive research, the author has been unable to trace it and it certainly was not published in *Neos Kosmos* of that year. The only letter from Markos during the de-stalinisation period, dated 10th July 1956, was addressed to the Committee of the Fraternal Parties which was investigating Zachariadis' past record and its contents bear no resemblance to that cited by Eudes. (This letter was published in the Athens daily, *Akropolis*, on 21st December 1976.) Markos was at that time still expelled from the party and therefore addressed himself in writing to this committee.

    A closer look at Eudes' wording shows that his quotations must originate from Markos' speech to the Seventh Plenum of 1957. Though both deal with the same subject, they in fact refer to two different episodes. The first refers to the time of Zachariadis' visit to Salonica and reads in translation from the original Greek: 'The Macedonian Party Bureau stated that its party organisation was in a position to arm and make ready 25,000 fighters in the villages and most important towns within two months. This raises the issue of our being given the order by the party to arm the Groups of the Persecuted and to begin military organisation of the popular forces. Both party secretaries persistently refused to give the order for arming these groups.' (Markos Vafiadis, 'Omilia pano sto proto thema',

p. 52.)

The second quotation we have already referred to in connection with the Second Plenum (see p. 488). In order to facilitate comparison we repeat Markos' original wording. 'However, when the Macedonia-Thrace Provincial Bureau reported a few weeks later to the Political Bureau that it had the ability to organise a force of 25,000 armed men, Zachariadis replied: "Stop it! The whole business was a bluff to force the government to give way".' Markos Vafiadis, *op. cit.*, p. 50. Apparently Eudes conflated these two statements and added the reference to Litochoro on his own authority—historically a more than questionable proceeding. Eudes' tendency to transpose material published in *Neos Kosmos* into direct speech for the sake of liveliness or to create the impression that he had actually interviewed Markos can often prove misleading. Smith shows how, in this context, even Woodhouse fell victim to Eudes' method; see Woodhouse, *Struggle for Greece,* p. 169 and Smith, *op. cit.*, p. 22.

58. Markos Vafiadis, 'Omilia pano sto proto thema', p. 52.
59. *Ibid.*, see p. 488.
60. Georgiou, *Eleftherotypia,* 23rd December, 1979.
61. Dimitris Gousidis. *Markos Vafeiadis: Martyries* (Thessaloniki: Epikairotita, 1983), p. 27.
62. Kousoulas, *Revolution and Defeat,* p. 232.
63. Bartziotas, *Voithima,* p. 236.
64. Ole Smith, *op. cit.*, p. 21.
65. Woodhouse, *Struggle for Greece,* p. 170.
66. *Rizospastis,* 21st and 22nd March, 1946; also 3rd, 4th, 10th and 11th April, 1946.
67. Partsalidis, *Dipli apokatastasi,* p. 199; Hajopoulos, *op. cit.*, p. 174; Solaro, *op. cit.*, p. 183.
68. Partsalidis, *op. cit.*, p. 199.
69. *Ibid.*
70. *Ibid.*
71. *I Avghi,* 27th, 29th, 30th January, 1980.
72. *Rizospastis,* 21st, 23rd, 24th March and 2nd April, 1946.
73. *I Avghi,* 27th January, 1980.
74. Vlandas, *Emfylios Polemos* Vol. II, pp. 424 ff. Vlandas is mistaken in speaking of two meetings between Zachariadis and Stalin.
75. *I Avghi,* 27th January, 1980.
76. *Ibid.*, 24th February, 1980.
77. *Rizospastis,* 3rd April, 1946.
78. Zachariadis, 'I katastasi sti Notioanatoliki Evropi', pp. 207-12.
79. See p. 254.
80. Markos Vafiadis, 'Omilia pano sto proto thema', p. 52; and Kikitsas in *I Avghi,* 3rd February, 1980.
81. See p. 530.
82. Kikitsas in *I Avghi,* 3rd February, 1980.
83. Markos, *op. cit.*, p. 52.
84. *Rizospastis,* 16th April, 1946.

THE ESCALATION OF VIOLENCE

From the moment Sofoulis resigned (1st April) evolution towards civil war accelerated at breath-taking speed. As this process belongs to the next period of Greek history, to the Civil War, only the outlines of this tragic development can be given here; its full story will be presented in an ensuing study on that subject.

Even before the elections Bevin had sent instructions to Ambassador Norton regarding the composition and programme of the future Greek government. Norton should convey to the Populist leaders Bevin's views: he desired a stable, broadly-based coalition government. Such a government could count on the continuation of present British support.

'In return we shall expect them to press on with the economic programme laid down in my exchange of letters with M. Tsouderos, to maintain parliamentary institutions and constitutional liberties, to suppress illegal armed bands, and to refrain from raising the issue of the monarchy immediately following elections. You will bear in mind that I suggested March 1948 as the date of the Plebiscite, and it was accepted. This is very important if Greece is to avoid civil strife and outside intervention.'[1]

On the eve of the elections Bevin repeated this: Norton should put the Populist leaders in possession of his views before they could commit themselves too publicly to an attitude which conflicted with them.

'As regards the date of the plebiscite, I realise that it will be difficult for the Populists to accept at this stage the date of March 1948 which they have already rejected. You might therefore suggest to them that they should themselves propose a postponement of the plebiscite until the economic programme laid down in London Agreement has made sufficient progress for it to be possible to say that conditions of normal tranquillity have been restored.'[2]

Norton conveyed Bevin's views to Damaskinos. He promised to pass them on to the Populist leaders and to advise them to consult Norton.[3] This was done when the four Populist leaders (Tsaldaris, Mavromichalis, Stefanopoulos, Theotokis) visited him on the 2nd April and informed him that they were in no hurry to form a government. In the afternoon of the same day Tsaldaris called on Norton who spoke to him strongly on the lines laid down by Bevin. Tsaldaris agreed to everything except the monarchy issue, where he obstinately refused to submit to any postponement of the plebiscite.[4] This prompted Bevin to send a further telegram to Norton in which he insisted on his views.

'I note that Tsaldaris told you he was anxious to work in full agreement with us. This will not be possible if he presses for an immediate plebiscite. I should have thought that the time to consider the question of the plebiscite would be when the new Government has had a chance of studying the problems which face Greece and has realised the heavy responsibilities which lie upon it and when the new Parliament has got down to work. I shall then be quite prepared... to discuss this question... but it would be disastrous if binding commitments were entered into by the new Greek Government in the meantime.'[5]

Norton thereupon briefed Venizelos, Kanellopoulos and Themistoklis Tsatsos (representing Papandreou) on Bevin's stand and they fully agreed.[6] On the 3rd April Norton received the four Populist leaders and in a long conversation he pressed Bevin's views home to them, but they remained obstinate.[7] Bevin, however, continued to attach the greatest importance to the postponement of the plebiscite and to the formation of a coalition government. On the 4th April he telegraphed to Norton.

'I do not think we should be deterred from pressing these points on the Greek leaders by the possibility that they will prove unacceptable and that the Populists will form a government on their own which will disregard our advice or that they will in fact refuse to form a government at all. Should that occur a new situation would arise and I do not think it is necessary for His Majesty's Government to commit themselves to the actions they would take in such circumstances.'[8]

Norton's pressure and the refusal of Venizelos, Kanellopoulos and Papandreou to enter the government unless the Populists dropped the idea of an immediate plebiscite led to a temporary compromise: the plebiscite date would be fixed after consultations with Bevin. Thereupon the new government was formed under the judge Panayotis Poulitsas. This was necessary because the Populists did not yet have an elected leader but were controlled by a governing committee composed of Tsaldaris, Mavromichalis, Stefanopoulos and Theotokis. The future party leader was to be elected at a conference of their parliamentary deputies in a couple of days; the winner would then become Prime Minister as well. The Poulitsas Cabinet consisted of Tsaldaris (Foreign Affairs), Mavromichalis (War), Theotokis (Interior), Stefanopoulos (Finance), Alexandris (Economy) and Gonatas (Public Works). Venizelos, Papandreou and Kanellopoulos became Ministers without Portfolio. It was stated that the Cabinet was on a temporary basis only and that Poulitsas would be replaced by the newly-elected Populist leader.

However, agitation for an immediate plebiscite continued among the elected Populist deputies with the silent connivance of the Populist leaders. On the 12th April 150 of them sent a telegram to the king which contained a veiled protest against the continuation of the Regency and an attack on the Papandreou trio, which almost caused their resignation. On the 15th April the Populist deputies met and elected Tsaldaris leader of the party with an overwhelming majority. On the 17th the trio resigned when it became obvious that their coalition partner was not prepared to allot them a proportionate share of portfolios and was insisting that the plebiscite question should be determined by the National Assembly.

On the same day Poulitsas handed in his resignation and on the 18th April Tsaldaris and his new government were sworn in. Of the twenty-four ministers and assistant-ministers all were Populist except the National Liberal Gonatas with one of his followers and the Reformist A. Alexandris.[9] In other words, Bevin's first condition—a government on the basis of as broad a coalition as possible—had been nullified. Formally the new government was almost a one-party government; politically it was totally right-wing.

The second condition—the postponement of the plebiscite until 1948—was dropped, too. After some rearguard fighting Bevin acquiesced in holding the plebiscite earlier, provided the electoral lists were revised.[10] He justified his *volte face* by stating that there had been no official British commitment on the 1948 date and that in any case the British government were in no position to overrule an elected Greek government.[11] Apparently Bevin, too, had become an adherent of the *après moi le déluge* mentality, when he noticed that he was losing control of the Greek government. Sofoulis on the other hand commented that he would never have accepted office in November 1945, nor agreed to holding elections when he did, had there not been a clear undertaking by the British government that the plebiscite would be postponed until 1948 and consequently, he said, by 'their present complete reversal of policy' they had gone back on their word.[12] At the opening session of the Greek parliament on the 13th May it was announced that the plebiscite would take place on the 1st September. The change to Tsaldaris was much more than a simple change of government, it signalled that the Right had taken power for good. The previous governments had not steered a course particularly friendly to the communists, but they had not persecuted them officially. So far excesses had been mainly the work of the *parakratos*, which was outside the government's control. The new policy was aggressively anti-communist and the *parakratos* became a part of the government's repressive machinery. Another of Bevin's conditions—to suppress illegal armed bands—was applied exclusively towards the Left; the Right bands (*e.g.* those of Sourlas and Manganas) were left unmolested, as will be seen. Bevin's further desire that the Greek government should maintain parliamentary institutions and constitutional liberties was also frustrated.

On the 3rd May the Cabinet approved a Royal Decree bringing back into force old legislation which reinstated the notorious Security Committees of the Metaxas dictatorship and re-introduced the death penalty for illegal possession of weapons and brigandage.[13] At the same time thirteen out of twenty-three generals were found unfit for active service. On the 5th May two Populist deputies announced that as soon as parliament met they would demand from the government the arrest and execution of twenty-five to thirty EAM and KKE leaders.[14] In the ensuing weeks *Rizospastis* was full of reports on transgressions of the law by the authorities, but, as these cannot be verified, it is better to quote from the report of three Labour MPs who toured Greece from 26th April to 9th May 1946 and reached the following conclusions.

'Greece is rapidly becoming a fascist state. Under the facade of democracy, there exists a unilateral civil war, the war of the extreme Right against all democratic elements who dare to disagree with the government. Murder, illegal imprisonment, brutal assault and intimidation are the fate of thousands of victims. The gendarmerie and police are fascist and rotten to the core and take a foremost part in the criminal activities and openly collaborate with the 'X'-ites—the fascist terrorists. If a Greek citizen has the temerity to complain about the conduct of the police he is immediately beaten up and imprisoned, frequently without a charge being made against him, or sometimes on a trumped-up charge.

'The premises of Republican and Left-wing newspapers, Trades Union organisations, Youth Clubs, etc. are illegally raided in all parts of the country and are shut down. For instance, one hospital in Athens which was largely attended by wounded Resistance fighters, but which nevertheless, gave aid to all, has been closed.

'The judiciary works hand in hand with the gendarmerie and is viciously reactionary. Those judges who refused to collaborate with the Germans no longer hold their posts. On the other hand, the judges who received their pay from the quisling governments are still in office, and, as in the trial now proceeding at Patras, sit in judgement against the heroes of the Resistance Movement.

'The Security Committees which did such infamous work for the Metaxas dictatorship, are now being set up again as an instrument for breaking up the Labour movement and imprisoning and deporting political opponents of the present regime.

'Just as happened in Nazi Germany, anybody who disapproves of the present Government is immediately dubbed a "Communist". Even the Right wing Liberals, the party of Mr. Sofoulis, are characterised as Communists, as Mr. Sofoulis himself told us.

'British prestige and moral standing is falling rapidly in Greece. The presence of British troops on Greek soil is regarded as an unwarranted intervention by one ally in the affairs of another allied country. Indeed, the Greek people talk about their country being "occupied" by the

British.'[15]

The 62-page report describes all sorts of repressive measures of which the following are the most characteristic.

'1. The "Security Committees" which were used by the Dictator, Metaxas as a weapon against his political opponents are being revived by the new Minister of Public Order, Mr. Spiro Theotokis.

'These committees which consisted of the Chief of the Gendarmerie, the Prefect of the Province, the Public Prosecutor and a Judge, could decide if "public order and security" were threatened, and could exile those "convicted" from particular areas. Mr. Theotokis told us with pride that he had made them "more judicial" by adding another judge and taking the right to vote away from the Gendarmerie Chief; he said he had also added the right of appeal to the Governor-General; but he did not deny that the committees would be used to exile Left-wing leaders from their villages and towns, and he could not give us an assurance that the public would be admitted to the courts or a legal defence permitted...

'The political opponents of the Right have little enough protection from the law today, but at least they have the prospect (however distant) of trial in open court with legal defence on specific charges. The Security Committees short-circuit all this.

'2. The ban on collecting donations or subscriptions is a very real weapon for making the carrying on of "legal" organisations almost impossible. This method involves the arrest and beating up of collectors and the confiscation of the money collected by organisations ranging from the GCL (Greek TUC), to the EA (the Red Cross of the Resistance), and the Panhellenic Union of Democratic Associations...

'3. An attempt is being made to set aside the election of the administration of the GCL, held under the supervision of the British TUC, and declared valid by the World Federation of Trade Unions...

'4. We got an indication in Salonika that the gendarmerie was about to be purged of its few remaining democratic elements—all those who fought with the Resistance had already been eliminated; and thus transformed completely into a weapon of the Right for use against the Left...'[16]

Ambassador Norton and the Foreign Office had been watching the tour of the three MPs with indignation. Though even the Foreign Office had to admit that the state of law and order was unsatisfactory, they stuck to their preconceived opinion that the main danger to law and order came from communism. As they expected trouble from the report of the three MPs they advised early counter-measures.

'We may expect that the three M.P.s at present in Greece will make a great deal of play with this question on their return... I hope therefore that the News Department can be instructed to do all in their power to convey this impression to the British press at an early date.'[17]

Hayter especially complained that the *Times* did not have a better correspondent despite the efforts by the Foreign Office to induce the *Times* to replace their correspondent in Athens.[18] Apparently for the Foreign Office this question was a propaganda affair.

In Greece meanwhile tension was steadily mounting. On the 12th May a right-wing band of about one hundred armed men raided Megalopolis in the Peloponnese.[19] On the 15th Manganas (of the Kalamata incident) attacked the gendarmerie station at Pylos with a band of forty and shot three communists imprisoned there.[20] On the 17th *Rizospastis* reported that National Guardsmen had destroyed the offices and printing premises of the newspaper *Anagenisi* in Volos. But these events were only symptoms: the decisive events took place in the Greek parliament. On the 30th May some Populist deputies proposed a motion for the banning of KKE. Though this was not even voted on it prompted Security Minister Spyros Theotokis to submit a draft law on the 6th June. This Security Bill (1) set up summary courts, consisting of five Judges of Appeal, empowered to pass the death sentence; (2) established the death penalty for anyone participating in gangs advocating autonomy or attacking 'the organs of the state or its citizens'; (3) imposed imprisonment for attendance at meetings declared illegal by the government, as well as for strikes in industries 'of paramount importance for public prosperity, rehabilitation, and reconstruction'; (4) suspended constitutional decrees of *habeas corpus;* (5) empowered the authorities to enter and search any premises without a warrant.[21] Two days later Theotokis gave reasons for this bill: since 1st April almost two hundred persons had been killed and 'roaming communist bands had created a "desperate" situation in Macedonia, where. . . the Greek Communist Party was agitating for Macedonian autonomy in cooperation with communists active on the Slav side of the frontier.'[22] Tsaldaris added 'that he could no longer tolerate such a state of terrorism on the part of the enemies of the state'.[23]

Though the bill provoked protests from all sides it was waved through on the 17th June with 138 votes for, 24 against and 181 abstentions. This bill together with the earlier laws now revived supplied the government with an apparatus of repression which can only be compared with Hitler's emergency laws after the burning of the Reichstag *(Reichstagsbrandverordnung).*

On the 18th June a deputy of Zervas' party demanded annulment of the Varkiza Agreement.[24] On the 26th the Council of State *(Symvoulio Epikratias)* decided Makris' lawsuit in his favour and invalidated the decrees of the Minister of Labour of the 28th October and 28th December 1945 which had been the legal base for the GCL elections. The Council of State, however, abstained from pronouncing on the validity of these elections and the decisions taken by the Eighth GCL Congress. Therefore the elected GCL Executive maintained that only a regular judge had the power to do this and, since the time-limit prescribed for such an action had lapsed, it considered itself the sole legal representative of the GCL. Makris, however, in close cooperation with the Minister of Labour, consulted the Legal Council of the government which ruled that the Council of State's sentence implicitly annulled the GCL elections. Thereupon on the 25th July Labour Minister Andreas Stratos demanded that the elected GCL Executive resign within 48 hours. On the next day WFTU Vice-Chairman Léon Jouhaux came to Athens but in spite of his mediating efforts the government stuck to its course. On the 29th July officials of Stratos' ministry tried to occupy the GCL offices but Theos, Stratis, Paparigas and Arabatzis refused to quit and hand over the archives. Thereupon in the presence of Jouhaux they were arrested and on the same day a court sentenced them to four months imprisonment for resisting the authority of the state. On the 30th July Stratos appointed a new GCL Executive in which Makris had a majority.[25]

On the 27th June the government submitted another bill to parliament for a purge of the Civil Service which favoured ex-collaborators and discriminated against former Resistance fighters.[26] On 5th July a bill was published for the deportation of the families of all army deserters who had joined armed bands[27] and on the 14th July another bill proposed that all collaborators even if serving sentences, should have their cases reviewed and be released or sent for retrial by ordinary courts.[28]

In the meantime the Security Committees had begun their work and by the end of August they had sent over 1,200 persons into internal exile.[29] During the same month the first group of former ELAS officers was deported to various islands.[30] On the 1st July the summary courts started to function and on the 15th the executions began. On the 27th seven former Resistance fighters were executed at Yannitsa, among them the 24-year old woman teacher Eirini Gini, who thus became the first woman in Greek history to die before a firing squad. Further—almost daily— executions followed.[31]

At the same time the right-wing bands, too, increased their activities. Though Manganas was arrested (and treated rather mildly), a wave of 'X' terror swept over the Peloponnese. In Thessaly the notorious bandit Sourlas practically supplanted the local authorities and terrorised all non-royalists with his gang. In Macedonia and Thrace, where the armed *aftoamyna* movement was slowly growing, the repression was carried out by the gendarmerie and army units.[32] In short, from July 1946 an unprecedented wave of violence swept over Greece and at the same time the Greek armed forces began their first mopping-up operations against the armed groups in Macedonia and Thrace. The civil war was gaining impetus.

Throughout this period the Left continued its bifurcated course. On the day of Zachariadis' return to Athens (15th April) a three day conference of leading cadres began which later became known as the Panhellenic Organisational Conference. The sources for this conference are Zachariadis' two speeches, Ioannidis' account and the published conclusions.[33] Obviously this conference busied itself with the results of the Twelfth Plenum (end of June 1945 before the Seventh Congress) and with the Seventh Party Congress resolutions on organisational matters. The first day was devoted to stocktaking. On the second day Ioannidis summarised: the Twelfth Plenum had recognised the social composition of the party's membership as a central problem. Though the situation had been improved by dissolving the party's village organisations and signing the members over to AKE this was not enough.[34] The Seventh Congress had talked about the separation of the leadership and the rank-and-file; and here, too, not everything necessary had been done to overcome this difficulty. Many leading cadres were still applying bureaucratic methods and did not control whether their orders were really executed. The main problem at the moment was to augment the number of qualified cadres, so that leading cadres did not have to do everything themselves. New leading echelons had to be raised from the rank-and-file, who had experience of practical work. On the ideological front the situation was not much better. Despite thousands of new members, only those who had entered the party before 1936 had ideological training and their number amounted to less than a thousand. The new members had only vague ideas about ideology. As learning by private study was excluded, party schools had to be founded. There were too many illiterates and others who were barely able to read. The books published by the party were often too difficult and therefore not understood. Educational work was badly needed. The leading cadres should know the abilities and the weaknesses of each single member. At least the members should be able to read *Rizospastis*. The educational work should not try to make them philosophers or professors *(profesores)*, but certain basic knowledge had to be taught.[35]

Only an ideologically-armed party could compete successfully with the ideology of the adversary. Constant vigilance against internal and external enemies was very important. Ioannidis then spoke about the line of the Second Plenum: the party struggled with all its might for a normal democratic evolution, but things did not take the desired course. There were only two ways: one could submit to the British occupation or fight against it. The latter course would naturally be followed. There were two methods: legal and 'higher forms'. At present the party struggled by the *aftoamyna* of the masses. However, should it become necessary, the enemy would be fought with his own weapons. For this the party must be prepared, as the Second Plenum had demanded. The creation of an intelligence apparatus would be decisive. As regards the further organisational preparations demanded by the Second Plenum, only the Macedonian Party Organisation had solved this problem (here Ioannidis obviously referred to the military stocktaking).[36]

In other words, the internal crisis of KKE had by no means been overcome, indeed, it had deepened. Even if KKE had wanted to go over to the higher form of struggle—the armed one—the organisational mess forbade it. Nefeloudis remembers:

'One year after Varkiza the party had recovered somewhat. It had reconstituted part of its forces especially in the big towns and the provincial towns. In the countryside, however, the party organisations had suffered heavily. The arrests and imprisonment of ELAS fighters, the terror orgy and the flight of the persecuted to the mountains had turned the organisations into shadows of their former selves. The organisations of the Peloponnese had in fact been dissolved and efforts were made to rebuild at least the leading echelons. The conclusions of the Panhellenic Organisational Conference reveal—in spite of the usual effort to gloss over the situation—that the pace of the party's redeployment did not correspond to the demands of the time nor to the respective "organisational decisions" of the Political Bureau.'[37]

Nefeloudis' criticism was fully justified. In large areas of Greece local functionaries of KKE had bureaucratically dissolved the party organisations in the villages and had not cared what happened to the peasant members afterwards, though it was obvious that KKE did not have the organisational facilities to register and integrate them. Thus the policy to improve KKE's social composition led objectively to a serious weakening of the party. But even those members who were considered socially suitable for KKE underwent a scrutiny which came close to a kind of purge.

At the Third Party Conference in 1950 Bartziotas held forth on this. During the Occupation KKE had pursued a wrong cadre policy, when many petit bourgeois elements and intellectuals were admitted. Many important functions were performed by persons who had signed one of Metaxas' repentance declarations (*dilosi;* in KKE's jargon a person who had signed such a *dilosi* was called a *dilosias,* plural *dilosies*). Control and supervision from above did not exist. After the dissolution of the Comintern the party had abandoned its Leninist principles and had opened its doors to everyone. Petit bourgeois elements had even advanced to leading positions in the hierarchy.[38] Only after the Twelfth Plenum was this altered and, inspired by two theoretical excursions of Zachariadis on this topic,[39] KKE steered a correct course in its cadre policy.

The first victims of this new cadre policy had been the *dilosies.* It is unknown how many of these were expelled from the party after the Twelfth Plenum and the Seventh Congress, but Bartziotas gives a hint when he asserts that during the Occupation sixteen out of seventeen Athens *achtida* (districts) secretaries had been *dilosies,* as well as the majority of the kapetans of ELAS divisions and brigades.[40] Though the number seems a bit exaggerated, the mere fact that a great number of these alleged traitors had been able to climb back so high in the hierarchy proves their quality as leaders and Resistance fighters, *i.e.* Zachariadis' new cadre policy was going to deprive the party of its most experienced and courageous members.

But the scrutiny was by no means confined to this category, it was extended to cadres and members who had criticised the Varkiza Agreement and had not been ready to submit to Zachariadis' claim to absolute power. The most prominent among these was Yannis Petsopoulos, a party member for many years and once editor of *Rizospastis*. Petsopoulos had continued to attack KKE's leadership and had requested them to discuss problems openly. They had, however, avoided this and Zachariadis had had him and his sympathisers expelled from the party by the newly created Control Committee after the Seventh Congress. Petsopoulos thereupon started a counter-attack in the form of an almost 500 pages long Open Letter in which he settled his accounts with Zachariadis.[41]

Petsopoulos wrote about the deeper causes of the conflict.

'The ELAS [kapetans] were the first who raised their voices against the betrayal of Varkiza. From the time of the first guerrilla struggle they were accustomed to each problem being put up for discussion to the guerrilla assembly and to decisions being taken democratically.'[42]

But open criticism and internal democracy were now no longer in fashion and Petsopoulos wrote bitterly in May 1946:

'The party is neither yours [Zachariadis'] nor comrade Siantos' personal fief *[tsifliki]* nor are the members tenant farmers *[kolligades]* whom you can chase away at random from one day to the next. Our party is the party of all those who fight for the people, it is their home in which all have equal rights and opinions of equal weight. If you don't like it that the party members have opinions of their own, then it is you who must leave the party not they... And among these members are especially those officers whom you insulted yesterday as *putschists* and agents.'[43]

The officers referred to in this way were leaders of the first armed *aftoamyna* groups in Macedonia who had taken to the mountains on their own initiative. Obviously Zachariadis regarded them as provocateurs.[44]

Zachariadis' line was confirmed by the Central Committee at the end of the Panhellenic Organisational Conference on the 18th April. The catchwords were reconciliation *(symfiliosi)* and unarmed self-defence *(aftoamyna)* by the masses;[45] the efforts of Petsopoulos were officially condemned.[46] Zachariadis expressly prohibited[47] armed *aftoamyna* after his return from abroad.

In the following weeks KKE stuck to this course. On the one hand KKE and EAM protested continually to the government and the Allied ambassadors against the mounting repression, and sent protest telegrams to the United Nations and to the Peace Conference in Paris; and on the other hand they organised the *symfiliosi* campaign. *Rizospastis* referred only once to the initial activities of the armed *aftoamyna* groups in Macedonia (ODEK) which had taken to the mountains on their own initiative, when it published a letter from such a group on the 26th May. But *Rizospastis* was full of stories about transgressions of the law by the gendarmerie and armed right-wing bands. In the leading article on the 1st June Zachariadis himself railed against the intention of those Populist deputies to have KKE banned.[48] On the 8th June *Rizospastis* condemned Theotokis' draft Security Bill of the day before with the following headline:

'This fascist Bill leads to civil war. *Symfiliosi* of the people will save Greece! Everyone into the pan-popular *(pallaiko)* democratic front! The British occupation and monarcho-fascism exclusively responsible for the hopeless situation. Forward Greeks, foil the colonial exploitation of our country!'[49]

On the 11th June Siantos, Partsalidis and Zevgos saw Tsaldaris and protested against the Bill and the increasing terror but the Prime Minister was not disturbed by this. Further escalation of violence was countered with the intensification of the *symfiliosi* campaign, and also by a decision by Zachariadis which had far-reaching consequences.

By mid-June Zachariadis set out again for Salonica to take part in the Third Plenum of the regional committee of Macedonia–Thrace. On the 16th June the tough local situation and the imminent ratification of the Security Bill (on the following day) prompted Zachariadis to approve the limited armed *aftoamyna*.[50] There are two independent sources for this decision. The first is a Foreign Office memorandum.

'It has been reported from a pretty good secret source that at the special meeting of the Greek Communist Party (K.K.E.) Salonika on June 16th it was decided to issue instructions for the Party to be ready for active guerilla operations to begin at the end of July, with the assistance of newly mobilised units of ELAS, the Macedonian Autonomists and ELASites at present in Yugoslavia. Incidents could be staged which would justify Yugoslav military intervention in Greek internal affairs. Meanwhile, the Party was to establish a state of terror by means of frequent murders of non-Communist leaders. Gendarmerie stations were to be regularly attacked.'[51]

Obviously this memorandum contains some elements which should be regarded with caution since they are in fact interpretations and deductions (*e.g.* movement of the autonomists or the re-mobilisation of ELAS units), but the basic information seems to be correct. The statement about a potential Yugoslav intervention is probably an imprecise account of the records of that meeting; however, if intervention is replaced by assistance it makes sense. It must be stressed though that Zachariadis authorised only a *limited* armed *aftoamyna,* not the beginning of full-scale guerrilla war. This interpretation is confirmed by the account of Leonidas Stringos at the Seventh Plenum in 1957. In 1946 he belonged to the Macedonian Party Bureau.

'In June 1946 we—in the secretariat of the province of Macedonia-Thrace—analysed the situation of the armed *andarte* groups existing in the province of Macedonia. We suggested that these forces be quickly increased, but this suggestion was not then accepted by the Political Bureau—or more precisely by Zachariadis. . . Zachariadis told us that our forces in Macedonia at that time should be limited to 2,000 men at most.'[52]

Stringos' account is essentially confirmed by Markos except for the date, but a closer look shows that Markos, too, is talking about this meeting with Zachariadis[53] since only one such meeting took place in June. The same holds good for the dates given by Kissavos[54] and Gousias.[55] Markos tells about the instructions given by Zachariadis: he had ordered Markos to hand over his post as organisational secretary to Bartziotas and told both of them to come to Athens to a Political Bureau meeting *(klimakion).* There they would analyse the existing *possibilities* from all angles. Meanwhile he should take the relevant measures on the basis of the existing armed groups, but the increase of their numbers should be on a purely voluntary basis. Complete army units wanting to desert should on no account be accepted, only individuals. Actions should be confined to strikes against armed bands of the Right; conflicts with units of the armed forces should be avoided. The actions should have a clearly defensive character and no party organisations should be established within the *andarte* units. The policy of the party was still *symfiliosi* and peaceful solution of the internal problems of the country. The armed actions should be confined to assisting this. When Markos and the other provincial cadres expressed the opinion that the party should resolutely prepare itself for the armed struggle by mobilising all its forces, Zachariadis refused to listen.[56]

Zachariadis stuck to his conception of a limited armed *aftoamyna.* In order to block any effort for an undesired spread and increase of the *aftoamyna* he placed personal henchmen as watchdogs in the regional bureaus of Macedonia-Thrace and Epirus (Bartziotas and Gousias), whereas many old middle-rank cadres were sent to the mountains where they were isolated and had no influence on the course of events within the party.[57] Others, as for instance the high-ranking ELAS officers from Salonica, were ordered to await arrest.[58] From ideological motives Zachariadis obviously did not want a revival of ELAS which with its peasant character, its internal democratic structures and its independent military opinions would have endangered his bid for absolute authority. Apparently he was waiting for the withdrawal of the British forces as the suitable moment for that armed uprising in the towns. The interval he wanted to bridge with intensification of the *symfiliosi* campaign. At the beginning of July this campaign reached such proportions that it in turn provoked even more drastic repressive measures by the government authorities and the right-wing armed bands, thus creating a vicious circle. The first armed actions by the ODEK guerrillas towards the end of July proved that Zachariadis' concept was absurd: instead of striking at right-wing bands they found themselves in conflict with the gendarmerie, a fact not astonishing in view of the close relations between these bands and the gendarmerie. And, when the gendarmerie proved too weak, regular army units were soon deployed against the *andartes,* creating a second vicious circle of escalating violence. But Zachariadis had not been and was not the active mover in this process. Since Tsaldaris had taken over, the initiative had been on the government side. Zachariadis had only reacted and this in such a way that the government retained the initiative and the trump cards in this power game. KKE thus stumbled into civil war without any clear perspective. One might almost say that, had Zachariadis had the intention to ruin his party and the whole Left movement he could not have set about it more efficiently.

In this situation of escalating violence a British all-party Parliamentary delegation arrived in Athens on 16th August. It had been officially invited by the Greek government to counteract the 'biased' report of the three British Labour MPs who had criticised Populist tactics. But the Greek government's intention misfired. The delegation's findings probably form the least partisan, most balanced account of the situation in Greece in the summer of 1946.

The delegation spent six days in Athens and then for another six days its members split up to visit other places: Patras, Corinth, Tripolis and Sparta in the Peloponnese, Salonica and Edessa in Macedonia, Larissa in Thessaly, Kavala and Xanthi in Thrace, and Crete. They saw Damaskinos, Sofoulis, Papandreou, Kanellopoulos, Sofianopoulos, Tsirimokos, Partsalidis and Zachariadis as well as the elected and the appointed GCL Executives. They visited prisons, hospitals, factories and various public institutions. They had conferences with UNRRA chief Maben, Lt-Gen. Clark and Sir J. Nixon of the British Economic Mission, British Police Mission Chief Wickham, British Military Mission chief Maj-Gen. Rawlins, the C-in-C of British Land Forces Lt-Gen. Crawford, and of course the Greek government and its subordinate officials. In short, they tried to base their account on the broadest evidence possible. They concluded[59] the following:

'The political state of the country is very distressing. Whilst the bulk of the people—perhaps 85 per cent of the population—only wish to live a peaceful life, extremists on both sides are engaging in acts of violence and terrorism to the great disturbance of civil order. Although the feelings of hatred, fear, revenge and discontent resulting from the events of December 1944 have by no means died away, it is clear that acts of violence by both sides have considerably increased since the advent of the present Government. In parts of Macedonia and the mountainous areas of Thessaly, especially around Mount Olympus, there is proceeding what almost amounts to a miniature civil war between Left-wing bands and the gendarmerie... There is evidence that amongst these bands are many Left-wing supporters who have fled to the mountains to escape terrorism exercised by the extreme Right. On the other hand, many Right-wing partisans have been shot by the Left, and this has given rise to acts of retaliation and revenge. Unofficial statistics are unreliable and it would be impossible without prolonged investigation on the spot to estimate the decree of culpability to be attached to the respective sides...

At Larissa
'In some parts of Thessaly, especially in the Larissa–Volos–Pharsala triangle, armed Right-wing bands are operating with the utmost audacity. One day in August a notorious Right-wing bandit named Sourlas actually entered the town of Larissa, headquarters of the 2nd Greek Army Corps, and remained there for some time without being arrested. On another day the political correspondent of... *Rizospastis...* Vidalis, was taken out of the railway train near Volos by bandits and shot in the presence, it is said, of gendarmes. As far as the Delegation know no arrests were made.

'These armed bands are apparently tolerated by the authorities and no attempt is made to suppress them. Although it is claimed in certain quarters that their object is to prevent the spread of Communism, the fact is that they never engage the Communist bands in battle but devote themselves to terrorising the villages and exacting blackmail from anyone rich enough to pay it. In the area south of Lamia, we were told, the Right-wing bandit leader levies a toll of one per cent upon the production of the district. Although it is unlawful to bear arms this law is only enforced against members of the Left. In certain districts in Thessaly the Government are supplying arms to their civilian supporters. British officials are disturbed at the possible consequences of this.

The Peloponnese
'In the Peloponnese the peasants are traditionally Monarchist and the Left-wing allege that, being in a minority, they have been subjected to violent persecution and terrorism exercised by 'X'-ites and armed bandits, with the connivance, if not actual cooperation, of the gendarmerie. They state that as a result of this persecution thousands of Left-wing supporters have fled from Laconia and Messinia and taken refuge

in Athens, Tripolis and other towns. An E.A.M. delegation, seen at Tripolis, stated that although there had once been a strong Republican party in the port of Kalamata it was now impossible to send any E.A.M. leader there for fear he would be killed on the way. The staff of their newspaper had recently been arrested and the journal had ceased publication. It was alleged that no one who had taken part in the Resistance movement was safe...

'Whilst the Delegation were at Tripolis an ex-ELAS officer was shot dead outside the headquarters of the gendarmerie. It was suggested that this man had been murdered by his own side in order to convince the Delegation that a state of violence existed in the town. Although the Delegation cannot say this is an impossible explanation, they do not feel that it is a very probable one...

'During their brief visit to the Peloponnese the Delegation had no opportunity of verifying the accuracy or otherwise of the various charges and counter-charges made... They can only say—
(1) That the charges made by the Left were far more numerous and detailed... than the counter-charges made by the Right which, on the whole, were vague and general.
(2) That as the Right appeared to be in a large majority and had behind them the coercive powers of the security committees and the gendarmerie, they had far more opportunities of intimidating the Left than the Left had of intimidating the Right.

'The Delegation are of the opinion that these opportunities have not been entirely neglected.

Athens

'In Athens, comparative order and security prevailed...
  The Security Measures
  The Government have taken exceptional measures... Security Committees have been set up in every province and under the regulations people can be arrested, put in prison and detained indefinitely without trial... The Security Committees also have the power of deporting people to the islands on the grounds that "they are dangerous to public order". It may well be that by now over 1,000 persons have been deported and these include members of EAM local committees and editorial staffs of Left-wing newspapers. They also include women, some with children. Allegations have been received to the effect that some of these islands are arid and barren, with scanty water supplies.

'In addition to these committees, courts-martial have been set up in Macedonia, Thrace, Epirus and Thessaly... These... have the power in certain cases of inflicting the death penalty which is frequently carried out within a week of the sentence...

The Plebiscite

'. . . Persons of considerable responsibility endeavoured to make it clear that the Government intended to take few chances in that matter. . . For example, Liberal deputies complained that owing to Right-wing banditry they were unable to get to their constituencies. It is only fair to say that a Populist deputy for the Olympus area said that he was unable to get to his constituency either. And one former Liberal Cabinet Minister stated that if he went outside Athens he was afraid he would be shot. . .

'It was alleged that many thousands of Left-wing supporters had been driven from their villages by intimidation and dared not return to vote. . .

'The utilisation by the Government of all available means for Monarchist propaganda, including the radio and the display of posters in every Government department, the presence of an active pro-Monarchist gendarmerie, and the fact that, owing to the Nomarch system, all local officials were supporters of the Government and all the machinery of provincial administration was in their hands, inevitably handicapped the Opposition. . .'

There followed chapters on British Responsibility, Policy of Reconciliation, Friendship for Britain, British Troops in Greece, Local Government, Position of Women, Over-Reliance on Britain, Material Conditions, Agriculture, Economic and Social Conditions, Black Market, Civil Service, Tax-Free Rich, Budget Unbalanced, Balance of Trade, British Missions, and Conclusions. The report ended with a list of nineteen recommendations:

'(1) That the opportunity given by the return of the King should be used to initiate an entirely new policy in and towards Greece.
 (2) That an All-Party Government should be formed, with the support of Great Britain, to include all sections with the possible exception of the extreme Left.
 (3) That this Government, should it not be practicable to declare a general Amnesty, should at least adopt a generous policy of clemency towards political offenders.
 (4) That the first object of this Government should be the establishment of law, order and internal peace and the restoration of constitutional liberties.
 (5) That the special security decrees should be cancelled and all persons who, by order of the security committees, have been exiled to the islands for political reasons should be allowed to return to their homes.
 (6) That all persons surrendering their arms by a given date should be freed from the penalties attached to the illegal possession of arms.

(7) That further steps should be taken to improve the conditions in the prisons.
(8) That after a certain defined period new elections should be held on an up-to-date register.
(9) That subject to considerations of strategy and high policy the British troops should be withdrawn at an early date.
(10) That the action of the Government in appointing a new General Council of Labour and nominating new trade union executives should be rescinded and that pending new elections the former elected representatives should be allowed to return to their duties.
(11) That as soon as possible new trade union elections should be held under the supervision of the T.U.C. or the W.F.T.U. and that the good offices of the latter organisations should be utilised to amalgamate the 2,225 small trade unions in Greece into larger units.
(12) That it is urgently necessary that some plan should be devised to meet the situation which will be created when UNRRA ceases to operate at the end of the present year, and that the Greek Government should be pressed to appoint a representative to press Greece's claims for food allocations before the International Emergency Food Council.
(13) That concrete plans for reconstructions, with priority for harbours, railways, and roads, should be adopted and pressed forward with the possible help of the International Bank for Reconstruction.
(14) That any further loans to Greece should only be granted on condition that the powers of the British Economic Mission are strengthened and that it be advisable to ask the Greek Government to accept appointment of a British Financial Adviser with the duty of recommending a drastic reform of the present system of taxation.
(15) That a system of price regulation and rationing is urgently needed.
(16) That a drastic re-organisation of the Civil Service is called for and that, if possible, a British Civil Service Mission should be sent to Greece to assist in the work.
(17) That every possible assistance should be given to enable Greece to replace her merchant ships which were lost in the war.
(18) That the Greek people should be more closely associated with the work of local administration and government.
(19) That the establishment in Greece of any regime which resembled a dictatorship would have fatal consequences.'

If one disregards the diction, the findings of the British Parliamentary Delegation are almost identical with those of the three Labour MPs of

May 1946 and if one looks at the remedies suggested one discovers that they, too, were repetitions of suggestions made before. If they had been applied they would have certainly altered the course of Greek history, but as they were not, the vicious circle of violence and counter-violence continued to escalate towards full-scale civil war.

Conclusions

Ending this study of one of the most crucial periods of Greece's contemporary history, it seems useful to recapitulate some of the most important developments and draw some conclusions.

The analysis began with a description of the armistice dealings and the bargaining for the Varkiza peace treaty which brought an end to the armed British intervention and the civil war of December 1944. It closed with an account of the escalation of violence leading inevitably to the Civil War of 1947-49. The reasons for this cyclic development are manifold.

Nevertheless it seems necessary to refute once more a hard-dying Cold War myth: the Greek Civil War was by no means the result of a conspiracy, either from the Left or from the Right. The thesis that a democratic Greece became the victim of a sinister communist aggression devilishly premeditated in Moscow is a survival of Cold War propaganda: Greece in 1945/46 was far from being a democratic state and Moscow was against civil war—Greece, after all, belonged to the British sphere of interest and Stalin had written off his Greek comrades as had been proven by his behaviour in December 1944.

Similarly there was no masterly right-wing conspiracy against the liberties of the people which was in its turn directed by the sinister forces of capitalism from abroad, as the Greek communists have asserted. The central motives on this side of the fence were revenge and anti-communism on the part of the Greek Right and an intention to restore pre-war domination and to contain communism on the part of the British.

There were other factors which contributed to this development such as war devastation, uprooting of large sections of the population, hunger and misery, fear and hatred of the opponent, economic and financial ruin, galloping inflation, fiscal bankruptcy, administrative chaos, class conflicts, etc. Although these factors increased the tensions and led Greek society and the Greek state to ruin, alone they would never have triggered civil war.

Not even the rank-and-file extremists of the two opposing political camps who were eager for a shoot-out would have done much damage had not the deteriorating political situation told in their favour.

The British intervention of December 1944 had overthrown the existing balance of power. At the time of liberation the Left had been the strongest force in the political spectrum and the Right had been a minority discredited by its pre-war adherence to the fascist dictator Metaxas and its partial collaboration with the Axis and Nazi Occupation forces. The December events, however, reversed this order: from now on the Left was under duress and the Right was in the ascendant. The final outcome, however, was not inevitable.

The Varkiza peace treaty was a reasonable compromise. Had both sides fulfilled its letter and spirit a peaceful development would have been assured. This, however, would have required a strong and moderate political leadership seeking compromise and reconciliation. But even before Metaxas, the majority of Greek political leaders had been anti-communist. Both the success of the Left during the Occupation and the December events had intensified this fear and turned it into pathological hatred. Even reasonable moderate politicians avoided conciliatory solutions because they, too, feared the communists on the one hand and were afraid of being called fellow-travellers on the other. Thus the first two prime ministers after Varkiza—both from the armed forces and anti-communists— let things drift and turned a blind eye to the ever-increasing persecution not only of the Left but quite often of all other opponents of the Right, including their own following. This attitude in turn encouraged the Right to intensify its anti-communist campaign. At the same time it crept back into the centres of power in two ways: officially in the armed forces and the gendarmerie/police and unofficially in that power structure, which has been described as the *parakratos*. The more power the Right controlled the more it intensified its hunting-down of the Left. The result was a process of escalating violence of which the victims were the forces of moderation: the Centre and the Centre-Left parties. The political spectrum began to polarise. Many of the disastrous developments before summer 1945 and later were thus the outcome, not of deliberate political moves by the various Greek governments, but rather of this kind of *laissez-faire* policy for which, nevertheless, these governments must bear the historical responsibility.

Until summer 1945 this process was by no means irreversible. A clear statement from the Churchill government of their political aims in Greece could have changed the course of events. But as such guidance was missing the Greek politicians interpreted British policy in their own particular way: they had seen how during the Occupation, Churchill and the Foreign Office had supported the king. The armed intervention in 1944 had left them with a suspicion which was shared by the Left: British policy makers wanted the Populists in power in order to restore the king. This impression, combined with a traditional attitude of submission to the protecting power, encouraged the *laissez-faire* attitude of the various Greek governments, their total disregard of the Varkiza Agreement provisions, the ever increasing persecution of the Left and the ever more intransigent, more uncompromising and more militant line pursued by the Right.

The communists on the other hand had at first been ready to compromise and to integrate into the parliamentary system. But this 'revisionist' line was rebuffed and their rank-and-file became the victims of right-wing persecution. Nevertheless Secretary-General Zachariadis stuck to the chosen line until the Twelfth Plenum when he permitted the organisation of unarmed mass self-defence. But even this mild retaliation provoked a further intensification of the massive persecution. The vicious circle of violence and counter-violence was gaining momentum.

This expanding cycle could have been interrupted if the Churchill government had intervened once more. The instruments for intervention were to hand: Ambassador Leeper as 'High Commissioner' hand-guided the Greek governments. The various British Missions had penetrated the country to such a degree that they could have easily reversed the situation. However, Churchill saw no reason why he should help the communists on the one hand—he preferred the Greek collaborators—and on the other he did not want to get too deeply involved in Greece's internal affairs. For him the main thing was that Greece remained in the British sphere of interest. And a second intervention might have risked his ultimate aim of restoring the Greek monarch.

This legacy of muddle, misunderstanding and misconceptions was inherited by the Labour government when it took office in August 1945. A clear statement by Bevin and a few energetic measures by the omnipresent British Missions could still have broken the cycle. But Bevin refrained from tackling the causes of the Greek problem and confined himself to a few isolated measures which were at best remedies for the symptoms. On 20th August Bevin stated that he would continue the policy worked out by the Churchill government, *i.e.* an anti-communist policy and therefore a policy 'most acceptable' to the Tories.[60]

Thus, when Sofoulis took office and there was another chance for a change of policy, the British did nothing decisive to assist Sofoulis when he tried to tackle the root problems. Therefore the suspicion that the British wanted the Populists in power slowly grew into a conviction, crippling Sofoulis' efforts: each time he or his ministers tried to act impartially or decisively or independently they met with stern opposition from the British Missions in Greece who pulled the rug from under their feet. A last-minute chance (the Manganas incident) might have prompted Bevin to change his course, but international entanglement and confrontation with the Soviet Union in the UN over Greece frustrated even this hope: Bevin's public statements in that body even prohibited a postponement of the elections, the last chance to avoid civil war. From that point the count-down to civil war began.

During the same period the Greek Communist Party's leadership continued their blunders. Instead of sticking to one line of policy, they vacillated between concepts of integration and confrontation. Their half-hearted counter-measures against right-wing terrorism only provoked the Right to an even more brutal persecution of the Left. Zachariadis, however, was not disturbed by this. He believed that the deteriorating situation would lead to the great crisis prescribed by his ideology and to revolution which would take place in the cities and would be won by the armed proletariat. In view of this ideological blindness, it is scarcely to be wondered at that he led his party to the capital mistake of abstention from the elections. In this way he forfeited all his assets and strengthened the 'democratically-elected legitimate' Greek government. From now on the initiative passed to the latter. Zachariadis and his henchmen stumbled into the civil war without any perspective, when they did not have the slightest chance of getting either enough national or international support.

From the elections on, the Foreign Office washed its hands of Greek affairs and after the elections Bevin acquiesced in the new Greek government's policy which went contrary to his own previous orders. He even silently accepted Tsaldaris' abolition of the few remnants of democracy in Greece. Criticism of his course by the Labour Left and the TUC did not move him. What counted for him was the fact that the Greek government was a reliable ally in the mounting Cold War, ready to steer an uncompromising anti-communist course—why should he bother with the internal political system of an under-developed, dependent country like Greece. For Bevin, Britain's rights, prestige and power were prime motives.[61] But for Britain's financial problems, he would probably have continued his protectorate even during the Civil War but, as things were in early 1947, he was obliged to hand his responsibilities over to the United States. More than one hundred years of British tutelage over Greece had come to an end.

Fortunately for the British government, the eager Americans were all too ready to take over. From now on Greece was to be *their* headache.

NOTES

1. Foreign Office to Norton 13th March, 1946 (R 3748/1/19).
2. Foreign Office to Norton 30th March, 1946 (R 4757/1/19).
3. Norton to Foreign Office 31st March, 1946 (R 5023/1/19).
4. Norton to Foreign Office 2nd April, 1946 (R 5170/1/19).
5. Foreign Office to Norton 3rd April, 1946 (R 5170/1/19).
6. Norton to Foreign Office 3rd April, 1946 (R 5213/1/19).
7. Norton to Foreign Office 3rd April, 1946 (R 5246/1/19).
8. Foreign Office to Norton 4th April, 1946 (R 5247/1/19).
9. The Cabinet consisted of:
    K. Tsaldaris: Prime Minister, Foreign Minister.
    P. Mavromichalis: War Minister and temporarily Navy and Air Force Minister.
    I. Theotokis: Interior Minister.
    S. Stefanopoulos: Minister for Coordination.
    D. Chelmis: Finance Minister.
    P. Hajipanos: Justice Minister.

S. Gonatas: Minister for Public Works and temporarily Reconstruction Minister.
N. Avraam: Mercantile Marine Minister.
D. Papadimitriou: Transport Minister.
A. Perrotis: T.T.T. (Post & Telecommunications) Minister.
A. Papadimos: Education Minister.
A. Papathanasis: Minister for Agriculture.
A. Alexandris: Economics Minister.
D. Stefanopoulos: Supply Minister.
G. Lazanas: Minister for Social Welfare.
A. Kalantzakos: Health Minister.
A. Stratos: Labour Minister.
S. Theotokis: Public Order Minister.
G. Paravantis: Assistant-Minister to the Prime Minister.
F. Dragoumis: Assistant-Minister Foreign Affairs.
M. Alianos: Assistant-Minister Coordination.
A. Antonopoulos: Assistant-Minister Finance.
L. Eftaxias: Assistant-Minister Agriculture.
N. Baltatzis-Mavrokordatos: Assistant-Minister Press and Information.
10. Norton to Foreign Office 10th May, 1946 (R 7099/1/19).
11. Foreign Office to Norton 28th May, 1946 (R 7716/1/19).
12. Norton to Foreign Office 23rd May, 1946 (R 7716/1/19).
13. Norton to Foreign Office 13th May, 1946 (R 7350/1/19). Norton added: 'The Decree was ratifiable by the Chamber, but this is presumably a foregone conclusion.'
14. *Rizospastis,* 6th May, 1946.
15. Dodds, et al., *op. cit.,* pp. 61 ff.
16. *Ibid.,* pp. 58 ff.
17. Hayter's Minute 11th May, 1946 (R 7098/1/19).
18. *Ibid.* In a telegram Norton had deplored 'that a newspaper of the standing of the *Times* should continue to depend on an unintelligent and unreliable Greek for its news from this country'. Norton to Foreign Office 9th May, 1946 (R 7098/1/19). For the earlier treatment of the 'Times' question see p. 370.
19. Norton to Foreign Office 16th May, 1946 (R 7411/1/19).
20. Norton to Foreign Office 21st May, 1946 (R 7667/1/19).
21. Quoted from Keesing's Contemporary Archives, p. 8026.
22. *Ibid.*
23. *Ibid.*
24. *Rizospastis,* 19th June, 1946.
25. *ILO Report,* pp. 237-244; *Greek Trade Unions in Chains, passim; Greek News* 1:6 (August 1946), p. 1, and 1:7 (September, 1946), p. 1.
26. *Greek News* 1:6 (August 1940), p. 5.
27. *Ibid.,* p. 6.
28. *Ibid.*
29. *Greek News* 1:7 (September 1946), p. 2.
30. *Ibid.,* p. 3.
31. *Ibid.* Until the 31st August these courts-martial in Macedonia and Thrace sentenced thirty-five to death (all executed), forty-six to life imprisonment and two hundred and forty-five to various terms of imprisonment totalling 750 years. *Greek News* 1:9 (November 1946), p. 3.
32. *Ibid.,* 1:7 (September 1946), p. 3.
33. *I panelladiki organotiki syskepsi,* (Athens: KKE Central Committee, 1946).
34. *Ibid.,* p. 17.
35. *Ibid.,* pp. 17-28.

36. *Ibid.*, pp. 29-32.
37. Nefeloudis, *Stis piges tis kakodaimonias*, pp. 278 ff.
38. Bartziotas, 'I politiki mas ton stelechon sto KKE ta teleftaia deka chronia', *Neos Kosmos*, (September 1950), pp. 560-3.
39. Zachariadis, 'Ya tin kommounistiki organosi Thessalonikis', *KOMEP*, (October 1945), pp. 30-4; Zachariadis, *O kommounistis, laikos agonistis, melos tou KKE*, (Athens: KKE Central Committee, 1946).
40. Bartziotas, *op. cit.*, p. 561.
41. Yannis Petsopoulos, *op. cit.*
42. *Ibid.*, p. 13.
43. *Ibid.*, p. 417.
44. *Ibid.*, pp. 434 ff.
45. 'Apofasi tis K.E. tou K.K.E. pano stin politiki katastasi', *KOMEP*, (May 1946), pp. 205 ff.
46. Yannis Zevgos, 'I kainourya antikommatiki prospatheia', *KOMEP*, (June 1946), pp. 282 ff.
47. See p. 490.
48. See p. 524.
49. *Rizospastis*, 8th June, 1946.
50. *Ibid.*, 12th June, 1946.
51. Hayter's Memorandum of the 24th July 1946 'Law and Order in Greece' (R 10399/1/19).
52. Leonidas Stringos, 'Omilia pano sto proto thema', p. 86.
53. Markos Vafiadis, 'Omilia pano sto proto thema', p. 52.
54. Blanas-Kissavos, *op. cit.*, p. 75.
55. Vontitsos-Gousias, *Oi aities* Vol. I, pp. 137 ff.
56. Markos Vafiadis, *op. cit.*, pp. 52 ff.
57. Vontitsos-Gousias, *op. cit.*, Vol. I, p. 139, *e.g.* Yannoulis, Lassanis, Ypsilantis, Liakos, Kartsounis, Kartsiotis, Alevras, Agrafiotis, Belis, et al.
58. See pp. 512-13.
59. *Report of the British Parliamentary Delegation to Greece, August 1946*, (London: HMSO, 1947).
60. Woodhouse, *British Foreign Policy*, p. 201.
61. *Ibid.*, p. 202.

ACRONYMS

AAA	Archiyion Apeleftherotikou Agonos (Liberation Struggle Command) or Agon-Anorthosis-Anexartisia (Struggle-Reconstruction-Independence). Both interpretations were in use.
AGIS	Anglo-Greek Information Service
AIS	Allied Information Service
AKE	Agrotiko Komma Elladas (Agrarian Party of Greece)
AMFOGE	Allied Mission for Observing Greek Elections
AMM	Allied Military Mission
BLO	British Liaison Officer
BMM	British Military Mission
DSE	Dimokratikos Stratos Elladas (Democratic Army of Greece)
EA	Ethiniki Allilengyi (National Solidarity)
EAM	Ethniko Apeleftherotiko Metopo (National Liberation Front)
EDES	Ethnikos Dimokratikos Ellinikos Syndesmos (National Democratic Greek League)
EEAM	Ergatiko Ethniko Apeleftherotiko Metopo (Labour National Liberation Front)
EKKA	Ethniki kai Kinoniki Apeleftherosis (National & Social Liberation)
ELAS	Ethnikos Laikos Apeleftherotikos Stratos (National Popular Liberation Army)
ELD	Enosi Laikis Dimokratias (Union of Popular Democracy)
ENA	Enosi Neon Axiomatikon (Union of Young Officers)
EP	Ethniki Politofylaki (National Civil Guard)
EPON	Ethniki Panelladiki Organosi Neolaias (National Panhellenic Youth Organisation)
ERGAS	Ergatikos Antifasistikos Synaspismos (Labour Anti-fascist Coalition)
ESSAK	Epitropi Synergasias Sosialistikon kai Agrotikon Kommaton (Co-operation Committee of Socialist & Agrarian Parties)
ETA	Epimeleitia tou Andarti (Guerrilla Commissariat)
GSEE/GCL	Geniki Synomospondia Ergaton Elladas (General Confederation of Workers of Greece, usually referred to by its English title of General Confederation of Labour)

IDEA	Ieros Desmos Ellinon Axiomatikon (Sacred Bond of Greek Officers)
ILO	International Labour Office
KKE	Kommounistiko Komma Elladas (Greek Communist Party)
KOA	Kommatiki Organosi Athinas (Athens Party Organisation)
KOMEP	Kommounistiki Epitheorisi (Communist Review)
KUTV	Kommunisticheskii Universitet Trudyashcshya Vostoka (Communist University for Eastern Workers)
ML	Military Liaison
NCO	Non-Commissioned Officer
NOF	Narodni Oslobodilački Front (National Liberation Front)
ODEK	Omades Dimokratikon Enoplismenon Katadiokismenon (Bands of Armed Persecuted Democrats)
OKNE	Omospondia Kommounistikon Neolaion Elladas (Federation of Communist Youth of Greece)
OPLA	Organosi Perifrourisis Laikon Agonon (Organisation for Safeguarding the Popular Struggle)
OWI	Office of War Information
PAS	Panellinios Apeleftherotikos Syndesmos (Panhellenic Liberation League)
PEEA	Politiki Epitropi Ethnikis Apeleftherosis (Political Committee for National Liberation)
RAN	Roumelia—Avlona—Nisa
SAN	Syndesmos Axiomatikon Neon (League of Young Officers)
SEKE	Sosialistiko Ergatiko Komma Elladas (Socialist Labour Party of Greece)
SKE	Sosialistiko Komma tis Ellados (Socialist Party of Greece)
SOE	Special Operations Executive
TUC	Trades Union Congress
UNO	United Nations Organisation
UNRRA	United Nations Relief & Rehabilitation Administration
WFTU	World Federation of Trade Unions

BIBLIOGRAPHY

1. Greek Official Sources

Directorate of Press and Information Diefthynsi Typou kai Pliroforion, *I symfonia tis Varkizas: Ola ta schetika keimena* (Athens, February 1945).

Ministry to the Prime Minister's Office, *Efimeris tis Kyverniseos (Government Gazette)*.

——————————————— *Appeals to the electorate in Greece since the end of the Second World War* (Athens, 1961).

National Statistical Service of Greece, *Synoptiki statistiki epitirisis tis Ellados 1954* (Athens, 1955); *Ib. 1966* (Athens, 1967).

——————————————— *Concise Statistical Yearbook of Greece 1962* (Athens, 1963).

2. Greek Communist Party (KKE)

To KKE apto 1931 os to 1952 (vasika dokoumenta) (n.p.: KKE Central Committee, 1953).

Chroniko tou agona (1878-1951). Dokoumenta kai ylika apo tin istoria tou laïkou mas kinimatos (n.p.: KKE Central Committee, 1952); re-print (Athens: Na ypiretoume to lao, 1975).

Voïthima ya tin istoria tou KKE (KKE Central Committee, 1953); reprint (Athens: Ekdoseis tou laou, 1975, 2nd ed.).

Episima Keimena, III, *1929-1933* (n.p.: Politikes kai logotechnikes ekdoseis, 1966).

Episima Keimena, IV, *1934-1940* (n.p.: Politikes kai logotechnikes ekdoseis, 1968).

Episima Keimena, V, *1940-1945, To Kommounistiko Komma Elladas sto polemo kai stin antistasi* (n.p.: KKE/ESOTERIKOU, 1974).

40 chronia tou KKE 1918-1958 (n.p.: Politikes kai logotechnikes ekdoseis, 1958).

Deka chronia agones 1935-1945. To KKE stis apofaseis ton synedrion, ton syndiaskepseon kai ton olomeleion tis Kentrikis Epitropis (Athens: KKE Central Committee, 1945).

I panelladiki organotiki syskepsi (15-17 Aprili 1946) (Athens: KKE Central Committee, 1946).

Pros tin 6i syndiaskepsi tis komm. organosis Athinas (Athens: Ekdoseis KOA, 1945).

I 6i syndiaskepsi tis komm. organosis. Athinas 28-29 Septemvri 1945 (Athens: Ekdoseis KOA, 1945).
To 7o synedrio tou KKE, 5 v. (Athens: KKE Central Committee, 1945).
To 8o synedrio tou KKE (n.p.: Politikes kai logotechnikes ekdoseis, 1961).
Apofasi tis 12is olomeleias tis Kentrikis Epitropis tou KKE (Athens: KKE Central Committee, 1945).
'Apofasi tis 2is olomeleias tis KE tou KKE. I katastasi stin Ellada. Ta provlimata tou dimokratikou agona kai ta kathikonta tou KKE', *KOMEP* (March, 1946), and *Rizospastis* (17th February, 1946).
'Apofasi tis KE tou KKE. Pano sti politiki katastasi', *KOMEP* (May 1946).

Leading articles from *KOMEP*
'Proschedio programmatos tou KKE', *KOMEP* (September, 1945).
'To kentriko provlima', *KOMEP* (November, 1945).
'O Dekemvris stathmos kai nea afetiria tou agona ya tin anexartisia kai ti dimokratia', *KOMEP* (December, 1945).
'Oi dyo dromoi', *KOMEP* (February, 1946).
'Chroniko: Apo to Litochoro os to Grammo kai to Vitsi. O dromos pros ti niki', *Dimokratikos Stratos* (November, 1948).

Articles from *Neos Kosmos*
'I antikommatiki likvidaristiki platforma tou Kosta Gyftodimou (Kara-giorgi)', *Neos Kosmos* (August, 1950).
'I opportunistiki platforma tou Markou Vafiadi' *Ib.*
'Stoicheia pano stin prodotiki drasi tou G. Siantou', *Neos Kosmos* (February, 1951).
'Ap' aformi tis efthynes ya ti Varkiza', *Neos Kosmos* (February, 1957).

From *Rizospastis*
'Ta trechonta organotika provlimata tou KKE. Apofasi tou PG tis KE tou KKE', *Rizospastis* (16th December, 1945).

From *I Avghi*
'To ypomnima tou Zachariadi ston Stalin', *I Avghi* (14th December, 1980).

3. Ethniko Apeleftherotiko Metopo (EAM)
Lefki Vivlos: Mais 1944–Martis 1945 (Trikala, 1946); re-print (Athens: Klepsydra, 1975).
White Book: May 1944–March 1945 (English ed. of above published by Greek–American Council, New York, 1945).
Lefki Vivlos: Paravaseis tis Varkizas Flevaris—Iounis 1945 (Athens, June, 1945); re-print (Athens: Ellinika Themata, 1975).

Lefki Vivlos: 'Dimokratikos' neofasismos Ioulis-Oktovris 1945 (Athens, October, 1945).
Mavri Vivlos: To eklogiko praxikopima tis 31 Marti 1946 (Athens, May, 1946).
Oi pragmatikes aities tou ellinikou dramatos (Athens, 1947).

4. 'Provisional Democratic Government'

La verité sur la Grèce: Livre Bleu. Sur l'occupation americano-anglaise, sur le régime monarcho-fasciste, sur la lutte du peuple grec (n.p.: August, 1948).
For Peace and Democracy in Greece: Second Blue Book. On the Anglo-American intervention, on the monarcho-fascist regime, on the people's struggle for liberty (n.p.: August, 1949).

5. Other parties and organisations

Democratic Organisations of Greece. *For Peace and Democracy in Greece: Third Blue Book*. On the Anglo-American intervention, on the monarcho-fascist regime, on the struggle for liberty (n.p.: 1950).
Enosi Laikis Dimokratias (ELD), *Theseis ya ta Dekemvriana. Apofasi tis Kentrikis Epitropis tis 15 Martiou 1945* (Athens, 1945).
Ethnikos Dimokratikos Ellinikos Syndesmos (EDES), *Idrytikon (1941), Programma (1943), Ya mia nea politiki zoï (1943)* re-printed (Athens: Ellinika Themata, 1974).
Sosialistiko Komma tis Ellados (SKE), *To kommounistiko kinima 1944-1945* (Athens, 1945).
I ekthesi ton anglikon syndikaton. O syndikalismos kai i katastasi stin Ellada meta tin katochi (Athens: Sideris, 1977).

6. British Official Sources

Documents regarding the situation in Greece (London: HMSO, 1945), Cmd. 6592.
What we saw in Greece: Report of the TUC Delegation (London: Trades Union Congress, February, 1945).
Report by the Supreme Allied Commander Mediterranean to the Combined Chiefs of Staff on Greece 12th December 1944 to 9th May 1945 (London: HMSO, 1949).
Report of the British Legal Mission to Greece (London: HMSO, 17th January 1946), Cmd. 6838.
Report of the Allied Mission to observe the Greek Elections (London: HMSO, 1946), Cmd. 6812.
Foreign Office, *Report of the British Parliamentary Delegation to Greece, August 1946* (London: HMSO, 1947).
Trades Union Congress. *Annual Reports* (London, 1945, 1946).

7. United States of America;
The Foreign Relations of the United States, 1945, VIII: The Near East and Africa (Washington: Government Printing Office, 1969).
Foreign Relations of the United States 1946, VII: The Near East and Africa (Washington: Government Printing Office, 1969).

8. United Nations Organisation
UN—Security Council, *Official Records,* First Year: First Series, Supplement No. 1 (London, 1946).

9. International Labour Office
Labour Problems in Greece: Report of the ILO Mission to Greece, October-November, 1947 (Geneva: ILO, 1949).

BOOKS
Alexander, George M., *The Prelude to the Truman Doctrine: British Policy in Greece 1944-1947* (Oxford: Clarendon Press, 1982).
Amen, Michael Mark, *American Foreign Policy in Greece 1944-1949: Economic, Military and Institutional Aspects* (Bern, Las Vegas: Peter Lang, 1978).
American Council for a Democratic Greece, *Facts on Greece* (New York, 1949).
Anderson, Terry, *The United States, Great Britain, and the Cold War* (London: Columbia, 1981).
Apostolou, Lefteris, *I parodia tis dikis ton dosilogon kai i aftokatadiki tis Dexias* (Athens: O Rigas, June 1945); re-print (Athens: Ellinika Themata, 1974).
Arkadinos, Polyvios (pseudonym), *I esoteriki krisi tou KKE (1945-1955). Vol. III. Kostas Karagiorgis i 'Liaskovos'* (Gyftodimos), (Athens, 1955).
Averoff-Tositsas, Evangelos, *By Fire and Axe. The Greek Communist Party and the civil war in Greece 1944-49* (New Rochelle N.J.: Caratzas, 1978).
Barry, Gerald, *Report on Greece* (London: News Chronicle Publications, 1945).
Bartziotas, Vasilis, *O agonas tou Dimokratikou Stratou Elladas* (Athens: Synchroni Epochi, 1981).
Blanas, Giorgis (Kapetan Kissavos), *Emfylios Polemos 1946-1949 (Opos ta ezisa)* (Athens, 1976).
Bokotas, Rizos D., *Etsi chathike o Aris* (Athens: Kodros, 1976).
Bullock, Alan Louis Charles, *The Life and Times of Ernest Bevin,* Vol. II. *Minister of Labour 1940-1945* (London: Heinemann, 1967).
Byford-Jones, W., *The Greek Trilogy: Resistance, Liberation, Revolution*

(London: Hutchinson, N.D. [1947]).
Capell, Richard, *Simiomata: A Greek Notebook 1944-1945* (London: McDonald, 1946).
Chandler, Geoffrey, *The Divided Land: An Anglo-Greek Tragedy* (London: Macmillan, 1959).
Churchill, Winston Spencer, *The Second World War*, Vol. VI (London: Cassell, 1954).
Couloumbis, Theodore and Hicks, Sallie (ed.), *US Foreign Policy towards Greece and Cyprus: The clash of principle and pragmatism* (Washington: Center for Mediterranean Studies and the American Hellenic Institute, 1975).
Dafnis, Grigorios, *I Ellas metaxy dyo polemon 1923-1940* (Athens: Ikaros, 1955).
Dimitriou, Panos (ed.), *I diaspasi tou KKE*. 2 v. (Athens: Politika Provlimata, 1975).
Dodds, Norman, Solley, Leslie and Tiffany, Stanley, *Tragedy in Greece* (London: League for Democracy in Greece, 1946).
Eden, Anthony, *The Eden Memoirs. The Reckoning* (London: Cassell, 1965).
Eudes, Dominque, *The Kapetanios: Partisan and Civil War in Greece 1943-1949*, English ed. (London: New Left Books, 1973).
Fleming, D.F., *The Cold War and its origins 1917-1960.* 2 v. (London: Allen and Unwin, 1961).
Gousidis, Dimitris, *Markos Vafiadis: Martyries* (Thessaloniki: Epikairotita, 1983).
Greek-American Council, *Challenge to Freedom. The Story of what happened in Greece from the Reports of Leland Stowe and Constantine Poulos.* (New York: March, 1945).
Grigoriadis, Foivos, *Istoria tou Emfyliou Polemou*. 4 v. (Athens: n.d.).
Grigoriadis, Solon, *O Emfylios Polemos. I Ellada tou 1945-1949*.Vol. I. (Athens: Fytranis, 1979).
Hajipanayotis, Yannis (Kapetan Thomas), *I politiki diathiki tou Ari Velouchioti* (Athens: Dorikos, 1976).
Hajopoulos, Achilefs, *Oi prostates 1943-1949* (Athens: Papazisis, 1977).
Iatrides, John O., *Revolt in Athens: The Greek Communist 'second round' 1944-1945* (Princeton N.J.: Princeton University Press, 1972).
Ieros Desmos Ellinon Axiomatikon (IDEA), *Vol. I. Apokalypsis tou typou (1951-1952)* (Athens: Ellinika Themata, 1975).
Jecchinis, Christos, *Trade Unionism in Greece: A study in political paternalism* (Chicago: Roosevelt University, 1967).
Kanellopoulos, Panayotis, *Ta chronia tou megalou polemou 1939-1944: Istoriki anadromi kai keimena* (Athens, 1974, 2nd ed.).
Karagiorgas, Giorgios, *Apo tin IDEA stin Chounta i pos fthasame stin 21i Apriliou* (Athens: Papazisis, 1975).

Karagiorgis, Kostas, *Apo ti Varkiza os ton emfylio polemo. Vol. I. 1945* (Athens: Dialogos, 1977).
Karayannis, Giorgios, *To drama tis Ellados 1940-1952* (Athens, 1964).
Katsoulis, Giorgis, *Istoria tou KKE*. 7 v. (Athens: Nea Synora, 1976-1978).
Kissavos, see Blanas.
Kolko, Gabriel, *The Politics of War: The World and US Foreign Policy 1943-1945* (New York: Vintage, 1970).
Kolko, Joyce and Gabriel, *The Limits of Power: The World and United States Foreign Policy 1945-1954* (New York: Harper and Row, 1972).
Koppel, Helga, *Partito Communista Italiano: Die Entwicklung der Italienischen KP zur Massenpartei* (Berlin: Verlag für das Studium der Arbeiterbewegung, 1976).
Kousoulas, Dimitrios George, *Revolution and Defeat: The Story of the Greek Communist Party* (London: Oxford University Press, 1965).
League for Democracy in Greece, *Greek Trades Unions in Chains* (London: 1946).
Leeper, Reginald, *When Greek meets Greek* (London: Chatto and Windus, 1950).
Mackenzie, Compton, *Wind of Freedom: The story of the invasion of Greece by the Axis Powers* (London: Chatto and Windus, 1943).
Maclean, Fitzroy, *Eastern Approaches* (London: Cape, 1949).
Macmillan, Harold, *The Blast of War 1939-1945* (London: Macmillan, 1967).
McNeill, William Hardy, *The Greek Dilemma: War and Aftermath* (London: Victor Gollancz, 1947).
Malagardis, Antonios, *Geniki kodikopoïsis tis ischyousis ellinikis nomothesias apo tis systaseos tou ellinikou kratous mechri simeron* (Athens: 1934).
Manousakas, Yannis, *Akronafplia: Thrylos kai pragmatikotita* (Athens: Kapopoulos, 1975).
———— *Chroniko apo tin Antistasi (meta tin Akronafplia)* (Athens: Kapopoulos, 1976).
Mathiopoulos, Basil P., *Die Geschichte der sozialen Frage und des Sozialismus in Griechenland 1821-1961* (Hannover: Verlag für Literatur und Zeitgeschehen, 1961).
Matthews, Kenneth, *Memories of a Mountain War* (London: Longmans, 1972).
Meynaud, Jean, *Les forces politiques en Grèce* (Montreal, 1965).
Millis, Walter (ed.), *The Forrestal Diaries* (New York: Viking Press, 1951).
Myers, E.C.W., *Greek Entanglement* (London: Hart-Davis, 1955).
Nefeloudis, Pavlos, *Stis piges tis kakodaimonias: Ta vathytera aitia tis diaspasis tou KKE 1918-1968* (Athens: Gutenberg, 1974).
Nefeloudis, Vasilis, *Achtina IX: Anamniseis 1930-1940* (Athens: Olkos,

1974).
Neubacher, Herrmann, *Sonderauftrag Südost* (Göttingen: Musterschmidt, 1956).
O'Ballance, Edgar, *The Greek Civil War 1944-1949* (London: Faber; New York: Praeger, 1966).
Othonaios, Alexandros, *Treis Logoi dia tin dimokratian* re-printed (Athens: Ellinika Themata, 1976).
Papakongos, Kostis, *Grammata ya ton Ari* (Athens: Papazisis, 1976).
Papastratis, Procopis, *British policy towards Greece during the Second World War 1941-1944* (London: Cambridge University Press, 1984).
Partsalidis, Dimitrios, *Dipli apokatastasi tis Ethnikis Antistasis* (Athens: Themelio, 1978).
Patatzis, Sotiris, *Ioannis Sofianopoulos: Enas epanastatis choris epanastasi* (Athens, 1961).
Pavlopoulos, Athanasios, *Istoria tou kommounismou en Elladi* (Athens: Geografiki Ypirisia Stratou, 1971).
Peponis, Ioannis, A. *Nikolaos Plastiras sta gegonota 1909-1945*. 2 v. (Athens: 1947).
Petsopoulos, Yannis, *Ta pragmatika aitia tis diagrafis mou apo to KKE: Kritiki mias politikis kairoskopias kai prodosias. Anoichti epistoli* (Athens, July 1946).
Poios einai poios eis tin Ellada. *Viografiko Lexiko* (Athens, 1958). [A Greek Who's Who.]
Provatas, Alkiviadis, *Politiki istoria tis Elladis 1821-1980: Nomothetika kai ektelestika somata* (Athens, 1980).
Puryear, Edgar F. Jr., *Communist negotiating techniques: A case study of the United Nations Security Council Commission of Investigation concerning the* Greek frontier incidents*, unpublished dissertation: (Princeton, 1959).
Richter, Heinz, *Griechenland zwischen Revolution und Konterrevolution 1936-1946* (Frankfurt: Europäische Verlagsanstalt, 1973).
———— Greece and Cyprus since 1920. Bibliography of contemporary history. (Heidelberg: Wissenschaftliche Verlag Nea Hellas, 1984).
Rosenau, James N., *The Scientific Study of Foreign Policy* (New York: Free Press, 1971).
Rousos, Petros, *I megali Pentaetia 1940-1945: I Ethniki Antistasi kai o rolos tou KKE*. 2 v. (Athens: Synchroni Epochi, 1978).
Rousseas, Stephen, *The Death of a Democracy: Greece and the American Conscience* (New York: Grove Press, 1967).
Sarafis, Stefanos, *ELAS: Greek Resistance Army*, English ed. (London: Merlin Press, 1980).
———— *Meta ti Varkiza* (Athens: Epikairotita, 1979).
Seferis, Kostas, *Elliniko syndikalistiko kinima 1860-1975* (Athens: Neo

syndikalistiko kinima, 1976, 2nd ed.).
Sheppard, A.W., *Britain in Greece* (London: League for Democracy in Greece, 1947).
Smothers, Frank; McNeill, William Hardy; McNeill, Elizabeth Darbishire, *Report on the Greeks: Findings of a Twentieth Century Fund team which surveyed conditions in Greece in 1947* (New York: The Twentieth Century Fund, 1948).
Sofianopoulos, Ioannis (John), *How to save Greece* (London: League for Democracy in Greece, 1946).
Solaro, Antonio, *Istoria tou Kommounistikou Komma Elladas* (Athens: Pleias, 1977).
Stavrianos, Leften Stavros, *Greece: American Dilemma and Opportunity* (Chicago: Regnery, 1952).
Stavrou, Nikolaos, Pressure Groups in the Greek political setting, unpublished thesis (George Washington University, 1970).
Stowe, Leland, *While Time Remains* (New York: Alfred Knopf, 1947).
Theodoropoulos, Spyros, *Ap'to 'Dogma Trouman' sto Dogma 'Chounta'. I 'Pax Amerikana' strangalizei tin Ellada* (Athens: Papazisis, 1976).
Theos, Kostas, *Ta ellinika syndikata stin pali enantia sto fasismo kai ya tin anexartisia tous* (Athens, 1947).
Vlandas, Dimitrios, *1950-1967. Tragodia tou KKE* (Athens, 1976).
——————— *I prodomeni epanastasi 1941-1944* (Athens: Evangelios, 1977).
——————— *Emfylios Polemos 1945-1949. Vol. I.* (Athens: 1979); *Vol. II.* (Athens: Grammi, 1981).
Vontitsos-Gousias, Giorgios, *Oi aities ya tis ittes, ti diaspasi tou KKE kai tis ellinikis Aristeras*, 2 v. (Athens: Na ypiretoume to lao, 1977-8).
Vukmanović, Svetozar (Tempo), *How and why the people's liberation struggle of Greece met with defeat.* English ed. (London: 1950, reprinted Merlin Press, 1985).
Woodhouse, C.M., *Apple of Discord: A survey of recent Greek politics in their international setting* (London: Hutchinson, n.d. [1948], reprinted Reston, Virginia: W.B. O'Neill, 1985).
——————— *British Foreign Policy since the Second World War* (London: Hutchinson, 1961).
——————— *The Struggle for Greece 1941-1949* (London: Hart-Davis, 1976).
——————— *Something Ventured* (London: Granada, 1982).
Wright, Colin, *British soldier in Greece* (London: Lawrence and Wishart, 1946).
Xydis, Stephen, *Greece and the Great Powers 1944-1947: Prelude to the 'Truman Doctrine'* (Thessaloniki: Institute for Balkan Studies, 1963).
Yergin, Daniel, *Shattered peace: Origins of the Cold War and the National Security State* (Boston: Houghton-Mifflin, 1977).

Zachariadis, Nikos, *Epilogi Ergon* (Athens: Protoporos, 1974).
——————— *O kommounistis, laïkos agonistis, melos tou KKE* (Athens: KKE Central Committee, 1946).
——————— *Ta provlimata kathodigisis sto KKE* (Athens: Poreia, 1978, re-print).
——————— *Syllogi ergon N. Zachariadi* (KKE Central Committee, 1953).
For articles re-printed as pamphlets see heading under ARTICLES)
Zachariadis, Nikos, Karagiorgis, Kostas et. al., *La trahison de Tito envers la Grèce démocratique* (N.P., N.D.).
Zalokostas, Christos, *To chroniko tis sklavias* 2nd ed. (Athens: Estia, N.D.)

ARTICLES

Baerentzen, Lars, 'The demonstration in Syntagma Square on Sunday, 3rd of December, 1944', *Scandinavian Studies in Modern Greek* 2 (1978).
——————— 'The liberation of the Peloponnese' in John O. Iatrides (ed.), *Greece in the 1940s: A nation in crisis* (Hanover: University Press of New England, 1981).
Barker, Elisabeth, 'Greece in the framework of Anglo-Soviet relations 1941-1947' in Marion Sarafis (ed.), *Greece. From Resistance to Civil War* (Nottingham: Spokesman, 1980).
Bartziotas, Vasilis, 'Agonas 33 imeron', *KOMEP* (February, 1945).
——————— 'Ta organotika provlimata tou KKE', *Ib.* (March, 1945).
——————— 'O pallaikos charaktiras tou Dekenvri', *Ib.* (December, 1945).
——————— 'I politiki mas ton stelechon sto KKE ta teleftaia deka chronia', *Neos Kosmos* (September, 1950).
Burks, R.V., 'Statistical profile of the Greek Communist', *Journal of Modern History* 27 (1955).
Fields, Allen D., 'Kolonaki and the others', *Nation,* 164 (29th March, 1947).
Georgiou, Vasos, 'Poioi kai pos mas odigisan ston Emfylio', *Eleftherotypia* (23rd December, 1978).
'Greek Balance Sheet' *New Statesman* and *Nation,* 35: No. 1 (12th June, 1948).
Hajivasiliou, Chrysa, 'Palia provlimata se kainourya fasi', *KOMEP* (February, 1945).
——————— 'Oi ellinides sto Dekemvri', *Ib.* (December, 1945).
Iatrides, John O., 'The Truman Doctrine: The beginning of United States penetration in Greece' in Theodore Couloumbis and Sallie Hicks (ed.), *US Foreign Policy towards Greece and Cyprus. The clash of principle*

and pragmatism (Washington: Center for Mediterranean Studies and the American Hellenic Institute, 1975).

Ioannidis, Yannis, 'Logos tou Y. Ioannidi', *Neos Kosmos* (November-December, 1950).

Kaiser, Robert, 'Churchill-Stalin accord reported on East Europe takeover', *International Herald Tribune* (25th August, 1977).

Karagiorgis, Kostas, 'To elliniko provlima ston pankosmio stivo', *KOMEP* (February, 1945).

——————————— 'Merika viografika stoicheia tou Nikou Zachariadi', *Ib.* (November, 1946).

Karandonis, Dimitrios, 'Episkopisi tis politikis katastasis', *KOMEP* (March, 1945).

Koutoulas, Panayis, 'Mia palia kai nea theoria 'sfaires epirrois kai yperdynameis', *KOMEP* (May, 1975).

League for Democracy in Greece, *Greek News*, Vol. 1 (1946).

Lehrman, Hal, 'Athens calling', *Nation*, 160 (5th May, 1945).

Massingham, Hugh, 'Greece: After the polls', *The Observer* (7th April, 1946).

Mavromatis, Panayotis, 'Omilia pano sto proto thema tis imerisias diataxis', *Neos Kosmos* (April-May, 1957).

Partsalidis, Dimitrios (Mitsos), 'Omilia M. Partsalidi stin 7i olomeleia tis KE tou KKE (14-18.5.1950)', *Neos Kosmos* (August, 1950).

——————————— 'Analytiko simeioma M. Partsalidi (14.2. 1950)'.

Porfyrogenis, Miltiadis, 'Oi omiroi', *KOMEP* (February, 1945).

Poulos, Constantine, 'Rule Britannia', *Nation*, 159 (23rd December, 1944).

——————————— 'Greek Tragedy 1945' *Ib.*, 161 (3rd November, 1945).

——————————— 'The American Observers', *Greek News*, I, No. 3 (May, 1946).

Richter, Heinz, 'O rolos tou G. Papandreou kata tin apeleftherosi', *Anti*, Vol. II, 58-61 (November-December 1976).

——————————— 'Ta praktika tis 'Megalis Syskepsis', Athina 26-27 Dekemvri '44', *Ib.* 61-2 (December 1976-January 1977).

Rodakis, Periklis, 'Giorgis Siantos itan prodotis;', *Tote...* 5 (1983).

Rousos, Petros, 'O ellinikos Dekemvris kai i diethnis thesi tou', *KOMEP* (December, 1945).

——————————— 'Omilia pano sto proto thema tis imerisias diataxis', *Neos Kosmos* (April-May, 1957).

Siantos, Giorgios, (I simasia tis politikos metavolis tis 21.11.45', *KOMEP* (January, 1946).

Smith, Ole L., 'On the beginning of the Greek Civil War', *Scandinavian Studies in Modern Greek*, No. 1 (Copenhagen, 1977).

Sofianopoulos, Ioannis (John), 'Greece needs an all-party Government to

end terrorism', *News Chronicle* (28th July, 1945).
———————————————— 'Why I left UN and returned to Athens', *Ib.* (4th February, 1946).
———————————————— 'Le problème grec', *Politique Etrangère,* 12:4 (September, 1947).
———————————————— 'How to end the Greek tragedy', *Nation,* 167 (25th December, 1948).
———————————————— 'Greece. Prescription for peace', *Ib.* (2nd July, 1949).
Stavrianos, Leften Stavros, 'Greece: The EAM White Book', *Nation,* 161 (15th December, 1945).
———————————————— 'Vacuum in Greece', *New Republic* 113 (24th December, 1945).
Stringos, Leonidas, 'Omilia pano sto proto thema tis imerisias diataxis', *Neos Kosmos* (April-May, 1957).
Thorez, Maurice, 'I ethniki apostoli tou gallikou Kommounistikou Kommatos', *KOMEP* (March, 1945).
Vafiadis, Markos, 'I alitheia ya tin esokommatiki politiki', *Neos Kosmos* (November, 1956).
———————————— 'Omilia pano sto proto thema tis imerisias diataxis', *Ib.* (April-May, 1957).
———————————— 'O Markos Vafiadis apanta sto Mitso Partsalidi ya tin synantisi me ton Stalin, ti Varkiza kai tin katangelia Zachariadi', *Anti,* Vol. II, 53 (4th September, 1976).
———————————— 'Apostoli sta Ouralia', *Epikaira* (16th December, 1976).
Vetas, Fokos, 'Pano stis apofaseis tis 6is plateias olomeleias', *Neos Kosmos* (September, 1956).
Wilkes, Lyall, 'British Missions and Greek Quislings', *New Statesman* and *Nation,* 33:832 (1st February, 1947).
Woodhouse, C.M., 'I elliniki Ethniki Antistasi opos tin ezisa me tous andartes tou EDES kai tou EAM/ELAS, *Akropolis* (11th April-9th June, 1965).
Zachariadis, Nikos, 'Ya tin kommounisitki organosi Thessalonikis', *Kommounistiki Epitheorisi* (October, 1945).
———————————— 'I simerini oikonomiki kai politiki katastasi stin Ellada kai ta provlimata tou dimokratikou kinimatos kai agona', *Rizospastis* (24th February, 1946).
———————————— 'Brosta ston kindyno tis dimokratias', *Ib.* (7th March, 1946).
———————————— 'I katastasi sti notioanatoliki Evropi kai i thesi tis Elladas', *KOMEP* (May, 1946).
———————————— 'Kainourya katastasi, kainourya kathikonta: Oi diapistoseis, i grammi kai oi apofaseis tis 6is olomeleias tis Kentrikis Epitropis tou KKE, 9 tou Octobri 1949' in Zachariadis, *Epilogi Ergon*

(Athens: Protoporos, 1974); published as pamphlet, Nicosia, 1950.
─────────────── 'Deka chronia palis: Symperasmata, didagmata, kathikonta (pros ti syndiaskepsi tou KKE)', *Neos Kosmos* (August-September, 1950), re-printed as pamphlet, 1950.
─────────────── 'Eisigisi stin Triti Syndiaskepsi tou KKE' in *Syllogi ergon N. Zachariadis* (KKE Central Committee, 1953).
─────────────── 'Theseis ya tin istoria tou KKE' in N. Zachariadis, *Epilogi Keimenon* (Athens: Poreia, 1974).
─────────────── 'Provlimata tis krisis tou KKE', *Kokkino Asteri*, 9 (July, 1976).
Zevgos, Yannis, 'I kainourya antikommatiki prospatheia', *KOMEP* (June, 1946).
Zografos, Zisis, 'Merika zitimata tis politikis mas grammis', *Neos Kosmos* (September, 1950).
─────────────── 'Provlimata schetika me to esokommatiko mas kathestos', *Ib.* (December, 1956).

FOREIGN OFFICE & PUBLIC RECORD OFFICE REFERENCE CONCORDANCE

All diplomatic papers arriving at or being despatched from the Foreign Office were registered and filed there on a code system by which the first number indicates the individual file, the second the group of files and the third the country (in this case Greece), *e.g.* R 721/4/19, R 465/1/19. As the content of each file is restricted, it is easy to trace an individual document.

When the F.O. files were transferred to the Public Record Office they were adapted to the PRO filing system: Considerable numbers of F.O. files were now combined in bigger files which, in addition, received a PRO filing number, *e.g.* the F.O. files from R 721/4/19 to R 926/4/19 became PRO F.O. 371-48.246. Each PRO file thus contains several hundred individual documents which complicates the retracing of an individual document.

To simplify this retracing and reference process, the author has adhered to the original F.O. registration system by quoting the F.O. 'R'-system. The following concordance for the F.O. code and PRO code will further simplify reference efforts.

The vast majority of the documents quoted stems from two groups of files, *i.e.* from **PRO F.O.** 371, Southern, *1945,* Greece, File No. 4 and from **PRO F.O.** 371, Southern, *1946,* Greece, File No. 1. Their individual F.O. 'R' code file numbers appear in the left-hand column and their PRO counterparts in the right hand column. At the end of each column there are some special groups of F.O. files and their PRO equivalents, *e.g.* R 6.627/73/19 = PRO 43.706.

PRO F.O. 317, Southern, *1945,* Greece, File No. 4.

F.O. 'R' code			*PRO code*
R	721 –	926	48.246
R	936 –	1.297	48.247
R	1.302 –	1.491	48.248
R	1.524 –	1.782	48.249
R	1.784 –	2.094	48.250
R	2.095 –	2.291	48.251
R	2.304 –	2.543	48.252
R	2.544 –	2.667	48.253

F.O. 'R' code	PRO code
R 2.684 — 2.874	48.254
R 2.882 — 3.198	48.255
R 3.217 — 3.399	48.256
R 3.400 — 3.784	48.257
R 3.804 — 4.185	48.258
R 4.187 — 4.563	48.259
R 4.614 — 4.927	48.260
R 5.024 — 5.359	48.261
R 5.362 — 5.652	48.262
R 5.702 — 5.994	48.263
R 6.063 — 6.477	48.264
R 6.514 — 6.696	48.265
R 6.721 — 6.985	48.266
R 7.018 — 7.597	48.267
R 7.618 — 7.904	48.268
R 7.928 — 8.588	48.269
R 8.600 — 9.299	48.270
R 9.322 — 10.082	48.271
R 10.122 — 10.908	48.272
R 10.915 — 11.378	48.273
R 11.410 — 12.288	48.274
R 12.324 — 12.968	48.275
R 13.007 — 13.691	48.276
R 13.726 — 14.290	48.277
R 14.301 — 14.941	48.278
R 14.970 — 15.679	48.279
R 15.749 — 16.294	48.280
R 16.303 — 16.594	48.281
R 16.619 — 17.191	48.282
R 17.247 — 18.486	48.283
R 18.501 — 19.491	48.284
R 19.512 — 19.895	48.285
R 19.900 — 20.294	48.286
R 20.311 — 20.792	48.287
R 20.809 — 21.278	48.288
R 21.310 — to END	48.289

Special files:
| R 9.722 — 14.520/8.001/19 | 48.419 |
| R 6.627/73/19 | 43.706 |

PRO F.O. 371, Southern, *1946,* Greece, File No. 1.

F.O. 'R' code			PRO code
R	1 —	397	58.667
R	444 —	821	58.668
R	826 —	1.076	58.669
R	1.093 —	1.295	58.670
R	1.307 —	1.512	58.671
R	1.514 —	1.888	58.672
R	1.905 —	2.018	58.673
R	2.019 —	2.316	58.674
R	2.349 —	2.633	58.675
R	2.634 —	3.039	58.676
R	3.042 —	3.456	58.677
R	3.457 —	3.720	58.678
R	3.731 —	4.201	58.679
R	4.219 —	4.542	58.680
R	4.552 —	4.852	58.681
R	4.859 —	5.125	58.682
R	5.126 —	5.277	58.683
R	5.318 —	5.438	58.684
R	5.445 —	5.559	58.685
R	5.561 —	5.962	58.686
R	5.967 —	6.478	58.687
R	6.493 —	6.804	58.688
R	6.871 —	7.071	58.689
R	7.076 —	7.266	58.690
R	7.267 —	7.556	58.691
R	7.571 —	7.878	58.692
R	7.892 —	8.244	58.693

Special files:
R   2.262, 2.263 — 3.873, 3.967/130/19   58.770

VARKIZA AGREEMENT

ARTICLE I. LIBERTIES
The Government will secure in accordance with the Constitution and the democratic principles everywhere recognized, the free expression of the political and social opinions of the citizens, repealing any existing illiberal law. It will also secure the unhindered functioning of individual liberties such as those of assembly, association and expression of views in the Press. More especially, the Government will fully restore trade union liberties.

ARTICLE II. RAISING OF MARTIAL LAW
Martial law will be raised immediately after the signature of the present agreement. Simultaneously with this action there will be brought into force a Constitutional Act similar in all respects to Constitutional Act No. 24, whereby the suspension of those articles of the Constitution to which reference is made in Act 24 shall be permitted.

Articles 5, 10, 20 and 95 of the Constitution shall be suspended forthwith throughout the country. This suspension shall continue until the completion of disarmament, and the establishment of administrative, judicial and military authorities throughout the country. As regards Article 5 in particular, this suspension shall not take effect in the cities of Athens and Piraeus and their suburbs. Especially, however, as regards persons arrested up to the present day it is agreed that Article 5 of the Constitution is not in force, and that they will be liberated, within the shortest possible period of time, the necessary orders to this effect being given to the competent authorities.

Followers of EAM who may be held in captivity by other organizations shall be set free as soon as possible.

ARTICLE III. AMNESTY
There shall be an amnesty for political crimes committed between the 3 December, 1944, and the publication of the law establishing the amnesty. From this amnesty shall be excluded common-law crimes against life and property which were not absolutely necessary to the achievement of the political crime concerned. The necessary law will be published immediately after the signature of the present agreement. From this amnesty will be excluded any person who, being under obligation to surrender their arms

as being members of the organizations of ELAS, the National Civil Guard or ELAN, shall not have handed them over by the 15th March, 1945. This last provision concerning exclusion from the amnesty shall be annulled after verification of the fact that the disarmament of ELAS has been effected, since there will then be no further cause and justification for it. Guarantees and details of the amnesty to be provided are contained in the draft law attached to the present agreement.[1]

ARTICLE IV. HOSTAGES

All civilians who have been arrested by ELAS, or by the National Civil Guard (EP), irrespective of the date on which they were arrested, shall be set at liberty immediately. Any who may be held on the charge of collaboration with the enemy or of commission of any crime shall be handed over to the justice of the State for trial by the competent courses according to law.

ARTICLE V. NATIONAL ARMY

The National Army, apart from the professional officers and NCOs, shall consist of the soldiers of the classes which shall from time to time be called up. Reserve officers, NCOs and other ranks, who have been specially trained in modern weapons, shall remain in service so long as there is a formation requiring them. The Sacred Squadron shall remain as at present, since it is under the immediate orders of the Allied High Command, and shall thereafter be merged in the united National Army in accordance with the above principle. The effort will be made to extend regular conscription to the whole of Greece in accordance with the technical facilities existing and the necessities which may arise. After the demobilization of ELAS, those men who belong to classes which are to be called up shall report for enrolment in the units already existing. All men who have been enrolled in the units now existing without belonging to the classes being called up, shall be discharged. All members of the permanent cadres of the National Army shall be considered by the Councils for which provision is made in Constitutional Act No. VII. The political and social views of citizens serving in the army shall be respected.

ARTICLE VI. DEMOBILISATION

Immediately on the publication of the present agreement the armed forces of resistance shall be demobilised and in particular ELAS, both regular and reserve, ELAN and the National Civil Guard. The demobilisation and surrender of arms shall take place according to the detailed provisions of the protocol drawn up by the Committee of Experts.

The State will settle all questions arising out of requisitioning carried

---

1. Not included here.

out by ELAS. The goods requisitioned by ELAS, including beasts, motor vehicles, etc., which will be handed over to the State according to the detailed provisions of the protocol which has been drawn up, will be regarded thereafter as having been requisitioned by the Greek State.

ARTICLE VII. PURGE OF CIVIL SERVICE
The Government will proceed, by means of committees or councils, to be established by a special law, to the purging of the personnel of the public services, officials of public companies, local Government officials, and those of other services dependent on the State or paid by it. The criteria of which the purge will take account will be either professional competence, or character and personality, or collaboration with the ememy or the utilisation of the official as an instrument of the dictatorship. Officials of the above services who, during the occupation, joined the forces of resistance will return to their positions and will be considered in the same manner as other officials. The above-mentioned councils will also consider the cases of officials who have taken part or collaborated in the manifestations which have taken place between the 3rd December, 1944, and the date of signature of the present agreement. Those of them who are found to have been concerned may be placed at the disposal of the State as provided by law. The final disposal of such officials will be decided by the Government which shall result from the elections to the Constituent Assembly. Officials who have already been placed *en disponibilité* by decisions of the ministers, will be submitted to the decision of the council above mentioned. No official will be dismissed solely on account of his political opinion.

ARTICLE VIII. PURGE OF SECURITY SERVICES
The purge of the Security Services, the Gendarmerie and the City Police will be carried out as soon as possible by the special purge committee on the same basis as the purge of the civil service. All officers and other ranks of the above corps who fall under the provisions of the Amnesty Law, who during the period of the occupation joined the ranks of ELAS, ELAN, or the National Civil Guard, will return to their positions and will be considered by the purge councils in the same manner as the rest of their colleagues. All the officers and other ranks of the above corps who left their positions between the 3 December, 1944, and the date of signature of the present document shall be placed *en disponibilité,* their final disposal of the councils to be constituted by the Government arising from the elections.

ARTICLE IX. PLEBISCITE AND ELECTIONS
At the earliest possible date, and in any case within the current year, there shall be conducted in complete freedom, and with every care for

its genuineness, a plebiscite which shall finally decide on the Constitutional question, all points being submitted to the decision of the people. Thereafter shall follow as quickly as possible elections to a Constituent Assembly for the drafting of the new Constitution of the country. The representatives of both sides agree that for the verification of the genuineness of the expression of the popular will the great Allied Powers shall be requested to send observers.

Of this present agreement two identical copies have been made, whereof the one has been received by the Government Delegation and the other by the Delegation of EAM.

In Athens, at the Ministry of Foreign Affairs, 12 February, 1945.

Signed: I. SOPHIANOPOULOS   G. SIANTOS
         P. RALLIS   D. PARTSALIDHIS
         I. MAKROPOULOS   E. TSIRIMOKOS
         for the Hellenic Government   for the Central Committee of EAM

(reprinted from C.M. Woodhouse, *Apple of Discord*, pp. 308-10)

INDEX OF PROPER NAMES

(footnote references are given only where they contribute information; footnotes which are simply source references are not included)

Acheson, Dean 215, 216, 359, 361
Acland, Sir Richard 22-5
Agnidis, Athanasios 193, 389, 393, 394, 398, 400, 472
Alanbrooke, Viscount 294
Alexander, George 285, n. 148, 492 n. 9
Alexander, Field-Marshal Lord 1, 3-7, 49, 50, 64, 65, 79, 89-91, 149, 158, 319 n.19
Alexandris, Apostolos 89, 104 n. 39, 183, 224, 374, 385 n. 160; 403 n. 14; 452, 520-1, 540 n. 9
Alexandris, Georgios 121 n. 3
Alexandris, Konstantinos 318 n. 3
Alianos, M. 540 n. 9
Altenburg, Günther 98
Anastasiadis, Stergios 277, 280 n. 50; 284 n. 116
Angelopoulos, Angelos 25, 160
Antonios, Bishop of Elis 160
Antonopoulos, Achillefs 454, 540 n. 9
Antypas 130
Arabatzis, Nikos 353, 525
Archer, Laird 205
Argyropoulos, P.I. 385 n. 160
Askoutsis, Nikolaos 170 n. 63; 246
Athanasiadis, Bodosakis 110, 208
Athanasiadis-Novas, Georgios 309
Athinellis 7
Attlee, Clement 162, 182, 263-4, 265, 295, 298, 402
Averoff-Tositsas, Evangelos 476 n. 68; 478
Avraam, N. 540 n. 9
Avramidis, Christos 157
Avyeropoulos, Gerasimos 156

Baelen 2, 222, 223
Bagnall, George 351, 352-4, 382 n. 97
Bakirjis, Evripidis 84, 156
Bakos, Georgios 141-2
Bakos, K. 170 n. 59

Bakoyannis, D. 141-3, 170 n. 59; 171 n. 72
Balanos, Dimitrios 120 n. 2
Balfour, David 320 n. s, 45, 57
Baltatzis-Mavrokordatos, N. 540 n. 9
Barker, Dudley 441
Barnes, Tom 299
Barry, Gerald 18 n. 34; 27, 28, 30
Bartlett, Vernon 442
Bartziotas, Vasilis 240-1, 245, 249, 262, 266-7, 269, 277, 280 n. 50; 284 n. 116; 488, 491, 494 n. 54; 507, 509, 527, 530
Belingratis 150
Bevan, Aneurin 24, 26
Bevin, Ernest 163-5, 176 n. 150; 180, 184-90, 193-7, 198 n. 35; 207, 216-7, 226, 231, 232-3, 264-5, 295, 298, 300, 305-7, 312-7, 327-8, 336-7, 343-4, 355-6, 358, 364, 365, 289-90, 396, 397-9, 400-2, 405, 408-17, 419, 426, 427, 429, 432-7, 449, 450, 470, 472, 503-4, 519-21, 538-9
Bidault, Georges 196-7, 401
Bitsanis, General 173 n. 94
Blanas, Giorgis (Kissavos) 242, 244-5, 276, 277, 486, 488, 530
Board, Sir Vivian 359, 362, 364
Bourandas 170 n. 65
Bourdaras, Georgios 321 n. 82; 431
Buckley, Christopher 442
Byrnes, James F. 186, 190, 194, 196-7, 207, 213, 216-7, 295, 298-9, 333, 363, 365, 435

Caccia, Harold 52, 80, 110, 152, 155, 179-82, 184, 186, 189, 190, 192-3, 195, 205, 214, 258
Cadogan, Sir Alexander 79, 91, 115, 204, 393
Chandler, Geoffrey 509

Chatziskos, Dimitrios 99
Chavinis, Theodoros 309, 317
Chelmis, Dimitrios 105 n. 39; 539 n. 9
Chiang Kai-Shek 241
Chronaios 149-50
Chrysanthopoulos, K. 167 n. 17
Chrysanthos, Archbishop 407
Churchill, Sir Winston vii-ix, xi, xii n. 7; 1-3, 19 n. 58; 22-7, 29, 30, 39, 41-2, 64-6, 79, 90-3, 96, 102 n. 1; 106 n. 84; 114-9, 120, 142, 153, 162, 166, 180, 186-7, 189, 202-4, 232, 243, 244, 260, 264, 314-5, 432, 443, 460-1, 472, 537-8
Citrine, Sir Walter 25, 27-30, 39-42, 45 n. 44; 46 n. 58; 128-30, 353, 355, 398-9
Clark, General 367, 531
Cocks, F. Seymour 189, 399, 439 n. 72
Crawford, Lt.-General 531
Cromer, Lord 91, 423

Damaskinos, Archbishop xi, 1-4, 6, 11, 14, 27-8, 49-53, 54 n. 1; 63-7, 81, 87-97, 99-100, 101, 103 n. 18; 105 n. 51; 106 n. 66; 109-10, 113-6, 126, 141, 154-5, 162-4, 176 n. s; 146, 150; 178-80, 181-2, 184-6, 190-5, 196-7, 199 n. 38; 214-5, 221-5, 229-232, 263, 272, 291-4, 297, 300, 305-13, 314, 329-30, 343, 371-4, 390, 393, 395-6, 405-10, 417, 427, 430-1, 434, 437 n. 3; 458, 462, 468-9, 472, 519, 531
Davidson 320 n. s 45, 57
De Gaulle, General 197
Delmer, Sefton 441
Delmouzos, Andreas 170 n. 63
Demestichas, G. 141, 170 n. 59; 171 n. 72
Dendramanis, Vasilios 199 n. 37; 221
Despotopoulos, Konstantinos 247
Dialetis, Dimitrios 170 n. 59, 171 n. 72
Diamantopoulos, Symeon 213, 216, 333
Dimitrakopoulos, Anargyros 120 n. 2; 199 n. 37; 229
Dimitratos, Aristidis 36-7, 39, 128-9
Dimitriou, G. 349, 353
Dimitroff, Georgi 65, 464
Doganis, Theodoros 471
Dragoumis, F. 403 n. 14; 540 n. 9
Drakos, Markos 121 n. 3; 178
Dromazos, Georgios 329

Edelman, Maurice 399
Eden, Sir Anthony viii, 1, 23-5, 27, 52, 65-6, 79, 81, 83-4, 89, 91, 92, 98, 100, 103 n. 18; 114-5, 116, 118, 150, 180, 181, 188-91, 203-4, 232, 254, 314, 317
Efstathopoulos, Konstantinos 454
Eftaxias, L. 540 n. 9
Eisenhower, General 143
Eleftheriou, Leftheris 485, 510-1
Eudes, Dominique 235, 475 n. 30; 478, 507, 516 n. 57
Evelpidis, Chrysos 309, 317
Evert, Angelos 5, 160
Evripaios, Petros 321 n. 82
Exindaris, Georgios 231, 320 n. 60; 392, 394

Faringdon, Lord 439 n. 72
Feather, Victor 128, 132, 348
Fodor, M.W. 44 n. 30
Foot, Michael 189
Forrestal, James 474
Fosteridis, Antonios (Tsaous Andon) 151
Fowle, Farnsworth 44 n. 30
Frazer, Peter 433

Gale, Sir Humfrey 292-5, 297
Gavriilidis, Kostas 51-3, 55 n. 17; 183, 281 n. 58; 284 n. 113; 320 n. 60; 433, 462, 501
Georgakis, Ioannis 110, 317-8, 431-2
Georgalas, Georgios 51-3, 55 n. 17; 160, 183, 281 n. 58; 461, 463, 466
George II x, xi, 1, 3, 36, 96, 97, 106 n. 84; 113, 119, 151, 177, 189, 193-4, 196-7, 199 n. 38; 226, 228, 229, 258, 309, 313-8, 321 n. 90; 322 n. s 91, 92; 323, 379 n. 6; 418, 424, 428, 462, 536
George VI 424
Georgiou, Vasos 126, 485, 508, 514 n. 10
Georgoulis, Spyridon 290, 318 n. 3; 328-9
Gerakinis, Christos 174 n. 109
Gerondas, Agesilaos 171 n. 72
Gikas, Solon 85
Gini, Eirini 525
Glavanis, Ioannis 17 n. 6
Glezos, Manolis 172 n. 87
Goebbels, Josef 188

INDEX OF PROPER NAMES

Gonatas, Stylianos 50, 55 n. 11; 84, 95–6, 98, 107 n. 104; 141, 182, 224, 333, 374, 383 n. 160; 403 n. 14; 452, 520–1, 540 n. 9
Gotzamanis, G. 438 n. 36
Gounarakis, Petros 189, 199 n. 37
Gousias *see* Ventitsos-Gousias
Gousidis, Dimitris 508
Gowran, Clay 44 n. 30
Grady, Henry F. 325, 330–2, 434–5
Grapsas, Konstantinos 170 n. 64
Greenwood, Arthur 24, 26, 399
Grew, Joseph G. 213
Grigorakis, Ioannis 170 n. 59; 171 n. 72
Grigoriadis, Foivos 478, 502–3, 507–8
Grigoriadis, Neokosmos 266, 281 n. 58; 284 n. 133; 463, 497, 502–4
Grivas, George 10, 147, 167 n. 7; 376, 378, 469
Gromyko, Andrei 387, 466, 497
Grove, Edward 359, 362, 364

Hajibeis, Stamatis 281 n. 58; 433, 467, 472, 501, 502–3
Hajidimitriou, Simos 37–41, 47 n. 69; 128–32, 138, 168 n. 30; 169 n. 36; 350
Hajikyriakos, A. 385 n. 160
Hajimichalis, Platonos 170 n. 59; 171 n. 72
Hajipanos, Panos 539 n. 9
Hajis, Thanasis 483, 515 n. 20
Hajivasiliou, Chrysa 240, 242, 245, 277, 280 n. s 41, 50, 55; 284 n. 116; 483, 489, 494 n. 54; 498, 500, 504
Halifax, Lord 152, 363, 435
Hallsworth, Sir Joseph 356
Hammond, Nicholas 299
Harriman, Averell xii n. 7
Harrison, Joseph 44 n. 30
Hayter, William 115, 116, 118, 192, 194, 203, 247, 295, 298, 320 n. 45; 328, 412, 418–9, 425, 524
Henderson, Loy 298–9
Henderson, Mr. & Mrs. 43 n. 22
Hill, Henry 350–2
Hill, Sir Quintin 110, 205, 296–7, 320 n. 45; 357
Hitler, Adolf 61, 98, 296, 491, 524
Hoare, Geoffrey 373
Hogg, Quintin (Lord Hailsham) 24
Hopkins, Harry xii n. 7
Hoskins, Harold B. 207, 217

Hourmouzios, Stelios 42
Howard, D.F. 98, 115, 116, 118, 203
Hoxha, Enver 299

Iasonidis, A. 309
Ingraham, Reg 44 n. 30
Ioannidis, Yannis 5, 236, 239–40, 242, 245, 247, 266–72, 276, 277, 280 n. 50; 284 n. 116; 486–7, 491, 494 n. 54; 497, 502, 504, 508, 526–7
Ismay, Hastings viii

Jackson, Commander 217, 292–5, 298
Janssen, Guthrie 44 n. 30
Joachim, Bishop of Kozani 160
Jouhaux, Léon 525

Kafandaris, Georgios 88, 93, 97, 113, 162, 178, 180, 182, 222, 224, 227, 229, 308, 317–8, 320 n. 60; 325, 330–2, 334, 403 n. 14; 407, 410, 413, 415–7, 429, 431–2, 438 n. 36; 468, 501, 505
Kaklamanos, D. 89, 90
Kalantzakos, A. 540 n. 9
Kalkandis 150
Kallergis 326
Kallias, Konstantinos 318 n. 3
Kallidopoulos 502
Kalomoiris, Ioannis 26–7, 34–5, 37, 39, 51, 128–37, 347–51, 353, 355
Kalyvas, N. 128–9, 167 n. 14; 170 n. 59
Kambas, Konstantinos 121 n. 3
Kanakousakis, E. 170 n. 59; 171 n. 72
Kanellopoulos, Panayotis 81, 86, 100, 140, 183, 232, 289–92, 294, 297, 299–302, 304–5, 307–12, 318 n. 3; 332, 358, 372, 374, 385 n. 160; 403 n. 14; 407, 414–6, 430, 441, 450, 453, 461–2, 520, 531
Karagiorgis, Kostas 236, 240, 242–3, 246, 250, 278 n. s 5, 6; 279 n. 24; 281 n. 67; 461, 471, 494 n. 54; 501, 504
Karamanlis, Konstantinos 37
Karandasis, Tryfon 121 n. 3
Karapanos, V. 170 n. 59; 171 n. 72
Karayannis, Georgios 85
Kardaras 198
Kartalis, Georgios 167 n. 11; 183–4, 309, 311, 323, 334–5, 345, 357, 362–4, 368, 372, 284 n. 135; 391, 404, 414, 417, 429, 431–2, 505

Karvounis, Nikos 463
Kasimatis, Grigorios 121 n. s 2, 3; 199 n. 37; 290, 292, 295-7, 302-5, 318 n. 3; 361-2
Katavolos, Dimitrios 318 n. 3
Katsimitros, Charalambos 141
Katsimitros, G. 170 n. 59; 171 n. 72
Katsotas, Pavsanias 5, 86, 290, 318 n. 3
Katsoulis, Giorgis 482
Kazantzakis, Nikos 317, 321 n. 82; 345, 467
Kessel, Dimitri 44 n. 30
Kikitsas, Georgios 494 n. 57; 507, 508, 512-3, 516 n. 56
Kirk, Alexander C. 121 n. 11; 295
Kissavos see Blanas, Giorgis
Kitsikis, Nikolaos 160
Klaras, Babis 255
Klaras, Thanasis see Velouchiotis, Aris
Kohler, Foy D. 106 n. 64; 330, 332
Kokkalis, Petros 160
Kolko, Gabriel viii
Kollias, Konstantinos 258
Kolyvas, Nikolaos 17 n. 6; 138, 140
Kondostanos, G. 174 n. 109
Kondylis, Georgios 326
Kosavras 244
Kostopoulos, K. 344
Kostov, Traicho 65
Kotzamanis, S. 143, 170 n. 59
Kouloumbis 130
Koundouriotis, Th. 17 n. 6
Kousoulas, D. George 60, 68 n. 7; 239, 464, 478, 509
Koutsomitopoulos, Petros 17 n. 6; 121 n. 3; 199 n. 37
Kouzentzis 130, 347
Kritikas, S. 183, 281 n. 58; 320 n. 60; 433, 467, 501
Kritikos 148
Kritsas 347
Krokos 26, 39
Kypriadis, Epaminondas 318 n. 3
Kyriakopoulos, Vasilios 162, 165, 199 n. 37
Kyrkos, Michail 183, 281 n. 58; 284 n. 133; 433, 467, 501
Kyrou, Achillefs 170 n. 63

Lambou 144, 308
Lambrianidis 86
Lambrinopoulos, Georgios 121 n. 2; 199 n. 37

Lancaster, Osbert 44 n. 30
Laparre, Arnaud 330
Lascelles 215, 320 n. 45; 429-32
Laskaris 26, 134-5, 347, 349
Laskey, Denys 91, 98, 192, 364, 394
Laski, Harold 23, 26, 187, 265
Lavrentiev 497
Lazanas, G. 540 n. 9
Leeper, Sir Reginald 1, 2, 4, 5, 10, 12, 15, 19 n. 61; 21-30, 39-41, 43 n. 22; 49-50, 52-3, 63-8, 79, 81, 87-97, 99-101, 103 n. 18; 106 n. 66; 109-19, 125-6, 140-1, 152-5, 157, 162, 164-6, 185, 192-3, 196-7, 202, 205, 211, 215, 221-32, 246-7, 253, 254, 289, 291-2, 295, 300, 305-12, 313, 315, 317, 320 n. s 45, 57; 324-5, 327, 334-6, 343, 357-8, 362-6, 370-6, 378, 390-1, 393-6, 405-10, 413-7, 419, 421, 424-5, 427-30, 461, 462, 473, 509, 538
Lehman, Herbert 207, 217, 292-3
Lehrman, Hal 152, 157
Lenin 73, 490
Levy, Benn 439 n. 72
Liosis, Evstathios 157, 258
Livieratos, Antonios 170 n. 59; 171 n. 72
Logothetopoulos, Konstantinos 138, 143-4, 170 n. 59
Loulakakis, Emmanouil 170 n. 59; 171 n. 72
Loules, Kostas 244
Loulis, Alkiviadis 183, 281 n. 58; 320 n. 60; 462, 463, 497
Louvaris, Nikolaos 141, 170 n. 59; 171 n. 72
Lumby, Christopher 117
Lunet 351, 353-4
Lychnos, Gerasimos 503
Lyttelton, Oliver 203

Maben, Buell F. 205-6, 216 n. 24; 364, 531
Machairopoulos, Christos 349
Machas, Dimitrios 199 n. 37, 309
Mackenzie, Sir Compton 41, 42, 439 n. 72
Macmillan, Harold 1-2, 4-8, 21, 49-53, 57, 59-60, 63-7, 79-81, 89-95, 101, 109-11, 115, 117, 119-20, 165-6, 205
McNeil, Hector 231, 295-6, 298, 299-

INDEX OF PROPER NAMES

312, 317, 320 n. s 45, 57; 357-8, 362, 364, 369-70, 407, 412, 419, 425, 461-2, 465-6, 468
McNeill, William Hardy 127, 145, 289-90, 509
MacVeagh, Lincoln 2, 43 n. 30; 110, 115, 180, 182, 190-3, 202, 205-7, 209, 213, 215-6, 222-5, 295, 297-8, 301-2, 305, 312-3, 357-67, 434
Mainwaring, Brigadier 7-9, 12-3, 17 n. 23; 66
Makin, Norman 402
Makridis, Theodoros 7-8, 277, 486-8
Makris, Fotis 37, 38-9, 132-8, 169 n. s 36, 37; 347-56, 382 n. 80; 524-5
Makropoulos, Ioannis 51, 87
Malamidas, Efstathios 321 n. 82
Maloney, Henry J. 330
Mandakas, Emmanouil 156
Manetas, Konstantinos 95
Manetas, Theodoros 309, 317, 324-6, 328-9, 345
Mangakis, Giorgios V. 318 n. 3
Manganas 377, 385 n. 189; 429, 442, 521, 524-5, 538
Maniadakis, Konstantinos 154, 249, 299
Manousis, Nikolaos 321 n. 82; 347
Mantzavinos, Georgios 120 n. 2; 199 n. 37; 211, 214-5, 319 n. 10
Mao Tse Tung 489, 490, 491
Marangos, G. 284 n. 133
Mariolis, Dimitrios 27, 39, 51, 349
Markezinis, Spyros 96
Markos see Vafiadis, Markos
Markou, N. 170 n. 59; 171 n. 72
Mastroyannakos, S. 167 n. 17; 346, 349, 353, 354
Matesis, Spyridon 120 n. 2; 199 n. 37
Matorikos, P. 349
Matthews, Major 80
Mavrikis, Panos 214
Mavrogordatos, Michail 17 n. 6
Mavromatis, Panayotis 483, 485
Mavromichalis, Petros 180, 182, 224, 320 n. 60; 374, 385 n. 160; 452, 519, 520, 539 n. 9
Mavros, Georgios 161, 321 n. 82; 335, 381 n. 58
Maximos, Dimitrios 105 n. 39; 113, 140, 403 n. 14
Melas, Giorgios 17 n. 6; 320 n. 60; 403 n. 14
Mercouris, Stamatis 162, 307, 309, 317,

320 n. 60; 327-8, 330, 409-10, 413, 415, 429, 431
Merenditis, Alexandros 158, 190, 199 n. 37; 221-3, 309
Metaxas, Ioannis 10, 36, 37, 38, 39, 40, 54, 57, 58, 70 n. 36; 84, 86, 87, 120, 125, 126, 129, 130, 131, 132, 134, 138, 147, 154, 156, 159, 160, 177, 231, 236, 238, 255-6, 268, 289, 290, 291, 316, 341, 343, 407, 438 n. 36; 445, 458, 522, 523, 527, 537
Metaxas, Pierre 97, 107 n. 92
Meynaud, Jean 449, 455
Mikoyan, Anastas 203
Millington, Ernest 187
Mitropoulos 150
Moatsos, Ioannis 107 n. 92
Molotov, Vyecheslav viii, 179, 186, 498, 510
Morgan, General William 294-5, 319 n. s 19, 20; 326, 329
Morphopoulos, Panos 44, n. 30
Mousterakis, Yannis 513
Moutousis, Sotirios 170 n. 59; 171 n. 72
Mylonas, Alexandros 106 n. 86; 162, 170 n. 63; 178, 224, 227, 229, 309, 311, 320 n. 60; 357, 359, 362, 429, 431-2, 438 n. 36; 453, 527

Nefeloudis, Pavlos 237, 249, 488, 498
Nefeloudis, Vasilis 246, 347, 349
Nelson, Donald 203-4
Neubacher, Herrmann 296, 304
Neyman, Jerzy 444
Nikolaïdis 131
Nikoloudis, Theologos 291
Nixon, J. 19 n. 40; 531
Noble 377
Noel-Baker, Francis 298
Noel-Baker, Philip 163-4, 193, 194-6, 230, 233, 320 n. 45; 328, 380 n. 20; 393, 425-6, 465
Norton, Sir Clifford 419, 436, 503, 519-20, 523, 540 n. 18

O'Ballance, Edgar 464, 478, 509
Oikonomopoulos, Grigorios 318 n. 3
Oikonomou, G. 183, 281 n. 58; 433, 462, 501
Oikonomou G. (Major) 174 n. 109
Oikonomou G.N. 199 n. 37
Oikonomou, Rear-Admiral 141, 171

n. 65
Orr, Major 148
Othonaios, Alexandros 86, 91, 104 n. 22; 105 n. 51; 272, 376, 416, 469, 475 n. 57; 502
Outrillo 320 n. 61

Pamboukas, Georgios 170 n. 59; 453
Panagakos 141, 170 n. 65
Pangalos, Theodoros 34
Panos 507, 508
Papadaki, Eleni 45 n. 52
Papadakis 142-3
Papadimitriou, D. 540 n. 9
Papadimos, A. 540 n. 9
Papadongonas 156, 158, 344
Papadopoulos, Georgios 104 n. 28; 170 n. 63
Papadopoulos, I. 170 n. 59; 171 n. 72
Papadopoulos (nomarch) 149-50
Papadopoulos (officer) 141
Papaligouras, Panayotis 318 n. 3
Papanastasiou, Alexandros 110, 416, 438 n. 36
Papandreou, George 2-3, 39, 46 n. 67; 54, 59, 85, 95, 100, 106 n. s 74, 89; 138-9, 141, 145, 160, 170 n. 63; 177, 183, 190, 222, 243, 289, 291, 297, 306, 308-12, 320 n. 60; 332, 372-3, 377, 385 n. 160; 403 n. 14; 407, 414-7, 427, 430, 441, 450, 453, 491, 501, 504, 520-1, 531
Papanikolaou 150
Papapolitis, Savvas 66
Papapolyzos, Dimitrios 454
Paparigas, Dimitrios 353, 525
Papastamatiadis, Nikolaos 160, 175 n. 126
Papathanasis, Athanasios 540 n. 9
Pappas, G. 431-2
Pappou (Capetan Tzavellas) 507
Papworth, A.F. 128, 132, 211, 356
Paraskevopoulos, Ioannis 121 n. 3; 199 n. 37; 214, 215
Paravantis, G. 540 n. 9
Partsalidis, Dimitrios (Mitsos) 5, 7, 51-3, 55 n. 17; 64, 71-3, 74-5, 77, 92, 94, 126, 235, 242-3, 245, 247, 263, 269, 271, 272-5, 277, 280 n. 50; 284 n. s 116, 133; 320 n. 60; 369-70, 433, 462, 463, 483, 485, 489-90, 497-502, 504, 509, 510-1, 513 n. 10; 514 n. s 11, 17, 20

Passadakis, I. 170 n. 59; 171 n. 72
Passalidis, Ioannis 266, 281 n. 58; 349
Patatzis, Sotiris 390, 396
Pavlakis, Panayotis 134, 141
Pavlopoulos, Athanasios 239, 478
Peck 155
Peltekis, Ioannis 312, 317, 321 n. 82; 382 n. 74; 427-9, 501
Perrotis, A. 540 n. 9
Pesmazoglou, Michail 121 n. 3
Petimezas, Iraklis 312, 321 n. 92; 427, 429, 501
Petrov 497-8
Petsopoulos, Yannis 528
Piniatoglou, L. 170 n. 63; 221
Pipinellis, Panayotis 229
Pistolakis, Stelios 107 n. 92
Plastiras, Nikolaos 1, 2, 4, 6-7, 16 n. 6; 19 n. 61; 21, 49-50, 55 n. 11; 59-60, 66, 81, 86-99, 100-2, 103 n. 18, 104 n. 30; 106 n. s 64, 66; 107 n. s 90, 92, 98, 99, 105; 109, 110, 113-7, 121 n. 6; 126-7, 141, 145, 162, 177-8, 180-2, 229, 237, 266, 297, 316, 328, 403 n. 14; 426
Ploumbidis, Nikos 280 n. 50; 284 n. 116
Politis, Ioannis 199 n. 37; 403 n. 14
Polydoropoulos, M. 349
Polyzos, D. 170 n. 59; 171 n. 72
Popov, Grigori 2, 65
Porfyrogenis, Miltiadis 5, 38-40, 51, 53, 55 n. 17; 126, 162, 240, 253, 468, 502
Poulitsas, P. 104 n. 39; 520-1
Poulos, 342, 344
Poulos, Constantine 44 n. 30; 201, 209, 443-4
Pournaras, K. 170 n. 59; 171 n. 72
Proïmakis, Manolis 281 n. 58; 468
Psarros, Charalambos 318 n. 3
Psarros, Dimitrios 75, 78 n. 9; 84, 290
Psiarris, General 160
Pyromaglou, Komninos 28-9, 141, 183, 380 n. 32
Pyrounakis, G. 170 n. 59

Rallis, Ioannis 45 n. 52; 97-9, 107 n. 101; 138-9, 141-3, 156, 170 n. 59; 438 n. 36
Rallis, Periklis 50, 51, 63, 66, 87-8, 104 n. 30
Rallis, Petros 17 n. 6; 91
Rangavis, Alexandros 170 n. 59; 171

… n. 72
Rankin, 296, 434-5
Rapp 21-2, 25, 173 n. 94
Rawlins, General 221, 324, 326-9, 379 n. 6; 531
Rendis, Konstantinos 162, 309, 317, 320 n. 60; 327, 330, 334-6, 344, 395, 403 n. 14; 408-10, 412-3, 415, 426
Renzies, I. 167 n. 17
Roberts, W. 439 n. 72
Robertson, General 69 n. 25
Rodionov, Konstantin 372, 464
Rodokanakis 170 n. s 64, 65
Roosevelt, Franklin D. viii, xii n. 7; 114-5, 202-5
Roper, James 44 n. 30
Rosenberg, Alfred 317
Rousopoulos, Athanasios 170 n. 59; 171 n. 72
Rousos, Petros 245, 264, 277, 280 n. 50; 284 n. 116; 458, 466, 483

Saillant, Louis 348, 350-2
Sakellariou, Alexandros 385 n. 160; 452
Sakellaropoulos, Loukas 17 n. 6
Salusbury, F.H. 78 n. 10
Sandas, Apostolos (Lakis) 172 n. 87
Sarafis, Marion 29
Sarafis, Stefanos 52, 70 n. 36; 84, 85, 156, 160, 175 n. 126; 236, 278 n. 9; 493 n. 27
Sargent, Sir Orme 91, 97, 115, 116-8, 180, 181, 192, 193, 203, 315, 364, 389, 412-3, 415, 419, 421, 425
Saukel 37
Sbarounis-Trikorfos, Nikolaos 120 n. 2; 121 n. 3; 171 n. 63
Schimana 462
Scobie, Lt.-General Sir Ronald vii, 3, 4, 5, 6, 7, 8, 12, 18 n. 29; 19 n. s 40, 61; 27, 30, 43 n. 30; 64, 79, 80, 83, 86, 102 n. 4; 106 n. 65; 109, 110, 202, 203, 206, 329, 430, 461
Sedgwick, A.C. 30, 44 n. 30; 45 n. 56
Sedgwick, Roxane 30, 41, 45 n. 56
Seferiadis (George Seferis) 105 n. 51; 290, 305, 320 n. 57
Sheppard, A.W. 153, 155, 173 n. s 98, 105; 324
Siantos, George 5, 39, 52, 53, 58, 60, 62, 63-4, 65, 66, 67, 68, 69 n. 18; 72, 73, 76, 77, 92, 94, 126, 183, 235-6, 238, 240-2, 245, 246-7, 250, 255, 256, 266, 271, 277, 278 n. 7; 279 n. 27; 280 n. s 50, 55; 284 n. 116; 391, 461, 467, 468, 483, 488-90, 494 n. 54; 498, 500, 502-4, 528, 529
Sideris, Georgios 17 n. 6; 39, 40, 41, 81, 96, 103 n. 18; 129, 130
Smallwood, Major-General 110, 111, 146, 157, 171 n. 81; 174 n. 108; 181
Smith, Ole L. 478, 509
Smith-Dorien, Brigadier 80
Sklavainas, Stylianos 385 n. 163
Sofianopoulos, Ioannis (John) 4, 5, 16 n. 6; 50-3, 57-60, 62-6, 68, 77, 78 n. 2; 81, 87-90, 91, 96, 101, 105 n. 51; 107 n. 102; 116, 121 n. 3; 138, 170 n. 56; 178-80, 183, 250, 308, 317, 318, 320 n. 60; 323, 327, 330, 332, 333, 334-6, 344-5, 372, 389-96, 399, 400, 402, 413, 417, 426, 433, 467, 470, 501-2, 504, 531
Sofoulis, Themistoklis 92, 94, 97, 100, 113, 139, 158, 162, 178, 180-2, 222, 224, 227, 229, 266, 307-13, 317, 318, 320 n. 6; 323-36, 341, 343, 345, 369-74, 376, 377, 385 n. 163; 390, 392-6, 403 n. 14; 405, 470-10, 412-8, 426, 427-32, 434-6, 438 n. 36; 441-2, 450, 453, 457, 462-3, 465, 467, 468-9, 501, 503, 519, 521, 522, 531, 538
Solaro, Antonio 478
Soliotis, Sotirios 121 n. 3
Someritis, Stratis 161
Sourlas, Grigorios 151, 254, 375, 400, 521, 532
Spaïs, Leonidas 17 n. 6; 66, 70 n. 36
Spanopoulos, Andreas 157
Spencer, Floyd A. 509
Spiliotopoulos, Panayotis 86, 104 n. 26; 141-2, 158
Sprigge, Sylvia 265
Spyridon, Bishop of Yannina 141, 142, 160
Stalin, Josef, viii, xii n. 7; 2, 65, 71, 79, 102 n. 1; 162, 204, 240, 372, 398, 464, 467, 473-4, 477, 484, 490, 492 n. 2; 498-9, 510-1, 514 n. 12; 536
Stavrianos, L.S. 11
Stavropoulos, S. 349
Stavrou, Nikolaos 85

Stefanakis, Georgios 134
Stefanopoulos, D. 540 n. 9
Stefanopoulos, Stefanos 182, 224, 311, 320 n. 60; 385 n. 160; 519, 520, 539 n. 9
Stettinius, Edward R. 110, 115, 399, 401-2
Stowe, Leland 44 n. 30
Stratis, Dimitrios 22, 27, 35, 37-8, 39, 51-3, 59, 66, 128-9, 132-4, 136-7, 246, 346-53, 525
Stratos, Andreas 540 n. 9
Stratos, G. 170 n. 64; 438 n. 36
Stringos, Leonidas 271, 272, 277, 280 n. 50; 284 n. 116; 483, 485, 508, 530
Svolos, Alexandros 5, 22, 51, 55 n. 17; 59, 160, 170 n. 63; 177, 183, 224, 227, 229, 246, 391, 395, 426, 433, 502
Symeonidis, V. 170 n. 59

Tavoularis, A. 170 n. 59; 171 n. 72
Tavoularis, Major 174 n. 109
Tempo *see* Vukmanović, Svetozar
Tewson, Vincent 42, 128-32, 167 n. 17; 382 n. 92
Thälmann, Ernst 251
Thanasekos, Georgios 183
Theodorakopoulos, Ioannis 318 n. 3
Theopoulos 347
Theos, Kostas 26, 27, 34, 37, 39, 51, 128-30, 132-7, 347-9, 353, 382 n. 80; 525
Theotokis, Ioannis 141, 182, 222, 224, 374, 403 n. 14; 438 n. 36; 452, 519, 520, 539 n. 9
Theotokis, Spyridon 523, 524, 529, 540 n. 9
Thorez, Maurice 76, 241, 509
Tito, Josip Broz ix, x, 65, 73, 248, 396, 489-91, 509-12, 515 n. 20
Togliatti, Palmiro 509
Tourkovasilis, Theodoros 438 n. 36; 453
Triantafyllopoulos, Konstantinos 91, 105 n. 51; 170 n. 63
Truman, Harry S. 115, 162, 213, 295, 299, 361-2
Tsakos, A. 130
Tsaldaris, Konstantinos 99, 104 n. 39; 177, 180, 182, 224, 311, 320 n. 60; 369, 371-2, 374, 385 n. 160; 410, 441, 452, 519-21, 524, 529, 531, 539, 539 n. 9
Tsaldaris, Panayotis 35, 95, 177
Tsambasis 150
Tsantis, Michalis 485, 486-7, 495 n. 58
Tsaous Andon *see* Fosteridis, Antonios
Tsatsos, Konstantinos 91, 105 n. 51; 109, 119, 121 n. s 2, 3; 127, 162, 172 n. 87, 178, 181, 183, 186, 240-2, 290, 292, 308, 310, 318 n. 3
Tsatsos, Themistoklis 91, 105 n. 51; 138-9, 291, 373, 520
Tsatsou, Ioanna 105 n. 51; 290
Tsigantes, Ioannis 85
Tsiklitiras 160-1, 175 n. 126
Tsirigotis, L. 170 n. 59; 171 n. 72
Tsirimokos, Ilias 5, 22, 43 n. 10; 51-4, 55 n. s 17, 32; 58, 59, 60, 63-6, 77, 94, 126, 177, 183, 227, 235, 246, 320 n. 60; 467, 501, 531
Tsironikos, S. 143, 144, 170 n. 59
Tsolakoglou, Georgios 138, 141, 142, 143, 170 n. 59
Tsouderos, Emmanouil 85, 89, 90, 99, 107 n. s 92, 103; 126, 132, 143, 152, 162, 177, 178, 182, 223-5, 227-9, 234 n. 25; 289, 292, 308, 311, 317, 320 n. 60; 321 n. 71; 323, 334, 357-9, 362-4, 368, 372, 284 n. 135; 391, 395, 420, 427-9, 432, 501, 505, 519
Turner, Admiral 110
Tuttle, Wing-Commander 110
Tzavellas *see* Pappou
Tzimas, Andreas 271

Vafiadis, Markos 145, 195, 242, 243, 247-50, 254-5, 271, 483-91, 494 n. 54; 499-500, 507-8, 512-3, 516 n. s 56, 57; 530
Varga, Eugen 488
Varvaressos, Kyriakos 83, 87, 91, 96, 97, 109, 112, 121 n. 4; 182-3, 195, 199 n. 37; 202, 206, 207, 210-5, 221, 223, 228, 253, 256, 300-1, 361, 393
Varvoutis, Giorgios 320 n. 60
Vasiliadis 128
Velichansky 257
Velouchiotis, Aris (Thanasis Klaras) 5, 74, 175 n. 126; 236, 240, 241, 245, 255-6, 261, 264, 268, 278 n. s 7, 11; 441
Vendiris, Konstantinos 84-6, 104 n. 22;

INDEX OF PROPER NAMES

127, 157-8, 174 n. 116; 258, 325
Venetsanopoulos, Thomas 159-60, 174 n. 121
Venizelos, Eleftherios 30, 31, 33, 35, 68 n. 4; 105 n. 39; 166 n. 3; 234 n. 36; 438 n. 36
Venizelos, Sofoklis 90, 91, 94, 231, 234 n. 36; 297, 308-10, 320 n. 60; 371-4, 403 n. 14; 405-6, 410, 415-7, 430, 438 n. 36; 4,50, 452, 467, 520
Verret, A. 348
Veshnikov 352-3, 354
Vidalis, Kostas 532
Vilos, Petros 17 n. 6; 105 n. 39
Vlachos, Simos 84, 87, 88, 104 n. 30; 126
Vlandas, Dimitrios 484-6, 491, 494 n. 54
Vlavianos, B. 89
Voigt, F.A. 509
Voilas, Vasilios 199 n. 37; 318 n. 3
Volotas 128
Vontitsos-Gousias, Giorgios 483, 485, 486, 488, 491, 494 n. 54; 499, 530
Voraxanis, Georgios 309
Voulgaris, Petros 91-2, 96, 100, 105 n. 51; 109-12, 120 n. 2; 126, 127, 137, 143, 157-8, 162, 177-86, 189, 194, 199 n. 37; 208, 211, 214-5, 216, 221, 222, 223-5, 229, 230, 258, 263-4, 292, 317, 325, 373, 403 n. 14; 457
Vovolinis, Konstantinos 141, 170 n. 63
Voyatzis, Apostolos 281 n. 57
Vukmanović, Svetozar (Tempo) 73, 74, 252, 255
Vyshinsky, Andrei 396-9, 400-2, 472

Waley, Sir David 79, 81, 82, 110, 364
Warner, Edward 98, 99, 107 n. 92; 425
Weller, George 44 n. 30
Wickham, Sir Charles 156, 173 n. 107; 327, 328, 409, 413-4, 426, 531
Wilkes, Lyall 161, 188, 230-1, 329, 399
Williams 394
Winant, John 193
Windle, Richard 330, 370, 412
Woodhouse, C.M. 37, 85, 144, 148-51, 156, 172 n. 90; 183, 247, 299, 310, 342, 444, 456 n. 8; 461, 464, 478 509
Wright, Colin 29

Yannikostas, Ioannis 502
Yannopoulos, D. 170 n. 64
Yanoulopoulos, Yanis 173 n. 105
Yergin, Daniel viii
Ypsilantis 507, 508, 541 n. 57

Zachariadis, Nikos 71-5, 240, 243, 246-57, 258, 259-61, 262, 263-9, 270-5, 277, 279 n. 27; 280 n. 55; 281 n. s 72, 79; 282 n. s 79, 80, 81; 283 n. s 83, 112; 284 n. 116; 375, 398, 457-8, 463-4, 467-8; 471-2, 477-9, 482-91, 492 n. 2; 494 n. 54; 498-513, 515 n. 20; 526, 527-8, 529-30, 531, 538-9
Zakkas, Andreas 121 n. 3; 132-7, 199 n. 37; 346, 352
Zakynthinos, Dionysios 121 n. 2; 127
Zannas, A. 105 n. 39
Zervas, Napoleon 149, 183, 311, 333, 372, 374, 380 n. 32; 385 n. 60; 425, 453, 524, 534
Zevgos, Yannis 3, 5, 7, 9, 12, 13, 14, 16, 17 n. 23; 18 n. 29; 236, 242, 243, 245, 277, 280 n. s 41, 55; 284 n. 116; 317, 376, 378, 468, 529
Zhdanov 510
Zografos, Zisis 242, 263
Zoumboulakis, Ilias 141